THINKING ABOUT CONGRESS

Observing the polarized, debilitating politics of today's Congress, one wonders whether change is possible on Capitol Hill. In *Thinking about Congress*, Lawrence Dodd reminds us that Congress seemed equally intransigent at times in the past, yet change and rejuvenation came. Reading his classic essays, one sees Congress move from Committee Government in the mid-twentieth century to Liberal Democratic reforms in the 1970s to the 1994 Republican Revolution to Party Government today. Simultaneously, one proceeds with Dodd to an ever-deeper understanding of the dynamic character of Congress.

Across forty years of watching paralysis give way to change, Dodd crafts a theory of congressional cycles – essay by essay – that explains why Congress evolves. However permanent periods of intransigency appear, the theory argues, they can and do give way to growing concern by legislators and parties for the collective public interest; to citizen demand for change generated by social crises; and to innovative ideas about politics and policy. With these developments come policy breakthrough, institutional renewal, and enormous social progress.

A rare book, *Thinking about Congress* holds out hope for the future while illuminating both the process and object of inquiry.

Lawrence C. Dodd holds the Manning J. Dauer Eminent Scholar Chair in Political Science at the University of Florida. His books include *Coalitions in Parliamentary Government*, *Congress and the Administrative State*, *Learning Democracy*, and nine editions of *Congress Reconsidered*. The university selected him as 2007 Teacher/Scholar of the Year, its highest faculty honor.

THINKING ABOUT CONGRESS

Essays on Congressional Change

Lawrence C. Dodd

Routledge
Taylor & Francis Group

NEW YORK AND LONDON

First published 2012
by Routledge
711 Third Avenue, New York, NY 10017

Simultaneously published in the UK
by Routledge
2 Park Square, Milton Park, Abingdon, Oxon OX14 4RN

Routledge is an imprint of the Taylor & Francis Group, an informa business

© 2012 Taylor & Francis

Library of Congress Cataloging-in-Publication Data
Dodd, Lawrence C., 1946–
  Thinking about Congress : essays on Congressional change / Lawrence C. Dodd.
  p. cm.
  Includes bibliographical references and index.
  1. United States. Congress—History—20th century. 2. United States.
  Congress—History—21st century. 3. United States—Politics and
  government—1945–1989. 4. United States—Politics and government—1989–
  I. Title.
  JK1041.D63 2011
  328.73—dc23
  2011044267

ISBN: 978–0–415–99155–1 (hbk)
ISBN: 978–0–415–99156–8 (pbk)

Typeset in Bembo
by Swales & Willis Ltd, Exeter, Devon

For Meredith, Christopher and Leslie

CONTENTS

FIGURES

FOREWORD

Eric Schickler

UNIVERSITY OF CALIFORNIA-BERKELEY

This volume brings together many of the important contributions by Larry Dodd to the study of Congress over the past thirty-five years. Although Dodd's under-standing of Congress has evolved over this period—along with the institution itself—a central innovative move is evident in the earliest work, which runs through each of the individual contributions and has made a singular contribution to the development of the Congress field. Dodd showed scholars how to combine historical and rational choice approaches to the study of Congress, demonstrating that the combination of multiple theoretical lenses can lead to a richer under-standing of the legislative branch.

The dominant approach to the study of Congress in the 1960s had been behavioral and norm-oriented, focusing on how Congress works as a social sys-tem. Starting in the mid-1970s, David Mayhew, Richard Fenno, and Morris Fiorina transformed the field by shifting the focus to individual, goal-oriented action. They asked: what kind of institutions and policies would rational members of Congress design to suit their particular interests? This question then became the dominant orientation in the field, generating considerable theoretical and empirical traction. But just as the "sociological" work of the 1960s tended to treat Congress as a relatively static system, the rational choice scholarship of the 1970s to 1990s generally treated Congress as an "equilibrium" institution. Congress was well-designed to achieve members' interests. In the absence of a major exogenous shock, stability was to be expected. As a result, this work shared with the socio-logical tradition a general lack of attention to historical development.[1]

---

1 There were, of course, exceptions. Polsby's studies of institutionalization and the seniority system were historical works in the sociological tradition, and there were a handful of rational-choice-oriented scholars who incorporated historical perspectives (e.g. Brady on realignment; Cooper and Brady 1981).

In "Congress and the Quest for Power" (1977), Dodd adopts the individualistic, goal-oriented approach that was just emerging from rational choice work on Congress, but unlike most other scholars working at the time, he connects this goal-oriented framework to a historical, developmental approach. Dodd takes as a given that members seek to design Congress in ways that promote the realization of their individual goals. But he argues that these goals do not generate a single stable solution. Dodd begins with the assumption that members of Congress seek individual power. The most obvious way to gain individual power is to decentralize: give power to committees and subcommittees, and then spread influence within those units to many backbenchers. The problem, Dodd notes, is that this fragmentation weakens Congress as an institution over the long term, inviting executive aggrandizement. As Congress loses power to the White House, the value of the many individual power bases within the institution erodes. What good is it to be a subcommittee chair if agenda-setting and policy-formation drift from Congress's committee system to the executive branch? This erosion gives power-seeking members of Congress an incentive to recentralize, empowering the leadership. The result is a cyclical dynamic, in which Congress oscillates between bouts of fragmentation and centralizing reform. Dodd notes, however, that even as members centralize, they are loath to give up too much influence to the leadership, and thus often build in decentralizing features even as they attempt to foster greater coordination. The budget process that emerged with the Congressional Budget and Impoundment Control Act of 1974 is a signal example.

As the successive chapters make clear, Dodd has refined this view over the years. Rather than simply an internally-driven cycle, he has come to emphasize the interplay of internal and external forces. He has also placed greater emphasis on political learning and experimentation as keys to the reform process. Yet the core insights from the 1977 article endure and continued to animate Dodd's subsequent contributions.

One sees the impact of Dodd's framework in the burgeoning literature on "Congress and History" since the 1990s. Dodd demonstrated that considerable leverage can be gained by integrating a focus on individual goals with a historical perspective. The result is to enhance both rational choice and historical scholarship. Dodd pushed scholars to see that individual "rational" action need not generate a stable equilibrium institution that is satisfying to most members. Instead, the result may well be a messy institution that combines elements of centralization and fragmentation, and that fails to gain the trust of the American public or to satisfy members' goal of exercising effective influence. It is through the study of historical development that one can identify the forces generating these conflicting reforms. Yet the historical scholarship is not simply motivated by the goal of understanding each particular episode, but rather it is in the service of gaining a broader theoretical understanding of how Congress works (or fails to work) and how the institution fits into our broader political system.

When I started working on my dissertation in the mid-1990s, I gravitated to

Dodd's "Quest for Power" and his later work because it provided a lesson in how one can address big questions about institutional development while attending to the importance of individual goal-oriented action. Since then, I have appreciated the influence of Dodd's works as it permeated the scholarship of many of my fellow Congress scholars. The idea of bringing multiple theoretical lenses together in a disciplined manner was a key innovation when Dodd joined historical and rational choice approaches in the 1970s. Today, it is part of the established repertoire of Congress scholars, itself a testament to Dodd's impact on the field. At the same time, the vitality of Dodd's more recent contributions suggests that linking history and rational choice is not so much the "answer" as a tool for continued exploration and refinement of our understanding of Congress.

PREFACE

The Origin, Development and Plan of the Book

The enclosed essays chart the evolution of Congress and my understanding of it across four decades of remarkable change. When I entered graduate school in the late 1960s, the Textbook Congress was in full sway on Capitol Hill. The literature on Congress assured my colleagues and me that the world of committee government, weak political parties, the conservative coalition, domineering committee chairs, subsystem politics, a disorganized and uncoordinated policy process—all of this was here to stay, enshrined by the very nature of the constitutional system, the organizational necessities of institutional governance, the office-seeking goals of members, and the segmented policy concerns of citizens. The Democratic Party appeared to have a permanent lock on control of Congress, combining its historic support from the Solid South with growing loyalty from northern constituencies supportive of the party's social programs.

Amid the factionalized nature of party politics and the fragmented nature of committee power, effective policy activism in Congress appeared dependent on strong presidential leadership and united party government. Reliant on strong presidents and preoccupied by local politics and personal reelection, members of Congress were hesitant to challenge the authority of presidents, even during an unpopular war.

Contemporary analysts were so frustrated with Congress that they proposed the nation consider a move to formal reliance on presidential policy making, with Congress left to conduct oversight of the executive and ratify presidential policy initiatives (Huntington, 1965; Burns, 1963, 1965). The creation of a congressional budget process and formal budget committees, the enactment of a war powers act, limitations of the norm of seniority in the selection of committee chairs, the weakening of the power of committee chairs, the strengthening of subcommittee autonomy, the reactivation of congressional party caucuses, the empowerment of party leaders to dominate the selection of committee members and committee chairs—none of these reforms appeared remotely possible within the dominant perspectives of the day.

Yet change and reform came and did so on a massive scale.

Within a decade all of the impossible reforms were enacted (Dodd and Schott, 1979; Sundquist, 1981). The congressional elections of 1974 in particular yielded a reformist surge on Capitol Hill that pushed forward the weakening of committee power and the strengthening of party leadership. Within twelve years Democratic dominance of the Senate would collapse, in the wake of the Reagan Revolution of 1981, preparing the way for Newt Gingrich and the Republican Revolution of 1994. Within roughly a quarter century a transition to party government in Congress would be so far advanced in nature and appear so inherent to American politics that analysts in the mid-1990s would come to doubt whether committee government had actually existed on the Hill, so difficult was it for those coming of age in the era of polarized partisanship to imagine a world of genteel bipartisan cooperation and committee government.

For those of my generation, coming of age as young political scientists amid the reform upheavals, the challenge came in understanding how and explaining why the politics of the Textbook Congress had collapsed, so inherent had it seemed in the very essence of American politics during our doctoral studies, and determining the character, consequences and implications of the new order on Capitol Hill. The essays in this volume emerged from my effort to respond to this challenge.

I. The Origin of the Book

As with my fellow political scientists, I was caught off guard by the upheavals in Congress. In truth, I had become disillusioned by Congress and American politics in the late 1960s. Though I had entered graduate school with the express intent of studying Congress and the presidency, the Vietnam War, the assassinations of Martin Luther King, Jr., and Robert F. Kennedy, the riots and societal disarray, the unwilling of Congress to push for an end to the War—all led me to wonder whether other approaches to democratic governance might be preferable to our own. In addition, while I had sat in on an undergraduate course on Congress taught by my early graduate mentor John C. Pierce during an introductory year of graduate studies at Tulane University, there were no courses on Congress or congressional–executive relations during my three years at the University of Minnesota, starting in the fall of 1969. And so I concentrated my studies on comparative politics and political theory, treating the United States as one of my area studies and focusing in-depth on European and British Commonwealth politics.

A dissertation on coalition politics in parliamentary democracies dissuaded me of the prospect that a magic solution existed elsewhere to the rigors of democratic life. A teaching position at the University of Texas-Austin in the fall of 1972 allowed me to return home to my beloved Southwest if only I would teach Congress. A Congressional Fellowship in 1974 offered an opportunity to move my young family to Washington and learn something up close and personal about the topic I was teaching. And so in the months following the Watergate election of 1974 I found myself on Capitol Hill and working in the House Democratic Whip Office as their resident Congressional Fellow.

It is difficult to convey today the awe, disorientation and excitement I experienced in December of 1974 and January of 1975 as I witnessed first hand the greatest congressional insurgency since the revolt against Speaker Joseph Cannon in 1910 and one of the most consequential restructurings of congressional power in American history. Everything that I had read about Congress and now was teaching my students seemed to collapse before my eyes. An institution that was said to be impervious to rapid change and innovation, with committee intransigence, gradualist tinkering and bipartisan conservative dominance the name of the game, appeared to be moving rapidly toward assertive partisanship, organizational and procedural transformation, and liberal dominance of congressional governance. Watching the response of the established committee and party leaders who flowed through the whip office in the early months of the new Congress, it was clear that the upheavals were real, with anxiety and uncertainty about their hold on power ever present on their faces.

Imbued by the excitement of the times, and inspired by research on the history of Congress by Joseph Cooper and David Brady (Cooper and Brady, 1973), I began scouring the Library of Congress and reading avidly on congressional history, trying to understand contemporary developments by putting them in a broader historical perspective (Dodd, 1980, 1987). Simultaneously, I focused substantial research attention on the whip system itself, witnessing and documenting a party leadership that was already more activist in vote-gathering by the early 1970s than scholars had previously realized (Dodd, 1979, 1983). And when I changed assignments as a Congressional Fellow in April of 1975, I switched to the Congressional Office of Bob Eckhardt of Texas, a Southern Democratic liberal deeply active in the reform-oriented House Democratic Study Group, which allowed me access to DSG meetings.

Additionally, I talked often with the other Congressional Fellows in my class, including John Ellwood, Bob Filner (now a member of the House), Michael Lyons, Bruce Oppenheimer, Cathy Rudder and Marcia Whicker Taylor, and also with recent Fellows still in Washington, particularly Norm Ornstein and James Thurber, getting their collective take on the events of the time. These discussions deepened my grasp of the extensive changes underway on the Hill and led to the decision by Bruce and me to prepare an edited volume on the ways in which the reforms were changing Congress. That decision produced the first edition of *Congress Reconsidered* (Dodd and Oppenheimer, eds., 1977), an edited volume of original scholarly essays that has traced the evolution of the reform and post-reform Congress across almost forty years and nine editions, with the tenth now in the works. Perhaps most critically, I began to reflect seriously on the failure of the existing verities about Congress and American politics to foresee the reform upheavals or to provide retrospective explanation of their occurrence.

A devotee of the behavioral revolution in political science, I was imbued with the belief that systematic study of and theorizing about the observed behavior of individuals, groups and institutions would enable scholars to uncover regularities in politics, thereby foreseeing and understanding critical shifts in social and political relations (Eulau, 1967; Kaplan, 1964). I thus found the failure of political science to anticipate the upheavals in Congress deeply troubling. If we as a discipline could fail so miserably in foreseeing such dramatic and broad-ranging changes, of what use were our empirical studies, theoretical perspectives, analytical models, philosophical musings, normative critiques and reformist debates? What authentic grounding did we actually have in a reliable and dynamic understanding of political reality? If our theories and studies of Congress not only missed the boat, but actually proposed that the developments occurring on Capitol Hill were essentially impossible in their breadth and depth, perhaps political science could not deliver on the promises made by our behavioral fathers. Perhaps I should just do political history, or engage in contemporary political commentary, or continue with my study of coalition politics in parliamentary democracies, or return to Austin and enter politics. At this point my experience studying European and British Commonwealth parliaments provided an instructive perspective, cautioning restraint in my rush to judgment.

My investigation of coalitional politics in twenty parliamentary democracies had convinced me that the behavioralists' goal of a science of democratic politics held out true promise. Guided by the work of such scholars as Anthony Downs, William H. Riker, Harry Eckstein, Seymour Martin Lipset and Stein Rokkan, I had constructed and tested a theory of coalitional politics that appeared to uncover significant regularities in coalition dynamics across eighty years of parliamentary politics (Dodd, 1976a), accounting for general patterns of coalition politics and for change in those patterns between the pre-war and postwar eras. Simultaneously others—Robert Axelrod, Robert Dahl, Hugh Heclo, Ron Inglehart, Arend Lijphart, Robert Putnam to name only a few—were investigating additional dimensions of parliamentary politics, to great effect, so that a broad theory of parliamentary democracy seemed imminent, a promise that has for the most part been realized (Almond, Powell, Dalton, and Strom, 2009; Loewenberg, 2011).

The success of parliamentary scholars in generating simple and yet empirically compelling analyses of electoral and institutional politics was inspiring, holding out hope that a science of democracy might yet be possible, but it also served to put the challenge confronting students of American politics in perspective. Virtually all well-established democratic regimes were parliamentary in character, so that there were numerous experiences to compare and contrast in creating a theory of parliamentary democracy. And in truth the basic logic of parliamentary politics was relatively straightforward, at least by comparison with politics in the United

States. The central task of the parliament was to choose and oversee the Prime Minster and Cabinet government, with most parliamentary democracies leaving policy crafting largely if not entirely in the hands of the executive. As a result, national politics revolved around the selection and durability of governing parties or coalitions in ways captured well by Downs' goal-centered theory of party politics and electoral democracy in *An Economic Theory of Democracy* (1957).

In contrast to parliamentary politics, the American constitutional system of separation of powers, checks and balances, federalism, and a bicameral policy-making legislature was unique among major established industrial-era democracies and quite complex in its operation, much more complex than grasped by Downs in his treatment of American politics. Moreover, the United States was the most powerful nation-state democracy in the world, with its responsibility for the security of the West in the face of Cold War animosities adding greatly to the stresses of its politics.

On reflection, the problem confronting students of American politics appeared to lie not with the behavioral vision of our discipline but with the unique challenges posed by studying such a complex and one-of-a-kind political system. If this were so, the critical challenge facing devotees of the behavioral persuasion lay in constructing a theoretical vision, a way of thinking about this most powerful and distinctive democracy that could uncover a simple and dynamic order amid the vast complexities of its politics. Moreover, a key to such an enterprise, perhaps *the* key to it, could lie in addressing the issue at hand: charting and explaining the extensive, unforeseen patterns of change in congressional politics evident during the early to mid-1970s.

With this epiphany, and nudged by the questions and insights of my undergraduate and graduate students as I returned to teaching in the summer and fall of 1975, I set out on the journey charted in the essays in this book—the effort to fashion a dynamic yet parsimonious perspective on Congress that could account for the upheavals of the 1970s, make sense out of previous periods of institutional change, and provide prospective foresight on the direction of Congress and American politics into the future. In this endeavor I joined the many other scholars of my generation fascinated by the politics of Congress and concerned to understand why the reforms had occurred and what their implications and effects were. That generation, composed of those political scientists who began publishing on Congress during and immediately following the reforms of the 1970–1975 period, included Abramowitz, Aldrich, Arnold, Asher, Bond, Brady, Carmines, Cover, Deering, Ellwood, Erikson, Ferejohn, Fiorina, Fisher, Fowler, Hershey, Jacobson, Kernell, Kostroski, Loomis, Malbin, Mann, Nelson, Oppenheimer, Ornstein, Parker, Peters, Price, Rohde, Rudder, Shepsle, Sinclair, Smith, Stimson, Thurber, Uslaner, Weingast, Weisberg, Wright, and many others. Focusing their attention like a laser beam on the reform and immediate post-reform period, they produced the most in-depth analysis of reformist upheaval and immediate post-reform politics that exists in the annals of legislative studies, with their work providing me a deep grounding in empirical reality as I pushed forward on my effort to construct a theory of institutional reform and change.

I then benefitted as well from the generations of scholars coming into congressional studies in the 1980s and thereafter, a vast group that includes among its many fine scholars such gifted analysts as Adler, Alford, Ansolabehere, Arnold, Baker, Baumgartner, Bensel, Berkman, Bianco, Bickers, Binder, Bosso, Brunell, Burden, Cain, Cameron, Canon, Carson, Clinton, Collie, Cox, Currinder, DeGregorio, Dion, Evans, Farrier, Flower, Frisch, Gamm, Griffin, Hall, Hansen, Herrnson, Heitschusen, Hibbing, Howell, Humes, Jenkins, Jones, Kahn, Kelly, King, Koger, Krehbiel, Kriner, Krutz, Lawrence, Lee, Lewis, Lipinski, Maltzman, Mayer, McCarty, McCubbins, McKee, Morris, Nokkan, Oldmixon, Owens, Pearson, Peterson, Poole, Powell, Quirk, Roberts, Raven, Rosenthal, Rybicki, Sala, Sanders, Schiller, Schickler, Schraufnagel, Sellars, Stewart, Stein, Stone, Strahan, Sulkin, Swain, Swift, Tate, Theriault, Volden, Von Houweling, Wawro, Wilkerson and Young. These scholars and numerous others have provided my reform-era colleagues and me a deeper awareness of the historical and developmental forces operating on and within Congress, a clearer sense of the party dynamics engulfing the contemporary Congress, more detailed understanding of the cyclical tensions and processes at work in Congress, and a greater appreciation of the policy dynamics driving congressional politics.

And all of us, including those of the reform generation of scholars and those who followed, owe a huge debt to the extraordinary generation of early postwar scholars who played such a critical role in etching out the details of the Textbook Congress. These scholars, including Burns, Clauson, Cooper, Davidson, Dexter, Eulau, Fenno, Froman, Hammond, Hinckley, Huitt, Jones, Key, Kingdon, Lowi, Maass, Manley, Matthews, Mayhew, Ogul, Oleszek, Patterson, Peabody, Polsby, Price, Rieselbach, Ripley, Sundquist, Truman, Turner, Wildavsky, Wolfinger, Young, and others, provided an invaluable portrait of the committee government and bipartisan politics that dominated the early postwar period, with several of its members also linking this politics to the historical development of Congress. Without their detailed portrait of the postwar Congress, it would have been impossible for my generation to grasp so readily the dramatic nature of the changes occurring on Capitol Hill in the 1970s.

Finally, as detailed elsewhere (Dodd, 2001b), my work on Congress and change would have been impossible, at least in the form that it took, without the era-defining book, *Congress: The Electoral Connection*, by David Mayhew (1974b). Coming of age in political science just as the Textbook Congress was about to give way to the new Reformed Congress, David drew on his immersion in the literature on the Textbook era and his experience on Capitol Hill as a Congressional Fellow in the late 1960s to craft a broad, speculative theory of Congress. Building on Downs' *Economic Theory of Democracy* and Richard Fenno's (1973) study of legislators' goal-oriented behavior in congressional committees, *Congressmen in Committees*, Mayhew proposed that scholars could best explain the overall character of congressional politics by focusing on members' obsession with reelection. In seeing congressmen as 'single-minded seekers of reelection,' we then could explain the strategic and self-serving character of legislators' behavior, the apparent weakness of political parties, the decentralized and committee-oriented structure of congressional organization, the distributional nature of congressional policy making, the institution's resistance to reform and innovative policy change, and also its remarkable persistence and resilience as a representative assembly.

Reading *The Electoral Connection* amid the upheavals on the Hill, and then grappling with it in my undergraduate and graduate courses back in Austin, I found Mayhew's theory of Congress mesmerizing as a model of the kind of simple and elegant yet comprehensive argument to which I aspired in my work. Yet I also sensed that it was limited in its capacity to explain the processes of change under way in Congress. The critical issues troubling me found their clear articulation in a question from an undergraduate student in the first course I taught after returning to Austin: how could the reelection motive, so powerful in explaining the decentralized, individualized and particularized politics of the early postwar Congress explain the recentralized, party-oriented and collective policy-making orientation of the reformed Congress? This question, stated in a starkly simplified and pointed query in front of 200 undergraduates—who had heard me lecture at length first on *The Electoral Connection* as the core explanatory perspective of the course and then on the centralizing reforms I had witnessed the previous year—left me red-faced and speechless. I had no answer at hand.

With this question, the central puzzle at the heart of the work in this volume emerged. To this day I reflect on the pivotal effect of that moment on my life and career, continuing to wonder if I would have seen as clearly and powerfully this puzzle without the question posed so innocently by that undergraduate—whose name I never learned but to whom I remain so deeply indebted. What is clear is my great debt to David Mayhew. His stimulating effort to develop a goal-oriented theory that could explain the politics, organizational structure, and policy processes of Congress pointed me towards a goal-oriented approach to explaining changes in its politics, structure and policy processes. At issue was how best to craft, develop and expand such a perspective.

II. The Development and Plan of the Book

My theoretical pilgrimage—my effort to build a theory of congressional politics that might have the elegant simplicity of a Downs or Mayhew while also being true to the complexity and dynamics of American politics—began with the articulation of a simple paradox. Politicians run for Congress, I proposed, in order to acquire power and policy-making influence within it, with reelection to Congress being essential to gaining power and policy-making influence but a relatively empty and limited goal without it. To aid in acquiring personal policy-making power, I maintained, members decentralize organizational power and resources within Congress, thereby increasing their prospect of rising to positions of influence while also gaining resources and visibility that can aid their reelection. And yet if they decentralize Congress too much, in efforts to maximize their personal reelection, policy influence, and power concerns, they upend its capacity for strong and coordinated action. In doing so, they undermine the governing power of Congress and thus the value of their power within it.

Struggling with the inherent tradeoff between personal power and the power of the institution, legislators will push initially for decentralization of Congress in order to serve their personal power and reelection concerns, doing so across decades of time somewhat unaware of the longer term consequences of their efforts. As they relentlessly push fragmentation and decentralization they put the constitutional authority and governing capacity of the institution at risk. Then over the long-run, confronted with presidential aggrandizement of power amid the weakening of Congress, members eventually move to recentralize power within Congress and resuscitate its constitutional authority. In doing so, they accept broad limits on members' personal power prerogatives and electoral resources in order to strengthen the institution. Ironically, they also invariably maneuver to protect their own special constituency interests, policy concerns and power bases, so that multiple goals across innumerable members and factions in Congress constrain and complicate centralizing reform, building glitches into the reforms that subsequently insure their unraveling.

Across time, fueled by members multiple contending goals and the contradictory purposes built into the reformed structure of Congress, organizational fragmentation will recur and future generations must again reform the institution, so that cycles of fragmentation and centralization become the defining attribute of congressional change. Moreover, I proposed, careerist legislators will likely generate increased levels of fragmentation, cycle by cycle, so Congress will drift across reform eras towards increased decentralization, progressively eroding its policy-making capacity unless institutional centralization is shored up through well-designed constitutional reforms.

The power paradox and the cyclical argument that flows from it—first presented in "Congress and the Quest for Power" (Chapter Two, published in 1977)—constituted my attempt to answer the question posed by my undergraduate student. In the decades prior to the 1970s, from this perspective, power-seeking legislators had generated growing decentralization and fragmentation in Congress, undercutting its capacity for coordinated leadership and thereby making it susceptible to presidential intrusion into its power prerogatives. The result was the imperial presidency of Richard Nixon, which so clearly seemed to challenge the foreign and domestic policy influence of Congress (Schlesinger, 1974). The reforms of the 1970s were efforts to recentralize congressional power and strengthen its institutional authority, enhancing both the power of Congress and the value of long-term service in it by placing limits on the personal autonomy, power and resources of individual members.

Initially I believed that "Quest" provided the simple, elegant and yet dynamic theory of Congress that I was seeking. My students and professional colleagues soon convinced me otherwise. Over the subsequent thirty-five years or so their critiques and queries posed one overarching challenge: *Just how Determinative and Predictable are the Cycles of Fragmentation and Recentralization in Shaping and Reshaping Congress?* This overarching challenge has generated four broad subsidiary questions:

1.   Does historical context and bicameralism matter?
2.   Do political parties and interparty competition foster change?
3.   Where is the role for human agency, ideas and creative innovation?
4.   Can the answers to these questions be integrated into an empirically credible theory?

In retrospect, these questions grabbed my attention in a sequential manner, generating a series of theoretical essays that gradually expanded the theory of cycles in a step by step and staged—if unanticipated—manner. This volume presents ten core essays that chart this development, organizing them into four parts that reflect the four questions above. The essays are presented by date of initial publication.

Each of these previously published essays will be preceded in this volume by an Abstract that summarizes the essay's argument and followed by a section entitled "Additional Perspective." These sections provide a third-person retrospect which details the concerns I had in writing the essay, the scholarly work I built on in crafting it, subsequent publications by other scholars that speak to the issues raised in the essay, and suggestions for ways in which the essay can be incorporated into undergraduate classes and graduate seminars. The Abstracts and Additional Perspectives provide a more extensive framing of each chapter and its place in the development of my work than I can present in this Preface. Here simply let me provide a broad roadmap.

Part One: Member Goals and Institutional Context

The first question that occupied me following the publication of "Quest" dealt with the role of context in congressional change. "Quest" had situated my cyclical argument in a time and place, focusing on the politics of the mid-twentieth century and linking the cycles back to the late nineteenth century. But it did not explicitly address the role that changes in social, constitutional or institutional context play in shaping the cycles or in influencing their outcome.

Written and published between 1975 and 1985, the essays in Part One examine the interplay between the careerist goals of legislators and historical-contextual factors generating and impinging on cyclical change. As noted, Chapter Two, "Congress and the Quest for Power" (1977), is the foundation essay of the book. It describes the reforms of the 1970s and presents the initial formulation of the cyclical theory designed to explain their occurrence. Chapter Three, "Congress, the Constitution, and the Crisis of Legitimation" (1981), puts the reforms in a broader historical, constitutional and social perspective. It stresses the ways in which industrialization and the emergence of a powerful national government fostered the rise of a careerist Congress. The pursuit of institutional power by the growing number of careerist legislators fueled the cycles of fragmentation, institutional decline and recentralization.

"Legitimation Crisis" raises the prospect that the coming of post-industrialism will pose severe policy challenges that the reformed Congress will be unable to address, given inadequacies built into the reforms by the multiple and countervailing motives of legislators, so that the contemporary Congress could prove even more conflictive, deadlocked and unpopular than the Congress of previous eras. Chapter Four, "Bicameralism in Congress," written with Edward Carmines (1985), argues that reforms such as those creating the new congressional budget process could exacerbate tensions between the Senate and the House, when combined with the effects of post-industrialism, further undermining the resurgence of Congress.

Taken together, the three essays of Part One portray Congress as a dynamic institution subject to reform and resurgence as well as to fragmentation and decline. But they worry that the reformed Congress of the late twentieth century, governed by recentralized but flawed institutional structures and procedures, would prove too weak and conflictive to address the issues posed by post-industrialism.

Part Two: Political Parties, Institutional Cycles and Era Transformations

The essays in Part Two, written and published between 1982 and 1986, step back from the focus on specific historical contexts present in Part One and develop the theory of congressional cycles in a more analytically detached manner. The goal of Part Two is to think through the theory of cycles more fully, being more explicit about the ways in which legislators' quest for power shapes institutional politics. In doing so, I introduced a critical shift into my perspective on Congress: I began to take political parties and interparty competition for control of Congress seriously.

With this shift, I proposed that legislators' quest for power proceeds in different ways, according to whether they are members of a majority party (or faction) controlling Congress, particularly a long-entrenched majority, or members of a minority party (or faction) seeking to gain control. Members of an entrenched majority will push for great fragmentation of power, as they come to take control of Congress for granted and seek to benefit from it in direct, personal ways. In contrast, members of a minority are more likely to support organizational centralization, particularly centralization within their party or faction, in efforts to coordinate the pursuit of institutional control. As a result, interparty competition

for control of Congress can introduce processes that foster heightened centralization of power in ways that I had overlooked when thinking about Congress in a
highly individualistic manner.

The first statement of this shift in perspective, Chapter Five, "The Cycles of
Legislative Change" (1986a), argues that the cycles of congressional change tend
to be driven or reinforced by cycles of partisan or factional shift in control of Congress. In this view, majority parties (or dominant factions) in Congress invariably
become fragmented and overconfident in their exercise of governing responsibilities, as their members concentrate on the personal power and policy influence
that can come with majority status. In contrast, minority parties (or factions)
tend to move towards more centralized, coordinated and cohesive politics, and
to become more attentive to new policy issues as they compete to win majority
control. As the majority becomes progressively more fragmented, the more centralized, coordinated and cohesive minority eventually overwhelms and defeats it,
bringing a new 'policy image' and greater centralized leadership to Congress in
ways that help to break policy deadlock, reassert the policy roles of Congress, and
reenergize national politics.

Chapter Six, "A Theory of Congressional Cycles" (1986b), expands the partisan perspective on congressional cycles. It argues that short-term swings in the
partisan or factional control of Congress, as addressed in Chapter Five, are nested
within longer multigenerational swings in its organizational fragmentation. In
this view, the organizational fragmentation of Congress will expand progressively
across two generations in time, with a dominant partisan regime generally able to
sustain broad support among voters and control the politics of Congress through
the continued popularity of and expansion in its initial innovative agenda. Its
lengthy hold on power will be aided, as argued forcefully by Morris Fiorina in
Congress: Keystone to the Washington Establishment (1977b), by the personal loyalty
constituents show to their legislators, who use their resources in Congress to
insure that the regime's programs directly benefit the citizens in their constituencies. Simultaneously, the regime will ignore new kinds of problems and concerns
at odds with its aging agenda.

The regime's dominance of Congress will collapse towards the end of the
second generation, falling victim to the fragmented politics and outmoded issue
politics that its long-term dominance of Congress has fostered. The collapse of
the existing regime sets in motion extensive interparty or inter-factional conflict
for control of Congress, increased electoral competition, the rise of new and
festering policy issues ignored by the previous partisan regime, and the eventual
emergence of a new partisan or factional regime together with a newly invigor-
ated Congress.

The two essays in Part Two, taken together, propose that periods of great
agenda shift in national politics, as with the rise of postindustrial issues to national
salience in the post-World War II period, bring with them the collapse of dominant but aging partisan regimes committed to an outmoded agenda geared to

the previous historical era. Regime collapse will set in motion serious interparty competition and shifts in partisan or factional control of Congress, as the nation searches for a new regime capable of addressing the policy issues of the new era. During such periods, the party or factional coalition more successful in generating a well-coordinated, innovative, and effective problem-solving approach to politics will win out over its less adaptive opponent. The capture of Congress by a better organized and problem-oriented party or faction will then help sustain and reinforce the centralizing tendencies produced by congressional reforms that accompany such periods of agenda shift. From this perspective, the reforms of the 1970s would be saved and augmented by growing interparty competition for control of Congress, giving rise to a new, assertive partisan regime in Congress and a new era of policy innovation in national politics. There was, of course, one glitch.

The hopeful arguments in Part Two, foreseeing vibrant interparty competition for control of Congress and a move towards a more centralized and activist Congress, seemed almost jarring and fantastical in light of the realities of Congress in the mid- to late 1980s. The vision of Congress portrayed in Part One—an institution descending into a dark night of heightened organizational disarray, weakened parties, policy intransigence and governing illegitimacy—seemed far more applicable to the contemporary Congress than did the vision of expanded centralization, heightened party competition, the emergence of a new issue-oriented politics, and rise of a more assertive Congress theorized in Part Two. If in fact the arguments in Part Two were in some sense 'true,' why did the politics of the 1980s appear so hopeless, looking more like the forecasts tendered in Part One than the resilient processes identified in Part Two?

Part Three: Societal Change, Social Learning and Political Renewal

Written and published between 1988 and 1995, the essays in Part Three introduce the role that ideas and human innovation play in congressional change. Chapter Seven, "Congress, the Presidency and the American Experience" (1991), argues that processes of renewed partisan competition, organizational restructuring and agenda change that appear highly determined in abstract theory, as in Part Two, depend for their effective operation on the success of real-world political actors in discovering new ways of seeing society and governance appropriate to the distinctive conditions of their time. This is a daunting challenge that builds indeterminacy and human agency into politics. In this view, tight rational choice theories, such as those presented in Part Two, work in actual practice only in so far as political actors learn 'updated' ways to pursue their self-interested goals that are appropriate to the realities of the historical context confronting them.

Chapter Eight, "Congress and the Politics of Renewal" (1993), argues that the Congress of the 1980s and early 1990s was failing to respond adequately to the challenges of post-industrialism because it was hindered both by industrial-era organizational politics and by outmoded ideas about national governance. It particularly highlighted the ways in which representational and deliberative processes that had emerged in the industrial era were hindering the capacity of Congress to learn new perspectives on society and politics appropriate to postindustrialism. The chapter is critical of the governing Democratic Party, my own party, seeing congressional Republicans as more attentive to post-industrial issues and to new ideas about governance than were the highly entrenched congressional Democrats.

Chapter Nine, "The New American Politics" (1995a), portrays a national citizenry in the mid-1990s moving rapidly away from the orthodoxies of the Cold War and industrial-era politics and toward new forms of citizen engagement in politics and new strategies of governance. Written in the spring and summer of 1994 and forecasting a probable Republican victory in the 1994 elections or soon thereafter, the essay was rewritten in the aftermath of the 1994 elections, immediately before going to press, to report the Republican victory and provide an initial assessment of its significance.

Part Three marks another substantial shift in the theoretical focus of my work. I continued to think as a rational choice scholar, looking to the multiple actor goals and tradeoffs driving politics, and also continued to attend closely to social, institutional and environmental context when assessing how the goal-oriented behavior of legislators will play out across time. But Part Three signals my growing sense that ideas, innovation and learning—or their absence—also play critical and independent roles in congressional politics that must be acknowledged, respected and incorporated into political inquiry.

From this perspective, Congress in the 1980s had been stymied in the emergence of vibrant interparty competition and a new agenda politics by the slowness of both congressional parties to experience generational change in leadership, to embrace less fragmented and more coordinated internal politics, and to move towards new ideas and innovative issue agendas attuned to post-industrial policy concerns. In contrast, by the early to mid-1990s Republicans appeared to be moving more rapidly in these directions than did Democrats, a move in keeping with the theory of partisan cycles presented in Part Two, which stresses the greater capacity of minority parties to innovate when contrasted with long-serving and entrenched majorities.

Part Four: The Multiple Dimensions and Processes of Change

The essays in Part Four, written and revised between 1995 and 2005, consider the extent to which the foregoing arguments served to foreshadow and explain the Republican Revolution of 1994, thereby demonstrating the utility of the effort to build a theory of congressional change. They also highlight new perspectives on congressional politics that require additional scholarly attention.

Published in 2001 and updated following the 2004 elections, Chapter Ten, "Re-Envisioning Congress: Theoretical Perspectives on Congressional Change— 2004" (2001a, 2005a), argues that the Revolution resulted from three broad factors: (1) an effective, well organized minority party challenge to an overconfident majority party, in ways resembling the arguments of Chapter Five; (2) festering post-industrial tensions and difficulties that the majority party had failed to adequately address, a failure that provided the minority party critical electoral opportunities, along the lines outlined in Chapters Three, Six, and Eight; and (3) citizens' willingness to consider new ideas about the sort of programs and governing strategies appropriate to a new economic, social and global environment, in ways resembling the arguments of Chapter Six, Seven, and Nine. The chapter closes by surveying the accomplishments of the majority party Republicans from 1995 through 2004 and highlighting potential limits to Republican governance that Democrats could exploit to regain congressional control.

From the perspective of theory development, the essay points to a broader and more multidimensional perspective on Congress than seen in other essays in the book or in other theories of congressional politics. In order to understand, foresee and explain institutional change, it proposes, analysts must attend not only to the foreground game of politics, looking at the multiple goals and goal-tradeoffs that drive the cycles of fragmentation and centralization within Congress. They also must incorporate into their analysis close attention to social and economic developments in background societal context and a sensitive awareness of shifting ideas about public policy and national governance within the nation at large.

The multidimensional perspective presented in "Re-Envisioning Congress" yields a simple and empirically testable proposition: in order for the foreground game of congressional politics to effectively address the nation's policy problems, sustaining the institution's central role in national governance, legislators and their parties must generate organizational arrangements, policy processes and agenda priorities within Congress congruent (1) with the shifting societal challenges facing the nation, and (2) with ideas about governance acceptable to and embraced by the nation's citizens.

Informed and foresighted analysis of Congress requires close and integrated attention to all three dimensions of politics and to the cyclical dynamics inducing long-term change within and across them.

Published in 2002, Chapter Eleven, "Making Sense Out of Our Exceptional Senate" (2002), closes the book by assessing the role that bicameralism plays in shaping and sustaining the cyclical processes of change. It argues that constitutional, institutional and career-centered differences between the two chambers enable each to play a vital and distinct role in aiding congressional response to new historical conditions. The Senate plays a critical role in insuring the cyclical adaptation of Congress to new societal challenges while the House helps sustain its long-term and routinized attention to them.

The Introduction: "Congress as Public Mirror"

Finally, the first chapter of the book, written specially for this volume, serves both to introduce its broad themes and to provide a new theoretical synthesis of them. As such, it can be read both as an opening and a closing chapter.

As an opening chapter it argues that congressional change has been one of the most critically important yet poorly understood topics of American politics over the past two centuries. This misunderstanding comes in part through oversight, with scholars too often failing to study periods and processes of change. But it also results from the focus by scholars, citizens and journalists on overly simplistic conceptions of the motives of political actors. To truly understand Congress, foreseeing its long-term cyclical and developmental trajectories, we must see legislators and citizens in their full human dimensions. We must focus not just on their short-term maximization of personal self-interest—Congress and the country be damned—but also on their broader concerns with collective self-interest.

This argument, presented in forceful manner, is intended to counterbalance the cynicism that characterizes so much of the analysis of the American Congress, a cynicism undermining public appreciation of it and driving undergraduate and graduate students away from serious study of it. The chapter reminds us that cynicism is not science—nor is naïve idealism. It is as we recognize and appreciate the multiple goals and complex motives that characterize citizens and the legislators they send to Congress, granting them the humanity we grant ourselves, that we truly understand the dynamic, flawed and yet resilient character of congressional politics.

Read as a concluding essay, the first chapter highlights more clearly than past essays the role that citizens play in congressional change. In doing so, it stresses the important contribution that 'the politics of attention' makes to congressional change (Jones and Baumgartner, 2005; Jones, 1994, 2001; Stimson, 1991; Hirschman, 1982; Burns, 1949): It is as legislators and constituents concentrate on short-term issues of personal and group goals and segmented policy preferences that Congress becomes mired in fragmentation, policy deadlock, and governing crisis. And it is as they shift their focus to the general institutional performance of Congress and collective concerns about the nation, a shift that generally comes amidst a growing sense of institutional paralysis and national crisis, that substantial change in the institution and its policy performance becomes possible. This synthesis integrates the enclosed essays and highlights new directions for thinking about Congress.

Future Directions

Looking to the future, my theoretical work on Congress and change continues, but with a difference. Over the past year I have returned to the work of Anthony Downs, which influenced my dissertation on parliamentary politics so strongly, and am reassessing the applicability of *An Economic Theory of Democracy* to Congress and American Politics. This new work (Dodd, 2011), still in progress and tentatively entitled "Congress in a Downsian World," will look forward and imagine the dynamic processes of electoral and partisan change likely to shape the Congress and its organizational politics into the mid-twenty-first century.

With this new direction, the time seems right to publish the essays contained in this volume as a unit. In making the essays available in one volume, I hope they can help inform classroom discussion of congressional politics of the early twenty-first century by highlighting its roots in reforms and partisan dynamics of the late twentieth century. The essays also help make clear that periods of deadlock and frustration on Capitol Hill are not permanent, but can and do give way to shifting actor goals and tradeoffs among them, to new societal contexts, partisan agendas and generational change, and to innovative ideas and social learning. I also hope the essays will help push forward the debate in the classroom and the discipline over how best to think about and theorize about Congress and American politics. And this book also affords me the opportunity to acknowledge publicly the great debts I owe so many individuals and institutions as I have pursued my work on Congress.

ACKNOWLEDGEMENTS

Let me begin by extending my deep appreciation to Michael Kerns, my editor at Routledge Press, for proposing this volume and standing by me during its preparation. The book simply would not have existed without his initiative, enthusiasm, resolute persistence, and sustained support as I worked to complete it while keeping various other balls in the air. Michael is a gifted, patient, industrious and innovative editor who enjoys my greatest admiration and appreciation. Sincere thanks also go to his associates at Routledge, in particular Mary Altman, Tom Newman, Felisa Salvago-Keyes, and Richard Willis for their excellent assistance in preparing the manuscript for publication. My heartfelt appreciation as well to the three anonymous reviewers for their thoughtful suggestions and assistance in determining how best to design the book and shape up the introductory chapter. The book is much better for the close attention all three gave to the review process. Finally, my great thanks to Eric Schickler for preparing the Foreword. A scholar of rare breadth, depth and theoretical acumen, it is a privilege to have Eric introduce the volume and do so in such a deft and gracious manner.

The essays in this book go to great length to acknowledge the numerous individuals who have contributed to their separate development. I encourage readers to attend closely to the acknowledgements contained in each essay and to the discussion in the "Additional Perspective" section that follows each essay. I have benefited beyond measure, essay by essay, from the support, encouragement and challenges offered by the extraordinary body of scholars, colleagues and students with whom I have been associated during the past four decades in studying Congress, a fact I hope is fully evident in the acknowledgements within these various essays. I absolve them all of any responsibility for the shortcomings of these essays while gratefully sharing with them any and all credit earned.

Here let me highlight individuals and institutions that were vital to the overall development of this book. First and foremost, my greatest professional debt goes to my friend, coauthor and coeditor Bruce Oppenheimer of Vanderbilt University, who was there at the beginning of the journey documented in the essays and then at every subsequent stage along the way, not only bantering with me about life and politics, and listening to my musings about Congress, but also helping insure that so many of these essays saw the light of day. Five of the essays were published in our co-edited volume, *Congress Reconsidered*, and a sixth appears in his wonderful solo edited volume, *U.S. Senate Exceptionalism*. I know of few professional partnerships that have been as long lived and productive as mine with Bruce, an experience for which I am deeply grateful.

Second, I have a very special debt to Joseph Cooper, who has served as my most sustained mentor and teacher of Congress for almost four decades now. Never Joe's formal student I have nevertheless learned enormously from him, about Congress, the profession and life. My life and my work would have been much the poorer without Joe. His support for this volume, in particular, has been heartwarming.

Third, I continue to benefit from the year-long course on Contemporary Political Theory taught by Edwin Fogelman during my graduate studies at Minnesota. Spanning all the major theoretical perspectives on politics published during the early post-war era, whether economic, sociological, social psychological, organizational, system-centered, cybernetic or anthropological in nature, and also highlighting the role of theory construction as a form of inquiry on par with empirical research—this course has kept on giving and giving, year in and year out across my career. The rigorous and pluralist training in theory Fogelman provided in that course, broadened to include issues of research design and theory testing when William Flanigan joined in teaching the third quarter of the course, proved essential to the movement across theoretical domains evident in this volume. My course on "Empirical Theories of Politics" at the University of Florida is an effort to make such an experience available to UF's doctoral students.

Fourth, let me thank several colleagues who were vital in the development of the work at critical moments. The essays in Part One benefitted from my close friendship and scholarly interaction with Richard L. Schott of the Lyndon B. Johnson School of Public Affairs. Together we co-authored *Congress and the Administrative State* (1979), an experience which deepened my appreciation of congressional–executive relations and my grasp of American political history. Edward Carmines of Indiana University-Bloomington aided my grasp of the interplay of elections, parties and congressional politics and also engaged with me in co-authoring Chapter Four in this volume, "Bicameralism in Congress." My great appreciation goes to Ted for his friendship and scholarly stimulation and for supporting the reprinting of our joint essay in this volume. I also benefited from collaboration with Gerry Wright and Leroy Rieselbach in planning the 1983 conference at Indiana University entitled "Congress and Policy Change" and co-editing with them the book that emerged from it (Wright, Rieselbach, and Dodd,

1986). The conference and the book allowed me to present the theoretical work in Part Two in a supportive environment. Let me note as well my great appreciation to Leroy Rieselbach for the mentoring he has provided me at critical points in my career. Finally, my appreciation goes to Cal Jillson for working with me in planning the 1992 conference at the University of Colorado on "The Dynamics of American Politics" and co-editing the two books that emerged from it (Dodd and Jillson 1994a, 1994b). The conference and books helped me formulate the ideas developed in Part Three, as seen in my essay from the conference, "Political Learning and Political Change" (Dodd, 1994).

Fifth, let me acknowledge the broad debt I owe to the universities and institutions in which I worked while developing these essays, together with colleagues and students at each. In doing so, let me note that the shifts in the questions and theoretical focus dominating my work largely parallel my movement across four of the nation's great public universities.

My decision to focus on Congress and the issue of change, the writing of "Quest," and then the first broad question challenging my cyclical perspective all came during my years at the University of Texas-Austin (1972–1980). The first two essays in Part One were written or drafted at UT-Austin. The two essays in Part Two were conceived and written during my years at Indiana University-Bloomington (1980–1986), a period which also saw me co-author the third essay in Part One, "Bicameralism in Congress," with Edward Carmines. The three essays in Part Three came during the nine years at the University of Colorado-Boulder (1986–1995). Finally, the two essays in Part Four together with the introductory essay came during my seventeen years (and counting) at the University of Florida in Gainesville (1995-present).

During service at and movement across these universities I also benefited from a Congressional Fellowship (1974–75), awarded by the American Political Science Association while at UT-Austin; a Hoover National Fellowship (1984–85) at Stanford while at IU-Bloomington; a University Fellowship (1993–94) while at UC-Boulder; and a Fellowship at the Woodrow Wilson International Center for Scholars in Washington, D.C. (2003–04) while at Florida.

It is doubtful that I could have engaged in the extensive shifts in theoretical perspective evident in the essays in this book without the movement across and stimulation provided by these four universities, together with the research opportunities provided by competitive national or university fellowships during my service at each. It is hard to know whether the shifts came because I moved, or I moved because I was going through a paradigmatic shift, or some of both. Whatever is true, my strong sense is that such academic moves open up great opportunities to see the world in new ways, with physical shifts in location unlocking one from established routines in one's life and thus opening the way for shifts away from habituated ways of thinking in one's work.

I am also convinced that I benefited in distinctive and essential ways from the environments, faculty and students of each university and am greatly appreciative of their contributions to the essays in this volume. Thus the roiling debates over political science underway in the Government Department at UT-Austin provided the stimulus I needed to broaden beyond my early rational choice orientation and consider the role of context in politics, as seen in Part One. Simultaneously, my interactions with the Lyndon B. Johnson School of Pubic Affairs and the LBJ Presidential Library, both on the Texas campus, enriched my grasp of contemporary American politics by introducing me to various movers and shakers of the time. The development of the partisan perspective on Congress in Part Two benefited from the open and stimulating intellectual environment at IU-Bloomington in the early to mid-1980s and from the presence of a large group of gifted legislative scholars and doctoral students involved in crafting a myriad of cutting edge perspectives on legislative behavior. During these years the experience at the Hoover Institution also helped shore up my comfort-level with the cyclical theory of change, with the Hoover economists, in particular, supportive of the essays in Part Two.

And then my movement in Part Three to look at the effect of ideas, innovation and human agency on congressional change was aided by the presence in the Colorado department of an array of faculty and doctoral students concerned with such issues as deliberation and discourse in politics, the role of ideas in the American founding, punctuated equilibriums in politics, and policy innovation in American politics. I benefited as well from the opportunity to create and teach the department's core doctoral seminar on "The Scope and Epistemologies of Political Science," which allowed me to grapple with epistemological issues created by the presence of contingency and indeterminacy in politics.

The development of the essays in Part Four, and the preparation of the introductory essay, benefited from the extraordinary opportunity I have had at the University of Florida to expand my role in graduate training. This has enabled me to teach "Congress" and "Scope and Epistemologies" and to create new courses on "Empirical Theories" and "American Legislative Development." Taken together, these courses aided the sharpening of my dynamic perspective on Congress and my ability to visualize politics in a more multidimensional manner. Along the way I have benefited from the strong and heterogeneous faculty in American Politics at UF, which includes substantial strength in political behavior and public policy as well as political institutions. My work has also been enhanced by the emergence at UF of a young, dynamic faculty across disciplinary fields in touch with the frontiers of the discipline and by the presence of a truly gifted group of doctoral students prepared to challenge themselves and me to ever higher standards of theoretical inquiry and empirical research.

The experience at the Woodrow Wilson International Center for Scholars likewise helped immensely, not only in getting me to Washington, D.C. and more in touch with the real world of early twenty-first century politics but also in engaging me with leading scholars in the nation. The group of political scientists and historians serving as Fellows during my year at WWICS was extraordinary in its breadth, depth and intelligence, and deeply probing in their responses to my work. "Congress as Public Mirror," the new project "Congress in a Downsian World," and the integrated perspective on my work presented in the Preface all have deep roots in my reading, group interactions and colloquia at the Center. I thus extend my great appreciation to Lee Hamilton, Phillippa Strum, Don Wolfensberger, and all the great people at WWICS during my year there.

Regrettably, I am unable to express appreciation here to all of the many people—students who challenged me in the classroom to address new dimensions of change as well as colleagues who supported and challenged and nudged me forward—across these universities and institutions. The list I have developed would constitute more than a page in this volume. Simply know that that my appreciation is continuous and heartfelt. And many of you find your way into acknowledgements in the enclosed essays. I have had a rare and stimulating journey across these great universities and institutions, a journey that seemed improbable if not impossible forty years ago. I am humbled by it and deeply appreciative of all the students and colleagues who fostered my passage along the way.

I must, of course, thank here individuals who helped insure the book's completion. Thus let me extend special thanks to my wonderful colleague, Beth Rosenson, for going way beyond the call of duty in vetting all new material published in this volume since I joined UF, including the essays in Part Four, the introduction, the abstracts, and the additional perspectives for each essay. I extend my deep appreciation as well to close friends Rodney Hero, Bryan Jones, Dianne Pinderhughes, Anne Pitcher, and Scot Schraufnagel for their invaluable support—over breakfast, lunch or dinner at various conferences and by phone or email—as I worked to complete this volume, raising my spirits when they lagged. Finally, senior doctoral student Josh Huder read and vetted the Preface and "Congress as Public Mirror" one last time immediately prior to my sending them to press, and Dr. Jordan Ragusa of the College of Charleston provided invaluable assistance in helping prepare the electronic manuscript for final submission. My great appreciation to both.

My great appreciation as well to the University of Florida for the competitive sabbatical leave that aided completion of the book manuscript, including the support for the sabbatical offered by my chair, Steve Craig, and by the Dean of Liberal Arts and Sciences, my fellow political scientist Paul D'Anieri. And my continuing thanks to my department colleagues and university for awarding me the Manning J. Dauer, Jr., Eminent Scholar Chair in 1995 and providing an environment where I could flourish over these years, with special thanks to Peggy Conway and Ken Wald for their roles in making all of this possible.

I also want to underscore how vital intimate friends and family have proved over the years this work was underway, and no more so than in this recent period. So my deep affection and great appreciation go to Cloyd and Robbie Dodd, to Michael, Mary, Rachel, Adrienne and John Dodd, to John and Andy Wotman and John's extended family, to Cheryl Staats and the extended Staats family, to

Carl and Linda Pierce and the extended Pierce family, to Allen Germano and Joan Fiore, to Cheryl and Randy Winter, to Lyle and Theresa Sherfey, to Jim Johnson and Susan Orr, to Ann Lane and Kevin True, to Kelly and Ray Barber, and to Chris and Helen Braider together with all of my friends in the Society of Friends in Boulder.

Finally, and at long last, I am in a position after almost four decades to dedicate this volume to the three individuals most critical in sustaining my energy, creativity and life force over most or all of the years in which the work gathered here emerged. My daughter Meredith was there from the beginning, just over a year in age on the 1974 journey to Washington and four years old when "Quest" was published. Her early words, "Papa go to Metro bus" still bring joy to my heart, as does her deep creativity and passion for life. My son Christopher entered my life a year after "Quest" and just in time to hear the phrase "Legitimation Crisis" bantered endlessly around the house. Cris has been blessed, and has blessed me, with life's most infectious smile, combined with a truly extraordinary capacity for friendship and empathy. And my wife Leslie Anderson and I joined together in mid-journey, with Leslie reading all of my published work as courtship ritual in the late 1980s and then bringing her incisive intellect, close editing and good humor to the critique of all subsequent essays. In the process she has held up before me that rarest of gifts, a true mirror. How fortunate I have been.

Boulder County, Colorado
July 4, 2011

Introduction

1

CONGRESS AS PUBLIC MIRROR

Congress is a deceptive institution.

A city unto itself, it rises luminous on Capitol Hill, towering above the teeming workaday life of Washington, D.C., monumental in appearance and steady in the beacon light of hope it provides the nation and the world. Strength, stability, grandeur, and permanence radiate outward, assuring us that America's noble experiment in representative self-government is alive and well. Our dreams of peace, prosperity, and progress for all appear safe and secure in the enlightened hands of the men and women—red and yellow, black and white; Jewish, Muslim, Christian, agnostic—who gather in the Capitol daily to do the work of the people. And indeed few experiences are as moving as driving slowly on a moonlit night from the Lincoln Memorial to the Reflecting Pool at the base of the Capitol where, pausing to glance upward, one can recall the great trials the nation has endured and the great promises it has fulfilled across two centuries of stewardship by this remarkable representative assembly.

Yet for anyone immersed in the daily life of Capitol Hill, a different reality slaps one in the face. At the sidewalk newsstands in the shadow of the Dome, headlines lament the nation's inability to end a dire social or moral injustice, a lingering war, egregious poverty, a deep recession or deficit spending because an entrenched power structure on Capitol Hill will not allow critical votes to proceed. Inside the newspaper an editorial laments a Congress impervious to electoral change owing to the special financial and political advantages of incumbency. In the bookstores on the Hill, proliferating with volumes on Congress old and new, the titles are bleak—*Congress on Trial, Congress: The Sapless Branch, Congress Against Itself, Congress Reconsidered, Congress as Public Enemy, Congress and the Decline of Public Trust, Congress: The Broken Branch.*[1] The books are filled with statistics certifying the high rate of incumbent victories and the low esteem in which citizens hold the institution; arguments that the legislators care only about reelection, personal power, and career advancement; predictions that Congress is in permanent decline; proposals that the nation should just cut its losses and embrace presidential government.

At congressional committee hearings lobbyists testify on behalf of well-heeled clients, as legislators interrupt to signal their approval of yet another tax break, anticipating corporate donations to their next election campaign. During floor deliberations the ten or fifteen members in attendance wander aimlessly, doze, or rifle through papers while a legislator drones on about the need for a "National Square Dance Day," a debate on the headlined issues nowhere to be heard. When debate does finally come it seems marked more by posturing and thirty-second sound bites than by a deliberative pursuit of mutual understanding and common ground. And far too often the nightly news reports another member indicted and possibly jailed for having served personal advantage and the moneyed interests rather than the people's interest and collective good.

On any given day, in snapshot form, Congress can seem less an ennobling and enduring temple of popular self-government than a tragi-comic farce—a farce in which protagonists and antagonists battle breathlessly on behalf of good and evil; inspiring soliloquies, humorous quips, and bitter barbs are flawlessly rendered; great elections are won, and great power is amassed; and yet nothing meaningful ever happens, nothing fundamental ever changes, nothing worthwhile ever emerges.

Amidst much ado about nothing, Congress appears as a comedie noir testifying to the profane avarice and tedious highhandedness that emerge when we humans—political animals all —give full and free rein to the self-serving and factious angels of our nature. One is left wondering whether to pay attention to it at all, whether Congress is worth the effort to understand it and take seriously the exercise of its constitutional authority.

There is, however, another way to probe the truth about Congress.

I Studying Congress I

Turn off CNN or Fox News and take a few minutes to clear your head before you rush to judgment. Let go of the need to idealize Congress and hold its members to noble standards that none of us can meet. Similarly, set aside the cynical certainty that the behavior of others—particularly politicians—is rooted solely in corrupt, self-serving motives and is thereby lacking in constructive potential.

Think for a moment about your deeper knowledge of yourself, your own complex psychology and behavior: your special blend of good intentions, aggressive impulses, self-serving rationalization, sensitive understanding of others, and personal self-absorption; your moments of sincerity, broken promises, frustrating failures, and sudden epiphanies of learning and self-correction.

Consider the difficulties you face in balancing, on the one hand, your desire to leave the world a bit better off than you found it and, on the other, your aspirations to better your own self in the world. Consider the stress you experience with life choices and problem-solving in the real world. Knowing the right thing to do, balancing your ideals and your self-interest, understanding and respecting others and their goals while attending to pursuit of your own can be tough out in the rough and tumble of daily experience.

Now hold on to this self-reflection and turn back again to Congress. Consider the realistic perspectives one might bring to the assessment of Congress and its members—should you grant it and them the humanity that you grant to yourself.

Perhaps its members struggle with the same conflicted tensions that you struggle with—the desire to do good in the world and the desire for personal security and self-advancement in their own life. As with you, your friends, your co-workers, their conflicted desires may be mutually intertwined. Doing good in the world, after all, can be closely linked to gaining some degree of personal security and self-advancement, with having the sustained opportunity, resources, and incentives for "doing good." Moreover, as with you and your associates, perhaps they come to understand with experience that "doing good" is itself an elusive goal, that one person or group cannot always know what "the good" really is, that listening to others with different views may raise questions and issues, generate useful perspectives, point towards common ground or mutually beneficial bargains that would never be seen as clearly by a solitary actor absorbed in his or her singular view of life.

The challenge for Congress and its members, as with all of us, is how to strike the balance: how to ensure that the pursuit of personal self-advancement by legislators also fosters the performance of the institution's critical tasks; how to enable legislators to present their own special perspective on good public policy, informed by the interests and ideologies of their constituents, while also encouraging members to consider the alternative perspectives of other members and their constituencies, thereby looking to the broad collective good beyond their narrow personal political considerations. They must find this balance amidst disorienting cross-pressures, shifting contexts, limited knowledge, and immense time constraints. As they confront these pressures and constraints, they also struggle with the same tendencies to become habituated in their behavior, stuck in their ideas and assumptions, and myopic in their perspectives that characterize you and me. As with us, they too often hold to old certainties and outmoded mindsets even amidst unforeseen problems that require thinking in new ways and embracing new understandings of social reality.

With them as with us, change comes hard, often requiring crisis and personal challenge, patience and risk, mutual cooperation and long-term commitment. As with us in our private lives and personal choices, they in their public roles engage in trial and error experimentation, trying one approach to problem-solving, coalition-building, institutional politics, or national governance and then another, balancing self-interest, public responsiveness, moral vision, and close attentiveness to "what works."

Seeing Congress through the reflected mirrors of our own self-awareness, it becomes less difficult to understand why it is such a deceptive institution. It is deceptive at least in part because we humans are complex and conflicted beings, desirous of doing good yet tending towards self-aggrandizement—quite often doing good primarily for ourselves unless called to task for it by others. And it is also deceptive because its tasks are enormously challenging and multifaceted, so that at any given moment it does truly seem engaged in political actions, institutional processes, and policy prescriptions totally at cross-purposes with one another as members balance contending concerns and pressures.

What is difficult to understand is why anyone would entrust such a demanding task as governing a large nation-state to a representative assembly that relies for its selection and its operation on humans as complex and frail as you and I are. And how could such an institution, even if invented and effectively employed by a very special generation operating amid very special conditions, survive and adapt as its gifted founders fade away, as new and unforeseen conditions arise, and as lesser mortals such as you and I come on the scene?

II Why Congress?

The genius of American democracy, and the genesis of America's Congress, lies in the clear-headed recognition by the nation's founders of the complexities of human nature.[2] Recognizing both our vain, self-serving, self-centered, combative propensities and our virtuous, self-corrective, sociable, cooperative capacities, they took a nuanced approach to crafting a governing regime. Left to our own solitary and singular devices, without some form of governing process to mediate among us, we seemed prone to dissolve into civil strife, perhaps even into a war of all against all, as Hobbes had written.[3] Thus government appeared necessary. Yet placing the power to establish and maintain order in the hands of an autonomous and all-powerful monarch or dictator risked leaving our fate to the aggrandizing tendencies of someone just as human and frail as we are, an imperious or willful or insecure or arrogant Caesar who, feeling thwarted in desires or opportunistic in ambitions, might turn the sword against the citizens rather than protect and nurture them.

Given the deeply engrained complexity of humans—not just a few of us, or most of us, but all of us—they envisioned no such thing as a benevolent despot—not even a benevolent elected king chosen from among themselves. With age and experience individuals may grow somewhat broader and more tempered in perspective and awareness, but no one fully outgrows private ambitions, willfulness, or the capacity for arbitrary and self-serving action. Thus relying on the one to govern the many seemed foolhardy. But given humans' sociable nature as well as self-interested concerns, perhaps the many could be brought together in a virtual if not literal assembly of citizens and empowered to govern themselves collectively, as a way to avoid tyranny by the one and ensure a measure of order, peace, and even prosperity for all.

Faced with history's dire testimony as to the aggrandizing qualities of rule by a powerful executive, our forebears set out on a distinctly new path—a path that sought to utilize our individual complexities and frailties as the basis for designing a constitutional order in which we might all flourish—transforming our separate weakness into a collective strength. They determined to place the central mediational roles and policymaking capacities of government in an assembly of elected representatives, with no pretense that they were divinely ordained and endowed with special select qualities. Their legitimacy would come, instead, from their election and reelection by us, with American democracy trusting to the capacity of the people to discern who best among them could adequately perform these mediative roles.[4] These representatives would mirror the composition of society at large—reflecting our divisions of perceived self-interest and also our contentiousness, fleeting passions, deceitfulness and shams, even our obsession with personal security and autonomy of action. Yet they would also mirror our inherent capacity to learn through experience and example, to reason and talk things out, to understand and bond with one another in communities of mutual regard and shared interests.[5] And, when confronted with dangers to public wellbeing, they would work to balance short-term personal and factional desires with long-term and generalized interests, much as we do in our private worlds.[6] The path to a meaningful, secure, and mutually enhancing peace among the individuals within society came in trusting that such representatives could meet in a powerful collective assembly, effectively mediate societal differences, and govern in a more just, effective, responsive, and broadly accepted manner than would result from reliance on a single executive.[7]

Key to this experiment was the founders' perception, as articulated by James Madison in Federalist #10, that we humans could best be seen within the public realm not as solitary individuals possessed of unique and separate interests but as factions of citizens, with each faction composed of individuals sharing similar interests. Thus the task of mediation within society did not involve deliberation among all individuals, a process that could be impossible on a national scale, but mediation among elected representatives of society's factions. The choice facing the founders was not between an executive dictator and anarchy. Rather, it included as well the possibility of constructing a government that would bring together representatives of the distinct factions of society and, in fostering effective mediation among them within a well-designed Congress, could prove more effective and legitimate than any previous national government in history.[8]

Implicit in this vision was a sense that citizens possessed numerous salient concerns and that these concerns would cut across the citizenry in complex ways, creating "a complex weave of interests."[9] Citizens of New England would not be opposed in all respects to those of the Middle Atlantic nor to those from the South. Rather, concerns about religion, social class, inland agriculture versus seacoast trade, and so forth would create numerous factional groups within and across regions. Ideally, there would be no majority faction, composed of totally like-minded citizens distinctly different from all other citizens and prepared to tyrannize the rest. Rather, the members of any given faction would look out on a society in which each individual in the faction also shared some concerns with citizens from other factions. These cross-cutting ties would bind various members of one faction with members of other factions, thereby facilitating empathic understanding and mutual regard. This intermingling of factions would "strengthen the Union of the Whole," as Madison put it, tying it together, stabilizing it, and providing it the time and conditions necessary for Congress to generate compromise on difficult societal issues.[10]

Also central to the founders' vision, as it came into clearer relief through deliberation and national debate, was an agreement that the civil liberties of all actors in the public realm would be respected and protected. This agreement applied even to those holding minority positions and losing out in elections to Congress or during mediation and policy choice within it. Politics would be an iterative game, in which winners and losers would live to contend among themselves another day, with no point reached at which the rights of one group could be so threatened as to upend their lives and liberties. An electoral calendar would be formalized and honored, no matter what the contingencies of the moment, so that elected representatives could be held accountable in the next election for how well their mediated solutions worked in practice. The assembly could be renovated across time through the selection of new members and through the emergence of new leadership teams and organizational arrangements more attentive to and responsive to the citizens.

With the rights of all citizens respected and the security of all assured, our forebears hoped that citizens and factions would commit to the legitimacy of conflict mediation through legislative bargaining, negotiation, and decision making, rather than taking their grievances to the battlefield. They would do so because mediation in legislative assembly, even should it take considerable periods of time to produce broadly acceptable changes, would be preferable to the costs of civil strife.

Our elected Congress exists not because the founders expected that its members would be better than the rest of us, but because they believed our representatives would be very much like us. They could represent our grievances, express our contentious and passionate feelings, barter hard for our separate positions, hear each other out over and over again like an extended family returning to well-trod grievances, hoping that some breakthrough might yet allow a reduction of mutual animosities and movement forward on shared interests. Of course, the founders knew that family stories do not always have happy endings, that resolution of deep strife often requires the patience of Job, and that failure is a distinct possibility, followed by the dissolution of family ties. Creating a Congress was no guarantee of effective governance and national survival, but it seemed a better path than the governing systems of the past.

They hoped that, with patience and reasoning, with forbearance and empathy, with the coming of a new leadership team or a new generation, with the recognition of old errors and discovery of new ways of thinking, breakthroughs would occur and progress would be made on the issues of the day. With success, Congress would work in the short-run, survive into a next generation, and perhaps prove sufficiently adaptable and successful in its tasks as to generate a deep and abiding loyalty among citizens that could sustain it in perpetuity thereafter.

The question for the founders was whether the creation of a Congress was sufficient to ensure effective representative government and a viable nation-state. Should the Constitution simply empower Congress, and leave it to invent ancillary institutions a government might require, as they proved necessary, or should the Constitution spell out such institutional arrangements?

III Congress and the Constitutional Design

Because representative government built around a strong policy-making assembly was a new development in the late eighteenth century, the founders could not know how Congress would operate in practice, and they were apprehensive about leaving the fate of the national government solely in its hands. They had thousands of years of experience with executive rule, under numerous guises and in varied contexts, with which to gauge how centralized rule by an all-powerful leader proceeds. This experience left them with little doubt as to the long-term aggrandizing and tyrannical tendencies of individual rule, however benevolent any one ruler might seem in the moment. It was for this reason that they sought to avoid monarchy or any form of executive government, looking instead to Congress for policy leadership and social mediation. Yet the dynamic tendencies of legislative assemblies were an open question.

The historical record provided little guidance in determining whether and when such an assembly might pose tyrannical threats to public liberty, particularly when invested with the kind of enumerated powers and policy-making roles they intended to give to Congress. The founders thus found themselves largely on their own,[11] attempting to learn from recent experiences on American soil as they sought to craft a government built around a national representative assembly.

The Continental Congress under the Articles of Confederation had demonstrated no tendency towards tyranny, but then it had been virtually devoid of leadership and unable to mediate or act, with its members being unelected and its explicit powers quite weak.[12] However, strong Speakers had emerged in some elected state legislatures, raising the possibility that a legislative assembly could yield its own version of one-man rule.

Of particular concern to the founders was the prospect that a demagogue could unite a majority of the legislature to act rapidly and rashly in response to citizen passions, bringing instability into government and imposing poorly considered and unwise legislation. Such a legislative dictator might use control of the Congress to engage in majority tyranny over a minority, possibly appealing to the mass citizenry to convince the legislature to support redistribution of property, for example. Rather than the legislature being a forum for the mediation of societal conflicts among citizens and factions, it could become a power base from which a legislative dictator, empowered by popular support and the legislature's acquiescence, could exploit social divisions and consolidate personal control of government.

The great question for the founders was whether a tendency to one-man rule would be likely to arise in the American Congress. And were it to be prone toward legislative dictatorship, how best should they proceed in defusing such tendencies?

As they considered these issues, the founders believed it was essential to give the Congress control of the purse, and substantial policy-making authority, so that it could operate as a serious mediator of national conflicts and enact meaningful national policies, as in the area of interstate and foreign commerce. And its members should be elected so that it could adequately represent the relevant factions of the nation and be seen as a legitimate instrument of social mediation and national governance. The experience with the Continental Congress had convinced them of these necessities. But the Continental Congress also had shown them how difficult it could be to attract and keep hard-working members in a national assembly at a time when there were limited transportation and communication facilities to aid close connection with home and family. Most legislators also needed to attend to plantations, farms, and local business for their livelihoods and to sustain their families. Additionally, local and state concerns dominated social and political life in the agrarian world of the late eighteenth century, especially the regulation of intra-state commerce and the building of local infrastructure, so that there were good reasons for public servants to concentrate their attention on service in state legislatures and local government. With few politicians willing and able to spend time attending to the business of a national legislature, the national assembly might be especially prone to dominance by a central leader and a few lieutenants.

A skillful legislative leader, popular with citizens, dominating distant and inattentive congressional colleagues, controlling the power of the purse, and with the capacity to raise a national army, could wield the authority of the national government as a powerful sword and lead a new social and political revolution. Even were tendencies toward strong legislative leadership to stop short of military rule, one could imagine a Congress pushed hither and yon session by session, as new passions arose in the public sphere, as new elections brought new majorities into Congress, and as new powerful Speakers and leadership teams dominated the assembly. Such developments could introduce continuous processes of radical policy change into Congress and political destabilization into the national government.

Faced with the prospect of a national Congress characterized by continuous and rapid change, and with a tendency towards legislative dictatorship always looming in the background, the founders chose to design a Constitution characterized by two powerful countervailing tendencies. It would empower the Congress to mediate social conflicts and craft public policy, making it the first branch of government, the institution possessed of specific enumerated powers, and the institution most reflective of the people in their vast regional, economic, and social diversity. Congress would be the central policy-making institution of American democracy. Yet simultaneously, the Constitution would constrain the capacity of Congress to move rapidly, rashly, and unilaterally in doing the people's work and imposing its decisions on the nation.

Seeking both to empower popular representative government and to restrain it, the founders constructed the elaborate system of dispersed and mutually constraining powers that has survived now for more than two centuries. This system includes enumerated powers for the Congress, separation of the executive and judicial powers from the legislature, checks and balances between the branches of government, and federal division of policy responsibilities and governing authority.

With this constitutional design, legislative power at the national level was accorded to Congress, but with the president as chief executive and the Supreme Court within the judicial branch able to check and constrain the Congress in a variety of ways. These checks included presidential veto of legislation and, as the power of the judiciary evolved, judicial review of legislation. Similarly, federalism left states intact and engaged in overseeing most governing activities affecting the daily lives of citizens, thereby acting as constraints on the reach of Congress and the national government.

Additionally, both to build internal constraints within the Congress and to address important issues of state representation and power, the Constitution created a bicameral Congress in which the House of Representatives and the Senate would have to agree on legislation for it to become law. Moreover, the House of Representatives would be elected directly by the enfranchised citizens of a state, with the number of seats accorded to each state determined by state population. But the Senate was to be chosen by states, two members per state and according to procedures created by each state, with no provision for direct election of senators by enfranchised citizens.

Public officials from across different branches and levels of government would compromise and converge on viable policy plans and government programs in order to sustain the political system in which they had accrued great personal power, just as social factions would compromise or even accept defeat in the moment in order to sustain a political system that protected their basic rights and liberties. Particularly on serious, system-threatening issues, or so the founders hoped, all factions and institutional elites would approach the bargaining table prepared to mediate, negotiate and compromise in good faith, recognizing that they were better off keeping the system intact and working within it. However serious the issue at hand, the ultimate inducement to sealing collective bargains and moving the nation forward thus would be the desire among all factions and institutional elites to ensure the survival of the collective processes of mediation, negotiation, and shared governance—lest they otherwise face a breakdown in the system, a dissolution of governing authority, and the anarchy and social strife which would follow.

It would be sustained deadlock and disorder, not the sudden capture of governing power by a dictator, that would threaten the persistence of such a dispersed system of governing power. This reality provides strong inducement to bargaining and compromise, but an inducement operating within very special political conditions and constitutional parameters.

The driving force of the bargaining system would be the Congress, where enumerated policy powers and broadly representative processes of democratic legitimacy were vested and where day-to-day political leadership was assumed to reside. But Congress, its leaders, and their mediated solutions would necessarily be tempered by practical realities.

Far from wanting a Congress that could respond rapidly to the majoritarian concerns of a broadly represented mass public, the founders sought a government that would move with deliberate speed in addressing the issue concerns of a relatively privileged electorate, largely composed of white and propertied men. Congress thus would carefully mediate conflicts—attending closely to the rights of minority factions within that electorate; respecting the roles, authority, and constraints imposed by other branches and levels of government, with special regard for the states; and demonstrating dutiful deference to the dominant social structures and cultural mores within and across the diverse regions of the nation. Stability, order, and freedom—freedom from majority tyranny and from radical experimentation, as well as freedom from the tyranny of a dictator—were paramount concerns.

The constitutional system would work, the founders assumed, because they as practical men of politics had carefully crafted it to fit with political and societal realities they expected to persist far into the distant future. They foresaw the nation changing gradually in its social arrangements and issue conflicts while remaining closely linked to its rural roots, agricultural base, and contemporary technologies. They also expected that the new nation would remain closely linked to the Eastern seaboard, with Jefferson musing that it would take a thousand years to explore and populate the great continent extending before them. The social issues of the foreseeable future would thus be similar to the immediate past and the social bases of politics would be similar in their relatively elitist character to those evident in the regional power structures of their time.

In reality, already rumbling under their feet were great social revolutions that would repeatedly test the adaptive capacities of Congress and the constitutional order. On the American continent citizens embraced the ethos of equality and democracy and, believing themselves to be as good as any man, looked west-ward toward unfettered opportunity.[13] Propelled by equality of opportunity, they began the great march toward the Pacific Ocean, which they would complete in less than a century, leaving great cities and scattered outposts of civilization along the way. In the process, as detailed by Alexis de Tocqueville,[14] they created a far more radical and egalitarian conception of democracy than the founders thought possible or desirable. And on the British Isles, a fascination with the mechaniza-tion of industrial production was generating innovations that would transform agrarian society world-wide, opening up new conceptions of mass production of agricultural and industrial goods, mass transportation of individuals, and mass communication within societies and across nations.[15] With these innovations, new kinds of factional conflicts, issue concerns, and citizen aspirations would emerge on the American continent, together with new kinds of politics and new expectations of government.

Would the Congress be up to unforeseen challenges beyond the founders' imagining? Would an institution designed to govern an agrarian society of limited suffrage adapt effectively to a radical egalitarian conception of democracy and to an increasingly industrial and then postindustrial world?

IV The Puzzle of Congressional Change

The puzzle of congressional change—whether the Congress can adapt to shifting contexts in ways sufficient to the challenges of the time—has haunted the nation across the subsequent two centuries of existence, pressing in upon it yet again in our own time. The repeated concern has been with whether or not Congress, faced not only with constitutional constraints but with vastly different social con-ditions and policy dilemmas from those envisioned by the founders, can change in a sufficiently rapid, responsive, and appropriate manner to ensure the mediation of pressing conflicts and fulfillment of its democratic purpose.

In the first 40 to 50 years, Congress experienced periods of relatively assertive Speakers in the House of Representatives and utilized political parties in organiz-ing majority and minority forces to aid internal governance and policy making.[16] The founders might well have considered both developments to be validations of their fear of centralized leadership and a tendency to majority tyranny. Yet Congress also created a committee system that dispersed policy-crafting and over-sight responsibilities among members in ways that somewhat attenuated power centralization as strong leaders and activist parties emerged; and the House and Senate embraced early rules and procedures to bring some order to deliberations, moving toward the protection of minority rights amid majority rule.[17] Addition-ally, the Senate reconstituted itself into a more democratic institution than the founders had planned, adjusting to the democratic ethos that swept the nation in the decades following the founding era.[18] And the states moved steadily to remove property qualifications for voting among white men, so that Congress began to reflect a truer cross-section of society and respond to a broader array of factional concerns.[19] Across these decades Congress succeeded initially in stabilizing the national government and moving it to the District of Columbia, rebuilding and reasserting itself after the War of 1812, addressing the issue of slavery in the Missouri Compromise (it hoped for generations to come), and fostering a period of great national expansion.[20]

Yet somewhere in the late 1830s or early 1840s it seemed as if time shifted into fast-forward mode. The combined effects of the industrial revolution and westward trek pushed North and South forward on rapidly different developmental paths in their economies, social structures, and ideologies.[21] The free population of the North grew more rapidly than the South's, yet the slave states of the South and border region exercised power in Congress beyond their proportion of the nation's free population. This disproportionate power owed both to the guarantee of two seats to each state in the Senate, regardless of population size, and to the "peculiar" system of proportional representation created by the Constitution, which counted each slave as three-fifths of a person for apportioning seats to states in the House of Representatives.

Amid rising regional tensions, and seeking to forge yet another compromise over slavery in 1850, Congress struggled over whether it had the authority to regulate slavery, or even to discuss it. The old party system of Whigs versus Democrats teetered and then collapsed, loosening the political bonds holding North and South together. A new "replacement" party emerged in the North in the mid-1850s, the Republican Party, fueled by growing opposition to slavery. The South, surveying the shifting demographics in the nation and unnerved by the Republican Abraham Lincoln's capture of the presidency in 1860, became convinced that it was no longer better off inside the Union, mediating its differences with northern factions, than outside of it.

The subsequent Civil War, taking six hundred thousand lives, demonstrated the costs that can accrue when Congress fails to fulfill its mediating roles on the critical national issues of an era. The terrible cost of the Civil War highlighted how vital it is for Congress to possess the clear authority and governing processes by which to address national issues and how essential it is that Congress accurately reflect emerging policy divisions within the citizenry. Instead, reflecting southern slave interests in magnified dimensions, and divided over issues of constitutional authority, the antebellum Congress failed to heed the growing northern opposition to slavery until it was too late.

The victory of Union forces on the battlefield asserted the sovereignty of the national government over the states, and in doing so reasserted the mediative role of Congress. The Fifteenth Amendment to the Constitution, enacted during Reconstruction, prohibited the states and federal government from limiting citizens' voting rights "on account of race, color, or previous condition of servitude," signaling thereby a dawning awareness that the nation should attend to the participatory rights of citizens in order that Congress more accurately reflect festering factional conflicts within society. Yet these were merely the opening rounds in the struggle to clarify the actual authority Congress could draw upon in addressing national policy issues and in determining who should be accorded rights of participation in national politics.

Over the coming century and a half, and particularly during the Great Depression of the 1930s and World War II, the enumerated powers of Congress would be interpreted in an ever broader manner, amid elbowing and bargaining among the institutions of government, so that the policy reach of the national government would expand into virtually all sectors of domestic life.[22] And step by step, from the Progressive era through the Liberal Democratic era of the 1960s and 1970s, reform movements would push the separate states and the nation to broaden citizen participation in politics.[23] This action included state moves to ensure secrecy of the ballot and fairness of election processes, Constitutional amendments to provide for popular election of senators and women's suffrage, and national statutory and constitutional moves to ensure civil rights and practical enfranchisement of all adult citizens, regardless of race or ethnicity, so long as they were at least eighteen years old.

At least in principle, Congress appeared increasingly able to mirror and mediate the emerging national conflicts of the day, however complex and daunting they might appear. Yet just as such developments seemed to assure the ability of Congress to change in response to new policy challenges, unforeseen dilemmas emerged that threatened its adaptive capacities in new and potentially fatal ways.

The first dilemma centered on the ways in which the growing power of the national government altered the calculus of political ambitions within the nation.[24] Once the Civil War made clear the dominance of the national government, turnover among members of Congress began to decline, with ambitious politicians preferring to build their political careers in Washington, where the power and action were, and with the city machines and constituents anxious to keep them there so as better to serve localized interests.

Wanting respect for their own expertise in specialized areas within congressional committees, and also seeking the freedom to respond to special localized interests of their districts and states, members moved during the first decade of the twentieth century to constrain the power of congressional parties and party leaders. This effort resulted, most famously, in the success of progressive insurgents in the House of Representatives in stripping the Speakership of its major powers in 1910, a move that caught Speaker Joe Cannon and virtually all political observers off-guard.[25] By the 1920s members of Congress had put in place a system of committee government, spreading power and autonomy widely among themselves in ways that created a highly decentralized institution. In doing so, they upended the centralized leadership processes that had helped Congress mediate factional conflicts and perform its policy-making roles.[26]

The second dilemma emerged as the growing power of the national government began to alter constituents' expectations of their representatives in Congress. There had always been individualized and local dimensions to the representative function of national legislators, starting with the benefits given by Congress to veterans of the Revolutionary War.[27] But following the Civil War and mounting thereafter, the ways in which the national government could impact individuals and localities increased substantially. For example, it determined the benefits for widows and orphans as well as for veterans of the War, and decided on the location and regulation of railroads.[28] Additionally, particularly from the turn of the twentieth century onward, members of Congress came to have personal offices and some staff assistance on Capitol Hill. These developments increased their capacity to answer constituent letters and meet with them in Washington, thereby staying attuned to their personal concerns. They also increased members' ability, either personally or working through staff members, to serve as intermediaries between constituents and the national government, contacting government agencies on behalf of constituents to insure that they respond to constituent inquiries and concerns.

With these varied developments, citizens increasingly came to see members of Congress as their "special agents" in Washington, responsible for providing personal services to them as individuals and providing their districts and states with federal largesse.[29] By the 1920s close observers of Congress such as George Rothwell Brown saw such developments as threatening Congress's capacity to fulfill its constitutional roles, diverting attention of members from their critical legislative work. This potential, present but muted in the first decades of the century, became pronounced in the aftermath of the Great Depression and World War II.

In the 1930s and 1940s, in the effort to save the nation from economic collapse and military defeat, the national government so expanded its roles in the life of the nation that political scientist Theodore Lowi,[30] writing three decades later, argued that this period should be considered the start of America's Second Republic. In this new world, apprehensions about Congress and its continuing role as a powerful representative increased substantially. The expansion of federal government programs brought with it a vastly increased opportunity for legislators and their staffs to focus their energies on serving as special agents, working to ensure that their constituents received maximum federal benefits, from social security and veterans' benefits to local military bases. Their personal incentive was reelection: the more services they provided their constituents the better their chances of returning for another term. But what about the consequences of these developments for the Congress and its historic policy-making roles? Would it take seriously its expanded responsibility to address new and pressing national issues, mediating effectively among the contending factions committed to different perspectives on government priorities? Or would it become preoccupied with the politics of constituency service?

From James MacGregor Burns' 1949 work, *Congress on Trial*, to E. Scott Adler's *Why Congressional Reforms Fail* in 2002, the dominant scholarly interpretation of Congress that emerged in the postwar era stressed legislators' growing focus on shoring up their reelection security through preoccupation with local constituency concerns.[31] In Burns's pithy phrase, this preoccupation was seen as "the root evil," undercutting all efforts at institutional change and reform in Congress and inhibiting its capacity to focus on national policy issues.[32]

The reelection perspective took center stage in political science with the 1974 publication of *Congress: The Electoral Connection*, by David Mayhew. A speculative theory of what Congress would look like, were we to suspend disbelief and see its members as "single-minded seekers of reelection," *The Electoral Connection* came to be seen by many if not most students of Congress as a description of what the institution was really like.[33] In this view, members of Congress spent much if not most of their time advertizing themselves to constituents through use of the resources of their office and claiming credit for government benefits through their roles as special constituent servants in Washington. Insofar as they focused on Congress as an institution, they were committed to maintaining a decentralized and poorly coordinated congressional structure designed to aid their service to their separate constituencies, rather than addressing the government's expanded policy responsibilities for the nation at large.

Initial support for Mayhew's arguments came from Morris Fiorina, in *Congress: Keystone of the Washington Establishment*, published in 1977.[34] Fiorina made a compelling case that the postwar decline in the competitiveness of congressional elections owed to the growth in the federal government and to the consequent capacity of members of Congress to engage in constituent service activities, giving them the opportunity to claim credit for the particularized benefits that constituents received from the government.[35] The members' increased attention to casework, Fiorina argued, generated an incumbent advantage in reelection campaigns, a phenomenon previously highlighted by congressional scholar Robert Erikson.[36] In this view, as expanded by Cain, Ferejohn, and Fiorina,[37] citizens were increasingly casting "personal votes" for incumbents out of appreciation for good constituent service, irrespective of other considerations. Projecting these results into the future, students of American politics began to foresee the growing irrelevance of agenda politics in elections to Congress, an obliteration of party competition in congressional elections, and the institutionalization of Democrats, as the party of the service state, in permanent control of Congress, particularly in the House of Representatives.[38]

Congress appeared to be sliding into long-term irrelevance as a policy-making body, unable to mirror the public's views on the great issues of the day because of the new character of electoral politics, and unable to mediate among differing public factions because constituency service concerns reinforced the decentralized nature of Congress. Congress seemed forever mired in the politics of constituency service, unable to reform itself in order to regain its governing capacity, constrain power aggrandizement by the executive, and reassert its policy relevance. Nor were citizens likely to demand that it do so through voting for better long-term institutional performance on national policy issues, given their desire for the immediate delivery of particularized constituent service benefits.

As argued by scholars such as Burns and Samuel P. Huntington,[39] the only recourse for protecting the welfare of the nation as a whole appeared to be through yielding policy-making power to a strong executive, the presidency, selected through the one national election process that might focus on national issues of collective well-being. Embraced by much of the public,[40] this argument reinforced a fascination with presidential government that had engulfed the discipline of political science and the nation at large from the presidency of Franklin Roosevelt onward. It also undercut serious attention to the resilient qualities of the Congress and to the substantial roles it had played in initiating, crafting and enacting the policy innovations associated with the New Deal and New Frontier/Great Society eras.[41]

During the subsequent decades of research into the electoral connection, scholars have repeatedly documented the pervasive nature of reelection concerns and incumbent advantage among postwar members of Congress, leaving no doubt that legislators' reelection obsession is a central influence on the contemporary Congress.[42] Nor is there much doubt that the incumbent advantage that has emerged during the postwar years has introduced a substantial drag factor into efforts at reform and institutional adaptation.[43]

Yet despite the ubiquitous nature of reelection concerns among postwar legislators, the Congress has engaged in repeated reform of the institution over the past sixty-five years. The implementation of extensive centralizing reforms during the 1970s led Brookings scholar James Sundquist to write of the "resurgence" of Congress.[44] Subsequently, there has been more meaningful party competition for control of Congress than appeared conceivable within the arguments propounded by electoral incentive theorists, with such competitiveness highlighted by the Republican takeover of the Senate in 1980, the Democrats' resurgence in the Senate in 1986, the Republican takeover of Congress in 1994, the Democrats' return to power in 2006, and then the Republicans' return to control of the House of Representatives in 2010. Moreover, this inter-party competition has involved considerable debate over the institutional performance and policy directions of Congress.[45] Finally, while the postwar Congress has witnessed periods of policy deadlock, it also has seen substantial phases of landmark policy innovation.[46]

So what is the truth about the contemporary Congress? Is it entrapped in permanent and irreversible decline, despite surviving the great challenges it overcame in the nineteenth and early twentieth centuries? Or does it maintain capacities for adaptation, offering hope for the persistence of representative government? These are the central issues raised by the essays in this volume.

V Legislators, Constituents, and the Changing Congressional Context

The enclosed essays argue that the fate of the contemporary Congress, and thus the future of America's democracy, remains an open question. The future remains open, subject not only to grievous threats that can upend Congress but to ongoing opportunities for institutional resilience and resurgence, because processes of change and transformation are deeply engrained within it, today as in past historical eras. Moreover, these processes are particularly powerful in the contemporary era owing to the paradoxical effect that the growth in the power and responsibilities of the national government has had on the politics of Congress.

The increased policy reach of the national government has not only increased the difficulties with which Congress must contend, including the difficulties that legislators' reelection obsession creates for it. The growing role of government also has vastly increased legislators' capacity to exercise influence on the vital policy issues confronting the nation and citizens' capacity to shape the broad direction of the nation on these issues through their votes for legislators and their lobbying of Congress.

Largely unconstrained by great constitutional controversies over the policy-making authority of the national government, and with a broader array of citizens enfranchised and able to participate in congressional elections than ever before, contemporary legislators and citizens have an extraordinary opportunity to use government to address national policy dilemmas, if only they can get their collective act together. Moreover, there is good reason to believe that legislators and citizens will rise to the challenges facing them, enabling Congress to find its way forward into the future.

In making these arguments, the essays ask you to think about Congress and congressional change, as did Madison and the founders, by focusing on the broader political aspirations of legislators and the broader policy concerns of citizens. As in Madison's day, politicians enter public life in order to influence the great issues shaping the lives, liberties, and general welfare of citizens, particularly the citizens they represent. Thwarted in this quest, a lifetime of reelection becomes a meaningless charade.[47] And citizens engage in the public sphere seeking to foster those government actions that enhance long-term life opportunities for themselves, their loved ones, and their communities of shared interest—opportunities without which the occasional receipt of casework benefits dissolves into fool's gold.[48]

The broader goals of autonomous personal influence and long-term life enhancement were the ones dominating the public sphere in the late eighteenth century, as epitomized in the lives of the founders and their citizen cohorts, goals sufficient to justify fighting a revolution. And they are still the goals that dominate it, sufficient to justify expanding, refining and reformulating the roles of national government amid depression, amid grievous threats to national security, and amid global financial collapse. It is not the goals of politicians or of constituents that have changed across the past two hundred and twenty years of national life. It is the context within which they pursue those goals that has changed.

The fundamental truth of the postwar years is that, while the American Congress may remain imperfect in its representational character, and its authority may be under siege within the separation-of-powers system in which it operates, it is today the most powerful national representative assembly in the history of the world, with extraordinary policy reach, constitutional authority, and actual influence on the life of the nation and on the international community.

The vastly increased policy reach of Congress, coming in response to industrialization and globalization, has ensured that it is composed of large numbers of ambitious legislators who seek to make a difference in national policy-making through the acquisition and exercise of personal power and influence within Congress. These legislators do attend closely to reelection politics, both to stay attuned to the constituencies they represent and to stay in the power game on the Hill, with the desire to stay in office and in pursuit of power accentuated by the extensive policy influence members can exercise through career advancement within the Congress. In attending to reelection, they give great attention not just to credit-claiming and personal advertising but also to the positions they take on the policy issues salient to their constituents, as Mayhew also argues in *Congress: The Electoral Connection*.[49] Because innumerable issues are salient in light of the vast roles and responsibilities of the federal government, they engage in position-taking on a vast array of issues. As a result, contemporary legislators probably mirror their constituents' values, priorities, and interests more closely and act to honor their positions once in office more fully[50] than ever in the past, aided by technological innovations in transportation, information availability, and survey research.[51]

Given the range, complexity, and changing saliency of national problems, issue-based politics poses a particular danger to incumbents, since challengers can always find an explosive hot-button topic around which to fashion an effective campaign, perhaps aided by a controversial roll call vote cast by a member. Such reelection dangers encourage incumbents to embrace the constituency service opportunities available to them, in an effort to generate personal loyalty from constituents that may help counterbalance the difficulties associated with issue politics. Members thus have become quite adept at constituency service. But members of Congress view constituent service not as the essence of their legislative life, but as a way to help defuse dangers that position-taking can pose to career advancement, providing them some leeway on the policy positions they take as they pursue careers on Capitol Hill.[52]

The essence of members' work in the Congress comes in their concentration on acquiring positions of power within committees and party caucuses, gaining mastery of policy-making skills and leadership roles, and engaging in the exercise of influence on major and controversial national issues.[53] In order to acquire real power and exercise substantial policy influence, members seek to ensure that the political party to which they belong gains and maintains majority control of their chamber within Congress, since the majority party controls organizational resources in each chamber.[54] They also seek to ensure that a sufficient number of positions of power and influence are available within the committee system and party organizations, so that they have a realistic chance to gain and exercise power, an effort that gives members considerable personal incentive to support a decentralized organizational structure. This push is reinforced by the ways in which a decentralized organizational structure helps divide up the workload of Congress, as Joseph Cooper reminds us,[55] a workload that is particularly crushing in light of the responsibility of the modern Congress to craft policies across a broad array of issue areas and to oversee bureaucratic implementation of the policies.[56] The push towards power decentralization is further reinforced by the ways in which reelection incentives encourage a decentralized congressional structure.

The momentum towards power decentralization in Congress is a strong one, but it ultimately operates amid substantial countervailing pressures. Legislators and their parties must resolve intra-institutional conflicts on policy issues, so that their hard work pays off in actual policy impact. The resolution of internal conflict and the push to policy enactment amid complex policy issues requires centralized leadership, coordination, and compromise.[57] Moreover, legislators must engage in oversight and surveillance of the laws they enact, which again requires attention to coherent rather than conflictive strategies of legislative action.[58] And the legislators and their parties must resolve external conflicts with the executive, who can block legislation unless two-thirds of the members of both houses vote to override his veto.[59] The ability of Congress to negotiate forcefully with the president or override a veto requires strong leaders who can engage effectively in such negotiation; it also requires strong support for Congress from the nation's citizens, support that comes from a history of effective policy-making.

Members of the contemporary Congress thus must balance an enormous array of concerns in order to exercise influence, including attention not only to their electoral security but also to their access to power within the institution, to the capacity of their party to gain and hold control of Congress, and to the policy-making capacity and popular legitimacy of the institution. As members grapple with these multiple countervailing pressures and demands, the expanded policy roles of the federal government in national life help ensure that constituents, or some substantial portion of them, are paying close attention. Their attentiveness is aided by the extraordinary access to information about Congress provided to citizens through the telecommunication and internet revolutions of the contemporary era.[60]

Citizens do want their legislators to serve as special agents in Washington, intervening with the federal bureaucracy on their behalf when necessary. But citizens are also deeply concerned that their legislators promote their values, group interests, and priorities as Congress crafts its major policies, doing so effectively through the use of power and influence acquired by skillful career advancement in Congress.[61] And they are concerned ultimately that Congress address those issues in definitive and system-enhancing ways, moving the nation beyond festering conflicts and crises before policy problems surge out of control, even if its policy actions are not entirely to their liking.

Citizens thus want a Congress that mirrors their own deep desire for effective public resolution of conflicts, with this desire particularly pronounced in the modern era when the nation faces so many pressing policy issues. This concern means that citizens pay attention to the role of parties, factional groups, and individual legislators in aiding or hindering congressional performance, not just to their role in delivering particularized benefits to individuals and groups or their grandstanding on controversial issues. Thus do citizens as well as legislators confront difficult balancing acts as they engage as actors in the congressional arena.

Though it may not always seem so, as legislators and citizens pursue their personal goals and engage in a complex balancing of multiple and countervailing pressures, they have considerable incentive to generate change, adaptation, and renewal in the contemporary Congress—as long as one looks at their behavior across time instead of in snapshots in time.

VI Congress and the Cycles of Change

Operating across time, citizens and legislators focus not simply on the immediate and particularlized benefits they receive from engagement with Congress, as seen in constituency services for constituents and electoral security for their representatives. They also pay close attention at critical moments in time to the overall performance of Congress as a policy-making institution. This process of attention-shift across time by citizens and legislators sets in motion the cyclical changes within Congress that foster its adaptation to the contemporary world. But in order to recognize these processes and their adaptive consequences, we must distinguish between the short-term focus by members and their constituents on their immediate personal goals and their longer-term focus on broader shared interests.[62]

Very much like you and me, constituents and their representatives are capable of being obsessive and narrowly instrumental in pursuit of immediate short-term personal desires. Thus when times are calm, constituents may obsess on the delivery of benefits promised by existing programs, on the purity of legislators' policy positions, and on legislators' use of power and influence to push constituents' values and views, even at the expense of effective mediation and compromise on Capitol Hill. And during such periods legislators may obsess on reelection, attending avidly to casework and position-taking, and on the single-minded pursuit of personal power, even at the risk of fragmenting Congress in ways that undercut its capacity for policy leadership and coordination. To aid their visibility and prestige, enhance their reelection chances, and facilitate their rise to power, legislators may highlight new or seemingly dormant national problems that deserve attention from government and introduce important new ways of thinking about and addressing such issues.[63] In avid, relentless pursuit of such policy issues, stressing their own unique solutions to them and the ways those solutions aid specific values and interests, legislators can become as obsessive in policy activism as they are in stressing constituent service.

The intense pursuit of personal interests and priorities by constituents and legislators is a natural and useful dimension of political engagement. It can ensure that members attend to specific constituent needs and parochial policy concerns, so that constituents realize the benefits of government programs in their lives. The incumbent advantage members derive from constituent service also provides them the time to gain influence, skills, and a mastery of legislative politics. Similarly, in making new issues and their positions on them the centerpiece of their vote decisions or legislative careers, citizens and legislators can highlight critical national policy dilemmas and innovative approaches to them. Yet such intense efforts, taken to the extreme, can also have their drawbacks.

Sustained and single-minded obsession with individualized and self-serving goal pursuits, whether it involves gaining particularized benefits, securing reelection, acquiring institutional power, or pushing policy innovations, fosters deeply engrained institutional deadlock on the Hill as political actors seek to maximize their personal advantage at the expense of all other considerations. So long as members and their constituents insist on their idealized preferences and personal priorities, there is little chance for cooperation with leaders in policy planning, compromise on policy controversies and support for vital congressional reforms. In such conditions, national problems fester and governing crises mount, encouraging executive intervention into congressional prerogatives. Fortunately, this is not the end of the story.

Faced with deepening crisis and rising anxieties, legislators and citizens have a deeply engrained capacity to recognize their threatening predicament, shift their attention to the broad and collective consequences of their narrow and private obsessions, and seek to make amends.[64] As they do so, they have incentive to compromise and embrace collective efforts at institutional change and effective policy mediation.

With respect to legislators, their reelection can be undermined amid citizen unrest and a decline in the perceived legitimacy of the institution, thereby encouraging legislators to take crises seriously and push Congress to resolve them, lest citizens turn their fury against them at the ballot box.[65] Their own families and fortunes are put at risk amid social instability and upheaval, so that real solutions to pressing crises can be as important to them as to anyone else.[66] Success in their personal efforts within Congress to foster crisis resolution can aid their advancement to power within the institution, encouraging them to work hard to redress crises.[67] And the value of the personal power they possess within Congress—or hope to possess—depends on sustaining the power of Congress as an institution.

The close connection between the aspirations of legislators and the sustenance of the authority of the institution helps insure that, as governing crises mount, members of Congress will take their collective governing responsibilities seriously, even to the point of limiting their own prerogatives and power within Congress in order to foster the power and performance of the institution.[68]

Likewise, citizens have substantial incentive to pay close attention to the performance of Congress and to act to improve its performance.[69] This incentive can arise from direct difficulties that policy failures cause for individual citizens or their loved ones. It can emerge from partisan and ideological frustrations, with citizens believing that their own party or ideological persuasion could do better if in power. And citizens have incentive to engage in close and critical attention to the institutional performance of Congress, even if their immediate personal issues or partisan and ideological preferences are not at stake, because their ability to build a good life depends on broader societal well-being and on the maintenance of responsive democratic institutions as part of that well-being.

While this awareness may not be at the forefront of citizens' minds day-in and day-out, their concern for the general policy performance of Congress can surge forward in periods of national crisis, emerging as a broad socio-tropic assessment of the performance of Congress. Citizens know when Washington is broken, or a substantial attentive portion of them do. And they know that Congress has responsibilities to fix things. Such awareness can be heightened by their fear of the rise of powerful, willful, and imperial executives, as during the presidencies of Franklin Roosevelt, Lyndon Johnson, Richard Nixon, and George W. Bush, generating citizen desire for a Congress that can constrain executive aggrandizement.

By observing Congress across time, we can see it as subject to cyclical shifts in the political concerns of legislators and citizens, with both groups moving from particularized and personal concerns in periods of "normalcy" to more generalized and collective concerns amid a growing sense of national crisis. Such shifts in attention often come first among politicians and citizens less strongly attached to the dominant forces in Congress, with such insurgents highlighting problems of institutional performance both out of concern for the nation and to aid their power quests and group interests. Those in power can be slow to recognize disenchantment with their policy performance, preoccupied with governing and trusting unduly to the electoral advantage enjoyed by powerful incumbents in more quiescent times, thereby allowing insurgents to catch them by surprise and defeat them. As legislators and citizens shift their attention to national issues and the institutional performance of Congress, they thus can generate sudden, unexpected, and successful moves to change and reform Congress, moves that come through electoral upheaval, internal organizational revolution, or both.

The cycles of congressional change generate moments of sustained national arousal in which the institution can respond to pressing national problems, adapt itself in organizational ways to ensure adequate and sustained response to such problems, and renew its popular legitimacy among the citizenry.[70] Such change can include the rise of new partisan or ideological regimes in Congress; the embrace of innovative policy agendas responsive to citizens' unaddressed issue concerns; the restructuring and recentralization of organizational power within Congress; and constitutional or statutory changes regulating congressional–executive relations.

Amid major societal and international upheavals, citizens and legislators also may engage in extensive reassessment of the epistemological mindsets or paradigms by which they understand the social and political world, experimenting with new ways of seeing society and politics and with new strategies of governance.[71]

The embrace of change within Congress comes through the complex balancing of personal and political considerations, within and across individuals, groups, and parties. As a result, multiple goals, varied institutional pressures, numerous logrolling ploys, and creative justifications shape the policies, reforms, and ideational shifts that engulf Congress amid upheaval and change.[72] Such complex considerations can generate extensive policy innovation, with the origin and crafting of much of that innovative policy coming from the Congress, exemplified by the New Deal and the New Frontier/Great Society. Yet faced with dire crisis and limited time to respond, legislators and citizens are likely to settle for problem-solving approaches that are "good enough" to move the nation forward beyond the current moment, leaving to the future the refinement, expansion, and improvement of policy programs and organizational reforms.

In developing these arguments, the essays highlight three major periods of cyclical change across the past century: 1910s to 1946; the late 1940s to 1980; and 1980 to present. During each period Congress struggled early on with differing forms of organizational fragmentation, experienced some limited internal movement toward centralized reassertion, and yet found itself engulfed even more powerfully with centrifugal forces of factionalization and fragmentation. During the first two periods Congress then experienced definitive moments of governing crisis, policy innovation, presidential aggrandizement of power, and subsequent efforts at reform (1929–46; 1961–80), including substantial organizational restructuring in Congress and constitutional or statutory constraints on the executive. The current third period could well be in the midst of its defining crisis, a severe global recession combined with structural readjustment in the domestic economy, as this essay goes to press.

Over the past century, Congress has contributed greatly to the policy-making innovations that redressed pressing societal problems, as in the New Deal/Fair Deal era and the sustained liberal Democratic era of the 1960s and 1970s. It has also shown a willingness to recognize the ways its governing problems allowed such problems to fester, and to address these problems through meaningful organizational reform that limited the autonomy and power of members.[73] Yet owing to the complex cross-pressures that constrained members as they engaged in reform, the results of their endeavors have fallen short of the changes needed to solidify the governing capacities of Congress,[74] especially with respect to budgetary planning, congressional control of war-powers, adequate mechanisms for bicameral coordination of policy crafting, and sustained, politically secure and skillful leadership.

Struggling over the past several decades with imperfect decision-making structures and processes, new and challenging domestic and international conditions, increasingly severe policy problems, and the complex political calculations of its members and political parties, Congress has allowed critical issues to fester so extensively that the nation now faces policy crises as severe in magnitude as any in its history. These issues include severe economic woes, the fiscal disarray of the government and the nation, long-term entrapment in debilitating foreign wars, continuing inadequacies in the regulation of financial institutions, inadequate health care provision for citizens, energy dependence on foreign nations, global environmental degradation, and limited inclusion of and responsiveness to women, the poor, and ethnic and racial minorities in national policy-making processes.

In the face of such difficulties, it is tempting to rush to presidential government.[75] And of course presidential leadership matters enormously in addressing national crises.[76] Yet insofar as we bet the ranch on presidential leadership, in turning away from the Congress, we forget the long-term dilemmas that attend rule by a powerful executive and his lieutenants.[77] We forget the limited time that any one president, however charismatic and brilliant, has in office. We forget the inherent limits on presidential power.[78] And we also overlook the substantial ways in which presidents contribute to policy dilemmas, including the embrace of bad domestic policy and unwise unilateral intervention abroad.[79]

Given the drawbacks associated with reliance on presidential leadership, it is useful to remember that there is a powerful and salutary cyclical logic driving congressional politics, one deeply rooted in the goals and decision-making processes of millions of citizens and hundreds of members of Congress. As part of this cyclical logic, Congress does play a substantial role in generating our policy dilemmas, moving slowly in its mediation and deliberation processes, building imperfections into its policy solutions and organizational reforms, and hesitating to act decisively until the emergence of severe crises mobilize citizens to accept compromise and embrace change.

Congress moves slowly in large part because the founders created a constitutional system designed for slow, careful, deliberate action that could generate support from a broad array of institutions and citizens, preferably involving a super-majoritarian coalition of factions. This complex constitutional design imposes severe external constraints and a multitude of public pressures on Congress and its members as they deliberate policy innovations. Congress moves slowly, within these constraints and pressures, because of the complex organizational structures and procedures it has created to represent a diverse citizenry while addressing a vast array of complex policy issues, governing arrangements made more complicated by bicameralism. And Congress moves slowly, as well, owing to contemporary factors that can subvert our politics, from a highly professionalized, entrenched and debilitating interest group politics to the computerized gerrymandering of congressional districts to the expanded role of money in politics to our highly polarized and uncivil politics to the distorted and demeaning view of Congress generated by the media.[80] We need to recognize, study and find ways to address each of these developments, lest they undercut the popular legitimacy of Congress and generate a sustained downward spiral in its institutional performance.

Yet Congress and its members also have substantial and multiple incentives to act and change amid crisis, even in the face of debilitating constraints and complications.

The multiple incentives for congressional action include not only electoral and partisan pressures to respond to the concerns of citizens but also the concern to protect and enhance institutional power of Congress itself, thereby protecting the value of members' power within it. These and numerous other incentives, including their own genuine concern about the nation and its citizens, provide members with substantial impetus to experiment with and learn new and more appropriate ways of understanding social and international conditions, to construct new programs of action guided by their new perspectives, and to craft new organizational arrangements to aid and sustain action.[81] And once committed to activism, Congress and its members can maintain this commitment for some considerable time, even across multiple presidencies and during divided as well as united government, as in the 1960s and 1970s.[82]

This cyclical activism and resurgence of Congress has played a major role in ensuring the resilience of our politics and the resolution of pressing policy crises. And it has done so in sustained ways that ensure the rights and liberties of the citizens.

The resilient power of the congressional cycles flows from the ways in which the contemporary Congress mirrors the citizenry, allowing the concerns of a heterogeneous public to be reflected in the policy agendas of the Congress, and from the willingness of the Congress to engage in the changes and reforms necessary to mediate and resolve those policy conflicts as they rise to pressing salience within the nation. The mirroring process is of course a complex one.[83] Deadlock in Congress may in fact reflect and exacerbate a divided and polarized society.[84] Congress and the citizenry then may move from deadlock to periods of breakthrough in a kind of mutual and interactive learning process. The citizens, seeing themselves reflected in their divisions by a deadlocked Congress, may dislike what they see and move to shift and moderate their attitudes and behavior in ways that induce change in Congress.[85] And Congress, seeing the social disarray within society that its entrenched power arrangements and policy deadlock help to foster, can move at critical moments to provide leadership that generates agendas of action around which citizens can unite.[86]

These mutual and interactive learning processes, linking legislators and citizens together in collective swings toward policy activism during critical historical moments, enable Congress to fulfill its daunting policy-making tasks. These learning processes, facilitated by the cycles of change, are critical and ameliorative features of the Congress that must be continually at the forefront of scholarly and public awareness as observers assess the institution, especially in times of crisis.

VII Conclusion: Studying Congress II

In order to see and study the capacities of the members of Congress and their constituents to engage in learning and adaptive change, as well as in obstreperous resistance and deadlock, it is necessary to remember one very critical factor: they mirror you and me in our shared and complex humanity. The actors on the congressional stage are deeply human participants in that common drama, "the human heart in conflict with itself," that is at the core of our collective experience.[87] They swing as we do between obsession with private desire and recognition of a shared fate. Manifest dramatically within the Congress, this cyclical drama is proceeding at the highest level of human endeavor, our effort to engage in collective self-government.

Amid this human drama, how we think about Congress and how we study it matters enormously. If we idealize Congress and its members, underestimating the challenges to the institution, we risk setting it up for failure through naïve and magnified expectations. Yet if we accept cynical caricatures of Congress, we risk creating self-fulfilling prophecies, limiting what we will see as possible and thus failing to study the mechanisms and processes that can help realize its potential. We may even convince legislators and citizens that the institution is truly irrelevant, in light of our caricature, so that they cease to take it seriously, ensuring its collapse.

The abstracted actors we visualize as operating within the congressional arena—the legislators, the constituents, and all the other players we posit as influential movers and shakers—are in truth deeply human participants in an historic and fragile experiment with representative self-government. They become entangled as with all of us in obsessive, habituated, and single-minded pursuit of heart's desire that, unregulated and un-tempered, becomes self-destructive. They also reason, feel, intuit, experiment and reflect attentively on the world around them. They are susceptible to learning, to epiphany and change, and even to those moments of collective awareness and mutual concern that constitute the deeper aspects of self-interest, rightly understood.

In acknowledging the human complexity of the actors operating within and upon Congress, we gain the capacity to understand and explain the dynamics of Congress with much greater accuracy, mirroring the institution's true dimensions in our study of it.[88] With this capacity, we then can more clearly identify the structural mechanisms and processes that help generate adaptive change in Congress and clarify the ways in which new mechanisms and processes might improve institutional adaptation in the future. Motivated by such enormous payoff, the challenge comes in constructing theories of congressional politics that are sufficiently simple and abstract that we can think in systematic and reasoned ways about the Congress, while also crafting theories sufficiently true to the complexity of the human actors and processes operating within it that we grasp both its debilitating pressures and its resilient potentialities.

The essays in this book present one scholar's evolving perspective on how to make theoretical sense out of the contemporary Congress in ways that recognize its capacity for change and resilience while also being true to its difficulties and recurring dilemmas. They are, in Mayhew's sense, theoretical speculations about Congress and change, speculations to be challenged and built upon, not treated as pronouncements of certified truth. In pointing to the dynamic qualities of Congress, these speculations are not intended to ignore the difficulties facing it, or the ways in which it might fail miserably and lose relevance. You will find warnings aplenty about Congress and its future as you read on, warnings that encourage the reader to consider how better to organize and conduct congressional politics. The essays are meant to caution against the tendency to focus intently on one or two features of Congress that push it towards stasis, deadlock, and demise, or towards innovation and adaptation, seeing these effects as absolute and determinative of the future. Rather, we must continually work to bring breadth and informed judgment to our assessments, weighing in the balance both the difficulties and constraints that confront Congress and the countervailing incentives and processes capable of fostering institutional responsiveness and change.

Taken as a whole, the essays remind us that Congress has proved to be a remarkably dynamic institution across the past two hundred and twenty years, more resilient than we often realize. It has failed miserably at times, particularly in the decades leading up the Civil War. But it has also succeeded, helping foster and sustain the nation's extraordinary rise to international prominence over the past century and a half, and doing so in the face of system-threatening crises. It is thus an institution to which we must accord great respect and continuing study, alert lest it fool us once again in its deceptive character and deeper capacities for institutional renewal. Looking to the future, it is useful to remember that Congress is most likely to resurge precisely when it and the nation appear on the verge of collapse. Nor should this surprise us. It is, after all, as we the people who elect the Congress see social and political breakdown just over the horizon that we become willing to let go of our ideal policy preferences and ideological certainties and move forward toward compromise and resolution on the great and festering issues of the day.

Faced with the alternative of societal breakdown, we compromise, stay in the game, and recommit to long-term processes of congressional mediation—as long as we are assured that the game will continue with our rights and liberties intact, and that a powerful Congress will retain the capacity to protect these rights and liberties and mediate our future policy grievances in a broadly responsive and effective manner. We study Congress, the linchpin of America's democracy, hoping to better understand and perfect its processes of mediation and adaptation and thereby to aid the survival and sustenance of our democratic politics far into the future.

Notes

Acknowledgements: My appreciation to the Woodrow Wilson International Center for Scholars for a residential fellowship during the 2003–04 academic year that aided in the early preparation of this chapter. And I owe a great debt to all of those at the Center who provided comments and critiques during presentation of early versions of it there, including Vinnod Aggarwal, Constantin Fasolt, Emily Goldman, Fred Harris, Michael Jones-Correa, Rey Koslowski, Enrique Peruzzotti, Dianne Pinderhughes, Anne Pitcher, Donald Wolfensberger and Nancy Beck Young. Let me also note my special appreciation to Anne Pitcher for her continuing support for me and my work in the years following the Wilson Center, with Anne urging me forward at critical points in the development of this essay and volume, when my resolve and focus wavered, insuring their completion. And I owe heartfelt thanks to Congressman David Price, Democrat of North Carolina and also a member of the Duke University faculty, for our dinners and talks together in Washington while I was at the Center, which greatly aided my understanding of contemporary congressional politics, my complex perspective on the goals and careers of legislators, and my enjoyment of the Capitol scene.

As I refined my analysis and prepared the final draft of the essay, I benefited greatly as well from comments by Leslie Anderson, Stephen Boyle, Lorna Bracewell, Dan Cicenia, Wendy Whitman Cobb, Sharon Damoff, Amanda Edmiston, Dustin Fridkin, David Glass, Will Hicks, Josh Huder, Jason Kassel, Daniel O'Neill, Susan Orr, Jamie Pimlott, Paulina Riperre, Jordan Ragusa, Beth Rosenson, Rob Scharr, Hans E. Schmeisser, and Tristan Vellinga. I also note the extensive and invaluable assistance with final editing provided by Jamie Pimlott. My thanks to all.

1 James MacGregor Burns (1949), *Congress on Trial*; Joseph S. Clark (1964), *Congress: The Sapless Branch*; Roger H. Davidson and Walter J. Oleszek (1977), *Congress Against Itself*; Lawrence C. Dodd and Bruce I. Oppenheimer, eds., (1977), *Congress Reconsidered*; John R. Hibbing and Elizabeth Theiss-Morse (1995), *Congress as Public Enemy*; Joseph A. Cooper, ed., (1999), *Congress and the Decline of Public Trust*; Thomas E. Mann and Norman J. Ornstein (2008) *Congress: The Broken Branch*.

2 The interpretation of the ideas of the founders presented in this essay benefited from numerous works on the topic, including *The Federalist Papers* by Alexander Hamilton, James Madison, and John Jay (1961), particularly #10, #48, #53, and #63; Wood (1969), particularly Parts V and VI; Dahl (1956); Ellis (2001); Anderson (1993); Jillson (1988); Bessette (1994), particularly Chapters One, Two and Three; and Wirls and Wirls (2004). For a good short summary of how the founders' ideas shaped the Congress, see Stewart III (2001), Chapter Two.

3 Hobbes (1962).

4 As Madison put it, "I go on this great republican principle, that the people will have virtue and intelligence to select men of virtue and wisdom ..., so that we do not depend on their virtue, or put confidence in our rulers, but in the people who are to choose them." Jensen et al., eds. (1976: 471).

5 Madison, in particular, was aware of the ways in which experience within deliberative assemblies could broaden representatives' perspectives on issues of public policy. As

Wills notes: "When (Madison) went to the Continental Congress, he was impressed by many of those he met and he learned to cooperate with people from other regions, to support things not envisaged by those who elected him—as when he worked with Hamilton to strengthen the Articles, and then to supplant them. Even when he resented the agents of other interests, as in the case of Virginia's cession of western lands to Canada, he had to compromise with their interests, and he came in time to see some of the reasons behind them." Wills (2002: 34).

6 Thus, as Wills (2002: 36) argues, "When Washington and his fellow Virginians chose an arbiter to settle disputes, they were relying on a code of gentlemen; but Madison said that ordinary citizens can [*also*] rise above narrow interest, trusting their delegates to make the best bargain for them, in conjunction with the just claims of others." Emphasis added by the author.

7 In this interpretation of Madison, I join with Garry Wills (2002: 35), in his biography of Madison. "It is often said that the Constitution, and Madison as its framer, expressed a pessimistic view of human nature, as something that cannot be trusted with power. That would more aptly describe Patrick Henry. Madison claimed, on the contrary, that republican virtue is precisely the willingness to let a disinterested spokesman do all he can do for one's interest *in an arena of just arbitration*." Emphasis in the original.

8 Because Madison appreciated the mediative dimension of legislatures, and in fact lived, worked and flourished amid the great deliberative and mediative American assemblies of his time, he approached the design of the Constitution not simply in terms of constraining Congress and its members, but perhaps first and foremost as an effort to create conditions that would foster effective deliberation, fair and just mediation among groups, and sustainable compromise, "This meant separating the officials, in some measure, from their local ties, freeing them to be impartial ("indifferent"). That is why the Constitution gives elected officials long terms (relative to expectations at the time), no rotation, no recall. ... In an extended sphere, moreover, where the representatives both traveled from their base and met a broad mixture of other regions' spokesmen, conditions would encourage men to adjudicate matters on their merit. The motive for choosing a man of probity to bargain with others would be the same as if Madison and Jefferson were choosing a mutually acceptable arbiter to set the price on a horse. The electors would already be balancing their interest against their regard for justice in choosing such a person. In that sense, a republic is a school of virtue—as opposed to direct democracy, where the representatives must be slaves to the interests of those sending them." Wills (2002: 33–34).

9 Wills (2002: 34).

10 See Matthews (1995: 232–233). The quote is included in the Matthews text. It comes from a query by Madison to Robert Walsh, November, 1819, as he reflects on the Missouri Compromise. In it he expresses his fear of the possible calamities that could attend the breakdown of cross-cutting factional cleavages and their replacement by political parties "founded on geographical boundaries and other Physical and permanent distinctions which happen to coincide with them," Both Matthews and Wills see Madison as struggling in the last years of his life with the legacy that slavery was leaving the nation, much as was the case with Jefferson (Kennedy, 2003), increasingly dividing its politics by geographical regions and thereby negating the value of a large republic (a fear evident to some extent in Federalist #63: See Rossiter: 385). In Matthews' language (1995: 233), the slavery issue was the ultimate "problem Madison's system could not defuse." See also Wills (2002: 161–164).

11 The great exception of course was Madison, who was a close student of ancient republics and devoted considerable time prior to the Constitutional Convention to the history of representative assemblies in earlier times. But none of the founders had access to the kind of information and knowledge about the politics of representative assemblies we possess in contemporary times, since such knowledge simply did not exist. This

realization makes all the more impressive their willingness to embrace the Congress as the centerpiece of national governance and their foresighted understanding of the political dynamics likely to characterize it.

12 Wood (1969), Part IV; Jillson and Wilson (1994).
13 Wood (1992), Part Three.
14 Tocqueville (1835/1969)
15 Howe (2007).
16 For useful overviews of the early Congress, see Young (1966) and the essays in Part I of Zelizer (2004b). On the rise of the early Speakership, see Peters (1990) and Swift (1998). On the rise of early political parties in Congress, or variants thereon, see Hofstadter (1969); Formisano (1971, 1974); Hoadley (1980); Aldrich and Grant (1993); and Aldrich (1995a).
17 On the creation of standing committees, see Cooper (1970) and Gamm and Shepsle (1989). On the early development of rules and procedures, see Binder (1997), Chapters Three and Four.
18 Swift (1996); and Wirls and Wirls (2004), Chapters Seven and Eight.
19 Neale (1995: 2072).
20 Jensen (2003), Chapter Four; Kassel (2009).
21 My discussion of the coming of the Civil War and its consequences is informed, in particular, by Potter (1976); Holt (1978); McPherson (1988); Bensel (1990); Miller (1995); and Neely (2004).
22 Lowi (1969, 2009)
23 Neale (1995).
24 For a broad overview, see Rauchway (2004); see also Polsby (1968); Polsby, Gallagher, and Rundquist (1969); and Fiorina, Rohde, and Wissel (1975).
25 Hechler (1940).
26 In *Congressional Government*, Woodrow Wilson considered a strong Speaker in combination with a system of standing committees to be essential to the efficient working of the House of Representatives and thus to the preeminence of Congress in the late nineteenth century. See Wilson (1885) and the discussion in Dodd (1987). Writing in the aftermath of the revolt against Cannon, George Rothwell Brown (1922: 13) concluded that "No more paradoxical action has ever been committed by the American people than in the destruction of the power of the speakership in the name of popular liberty." Arguing that a strong Speakership which insured the organization and efficiency of the House had been essential to the success of "the American experiment in representative government" (page 15), Brown argues forcefully throughout *The Leadership of Congress* in behalf of a return to strong Speakers if the House and Congress are to function effectively.
27 Jensen (2003), Chapter Two; see also Swift (1987).
28 On post-Civil War social programs, see Skocpol (1992, 1994). On railroad policy, see Kerr (2004) and Harrison (2004).
29 More specifically, Brown (1922: 249–250) writes: "During the past two decades there has been a significant increase in what might be called the purely personal duties of Congressmen, who became, indeed, almost the special agents in Washington of their constituents. They came to be called upon, more and more, to attend to innumerable matters unrelated to their legislative functions, to obtain passports, to urge the granting of pardons, to secure the admission of aliens, to report on claims against the government, to do the errands of influential persons in their congressional districts, ... matters which came to be more and more a drain upon their time which should have been devoted strictly to the major business of law-making."
30 Lowi (1969, 1979).
31 Burns (1949) should be read by all students of Congress seeking to understand the postwar Congress, and also to assess the development of postwar scholarship. Virtually

all major substantive themes of the postwar scholarship are foreshadowed in this work. Adler (2002) makes a strong case for the continuing relevance of the reelection motive in the study of Congress.

32 Burns (1949: 141).

33 Mayhew (1974b: 5). For my 1978 review of *The Electoral Connection* in the *American Political Science Review*, see Dodd (1978a).

34 See Fiorina (1977b; see also 1977a). Yale University Press published a revised and expanded version of *Keystone* in 1989.

35 Mayhew (1974a) presents extensive statistical evidence demonstrating a growth in the number of 'safe seats' in the House of Representatives during the early post–World War II period, describing this phenomena as a case of 'the vanishing marginals.' Fiorina was responding to this evidence in developing his argument in *Keystone*, which also reprints some of Mayhew's data in Chapter One. Fiorina was also drawing on his own analysis of marginal districts in Fiorina (1974), and responding to Ferejohn (1977).

36 Erikson (1971, 1972).

37 Cain, Ferejohn, and Fiorina (1987).

38 Fiorina (1995a, 1995b) came to see Democrats' hold on the Congress, particularly the House of Representatives, as also reinforced by their hold on state legislatures, which he attributed in part to the professionalization of state legislatures and the way in which this attracted working class Democrats to legislative service at the state level. He argued that state legislative service gave Democrats an edge when they ran for Congress, enhancing their status as 'quality candidates' (Jacobson and Kernell, 1983). For a useful discussion of the Republicans' seeming permanence as a minority party in the House, see Connelly and Pitney (1994). For Fiorina's retrospective discussion of *Keystone*, initially prepared for the twenty-five year anniversary of its publication, see Fiorina (2004).

39 Burns (1949, 1965) and Huntington (1965, 1973).

40 Lowi (1985); Crenson and Ginsberg (2007).

41 On Congress and the New Deal, with suggested reading, see Maney (2004); and for the Great Society, see Berkowitz (2004).

42 For a twenty-five-year roundtable retrospective on *The Electoral Connection*, which includes essays by Mayhew, John R. Bond, John H. Aldrich, Alan A. Abramowitz, Patricia A. Hurley, and Lawrence Dodd, see *PSOnline*, June 2001, pages 251–266: www.apsanet.org. These essays gauge the broad affect of the reelection argument in congressional studies. Adler (2002, Chapter Two), provides a useful review of the literature on electoral incentive theory, or a "gains-from-exchange" theory, particularly as it relates to committee structure and change in Congress. His discussion includes an assessment of how the theory has been modified and extended to apply to the current era of conditional party government in Congress. On the latter developments, see also Aldrich and Rohde (1997, 2001).

43 See Erikson and Wright (2009: 81–83).

44 Sundquist (1981).

45 For overviews of the growth of party competition during the 1980s and 1990s, and the role that agenda politics and debate over the institutional performance of Congress played in the revitalization of party competition and Republican capture of Congress in 1994, see Critchlow (2004) and Zelizer (2004a), Chapter Twelve. On the role that policy issues played in the rebound of the Democrats in 2006, see, for example, Oppenehimer and Grose (2007) and Herrnson and Curry (2009).

46 Mayhew (1991); Kelly (1993); Binder (1999, 2003); Howell et al. (2000); Dodd and Schraufnagel (2009a).

47 Thus Richard Fenno (1989a) reports that Republican Congressman Dan Qualye was so frustrated by his party's seeming permanence as the minority party in the House that he chose to run for the Senate rather than remain in a safe House district, risking his

career in the process. Fenno (1992a) also demonstrates that casework prowess cannot save a candidate who is out of touch with his state and subject to scandal.

48 Thus, despite the existence of incumbent advantage in House elections, Erikson and Wright (2009: 92–98) also find that voters select the candidate to support based in part on which candidate is closest to their ideological views on issues.

49 Mayhew (1974b: 61–73). See also the essay by Patricia Hurley (2001) in the twenty-five year retrospective assessment of *The Electoral Connection* in *PS*. She notes that position-taking is a more complex phenomenon than credit-claiming and advertising, and can be seen in ways that undermine members' reelection chances as well as enhance it. My treatment of position-taking here reflects the roundtable discussion of position-taking, including Hurley's oral as well as written statements, and Mayhew's response. My appreciation to both.

50 The efforts of members to stay in close touch with their constituencies is documented most tellingly in Fenno (1978). See also Fenno (1997a and 2003) and Parker (1986). For intriguing discussions of member attentiveness to constituencies in earlier periods, see Swift (1987); Brown (1922: 13–14); and Burns (1949), Chapter One. For an inventive and insightful analysis of members' tendencies to make promises of policy support and then to keep them, see Sulkin (2009).

51 See Sellers (2002); Thurber and Campbell, eds. (2002); Schudson (2004); Thurber and Nelson, eds. (2004); and Zelizer (2004a), Chapter 11.

52 Cain, Ferejohn, and Fiorina (1987).

53 For examples of the attentiveness of senators to chamber and policy influence, see Fenno (1991a, 1991b). For the House of Representatives, see Price (2000).

54 Dodd (1986a) and Cox and McCubbins (1993).

55 Cooper (1970; 1977); Cooper and Mackenzie (1981); Dodd (1988).

56 Dodd and Schott (1979), Chapter Four/Five; Aberbach (1990).

57 Dodd and Schott (1979), Chapter Three/Four; Sundquist (1981), Chapter Thirteen; Mayer and Canon (1999).

58 Dodd and Schott (1979), Chapters Five and Six; Aberbach (1990); Ogul (1976); McCubbins and Swartz (1984); Talbert, Jones and Baumgartner (1995); Shipan (2003). See Mycoff (2007) for a fine review of the literature and intriguing empirical analysis of the conditions of effective oversight.

59 Cameron (2002).

60 See Barabas and Jerit (2009) for a discussion of the research literature on media coverage and citizens policy knowledge, and for evidence demonstrating a positive connection between them.

61 Considerable debate exists about what citizens know about national policy performance and how they respond in terms of attention and participation. For a useful and suggestive study, utilizing 2000–2002–2004 NES panel data, see Flavin and Griffin (2009). They find that citizens' policy views on Iraq and the 2001 federal tax cut did shape participation in national elections. They also provide a useful discussion of relevant literature. My effort in this essay is to indicate why I believe that significant citizen attention to Congress exists, as part of attention to national policy performance, particularly at key moments in time and on critical issues of institutional performance, and to make clear why such attention and engagement could matter for the adaptive capacities of Congress as an institution. Work such as that of Flavin and Griffin seem to support this line of theoretical inquiry.

62 Other cyclically-oriented perspectives on Congress, American politics, legislative politics or socio-political phenomena which have influenced the author's work include Blondel (1973); Burnham (1970, 1976); Hirschman (1982); Huntington (1981); Jones (1994, 2001); McClosky and Zaller (1984); Raven (2004, 2010); Stimson (1991/1999); Sundquist (1973, 1981); and Schlesinger, Jr. (1986), especially Chapter Two.

Raven's work, the newest of these studies, provides a very exciting perspective that stresses the role that institutional precedents and norms play in inducing organizational cycles in Congress. He argues that external punctuations upend the equilibrium politics of party government eras or committee government eras, followed by the use of precedents by legislative leaders and the development of norms among members that move the legislature towards the opposite form of institutional equilibrium, once its stability has been upended.

63 Mayhew (1974b: 68–69); Riker (1982b, Chapter Eight, 1986).

64 Thus Marcus, Neuman, and MacKuen (2000) discuss the ways in which crisis can facilitate a heightened level of citizen attentiveness and focus on politics, based on our neurobiological system, with anxiety in the face of difficult or threatening crises leading citizens to be open to new ideas and the possibility of political change. This finding helps us to understand the psychological processes that may underlie the substantial evidence that citizens do shift their attitudes and vote choice in difficult or threatening times, ranging from V. O. Key (1961, 1966) to Marcus and Mackuen (1993) to my own study with Leslie Anderson (Anderson and Dodd, 2005) of vote choice and citizen engagement in post-revolutionary Nicaragua. My involvement in the latter study has reinforced my sense (Dodd, 1994) that citizens—even quite poor citizens—are much more capable of attending to, comprehending and making reasonable decisions about politics in the midst of difficult circumstances than was generally recognized by early public opinion and vote studies in the United States, and that this capacity could extend to elections other than those for the presidency. For recent evidence supporting the general idea that economic conditions can affect congressional elections, during the mid-term elections and presidential elections, independent of vote for the president, see Fair (2009). For relevant studies of attention shift across time, see Hirschman (1982), Stimson (1999); and Erikson, MacKuen and Stimson (2002).

65 Jones and Baumgartner (2005) develop a theory of attention shift that applies to elite institutional actors such as members of Congress. Their general punctuation hypothesis would seem to correspond to the arguments presented here about the propensity of legislators to shift attention away from the routinized politics of Congress and to issues of broad institutional performance in periods of national difficulty or crisis. Moreover, they appear to find that congressional elections—particularly House elections—are subject to substantial punctuation effects amid difficult national circumstances, justifying members attentiveness at such times to issues of institutional performance. See also their discussion of the 'meaning' of their findings in Chapter 11. See also Tracy Sulkin's (2005) discussion of issue uptake, where members adopt important issues potentially threatening their reelection.

66 For an insightful work that stresses the ways in which members own values and personal concerns may shape their behavior as members, which could of course be extended to their concern for the general institutional performance of Congress, see Burden (2007).

67 The observation that members of Congress tend to run for office by running against Congress was first highlighted by Fenno (1975); see also Parker and Davidson (1979). For an extensive discussion of this phenomenon across electoral democracies, see Mayer and Canon (1999) and Loewenberg (2011: 80–84).

68 Consider, for example, Eric Schickler's analysis of the factors that shape institutional innovation and development across different periods of change. What is noteworthy in his work is the extent to which those factors we tend to believe 'explain everything' about Congress, such as reelection, have relatively limited influence at key moments of institutional innovation and shift, whereas issues of personal power, factional or ideological advantage, institutional capacity, party governance, chamber power and congressional prestige loom relatively large in such periods, as seen in Chapter Five.

69 Parker and Davidson (1979); Cain, Ferejohn, and Fiorina (1987, Chapter Eight); and Cooper (1999) all provide evidence that citizens pay general attention to the

performance of Congress and are prepared to evaluate it. In assessing such findings, in which they compare assessments of the Congress with those of the British Parliament, Cain, Ferejohn and Fiorina conclude: "That national legislatures are judged on their performance should surprise no one. What is more interesting is how little the individual members, in either country, appear to be judged on their contributions to the resolution of national problems" (page 204). My argument is that it almost certainly depends on when you examine the relationship between perceptions of institutional performance and the vote, with a connection between institutional performance and the vote more likely to be seen in a period of crisis or with a highly salient issue dominating national politics. See, for example, the findings in Jones and McDermott (2004, 2009). For a more general discussion of "public cognizance of changes in the political environment" and evidence that at least some portion of the public "updates its views of government when the political environment changes," see Gershtenson, Ladewig, and Plane (2006: 882). And for deep background, see V.O. Key (1966).

70 On the importance of 'windows of opportunity' to policy making, see Kingdon (1984, 1994).

71 For an argument that one of the major contemporary challenges facing the nation is with how citizens and leaders adjust and adapt their ideologies and conceptions of governance to new conditions, and whether they do so in ways that respect constitutionalism and democracy, see Lowi (1995).

72 Thus across time Schickler (2001) finds multiple factors shaping congressional innovation, with the factors shifting substantially, depending on conditions and pressures facing Congress and its leaders. Also, see Guelzo's (2003) discussion of the multiple maneuvers Lincoln employed in trying to gain congressional support for the Thirteenth Amendment, including the distribution of a good deal of patronage. And consider Evans' (2004) discussion of the general role pork barrel plays in building majority coalitions in Congress. See also Josh Huder's (2011) discussion of legitimacy crises that arise in congressional politics, shaping change.

73 Sundquist (1981).

74 Davidson and Oleszek (1976); Oppenheimer (1997); Mayer and Canon (1999); Mann and Ornstein (2006/2008).

75 See, for example, Cooper's (2009, 2001) discussion of the varied ways in which the contemporary limits of Congress play into the move towards a plebiscitary presidency.

76 Skowronek (1993); Burns (1965).

77 Schlesinger, Jr. (1974).

78 Neustadt (1960); Lowi (1985); and Skowronek (1997).

79 See Jones and Williams (2008) on domestic policy; and, on foreign interventions, see Howell and Pevehouse (2007); and Conley (2005).

80 On the debilitating role of interest group politics in Congress, see Wright (1996) and Johnson and Broder (1996). On the nature and troubling role of gerrymandering, see Cox and Katz (2002); and also see Brunell's (2008) imaginative argument about the ways in which systematic gerrymandering, packing like-minded partisans into homogeneous districts, might actually aid congressional responsiveness and public support. On the questionable role of money in congressional politics, see, for example, Hall and Wayman (1990); Currinder (2009); and Cann (2008). And on our uncivil and polarized politics see Bond and Fleischer (2000); Uslaner (1993); Loomis (2000); Theriault (2008); Smith (2007); and Dodd and Schraufnagel (2008). On the role of the media in creating a distorted view of Congress, see Shribman (1999). And for an argument maintaining that citizens are seeing the Congress only too well, picking up the cues, signals and messages Congress as well as the media are sending, see Brady and Theriault (2001).

81 As an example, see the discussions of the creation of the 1974 Budget and Impoundment Act by Schickler (2007) and Whittinton and Carpenter (2003).

82 Mayhew (1991); Binder (2003), Howell et al. (2000). Dodd and Schraufnagel (2009).
83 Thus Gerhardt Loewenberg (2011: 127–128) concludes as follows, in his masterful and broad-ranging survey of research on legislatures: "One plausible generalization derived from a range of studies on public perceptions of the legislature is that legislatures mirror the public's disagreements on issues. Legislatures constantly demonstrate that there is no easily discovered solution to most political issues and that the prospect of consensus on issues is often an illusion. The public therefore projects on the legislature its unwillingness to face dissensus and its despair about finding solutions. None of the more popular institutions of government provide similar mirrors to the reality of political controversy."
84 For a discussion of the complexities involved, see Fiorina, with Abrams and Pope (2005).
85 Thus consider the extraordinary story told by Miller (1995) about the role that citizens and the abolitionist social movement played in the 1830s and 1840s in pushing Congress toward action on slavery. In more recent times, consider the careful research by Sean M. Theriault demonstrating the capacity of contemporary citizens to exercise influence on legislators, as in issues of civil service reform, congressional pay, campaign finance and term limits.
86 See, for example, Schickler (2007); Strahan (2007); and Fowler (1994). For an intriguing discussion of the ways in which legislators' efforts to gain media attention for their policy positions can play a significant role in helping citizens learn about policy issues and debates in Congress, see Sellers (2010).
87 To place William Faulkner's phrase in context: "… the young man or woman writing today has forgotten the problems of the human heart in conflict with itself which alone can make good writing because only that is worth writing about, worth the agony and the sweat. He must learn them again. He must teach himself that the basest of all things is to be afraid; and, teaching himself that, forget it forever, leaving no room in his workshop for anything but the old verities and truths of the heart, the universal truths lacking which any story is ephemeral and doomed—love and honor and pity and pride and compassion and sacrifice. Until he does so, he labors under a curse. He writes not of love but of lust, of defeats in which nobody loses anything of value, and victories without hope and worst of all, without pity or compassion. His griefs grieve on no universal bones, leaving no scars. He writes not of the heart but of the glands. Until he relearns these things, he will write as though he stood among and watched the end of man." Faulkner delivered these words as part of his Nobel Prize Speech in Stockholm, Sweden on December 10, 1950. The speech can be accessed at Nobelprize.org: The Official Web Site of the Nobel Prize.
88 The complex range of motives, goals and personal considerations legislators bring to public service is particularly underscored by the masterful "Senate narratives" of Richard Fenno (1989a, 1990, 1991a, 1991b, 1992), which portray the experiences of five senators across roughly a decade of observation. For probing assessments of the implications of Fenno's narratives for our understanding of Congress, see the "Extension of Remarks" in the November 1992 issue of the *Legislative Studies Section Newsletter*. This issue of "Extensions," entitled "Making Sense Out of the Senate: The Narratives of Richard F. Fenno, Jr.," includes "Introductory Remarks" by Fenno (1992a) and five essays commenting on the narratives. The contributors include Donald Matthews (1992), Barbara Sinclair (1992), Bruce Oppenheimer (1992), Steven Smith (1992), and the author (Dodd, 1992).
    All five commentators emphasize the extent to which Fenno's narratives point towards the rich and human complexity of legislators' motivations and behavior. Barbara Sinclair (2002: 4) concludes as follows: "Fenno's Senate narratives, like his earlier work, thus point to the need for theory that allows the assumption of multiple goals. Assuming the single goal of reelection makes for easier theory building, but that is not

sufficient justification for adopting an assumption that leads to disastrously distorted propositions ... While building theory based upon the assumption of multiple goals is more difficult, the notion of balancing goals, of trade-offs among goals is likely to provide an important source of dynamism that the single-goal theories lack. The theories that result are likely to be more interesting as well as more descriptively accurate."

"Making Sense Out of the Senate" is available in the Archives for the *Legislative Studies Section Newsletter* on the Legislative Studies Section website of the American Political Science Association (www.apsanet.org), or from the author.

The complex and human character of legislators, and the role that their values and personal experiences can play in legislative life, are also documented forcefully in Barry Burden's excellent 2007 study of the *Personal Roots of Representation* and in Congressman David E. Price's (1992, 2000, 2004) detailed first-hand account of legislative politics.

Additional Perspective on "Congress as Public Mirror"

The mirror metaphor is used in this essay with some trepidation and yet also with great appreciation for the multiple dimensions of political, social, and psychological reality that it helps us to reference.

The trepidation comes in substantial part because of the role that the metaphor played in the great debate between the Federalists and Anti-Federalists during the ratification of the U.S. Constitution, as brilliantly portrayed by Isaac Framnick in his "Editor's Introduction" to *The Federalist Papers* (Kramnick, 1987: 40–47). The Anti-Federalists pushed for a government that would mirror the people as directly as possible. Thus Anti-Federalists such as Patrick Henry and Melancton Smith preferred a government based on direct assembly of the people or, failing this, a government constructed around representative assemblies sufficiently large in size to serve as "an exact miniature" or "true picture" of the citizenry in its varied social, economic and demographic characteristics. In contrast, Madison and the Federalists argued against such a precise mirroring and stressed, among other things, the way in which a relatively small national representative assembly would filter out "local prejudices" and "refine" and "enlarge" public views and the quality of the men chosen to express them (Kramnick, 1987: 42). Students of American political thought thus often will see the Congress as a relatively conservative institution, a warped and elitist mirror so to speak, and lament the failure of the Anti-Federalists' efforts to move the nation toward a larger representative assembly in which members were elected in much smaller constituencies and thus more nearly reflected the diverse character of the citizenry.

"Congress as Public Mirror" embraces the Anti-Federalist view that the Congress should be selected in ways that seek to ensure its broad representation or mirroring of the citizenry. Thus the broadening of citizen enfranchisement has been a critical element in sustaining the institution's effectiveness and legitimacy as a policy-making legislature. And much more remains to be done in ensuring that Congress, and American politics more generally, genuinely reflect the diversity of the nation (Canon, 1999; Cooperman and Oppenheimer, 2001; Haynie, 2005; Hero, 1992, 1995, 1998, 2007; Pimlott, 2010; Pinderhughes, 1987, 2011; Swain, 1993, 1997; Tate, 2003; Wolbrecht et al., 2005). But the essay also embraces the Federalist view that the construction of government is a serious proposition, so that attention must be given as well to those characteristics—such as a relatively modest and manageable number of members in each chamber—that help foster a workable national assembly capable of representing citizens effectively in the actual process of policy crafting and enactment. The Federalists designed a national representative assembly that has proven remarkably successful and durable in maintaining and exercising control over the policy-making processes of the national government. In contrast, the exceedingly large representative assembly proposed by the Anti-Federalists would almost certainly have confronted serious difficulties in sustaining control of policy making, with the cumbersome nature of contemporary policy making within a huge assembly composed of thousands of members likely to encourage assembly reliance on executive policy making.

Seen from the perspective of autonomous legislative policy making, there is much to applaud in the Federalist design. The American Congress is, in fact, the most radical participatory national policy-making legislature in history, with the members elected to it engaging more directly, autonomously and publicly in national policy making than is the case for any other durable national representative assembly among large nation-state democracies in the world. Put differently, the individuals who craft national public policy in the United States—the members of the Congress—more nearly reflect or mirror the actual citizens who will be governed by that policy than is the case in any other large democratic nation-state in history, with virtually all other well-established democratic regimes relying on executive/bureaucratic crafting of policy.

When contrasted with other national legislatures, Congress is aided in its control of policy making by separation of powers, the firm constitutional authority of the Congress over revenue and appropriations policy, and Senate advice and consent on executive nominations (Loewenberg, 2011: 85–86), all of which are constitutional features. This control of policy is then further aided by its well-developed system of standing committees (Loewenberg, 2011: 65–66; Cooper, 1970) and its deeply engrained procedures protective of both majority rule and minority rights (Loewenberg, 2011: 54–62; Binder, 1997). These varied factors, taken together, give the Congress greater actual leverage over national policy making than the leverage possessed by any other national legislature among large-scale national democracies. Close students of legislatures thus tend to see the U.S. Congress "as the most powerful legislature in the world" (Loewenberg, 2011: 2; Polsby, 1975).

Regrettably, all representative assemblies have drawbacks. Large ones inhibit authentic deliberation and close engagement of members in crafting policy. Small ones have difficulty in reflecting the full diversity of a nation's citizenry. Plurality electoral arrangements in the selection of legislators more nearly reflect geographic and district constituencies whereas proportional ones more nearly represent constituents in their political and partisan diversity. Nevertheless, all representative assemblies build a mirroring of citizen diversity into government decision-making that would be missing without them (Loewenberg, 2011: 127–128; Tate, 2003), with that mirroring process more pronounced during the policy-making process in the United States Congress than in any other large-scale nation-state democracy.

The autonomous role the Congress plays in national policy making allows the other dimensions of mirroring stressed in this essay to come strongly to the fore in American national governance. Put a bit more provocatively, policy making through a deliberative American-style elected assembly allows the interactive learning capacities and the sociable, empathic and discursive qualities of homo sapiens to come to the fore in government policy making more fully than is the case in any other form of large-scale national representative government.

This mirroring, it should be stressed, is greatly aided in the United States by constitutional provisions that ensure periodic and time-specific elections for Congress. These provisions include elections every two years for the House of Representatives that help keep the Congress updated on the shifting policy sentiments of citizens. Mirroring is also aided by widespread adoption of state-based public primaries for selecting the party nominees to stand in general elections for congressional office, insuring that citizens have relatively direct influence on the range of candidate choices they will face at election time. These two provisions are virtually unique among major nation-state democracies, providing an opportunity for citizens operating through electoral politics in the United States to generate a more rapid shift in the policy-making orientation of the Congress than is customary elsewhere.

PART I

Member Goals and Institutional Context

2

CONGRESS AND THE QUEST FOR POWER

1977

During the early decades following World War II, leading scholars of the U.S. Congress argued that it was a static, rigidly decentralized and outmoded institution, incapable of change and reform. Yet in the 1970s Congress embraced extensive centralizing reforms. Why?

"Congress and the Quest for Power" argues that a deep-seated tension exists between legislators' quest for personal power within Congress and their need to sustain the power of the institution. In the short-run members push to decentralize Congress in ways that serve their personal power and autonomy. But over the long-run their creation of a decentralized and poorly coordinated Congress undercuts its decision-making capacity. Policy crises in society and power aggrandizement by the president then convince members to recentralize the institution in order to reassert its policy-making power, lest their power within it prove meaningless.

The cyclical swings of Congress between decentralization and recentralization explain both the early postwar decades of institutional stasis and the congressional reforms of the 1970s. The essay thus portrays Congress as a dynamic institution capable of reform. On the other hand, it also sees Congress as an institution grappling with serious issues of internal governance and long-term power, with its careerist members hesitant to embrace "too much" centralization lest it impinge unduly on their personal power.

The postwar years have taught students of Congress a very fundamental lesson: Congress is a dynamic institution. The recent congressional changes picture an institution that is much like a kaleidoscope. At first glance the visual images and structural patterns appear frozen in a simple and comprehensible mosaic. Upon

Lawrence C. Dodd. "Congress and the Quest for Power." In Congress Reconsidered, 1st Edition. *Edited by Lawrence C. Dodd and Bruce I. Oppenheimer. New York, N.Y.: Praeger Publishers. 1977, pp. 269–312.*

closer and longer inspection the realization dawns that the picture is subject to constant transformations. These transformations seem to flow naturally from the prior observations, yet the resulting mosaic is quite different and is not ordered by the same static principles used to interpret and understand the earlier one. The appreciation and understanding of the moving image requires not only comprehending the role of each colorful geometric object in a specific picture, nor developing a satisfactory interpretation of the principles underlying a specific picture or change in specific aspects of the picture, but grasping the dynamics underlying the structural transformations themselves. So it is with Congress. To understand and appreciate it as an institution we must focus not only on particular aspects of internal congressional structure and process, nor on changes in particular patterns. We must seek to understand the more fundamental dynamics that produce the transformations in the congressional mosaic.

This essay represents an attempt to explain the dynamics of congressional structure.[1] Part I presents a general interpretation of the motives that lead members to organize Congress along particular lines, and attempts to specify the type of institutional structure and behavior that should flow from these motives. The model generated in Part I fits roughly with (and derives from a study of) congressional structure and behavior as represented by scholars of the era from the mid-1950s to the mid-1960s. That time period is treated as one observation point—much like one glance through a kaleidoscope. Part II argues that there is an inherent paradox within the motivational principles uncovered in Part I: to the extent that members of Congress try to maximize their personal goals in the short run, they create a congressional structure that undermines their ability to realize the personal goals over the long run. Members of Congress come to realize this fact in periods of institutional crisis and produce the type of structural reforms witnessed in the 1973–75 period. This tension between the short-term and long-term goal maximization generates the basic organizational dynamics of Congress. Part III argues that the pattern of change identified in Part II, a pattern that is cyclical in nature, does in fact characterize congressional organization and American politics generally, particularly in the twentieth century. Part IV argues that this cyclical theory allows us to predict the general fate of current congressional reforms. Part V considers the extent to which the overall cyclical pattern conforms to a Madisonian vision of American politics and the consequent implications for the future of Congress and American politics.

I

As with politicians generally, members of Congress enter politics in a quest for personal power. This quest may derive from any number of deeper motives: a desire for ego gratification or for prestige, a search for personal salvation through good works, a hope to construct a better world or to dominate the present one, or a preoccupation with status and self-love. Whatever the source, most members of Congress seek to attain the power to control policy decisions that impose the authority of the state on the citizenry at large.

The most basic lesson that any member of Congress learns on entering the institution is that the quest for power by service within Congress requires reelection. First, reelection is necessary in order to remain in the struggle within Congress for "power positions."[2] Staying in the struggle is important not only in that it provides the formal status as an elected representative without which an individual's influence on national legislative policy lacks legal authority; the quest for power through election and reelection also signals one's acceptance of the myth of democratic rule and thus one's acceptability as a power seeker who honors the society's traditional values. Second, reelection, particularly by large margins, helps create an aura of personal legitimacy. It indicates that one has a special mandate from the people, that one's position is fairly secure, that one will have to be "reckoned with." Third, long-term electoral success bestows on a member of Congress the opportunity to gain the experience and expertise, and to demonstrate the legislative skill and political prescience, that can serve to justify the exercise of power.

Because reelection is so important, and because it may be so difficult to ensure, its pursuit can become all-consuming. The constitutional system, electoral laws, and social system together have created political parties that are weak coalitions. A candidate for Congress normally must create a personal organization rather than rely on her or his political party. The "electoral connection" that intervenes between the desire for power and the realization of power may lead members to emphasize form over substance, position taking, advertising, and credit claiming rather than problem-solving. In an effort to sustain electoral success, members of Congress may fail to take controversial and clear positions, fail to make hard choices, fail to exercise power itself.[3] Yet members of Congress generally are not solely preoccupied with reelection. Most members have relatively secure electoral margins. This security stems partially from the fact that members of Congress *are* independent of political parties and are independent from responsibility for selecting the executive, and thus can be judged more on personal qualities than on partisan or executive affiliations. Electoral security is further reinforced because members of Congress personally control financial and casework resources that can help them build a loyalty from their constituents independent of policy or ideological considerations. The existence of secure electoral margins thus allows members to devote considerable effort toward capturing a "power position" within Congress and generating a mystique of special authority that is necessary to legitimize a select decision-making role for them in the eyes of their nominal peers.

The concern of members of Congress with gaining congressional power, rather than just securing reelection, has had a considerable influence on the structure and life of Congress. Were members solely preoccupied with reelection, we would expect them to spend little time in Washington and devote their personal efforts to constituent speeches and district casework. One would expect Congress to be run by a centralized, efficient staff who, in league with policy-oriented interest groups, would draft legislation, investigate the issues, frame palatable solutions, and present the members with the least controversial bills possible. Members of Congress would give little attention to committee work, and then only to committees that clearly served reelection interests. The primary activity of congresspeople in Congress, rather, would be extended, televised floor debates and symbolic roll call votes, all for show. Such a system would allow the appearance of work while providing ample opportunity for the mending of home fences. Alternatively, were only a few members of Congress concerned about power, with others concerned with reelection, personal finances, or private lives, one might expect a centralized system with a few leaders exercising power and all others spending their time on personal or electoral matters.

Virtually all members of the U.S. Congress are preoccupied with power considerations. They are unwilling—unless forced by external events—to leave the major decisions in either a centralized, autonomous staff system or a central leadership. Each member wants to exercise power—to make the key policy decisions. This motive places every member in a personal conflict with every other member: to the extent that one member realizes her or his goal personally to control all key decisions, all others must lose. Given this widespread power motive, an obvious way to resolve the conflict is to disperse power—or at least power positions—as widely as possible. One logical solution, in other words, is to place basic policymaking responsibility in a series of discrete and relatively autonomous committees and subcommittees, each having control over the decisions in a specified jurisdictional area. Each member can belong to a small number of committees and, within them, have a significant and perhaps dominant influence on policy. Although such a system denies every member the opportunity to control all policy decisions, it ensures that most members, particularly if they stay in Congress long enough to obtain a subcommittee or committee chair, and if they generate the mystique of special authority necessary to allow them to activate the power potential of their select position, can satisfy a portion of their power drive.

Within Congress, as one would expect in light of the power motive, the fundamental structure of organization is a committee system. Most members spend most of their time not in their district but in Washington, and most of their Washington time not on the floor in symbolic televised debate but rather in the committee or subcommittee rooms, in caucus meetings, or in office work devoted to legislation.[4] While the staff, particularly the personal staff, may be relegated to casework for constituents, the members of Congress sit through hearing after hearing, debate after debate, vote after vote seeking to shape in subcommittee, committee, and floor votes the contours of legislation. This is not to suggest, of course, that members of Congress do not engage in symbolic action or personal casework and do not spend much time in the home district; they do, in their effort at reelection. Likewise, staff do draft legislation, play a strong role in committee investigations, and influence the direction of public policy; they do this, however, largely because members of Congress just do not have enough time in the day to fulfill their numerous obligations. Seen in this perspective, Congress is not solely, simply, or primarily a stage on which individuals intentionally and exclusively engage in meaningless charades. Whatever the end product of their effort may be, members of Congress have actively sought to design a congressional structure and process that would maximize their ability to exercise personal power within Congress and, through Congress, within the nation at large.

The congressional committee structure reflects rather naturally the various dimensions that characterize the making of public policy. There are *authorization* committees that create policies and programs, specify their duties and powers, and establish absolute funding levels. There are *appropriations* committees that specify the actual funding level for a particular fiscal year. There are *revenue* committees that raise the funds to pay for the appropriations necessary to sustain the authorized programs. In addition, since Congress itself is an elaborate institution that must be serviced, there are *housekeeping* committees—those that provide for the day-to-day operation of Congress. In the House of Representatives there is also an *internal regulation* committee, the House Rules Committee, that schedules debate and specifies the rules for deliberation on specific bills.

These committees vary greatly in the nature and comprehensiveness of their impact on national policy making. The housekeeping committees tend to be *service* committees and carry little national weight except through indirect influence obtained from manipulating office and staff resources that other members may want so desperately as to modify their policy stances on other committees. A second set of committees, authorization committees such as Interior or Post Office, have jurisdictions that limit them to the concerns of fairly narrow constituencies; these are *reelection* committees that allow members to serve their constituencies' parochial interests but offer only limited potential to effect broad-scale public policy. A third group of committees are *policy* committees, such as Education and Labor or International Relations, that consider fairly broad policy questions, though questions that have fairly clear and circumscribed jurisdictional limits. A fourth set of committees are the *"power"* committees, which make decisions on issues such as the scheduling of rules (the House Rules Committee), appropriations (House and Senate Appropriations committees), or revenues (House Ways and Means or Senate Finance) that allow them to affect most or all policy areas.[5] Within a pure system of committee government, power committees are limited in the comprehensiveness of their control over the general policy-making process. No overarching control committee exists to coordinate the authorization, appropriations, or revenue process.

Because an essential type of legislative authority is associated with each congressional committee, members find that service on any committee can offer some satisfaction of their power drive. There are, nevertheless, inherent differences in the power potential associated with committees, differences that are tied to the variation in legislative function and in the comprehensiveness of a committee's decisional jurisdiction. This variation between committees is sufficient to make some committees more attractive as a place to gain power. Because members are in a quest for power, not simply reelection, they generally will seek to serve on committees whose function and policy focus allow the broadest personal impact on policy.

Maneuvering for membership on the more attractive committees is constrained by two fundamental factors. First, there are a limited number of attractive committee slots, and much competition will exist for these vacancies. Most members cannot realize their goal to serve on and gain control of these committees. For this reason, much pressure exists to establish norms by which members "prove" themselves deserving of membership on an attractive committee. Such norms include courtesy to fellow members, specialization in limited areas of public policy, a willingness to work hard on legislation, a commitment to the institution, adherence to the general policy parameters seen as desirable by senior members of Congress who will dominate the committee nominations process, and a willingness to reciprocate favors and abide by the division of policy domains into the set of relatively independent policy-making entities. Members who observe these norms faithfully will advance to the more desirable committees because they will have shown themselves worthy of special privilege, particularly if they also possess sufficient congressional seniority.[6]

Seniority is particularly important because of the second constraint on the process—the fact that service on the more powerful committees may limit one's ability to mend electoral fences. On the more comprehensive committees, issues often can be more complex and difficult to understand, necessitating much time and concentration on committee work; members may not be able to get home as often or as easily. Issues will be more controversial and will face members with difficult and often unpopular policy choices; members will be less able to engage in the politics of form over substance. The national visibility of the members will be greater, transforming them into public figures whose personal lives may receive considerable attention. Indiscretions that normally might go unreported will become open game for the press and can destroy careers. Thus, although it is undoubtedly true that service on the more comprehensive committees may bring with it certain attributes that can help reelection (campaign contributions from interest groups, name identification and status, a reputation for power that may convince constituents that "our member can deliver"), service on the more attractive committees does thrust members into a more unpredictable world. Although members generally will want to serve on the most powerful committees, it will normally be best for them to put off such service until they have a secure electoral base and to approach their quest for power in sequential steps.

Because of the constraints operating within a system of committee government, congressional careers reflect a set of stages. The first stage entails an emphasis on shoring up the electoral base through casework, service on constituent-oriented reelection committees, and gaining favor within Congress by serving on the housekeeping committees. Of course, the first stage is never fully "completed": there is never a time at which a member of Congress is "guaranteed" long-term reelection or total acceptance within Congress, so both constituent and congressional service are a recurring necessity. But a point is normally reached—a point defined by the circumstances of the member's constituency, the opportunities present in Congress, and the personality and competence of the member—when he or she will feel secure enough, or perhaps unhappy enough, to attempt a move to a second stage. In the second stage members broaden their horizons and seek service on key policy committees that draft important legislation regulating such national policy dimensions as interstate commerce, education, or labor. In this stage, representatives begin to be "legislators," to preoccupy themselves with national policy matters. Because of the limited number of positions on power committees, many members will spend most, perhaps the rest, of their career in this stage, moving up by committee seniority to subcommittee and committee chairs on the policy committees. As they gain expertise in the specific policy area, and create a myth of special personal authority, they will gain power in some important but circumscribed area of national policy. For members who persist, however, and/or possess the right attributes of electoral security and personal attributes, a third stage exists: service on a power committee—Rules, Ways and Means, or Finance, Appropriations, and, in the Senate, Foreign Relations. Service on these committees is superseded, if at all, only by involvement in a fourth stage: service in the party leadership as a floor leader or Speaker. Few individuals ever have the opportunity to realize this fourth and climactic step; in a system of committee government, in fact, this step will be less sought and the battles less bitter than one might expect,[7] considering the status associated with them, because power will rest primarily in committees rather than in the party. Although party leadership positions in a system of committee government do carry with them a degree of responsibility, particularly the obligation to mediate conflicts between committees and to influence the success of marginal legislation on the house floor, members will generally be content to stay on a power committee and advance to subcommittee and committee chair positions rather than engage in an all-out effort to attain party leadership positions.

This career path, presented here in an idealized and simplified fashion, is a general "power ladder" that members attempt to climb in their quest for power within Congress. Some members leave the path voluntarily to run for the Senate (if in the House), to run for governor, to serve as a judge, or to serve as president. Some for special reasons bypass one or another stage, choose to stay at a lower rung, are defeated, or retire. Despite exceptions, the set of stages is a very real guide to the long-term career path that members seek to follow. Implicit within this pattern is the very real dilemma discussed earlier: progress up the career ladder brings with it a greater opportunity for significant personal power, but also greater responsibility. As members move up the power ladder, they move away from a secure world in which reelection interest can be their dominant concern and into a world in which concerns with power and public policy predominate. They take their chance and leave the security of the reelection stage because of their personal quest for power, without which reelection is a largely meaningless victory.

The attempt to prove oneself and move up the career ladder requires enormous effort. Even after one succeeds and gains a power position, this attainment is not in itself sufficient to guarantee the personal exercise of power. To utilize fully the power prerogatives that are implicit in specific power positions, a member must maintain the respect, awe, trust, and confidence of committee and house colleagues; he or she must sustain the aura of personal authority that is necessary to legitimize the exercise of power. Although the norm of seniority under a system of pure committee government will protect a member's possession of a power position, seniority is not sufficient to guard personal authority. In order to pass legislation and dominate policy decisions in a committee's jurisdictional area, a committee chair must radiate an appearance of special authority. The member must abide by the norms of the house and the committee, demonstrate legislative competence, and generate policy decisions that appear to stay within the general policy parameters recognized as acceptable by the member's colleagues. Among reelection efforts, efforts to advance in Congress to power positions, efforts to sustain and nurture personal authority, and efforts to exercise power, the members of Congress confront an incredible array of cross-cutting pressures and internal dilemmas—decisions about how to balance external reelection interests with the internal institutional career, how to maximize the possibility of power within Congress by service on particular committees, how to gain and nurture authority within committees by specific legislative actions. The world of the congressman or congresswoman is complicated further, however, by a very special irony.

II

As a form of institutional organization, committee government possesses certain attributes that recommend it. By dividing policy concerns among a variety of committees it allows members to specialize in particular policy areas; this division provides a congressional structure through which the members can be their own expert advisers and maintain a degree of independence from lobbyists or outside specialists. Specialization also provides a procedure whereby members can become acquainted with particular programs and agencies and follow their behavior over a period of years, thus allowing informed oversight of the implementation of public policy. The dispersion of power implicit in committee government is important, furthermore, because it brings a greater number of individuals into the policy-making process and thus allows a greater range of policy innovation. In addition, as stressed above, committee government also serves the immediate power motive of congresspeople by creating so many power positions that all members can seek to gain power in particular policy domains.

Despite its assets, committee government does have severe liabilities, flaws that undermine the ability of Congress to fulfill its constitutional responsibilities to make legislative policy and oversee the implementation of that policy. First, committee government by its very nature lacks strong, centralized *leadership*, thereby undermining its internal decision-making capacity and external authority. Internally, Congress needs central leadership because most major questions of public policy (such as economic or energy policy) cut across individual committee jurisdictions. Since each committee and subcommittee may differ in its policy orientation from all others, and since the support of all relevant committees will be essential to an overall program, it is difficult, if not impossible, to enact a coherent general approach to broad policy questions. A central party leader or central congressional steering committee with extensive control over the standing committees could provide the leadership necessary to assist the development and passage of a coherent policy across the various committees, but committee government rejects the existence of strong centralized power. The resulting dispersion of power within Congress, and the refusal to allow strong centralized leadership, ensures that congressional decisions on major policy matters (unless aided and pushed by an outside leader) will be incremental at best, immobilized and incoherent as a norm. And to the extent that a Congress governed by committees can generate public policy, it faces the external problem of leadership, the inability of outside political actors, the press, or the public to identify a legitimate spokesperson for Congress on any general policy question. The wide dispersion of power positions allows numerous members to gain a degree of dominance over specific dimensions of a policy domain; all of these members can speak with some authority on a policy question, presenting conflicting and confusing approaches and interpretations. In cases where Congress does attempt to act, Congress lacks a viable mechanism through which to publicize and justify its position in an authoritative manner. Should Congress be in a conflict with the president, who can more easily present a straightforward and publicized position, Congress almost certainly will lose out in the eyes of public opinion. Lacking a clearly identifiable legislative leader in its midst, Congress is unable to provide the nation with unified, comprehensible, or persuasive policy leadership.

Closely related to the lack of leadership is a lack of *fiscal coordination*. Nowhere within a system of committee government is there a mechanism to ensure that the decisions of authorization, appropriations, and revenue committees have some reasonable relationship to one another. The authorization committees make their decisions about the programs to authorize largely independent of appropriations committee decisions about how much money the government will spend. The appropriations committees decide on spending levels largely independent of revenue committee decisions on taxation. Since it is always easier to promise (or authorize) than to deliver (or spend), program goals invariably exceed the actual financial outlays and thus the actual delivery of services. And since it is easier to spend money than to make or tax money, particularly for politicians, expenditures will exceed the revenues to pay the bills. Moves to coordinate the authorization, appropriations, and revenue processes are inconsistent with committee government, since such an effort would necessarily create a central mechanism with considerable say over all public policy and thus centralize power in a relatively small number of individuals. Committee government thus by its very nature is consigned to frustration: the policies that it does produce will invariably produce higher expectations than they can deliver; its budgets, particularly in periods of liberal, activist Congresses, will produce sizable and unplanned deficits in which expenditures far exceed revenues. The inability of committee government to provide realistic program goals and fiscal discipline will invite the executive to intervene in the budget process in order to provide fiscal responsibility and coordination. The result, of course, will be a concomitant loss of the congressional control over the nation's purse strings.

A third detriment associated with committee government, and one that is exacerbated by the absence of leadership and committee coordination, is the lack of *accountability* and *responsibility*. A fundamental justification of congressional government is that it allows political decision making to be responsive to the will of a national majority. Committee government distributes this decision-making authority among a largely autonomous set of committees. Since seniority protects each committee's membership from removal and determines who will chair each committee, a committee's members can feel free to follow their personal policy predilections and stop any legislation they wish that falls within their committee's jurisdiction, or propose any that they wish. Within a system of committee government, resting as it does on the norm of seniority, no serious way exists to hold a specific committee or committee chair accountable to the majority views of Congress or the American people, should those views differ from the views held within a particular committee. Because of the process whereby members are selected to serve on major committees—a process that emphasizes not their compatibility with the majority's policy sentiment but rather their adherence to congressional norms, general agreement with the policy views of senior congresspeople, and possession of seniority—the top committees (especially at the senior ranks) are quite likely to be out of step with a congressional or national majority. This lack of representativeness is particularly likely if patterns of electoral security nationwide provide safe seats (and thus seniority) to regions or localities that are unrepresentative of the dominant policy perspectives of the country. Responsiveness is further undermined because the absence of strong central leaders, and a widespread desire among members for procedural protection of their personal prerogatives, require reliance on rigid rules and regulations to govern the flow of legislation and debate, rules such as the Senate's cloture rule that allows the existence of filibusters. Under a system of party government, where limiting rules may exist on the books, strong party leaders can mitigate their effects. In a system of committee government, rules become serious hurdles that can block the easy flow of legislation, particularly major, controversial legislation, thereby decreasing the ability of Congress to respond rapidly to national problems. Committee government thus undermines the justification of Congress as an institution that provides responsive, representative government. Since institutions derive their power not solely from constitutional legalisms but from their own mystique of special authority that comes from their legitimizing myths, committee government undercuts not only Congress's ability to exercise power but also the popular support that is necessary to maintain its power potential.

The lack of accountability and the damage to Congress's popular support are augmented by a fourth characteristic of committee government—a tendency toward *insulation* of congressional decision making. This insulation derives from three factors. First, members of committees naturally try to close committee sessions from public purview, limiting thereby the intrusion of external actors such as interest groups or executive agencies and thus protecting committee members' independent exercise of power within committees. Second, the creation of a multiplicity of committees makes it difficult for the public or the press to follow policy deliberations even if they are open. Third, it is difficult if not impossible to create clear jurisdictional boundaries between committees. The consequent ambiguity that exists between jurisdictional boundaries will often involve committees themselves in extensive disputes over the control of particular policy domains, further confusing observers who are concerned with policy deliberations. By closing its committee doors, creating a multiplicity of committees, and allowing jurisdictional ambiguities, a system of committee government isolates Congress from the nation at large. Out of sight and out of mind, Congress loses the attention, respect, and understanding of the nation and becomes an object of scorn and derision, thus further undermining the authority or legitimacy of its pronouncements and itself as an institution.

Finally, committee government undermines the ability of Congress to perform that one function for which committee government would seem most suited— aggressive oversight of administration. According to the classic argument, the saving grace of committee government is that the dispersion of power and the creation of numerous policy experts ensure congressional surveillance of the bureaucracy. Unfortunately, this argument ignores the fact that the individuals on the committees that pass legislation will be the very people least likely to investigate policy implementation. They will be committed to the program, as its authors or most visible supporters, and will not want to take actions that might lead to a destruction of the program. The impact of publicity and a disclosure of agency or program shortcomings, after all, is very unpredictable and difficult to control and may create a public furor against the program. The better part of discretion is to leave the agency largely to its own devices and rely on informal contacts and special personal arrangements, lest the glare of publicity and the discovery of shortcomings force Congress to deauthorize a pet program, casting aspersions on those who originally drafted the legislation. Members of Congress are unwilling to resolve this problem by creating permanent and powerful oversight committees because such committees, by their ability to focus attention on problems of specific agencies and programs, would threaten the authority of legislative committees to control and direct policy in their allotted policy area. Committee government thus allows a *failure of executive oversight*.

In the light of these five problems, the irony of committee government is that it attempts to satisfy members' individual desires for personal power by dispersing internal congressional authority so widely that the resulting institutional impotence cripples the ability of Congress to perform its constitutional roles, thereby dissipating the value of internal congressional power. Members of Congress thus are not only faced with the daily dilemma of balancing reelection interests with their efforts at upward power mobility within Congress; their lives are also complicated by a cruel paradox, the ultimate incompatibility of widely dispersed power within Congress, on the one hand, and a strong role for Congress in national decision making, on the other. This inherent tension generates an explosive dynamic within Congress as an organization and between Congress and the executive.

In the short run, as members of Congress follow the immediate dictates of the personal power motive, they are unaware of, or at least unconcerned with, the long-term consequences of decentralized power; they support the creation of committee government. The longer committee government operates, the more unhappy political analysts and the people generally become with the inability of Congress to make national policy or ensure policy implementation. With Congress deadlocked by immobilism, political activists within Congress and the nation at large turn to the president (as the one alternative political figure who is popularly elected and thus should be responsive to popular sentiments) and encourage him (or her, if we ever break the sex barrier) to provide policy leadership and fiscal coordination, to open up congressional decision making to national political forces and ensure congressional responsiveness, and to oversee the bureaucracy. Presidents, particularly those committed to activist legislation, welcome the calls for intervention and will see their forthright role as an absolute necessity to the well-being of the Republic. Slowly at first, presidents take over the roles of chief legislator, chief budgetary officer, overseer of the bureaucracy, chief tribune, and protector of the people.[8] Eventually the president's role in these regards becomes so central that he feels free to ignore the wishes of members of Congress, even those who chair very important committees, and impose presidential policy on Congress and the nation at large.

The coming of a strong, domineering, imperial president who ignores Congress mobilizes its members into action. They see that their individual positions of power within Congress are meaningless unless the institution can impose its legislative will on the nation. They search for ways to regain legislative preeminence and constrain the executive. Not being fools, members identify part of the problem as an internal institutional one and seek to reform Congress. Such reform efforts come during or immediately following crises in which presidents clearly and visibly threaten fundamental power prerogatives of Congress. The reforms will include attempts to provide for more centralized congressional leadership, fiscal coordination, congressional openness, better oversight mechanisms, clarification of committee jurisdictions, procedures for policy coordination, and procedures to encourage committee accountability. Because the quest for personal power continues as the underlying motivation of individual members, the reforms are basically attempts to strengthen the value of internal congressional power by increasing the power of Congress vis-à-vis the executive. The reform efforts, however, are constrained by consideration of personal power prerogatives of members of Congress. The attempt to protect personal prerogatives while centralizing power builds structural flaws into the centralization mechanisms, flaws that would not be present were the significance of congressional structure for the national power of Congress itself the only motive. The existence of these flaws provides the openings through which centralization procedures are destroyed when institutional crises pass and members again feel free to emphasize personal power and personal careers. In addition, because policy inaction within Congress often will be identified as the immediate cause of presidential power aggrandizement, and because policy immobilism may become identified with key individuals or committees that have obstructed particular legislation, reform efforts also may be directed toward breaking up the authority of these individuals or committees and dispersing it among individuals and committees who seem more amenable to activist policies. This short-term dispersal of power, designed to break a legislative logjam (and, simultaneously, to give power to additional individuals), will serve to exacerbate immobilism in the long run when the new mechanisms of centralization are destroyed.

Viewed in a broad historical perspective, organizational dynamics within Congress, and external relations of Congress to the president, have a "cyclical" pattern. At the outset, when politicians in a quest for national power first enter Congress, they decentralize power and create committee government. Decentralization is followed by severe problems of congressional decision making, presidential assumption of legislative prerogatives, and an eventual presidential assault on Congress itself. Congress reacts by reforming its internal structure: some reform efforts will involve legislation that attempts to circumscribe presidential action; other reforms will attempt to break specific points of deadlock by further decentralization and dispersal of congressional authority; eventually, however, problems of internal congressional leadership and coordination will become so severe that Congress will be forced to undertake centralizing reforms. As Congress moves to resolve internal structural problems and circumscribe presidential power, presidents begin to cooperate so as to defuse the congressional counterattack; to do otherwise would open a president to serious personal attack as anticongressional and thus antidemocratic, destroying the presidency's legitimizing myth as a democratic institution and identifying presidential motivations as power aggrandizement rather than protection of the Republic. As the immediate threat to congressional prerogatives recedes, members of Congress (many of whom will not have served in Congress during the era of institutional crisis) become preoccupied with their immediate careers and press once again for greater power dispersal within Congress and removal of centralizing mechanisms that inhibit committee and subcommittee autonomy. Decentralization reasserts itself and Congress becomes increasingly leaderless, uncoordinated, insulated, unresponsive, unable to control executive agencies. Tempted by congressional weakness and hounded by cries to "get the country moving," the executive again reasserts itself and a new institutional crisis eventually arises. A review of American history demonstrates the existence of this cycle rather clearly, particularly during the twentieth century.

III

Throughout the nineteenth century, the national government was not immensely powerful. Most politicians were not drawn to longterm careers in Congress. Those who were drawn to Congress and were concerned with congressional power did struggle for power positions, a struggle that initially served to create a fledgling committee system.[9] The committee system was balanced by and guided by strong central leadership, particularly in the House of Representatives, where the Speakership offered a clear mechanism for legislative leadership. The central leaders were able to maintain considerable authority because they offered services—such as selection of committee members and chairpeople, policy development and guidance, mediation of parliamentary conflicts, scheduling of legislation—that were necessary to avoid the chaos implicit in the high turnover of members throughout most of the nineteenth century. The leaders' authority was challenged occasionally by other members who wanted greater independence and more autonomy for themselves and their committees. These challenges led to a "minicycle" in which forces of decentralization occasionally would assert themselves within Congress and attempt to disperse power.[10] Supporters of decentralization during the nineteenth century were never numerous enough to break the power of central leaders permanently, however, since the number of congresspeople committed to congressional careers of any significant duration was quite low.

Events of the late nineteenth century altered dramatically the nature of national power. The Civil War ended the ambiguities about the supremacy of the national government over the states and clearly established the hegemony of the national government in political affairs. The industrial revolution, whose effects began to multiply in the late nineteenth century, helped create an interdependent economy based on interstate commerce, thus expanding the power potential of the national government by confronting it with social and economic decisions of considerable magnitude that lay within its constitutional mandate. The industrial revolution also provided America (as well as other nations) with the technical means to span the oceans, conquer far-off lands, and gain international markets for American goods. America thus discovered the world, the world rediscovered America, and the national government discovered anew its constitutional responsibility for foreign policy and the regulation of American involvement in foreign commerce.

As these responsibilities served to strengthen the power of the national government over the lives of individual citizens, Congress became a center of national decision making. The Constitution gave to it the delegated powers to regulate interstate and foreign commerce, give advice and consent (on the part of the Senate) to treaties and ambassadorial nominations, control defense authorizations and appropriations, and declare war. Politicians who wanted to exercise these prerogatives had to go to Congress and stay there, which they did in ever-increasing numbers.[11] In the late nineteenth century congressmen attracted to long-term careers found power in the House centralized in the hands of a Speaker and power in the Senate centralized in the majority party leadership and majority caucus.[12] The centralized conduct of congressional operations denied the rank-and-file members the personal congressional power that growing numbers of them sought. Between 1910 and 1915 their numbers were sufficient so that these disaffected members successfully attacked the foundations of party government in both chambers, overthrowing both the Speakership and the party caucus and dispersing congressional power to the standing committees.[13] The system of committee government that emerged was held together by the institutional norms and rules that had been growing up over the preceding decades as congressional turnover had decreased, particularly the norm of seniority. As Congress moved to a system of committee government, the inherent problems began to emerge.[14] The presidency, which had benefited as an institution from the growth of an administrative state that it partially headed, from the visibility given it by the new nationwide system of mass communications, and from the rise of international relations, became increasingly free from congressional constraints and able to assert national dominance.[15]

From around 1910 to 1945 the presidency grew enormously in power, while Congress floundered. In 1921, in an act that recognized the inability of a decentralized Congress to provide policy coordination and a coherent budget, Congress created the Bureau of the Budget (BOB) and placed it in the executive branch. In the 1930s Roosevelt asserted strongly the role of chief legislator, with major laws drafted in the White House or executive agencies. Roosevelt also seized BOB—which was moved directly under his control—as a tool of presidential decision making. In addition, Roosevelt gained the authority to reorganize the executive branch and thus gained more direct control of the bureaucracy. By the early 1940s many congressional committees were overwhelmed by the executive: their staff work was conducted by staffs from the agencies; their legislation came from the president and the agencies; many committees would not consider legislation that was not approved by BOB; and the legislation that did pass Congress provided the executive broad rule-making authority.[16]

The Roosevelt presidency constituted such a direct threat to Congress—to its control over legislative decision making, the budget, and the bureaucracy—that its members moved to put their own houses in order by passing, in modified form, the 1946 Legislative Reorganization Act. In an attempt to resolve the problems of *leadership* and *accountability*, the act proposed the creation of party policy committees for each party in each house.[17] The House defeated this proposal and it was knocked out of the final act. As a means of providing for *fiscal coordination*, the act proposed and Congress approved the creation of a Joint Committee on the Budget to be composed of all members of the House and Senate Appropriations committees, the House Ways and Means Committee, and the Senate Finance Committee. A third provision of the act, passed by Congress, involved the reduction of the number of standing committees from 33 to 15 in the Senate and from 48 to 19 in the House, as well as a reduction in subcommittees. As part of this process, Congress tried to clarify jurisdictional boundaries between committees. These efforts were designed to reduce the degree of committee *insulation*, as well as to make leadership and coordination easier. Fourth, in an attempt to provide for greater *oversight* of the executive, the act directed the standing committees to exercise "continuous watchfulness" over the agencies under each committee's jurisdiction, thereby removing any doubt as to their role in bureaucratic surveillance, and also authorized each standing committee to hire professional staff members, setting a limit of four on all except Appropriations.

The 1946 Legislative Reorganization Act served to bring to a close the first twentieth-century cycle of organizational change within Congress and external struggle between Congress and the presidency. With the passage of the act, Congress was able to assert a greater degree of autonomy from the agencies and the president, particularly because of its increased staff resources. The greater congressional autonomy was assisted, however, by the fact that eight of the fourteen years following the passage of the act witnessed a divided government in which the majority party in Congress failed to control the presidency. The act itself actually did little to resolve the fundamental problems of Congress. In their attempt to protect fundamental personal prerogatives, members of Congress failed to take the really difficult steps that might have helped resolve structural problems within Congress. They left party leadership as weak after the act as before, ensuring that central party leaders would offer no threat to committee autonomy; congressional leadership and accountability remained weak. The members of Congress created a joint budget committee whose size was so large (over 100 members) that it was unworkable, whose membership had vested interests (as members of the appropriations and revenue committees) in protecting the power of outside committees, whose powers were nonexistent, and whose legislative timetable (a budget by the second month of a congressional session) was totally unrealistic. Within four years the new budget process had ceased to operate and the problems of fiscal coordination were free to reign. Third, the act did nothing to open committee meetings, to stop long-run proliferation of subcommittees, or to provide sure-fire centralized mechanisms that could enforce committee jurisdictions; the act did not defuse the problems of insulation. And the primary direct effort toward guaranteeing oversight, a provision encouraging its conduct, was a pathetic attempt at problem avoidance that left responsibility for oversight once again in the hands of those least likely to conduct it.

In the final analysis, the 1946 Reorganization Act did not replace the old order of committee government with a new order of congressional rule; the reorganization refurbished the old order and removed some of its most glaring shortcomings but in the end left committee government intact and strengthened. The new committees, by virtue of broader jurisdictions and increased staff resources, were actually stronger and more potent forces than before. Because the new committees were stronger entities, the committee chairpeople—whose prerogatives had not been reduced—emerged as even more powerful figures. The postwar system of committee government thus possessed all of the fundamental problems of the prior era. The 1946 act, moreover, contributed to the *isolation* of most members from congressional power. In streamlining the committee system the act left a relatively small number of autonomous positions that carried with them real power and status. The reform effort thus provided neither the benefits of decentralization (widespread expertise and policy innovation) nor the benefits of centralization (leadership and coordination).

Throughout the 1950s and 1960s, congressional policy making evidenced considerable deadlock. Part of the deadlock, no doubt, was due to the conservative orientation of its members. But part was clearly due to the nature of the postwar committee government, the most apparent attribute of which was the dominance of conservative committee chairpeople. Liberal Democratic activists, particularly in the House, organized to break this deadlock by breaking up the power of committee chairs and dispersing it to subcommittees and subcommittee chairs, thereby also increasing their potential ability to gain power positions. On a committee-by-committee basis they succeeded until the point that, in the early 1970s, they were strong enough to institutionalize a system of subcommittee government by altering the congressional rules. A similar breakthrough had come more informally and earlier in the Senate, so that by the 1970s power within Congress was far more decentralized than it had ever been in the period before World War II.

As liberal activists within Congress moved to decentralize its internal authority, the presidency again came to the fore as the dominant national institution. In the postwar era, under the rubric of national security, presidents gained control of a "secrecy system" in which they dominated (to the extent that any external institution did) the nation's intelligence community. Congress itself was so pluralistic—and its pluralism was increasing so steadily—that presidents and the agencies could easily "justify" ignoring Congress lest congressional leaks expose national "secrets." In foreign policy, "by the 1960s and 1970s, Presidents began to claim the power to send troops at will around the world as a sacred and exclusive presidential right," a right derived from the greater capacity of the executive branch to respond rapidly to international events and to create a coherent and rational foreign policy.[18] Domestically, Kennedy and Johnson asserted in Rooseveltian tradition the primacy of the president as chief legislator and chief budgetary officer, a role reinforced by the increasing desire of the country for a planned and prosperous economy. By the 1970s the presidency was again ascendant in American politics and undertaking political actions far in excess of its legitimate constitutional role. In Schlesinger's term, "constitutional comity" between Congress and the president had broken down. Vietnam, Cambodia, and Watergate were obvious symbols of this breakdown. But the most serious direct assault on Congress came with the attempts by Richard Nixon to impound duly appropriated funds.

The lack of fiscal coordination within Congress meant that in an age of activist legislators, and without external coordination by the executive branch, Congress would generate huge and unplanned deficits, these deficits being the result of dispersed and incremental decision making. With the coming of the Nixon years, both of these conditions were met: a liberal Congress and a divided government in which the liberal Congress faced a conservative president on whom Congress could not rely to provide a budget geared to liberal priorities. The result was huge budgetary deficits. Nixon's response was not to veto the appropriations, which for a variety of reasons seemed politically untenable and unwise, but to impound specific funds and refuse to spend them. He concentrated his efforts on the social legislation that he opposed, and "from 1969 to 1972 … impounded 17 to 20 percent of controllable expenditures…"[19] A final straw in the impoundment controversy was Nixon's assertion that impoundment was a constitutional right of the president. Nixon lost this argument in court battle after battle, but in the process he won his policy goals because his unconstitutional impoundments nevertheless succeeded in destroying or crippling the programs he opposed. And, politically, Congress could not move to impeach Nixon for his unconstitutional acts because he had the political trump card: his unconstitutional acts, so he could argue, were necessary to save the Republic from the economic disaster inherent in the budgetary deficits produced by the fiscal irresponsibility of the decentralized, leaderless, uncoordinated, unresponsive, insulated Congress.

Nixon's impoundment of duly appropriated funds confronted members of Congress with the ultimate dilemma implicit within a system of committee government in the twentieth century. The members of Congress could disperse power internally, play their power game, give half the members of each house a power position. The dispersion of power, however, created policies and budgets that the members of Congress could not defend rationally. The president was free ultimately to ignore congressional decisions if he so wished. He could not be threatened by impeachment because of unconstitutional impoundments, since impeachment is ultimately a political undertaking and the president had the political upper hand as a result of the irresponsible behavior on the part of Congress. Nixon thus presented members of Congress with the clearest message yet that the value of power within Congress depended on its ability to ensure the implementation of the policy results generated by internal congressional decision making. Nixon's actions, however, were "not an aberration but a culmination"[20] of forces at work in twentieth-century society, particularly the internal dynamics of Congress as an institution.

The response of Congress to the external threat that had been growing from the 1960s to the early 1970s, and that materialized most dramatically in the impoundment controversy, was to reform its internal organization and procedures once again. The move toward reform came largely in the Democratic party, which, as the congressional majority party, had the most to lose in a shift of power from Congress to a Republican president. Because the lower national status and visibility of House members made their personal power more dependent on the national power of their institution, and because the size of the House meant that problems of leadership, coordination, insulation, and responsiveness undermined more critically its internal decision-making capacity and consequent external authority, the House of Representatives led the reforms.

These reform efforts—from increased leadership power and fiscal coordination to alterations in oversight procedures—seem to have brought an end to a second cycle of internal organizational change and external congressional struggle with the executive branch. Few calls remain within Congress for further centralization of power. The internal struggle has shifted from planning centralized reforms such as the new budgetary process to an effort to implement and institutionalize them. Externally, the president seems less arrogant and aggrandizing in behavior than did Nixon or Johnson. As a result of these reform efforts, and the Watergate incident, the Congress appears resurgent. Is this true? Will it last?

IV

Congressional history during the era of strong national government can be characterized as cyclical in nature. The cyclical pattern derives from the implicit tension between the quest for power by individuals within Congress and the necessity of maintaining the external authority of the institution. The power motive is a very delicate phenomenon, resting as it does in the psyche of politicians who face incredible obstacles and personal demands in any attempt to realize their power drive. For several reasons, however, it seems unlikely that a significant and permanent decline will occur soon in the interest that politicians demonstrate toward congressional service. First, it seems unlikely that individuals preoccupied with political power can look outside of the nation-state for a realization of their quest. Within the nation-state all tendencies seem to indicate a continuing flow of authority away from local and state levels and toward a national level. Individuals preoccupied with attaining political power have no place to look but at the national level. Second, the recent reforms are the most dramatic alterations of internal congressional power relations since the overthrow of Cannon and have been hailed by James Sundquist as restoring the imbalance between congressional and executive power.[21] Politicians have even more reason than Sundquist to find these reforms successful, since this conclusion serves to convince them that service is worth it after all, and offers a means to attain their power goal. Third, electoral security of members of Congress has been increasing dramatically over the past decade or so. The demands of reelection should not be so great that members of Congress will feel that their reelection efforts will of necessity deny them the opportunity and time to seek and exercise congressional power. Finally, underneath the centralizing reforms, which might seem to make Congress less attractive for particular individuals, the dispersion of power of the 1947 to 1973 era remains, institutionalized by a Subcommittee Bill of Rights and augmented by further decentralization decisions that occurred as part of the 1973–75 era. Numerous subcommittee chairs and the resources that go with them, as well as an appearance of power and status, all exist to draw members back to Congress.

The thrust of these arguments is that no changes have occurred that alter the power motive underlying the internal congressional cycle. Can we therefore expect the cycle to continue to operate and the centralizing reform efforts to be undercut in the coming years? The answer to this question would seem to depend largely on the extent to which the reforms really did strengthen central policy organs. It could be that the recent institutional crisis was so severe that members did create central mechanisms so strong that those mechanisms cannot be easily undermined. Alternatively, 'members may have continued their preoccupation with personal prerogatives, even in the midst of external institutional decay. In the latter case, we would expect an examination of the reform attempt to demonstrate failure of action and, in situations in which reforms actually did pass, evidence of built-in structural flaws that will deflate the renewed congressional resurgence and aid the move toward decentralization. As selected illustrations will indicate, this latter interpretation is the more plausible one.

With regard to *leadership*, the Senate made no effort to restructure the institutional authority or roles of its party leaders. In the House, where serious attempts were made, the Democratic party leader's power (that is, the power of the Speaker in periods of majority party status) is still quite problematic. First, the rise of the caucus and the caucus chairperson, and the lack of a central role of the Speaker in the caucus, has served to dichotomize the power of the Democratic party leadership and has created a situation in which the Speaker may be opposed by a strong caucus chairperson, who can manuever the caucus against the Speaker. The inability of the Speaker to gain central authority in the caucus (for example, as its automatic chair) undercuts severely the authority of the Speaker and his ability to speak for and guide the party. This fragmentation within the leadership ranks continues in the Steering and Policy Committee where the Speaker (who chairs the meeting) and the caucus chairperson both sit, along with 22 other members. While the Speaker has the authority to select 9 of the 22, 12 are chosen by regional caucuses, not by the party caucus as a whole. The emphasis on regional selection of half of the Steering and Policy membership activates not the majority sentiments that might tie the Steering Committee and the party caucus together, but differences that can tear them apart. This is particularly true in light of the *juniority* rule in which Steering and Policy positions within each region must be rotated from Congress to Congress between junior and senior members of the region, even if only one junior member or senior member exists to be chosen. Under such decision rules it is quite possible to generate 12 members who—chosen because of regional affiliations and degree of congressional service rather than policy sentiments—are out of step with the majority of the party and can immobilize the Steering and Policy Committee. The Speaker's authority is also weak because the recent reforms have not given him greater procedural authority on the floor, or personal incentives that the Speaker can use to bargain and cajole with. In addition, in the summer of 1976 the House Democratic caucus defeated the most serious attempt to provide the Speaker with incentives he could use as inducements to party loyalty—the power to select Democratic members of the House Administration Committee and through them control resources such as office space.

The move toward greater *fiscal coordination*—the creation of the new budget committees and a new budget process—has been limited and perhaps crippled fatally by two efforts at protecting the power of existing House committees. First, 10 of the 25 members of the House Budget Committee must come from the House Appropriations and House Ways and Means committees, 5 from each. Second, all members of the House Budget Committee maintain membership on other committees (including Appropriations and Ways and Means) and are limited in service on the Budget Committee (though not on the other committees) to four years out of every ten. These two rules were the price that had to be paid in the House to gain passage of the Budget Act. Together, they help guarantee that the loyalty of House Budget Committee members is not to the Budget Committee, and thus to a centralized coordination of fiscal policy, but to their other committee assignments (particularly to the two committees, Appropriations and Ways and Means, whose fiscal authority and general status is most threatened by the Budget Committee), and thus to the protection of the autonomy and authority of the other committees. It is, after all, the other committees to which they must look for their long-term power, not the Budget Committee (because of the four-year service limit). It would be hard enough to make the new process work even with a united and cohesive Budget Committee; the internal divisions and weakness built into the House committee seem destined to destroy the process altogether.

The moves to increase *accountability* and *responsibility* did produce a mild change in the Senate cloture rule. Unfortunately, the other reforms—those that have focused on the ability of the caucuses (particularly the House Democratic caucus) to discipline committee chair-people and select chairs more in line with the policy sentiments of the caucus majority—have suffered from a severe irony. Committee power, and to a large extent congressional power, now rests with subcommittees and subcommittee chairs, not committees and committee chairs. The only subcommittee chair nominations that will be reviewed and ratified or rejected by the House Democratic party caucus are those on the Appropriations Committee. Selection of all other subcommittee chairs is left to the party caucus within the parent standing committee. The majority party caucus thus has gained the real power to hold committee chairs accountable at precisely the time that they matter least. The party caucus does not have a direct procedure to hold most subcommittee chairs accountable; there are, in fact, so many subcommittee chairs now that it would be practically impossible for the full caucus, or even the Steering and Policy Committee, to maintain even a cursory knowledge of their behavior. Since it is the committee caucuses that must constrain and guide subcommittee chairs, and ensure that they reflect the dominant sentiments of the House majority, it is increasingly important that committee caucuses be representative of the party at large and reflect its dominant sentiments in their policy jurisdiction. The representativeness of committees, and the accountability that would come from it, will be much harder for the party to ensure and maintain than the discipline of a small number of powerful committee chairs, if only because of the large numbers of members involved. Considering how hard it has been, and how long it has taken, for the party to evolve a system that would allow the disciplining of committee chairs, it may be a much harder and longer process to move to a system that would ensure a representative selection of committee members who could be trusted to reflect dominant party sentiments and discipline subcommittee chairs accordingly. The alternative, to centralize power within committee chairs who would then be held accountable by the new caucus rules, seems politically impossible in the near future, given the power motive that generated—and continues to generate—subcommittee power; such a move seems probable only if a new institutional crisis forces it (or an analogous move) on the members of the House and on Congress generally.

The effort to reduce congressional *insulation* has hardly fared any better. It has produced one victory of sorts—the sunshine rules that have opened virtually all committee meetings. The open hearings, and the widespread publicity of some meetings, may well have increased somewhat the public's respect for Congress, as in the Senate Watergate hearings or the House Judiciary proceeding on impeachment. Even this victory has had its price, in making committees more susceptible to intrusion by powerful external groups, particularly executive agencies, intrusion that may undermine congressional autonomy; but the sunshine has seemed worth it. Elsewhere, unfortunately, the moves against insulation have been far less successful in their initial passage, much less so in their final impact. The plan of the Bolling Committee to provide for clearer and more rational committee jurisdictions had the misfortune to come to the House floor only after years of power dispersion to subcommittees and the institutionalization of the power of subcommittee chairs. The Bolling plan would have undermined many of these new domains and cast uncertainty into the future of others. Most important, the Bolling plan hurt liberals as well as conservatives, throwing the former (who had supported many of the other reforms) into the arms of the latter, thereby producing a majority against the plan. The Bolling plan was defeated miserably. The cause of its defeat lay with the power motive and the desire of members of Congress, even under the greatest assault on the power of Congress in American history, to protect their personal power prerogatives. This concern for personal power prerogatives, and a widespread willingness to create even more power positions, also meant that no reform was proposed successfully to reduce the multiplicity of subcommittees. Instead, the desire to break up the power of committee chairs that had remained strong, particularly Wilbur Mills's power as chair of Ways and Means, led to a rule requiring all committees of more than 15 members to have subcommittees. The move to increase the number of subcommittees also was exacerbated by a provision of the Hansen plan that encouraged the creation of oversight subcommittees. Overall, to the extent that a multiplicity of committees and subcommittees contributes to congressional insulation, that insulation was increased rather than decreased.

Finally, there were the attempts to increase congressional *surveillance* or *oversight* of executive branch behavior. Once again Congress was unable to undertake strong action. This failure was painfully evident in the oversight hearings into intelligence activity of the federal government; Congress, particularly the House, became so bogged down in attempts by each member to assert her or his own policy perspectives that no overarching legislation or powerful oversight mechanism was produced. Less evident, but no less indicative, were congressional mistakes in the War Powers Act. With the War Powers Act, members of Congress wanted a procedure that would leave them each in control of a piece of the congressional decision; at the same time, they wanted a decision procedure that would leave open their option to exercise power, but a procedure that would not force them to do so if that exercise might prove costly in political terms. The desire of each member for a piece of the war power prerogative kept members from establishing a central Congressional Security Council, analogous to the National Security Council, that they could have mandated to exercise congressional prerogatives in a time of imminent emergency. Rather, they left the president free to act for up to sixty days on his own. In so doing, they also left themselves the protection of facing a decision only after public reaction to the president had become established. Although this might seem an astute move on the part of Congress, in effect it gave congressional war-making powers to the president for sixty days *unless* Congress chose to enforce them. Within sixty days, as any student of the modern presidency should know, a president can maneuver the country into a situation in which it is politically impossible for Congress to fail to support the president. And it is simply not the case that international relations are so complex, and events so fast-moving, that Congress had no alternative. If Congress can invest its war-making powers in a president, it can likewise delegate them to a small number of its own members whose advice and consent a president could be required to receive. After all, all modern presidents have had time to consult the National Security Council and key advisers before acting. Short of imminent nuclear attack, an extreme case whose possibility cannot be used to dictate the norm, a Congressional Security Council would be just as feasible as, and far more necessary for government in a democratic society than, the National Security Council. Members of Congress have failed to establish such a council, which could oversee presidential war making and defend congressional prerogatives, because members of Congress do not want to centralize congressional power. The continuing irony, an irony they truly fail to grasp, is that the unwillingness to structure congressional power in a manner that adjusts to the twentieth-century realities of foreign policy ultimately abrogates the war-making authority of Congress.

A concluding illustration of Congress's dilemma is its attempt to encourage oversight of the bureaucracy. The Senate essentially failed to act. The House, in attempting to act, stripped the most meaningful elements out of the Bolling Committee's oversight recommendations. In order to have serious oversight of the bureacracy, that authority must be taken from the legislative committees and placed in an oversight committee in each house that has real authority and power to investigate and to force Congress to react to the results of its investigation. The Bolling Committee recommended that the House strengthen the ability of the Government Operations Committee to be a real oversight committee by giving it privileged status to offer amendments to authorizing legislation, amendments that would result from its oversight investigations and present the House with the clear opportunity to incorporate the recommendations in the authorizing legislation. This recommendation was the test case of congressional willingness to have oversight activity. The move was defeated; it was a threat to the authority of the other standing committees. Instead, the Government Operations Committee was authorized to make a report on the planned oversight activities of the other committees. The attempt to create independent oversight activity turned to the creation of oversight subcommittees within existing legislative committees. Even this was defeated as a mandatory move and committees were merely told that they had the option of either creating such subcommittees or instructing the existing subcommittees to undertake oversight action. Less than half of the committees have turned to oversight subcommittees. The moral should be clear: Congress fails to conduct oversight of the bureaucracy not because there are no incentives to it (there are, power and publicity for those who conduct it) nor because it fails to help reelection (being a member of a powerful oversight committee would be a sure-fire method of ensuring widespread publicity). Congress fails to conduct oversight because most members of Congress *fear* its impact on the authority of their existing committee assignments and *fear* the power that a strong oversight committee would have in Congress and in national policy making. Because of the underlying power motive, Congress has failed, and continues to fail, to structure itself in a manner conducive to oversight of the bureaucracy.

As this review should demonstrate, Congress in the 1970s has attempted to act on the problems of leadership, coordination, accountability, insulation, and oversight; its actions in each area have been constrained by and ultimately crippled by a preoccupation of its members with personal power prerogatives. In light of this overview, it is quite sensible to expect the reform efforts of the 1973–75 period, the centralizing era, to be slowly but surely undermined as members reassert the exercise of their power prerogatives, thrusting the country into a new cycle. Much depends on the presidency and the willingness of presidents to show a greater sensitivity to Congress. In all probability, given the extensiveness of congressional reaction in the preceding few years, and the impeachment proceedings against Nixon, the high point of presidential aggressiveness during the postwar cycle was reached with Nixon in 1973. In the years immediately ahead, the country should witness a more cooperative presidency as presidents attempt to defuse the congressional resurgence, a phenomenon already witnessed partially in the Ford presidency. The seduction of Congress is most likely, of course, if an era of united government should dawn in which the individual in the White House is an ideological and partisan compatriot of members of Congress. With a less threatening presidency, the internal dynamics within Congress should lead once again to a push toward decentralization, with a maintenance and strengthening of the 1970–73 era reforms. With Congress not being confronted by apparent institutional crisis, the entity that would be the most probable and immediate victim of this move toward decentralization would be the congressional budget system, since it is the entity that can most severely constrain the autonomous decision-making authority of individual committees and subcommittees. The short-term survival of the budget process in its current form, and as an *autonomous* mechanism of congressional decision making, would seem probable only with the election of a president or a series of presidents who continued attacks on Congress analogous to those made by Nixon and would probably be most likely in an era of divided government.

When a period of quiescence does come, and as the personal power motives of congresspeople produce a move within Congress toward decentralized decision making, it is realistic to assume that the problems inherent in congressional decentralization will lead the nation to demand yet another resurgence of presidential power, unleashing again the momentum toward an institutional crisis in which a president or a series of presidents will overstep dramatically the bounds of political and constitutional comity. The resurgence of presidential power may even come through the centralized congressional mechanisms themselves. For example, the internal moves by self-interested members of Congress against centralized policy organs or against the decisions of those organs (such as the new budget process, the Speakership, or the Steering and Policy Committee) would provide a president with the opportunity to intervene forcefully in the congressional process and throw his weight behind the central policy mechanisms. In such a case we should expect Congress to pay a high price for its "salvation," with the president using and altering such mechanisms to meet the policy ends and power advantage of the president. A majority party president with strong policy commitments could begin the manipulation of the central policy mechanisms by use of a strong presidential liaison team to exert executive influence on the budget committees and budget resolution votes, through agency "cooperation" with and "assistance" to the Congressional Budget Office, and by presidential cooptation of congressional party leaders. We would eventually expect formal alterations in the congressional budget process that would institutionalize executive control of it (perhaps through "coordination" of the CBO with the OMB), thus allowing and formalizing an executive branch penetration of the congressional decision-making process far greater than ever before. Alternatively, Congress may overthrow the new centralizing mechanisms in form as well as reality, leaving in their stead a system totally based on sub-committee government and leaving the executive free to develop other means by which to more strongly coordinate and dominate congressional decision making.

Whatever the precise form of behavior, the logic of the power motive suggests another cycle involving internal moves toward decentralized policy making in Congress, presidential usurpation of congressional authority, and eventual warfare between Congress and presidents over public policy and institutional prerogatives. The immediate question, within the context of this perspective, is not whether a surge toward decentralization and institutional crisis is likely, but rather what such an occurrence will mean when it comes, and what the general cycle tells us about Congress and American politics generally.

V

In order to interpret the significance of the cyclical pattern of internal congressional change for the external struggle between Congress and the executive, we must return to the *Federalist Papers* and James Madison. Madison's analysis of the U.S. Constitution provides us with the most convincing justification of the Constitution and the most prescient projection of the behavioral patterns expected to flow from its institutional structure. The classic summary of his stance is in Federalist #51:

> In order to lay a due foundation for that separate and distinct exercise of the different powers of government, which to a certain extent is admitted on all hands to be essential to the preservation of liberty, it is evident that each department should have a will of its own ... .

> [T]he great security against a gradual concentration of the several powers in the same department consists in giving to those who administer each

department the necessary constitutional means and personal motives to resist encroachment of the others. The provision for defense must in this, as in all other cases, be made commensurate to the danger of attack. Ambition must be made to counteract ambition. The interest of the man must be connected with the constitutional rights of the place.[22]

The devices to which Madison refers here are a separation of powers among the legislative, executive, and judicial branches or departments and a system of checks and balances between these branches. Explicit in the Madisonian conception is an assumption that tension will exist between the branches of government, a tension deriving from the natural ambitions of the politicians within each institution. Ambition will naturally lead these politicians to aggrandize power for themselves by asserting a broad political role for their institution. Inherent in this conception of interbranch tension is the expectation of thrust and counterthrust between the institutions, particularly Congress and the presidency, with one branch asserting itself only to be constrained by the other.

From a Madisonian perspective, Congress should have no problem in asserting its "will" and checking executive aggrandizement. This ability will exist, in large part, because a "few of the members, as happens in all such assemblies, will possess superior talents; will, by frequent re-election, become members of long standing; will be thoroughly masters of the public business…" This tendency toward a few involved legislators would be reinforced in the U.S. Congress by the problems of service, "the distances which many of the representatives will be obliged to travel and the arrangements rendered necessary by that service…"[23] In fact, Madison saw the real problem of Congress not in a weakness of will but in a tendency toward too great an internal concentration of authority and too strong a congressional will. For this reason, Madison feared Congress as the primary threat to the Republic and directed the most attention to constitutional constraint on Congress, not on the executive.[24]

In a Madisonian interpretation, the congressional cycle is one additional element that helps the system of separation of powers and checks and balances work. It ensures that the health and vibrancy of the presidency is maintained in the face of the more threatening legislature, and that there will be struggle and compromise between the Congress and the presidency. Because each institution thus can maintain its autonomy and will, and because Congress is sufficiently restrained by both the external checks and its internal dynamics, the power shift between Congress and the presidency revolves around a constant center or balance point, and the parameters of the cycle are relatively constant, with neither institution ever allowing the other to proceed too far in power aggrandizement. When each cycle is complete, the constitutional powers of the two institutions are once again intact and in balance, a balance specified by the Constitution. During each cycle the rise of one institution and the decline of the other is maintained within clearly defined boundaries that are relatively similar from cycle to cycle. No tendency exists for the institutional excesses to increase in extensiveness or severity from cycle to cycle. The cycle thus can last indefinitely and is, in fact, a "good" thing. The current resurgence of Congress demonstrates its resilience as an institution, its ability to rise to the demands of the day. The failure of the centralizing reforms over the coming years will not be a "bad" thing but merely a natural process that is essential to the dynamics of the Madisonian system of government.

Throughout the nineteenth century, American politics probably did conform fairly closely to the Madisonian interpretation, with the minicycles discussed earlier a constraint on internal congressional ambitions and external aggrandizement. Congress probably was the greatest threat (from a Madisonian perspective) to the constitutional system and to property, and the dominant force in American politics. After a review of twentieth-century congressional behavior, there is good reason to suspect that the Madisonian interpretation no longer applies.

Madison assumed that each institution would sustain sufficient internal integrity that it could have an "institutional will" and would have the institutional capacity to exert that will and counteract the aggrandizing tendencies of other institutions. That assumption was central to Madison's argument and, in the case of Congress, rested on supporting assumptions of high turnover and unpleasant working conditions that would lead Congress naturally to invest its authority in a few select individuals. The alterations in American society and politics in the late nineteenth century that made Congress a more attractive place in which to serve (owing to the growth of national power) and an easier place in which to serve (owing to greater ease of travel and the existence of professional occupations that would mesh well with congressional service) undermined Madison's supporting assumptions, creating internal problems for Congress as an institution that were of a magnitude Madison never envisioned. These problems—of leadership, coordination, insulation, accountability, oversight—have crippled both the ability of Congress to know its "will" and its ability to assert its will. Simultaneously, the growth in societal complexity and international interdependence put a greater emphasis on the speed and efficiency of national decision making. The standard for congressional performance thus was raised at precisely the time that its capacity to perform was being undercut. Unfortunately for Congress, these same changes that hurt it served to highlight the attributes of the presidency—its ability to act quickly, coherently, and decisively; in fact, the coming of the mass media increased the capacity of the president to publicize his will and project a mystique of special authority that is essential to the exercise of power.

It is unrealistic to expect that this shift to presidential ascendancy can or will be altered by the Supreme Court. The power alterations result from inherent constitutional and institutional problems that the Court largely is unable to address. In addition, the judicial appointive process in the Constitution created an informal alliance between the Court and the presidency,[25] an alliance that should constrain the Court from serious innovative efforts to create conditions and interpretations that might subtly alter the formal Constitution so as to strengthen Congress.[26]

The institutional power struggles of the twentieth century thus are operating by a different set of principles, and toward a different end, than the dynamics of Madisonian government suggest. First, the presidency and the executive branch generally gain more authority or power with each cycle than they are forced to give up. During the cycle from 1910 to 1945, for example, the presidency gained dominance over the bureaucracy (that is, to the degree that any external institution dominates the bureaucracy), gained the legitimate role as the nation's chief legislator, and gained legitimacy as chief budgetary officer. With the resurgence of Congress in the postwar years, the presidency still maintained all of the roles—if not as strongly as in Roosevelt's case, certainly more strongly than before the Roosevelt era. At what appears to be the end of a 1945–73 cycle, the presidency has added to its earlier roles (1) a new and legitimized role as the nation's independent agent in war (as a result of the sixty-day provision of the War Powers Act); (2) a wider range of options with regard to control of the budget and the spending of funds (as a result of the Impoundment Act, which, while trying to limit presidential impoundments, succeeded in giving the president a political weapon, impoundment recommendations, to use against Congress and in legitimizing the president's prerogatives to propose a delay or rescission in spending for reasons other than financial efficiency); and (3) retained central authority over the intelligence community and the bureaucracy generally. At the same time that the balance of power seems to be shifting toward the presidency, a second trend seems also to be occurring: an overall increase with each cycle in the extremity of presidential transgressions. Recent presidents' illegal use of the nation's intelligence community, the expanding misuse of presidential war-making powers, and Nixon's unconstitutional impoundments are cases in point.

Existing factors suggest that these trends will continue and worsen. First, the domestic and international problems appear to be increasing in severity, rather than decreasing. The existence of these problems, and the necessity of national action to resolve them, will continue to draw politicians to Congress and sustain the power cycle. The severity of the problems, however, and the existence of congressional immobilism, will justify a continuing and increasing reliance on the executive. This move toward executive power will be reinforced by a second trend: the electoral difficulties of becoming president are so great, and are increasing so significantly with well-intentioned reforms designed to purify presidential politics, that there is an inherent self-selection and weeding process such that the people who rise to that office are, and increasingly will be, immensely power-driven individuals, a phenomenon reinforced by the pressures on and isolation of presidents. In addition, should presidents attempt to forsake proffered power, the structure of American politics and the presidential office probably will offer them no eventual alternative but to accept the expanded authority: with policy immobilism and a resultant economic and social crisis, it would actually be an act of immediate and contextual irresponsibility for presidents not to act in particular and desperate situations.

A final factor which suggests that the momentum toward presidential power will continue and increase is the internal power structure of the current Congress. Underlying the reforms of the 1973–75 era are the reforms of 1970–73. These earlier reforms created a dispersion of power within Congress that is truly unprecedented in American history. As the centralizing mechanisms of the 1973–75 era falter, congressional decision making (as an autonomous process) will depend on an institutionalized system of subcommittee government. Given the greater dispersion of power in that system, the problems of leadership, coordination, insulation, accountability, and oversight that face Congress will be of a magnitude beyond any we have witnessed thus far. The political immobilism implicit in this situation will be intolerable without a strong president. Presidents seeking to assert authority will not face relatively strong committee chairs like Wilbur Mills, who have authority over a moderate range of policy areas, but relatively weak and isolated subcommittee chairs who can at best dominate a small policy domain and thus will have less maneuverability and fewer resources to use in a congressional–executive struggle. Congress increasingly will be a primary justification for a strong presidency and increasingly an ineffective agent in the constraint of presidential imperialism.

The thrust of my argument, then, is that the Madisonian system is self-destructing. An age of strong national government magnifies the power motive underlying politics generally and sets in motion organizational dynamics within Congress that undermine its ability to perform its constitutional roles. These governmental roles are undertaken by a strong presidency whose institutional integrity and external authority are not decreased but actually increased by the complexities and technology of modern society. In light of human nature and the rules of the political struggle specified in the U.S. Constitution, this alteration in the conduct of governmental roles is a natural reaction of the relevant actors and institutions to the growth of the power of the national government. Seen in this context, the ongoing and continuing destruction of the constitutional system does not stem necessarily from evil motives or evil people. Politicians' quest for power within Congress can derive from the most noble of desires to serve humanity. Power aggrandizement on the part of presidents may be forced on them by the very nature of the political immobilism within Congress and the severity of social and economic crises in the country.

The source of constitutional destruction, and the decline of Congress, lies in the Constitution itself and its inappropriateness today as a guide to representative government. The separation-of-power system provides Congress with an autonomy, as is desirable, that allows it an internal organizational life independent of the executive branch. It also properly invests Congress with legislative authority, delegating it in clear and unmistakable terms. Yet legislative authority is a type of responsibility that can be decentralized and thus afflicted by the problems evident in a system of pure committee government. The Constitution provides no function or structure to Congress that would create internal congressional incentives supportive of power centralization, coordination, and institutional integrity. It merely assumes that these will be maintained by the natural operation of political life in a simple, agrarian society. When the latter assumption is no longer valid, when it is no longer true that policy problems will be simple and congressional life will draw only a few legislators committed to long-term congressional careers and power, there is no provision within the constitutional system—no incentive system—that will lead members naturally to sustain mechanisms of institutional centralization.

As a Congress composed of members who are concerned about public policy becomes increasingly and necessarily enmeshed in institutional immobilism—an immobilism that may result from the very genuineness of members' policy concerns—Congress faces the external checks and balances built into the Constitution. Ironically, since the Founding Fathers thought that Congress was the most dangerous branch, the really powerful checks, such as veto and judicial review, were given to the president and the Court to use against Congress. The inability of the legislature to know its will thus is exacerbated by the ability of the president and the Court, separately or in alliance, to debilitate any congressional will that may exist by throwing in front of Congress the requirement that it make legislative policy not by majority vote but by two-thirds vote.

In light of these considerations, a successful end to the debilitating cycles of the twentieth century requires that we direct attention not to internal congressional reform but to fundamental alterations of the constitutional system itself. We must create an incentive system within the Constitution that, while sustaining a degree of congressional decentralization that will allow for innovation and expertise, will lead members of Congress naturally to support centralizing mechanisms that can sustain institutional integrity. We also must reconsider the nature of the checks-and-balances system with the intent of strengthening the position of Congress. Simultaneously, we can redirect the values by which we wish institutional politics to be conducted, shifting from a politics of minority veto and policy inaction toward majority government and social justice.

It may be that changes within the confines of the current Constitution will be sufficient for our ends.[27] Perhaps constitutional specifications of certain electoral laws could ensure a more competitive electoral system at the congressional level which, by generating higher turnover and more internal institutional need for leadership by individual members, would force a greater degree of centralization. Constitutional provisions giving real authority to the Speaker of the House or the president pro tem of the Senate could give them real incentives to use in the creation and long-term maintenance of significant centralized policy organs in each house. The creation at a constitutional level of a Congressional Security Council that could exercise congressional authority under specific emergency conditions might help Congress regain constitutional control of war making. Finally, a revision of the veto provision (making overrides easier or vetoes harder) might help sustain congressional policy making by holding out the hope that congressional decisions eventually could become the law of the land. While some of the above perhaps could be handled legislatively, it is critical that the changes come at the constitutional level, the level most difficult for members of Congress to manipulate and undermine for personal advantage.

Finally, we must realize that the complex and demanding nature of contemporary life raises serious and fundamental questions as to the viability of Congress within a system of separation of powers and checks and balances. We should reconsider, therefore, our constitutional system itself and direct some attention toward assessing the viability of a new constitutional structure less geared to policy immobilism and institutional conflict. As we consider movement toward alternative constitutions we must realize that constitution making is serious and difficult business. It requires realistic and hard-headed assessment of human nature, of the implications of different institutional arrangements, of the social conditions within which politics is to be conducted, and of the consequences that will derive from the interaction of these three elements of political life. In many ways Madison's performance in the *Federalist Papers* is still the best guide to this type of undertaking. A proper respect for his intellect is always advisable. Yet we also must unlock ourselves from the infatuating clarity and logic of Madison's arguments that continue to exert a seductive hold on our imaginations long after the supporting conditions assumed by them have passed. The transformations of our society in the last century undercut the accuracy of his forecasts. The changes in our values, and hopefully the growth of a greater commitment to majoritarian government and popular justice, alter the goals to which a new or modified constitutional arrangement should be committed. The quest for democratic government demands that we throw off the Sisyphean preoccupation with internal congressional reform and reconsider the constitutional structure that today necessarily consigns Congress—our most democratic institution—to an increasingly weakened political role in an ever more powerful national government.

Notes

Acknowledgements: For critical assistance at various stages in the writing of this essay, I would like to thank Arnold Fleischmann, Michael N. Green, Bruce I. Oppenheimer, Diana Phillips, Russ Renka, Terry Sullivan, and numerous graduate and undergraduate students who shared with me their questions and insights.

1 The approach presented here builds on the work of Fenno (1973), Huntington (1965) and Mayhew (1974b).
2 By the power positions I mean those formal positions within the congressional institution that carry with them the legal authority over such prerogatives as parliamentary procedure, financial and staff resources, information collection and dispersal, and agenda setting, that are amenable to the control of policy making in a legislative assembly.
3 See Mayhew (1974b: 32–77).
4 A survey conducted during the 89th Congress under the auspices of the American

Political Science Association's Study of Congress found that the average congressperson spent only 5.6 days per month in the home district while Congress was in session (a phenomenon that increasingly covers the calendar year). Although the figure demonstrates that members do take care to return home (a fact that Fenno's research shows is partially related to the location of the family home), members clearly devote *most* of their time to work in Washington. While in Washington, the average member's work week stretches to 59.3 hours per week and has a clear legislative cast to it, with 22.5 hours devoted to work related to legislative research or committee activity, or to party and leadership activities; an additional 15.3 hours are spent on the floor; 7.2 hours are spent answering mail; 5.1 hours handling constituent problems and 4.4 hours visiting with constituents in Washington; 2.7 hours on writing chores, speeches, and magazine articles; 2.3 hours with lobbyists; 2.1 hours on press work, radio and TV appearances. See Tacheron and Udall (1970: 303–304); see also Fenno (1978).

5 This breakdown of committee types, and the idea of a set of career stages, derive from a very liberal reading of Fenno (1977), together with the literature on committee attractiveness and mobility between committees. For a good summary of this latter literature, see Rieselbach (1973: 30).

6 On the existence of congressional norms or folkways, see Donald Matthews (1960) and Asher (1973). On the committee selection process, see Masters (1961) and Rohde and Shepsle (1973).

7 See Peabody (1976). I am struck in Peabody's discussion by the small number of leadership challenges, the lack of bitter struggles, and the short amount of time and limited resources put into leadership battles.

8 Some of the major academic works that reflect these calls for presidential assertion are Richard Neustadt (1960); Harris (1964); and Burns (1963). The classic glorification of the twentieth-century presidency is Rossiter (1956).

9 Cooper (1970); and McConachie (1898).

10 This assertion is based on Brown (1922); and Bolling (1968).

11 The literature on decline in turnover includes Price (1975); Fiorina, Rhode, and Wissel (1975); and Polsby (1968).

12. On the House, see Brown (1922); on the Senate, see Rothman (1969).

13. See Hechler (1940).

14. Discussions of these problems in the 1920s are contained in Brown (1922) and Rogers (1926).

15. For a more general discussion of the rise of the presidency, see Burns (1965) and Schlesinger, Jr. (1973).

16. See Galloway (1946: 7–8, 53, 242–254).

17. Galloway (1951: 51).

18. Schlesinger, Jr. (1973: 298).

19. James P. Pfiffner, "Congressional Budget Reform, 1974: Initiation and Reaction," 1975 APSA convention paper, pp. 4–5; see also Fisher (1975: 147–201).

20. Schlesinger, Jr. (1973: 395).

21. Sundquist (1977) writes: "Viewed in the perspective of history, the changes in the executive-legislative power balance wrought by a single Congress—the 93rd—are truly momentous. Ever since the era of congressional government at the close of the Civil War …, the flow of power had been all one-way, in the direction of the president. In just two years, the trend of a hundred years was dramatically reversed. An extraordinary abuse of presidential power triggered a counteraction equally extraordinary, and the ponderous processes of institutional change were expedited." Sundquist seems to reflect an essentially Madisonian conception of the recent changes in congressional structure.

22 James Madison, Federalist # 51, in Hamilton, Madison, and Jay (1961: 321–322).

23 Madison, Federalist # 53, in Hamilton, Madison, and Jay (1961: 334–335).

24 Madison, Federalist # 48, in Hamilton, Madison, and Jay (1961: 309).
25 Scigliano (1971: 197).
26 Ibid., pp. 200–201.
27 For an intriguing dialogue on the Constitution and current problems, see Eckhardt and Black (1976).

Additional Perspective on "Quest"

"Congress and the Quest for Power" was written in the immediate aftermath of the congressional reforms of the mid-1970s and sought to explain their occurrence. In part the reform period served to increase fragmentation and decentralization in Congress, as with the increased autonomy given to subcommittees in Congress. The dominant scholarly literature of the early postwar era had stressed the committee-centered focus and decentralizing tendencies of Congress (Galloway, 1946; Burns, 1949, 1963, 1965; Gross, 1953; Huntington, 1965; Fenno, 1965, 1966, 1973; Polsby, 1968; Polsby, Gallagher and Rundquist, 1969; Huitt and Peabody, 1969; Goodwin, 1970; Manley, 1970; Cooper, 1970; and Mayhew, 1974b). Thus the move by members of Congress to increase decentralization within committees was not surprising. What was puzzling was the extent to which the reforms instituted centralizing procedures that fostered party government (as with the increased powers of the Speaker).

The contribution of "Quest" was to offer a cyclical "rational-choice" explanation for this puzzling development. The explanation sought to account for previous patterns of recentralizing and decentralizing change in Congress from the late nineteenth century to the 1970s while building on rather than negating the goal-oriented, organizationally based and constitutionally sensitive literature of the early postwar period. In its comparison of the centralizing reforms of the 1970s with those at the turn of the twentieth century, the essay pointed toward a renewal of party government.

The length of party resurgence and the timing of a future return to congressional decentralization were left as open questions. Rather, the essay noted that a sustained period of united party government (with reduced conflict between Congress and the president) probably would undermine the centralizing reforms relatively fast, working against party government and the new budget process in Congress; a sustained period of divided government (and the resulting conflict with the president) could work to sustain the immediate potency of centralizing reforms. Instead of predicting which of these outcomes would occur in the short-run, "Quest" focused on the troubling long-term dilemma posed by a gradual 'decentralizing drift' likely to characterize a careerist Congress across a series of organizational cycles. With careerist legislators ultimately more attuned to personal autonomy than to the institution's governing authority, Congress would gradually create a more decentralized organizational structure across cycles of change, despite recentralization at the end of each cycle. Cycles of institutional resurgence thus would be unable to redress the long-term erosion of congressional authority, so long as legislative careerism dominated the politics of Congress.

A more complete discussion of the ways in which considerations of power pushed Congress towards extensive reforms is provided in Lawrence C. Dodd and Richard L. Schott, *Congress and the Administrative State,* published in 1979. In particular, Chapter Four (pages 129 to 154) develops more fully the ways in which the reforms of the 1970s could foster party government, particularly in the House of Representatives. The chapter opens by stressing the role that elections, particularly the 1958 congressional elections, played in solidifying a relatively united and reformist liberal majority in Democratic caucuses of the two chambers. It ends with the Congress of the late 1970s positioned in "a delicate balancing act, a balance between dispersed and centralized power centers, between particularized and general policy interests. And, as the history of the past century should indicate, there is nothing inherently permanent about a new congressional order or the policy process that results from it," leaving the future direction of congressional development an open question (page 154).

Writing in 1989, Dodd and Oppenheimer saw the power balance in the House shifting strongly toward "consolidation of institutional power in a new House oligarchy composed of the majority party leadership and members of a few elite committees," concluding that "(a)s the 100th Congress drew to a close, power within the House was consolidated in a more centralized and concentrated manner than at any time since the days of Joseph Cannon." See Dodd and Oppenheimer, (1989: 39, 60). With the rise of party government, the pressing concerns for students of Congress centered on (1) interpreting the meaning and implications of this development, in light of social and political conditions of the late twentieth century; (2) gauging its implications for the role and power of Congress; and (3) assessing whether the shift to party government was likely to be permanent, as suggested by Gary Cox and Mathew McCubbins in the *Legislative Leviathan* (1993), or would eventually fall prey to the cyclical and decentralizing organizational dynamics outlined in "Quest." The subsequent essays in this book address these issues.

Foundation Work: "Congress and the Quest for Power" owes an enormous debt to David Mayhew's pioneering 1974 study, *Congress: The Electoral Connection. The Electoral Connection* provided the first explicit 'theory of Congress' to gain explanatory traction within political science. It did so by linking member motives, electoral and organizational politics, institutional structure, and policy making together in an effort to explain the institution's overall characteristics and adaptive survival. Mayhew's effort to visualize how the varied aspects of congressional politics 'fit together' in a simple and comprehensible manner, with the parts united into a comprehensible whole by members' 'single-minded pursuit of re-election,' was a transformative breakthrough in the study of representative assemblies. Dodd discusses Mayhew's influence on his work, and his decision to move beyond a focus on reelection and to stress the acquisition of power as members' central goal, in his *"Comments on David Mayhew's Congress: The Electoral Connection"* (Dodd, 2001b).

The author notes as well his huge debt to Richard Fenno's 1973 work, *Congressmen in Committees.* Without Fenno's masterful study of the multiple goals members bring to committee politics he almost certainly would not have envisioned members' step-level career movement through stages of reelection, policy making and influence, in which member frustration with slow ascent up the ladder becomes a driving force for organizational change in Congress. Highlighting members' multiple career goals and their frustration in achieving them greatly increased the plausibility and explanatory power of the 'power paradox' at the heart of "Quest." *Congressmen in Committees* and *The Power of the Purse* (Fenno, 1966), in combination, constitute the most extraordinary empirical study of legislative politics ever conducted and will remain 'must reading' for all future scholars of elective policy-making assemblies.

For a helpful discussion of "Quest," see Herbert F. Weisberg, Eric S. Heberlig and Lisa M. Campoli (1999), Chapter Two. For an assessment of the essay's contribution to the debate over rational-choice approaches to political inquiry, see Morris Fiorina (1995c), "Rational Choice, Empirical Contributions, and the Scientific Enterprise," and Donald P. Green and Ian Shapiro (1995), "Pathologies Revisited: Reflections on our Critics." This debate was focused and enhanced by the publication of *Pathologies of Rational Choice Theory,* by Donald P. Green and Ian Shapiro (1994).

Suggested Reading: Books, articles and essays that speak to, build on, test or assess the arguments introduced in "Quest" include Davidson and Oleszek (1976); Cooper and Brady (1981a); Sundquist (1981); Sinclair's extensive research (1983), (1989), (1995), (2001); Parker (1992); Shepsle (1989); Hibbing (1991); Rohde (1991); Cox and McCubbins (1993); Schickler (2001); Zelizer (2004a); Polsby (2004); and Cooper (2009).

Classroom Use: "Quest" can be used as an introduction to the mid-twentieth century politics of Congress and to the experience of being a legislator during that period. Additionally, it speaks to the reforms of the 1970s, dynamics of political change from the late nineteenth century to the 1970s, and the power struggles between Congress and the presidency.

For point/counterpoint contrasts, the essay can be paired with Samuel P. Huntington's 1965 essay, "Congressional Responses to the Twentieth Century," in which he stresses the incapacity of Congress to reform itself, whereas "Quest" highlights its reformist capacities. It can be paired with Mayhew (1974b) to explore contrasting ways to interpret congressional politics, with "The Electoral Connection" focused on the implications that members' reelection concerns have for Congress and "Quest" focused on the implications that flow from members' power concerns. It can also be paired with *Legislative Leviathan* (Cox and McCubbins, 1993), with students asked to contrast and assess the emphasis by Cox and McCubbins on the continuity of party cartels in dominating congressional politics (specifically the House), as opposed to "Quest," which stresses a cyclical perspective on party power. This contrast can be informed by Pearson and Schickler (2009) and Schickler and Pearson (2009).

3

CONGRESS, THE CONSTITUTION, AND THE CRISIS OF LEGITIMATION

1981

Chapter Three places the congressional reforms of the 1970s in historical perspective. It argues that the move from the agrarian world of the founders to the contemporary postindustrial era has created difficulties for Congress that the founders failed to anticipate.

Fearing that the citizen legislators of the agrarian era would invest dictatorial power in a central congressional leader, the founders focused their attention on constraining the Congress, withholding from its constitutional officers explicit powers they could use to lead it. In contrast, the concern in the postindustrial era is not with congressional dictatorship but with policy deadlock. This deadlock emerges from careerist politics within Congress combined with the daunting postindustrial policy challenges facing the nation. Despite the grievous problems associated with deadlock, there has been no effort to revise the Constitution in ways that would strengthen Congress and empower its leaders to lead. Congress is left struggling to reform itself, hindered by the very constraints on leadership power the centralizing reforms seek to address.

The essay concludes that the reforms of the 1970s were insufficient to ensure a strong Congress, given the severe policy challenges confronting it. It anticipates a more conflict-ridden, immobilized and unpopular post-reform Congress and reemergence of presidential imperialism. It closes by proposing constitutional changes that would enable Congress to generate strong leaders, better assert its "institutional will," and regain popular legitimacy.

The American Constitution was constructed upon a theory of politics, a theory most evident in the essays by James Madison in the *Federalist Papers*. The theory assumed that a basic motive driving politicians is a quest for power to control the

Lawrence C. Dodd. *"Congress, the Constitution, and the Crisis of Legitimation."* In Congress Reconsidered, 2nd Edition. *Edited by Lawrence C. Dodd and Bruce I. Oppenheimer. Washington, D.C.: Congressional Quarterly Press. 1981, pp. 390–420* policy decisions that impose the authority of the state on the citizenry at large. As power seekers, politicians crystallize the factional divisions that undergird any society and fuel the political strife in which faction seeks to dominate faction in order to maximize particularized interest. In the heat of political battle and the impassioned aftermath of victory, the power quest can be so all-consuming that the victorious faction and factional leaders overlook the general interest and civil liberties of the public.[1]

Because the power quest can pose such a fundamental threat to political freedom and stability, Madison argued that the best way to protect civil liberties and property was through a constitution that divides the power of the state among governmental institutions. With separation of powers, checks and balances, and federalism together dispersing power, little chance exists that one individual or faction can gain sufficient leverage to dominate the nation. Rather, governmental action will require cooperation among institutions that share power. In the act of cooperating, each institution should jealously guard its prerogatives.

Madison did not assume, however, that institutions would, in fact, jealously guard their prerogatives. After all, institutions have no autonomous being, but are only aggregations of individuals who act in the institution's name. Recognizing this problem, Madison concluded:

> In order to lay a due foundation for that separate and distinct exercise of the different powers of government, which to a certain extent is admitted on all hands to be essential to the preservation of liberty, it is evident that each department should have a will of its own ...[2]

The entire logic of the Constitution rests on this critical variable: *institutional will.* Should any one branch of government consistently fail to assert an institutional will, then the powers of that branch would be usurped by another branch, checks and balances would cease to operate, and "the preservation of liberty" would be jeopardized.

Because of the critical importance of institutional will, the founders were not content to hope blindly that each institution would be capable of developing and sustaining institutional cohesiveness. They saw the Constitution as an instrument that could structure institutions, nurture cohesiveness, and generate an institutional will. Madison stated this proposition quite clearly:

> ... [T]he great security against a gradual concentration of the several powers in the same department consists in giving to those who administer each department the necessary constitutional means and personal motives to resist encroachment of the others. The provision for defense must in this, as in all other cases, be made commensurate with the danger of attack. Ambition must be made to counteract ambition. The interests of the man must be connected with the constitutional right of the place.[3]

Based on this proposition, the founders created a single executive and gave to the president the power to nominate department heads. Similarly, they created a single Supreme Court composed of justices with virtual lifetime tenure. These and other devices were expressly designed to nurture the cohesiveness of the presidency and the Supreme Court. The founders wanted to ensure that the executive and judicial branches of government could assert their institutional wills.

When the writers of the Constitution came to the legislative branch, however, they lost their fervor for constitutional provisions that would nurture institutional cohesion. The constitutional provisions for Congress, such as bicameralism and separate selection procedures for the House and Senate, seem to generate internal conflict and weakness. There are several reasons why the founders failed to undergird the institutional will of Congress as they did the presidency and the Supreme Court.

Madison believed that the way politicians approach political institutions and seek power through them strongly depends upon the nature of the extant society and on political realities within it. The Constitution was written for an agrarian society in which political service at the national level was physically and economically difficult. Moreover, because the role of the national government was quite limited in an agrarian society isolated by the Atlantic from European wars, and because the federal Constitution left considerable power to state and local governments, Madison believed that long-term service at the national level would not be very attractive to politicians. Power would be pursued more easily and perhaps more effectively in local or state politics. At the national level of government, there would be a high turnover of elected officials. The few politicians who stayed on for long-term congressional careers would acquire expertise and would be relied upon as power wielders.[4]

Madison's great fear was that the Congress, in the context of an agrarian and isolated society, would come to rely on too few leaders, particularly the presiding officer of the House, to exercise power. The experience of the colonial assemblies suggested that a legislature in control of the power of the purse and guided by a strong-willed leader could come to dominate governmental affairs. Similarly, Congress could be an overly cohesive, aggressive institution using its taxing and spending power to dominate the other branches. Hence, the best constitutional course was not to reinforce the natural cohesiveness that Congress would derive from high turnover and centralized organizational power in an agrarian age, but to constrain Congress in order to equalize the balance of power between Congress, the presidency, and the Court.[5]

The Madisonian theory of politics thus envisioned a constitutional system in which each branch of government would be sufficiently cohesive to have an institutional will, assert itself in its own area of governmental authority, cooperate in areas of shared authority, and respond effectively to aggrandizing efforts by other branches. As long as the underlying premises held, the Madisonian model worked to a large extent as Madison had expected. But

Madison's assumptions did not hold indefinitely, not because politicians ceased to seek power or because the constitutional system of checks and balances or separation of powers was revised, but because the character and setting of the nation itself changed. As the environment changed, politics began to follow dynamic patterns unforeseen by Madison.

The general thesis of this essay is that the capacity of Congress to generate a cohesive institutional will and play a strong role in national politics is conditioned by the impact of external environmental factors on the ways in which politicians approach congressional service and organize institutional power. During the past two centuries, the United States has passed through three broad environmental eras in which distinct modes of electoral and organizational politics characterized Congress and influenced its power and role in American politics: the era of confrontation (1789–1860), the era of expansion (1876–1910), and the era of consolidation (1920–1965). Between these eras came periods of rapid and fundamental change in the nation's domestic and international life: the Civil War and Reconstruction (1860–1876) and the Progressive age and World War I (1910–1920).

Congress sustained its institutional cohesiveness and played a forceful role in national government during the eras of confrontation and expansion. Then, during the era of consolidation, as careerist legislators began to lobby for an ever more decentralized form of congressional organization, Congress experienced a long-term, cyclical decline in its capacity to generate authoritative leadership and institutional cohesion. As a consequence, the executive branch of government increasingly came to dominate Congress, although Congress was able to maintain a significant role in national policy making.

During the past two decades domestic and international developments have been occurring that may further alter congressional behavior and cripple the capacity of Congress to act. The 1960s and 1970s were a great period of protest that saw transformations as fundamental in their significance as those of the Civil War and Reconstruction or the Progressive age and World War I. As a result, the nation may be entering a fourth era of American politics, an era of reassessment characterized by greater electoral vulnerability, a decline in members' policy-making competence, and a personalization of their struggles for organizational power. Institutionally, Congress will become more fragmented, more variable in its policy commitments, more dominated by a professionalized staff, and more immobilized in its independent capacity to make innovative policy decisions.

The tension between the motives of ambitious politicians seeking power through congressional service and a highly volatile, complex, and threatening environment should produce an institution virtually incapable of generating strong leadership, sustaining an institutional will, or protecting its constitutional prerogatives. As a consequence, Congress and its members may lose public support. This essay concludes with a discussion of the conditions that could give rise to this crisis of congressional legitimation and suggests constitutional reforms designed to resolve the crisis. We turn first to a discussion of the historical dynamics that have generated the modern Congress.

THE CONGRESSIONAL ROLE IN NATIONAL POLITICS

The Era of Confrontation, 1789–1860

During the first 70 years of our history, the national government approximated the one foreseen by Madison. It was an era of confrontation. The nation struggled over the fundamental goals and values to which the new Republic would be committed—agrarian or industrial democracy; slavery or freedom; isolationism or a manifest destiny.[6] By and large, the economy remained agrarian, the citizenry was isolated from the immediacy of international affairs, local and state governments were strong, and the national government was out of sight and out of mind.[7]

Congress served as a great debating society, a forum for the far-reaching ethical and political struggles of the day. The leaders and careerists in Congress—the Websters, Clays, and Calhouns—were individuals gifted in debate, in identifying and articulating broad principles, and in compromise. Men such as these led elite caucuses that ran the House and Senate. Through positions of party and committee leadership (particularly on the revenue committees) and through informal personal influence, a few careerists dominated the organizational politics of Congress. Most members were content to serve for two to four years, follow the guidance of regional leaders, and return home to build state and local careers in business or politics.[8] With congressional power largely centralized in the hands of a small elite, Congress maintained relatively clear command of its role as legislative decisionmaker for the nation, but it was balanced by strong presidents such as Washington, Jefferson, Jackson, and Polk, and by an assertive Court.

The Era of Expansion, 1876–1910

Events of the 1860s and early 1870s altered the situation dramatically. The Civil War ended formal ambiguities about slavery and state supremacy and clearly established the hegemony of the national government in political affairs. The industrial revolution, the effect of which was exacerbated by the war, helped create an interdependent economy based on interstate commerce. It also provided America, as well as other nations, with the technical means to expand trade to far-off lands and gain international markets for domestically manufactured goods. America discovered the world, the world rediscovered America, and the national government discovered anew its constitutional responsibility for foreign policy and the regulation of American involvement in foreign commerce.

Congress became the center of the expanding activity of the national government because of its constitutional powers to regulate interstate and foreign commerce, to give advice and consent (on the part of the Senate) to treaties and ambassadorial nominations, to control defense authorizations and appropriations, and to declare war. Consequently, ambitious politicians focused more intently on Congress in the aftermath of the Civil War and Reconstruction. Voluntary turn-over of members began to decline as more and more politicians were attracted to congressional service as a means of exercising real power over important policy decisions. Committee work was taken more seriously, and significant committee reforms and changes were instituted. The formal party leadership began to assert itself, with the leaders gaining considerable authority because they offered serv-ices—such as selection of committee members and chairs, policy development and guidance, mediation of parliamentary conflicts, scheduling of legislation—that were necessary to avoid the chaos implicit in the changing Congress.[9]

The late nineteenth and early twentieth centuries thus constitute a second great era of American politics—the era of expansion, during which the national government extended its control over the economy, its sovereignty over the states, and its involvement in international politics.[10] Congress, led by strong cen-tral leaders and in control of the power of appropriation, taxation, and the tariff, could dominate the judicial and executive branches.[11] But this dominance was short-lived.

During the early twentieth century, the nation experienced a new dramatic upheaval in the underpinnings of its political and social life, an upheaval fueled by the Progressive movement and World War I. This period in American politics was as significant in many ways as the period of transformation during the Civil War and Reconstruction. The national government accepted critical new roles as regulator of the economic and social life produced by industrialization, roles greatly expanded by the Depression and World War II. During this period, the nation became convinced of its unlimited power—not only power nationally to secure a good life for its citizens but power internationally both to remake the world order and to make it safe for democracy.

The Era of Consolidation, 1920–1965

The coming of the Progressive movement and World War I refocused American politics, and the nation entered a new era, the era of consolidation. In this era the national government consolidated its control over the economy, its suprem-acy over the states, and its dominant role in international affairs. These decades were characterized by cooperative federalism, by a distributive politics in which major interest groups (particularly labor and business) fought for the spoils of government through partisan control of government, and by strong international involvement. Major changes in the character and role of Congress also character-ized this period.

CONGRESS DURING THE ERA OF CONSOLIDATION

In order to understand the changes in Congress during the era of consolidation, one must take into account the preceding congressional developments. During the era of national expansion, Congress experienced three internal trends. First, party leaders in both the House and Senate increased their power through control over committee appointments, selection of committee chairs, bill referral, parliamentary procedures, and other means. Second, with the expanding political responsibility of the national government, congressional committees grew in number and in influence. Third, more and more politicians were attracted to congressional service and ran successfully for election and reelection. With declining turnover, there emerged a growing number of career-oriented members seeking to sustain long-term congressional service in order to gain personal influence over national policy making.[12]

As the nation moved to consolidate major roles for the national government in both domestic and international affairs, these three trends within Congress became increasingly incompatible with each other. In the words of Cooper and Brady, Congress faced an "adaptation crisis."[13] Career-oriented members found that a centralized system of congressional government denied them the personal autonomy and policy influence they wanted. Somehow new organizational procedures, structures, and rules had to be created that would serve the career aspirations of members while nurturing sufficient institutional cohesion to protect the capacity of Congress to generate authoritative decisions and assert an institutional will. To a large extent, however, the adaptation process became an effort by career-oriented members to create procedures and structures that would maximize their immediate career interests, unguided by an awareness of the consequences for Congress as an institution.

Personal Goals of Members

Among the many career interests characterizing the new, professional members of Congress, three were paramount.[14] First, members became *electoral entrepreneurs* who developed a range of image-building and constituent-service enterprises designed to enhance their electoral security. With the rise of electoral entrepreneurship, dramatic and measurable patterns in congressional elections emerged.[15] In particular, members came to benefit from the growth of an "incumbent advantage," that is, a vote advantage over their electoral challengers.

The second career goal that grew to fruition during the age of consolidation was a widespread desire to gain a reputation for policy-making competence. This goal required that a member specialize within committees in particular areas of public policy, become expert in those areas, and be able to speak with authority on them. Policy competence came to entail not only knowledge in a policy arena, but sensitivity to the formal and informal norms and procedures governing the policy-making process, skill at legislative draftsmanship, and facility at legislative maneuvering.[16] The concern for policy-making success led members to form supportive coalitions of policy allies in Congress and to seek association outside Congress with interest groups and bureaucratic agencies that could provide critical information and assistance in policy debates and maneuvers.[17] The era of consolidation thus witnessed the development of members as *policy entrepreneurs*.[18]

Third, members wanted control over the formal organizational and parliamentary prerogatives governing policy making. This desire for significant power positions within Congress placed career-oriented members in direct conflict with the system of strong party leadership that had emerged during the era of expansion. Between 1905 and 1920, insurgent members of Congress stripped the Speakership of virtually all of its formal authority within the majority party and in the House rules, and they discarded the role of a powerful majority party leader in the Senate.[19] Increasing reliance on committee government during the era of consolidation meant that fundamental congressional policy-making responsibility was placed in a series of discrete and relatively autonomous committees and subcommittees, each having control over the decisions in a specified jurisdictional area. Members thus became *power entrepreneurs* who sought to obtain committee assignments early in their careers that would provide them with the broadest possible base for policy influence. Members also sought to nurture their seniority on those committees in order to gain personal control of the committees and key subcommittees.

These three goals—to enhance electoral security, to develop policy expertise, and to control positions of power in Congress—formed a sort of goal hierarchy for careerists. Before members had the time and emotional freedom to seek policy competence, they needed a reasonably secure electoral base. And before obtaining sufficient seniority to reach key positions of committee leadership, members normally would develop their reputation at policy competence. Hidden within the orderlines of this sequential progression, however, was an underlying tension. As congressional service became increasingly attractive and as incumbents became skilled as electoral entrepreneurs, newer members of Congress generally proved able to move through the earlier stages of career progression faster than more senior members left the Congress. Newer members often found themselves ready to direct policy making in key areas only to be constrained by senior members in positions of power. Because of the requirements of seniority, which seemed essential to avoiding the return of dominance by strong party leaders, members were prohibited from challenging a senior member for leadership of a committee. For this reason, unhappy members focused their attention less on removal of key occupants of the existing power structure and more on measures designed to reduce the authority of existing positions, to create new positions that would exercise this authority, and to spread the new positions among a wider number of members.

The Characteristics of Committee Government

The era of consolidation witnessed the spread of power from party to committee government and the proliferation of power positions within the committee system. For Congress and, ultimately, for the members of Congress, the costs of decentralized power were great. While committee government nurtured the development of legislative expertise and individualized policy creativity, it also undermined the ability of Congress to fulfill its constitutional responsibilities to make public policy and oversee executive implementation of that policy.

Four flaws of committee government were particularly critical. First, committee government lacked strong, central leadership. Second, committee government lacked fiscal coordination; the decisions of the authorization, appropriations, and revenue committees bore little relationship to one another. Third, committee government created problems of institutional responsiveness and democratic accountability; the decentralization of power within committees made it difficult for the public to hold any congressional majority accountable for policy decisions or nondecisions. Fourth, committee government led to a failure of objective, independent oversight of the executive branch; committees with oversight responsibility usually had close ties to lobby groups and bureaucratic agencies with a vested interest in the outcome of programs and policies.

Danger of Presidential Imperialism

All of these flaws, exacerbated by the continuing pressures for decentralization, created a tension between personal power and institutional power in Congress.[20] As Congress moved toward greater dispersion of organizational power within the institution, it became so immobilized on major policy questions that political activists turned to the presidency for policy leadership and for centralized control of the bureaucracy. As presidents became increasingly responsible for policy formulation and implementation, however, they sought power commensurate with their responsibility, often going beyond constitutional norms and usurping congressional power prerogatives.

Such presidential imperialism eventually provoked Congress into attempts to constrain the presidency and strengthen Congress. These efforts included congressional reforms to bolster centralized party leadership, improve budgetary and policy coordination, and strengthen congressional oversight of the executive.[21] Because the quest for personal power continued as the underlying motivation of individual members, the centralizing reforms became constrained by considerations of personal power prerogatives, building flaws into them that would provide openings through which the new procedures could be undermined as the crisis passed. Thus Congress was characterized by cyclical organizational dynamics; long periods of organizational decentralization were momentarily halted by short-lived periods of power centralization.

Conclusion

In essence, the era of consolidation was a period of American politics devoted to institutionalizing at a state, national, and international level American commitment to an industrial economic order. Government served to ensure proper functioning of the order by distributing special goods, regulations, and services to whichever of the two major groups within the economic order—business or labor—was momentarily capable of coalescing with other social and economic forces to capture Congress and the presidency and produce laws and regulations to nurture a productive industrial order. The security of the social order came through establishing minimal standards of governmental relief support to the poor, through economic regulation and defense preparedness, and through an activist involvement in international affairs and military conflicts.

The development of distributive policy commitments came largely through presidential leadership and the use of executive intervention to break policy deadlocks in Congress. In the process, the expectations and symbolic authority of the executive branch expanded dramatically. Simultaneously, much of the routine of government—marginal and incremental adjustments in national policy commitments—occurred in the interaction among the committees of Congress, the agencies of the national bureaucracy, and major interest groups.

Short-term attempts to centralize power during this period were eroded by renewed efforts at power dispersion. In the 1960s and early 1970s Congress began to institutionalize the most decentralized structure of subcommittee government in its history. Despite reforms that strengthened party leadership, budgetary coordination, and oversight capacity, subcommittee government appeared likely to become the dominant form of congressional organization, particularly in light of the environmental changes of the sixties and seventies.

THE AGE OF PROTEST, 1960s–1970s

Postindustrial Economic Order

While politics during the era of consolidation was preoccupied with presidential power, congressional routine, and distributive policy making, by the 1960s fundamental changes were occurring in the structural underpinnings of industrial democracy. Events were propelling the nation toward a postindustrial economic order. The economy remained one based on mass production and a strong agrarian base, but technological innovations of the postwar space age expanded both agrarian and industrial productive capacity while reducing reliance on a large domestic workforce.

The resulting vulnerability of the agrarian and industrial workforce focused greater attention on careers in education, technology, leisure industries, and public and private service delivery. It also created a growing body of citizens concerned with issues such as the fate of disadvantaged groups, health care, quality education, urban planning, mass transit, cultural affairs, and consumer and environmental protection.

While the dominant political forces remained fixated on struggles of industrial democracy—the classic partisan conflicts among business and labor and traditional efforts to generate tax breaks or jobs for the politically faithful—a growing segment of society was becoming concerned with issues of an interdependent, communal life in an increasingly urbanized, postindustrial world. The effective articulation of these policy concerns came to Congress largely through mass protest movements. The most important of these were the great civil rights movement, the consumer and environmental campaigns, and, above all, the protest against the Vietnam War.

As the new preoccupations of the sixties and seventies found legitimacy and increased salience, they altered the structure of political conflict. First, many of the new issues divided the traditional political groups internally. Questions of affirmative action created great factional strife within labor unions, for example. Second, the new programmatic concerns such as national health care were often so costly that their enactment would necessarily entail greater tax burdens on the affluent recipients of traditional distributive politics and necessitate a redistribution of resources from traditional programs and groups to new programs. Third, many of the new groups and issues of the sixties and seventies raised cultural and lifestyle concerns—feminism, gay rights, abortion, racial equality—that conflicted with codes of morality and religious beliefs among many traditional groups in society. The centrality of these cultural and symbolic issues often overshadowed the substantive issues of postindustrial change and led groups that might have been potential supporters of redistributive politics to see all issues proposed by new social forces as threatening cherished social and cultural values.

Emergence of Conflicting Factional Groups

The new policy concerns of the 1960s and 1970s thus produced a complex set of cross-cutting domestic issues that divided the public into a vast array of conflicting factional groups. In particular, these cross-cutting issues broke down the simplicity of labor-business conflict that had emerged during the era of consolidation and made difficult the building and sustenance of a national majority coalition that could encompass new and old issues alike.

The arguments of many if not most of the groups reflected a major change in the standards applied to policy debate and evaluation. Politics in the era of consolidation was justified by the canons of procedural democracy. In the 1960s and 1970s, however, the new concern was less with procedural legalities than with substantive consequences. The underlying standard of evaluation became *substantive justice*, the assertion that policies be evaluated in terms of substantive consequences for individuals, groups, and society as a whole, often regardless of procedural formalities. For example, it was unjust for citizens of one state or locality to be deprived voting rights, a good education, efficient mass transit, or a clean environment because the state or locality with legal jurisdiction over the problem had few fiscal resources or a repressive political structure. The application of this argument across a wide array of policy concerns necessarily led to calls for action by the national government, the one level of government capable of ensuring equitable treatment of groups regardless of the region, state, or locality in which they lived.

The New Federal Activism

With the move toward the politics of postindustrialism, then, came a second major change. Not only did a broad array of conflicting factional groups spring up, but in addressing many of the issues raised by the new political forces, the national government during the Johnson and Nixon presidencies took an increasingly activist role in policy domains traditionally or constitutionally left to state and local government, most notably, issues of suffrage (procedures for securing the voting rights of all citizens and standards for legislative apportionment) as well as health, education, law enforcement, and consumer and environmental protection.

The end result of these policy innovations was a qualitative change in state–federal relations. The new federal activism of the 1960s and 1970s did not constitute short-term intervention by the national government in state and local affairs, but long-term penetration of state and local policy activity. Once state and local governments accepted federal programs and federal money, their residents came to expect certain services. Without continued acceptance of federal programs and money, local and state governments had difficulty meeting these expectations.

Along with federal programs and federal money, however, came federal regulations and review covering policy questions entirely apart from the policy domain that a specific program was designed to address. For example, a state university accepting federal money for research might face federal threats to freeze those funds if the university failed to comply with federal affirmative action standards in admission or hiring or failed to provide specific types of ramps for the handicapped. Similar types of rules, across a wide range of federal concerns, were applied to local and state entities accepting federal funds.

Thus, in the 1960s and 1970s the nation moved from a *cooperative federalism* in which the national government occasionally intervened in state and local affairs to a *cooptative federalism* in which national concerns for substantive justice served to justify national dictation of state and local policies. In less than 20 years, state and local governmental units became constrained and guided, in many if not most major policy decisions, by federal regulations and actions. The national government penetrated the units of state and local policy making even in policy domains the Constitution clearly reserved to the states or the people. Yet precisely as the national government was expanding the scope of its programmatic and fiscal commitments, international developments undercut the nation's capacity to fulfill these responsibilities.

International Developments

On the international stage, the postwar years witnessed three significant developments: the end of overt colonialism and the rise of third world nationalism; the emergence of the United States as defender of the industrialized, noncommunist world; and the re-industrialization of Europe, particularly Germany, and Japan. During these years, the United States experienced a decreasing ability to influence the underdeveloped nations and ensure cheap access to the resources, such as oil, that third world nations possessed. Simultaneously, the United States became increasingly responsible for the defense of the western industrialized nations. This responsibility meant that a large portion of the national budget was devoted to defense and foreign policy commitments. Yet by accepting responsibility for the security of nations who then devoted less of their fiscal resources to military preparedness than they might have otherwise, the nation freed its allies to use their resources to nurture the development of their productive capacity.

With fewer defense constraints on their national budgets, many western nations developed extensive social services, such as national health care, while the United States continued to debate the economic feasibility of such programs. Simultaneously, the re-industrialization of Europe and Japan had serious economic consequences for the United States. In capturing a significant share of the market traditionally controlled by American industry, these nations severely curtailed American industrial employment and profits.

During the the 1960s and 1970s, these three international trends coincided to constrain America's fiscal capacity to continue distributive policies while responding to new postindustrial policy demands. The Vietnam War, together with a series of events ranging from the Bay of Pigs fiasco to the hostage crisis in Iran, conveyed the clear message that the economic and military power of an industrial giant does not necessarily translate into power over nonindustrial nation states. The nation thus confronted its growing incapacity to control the direction of world affairs.

The 1973 Arab oil embargo and the consequent rise of OPEC and cartel economics weakened America's international economic position by producing annual deficits in its balance of payments. Its domestic economy was also weakened by the greater relative capacity of other industrialized nations to sustain strong productive capacity despite the energy crisis. Thus the United States experienced runaway inflation and growing unemployment. These economic developments eroded the financial resource base on which the nation could draw to sustain economic productivity and generate the revenues to meet the growing programmatic and fiscal responsibility of the national government.

Simultaneously, the widespread deployment of American military forces at home and around the world, and the extensive responsibility of the United States for western defense, built into the national budget a large fiscal commitment that hindered the nation's flexible control of the revenues it could generate. This extensive and perhaps overzealous commitment to an international American military presence not only limited the flexible funds available for developing new and experimental forms of military hardware and defense capacity but also limited funds the United States had for its own re-industrialization, for the development of new energy sources, and for social programs that could respond to the new political forces and provide relief to the victims of inflation and unemployment.

The reverses that the United States experienced in the 1960s and 1970s on the international scene were intricately linked to the politics and policies that dominated the nation in the era of consolidation. Policies during this era had encouraged domestic energy entrepreneurs to "drain America first." These policies, which kept cheap foreign oil out of the country while American oil reserves were being exploited, built huge domestic fortunes and financed the careers of a generation of politicians who served the oil interests. Similarly, tax policies gave depreciation allowances and other incentives to industry under the assumption that such policies stimulated modernization. In actuality, however, such procedures allowed industries to divert huge sums of money into more immediately profitable endeavors or into salaries and fringe benefits, allowing American plants to deteriorate at the long-term expense of the nation's economic well-being. Analogously, the buildup of a permanent military force at home and abroad served the interests of domestic manufacturers of traditional military hardware, sustained local economies built around military installations, and supported the political careers of the politicians who fueled the preoccupation with unilateral American defense responsibility for the noncommunist world.

In all of these policy areas, the ethic of distributive politics, with its emphasis on short-term governmental rewards to those groups and factions that support victorious politicians and parties, diverted the nation from an assessment of its long-term needs and priorities.[22] Needless to say, the decision-making structure within Congress—with its emphasis on incremental, routinized decision making rather than on innovative and comprehensive policy formulation and aggressive policy surveillance—reinforced the tendency to respond to short-term political pressures rather than long-term policy needs. The end result was a nation ill-prepared to face the challenges of a postindustrial world of scarcity and international volatility.

Conclusion

Upon reflection, it would appear that the transformations produced by this period are just as dramatic as those unleashed by the Civil War and Reconstruction or by the Progressive movement and World War I. A nation that 20 years ago saw itself as dominant, autonomous, and secure in the world, possessed of virtually limitless resources, productive capacity, and military might, today finds itself increasingly dependent on the world community, painfully conscious of resource limits, questioning its economic capacities and governmental competence. We have a national government today that faces an expanding array of conflicting policy demands and has leverage over many of the state and local policy-making domains necessary to respond to these demands, yet is constrained by limited resources with which to meet the demands and support the programs for which the public holds it responsible.

Hard choices must be made about the relative weight to be given to the needs and demands of different groups and programs; about the type of policies to be undertaken to meet the challenge of the postindustrial era; about the means to be utilized to nurture and sustain our domestic economy and energy autonomy; and about the role and policies of the nation in the international community. These choices necessarily require a broad reassessment of domestic and international policy commitments and procedures. This reassessment should be made in a representative assembly with the capacity to make informed, authoritative decisions that are responsive to the American public. Unfortunately, today Congress may be far less capable of making such decisions than it was during the era of consolidation and committee government. This prospect exists because the emerging external and internal worlds of the contemporary Congress together create an environment that undermines the capability and incentives of career-minded members to unite in majority coalitions that can govern.

ERA OF REASSESSMENT: THE CONGRESSIONAL RESPONSE

As the nation moves into the era of reassessment, the external environment and internal organization of the contemporary Congress together create an exceedingly complex world for members. Externally, the nation is balkanized into special interest groups concerned not solely with the traditional broad issues of industrial democracy but with a myriad of general and particularized issues that suggest the coming of a postindustrial world of scarcity. Labor and business remain the two largest groups and thus define the general character of our electoral and partisan politics. Yet labor and business find themselves challenged by forces preoccupied with a wide range of new issues that do not fit neatly into their orthodox policy orientations. With cross-cutting issues thus splintering the public, parties and party leaders find it increasingly difficult to find a cohesive set of policy positions that can appeal to a majority of the public over an extensive time period.

Internally, congressional government is similarly fractured. Approximately 140 subcommittees in each house possess significant resources and decision-making autonomy independent of their parent committees. Yet subcommittee government does not exist in a vacuum. Significant formal authority also rests in central party leaders and, sporadically, in a central budget process. This bifurcated and balkanized congressional structure links up with the complex features of the external environment to create an extensive set of new pressures within Congress, pressures that undermine both its institutional integrity and the career aspirations of its members. In particular, the existence in the electorate of a wide range of narrow specialized interest groups creates strong external support for the institutionalized subcommittee government that has arisen.

In the new congressional world, the cross-cutting policy pressures on the individual members of Congress should be immense. They are pressured both by newly politicized special interest groups in their constituencies and by traditional economic groups that have long dominated local electoral politics. Simultaneously, members continue to face the paradoxical tension that exists between their immediate career aspirations and the long-term institutional interests of Congress. The decentralized system of subcommittee government provides a very real opportunity for individual members to gain a power position early in their careers and through it to seek personal influence over particular policy choices that fall within the jurisdiction of their subcommittees. Yet the decentralized subcommittee system makes difficult the broad-scale, comprehensive policy planning and program creation that seem required by the redistributive and corrective policy issues to which members increasingly must respond.

Thus the policy pressures from the external environment of Congress today, in combination with the continuing conflict between the career aspirations of members and organizational requisites of Congress as an institution, create serious new constraints on members of Congress that may well alter their patterned behavior and, as a result, the functioning of Congress. While it is admittedly difficult to forecast with any certainty the precise ways in which these various factors will interact, a useful beginning can be made by considering the impact that the new congressional world may have on members' capacity to realize their congressional career goals.

Electoral Vulnerability

First, consider the goal of reelection. During the period of committee government, both voluntary and involuntary turnover was low. Local party organizations and strong partisan identification among the public helped secure the reelection of incumbent members of dominant state and regional parties. Incumbents were able to build powerful supporting coalitions through attachment to dominant interest groups. Pork barrel and casework activity by members helped to offset the disruptive effects of an attractive challenger or an unpopular presidential candidate heading the party ticket.

In the new political world, all of these factors are becoming less influential in congressional elections. Political parties are disintegrating as objects of attachment and as mechanisms of organizational support. Likewise, labor and business are no longer the sole or primary interest groups in the electoral arena, but have been joined by groups that believe themselves left out of the mainstream of governmental life or unrepresented in policy making. Congressional elections are one of the most visible and potentially significant electoral arenas in which protest groups can strike. In particular, state and local groups seeking to influence the national government's actions regarding state and local policy should focus increased attention on congressional elections.

Likewise, attempts by incumbents to defeat electoral challengers through emphasis on the member's power within the Washington establishment may not prove as great an asset as in the past. It is exclusion from that establishment and its services that alienate many constituents. And many are also alienated by the decisions of the establishment that do touch them, particularly those affecting lifestyle concerns. In addition, "historical memories" of individualized services delivered by specific members of Congress may have decreasing electoral utility as constituents become increasingly mobile.

Seen in this context, congressional primaries and general elections increasingly should be characterized by protest efforts against incumbents, with incumbents caught in a peculiar bind, particularly in the Senate. Even a homogeneous constituency contains groups that believe themselves unrepresented by their members in Congress. The more heterogeneous the constituency, the more likely the rise and success of countervailing radical and reactionary protest movements that hold members accountable for policy stands. Likewise, it should become more difficult for members to build durable electoral coalitions and to develop a "home style" that works effectively over time across a complex, changing, and diverse constituency. Thus involuntary as well as voluntary turnover may begin to occur at a higher level than during the era of consolidation. The changes in the electoral environment and member turnover should be reflected in significant increases in the number of marginal districts, a decreasing statistical advantage of party and incumbency factors, and increasing electoral volatility (i.e., upset defeats of powerful and "safe" incumbents).

Decline of Policy-Making Competence

With members facing a more complex and volatile electorate and a more decentralized congressional structure, the level of their policy-making competence probably will decline. Electoral uncertainty will tempt members to emphasize reelection activity more than in the past; less time will be left for nurturing policy-making competence. Members will move to power positions earlier in their careers, reducing the time for apprenticeship and constraining their ability to gain policy-making expertise before entering leadership roles. In addition, the legion of autonomous subcommittees will give members the opportunity to move from subcommittee to subcommittee within a parent committee, changing policy specializations to increase electoral advantage or policy influence without giving up committee seniority. Such frequent movement could reduce the quality of legislators' policy-making expertise and increase reliance on a professionalized staff.

It could also increase the chance for seasoned committee chairs on committees characterized by high turnover in subcommittee leadership to reassert power. We thus could expect significant power struggles between committee and subcommittee leaders within such committees.

The greater variability in policy specialization of individual members over time also could have a second, corollary result. It may become increasingly difficult for programs and bureaucratic agencies to be assured of congressional support—not because the policies or agencies have been found wanting through systematic investigative oversight or have lost their initial congressional majority, but because key supporters have moved to greener pastures (or have been defeated). And new subcommittee leaders and members are concerned with different "pet" programs. A rise in the variability of subcommittee leadership and membership thus could lead to a decrease in the continuity of congressional policy commitments, reducing the probability that national programs will be implemented in accordance with congressional intent and probably threatening their long-term viability.[23]

The decline in policy-making competence and the increased discontinuity in congressional policy commitments should be exacerbated by the changing nature of coalitional politics within Congress. The addition to the political spectrum of cross-cutting issues raised by postindustrial change and concern over public morality should splinter the traditional coalitions without producing new, viable, and cohesive ones capable of generating stable majorities.

In general, we can expect to see more policy entrepreneurs who rise to power positions earlier than did their counterparts during the era of consolidation. These policy entrepreneurs, as subcommittee chairs, will have fewer real resources, less expertise and skill, and will face more complex legislative and policy decisions than their predecessors. Thus they will need assistance from central party leaders who can coordinate the efforts of the disparate factions and subcommittees. Yet they will approach the party leaders with fears of power aggrandisement and suspicions about the real utility of party leaders in legislative efforts. These fears and suspicions will be influenced by, and will influence, the congressional power structure.

More Personalized Power Struggles

In the era of consolidation, the struggles over power positions in Congress centered largely on conflicts about the proper authority of particular power positions and reform efforts to disperse power among a greater number of positions and members. Because committee seniority dominated the selection of committee chairs and maintained the viability of the decentralized power structure, conflict was largely depersonalized. In the future, conflict should become more personalized, however. First, key congressional power positions—party leadership posts and subcommittee chairs—have not been filled historically by following well-established norms of seniority. Conflict over the occupants of these positions therefore would not threaten the seniority norm.

Second, with so many power positions and with subcommittee chairs having some incentives to move to new positions, every Congress should start with a significant number of open positions, particularly subcommittee chairs. In these conflicts over subcommittee chairs, seniority claims may be emphasized, with some members stressing their subcommittee seniority and others stressing their committee or House seniority as bases for justifying their selection. Over time some form of seniority criteria governing subcommittee chair selection may develop within committees. However, given the more complex factional nature of Congress and the less critical historical importance of protecting the seniority norm at a subcommittee level, seniority criteria will almost certainly be balanced by such considerations as a candidate's ideological and regional orientation, policy-making competence, and electoral needs and security. Thus we can expect more overt conflict over and variability in the possession of power positions within committees.

Likewise, we can expect more conflict over party leadership positions. In the past, the selection of party leaders was not characterized by extensive and continuing conflict, in part because the positions did not carry extensive formal power, and in part because compromise among persistent dominant factions produced leadership teams that reflected party diversity. Today, however, party leadership positions carry significant formal authority, thus making them more attractive. Yet, with the greater factional complexity of the parties, it is less likely that stable leadership teams can be created that balance dominant factional interests and subdue conflict. Even the most skillful party leaders may face policy choices so complex and conflictual that viable policy-making majorities are impossible to produce or sustain. With party leadership positions thus potentially more valued, yet reliant on more complex and volatile intraparty coalitions, we may see greater conflict in the selection of party leaders and more rapid turnover in the occupants of leadership positions.

The problems faced by congressional leadership should be magnified by members' continuing quest for personal power, a quest that should produce even greater concern for personal autonomy. Greater electoral volatility will make members more attentive to constituent politics, more insistent on maintaining independence in roll call voting, and less willing to engage in compromises or to confront difficult policy choices. The greater pressures of particularized groups for attention to their special interests will reinforce members' own desires to have personal influence on policy making, thus sustaining the existence of numerous specialized subcommittees attentive to an ever-widening range of policy concerns.

Conclusion

The picture of Congress that emerges from a consideration of the concerns of individual members of nurture and protect their electoral maneuverability, policy influence, and power position acquisition is a chaotic one. Within Congress, we can expect the nature of careerism to change. The ever growing importance of the national government in this era of cooptative federalism will continue to attract ambitious politicians to Congress. Yet precisely because of the increased importance of national policy making to state and local affairs, congressional seats may become such focal points that the number and quality of serious challengers to incumbent officeholders will increase. As a result, we can expect more members to leave involuntarily owing to defeat or retire under the threatening cloud of defeat.

In addition, with less real personal power, more electoral uncertainty, and greater personal sacrifice characterizing congressional service, members will leave earlier in their careers than in the past in search of higher elective or appointive office or lucrative lobbying or legal consulting positions in the Washington establishment. Fourteen or more years in Congress, instead of 20 to 40, will constitute a realistic career expectation. Members will envision more readily than in the last 60 years a "life after Congress."

Thus a key characteristic of Congress in the future will be volatility. Congressional elections probably will produce more serious and potentially successful challengers to incumbents. Partisan majorities and party control of the House and Senate may fluctuate considerably more than in the era of consolidation. Coalition politics within Congress should become far less stable, with the conservative coalition and northern liberals ceasing to be the dominant cohesive groups shaping roll call behavior. Coalitional politics will be made even more difficult both by the cross-cutting complexity of the issues and by an increased variability over time in subcommittee policy entrepreneurs and congressional party leaders.

What are the consequences for Congress of the rising turnover and increased organizational chaos? Will a flight from subcommittee government toward elite or party government result as occurred during the nineteenth century? Probably not. First, the level of turnover is not expected to rise to the nineteenth-century norm of 50 percent, but simply range above the postwar levels. Career-oriented politicians will continue to see congressional careers as electorally possible, if not as easy to secure as in past decades. Second, subcommittee government should persist because members will see subcommittee autonomy and dominance as critical to the realization of their personal career aspirations.

Politicians will continue their quest for personal power within Congress, with the quest simply occurring in a shorter time span and a more volatile environment. In this environment, the persistence of subcommittee government may be reinforced by the emergence of a professional staff at the subcommittee level. Professional staff members, who may become the real long-term congressional careerists, could provide continuity and expertise in Congress somewhat analogous to the continuity provided by the civil service bureaucrats in the executive branch. We may be moving into a new period of legislative professionalism at the national level, with the staff being a critical core of the professional Congress. Unfortunately, while a professional staff can sustain Congress as a functioning organization, it will not be able to replace the members as professional actors or nurture the institutional power of Congress.

THE DECLINE OF CONGRESS: A CRISIS OF LEGITIMATION

Ultimately, the power of Congress rests on the ability of its elected members to legislate; to respond effectively to policy needs, interests and demands; in short, to act. Congress must generate leadership that can unite a majority of its members and speak for them authoritatively if it is to be an effective representative institution. And it must be able to coordinate its policy processes and ensure that the executive executes its policy decisions.

The Congressional Dilemma

The coming of committee government undermined all of these requisites of congressional power. The increased dispersion of power in subcommittee government and the greater volatility of the new political environment together should multiply the problems of congressional leadership, coordination, and oversight. Subcommittee government will not produce the large number of elected careerists and the long-term, powerful elected congressional experts who existed in the period of committee government and who served somewhat to counterbalance officials of the executive branch. Congressional professionalism will rest on a staff whose personal interests (such as staff dominance of institutionalized subcommittees) may conflict ultimately with the interests both of individual members and of the institution itself.

The expanded role of party leaders and the creation of a new budget process provide some centralized congressional capacity for constraining, directing, and integrating the policy actions at the sub-committee level. However, the powers of the party leaders and budget committees derive from the members of Congress whom they seek to constrain and direct. In light of the immense career pressures members are likely to feel in this new era and their concomitant desire for freedom of action in pursuit of immediate career aspirations, particularly electoral security, the increased authority of the party and budgetary leadership will appear thin straws on which to hinge considerable hope for strong, authoritative, forceful, and sustained congressional leadership. This is true particularly in light of the complex policy choices facing members of Congress, choices that would make leadership of a collegial body difficult under the best organizational circumstances.

The Consequences

As a rule, autonomous congressional policy making on major policy issues in this new era will be incremental at best, immobilized and incoherent as a norm. While on occasion we may see forceful congressional leadership and integrated policy making, such actions probably will occur primarily in the direst of crises and probably will exhaust the willingness of members to cooperate with the leadership on future major policy questions. The inability of the central party and budgetary officials to sustain forceful leadership will critically undermine the ability of Congress to act.

In the face of an increasingly immobilized Congress, the pressures for action by other institutions will be immense. Such conditions particularly tempt presidents to establish their popularity and power by bold strokes of leadership and by forceful efforts to "save the Republic." Thus we can expect severe incursions of presidents into the constitutional powers of Congress, incursions more severe and coming at a faster pace than in the era of committee government. This faster pace will occur in part because (1) Congress will move toward decentralization more rapidly as a result of the greater pressures by members for personal autonomy; (2) subcommittee government will create greater problems of immobilism than did committee government; and (3) the complex policy problems of the new era will create greater demands for rapid government action.

As a result, and assuming that there are no unforeseen countervailing changes in the systemic setting of national or international politics, we shall surely witness the further decline of Congress, the rebirth of the imperial presidency, and a severe constitutional crisis surpassing any previous one.

The great fear is that a point will be reached in this cyclical decline of Congress beyond which the citizenry no longer looks to Congress as a necessary participant in national governance, a point at which the slow transformation away from representative democracy becomes an institutionalized and popularly accepted reality. Unfortunately, various national surveys indicate that the public is increasingly doubtful of the capacity of Congress as an institution to act, particularly on the major policy concerns of the day.[24] As Richard Fenno has so aptly noted, citizens may love their representatives in Congress, but they do not love Congress.[25] And while similar patterns characterize other institutions, both in America and the West generally,[26] the congressional survey results are particularly troubling because Congress is so clearly the touchstone of American democracy, and executive government is so clearly the probable long-term consequence of congressional decline.

Ironically, as we move into a postindustrial world of scarce resources and complex policy choices, members of Congress may become ultimate victims of Fenno's paradox, as well as its immediate perpetrators. In the emerging world, they stand to lose electoral security, policy-making competence, and long-term personal control over significant power positions. In spreading organizational power so widely that Congress cannot act, members undermine not only the legitimacy of the institution but also the popular belief in the viability of congressional policy making. Given the severity of the policy problems raised by the coming of postindustrialism in contemporary America, it is doubtful that the citizenry will continue to "love" members of Congress simply because they cut bureaucratic red tape or deliver highways and dams. Congressional incapacity to act in the midst of severe crisis must ultimately delegitimate not only Congress but the individual members of Congress by challenging popular beliefs that they are effective, responsive representatives serving the fundamental needs of the people.

The Crisis of Legitimation

It would seem, then, that Congress has moved beyond a *crisis of adaptation* and now, in light of the probable characteristics of the new era into which we are moving, will face a serious and growing *crisis of legitimation*, a crisis that threatens the very foundations of American democracy.[27] Continued congressional immobilism on major policy problems in a postindustrial world of scarce resources necessarily will challenge popular belief in the viability and desirability of representative government that historically has served to legitimate Congress, to sustain popular support for its decisions, and to nurture popular insistence that its constitutional prerogatives be protected. This legitimation crisis flows from two interacting factors: *congressional organization* and *congressional environment*.

Organizationally, Congress has proven increasingly incapable of creating an internal structure that could produce decisive, innovative, independent, and authoritative policy decisions on major policy issues. Yet the severity of the legitimation crisis now descending on Congress, and more broadly on American politics, flows from more than the inability of Congress to resolve its adaptation crisis constructively and create a responsive organizational structure capable of providing sustained leadership, coordination, and oversight.

While the congressional incapacity to act would no doubt ultimately generate a crisis, it is augmented by the pell-mell rush of the nation into a new environmental setting. Congress today faces complex and seemingly intractable issues—redistributive politics amidst diminishing resources; national enforcement of substantive justice amidst growing unhappiness with a large national bureaucracy; sustenance of our international economic security amidst increasing dependence on expensive foreign resources and foreign goods; the solidification and modernization of our military defense capacity at a time when domestic social problems require considerable financial outlays. Organized to process incremental, routinized distributive policy choices, Congress now must confront a world in which most major policy decisions require comprehensive, innovative, and redistributive policy actions. Both in terms of its organizational structure and its environmental context, Congress's serious incapacity to act may lead to a widespread questioning of its legitimate role in national governance.

What we may be witnessing, then, is the self-destruction of the Madisonian system of government. This self-destruction is not necessarily the result of malevolence, evil motives, or evil people. The quest for power by members of Congress may derive from the genuine desire to serve humanity. The effort of members of society to seek a redress of personal grievances and protect personal interests is merely an articulation of their constitutional rights. Finally, presidential assertiveness and "imperialism" may derive from a very genuine presidential concern for economic stability or national security and from an accurate perception that Congress cannot act.

Nevertheless, the potential for self-destruction is real. Because of the cyclical nature of the power struggles and the occasional recentralization and resurgent periods within Congress, as in the 1970s, the long-term weakening of Congress is not as readily evident as it might be. Such short-term resurgence, however, simply diverts attention from the long-term momentum toward congressional impotence. In fact, when we examine the probable long-term characteristics that will emerge from the recent "reformed" Congress, in light of the concomitant changes in our national and international environment, what we foresee is greater congressional impotence and greater executive usurpation of congressional power.

The age of protest witnessed major transformations as significant in many ways as those that occurred during the Civil War and Reconstruction or the Progressive movement and World War I. Events of the 1960s and 1970s raised important questions of substantive justice and national purpose and unleashed new economic, social, political, and technological changes that are producing fundamental transformations in national life as great as those that arose with the emergence of industrial democracy in the late nineteenth century or its consolidation in the twentieth century. These transformations should produce a Congress of less secure incumbents and more immobilized policy making.

Proposals for Constitutional Change

With these changes, a new era is upon us, an *era of reassessment*. As in the other eras of American politics, policy questions will center on the nation's social and economic order, on the desired form of federalism, and on our role in international affairs. Yet unlike the earlier eras, today even more fundamental questions must be faced: Is representative government a central value that we wish to nurture? If so, how can we reassert and sustain representative institutions as we move into a postindustrial world? Failure to address these questions could lead to the end of representative government. Willingness to face the potential severity of the emerging legitimation crisis and act constructively to resolve it could introduce a creative transformation and rebirth of representative democracy.

In acknowledging the crisis facing Congress and moving to address it, we must recognize that the root of the problem lies not in Congress per se but in the Constitution, in its failure to provide constitutional provisions that nurture the organizational integrity of Congress in ways comparable to the Supreme Court and the presidency. In retrospect, it is understandable why the founders failed to provide specific functions and organizational structures for Congress that would help ensure its institutional integrity and help it generate an institutional will.

The founders were structuring a constitution for a very different world, a world in which Congress could be expected to maintain its organizational cohesion without constitutional assistance. But the rise of industrial America and the coming of the postindustrial era of scarcity have created conditions that undermine the ability of Congress to organize effectively, assert an institutional will, balance the other branches of government, and respond authoritatively to new policy challenges.

What is to be done? Clearly, it is time to reconsider the appropriateness of our constitutional structure to the problems and realities of our time. Perhaps a more effective representative government can be constructed by changes in the current constitutional structure. For example, constitutional amendments could give greater authority to the Speaker, Majority Leader, or other organizational leaders. Such authority might include significant responsibility to appoint committee members and/or leaders, greater procedural powers, and tightened control over congressional perquisites. Amendments of this kind would help redress problems of congressional leadership caused by committee and subcommittee government and give the congressional leaders "bargaining chips" they could use in coalition building analogous to the "chips" the president possesses, such as the veto power and the ability to make political appointments and nominate federal judges. Another constitutional amendment could create a Congressional Security Council that would help Congress regain constitutional control of war making under specified emergency conditions. To bridge the legislative division created by bicameralism, the Constitution could authorize or require joint congressional committees in key areas such as national security, budgeting, and oversight. Finally, a revision of the presidential veto authority could enhance congressional control of policy making by making overrides easier or vetoes harder.

All of these constitutional changes would be designed to mesh with the preexisting system of separation of power and checks and balances. Their intent would be to strengthen the ability of Congress to know and express its will authoritatively, creating a constitutionally supported incentive structure conducive to the creation of majority coalitions. The problem with accepting the basic constitutional design of Madison, however, is that it reasserts a separation of powers, checks and balances system.

Political analysts often lament that in a separation of powers system majoritarian politics is slowed by the force of institutional pluralism.[28] This argument is a strong one and suggests that one might wish to enact concomitant constitutional changes designed to nurture the capacity of national majorities to bridge the branches of government. For example, hand in hand with strengthening Congress could go a variety of reforms designed to strengthen the one organizational device that historically has shown some capacity to unite the separate branches in a responsive, accountable fashion: the political parties. In addition, the construction of some form of parliamentary government could be considered. For example, Congress could be given the power to pass a vote of no confidence that could remove the president and activate selection of a new president either through a specific institutional process or through new elections. Presidents also could be required to draw cabinet members from Congress (with members retaining their seat in Congress). Obviously, such proposals constitute a significant move away from Madisonian government.

A final proposal stems from the recognition that representative government entails more than a strong Congress at the national level. Strong representative assemblies that are close to the people yet have sufficient authority, scope, and financial resources to influence public policy are also needed. The creation of subnational, multistate regional governments might provide one means of sustaining our commitment to a federal system of government in which popular control of policy making would be invested in that governmental body closest to the problem yet possessed of sufficient jurisdictional authority to address it effectively. Similarly, new devices of representative decision making could be envisioned at the local level.

New and revitalized forms of regional and urban government would not only nurture representative democracy at local and regional levels and constrain the rise of cooptative federalism, but also would help Congress to address creatively those questions that are truly national in scope. Relieved of policy issues better left to regional assemblies, Congress might be less compelled to rely on bureaucratic expertise and rule making as a substitute for congressional deliberation and decision making on questions requiring national action.

In considering constitutional changes such as these, we must recognize, of course, that constitutional revision is a serious and difficult business. It requires a realistic and hard-headed assessment of human nature, of the implications of different institutional arrangements, of the social conditions within which politics is to be conducted, and of the consequences that will derive from the interaction of these elements of political life. In many ways Madison's performance in the *Federalist Papers* is still the best guide to this type of analysis. And certainly we must remember that the effects of large-scale constitutional change in any particular national environment are difficult to forecast.

Despite the problems of constitutional change, however, the nation cannot shy away from facing the legitimation crisis that confronts Congress and thus challenges the maintenance of representative government in America. A failure to face this crisis may result in the disintegration of our political order and the loss of meaningful democratic control over public policy. Facing the crisis squarely may not only revitalize Congress but liberate the nation to approach constructively the policy dilemmas and opportunities of the postindustrial world. If we successfully confront both the constitutional and policy dilemmas facing us, we may lay the foundations for a more equitable and democratic society. The era of reassessment could activate a great renewal and expansion of democratic government in America.

Notes

Acknowledgements: For their useful comments on this essay and assistance with crafting it, the author would like to thank Patricia Brown, Bruce Buchanan, Gary Freeman, Madeline McCully, Bruce Oppenheimer, Barbara Romzek, Fred Smoller, Terry Sullivan, and Al Watkins. In addition, he owes a continuing debt to the numerous graduate and undergraduate students who have shared with him their insights and questions regarding congressional politics.

1 James Madison, "Federalist #10," in Alexander Hamilton, James Madison, and John Jay (1961: 77–84). For interpretations of the Madisonian theory, see Robert Dahl (1956) and Ostrom (1971).
2 Madison, "Federalist #51," in Alexander Hamilton, James Madison, and John Jay (1961: 321–323).
3 Ibid.
4 Madison, "Federalist #48" and "Federalist #53" in Alexander Hamilton, James Madison, and John Jay (1961: 309, 334-335).
5 Ibid. See also Scigliano (1971) and Wood (1969).
6 For a complimentary interpretation of political eras in American history see Namenwirth (1973).
7 Young (1966: 13–37).
8 For statistical and documentary evidence, see Polsby (1968: 144–168); Ripley (1969b: 43); H. D. Price (1977); Fiorina, Rhode, and Wissel (1975).
9 On the House, see Brown (1922) and Bolling (1968). On the Senate, see Rothman (1969).
10 The major study of this era among contemporary political scientists is Brady (1973), *Congressional Voting in a Partisan Era.*
11 This was, in fact, the thesis of Woodrow Wilson's (1885) classic study of the era, *Congressional Government).*
12 Price (1977); and Polsby, Gallagher, and Rundquist (1969).
13 Cooper and Brady (1973: 46–52). See also Huntington (1965).
14 The approach taken here has been heavily influenced by Fenno (1973) and Mayhew (1974b).
15 On emerging patterns in congressional elections, see Cummings (1966); Kingdon (1968); Erikson (1971); Jones (1967); Hinckley (1970a, 1970b); Bullock (1972); Mayhew (1974b); Fiorina (1974; 1977a); and Mann (1978). For a discussion of how the economy affects election results, see Tufte (1978). On incumbents' approaches to district politics, see Fenno (1978).
16 See, for example, the discussion in Manley (1965).
17 Ripley and Franklin (1980); Arnold (1979); Dodd and Schott (1979).
18 For an earlier discussion of members of Congress as policy entrepreneurs, see Uslaner (1978).
19 See Hechler (1940) and John D. Baker (1973).
20 For earlier and more extensive development of the ideas presented here, see Dodd (1977, 1980).
21 For useful discussions of reform politics in the 1970s, see Davidson and Oleszek (1977) and Rieselbach (1977).
22 On the politics of oil, see Oppenheimer (1974); see also Manley (1970). On military politics, see Dexter (1969). For a broader interpretation, see Lowi (1969, 1979).
23 For excellent discussions of the impact of policy formulation and the congressional environment on policy implementation, see Pressman and Wildavsky (1973) and Michael N. Green (1978).

24 For a good summary, see Parker (1977).
25 Fenno (1975); see also Parker and Davidson (1979).
26 See, for example, Bruce Cain et al. (1980).
27 My interpretation has been influenced significantly by Habermas (1973).
28 Burns (1963).

Additional Perspective on "Legitimation Crisis"

"Congress, the Constitution, and the Crisis of Legitimation" shifts the focus of scholarly analysis away from the immediate politics of the 1970s and to a broader historical perspective on Congress. It assesses the likely outcome of the reforms of the 1970s by placing them within a clearer constitutional, historical, and developmental context. It does so to clarify the ways in which constitutional design, societal developments, political ambitions of legislators, and congressional rules, norms and structures interact across time, shaping and reshaping the character of congressional politics and the effectiveness of its policy making. Building on this assessment, the essay details probable consequences that should flow from the reforms of the 1970s, given their characteristics and the immediate historical context confronting the post-reform Congress.

In assessing the future of Congress, the essay foresaw growing citizen frustration with and distrust of government and a crisis of legitimacy for the institution. In essence, the post-reform Congress would prove inadequate to addressing the policy challenges associated with postindustrialism, leaving it mired in a growing political crisis of historic proportions. This crisis would entail increased political conflict and policy deadlock in Congress, the growing electoral vulnerability of powerful and long-term incumbents seen by voters as contributing to its policy failures, greater executive usurpation of congressional power, a potential turn of citizens against Congress, and a sustained challenge to the role of Congress in national governance. A dire prospect, one that appeared overly-pessimistic at the time and thus was largely ignored, "Legitimation Crisis" led the author to take ever more seriously the study of congressional change. His hope was that a clearer understanding of the dynamics of institutional change would help clarify how best to assess and attend to the crisis likely to engulf Congress in subsequent decades. The issues raised in "Legitimation Crisis" came front and center in American politics in the 1990s.

Foundation Work: The author's attentiveness to an historical perspective on Congress, and to the legitimacy of Congress as a governing institution, owes a tremendous debt to Joseph Cooper (1970), *The Origins of the Standing Committees and the Development of the Modern House*. This pioneering monograph was cited in "Congress and the Quest for Power" but proved even more relevant to the development of this essay. Also critical to Dodd's early work were "Strengthening the Congress: An Organizational Perspective" (Cooper, 1975) and "Congress in Organizational Perspective" (Cooper, 1977). The ongoing conversation between Cooper and the author, in their distinct efforts to understand Congress and its struggle for ongong relevance amid growing assertion of presidential power, will be evident throughout subsequent chapters. In this conversation, Cooper tilts toward an organizational theory perspective and Dodd toward rational-choice and then social learning perspectives, with remarkable similarities and, on occasion, consequential contrasts emerging in their separate interpretations. Cooper's most extraordinary contribution to this effort, to-date at least, is "From Congressional to Presidential Preeminence" (Cooper, 2009).

"Legitimation Crisis" benefited as well, in deep background, from the work of three visionary students of American politics. The first is George Rothwell Brown and his long-ignored classic, *The Leadership of Congress*, published in 1922, Brown's insightful analysis highlights the characteristics of party government in the early twentieth century and the consequences of dismantling it, as seen at the time by a close journalistic observer.

The second is James MacGregor Burns, whose prescient 1949 analysis in *Congress on Trial* (which Dodd and Schott (1979) built on extensively in Chapter Three of *Congress and the Administrative State*) foreshadowed virtually all of the major congressional developments and scholarly *foci* of the next sixty years. See, for example, Burns' attention to members' concern for reelection and their close constituency engagement, in Chapter One; members' concern for power and autonomy and its affect on institutional structure and policy making, in Chapters One, Three and Four; party system polarization and party government, in Chapters Three and Eleven; the complexities of committee politics, policy making and oversight, in Chapters Four, Five and Six; policy stalemate and political crisis, in Chapter Seven; power struggles between Congress and the president, in Chapter Ten; and institutional and party reform, in Chapters Eight and Eleven. His contrasts of congressional and parliamentary politics in Chapter Nine are also noteworthy. Also important were Burns' classics from the 1960s, *Deadlock of Democracy* (Burns, 1963) and *Presidential Government* (1965), which helped the author grasp the great issues at stake in party-building and executive-legislative relations in the politics of the 1950s and 1960s.

The third scholar is Theodore Lowi, whose 1969 masterwork, *The End of Liberalism,* helped the author grasp the full extent of the changes underway in twentieth-century America and their transformative affect on Congress. Additionally, Lowi's works on the presidency, as in *The Personal President* (Lowi, 1985), and on the role of ideas in American politics, as in *The End of the Republican Era* (Lowi, 1995) were of critical importance to his understanding of the power struggles between Congress and the presidency and the role of learning in American politics.

His long-term perspective on congressional change also benefited in essential ways from the pioneering work by Nelson Polsby (1968) on "The Institutionalization of the U. S. House of Representatives," and by Polsby, Gallapher, and Rundquist (1969) on "The Growth of the Seniority System in the House of Representatives." It benefited in a more immediate sense from Samuel P. Huntington's foresightful 1974 essay, "Postindustrial Politics: How Benign Will It Be?", which helped frame his understanding of the implications of postindustrialism for Congress. And his characterization of the emerging congressional crisis as a "Legitimation Crisis" owes to his reading of the 1973 work on the topic by

Jurgen Habermas, together with a sensitivity to the issue of congressional legitimacy as fostered by Joseph Cooper (1970). Key arguments in "Congress, the Constitution, and the Crisis of Legitimation" are foreshadowed in Dodd (1980). For an early discussion that frames the contribution of "Legitimation Crisis" to congressional studies, see Cooper and Brady (1981b).

Suggested Reading: Works that speak to, build on, test or assess arguments introduced in this essay include *The Decline of Comity in Congress* by Eric Uslaner (1993); Calvin Jillson (1994), "Patterns and Periodicity in American National Politics"; Joseph Cooper, ed., *Congress and the Decline of Public Trust* (1999); Kenneth R. Mayer and David T. Canon, *The Dysfunctional Congress? The Individual Roots of an Institutional Dilemma* (1999); Terry M. Moe and William G. Howell, "Unilateral Action and Presidential Power: A Theory" (1999); Charles M. Cameron (2000); Jon R. Bond and Richard Fleisher, *Polarized Poiltics: Congress and the President in a Partisan Era* (2000); Burdett A. Loomis, ed., *Esteemed Colleagues: Civility and Deliberation in the U.S. Senate* (2000); Joseph Cooper, "The Twentieth Century Congress" (2001); Kenneth R. Mayer, *With the Stroke of a Pen* (2001); Charles Stewart III, *Analyzing Congress* (2001), Chapters Two and Three; Eric Schickler, *Disjointed Pluralism* (2001); William G. Howell, *Power without Persuasion* (2003); Jasmine Farrier, *Passing the Buck* (2004); Matthew Crenson and Benjamin Ginsberg, *Presidential Power: Unchecked and Unbalanced* (2007); Thomas E. Mann and Norman J. Ornstein, *The Broken Branch*, (2008); Joseph Cooper, "From Congressional to Presidential Preeminence: Power and Politics in the Late Nineteenth-Century America and Today" (2009); and Jasmine Farrier, *Congressional Ambivalence: The Political Burdens of Constitutional Authority* (2010).

Classroom Use: "Legitimation Crisis" can be used as an interpretation of the environmental and institutional tensions pressing in on the Congress in the late twentieth and early twenty-first centuries; a perspective on how the experience of this period fits with societal developments, era shifts and congressional change from the late eighteenth century onward; an interpretation of how constitutional design, institutional politics and societal change have interacted across American history to alter the role and power of Congress; and as a 'blind forecast' in 1981 of how the interaction of such processes were likely to challenge and change Congress in the late twentieth and twenty-first centuries.

For point/counterpoint contrasts, "Congress, the Constitution, and the Crisis of Legitimation" can be paired with Madison's essay #10, and also essays #45 to #66 in *The Federalist Papers* (Hamilton, Madison, and Jay, 1961). This pairing highlights the kind of congressional politics the constitutional design was expected to generate, in contrast to the portrait of its historical development and likely future direction presented here. The essay can also be paired with James Sterling Young's classic work, *The Washington Community.* Young describes an early-nineteenth-century Congress remarkably at odds with that portrayed for the late twentieth and early twenty-first centuries. It could be paired in intriguing ways with Woodrow Wilson's pathbreaking 1884 book, *Congressional Government*, the first scholarly work to argue that societal change combined with institutional evolution could and was altering the role of Congress in the American political system. And it can be paired, to gain greater depth of historical perspective, with Joseph Cooper (2009), "From Congressional to Presidential Preeminence."

4

BICAMERALISM IN CONGRESS

The Changing Partnership

Edward G. Carmines and Lawrence C. Dodd

1985

Among the constraints on congressional policy making imposed by the Constitution, none has proven more potent than bicameralism. The constraining effects of bicameralism are seen, in particular, in the requirement that both the House of Representatives and the Senate pass legislation in identical form for it to be enacted into law, a requirement that can foster policy deadlock. Written with Edward Carmines, Chapter Four examines the changing nature of bicameralism and its affect on the governing capacity of the contemporary Congress.

In the early Republic, the House of Representatives tended to be the more prestigious and dominant chamber, aided by its status as an elected assembly and its special constitutional role in fiscal policy. But following the Civil War, and with growing momentum thereafter, the Senate grew in stature, aided by the growing importance of foreign policy and the move to an elective Senate. It thus became less likely to defer to the House in policy making.

During the early postwar decades, the chapter argues, bicameralism was again undergoing significant change. The House was becoming more cumbersome and parochial and the smaller Senate was emerging as more assertive and nationally-oriented. With these developments, combined with the budgetary reforms of the 1970s, the Senate seemed increasingly prone to challenge the preeminence of the House in fiscal policy. This challenge raised the prospect that a long-term power struggle between the two chambers would emerge, with growing conflict between the two houses further inhibiting the policy-making capacity of the contemporary Congress.

The U.S. Congress stands out as one of the most distinctive national legislatures in the world. This distinctiveness is evident in both its extensive policy-making

Edward G. Carmines and Lawrence C. Dodd. "Bicameralism in Congress: The Changing Partnership." In Congress Reconsidered, 3rd Edition. *Edited by Lawerence C. Dodd and Bruce I. Oppenheimer.* Washington, D.C.: CQ Press. 1985, pp. 414–416

role and its formal separation from the executive. Yet nowhere is the uniqueness of Congress seen more clearly and consequentially than in its bicameral nature: two separate chambers sharing legislative power.[1] While other national legislatures have two separate houses, their upper chambers have faded in importance and prestige, leaving the lower house the pre-eminent legislative institution.[2] In the United States, by contrast, the power and status of the Senate rivals and perhaps surpasses the House. It is this prominence of the upper house that gives our bicameralism special significance.

In this essay we will examine the bicameral nature of the U.S. Congress, focusing especially on the changing relationship between the House and Senate. How could the Senate, originally the less prestigious chamber, increase in power and prestige to such an extent that it challenges the House for legislative preeminence? The House is, after all, the legislature of the people, the body that is theoretically closer to the common man and more representative of the majority will. The ability of a less representative institution such as the Senate to challenge the more democratic body is an intriguing puzzle in an age enamored of democratic rule.

A related concern is the relative power and role of the two chambers today. Are the two houses equal partners, or are there forces favoring the power and prestige of one over the other? And what consequence does the bicameral relationship, whether an equal or unequal partnership, have for the operation of Congress? To address these questions, we shall look first at the constituional design of bicameralism and trace its historical evolution. We shall then examine the changing state of bicameralism in the contemporary period, giving special attention to its prospects in the emerging postindustrial era.

Bicameralism: The Constitutional Design

The fact that the U.S. Congress is composed of two chambers sharing power is hardly an accident or afterthought. It was a deliberate choice by the members of the Constitutional Convention in 1787 and an integral element of the theory of government articulated at the convention and outlined in the Federalist Papers.[3] The framers of the Constitution sought to create a national government strong enough to rule decisively and yet sufficiently limited so that it would not abuse its powers over the people. How to form a government that was both authoritative and nontyrannical—this was the great dilemma confronting the framers. Their solution was threefold.

First, they gave the national government extensive responsibilities for taxation, interstate and foreign commerce, and foreign policy, while reserving other powers for the states; this grant of power helped ensure a national government with strong but not exclusive policy-making authority. Second, they constructed a government in which authority and power did not reside in a single individual or institution but was dispersed widely throughout various institutions. Third, the framers placed the government on a popular, democratic base. Article II of the

Constitution thus granted the essential powers of government to Congress[4] and specified that the members of the House of Representatives be directly elected by the people.

The extensive policy-making responsibilities of Congress together with its democratic base made it the great institutional centerpiece of American government. Yet this very importance made Congress a focus of additional concern to the founding fathers. As Madison wrote, "A dependence on the people is, no doubt, a primary control on the government; but experience has taught mankind the necessity of auxiliary precautions."[5]

Madison and other founders feared that Congress, as an elective institution with taxing and spending powers, might accumulate governmental power in its own hands and dominate the executive and judiciary. Their concern thus shifted from how to separate governmental power among different branches of government to ways to build constraints into Congress itself. This concern led them to create a bicameral legislature. The framers of the Constitution decided that the way to control legislative authority was to divide it, just as they divided government itself.

Madison stated the rationale for separation this way:

> In republican government the legislative authority necessarily predominates. The remedy for this inconvenience is to divide the legislature into different branches: and to render them by different modes of election and different principles of action, as little connected with each other as the nature of their common functions and their common dependence on the society will admit.[6]

By dividing the Congress into the House and Senate and requiring that any legislation be passed by both chambers in an identical form, the framers again put into practice their basic principle of government: different institutions sharing power in order to check and balance one another. Bicameralism was one of the primary "auxiliary precautions" against unlimited governmental authority, in this case legislative authority.

As an auxiliary precaution, bicameralism was intended to control the behavior of the House of Representatives. From the beginning of the Constitutional Convention, the framers recognized that an elective and representative assembly—a House of Representatives—would be an essential element of the new government. When they discussed their fear of the legislature, they meant their fear of this elected representative assembly. The problem, as Hamilton put it, was that the House, as the sole legislative chamber, might be "a full match if not an overmatch for every other member of the government."[7]

If selected directly by the people, as seemed necessary given the democratic spirit of the American Revolution, the House might be overly responsive to popular sentiments and enact legislation that was both dangerous and unwise.

Moreover, like legislative assemblies in the colonies, the House of Representatives presumably would require a strong Speaker for proper leadership of its members and coordination of its activities. The Speaker's role would be further enhanced, Madison feared, by the dearth of legislators competing for power in the House.[8]

Because of the difficulty of long distance travel and communication in the rural, agrarian society of the late eighteenth century, and the importance of local as opposed to national issues, Madison expected most legislators to serve only one or two terms in Congress before retiring to state and local politics. A legislator interested in national politics and willing to remain in the capital faced few House colleagues interested in competing with him for influence or challenging the expansion of his power. An ambitious individual, confronting such a vacuum and skillful at building personal alliances, could win the Speakership and gather to it resources that would allow him to control the House. Such a Speaker, unconstrained by his colleagues, could use the taxing and spending powers of the House to dominate national politics itself.[9]

The founding fathers created the Senate to provide an internal congressional check on these potential tyrannical tendencies of the House and its Speaker. By having senators selected by state legislatures, not by mass electors, the founders hoped the Senate would provide a dignified, stabilizing counterforce to the House.

The vice-president was chosen to be the presiding officer of the Senate to facilitate closer ties with the executive branch. Senators were given lagged, six-year terms so they would have time to consider public policy carefully and offset any hasty actions taken by House members. Presumably because of their greater wisdom and maturity, senators were given prerogatives in the ratification of treaties and the approval of executive and judicial appointments. In sum, the Senate was to be an "anchor against popular fluctuations," the chamber that would act with "more coolness, with more system and with more wisdom, than the popular branch."[10]

The framers designed the House to be a truly representative institution. Its members, selected simultaneously for two-year terms, were elected from districts drawn in proportion to the nation's population. Only the members of the House could initiate revenue legislation, reflecting the framers' great concern that the people determine their own taxes. This provision gave the House a claim to preeminence in all financial matters.

The essence of bicameralism, then, was two distinct, independent chambers with different sizes, terms of office, constitutional responsibilities, and constituencies. The House seemed destined to be the most prestigious and powerful body because of its elective status, its preeminence in fiscal matters, and its presumed capacity to generate strong and forceful leadership. The Senate lacked full democratic legitimacy because the people played a more indirect role in the selection of its members. The Senate also lacked a strong, elected presiding officer.

Nevertheless, it did possess unique roles, particularly in foreign policy, that could sustain its power in legislative affairs.

These distinctions between the House and Senate rested in part on expressed constitutional provisions that could be changed only by amendment. A degree of stability thus was built into the operation of bicameralism, with the House and Senate unable to alter differences in their length of office, their modes of selection, or their distinct constitutional powers. But the actual operation of bicameralism also depended on the nature of the society in which it operated.

The existence of a rural and agrarian society led the framers to expect that the elected House would have high turnover, a strong Speaker, and potentially a tyrannical bent. These expectations fueled the drive for bicameralism and a nonelective Senate. They also convinced the framers that the House, despite its much larger size, would maintain a cohesive organization equal to and possibly superior to the Senate, particularly since the Senate would not have a strong presiding officer. Similarly, the framers assumed that America would remain relatively isolated by the oceans from foreign entanglements. Influence over foreign policy would be of modest importance, they thought, and thus could be given to the Senate without violating the principle of popular government.

Two centuries have now passed since the founding fathers designed the bicameral Congress. Their world—a small nation on the eastern seaboard, dominated by an agrarian economy and rural lifestyle, isolated by the oceans from foreign wars—has vanished. In its place is an industrial and, more recently, a postindustrial nation of continental size and great international power. These societal transformations have necessarily altered the operation of bicameralism and eroded the constitutional design.

The Evolution of Bicameralism in the Nineteenth Century

The evolution toward modern bicameralism began in the nineteenth century when the Civil War activated the move away from an agrarian economy and toward an industrial order. The response of Congress to these environmental changes tells us a great deal about the flexibility of our bicameral arrangements and about the types of factors most likely to produce substantial alteration in the roles of the House and Senate today.

The Agrarian Era

In the early decades of the Republic, the House eclipsed the Senate in status and influence, much as the founding fathers had expected. The Senate was seen as "an honorific nothing." In fact, prior to the Civil War one did not make a long-term career out of Senate service, "except perhaps as a fluke."[11] The House, by contrast, experienced perhaps its greatest period of preeminence during the

Speakership of Henry Clay. So prestigious was the House that John Quincy Adams chose a career there following his presidency.

The ascendancy of the House during the first half of the nineteenth century resulted from several factors. Senators' unelected status and statewide responsibilities naturally built a barrier between them and the public. The Senate lacked full democratic legitimacy, whereas the House was the very embodiment of democratic principles. In addition, the Senate did not develop a strong internal organization, whereas the House, experiencing the high turnover that Madison had predicted, invested great power in its Speaker. The strong organization of the House enabled it to provide legislative leadership to the nation, which reinforced the prestige it gained as the nation's most democratic institution.

There were other reasons for the ascendancy of the House during this period. First and foremost, the House drew its membership from every byway in the country and thus was close to the pulse of the people. The large number of House members gave the House and its leadership a capacity to gauge and influence public opinion that neither the Senate nor the president could match. The president, as one individual with a small staff, had no direct means to reach the public in a rural society that lacked modern man's communication and rapid transportation systems. Senators, unelected and serving states rather than small districts, were also more isolated from the public than were House members.

In these early years the constitutional power of the House loomed large. The Senate's distinctive constitutional powers over treaties and nominations were defused by the physical isolation of the nation and the small size of the government. By contrast, the primacy of the House in fiscal affairs allowed it to claim broad influence over budgetary politics and shape the domestic policies of the day. This more critical policy focus of the House—together with its greater prestige as an elected body, strong organization, and closeness to the public—made it the dominant partner in Congress.

The Civil War ended the first era of American politics, the agrarian era. The debates over slavery highlighted the importance of the Senate as a forum for the discussion of national issues, greatly increasing its prestige. The war and its aftermath spurred the rise of a mass production economy and new transportation systems such as the intercontinental railroad. The technological revolution also produced faster ships to cross the oceans and facilitate the trade of the goods made possible by industrialization. The Civil War thus drastically altered the environmental conditions presumed by the founders and unleashed a new period of American history, a period referred to by Samuel Huntington as the "post-agrarian era" of American politics.[12]

The Post-Agrarian Era

The post-agrarian era stretches roughly from the end of Reconstruction in the 1870s to the first decade of the twentieth century. For the first time the country was preoccupied with creating an industrial base, building its urban centers, developing a system of interstate and international commerce, and debating the proper role of the government in economic and foreign affairs.

Perhaps the most significant political impact of post-agrarianism was the increased power of Congress and greater attractiveness of congressional service. During the agrarian era many policy problems, even on national topics such as commerce, were local problems best addressed by local governments and state legislatures. But with the growth of industrialization and interstate commerce the country's policy problems became increasingly national in scope and subject to congressional regulation. Congress became more central to the daily lives of citizens and a more attractive arena in which to gain and exercise power. Therefore, politicians began seeking long-term careers in Congress and turnover declined.[13]

The new policy issues of the post-agrarian era influenced the Senate perhaps more than the House because of the Senate's constitutional prerogatives in foreign affairs and greater interest in national concerns. In addition, the expanding role of government increased the size of the federal bureaucracy and created many new governmental positions whose occupants were subject to Senate approval. The resulting expansion in the patronage controlled by senators made the Senate more influential in state and national politics.

Environmental changes in the late nineteenth century benefited the House as well. The rise in international trade made tariff legislation the most critical issue of the day. The House, with its special constitutional powers in revenue matters, thus was able to expand its role in national policy making. In fact, two chairs of Ways and Means, the revenue-writing committee in the House, were the only two members of Congress to be elected president during this period. The election of Representative James Garfield in 1880 and Representative William McKinley in 1896, together with the nomination of Representative James Blaine as the Republican party's presidential candidate in 1884, clearly demonstrate the high standing of the House at that time.

The late nineteenth century was a golden era for the bicameral Congress. As Woodrow Wilson wrote in 1885, Congress was in ascendancy in American politics, dominating the presidency and the courts.[14] Both the House and the Senate possessed constitutional powers that were critical to national policy making, and both were well organized.[15] Each asserted its unique constitutional powers and played a clear role in making national policy.

Congress thus was more dominant and bicameralism was more balanced than the framers had planned. Yet underlying this period of congressional ascendancy were forces that eventually would undercut the power of Congress and alter its bicameral partnership. For example, the House, adjusting to the doubling, tripling, and quadrupling of the nation's population, increased its seats from 243 in 1860 to 435 in 1913. During the same time the number of senators increased from 72 to 96, reflecting the admission of 12 new states to the union. By the early twentieth century the size of the House had greatly outstripped that of the Senate.

This made the House a much more difficult institution to manage and decreased the prestige associated with service in it.

Nevertheless, turnover declined and careerism increased in the House as well as in the Senate. The move toward careerism came first in the Senate, where the average length of service rose from four years in 1880 to more than eight years by the early 1900s.[16] In the House, careerism lagged behind by about 15 years until the 1896 realignment greatly increased the number of safe districts in the country.[17] In both chambers, careerism was accompanied by decentralizing pressures. The number of legislators who wanted to hold positions of power grew, and the dominance of party leaders was questioned. Careerism threatened to reverse the founders' assumption that high turnover would produce centralized congressional leadership and sustain the governing capacity of the House and Senate.

The calls for decentralization were largely unsuccessful in the late nineteenth century; the existence of strong national parties, the modest number of careerists, and the strong procedural powers of congressional leaders combined to thwart the reformers. Moves toward fragmentation of the committee system were early warning signals, however, of the difficulties Congress could face if turnover continued to decline.

The post-agrarian era thus was a paradoxical one. It was the great era of congressional power. Congress had the institutional cohesion and constitutional authority to dominate national policy. The growing importance of foreign policy and patronage enabled the Senate to emerge as a more equal partner to the House. It was also a time when the House extended its influence, tariff policy was the most important national issue, and the Ways and Means Committee served as an "incubator" for presidents.

In short, Congress had become a powerful force in domestic and foreign affairs. Yet the very rise of Congress to prominence was attracting careerist legislators whose desire for personal power threatened to fragment the institution and undermine its capacity to make decisions. Moreover, the nation's population explosion had swelled the size of Congress, which further complicated congressional policy making. These tensions erupted with the coming of the industrial era during the first two decades of the twentieth century.

Bicameralism in the Industrial Era

The Progressive movement and World War I spurred on the industrialization of America. The Progressives brought to national politics a great concern for the democratization and decentralization of government, thus providing a philosophical and reformist argument for careerist legislators who wanted to decentralize power in Congress. The Progressives also favored a more active and powerful role for the federal government, including protection of the environment, the regulation of industry as well as commerce, and the use of the individual income tax to raise revenues. This expanded role of government fueled a continued rise in the power of Congress and reinforced the attractiveness of congressional service.

World War I, like the Civil War, increased the nation's need for the rapid and reliable production of war materiel. The government's efforts to meet these needs strengthened the country's commitment to new technologies, the development of its industrial base, the urbanization of its citizenry, and the economic interdependence of its various regions. The war also solidified the view of the national government as an active force in international politics.

Thus, the first two decades of the twentieth century marked a second great watershed period analogous to the Civil War and Reconstruction. By 1920 the nation was an industrial and urban society in which government revenues, derived from an income tax, financed social programs to protect consumers, the young, and the environment. Internationalism versus isolationism was the central political debate of the period. Women, beneficiaries of the Progressives' commitment to democracy, had the right to vote. In short, the outlines of modern America were in place. The coming of this new America transformed both Congress and its bicameral arrangements.

Restructuring Bicameralism

The new political agenda of the industrial era made the Congress more critical to the daily life of the country than ever before and ensured that more politicians would seek long-term congressional careers. As a result of the growing number of careerist legislators and the Progressive's efforts to democratize government, party leaders in Congress in the early twentieth century faced serious threats to their centralized control of power. By 1910 the reformers were powerful enough to challenge the leadership and win. Speaker Joe Cannon was stripped of much of the authority that had enabled the Speakership to lead and coordinate the House over the preceding century. Senate leaders were also weakened during this period, although in a less public and formal manner.[18]

This weakening of the power of congressional leaders marked the end of bicameralism as the founders conceived it. They instituted a bicameral legislature in the late eighteenth century because they feared that the House would elect a strong leader and play too strong a role in American politics. Two legislative chambers, they felt, would provide the division of authority needed to rein in the power of the legislature. But with the demise of strong central leadership and the subsequent rise of committee government, fragmentation and immobilism resulted. Rather than a restraint on an aggressive Congress, bicameralism now became an inducement toward weakness, a constitutional provision that helped increase the leverage of the executive and judiciary over the legislative branch.

The decline of central leadership had its greatest influence on the procedures and power of the House.[19] With 435 members, the House could not operate effectively under informal procedures of cooperation and mutual adjustment. It needed formal mechanisms that could plan and coordinate the flow of business and rule with authority. Without strong central leadership, the House was faced with a variety of often competing centers of power—the weakened Speaker, the Rules Committee, the Ways and Means Committee, the Appropriations Committee, and numerous specialized substantive committees. The smaller Senate was better able to adjust to the weakening of party leadership and thus improved its leverage over the House.

The Senate also benefited from other developments. Passage of the Seventeenth Amendment in 1913 made the Senate an elective body and removed the most substantial constitutional difference between it and the House. The Senate was then able to claim full legitimacy as a democratic institution. The second development was the nation's emergence as an economic and military power with extensive international interests and responsibilities. As America's international involvement increased, the Senate's special constitutional role in foreign policy became more important. The Senate's power was demonstrated most notably by its rejection in 1918 of the Versailles Treaty, a decision based in part on President Woodrow Wilson's failure to consult the Senate adequately during his negotiation of the treaty. The rejection of the Versailles Treaty revealed more clearly than on any previous occasion the power of the Senate in foreign policy.

In earlier decades the large size of the House and its local access had enabled it to be the superior institution at communicating with and persuading the public, but the rise of new communication technologies—mass circulation national newspapers, radio, and eventually television—tilted the power of communication toward the Senate and the presidency. These mass media were drawn to the Senate because of its small size, which allowed them to focus on individual senators, and because senators' large constituencies and more national and international focus provided the media with a wider audience. Media attention made national personalities out of senators and a notable debating forum out of the Senate. Individual senators and the Senate as a body could convey their opinions to the public more easily than could the larger House and its more parochial and anonymous members.

The House, for its part, was not without its strategies of influence. What House members lacked in national prominence, for example, they tried to make up for by outstripping senators in technical knowledge about legislation. The special influence they lacked in the area of foreign policy, they sought to balance by asserting dominance over revenue and appropriations legislation. And the House remained the truest reflection of the nation's pluralistic population. It was the essential arena in which coalitions were built and compromises reached among the spokesmen for the nation's distinctive local and regional interests.

The very parochialism of the House provided it with a certain stability. House members knew their districts, cultivated personal ties with their constituents, and established long-term support that senators, riding above the fray, could not match. In the process of developing their careers, House members lost whatever tinge of radicalism they may have had in the early years of the Republic. Representatives became spokesmen for the dominant economic and social interests in their districts, and their politics tended to be conservative. Senators, in building coalitions among minorities throughout their states, often held more liberal and controversial views.[20]

Contrasting the House and Senate

Industrial America thus produced a bicameralism very different from that foreseen by the framers of the Constitution. They had expected a radical, elected, aggressive, and powerful House that would be constrained by a conservative and appointed Senate. The industrial era produced an elected and powerful Senate that was often better organized, more visible, and even on occasion more liberal than the large, unwieldy, and parochial House.

These unforeseen developments, arising from the constitutional and environmental changes early in this century, have led the House and Senate to develop in very different ways over the past 60 years. The differences in the day-to-day life of the two houses influence how new environmental changes will affect bicameral arrangements today. Thus, before examining the effects that postindustrialization have on bicameralism, we will compare the electoral and institutional politics of the House and Senate during the industrial era.

Electoral Politics

Electoral differences between the two houses since ratification of the Seventeenth Amendment are rooted first and foremost in the fact that representatives serve for two years and senators for six. House members thus must always be prepared to face public evaluation of their decisions. Senators, according to an old adage, have two years to be statesmen, two years to be legislators, and then two years to be politicians running for reelection. As a result of constant electoral pressures, representatives are presumed to be more responsive to short-term changes in public opinion than senators.

This responsiveness is reinforced by the small size of House districts, relative to states, which allows members (in fact, may require them) to engage in personalized campaigns and develop specialized home styles that fit their constituencies.[21] The small size and homogeneity of most districts lead representatives to stress local issues and constituency service. And the personalized and parochial nature of House campaigns produce relatively safe seats.[22] These factors inhibit the House from taking a national approach to issues and have thereby limited its leadership on national issues.

The electoral circumstance of senators is quite different. Senatorial candidates campaign statewide and run for office only every six years. They rely less than House members on personal campaign appearances and friendships. Their diverse and mobile audience is reached through extensive use of mass media.[23] As a result, the theme of Senate elections is more likely to be national in character. Over the past several decades, national political forces have had a reasonably strong impact on their electoral fortunes.[24]

The electoral differences between the House and Senate reinforce the effects of their constitutional differences. The Senate has benefited from the growing importance of foreign affairs, not solely because of its unique constitutional role in this area, but also because statewide elections provide Senate candidates with the incentive and opportunity to look beyond narrow local questions to national and international issues. Six-year terms also give senators sufficient freedom from short-term electoral politics that they can pursue wider interests.

House members, tied to local districts and facing reelection every two years, have a primary incentive to focus on local problems that affect their constituents rather than on national and international concerns. So long as the local constituency gets its federal funds and constituents receive satisfactory casework, House incumbents usually can win reelection without great difficulty. Questions of ideology and national policy thus are likely to affect Senate races more than House races.[25]

Institutional Politics

These electoral and constitutional distinctions between the House and Senate have led to quite different patterns of institutional behavior. Some of the characteristics of Senate elections—specifically, their tendency to be more ideological, policy-oriented, and national than House elections—help give the Senate a special role in national policy making. As Nelson Polsby has observed, "The essence of the Senate is that it is a great forum, an echo chamber, a publicity machine." He goes on to state that "in the Senate the three central activities are (1) cultivating national constituencies; (2) formulating questions for debate and discussion on a national scale (especially in opposition to the President); and (3) incubating new policy proposals that may at some future time find their way into legislation."[26]

It is the grand design of national public policy rather than the nitty-gritty details of legislation that is of prime concern to most senators. The detailed expertise on legislative matters that is needed to produce sound legislation is usually provided by the House. Its established division of labor—that is, the tendency of members to focus their main attention and energies on their few committee assignments—leads to technical expertise that far exceeds the more generalist Senate.

Thus, a related distinction between the two chambers concerns the basic organizational structure of the House and Senate. The House is predominantly a committee-centered body. With 435 members, it simply could not consider legislative matters on the floor without the extensive prior use of committees. Members get to know other members often through their being colleagues on the same committee. The consideration of legislation on the floor is usually dominated by members of the relevant substantive committee. Committees, in short, are essential to the workings of the twentieth-century House.

While the Senate also is organized around committees, they are far less important to the typical senator than to the typical House member. Not only do most senators serve on many more committees than representatives, but senators may develop an interest in an issue that lies beyond their committee assignments. Moreover, the Senate is a flexible enough institution that individuals find it easy to pursue wide-ranging concerns. In other words, if the House is organized to fulfill the goals of its members through committees, the Senate accommodates its members by its individualist orientation. It is the individual senator who is the essential driving force of the contemporary Senate.[27]

There is a final institutional difference between the House and Senate that partly orginates in their differing electoral environment and institutional character—the emergence of the Senate as a presidential incubator. This development no doubt reflects the media-dominated, national, and public-policy-oriented nature of Senate campaigns.[28] Given how most senators become senators—namely, by becoming television celebrities who can comment on any national or international problem—it is not surprising that many are seen as potential presidential material. Indeed, so many senators aspire to the presidency that Alan Ehrenhalt of Congressional Quarterly believes the Senate as an institution may be adversely affected. It is a substantial strain, he observes, to be in the Senate and running for president.[29]

Conclusion

As we have seen, the coming of an industrial society has generated a House and a Senate that differ greatly from those of earlier times and from each other. The Senate has emerged as the more prestigious and influential body. Its elected status, longer term, constitutional prerogatives in foreign policy, availability as a forum for national debate and leadership, and special role as a presidential incubator have combined to increase its prestige. The House has developed as a chamber devoted to technical expertise, personalized constituency service, and responsiveness to local political interests. The greater relative status of the Senate is shown, among other ways, in its tendency to dominate conference committee decisions despite the greater legislative expertise of House members.[30]

These patterns have been evident in the House and Senate for most of this century, and they remain strong today. But the history of bicameralism demonstrates that even the strongest and most dominant patterns are subject to change when the underlying social and economic environment is transformed. Postindustrialism appears to be precisely such a change. In the final section we will consider its effects on the electoral procedures, institutional politics, and policy agenda of the House and Senate.

Postindustrial Change and the New Bicameralism

Postindustrialism involves the rise of a high-tech society in which agriculture and industry are automated and most people work in service jobs in areas such as education, communication, and health care. The postindustrial revolution, which first took hold during the 1960s, is well underway in America today. The majority of the public is involved in service occupations, and technical advances are being made in mass communications, transportation, computer technology, and robotics.[31]

At the domestic level, these changes are associated with the growing call for government to facilitate the transition to a high-tech economy and to ensure a decent and equitable quality of life for an increasingly mobile population. They also are associated with a deep clash of political values over the moral choices that the technological advances of postindustrialism produce. At the international level, these changes involve the development of nuclear and space-age technologies. Postindustrialism also depends upon developing good relations with Third World nations whose cheap labor force and extensive natural resources are essential to the economies of postindustrial nations.[32]

As the history of earlier eras makes clear, societal transformations of the magnitude of these postindustrial changes will alter the conduct of politics and the nature of bicameralism. Such environmental changes introduce new policy problems, thereby potentially transforming the policy roles of one or both houses. They revolutionize campaign techniques, alter institutional procedures, and change the attractiveness of House and Senate careers. It is not yet clear whether postindustrialization will affect the House-Senate partnership as dramatically as did the moves from an agrarian to a post-agrarian to an industrial society. The postindustrial era is still in its early stages; the space race and Vietnam War in the 1960s spurred it on, but it is not yet fully consolidated as the dominant economic and social force in American life. Nevertheless, broad outlines of the impact of postindustrialism are becoming increasingly apparent.[33]

Postindustrialism has complicated congressional politics by dramatically increasing the number and widening the scope of issues that legislators must confront. The growing complexity and unfamiliarity of the policy agenda have led members to create specialized committees and subcommittees to deal with the new issues, thereby further fragmenting Congress. These changes, in turn, undercut Congress's ability to provide strong and coherent policy leadership and thereby created a demand for central committees to improve policy coordination in areas such as budgetary politics. Postindustrialism threatens to continue the decline, begun in the industrial era, in the policy influence of Congress. It confronts Congress with problems of organization and decision making that are far more difficult than those of the industrial era. Will the House and Senate respond to these new problems in constructive ways and with equal degrees of success?

Electoral Politics

Let us address this question by first examining elections and mass communications. The mass communications revolution of the postindustrial era provides House and Senate candidates with a greater opportunity than in the past to contact constituents. The expense of television somewhat limits its utility in House races, particularly since districts often fail to correspond to a natural media market. House candidates generally find a highly direct and personal campaign much more practical and efficacious than TV ads.[34] Television is far more efficient in statewide constituencies because it allows candidates to reach voters whom they probably could not contact through personal campaigning.[35] Television also influences Senate races through the greater coverage that it gives to the Senate as an institution and to the policy positions of senators. As we have already noted, television has made household names out of many Senate candidates. House members, by contrast, have remained more enmeshed in local politics.

House members' attention to their districts has been aided by developments in rapid transportation, mass mailing techniques, and the computerization of casework activity.[36] These developments allow House members to maintain an almost constant presence in and attention to their districts. Home several weekends a month, anxious to solve their constituents' problems with the federal government, members of the House are personal ombudsmen for their constituents in Washington.[37]

The recent technological advances in communication and transportation thus have had different implications for the House and Senate. Television has increased senators' visibility, status, and national orientation, and it has led them further away from a personalized relationship with their constituents. Yet television can prove to be a double-edged sword because it is a resource available not only to senators but also to their challengers who can afford it. In fact, television may so raise the prestige and visibility of Senate service that it increases the number of serious challengers and gives them a resource with which to defeat Senate incumbents.

With respect to House elections, the high-tech revolution has served primarily to strengthen incumbents rather than challengers. Their small districts, frequent trips home, and rapid response to casework allow incumbents to develop close ties with many constituents. Moreover, mass transportation, mass mailings, and computerized casework enable them to develop a personal relationship with constituents and provide a direct, personal service that challengers cannot match. House elections thus are typically less competitive than Senate elections.[38]

These basic differences between the House and Senate generate other contrasts. Because of senators' greater need for media advertising and larger constituencies, Senate elections are much more expensive than House campaigns. Unless the candidate is wealthy, he or she will require a major infusion of funds to run a competitive race. Under these circumstances, political action committees

(PACs), especially those with a national orientation, are likely to be key sources of funds and quite visible participants in the electoral process. In short, nationally organized groups are more likely to focus on Senate than House elections.[39] Therefore, the themes of Senate elections are national in character. More than House contests, they tend to center on the clash between the candidates' ideologies and national policy positions and are less likely to hinge on local issues and constituent service.

Thus, national political forces have a reasonably strong impact on Senate elections.[40] As a result, Senate elections are becoming more competitive and volatile while House races are experiencing a high degree of incumbent security. The decline in the competitiveness of House elections is tied, in part, to the greater ease with which members can return to their districts, to their increased resources for casework activity, and to their abilities to create home styles that mesh closely with the character of their districts. The greater competitiveness of Senate races, by contrast, is tied to the visibility of senators and the availability of mass communications resources to well-financed challengers. Home style and constituent service are bonds between House members and their constituents that challengers find hard to break. A senator's media image and policy visibility are viable targets for a well-funded challenger.

These contrasts between the competitiveness of House and Senate elections have great significance for careerism within the two houses and thus for politics within the two institutions. Members of the House, less threatened by electoral defeat, can concentrate on pursuing personal power within the House, thereby further fragmenting its centralized structure. Members of the Senate, more threatened by electoral challenge and more likely to be in their first term, must pay attention to getting reelected and are less free than they might otherwise be to build up personal power in the Senate. These differences in career behavior have significant consequences for the overall operation of the two institutions.

Institutional Politics

The Senate has historically been known as an individualized institution with a highly fragmented power structure. This characterization remains largely true today and can be seen in senators' use of filibusters to assert their policy stands. Nevertheless, significant recent developments orient the individualistic Senate toward more cooperation and compromise than one now witnesses in the House. For example, increases in Senate turnover limit power struggles within the institution. Junior senators bargain from positions of weakness and vulnerability rather than strength and dominance. As a result, they have an incentive to respond to the wishes of senior legislators and party leaders if they are to succeed in the Senate. This motivation increases the likelihood that senators will work together.

Senators' incentives to work with party and ideological leaders are reinforced by national lobby groups. Increasingly critical to the funding of Senate elections, lobbies encourage senators whom they have helped to operate as cohesive groups, often in support of key committee or party leaders. The intense pressure from lobby groups can inhibit the ability of senators to focus on parochial and idiosyncratic concerns and force them to be attentive to the national forces that helped elect them.

Finally, the growing competitiveness and cost of Senate elections have forced senators to concentrate more collective attention on financing elections. During the late 1970s the Republican party in the Senate skillfully used its congressional campaign committee to collect contributions for Republican incumbents who were in trouble and Republican challengers who had a chance of winning office. Through state-of-the-art fund-raising techniques the committee has been able to build a large war chest. This party-directed fund-raising campaign, now undertaken by Senate Democrats as well, encourages party members to cooperate with the leaders who dispense party funds and thus creates additional impetus for cohesiveness and cooperation in the Senate.[41]

These forces toward cooperation and cohesiveness do not negate the natural individualism of the Senate nor the policy conflict that has come with the rise of the postindustrial agenda. The Senate is undoubtedly a more complex and unwieldy institution than it was in earlier decades. Nevertheless, the foregoing factors, together with the Senate's small size, have saved it from being crippled by the effects of postindustrialism.

The experience of the House has been rather different. The effects of postindustrialism have been to decrease the competitiveness of House elections and increase incumbent security. These developments have freed members to pursue positions of power for themselves, thereby producing a highly fragmented system of committees and subcommittees and a weakening of its most vital Ways and Means Committee.[42] This fragmentation, together with the large size of the House, have made it a very difficult institution to operate.[43]

To streamline the legislative process, the House has turned to electronic voting procedures. These procedures, however, may have robbed House leaders of their flexible control of the voting process while producing formal means that dissidents can use to increase roll call votes and thereby obstruct House business. Furthermore, to improve its declining image and prestige, the House recently began to televise its proceedings. The TV broadcasts have given self-interested careerists and dissidents a powerful new resource for gaining personal visibility and engendering conflict.

Although the coming of postindustrial technologies has helped House members in their personal quests for reelection and power, it has eroded the governance of the House itself. Senators, by contrast, have suffered in terms of their personal electoral security while the Senate as an institution may have benefited. The consequences of these patterns can be seen by focusing on the changing policy roles of the two institutions, particularly in the areas of budgetary and fiscal policy.

The Changing Roles of the House and Senate

In response to the need for planning that grows out of postindustrial change, the contemporary Congress has created a centralized budgetary process. Budgetary reform was in many ways a more salient concern in the Senate than in the House, largely because of the Senate's greater interest in national policy and the House's reluctance to alter its existing committee system. As the Senate and House pursued their own political ends during the design of the new budget system in 1974, two very different budget committees emerged.[44]

In the House, legislators were quite concerned that the new budget committee might alter power relations among members and committees. As a result, a weak committee was created that lacked the capacity to act decisively. Requirements that members from key existing committees be included on the budget committee and that no member serve longer than four years weakened the new committee. Its members lacked a real incentive to establish the committee's power and develop strong control of the budgetary process. By contrast, the Senate created a committee with permanent membership that possessed the incentive to play a strong, cohesive role in budgetary affairs.

This contrast between the House and Senate budget committees has had important consequences for the power of the two houses. The Senate's well-organized structure and more cohesive membership have allowed it to develop a strong role in monetary matters and a fair degree of prominence in the area of revenue policy—an area that the Constitution sets aside as the greater responsibility of the House. Not only is postindustrial change aiding the Senate by magnifying the importance of foreign policy, but it also appears to be increasing the role of the Senate in fiscal affairs.

The expanded role of the Senate is seen not only in the general budget-making process but also in the actual initiation and drafting of revenue legislation. Going against all constitutional and historical precedents, the House in 1982 allowed the Senate Finance Committee to initiate a major revenue bill. Although there were several reasons for this decision, a major one was simply the difficulty of organizing and controlling the House Ways and Means Committee. Thus, a precedent was set, and the Senate added a growing role in revenue matters to its preeminence in foreign policy.[45]

Has overall control of revenue policy shifted from the House to the Senate? It is much too early to tell with any certainty, but the possibility of such a shift is disturbing. Historically, the House has taken a constitutional prescription that is rather limited in character—"all bills for raising revenue shall originate in the House" (Article 1, Section 7)—and built around it a justification for House preeminence in monetary matters and thereby in domestic legislation. This strong role of the House was made possible, at least in part, by its capacity to organize effectively and assert its authority. This was true both in the nineteenth century with a strong Speaker and in the twentieth century with strong Ways and Means and Appropriations committees. If the House now loses that organizational capacity, it has little to fall back on to ensure its policy dominance in this area—only a constitutional prescription to initiate legislation, a prescription that the Senate may find easy to finesse.

The vulnerability of the House becomes more apparent when one compares its revenue authority to the Senate's special powers. With respect to treaties and nominations, the Senate is given the sole congressional power of advice and consent. Even if the Senate has extensive problems handling this responsibility, the House cannot act in its stead. But the Senate faces no similar difficulty should the House become unable to operate effectively in budgetary and fiscal matters.

The Senate has all of the constitutional power of the House in monetary matters save the authority to initiate revenue legislation. Should the House face severe organizational problems, the Senate could increase its role dramatically by providing policy leadership in fiscal matters while taking care to abide by technical niceties in the formal introduction of final bills. Should the governing capacity of the House weaken and that of the Senate increase, the House could experience an erosion in its power that would be hard to contain since its historic dominance of budgetary and domestic matters is built on such a slender constitutional thread.

Conclusion

As we have seen, the history of bicamerialism is one of change. The Constitution outlines only the broad contours of the House-Senate partnership, contours that can be shaped by the ebb and flow of environmental forces. As society moved from the agrarian era of the founding fathers to an industrial order, the politics of bicameralism altered, with the Senate becoming a more equal and vital partner to the House.

Now the move into a postindustrial, hi-tech world again may be transforming bicameralism. The electoral and institutional changes fueled by the coming of postindustrialism over the past two decades appear to be weakening the governing capacity of Congress while strengthening the power of the Senate relative to the House. What are the possible consequences of this new relationship?

First, conflict between the House and Senate may increase. Previous alterations in the power relations of the two houses did not involve a struggle between them over their joint powers or a usurpation by one house of the power of the other. The historic rise of the Senate was largely tied to the growing importance of its unique powers in foreign policy. But now the Senate has reached into a domain that constitutionally and historically has been the province of the House—namely, fiscal and monetary policy. Even though this development comes in large part as a result of its own disorganization, the House may see it as unwarranted and unacceptable and try to obstruct and undermine Senate leadership in this area.

Second, the responsiveness of Congress to short-term shifts in public opinion may decline. The Senate, increasingly the more influential body and the one with more competitive elections, is reelected in full only every six years. The House, with its two-year terms that allow the public to register immediate displeasure, seems to be increasingly insulated from electoral upheaval and declining in its policy influence. The public thus confronts a weakened House whose two-year elections seem almost meaningless and a stronger Senate whose more competitive elections are spread out over six years. Neither institution appears to offer short-term control of public policy through the electoral process. Nevertheless, both institutions are subject to electoral change in the long run, and the focus of the legislature on long-term policy analysis may have its own benefits in terms of policy deliberations and risk-taking.

Finally, Congress may become more national in focus and deliberative in nature. The growing prominence of the Senate—in budgetary and fiscal matters, for example—may focus attention on the national and international consequences of social and economic policy. Similarly, the more deliberative nature of the Senate should focus attention more on debate over public policy and less on the technical details in the drafting of legislation.

Thus, Congress appears to be changing in important ways, moving toward a more conflict-ridden and nationally oriented institution. This institution will be relatively immune from short-term electoral change and preoccupied with deliberation over policy directions. The Senate will be the more dominant institution while the House will suffer from organizational problems. The challenge to the new Congress will be to ensure representation of and responsiveness to the people.

The rise of the Senate and the weakening of the House shift power away from popular representation based on population. This shift may be temporary, but it is significant. Congress is the nation's central democratic institution, and when alterations in the power and performance of the House and Senate undermine its representativeness and responsiveness, as would be the case with a decline in the influence of the House, it is cause for concern. Students of Congress must carefully examine the factors that underlie this decline and consider measures to reverse it. They also must study the Senate more closely than in the past and identify the norms and procedures that can best assist it in fulfilling its leadership role in the postindustrial era.

Notes

Acknowledgements: Larry Dodd wishes to thank the Hoover Institution at Stanford University for its financial and clerical support during the preparation of this chapter.

1 Blondel (1973); Loewenberg and Patterson (1979); Schwarz and Shaw (1976). For recent discussions of bicameralism in Congress, see Fenno (1982); Longley and Oleszek (1983); and Pressman (1966).

2 According to the comparative scholar David Butler, in a survey of 28 major democracies, "Only in the United States ... is the upper chamber as important as the lower chamber." See David Butler, "Electoral Systems," in *Democracy at the Polls*, ed. David Butler, Howard R. Penniman, and Austin Ranney (Washington, D.C.: American Enterprise Institute for Public Policy Research, 1981).

3 For interpretations of this theory of government, see Dahl (1956) and Ostrom (1971).

4 Eckhardt and Black (1976).

5 Alexander Hamilton, James Madison, and John Jay (1961: 322).

6 Ibid., p. 322.

7 Ibid., p. 403.

8 Ibid., p. 309, pp. 334–335.

9 Ibid. See also Scigliano (1971).

10 James Madison, *Notes of Debates in the Federal Convention of 1787* (New York: W. W. Norton, 1969), p. 83.

11 Price (1975: 5–7).

12 Huntington (1974: 163–192).

13 See Polsby (1968: 144–168); Ripley (1969b: 43); and Fiorina, Rohde, and Wissell (1975: 24–57).

14 Woodrow Wilson, *Congressional Government* (1885; reprint, Baltimore: Johns Hopkins University Press, 1981).

15 Brown (1922); Bolling (1968); and Rothman (1969).

16 Ripley (1969b: 43).

17 Price (1975: 9).

18 Hechler (1940: 27–82); Brown (1922: 195–197, 275).

19 Brown (1922: 106–107, 248–249).

20 For discussion of the Senate's greater tendency toward liberalism, see Froman (1967).

21 Fenno (1978, 1982: 12–25) and Jones (1967).

22 Fiorina (1977b).

23 Fenno (1978: 9–12).

24 Kostroski (1973).

25 Barbara Hinckley (1970b); and Mann and Wolfinger (1980).

26 Nelson W. Polsby (1971: 7).

27. Fenno (1973).

28 Peabody, Ornstein, and Rohde (1976).

29 Alan Ehrenhalt, "The Moulting Season in the U.S. Senate," Congressional Quarterly Weekly Report, March 15, 1983, p. 535.

30 See Vogler (1971); Ferejohn (1975); Strom and Rundquist (1977); and Longley and Oleszek (1983).

31 Bell (1973); and Huntington (1974).

32 Thurow (1980); and Dodd (1981: 400–411).

33 See, for example, Lenchner (1979) and Saloma, III (1969).

34 Robinson (1981).

35 Fenno (1982: 9–12).

36 See Frantzich (1979).

37 Fiorina (1977b); and Johannes (1984).

38 Hinckley (1970b); and Mann and Wolfinger (1980).

39 Hershey (1984).

40 Kostroski (1973).

41 *Congressional Quarterly Weekly Report*, November 1, 1980, pp. 32–38.

42 Smith and Deering (1984).

43 Sinclair (1983).

44 Ellwood and Thurber (1981); and Schick (1980).

45 Pamela Fessler, "Spending Cuts, Record Tax Hike Pass Senate," *Congressional Quarterly Weekly Report*, July 24, 1982, p. 1747.

Additional Perspective on "Changing Partnership"

Written with Edward Carmines, "Changing Partnership" seeks to assess the state of House-Senate relations in the aftermath of the reforms of the 1970s and amid the coming of postindustrial politics. It stresses the increased prominence of the Senate in bicameral relations, following the Civil War, and notes a variety of ways in which the two chambers were becoming more similar in electoral and organizational politics during the post-World War II era. The Senate, for example, appeared to be serving more and more as a sensitive electoral barometer of shifting public sentiment, a role Madison had envisioned the House as serving. "Changing Partnership" was not the only work of the early 1980s to recognize the growing convergence of the House and Senate in many of their broad behavioral attributes. Norman Ornstein makes analogous arguments in his 1981 essay, "The House and Senate in a New Congress." For an exploration of the convergence of the House and Senate during the postwar years in ways discussed in these two essays, particularly those arguments dealing with convergence in electoral politics, see John R. Alford and John R. Hibbing (2002), "Electoral Convergence in the U. S. Congress."

The more controversial theme in "Changing Partnership" was its stress on the likely increase of policy conflict between the two houses, fostered in part by the creation of an electoral Senate and ongoing electoral convergence between the House and Senate. This increase in bicameral conflict would occur, aside from electoral reasons, as a result of (1) the budgetary reforms of the 1970s, which could aid an increased Senate role in fiscal matters (Ellwood and Thurber, 1977, 1981), and (2) the ongoing emergence of postindustrial policy pressures, which would make budgetary politics increasingly central to congressional policy making (Huntington, 1974; Thurow, 1980). Such increased conflict could heighten policy deadlock in Congress and reinforce momentum towards a crisis of institutional legitimacy.

For a compelling work that documents growing policy conflict between the House and Senate in the subsequent decades, see Jordan Ragusa (2011), "Contemptible Compromise? Bicameral Disagreement and Reconciliation in the Post-Reform Congresses," Doctoral Dissertation, In Progress, Department of Political Science, University of Florida. What is particularly intriguing in Ragusa's analysis is his demonstration that this increased bicameral conflict over policy comes amid growing polarization between the two political parties in Congress. One might expect party polarization to bring a decrease in interchamber conflict owing to close cross-chamber cooperation by majority party members during periods of united party control of Congress. In fact, interchamber policy conflict has increased with party polarization in the late twentieth and early twenty-first centuries, suggesting that the pressures toward increased conflict are substantial in nature.

Suggested Reading: Works that speak to, build on, test or assess arguments introduced in this essay include Lawrence D. Longley and Walter J. Oleszek, *Bicameral Politics: Conference Committees in Congress* (1989); Ross Baker, *House and Senate* (1989); Samantha Durst, "Delay, Deadlock, and Deficits" (1991); William Riker, "The Justification of Bicameralism" (1992); James A. Thurber, "Centralization, Devolution, and Turf Protection in the Congressional Budget Process" (1997); David W. Brady and Craig Volden, *Revolving Gridlock*, (1998); Francis Lee and Bruce I. Oppenheimer, *Sizing Up the Senate: The Unequal Consequences of Equal Representation* (1999); Louis Fisher, *Congressional Abdication on War and Spending*, (2000); Barbara Sinclair, "Coequal Partner: The U. S. Senate" (1999); Eric Uslaner (2000); Bruce I. Oppenheimer, ed., *U. S. Senate Exceptionalism* (2002a); Daniel Wirls and Stephen Wirls, *The Invention of the United States Senate* (2004); Eric Patashnik, "Budgets and Fiscal Policy" (2005); Sean Gailmard and Jeffery A. Jenkins, "Negative Agenda Control in the Senate and House" (2007); Abhinay Muthoo and Kenneth A. Shepsle, "The Constitutional Choice of Bicameralism," (2008); and Bruce I. Oppenheimer (2009), "The Process Hurdles: Energy Legislation from the OPEC Embargo to 2008," pp. 305-306.

Classroom Use: "Changing Partnership" can be useful as an accessible overview of the shifting relationship between the House and Senate from the founding to the 1980s; a description and assessment of what bicameral politics looked like to close observers of the Congress in the years immediately following the reforms of the 1970s; and an assessment of how politics in the two houses was likely to converge and conflict in the foreseeable future.

In the same edition of *Congress Reconsidered*, Bruce Oppenheimer's 1985 essay, "Changing Time Constraints in Congress," provides an insightful assessment of how the new rules and conditions of the era were affecting the ability of the two houses to manage time pressures. Oppenheimer's essay is perhaps the first work to grasp fully the ways in which the new rules and conditions of the post-reform era were likely to foster an increased use of the filibuster in the Senate, leading to the emergence of a 60-Vote Senate in the 1990s (Sinclair, 2002). "Changing Partnership" and "Changing Time Constraints" should be combined for a fuller understanding of bicameralism in the immediate post-reform period of the late 1970s and early 1980s. Their combination with Ornstein (1981) could also prove useful.

For point/counterpoint contrasts, "Bicameralism in Congress" can be usefully paired with *Congressional Government* by Woodrow Wilson (1985) and *The Leadership of Congress* by George Rothwell Brown (1922), both of which look to a time in which the House of Representatives was the driving force in congressional politics. Additionally, it can be paired with Barbara Sinclair, "The 60-Vote Senate," in Oppenheimer (2002a), *U. S. Senate Exceptionalism*, to contrast the concerns about the Senate that preoccupied scholars in the late 1970s and early 1980s with those concerns they stressed in the first decade of the twenty-first century amid greatly heightened party polarization.

PART II

Political Parties, Institutional Cycles and Era Transformations

5

THE CYCLES OF LEGISLATIVE CHANGE

Building a Dynamic Theory

1986a

To better understand the dynamic character of Congress, Chapter Five shifts from an historical to a theoretical perspective on Congress. In developing a theory of change, the chapter builds on the cyclical argument presented in previous chapters, attempting to develop it in a more systematic manner. In doing so, it deviates from previous work in three key ways.

First, the essay emphasizes the struggle for party control of Congress as the central mechanism by which members seek personal power in Congress. Second, it sees members of a long-term minority party as so concerned to gain majority status that they eventually yield party leaders considerable power with which to coordinate challenges to the majority party. Minority party members will also stress their party's commitment to the increased governing capacity of Congress. Third, the essay sees members of a long-term majority party as tending toward over-confidence about their party's hold on power, given the incumbent advantages majority status provides them, and prone toward debilitating fragmentation of governing power. Long-term majority parties will thus be prone to unexpected and dramatic defeat, giving the minority an opportunity to assert its policy mandate, challenge presidential aggrandizement of power, and eventually reorganize the Congress to improve its governing capacity.

Party competition for control of Congress thus generates cycles of party-driven reform, providing an organizational mechanism for long-term attention to meaningful change.

The subject of legislative change first captured my attention in the summer of 1975. I was teaching a course on Congress; I had started the semester with the theoretical arguments of David Mayhew (1974b) and was ending with a review

Lawrence C. Dodd. *"The Cycles of Legislative Change: Building a Dynamic Theory."* In Political Science: The Science of Politics. *Edited by Herbert F. Weisberg. New York, N.Y.: Agathon Press. 1986, pp. 82–104.*

of the recent budgetary reforms. As the course drew to a close an exasperated student raised two questions: "Mayhew presents a static Congress; why is Congress changing? Mayhew describes a fragmented Congress; why is Congress centralizing?" I had no answer for the student, nor could I find one in the legislative literature. Scholars from Wilson (1885) to Huntington (1965) to Polsby (1968) had described congressional change and noted its critical implications. Parliamentary analysts such as Bryce (1924) and Bracher (1971) had treated change—the decline of legislatures—as one of the great themes of twentieth century politics. And Blondel (1973), surveying all contemporary legislatures, had found cyclical change to be legislatures' most widely shared characteristic. Yet none of these writers provided a coherent explanation of change.

The questions posed by the undergraduate student had uncovered a major flaw in the study of legislatures. The problem did not lie with inadequate methods. Legislative scholars had pioneered the use of mathematical models (Ferejohn, 1974; Fiorina, 1974; Shepsle, 1978), sophisticated statistics (MacRae, Jnr., 1970), and participant observation (Fenno, Jnr., 1966, 1973, 1978; Huitt and Peabody, 1969; Jones, 1961; Oppenheimer, 1974; and Peabody, 1976). The problem did not lie in a paucity of data; scholars had abundant access to roll call votes, election statistics, and first-hand interviews. Nor was the problem an absence of historical research. A solid body of literature existed by the mid-1970s that traced the outlines of congressional history in some detail (Bolling, 1965; Brady, 1973; Cooper, 1970; Ripley, 1969a, 1969b; Rothman, 1969; and Young, 1966).

The problem lay in the absence of theory. The student's questions—why change? why centralization?—demanded explanation, demanded theory. With theory the student could understand the movement of Congress from one organizational structure to another, and then hypothesize perhaps the emergence of a third. With theory legislative scholars could visualize and research the critical patterns of change that static analysts might overlook or misunderstand. But no theory of change existed to guide students or scholars.

A decade has now passed since the congressional reforms led my undergraduate student and others across the country to challenge the static nature of legislative theory. And today, just as in the 1970s, the creation of a theory of change remains an unfulfilled task (Rieselbach, 1984). A growing body of scholars focus on the historical research necessary for developing and testing theory (Aydelotte, 1977; Cooper and Brady, 1981a, 1981b). But legislative theory itself remains preoccupied with static models that bear little relationship to the turbulent change of modern legislatures.

Against this backdrop the purpose of this essay is to encourage scholars to build theories of change. Given the relative absence of theory perhaps the best way to provoke such work is to construct a theory. To this end let us first examine some major studies on which we can build.

The Intellectual Foundation

The theoretical work of Anthony Downs (1957), presented in *An Economic Theory of Democracy*, provides us a useful starting point. Downs is important not so much for what he says about legislatures as for the insights he provides into building theories of change. He focuses on the behavior of parties and elections in a world that closely resembles a British parliamentary system. Parties are goal-oriented teams of members seeking to gain power by winning elections. To win the support of the electorate, parties reflect dominant ideological positions of voters. As large groups of voters shift their ideological stands, the parties alter their policy positions. Such jockeying among parties can alter the number and size of parties in the party system.

Downs' theory demonstrates that the goals of political actors can shape and explain changes in their political behavior. Moreover, micro level motivations, such as actors' desires for power, can shape macro phenomena such as the changing structure of the party system. These conclusions suggest that legislative scholars, who after all are studying the same politicians as Downs, should examine the impact that legislators' goals have, not simply on elections and parties, but on the politics of the institution. Just as a focus on politicians' goals can generate a deductive theory of electoral and partisan change, it may also produce a coherent understanding of legislative change.

Downs' influence on general legislative theory is seen most clearly in the work of David Mayhew (1974b). In *Congress: the Electoral Connection*, Mayhew provides us the first full-fledged attempt to build an economic theory of legislative politics. He draws his inspiration from Downs' emphasis on the goal-oriented nature of politicians. Mayhew argues that the goals of legislators, specifically, their desire for reelection, shapes the structure and functioning of a legislature. The effort by members to gain reelection leads to common patterns of behavior such as credit-claiming and to the creation of a decentralized Congress designed to serve members' reelection needs.

Mayhew's work is a major step toward a general legislative theory. Unfortunately, his theoretical strategy suffers from two shortcomings (Dodd, 1978a). First, the book contains a logical flaw. In order for Mayhew to explain the existence of mechanisms such as the Rules Committee that keep Congress functioning, he argues that legislators receive side payments of power for service on these committees; these side payments induce members to serve on such committees even though service may limit their opportunity to pursue their reelection interests. The reelection motive by itself cannot account for the existence of these committees and thus fails to explain fully the organization of the legislature. A second problem, as noted above, is the static nature of Mayhew's Congress. He develops no argument to explain how or why the legislature may change.

These theoretical shortcomings should not mask the great contribution of Mayhew's work. Early efforts such as this to build a theory are bound to have conceptual and logical flaws; but the effort itself is a vital part of a process of theory building that will span several generations of scholars and explore many dead-end paths. The important point is that Mayhew directs us to a potentially fruitful strategy for studying legislatures: linking members' goals to institutional politics and structure. He also identifies an argument, the emphasis on reelection, that undoubtedly has widespread applicability in the legislative world.

Mayhew's work was published almost simultaneously with Richard Fenno's pathbreaking study of congressional committees (Fenno, Jnr., 1973). Fenno's empirical work directly addressed the central problems of Mayhew's theory. Whereas Mayhew focused on one narrow goal, Fenno introduced three goals: reelection, policy, and influence. Members pursue these by serving on committees that facilitate one or another of the goals. These findings suggest that legislators may in fact create different committees to serve these different career goals. An explanation of the structure of the committee system and thus of Congress must incorporate all three goals.

Fenno's analysis also suggests that a certain hierarchy of goals may exist among members. While Fenno does not develop the topic himself, the move from reelection to policy to influencing committees parallels an increase in the average seniority of committees' members and in the power and prestige of committees (Rieselbach, 1973; Smith and Deering, 1984). These patterns suggest that legislators may share some very general goal such as power that they pursue through orderly stages of career advancement, moving from a reelection to a policy to an influence stage (Dodd, 1977). The pursuit of power then would be the underlying factor determining the type and relative status of committees in the legislature.

Fenno's second contribution was to link legislators' goals with organizational change. This development comes in his exploration of the House Post Office Committee. In the postwar years, Fenno argues, the members of that committee pursued reelection goals so avidly—by raising civil service pay while keeping postal revenues low—that they undermined the fiscal integrity of the postal service. Their continued pursuit of the reelection goal eventually produced a fiscal crisis; in response, Congress stripped the committee of its jurisdiction and created a postal service commission. The uninhibited pursuit of members' short-term goals had crippled the committee's capacity to perform responsibly and had forced Congress to change the committee's role.

The tension evident in Fenno's micro-level analysis of the Post Office Committee is writ large in the ambitious work of a fourth scholar, Joseph Cooper (1975, 1977). Cooper argues that a key way to see legislatures and legislative change is from an organizational perspective (see also Davidson and Oleszek, 1976). Whereas Fenno sees tension between the individual and a committee, Cooper sees tensions involving the individual, the overall legislative structure, and the legislature's external environment. These tensions shape and constrain the individual's career development and thus the sort of structure and process he supports for the legislature.

Of the scholars discussed here, Cooper is the one for whom legislative change is really a major issue. Cooper is particularly concerned with macro change. Just as Downs is interested in changes in macro level phenomena (shifts from a two party to a multiparty system, for example), Cooper is interested in knowing why a legislature may change from a party dominated to a committee based structure. Cooper reminds us that our real explanatory task is to explain the institution itself: its broad patterns of organization, behavior, and change. We will possess an incomplete and unreliable understanding of legislative behavior until we can explain how the general structure and processes of the legislature shape the behavior of its members.

A similar concern with macrolevel analysis is reflected in the growing research into congressional realignments (Brady, 1978; Carmines and Stimson, 1986a, 1986b; Sinclair, 1982; and Sundquist, 1973). Key (1955) and Burnham (1970) saw realignments as the critical engines of electoral change; the students of congressional realignments see them as critically connected with policy decisions in the legislature. Such scholars demonstrate, for example, that the coming of realignments may be preceded by sustained shifts in the legislature's policy outputs. They also show that a realignment itself may produce policy changes in the legislature.

These studies invite us to look closely at the interconnection between electoral and institutional change. They suggest, first, that we explore the institutional consequences of realignment. When a realignment brings new members and a new policy agenda into the legislature, for example, it may generate presures for the legislature to reorganize so that it can better meet members' career goals and process their new policy proposals.

Similarly, consider the observation that policy shifts in the legislature foreshadow the coming of realignment. These patterns suggest that the legislature itself may play a role in the genesis of realignments, with the policy actions or inactions of the legislature fostering electoral upheaval. The research conducted by students of congressional realignment, though still at an early stage, could have important implications: realignments may arise from a legislature's internal politics and then spark change in the legislature itself.

This emerging concern with realignment reflects an increased attention to historical research on legislatures. The pathbreaking analyses of Bolling (1965), Huntington (1965), Polsby (1968), Ripley (1969a,b), and Young (1966) have brought to our attention the existence of different historical eras with very different patterns of organizational behavior. A second body of scholars (Bullock, 1972; Fiorina, Rohde, and Wissel, 1975; Kernell, 1977; King, 1981; Loomis, 1982; Price, 1975; and Rohde, 1979) stress the critical impact of careerism on legislative behavior. A third theme, seen in the work of Blondel (1973) and Sundquist (1981), is the cyclical nature of change. Legislatures tend to experience long periods of decline followed by short periods of resurgence and organizational reform.

Together these empirical and theoretical studies are moving toward a general theory of legislative change. They exhibit a common focus on the career goals of legislators (Downs, Fenno, and Mayhew). The goals shape the organizational structure and behavior of the legislature (Cooper and Mayhew). Yet legislators' pursuit of personal goals also may be in conflict with the maintenance of a viable decision-making process (Cooper and Fenno).

The consequent inability of the legislature to make responsible policy decisions can foster societal crisis (Bolling, Huntington, and Sundquist), provoke party realignment, and thereby alter the legislature's policy agenda and organizational structure (Brady and Sundquist). Tension between members' personal goals and their broader environment thus can reshape the fundamental operation of the legislature (Cooper). The resulting change tends to be cyclical in nature (Blondel and Sundquist).

Building A Cyclical Theory

The foregoing studies fit together in a suggestive way, pointing toward a theory of change. The key missing element is a proposition that can pull the discussion together into a structure of reasoned and logical argument. Such a proposition can be found, I suggest, by treating legislators as power seekers whose preoccupation with career advancement undermines the policy-making integrity of the institution.

In what follows, I develop this proposition into a theory of change. The theory begins with a micro-level discussion of legislators' goals and career cycles. It then details the impact of this micro-level behavior on the legislature at a macro level, focusing on the progressive emergence of fragmentation, realignment, and reform. The conclusion to the essay considers the empirical applications of the theory.

Legislative Goals and the Career Cycle

Let us assume that a politician enters a professional legislature to gain policy-making power. He or she enters a legislature in which all formal decision making is collective and based on formal equality among members. The legislature's rules establish the procedures and work groups through which policy is created and approved. These rules give special resources to a limited number of members who are to lead and coordinate the activities of the legislature. These resources are highly valued because they allow such members to have special power in policy making.

Career advancement is the process whereby legislators gain mastery over the resources that are necessary for this exercise of power (Muir, 1982). To become a successful power wielder, a legislator must exercise mastery of four types of resources: those associated with reelection, policy development, institutional influence, and organizational control. The quest for policy-making power is thus an extended pursuit of legislative mastery.

Legislative Goals and the Stages of Mastery

The development and exercise of mastery follows a certain natural order. A member first must ensure her reelection; the realization of all other goals depends on this goal. As a result, the newly elected legislator must focus extensive attention on reelection politics, gaining the resources and learning the skills that best nurture her security in her district (Fenno, 1978; Jacobson, 1983).

As the legislator gains mastery of reelection politics, her concern necessarily turns to policy making: advocating and presenting specific policy proposals. Policy making is an immediate concern in part because it is so closely linked to constituent concerns—to fulfilling specific promises (Clausen, 1973; Kingdon, 1973). It is also important, however, because it provides the legislator with the knowledge and experience she needs before she can address broader societal problems and before she can gain legitimacy in the eyes of the legislators whom she seeks to influence and lead (Matthews, 1960).

With reelection and policy-making mastery, the legislator can turn her concentration to influence over the members and control of the organization. Influence, the ability to persuade and bargain effectively with legislators, is generally required before a legislator has the support to win a position of organizational control. Influence will come as a member gains leverage over resources—campaign funds, information, constituency appropriations—that other members want. Control of the organization means authority to appoint members to the legislature's work groups, to schedule debates and votes on bills, to rule on parliamentary conflicts, and to regulate policy debates. Such control allows a legislator to shape the policy agenda and policy decisions of the legislature (Sinclair, 1983).

Legislators gain these four types of mastery primarily through membership and service in political parties. The resources of the legislature, such as staff, office space, and committee positions, are allotted to the parties according to their majority or minority status, with the majority party receiving a greater than proportional share. Each party distributes its resources in accordance with a well-established body of rules and norms. These rules and norms regulate the availability of the different types of resources.

Since the goal of each party is to govern, each seeks to use its resources to build a large group of supportive legislators who can help it gain and exercise institutional power. As a result each party spreads its reelection and policy resources widely, hoping to ensure members' electoral security and their satisfaction with the party. Yet precisely because a party seeks to govern, it must ensure that party leaders can coordinate the party's members and pursue the party's general interests. Thus party rules and norms create a small number of influence and control resources that generally go to long-term members who are knowledgeable, loyal, and electorally secure.

The rules and norms of legislative parties thus create a hierarchy of resources which parallels the goal hierarchy of members. Each party's quest for power leads it to distribute reelection resources widely among its members, followed in progressively smaller amounts by policy, influence, and control resources. Party rules thus create a set of resource stages that are similar to and reinforce the four stages of mastery. A complete legislative career will begin by focusing on reelection mastery, both because of the legislators' personal desire to solidify reelection and because the rules and norms of the legislature guide new members toward reelection activities. The legislators' goals and the legislature's resource structure then focus him progressively on policy making, organizational influence, and organizational control.

Movement from one career stage to the next generally requires a congruence between goals and resources: legislators must both want to achieve new goals and have access to the necessary resources before a new stage of mastery can be pursued effectively. The development of organizational mastery thus may involve tensions and frustrations, particularly when legislators pursue organizational goals but are denied access to appropriate resources. Such tensions are inherent in legislative life.

Organizational Resources and the Career Cycle

In a highly professional legislature, where a large proportion of the members seek long-term careers, the rules and norms restrict the availability of organizational resources and thus hinder rapid career advancement. While numerous reelection and policy-making resources are normally available so that most legislators can realize their early career aspirations, influence and control resources are limited in number and restricted primarily to more seasoned legislators. Because a large number of careerist legislators compete for a relatively small number of highly desirable resources, the career path, or career cycle, that legislators desire falls far short of the career cycle that they actually experience.

The legislators' desired career cycle is shaped by their aspirations to gain legislative mastery as early in their careers as possible. Otherwise the vagaries of electoral politics or the organizational success of other legislators may deny any one member his or her opportunity for power. The amibitious legislative profesional thus seeks the desired career cycle illustrated in Figure 5.1. He wants to move rapidly through the stages of career development, spending a short and concentrated amount of time gaining skills and resources necessary to master each stage. The bulk of his career can then be spent in the exercise of policy-making power.

In actual practice, the professional legislator spends the bulk of his career not in the exercise of mastery but in its pursuit. The rules and norms of the legislature control resources and severely limit the availability of influence. Such resources generally are possessed by senior legislators whose electoral and organizational mastery ensures their long-term reelection to the legislature and to its positions of power. Young and midcareer legislators thus face a long struggle in their pursuit of valued resources.

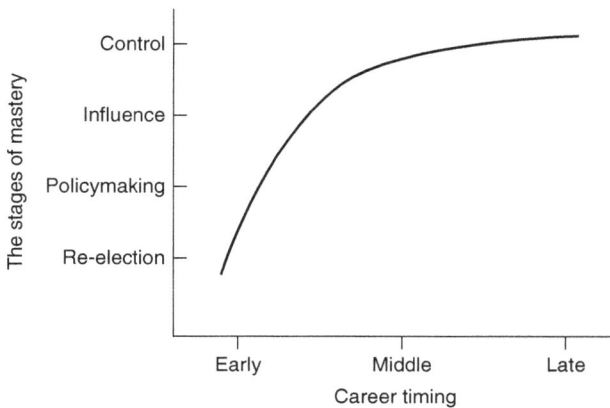

FIGURE 5.1   The desired career cycle.

Figure 5.2 illustrates the actual career path a professional legislator will experience. While the legislator may move rapidly through the reelection stage and into the policy stage, owing to widespread availability of resources, legislators then are caught in a midcareer stall that diverts them from influence and control; rather than a career focused on broad policies they spend the bulk of their time concerned with narrow and middle range issues, always under the influence and control of the more advanced careerists.

The basic message of Figure 5.2 is that the core of a professional legislator's career will be spent in frustration. Experiencing such frustration, younger and midcareer legislators will necessarily seek ways out of their predicament—ways to speed up their career advancement. The most obvious and direct way is to change the rules of the legislature and make the desired resources more available to the less senior members. The consequences of such efforts are clearest if we

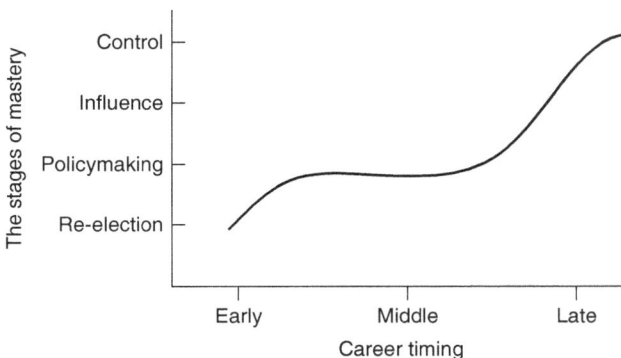

FIGURE 5.2   The actual career cycle

examine legislators' behavior beginning with the creation or reorganization of a legislature.

Career Goals and Organizational Fragmentation

Let us assume that a legislator enters a professional legislature with a large group of new professionals at a time when the legislature is reforming. A significant aim of this organizational reform is to strengthen the governing capacity of the legislature while securing the broad career interests of its members. The reforms create numerous reelection and policy resources to serve the large junior contingent. They establish a relatively limited number of influence and control resources to meet the career needs of the senior legislators and the coordination and leadership needs of the institution.

A new legislator will have few initial quarrels with this distribution of resources: it readily fulfills his reelection and policy-making interests. But as the new legislator, his cohorts, and succeeding classes seek access to the stages of influence and control they face a more difficult circumstance. The career advancement of the new generation is hindered by the limited number of available resources and by the dominance of senior legislators. To end their shared frustration and gain desired resources, these junior and midcareer legislators use their collective voting power and pass reforms designed to spread resources more widely among all members.

Over time, the legislature will experience the organizational fragmentation pictured in Figure 5.3. The period immediately following the creation or reorganization of the legislature will witness very little fragmentation. The new organizational structure and the career interests of legislators mesh fairly well. But with the aging of the new generation, the legislature will witness a steady rise in fragmentation, with the junior and midcareer legislators using their growing

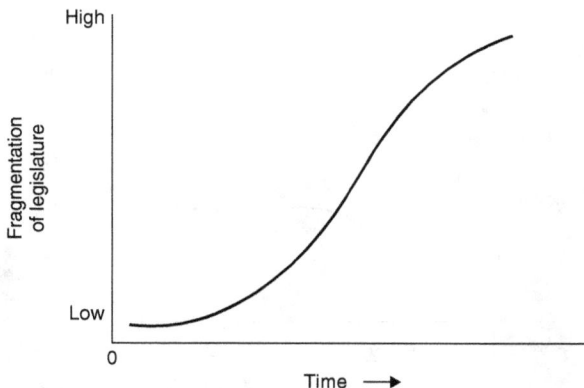

FIGURE 5.3 The pattern of legislative fragmentation.

numbers to pass the necessary reforms. The fragmentation process, however, will not occur in identical ways through all segments of the legislature.

Countercyclical Fragmentation Among Work Groups

The general pattern of fragmentation in Figure 5.3 is a composite of the specific patterns that characterize the diverse work groups of a legislature. When we characterize groups such as legislative committees according to the primary career goal they serve, we see the more complex fragmentation patterns of Figure 5.4. As this figure indicates, the pattern of legislative fragmentation will differ dramatically among different groups.

The move toward fragmentation occurs primarily in those work groups where new and midcareer legislators exist in large numbers, work groups which are most concerned with reelection and policy making. It is in these groups where a sufficient number of frustrated legislators exist to force the creation and redistribution of resources. Unable to move out of these work groups, legislators will attempt to use these groups and their resources as surrogates for the influence and control resources they lack.

The continued presence of legislators preoccupied with influence and control means that reelection and policy-making work groups will increasingly disintegrate over time. Their membership will be concerned with an incompatible mix of goals that undermines the work groups' capacity to establish coherent decision rules and perform their allotted tasks. The breakdown of such work groups, and the spread of their resources among uncoordinated individuals, makes it difficult for the majority party to maintain control of the electoral and policy making resources of the legislature.

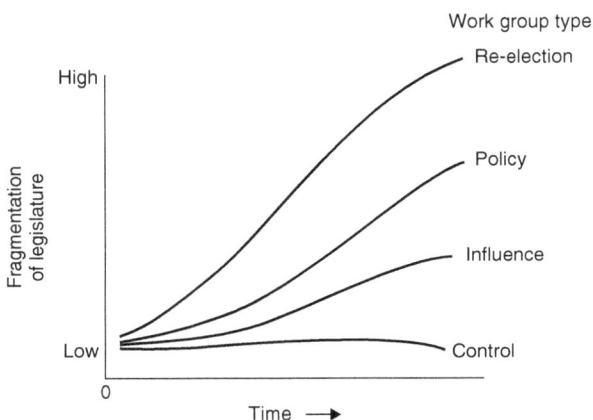

FIGURE 5.4   The pattern of work group fragmentation

The process of organizational change is quite different among the influence and control groups. Few early and midcareer legislators serve on such groups; thus it is difficult to reform the groups from within. Attempts to reform such groups from the outside are equally difficult because the senior members can use their parliamentary power to stop the passage of reforms through the legislature. In the fight against outside interference the members of these work groups may actually develop greater group cohesion.

Fragmentation and Crisis

Over time, then, work groups within a professional legislature experience a countercyclical pattern of change. Those groups most open to new and mid-career legislators, the reelection and policy groups, should fragment extensively. The groups most dominated by the advanced careerists, the influence and control groups, will fragment least and possibly centralize somewhat in their effort to offset the reformist assaults. The bulk of the legislative organization, the reelection and policy-making groups, thus disintegrates over time while the governing groups may actually experience increased integration.

The various groups direct their attention not toward working with each other but toward working against each other. The result is a breakdown in the mechanisms for coordination and leadership of the legislature. As the decision-making capacity of the legislature declines, the legislature increasingly loses its ability to make policy and govern. Severely immobilized, the government will have difficulty performing its most basic and seemingly routinized functions. Such extensive immobilism will generate or exacerbate serious national crises and set in motion a period of electoral upheaval.

The Institutional Genesis of Party Realignment

The foregoing pattens of fragmentation and policy immobilism are generated by the organizational ambitions of legislators. Members' success in their power quest rests on the ability of their party to provide them scarce legislative resources. The party's ability to provide such resources is tied to its effectiveness in gaining and maintaining control of the legislature.

In a two party (or two factional) setting, which we will assume here, the party that gains the attachment of the largest number of voters becomes the long-term governing party. The minority party continually challenges the governing party and is prepared to take power if the public loses faith in the government's performance. The performance of the governing party rests in part on how well organized the legislature is to make policy decision. The fragmentation of a legislature, thus, can have substantial consequences for the electoral fortunes of the majority and minority parties.

The Majority Party

The most obvious impact of legislative fragmentation is on the majority party, particularly the party's perceived performance. Because fragmentation immobilizes policy making, it limits the party's ability to fulfill its promises to the public. And because immobilism ultimately fosters societal crisis, it undermines public confidence in the party's ability to govern. Legislative fragmentation thus cripples the majority party's performance and erodes public support for the party.

Ironically, legislative fragmentation has a somewhat opposite effect on the immediate fate of majority party incumbents. As fragmentation undermines the capacity of the majority party to coordinate legislative resources, it increases the autonomous control that junior and midcareer party members have over resources, particularly those connected with reelection and policy making (Sundquist, 1973, 1981). This individual control of resources increases the capacity of majority party incumbents to engage in constituent services and strengthen their reelection chances (Fiorina, 1977b). Fragmentation thus aids the reelection of majority party incumbents and may actually increase their margins of victory.

In a fragmented legislature the apparent electoral strength of the majority party incumbents hides the party's increasing vulnerability and weakness. Because the party lacks coordinated control of its own resources, it can neither create a record that will elect its candidates nor provide campaign assistance to the candidates who could use it most effectively. The party's legislative majority depends on incumbents who are attractive for their constituent service rather than their policy views. Yet such legislators are particularly vulnerable when periods of extreme national crisis allow strong minority challengers to stress the overriding importance of the nation's policy problems.

The Minority Party

The experience of the minority party is quite different. The minority party lacks control of the legislature. Before minority legislators can gain extensive legislative resources, their party must win a legislative majority. To do so minority party members must focus their attention primarily on nurturing the electoral and policy success of the party (Jones, 1970). Minority party members thus will protect the cohesion of the party and oppose moves to fragment the organizational resources that it does control. Only after the party gains secure majority party status will party members focus their primary attention on personal competition for resources.

The cohesion of the minority party gives it an increasing electoral advantage as the legislature fragments. It can coordinate the electoral resources that it does possess within the legislature, utilizing those resources in the manner best designed to expand the party's delegation in the assembly. It can coordinate policy-making resources to create a coherent and visible party program that presents an image of party unity, policy competence, and governing capacity. Such a policy image, publicized by a well-coordinated and well-financed body of candidates, generates public support for the party and its legislative team. Minority party incumbents thus can win in increasing numbers (Cook, 1980; Light, 1980).

The General Pattern

During the period of fragmentation, then, the two parties follow very different paths. The majority party experiences an apparent increase in the security of its incumbents accompanied by a largely unseen *decline* in the public support for the party itself. The minority party members experience an increase in the electoral performance of its members accompanied by a *growth* in the party's public support. As incumbent security increases, and as the parties converge in the degree of public support they enjoy, the growth in legislative fragmentation leads the legislature deeper into policy immobilism and crisis.

The coming of severe national crisis provides the minority party a golden opportunity. The crisis highlights the inability of the majority party to govern effectively and encourages the public to voice its hidden discontent with the party. It also encourages normally inactive citizens to participate in politics and oppose the governing party. Such political upheaval casts a shadow over the electoral future of the majority party and encourages ambitious junior politicians to join the minority party. These attractive candidates then can mount effective campaigns on a nationwide basis by attacking the policy failure of the majority party and by dismissing the value of incumbent's constituent services in the face of national crisis.

The nationwide challenge by the minority party uncovers the underlying vulnerability of the majority party and produces its massive electoral defeat. The great fall of the majority party is not the result of sudden displeasure on the part of voters. The public had long ceased to identify with the majority party. The great fall occurs because the electoral strength of the party or dominant faction was more apparent than real, resting on incumbents who also were open to defeat when seriously challenged (Mann, 1978). The national crisis activates serious challenges, leading the public to throw the old rascals out, and gives the governing mandate to a new party.

We can talk, then, of the institutional genesis of electoral realignments. The fragmentation of the legislature leads to the rise of policy immobilism, a decrease in majority party support among voters, and the eventual national crisis that activates electoral upheaval. The electoral upheaval brings to the legislature a new majority party dedicated to new policy solutions. It also brings into majority status new legislators concerned with career advancement.

Organizing to Govern

Upon gaining majority status, the victorious party confronts the central dilemma that undercut the former majority party: it must organize the legislature so that it can govern effectively. In approaching this task, the party inherits the fragmented legislature created by the outgoing party. This organization can cripple the new majority party just as it undermined the governing capacity of the old party. Yet the severity of the national crisis demands immediate policy changes and allows little time for elaborate organizational reforms.

During the early days in power, the new majority party offsets legislative fragmentation by drawing on two distinct advantages. It possesses a relatively cohesive party organization within the legislature because it avoided extensive fragmentation when in the minority. In addition, the new party majority contains a large number of new legislators preoccupied with reelection and policy advocacy and not yet concerned with using resources to exercise influence and control. The party thus can govern effectively despite a fragmented legislature. It can move rapidly to end the crisis of immobilism.

Soon the honeymoon ends, however, and the new majority party faces the dilemmas of governing. The legislators elected during the realignment upheaval gain mastery of reelection and policy-making resources. They increasingly pursue the numerous resources available in the fragmented legislature and use these resources to gain influence and control. The capacity of the party to lead and coordinate its members declines, and within two to three elections the legislature experiences renewed immobilism (Patterson, 1967).

Policy immobilism after realignment is even more difficult for the legislature to resolve than before. The new majority party is hesitant to deny its members the legislative rewards for which they worked so hard while in the minority. The party members, concerned with their personal career success, fail to connect the policy failures of the party with their pursuit of personal power. The new party thus embraces the politics of fragmentation and watches its governing mandate flounder. Seeing the legislature stifled even with a fresh infusion of new members and new ideas, public disenchantment with legislative decision making grows.

Legislative immobilism and the public disillusionment invite the executive to usurp the policy-making power of the legislature in order to break policy immobilism and end the national crisis. The executive initially succeeds because the legislature is too fragmented and disorganized to oppose it effectively and because many members of the legislature and the public see executive intervention as necessary to save the Republic. As the executive attempts to consolidate power, however, legislators come to realize that the institution is on the verge of permanently losing its governing power. Such a loss would make members' resources and status in the legislature worthless. The legislators support for the strong executive thus turns to fear and opposition.

Executive intervention demonstrates to legislators that they must strengthen the legislature if they are to save their personal power. They respond by reducing fragmentation and creating a more coherent decision-making structure. With the reformed structure in place, the new majority party is now prepared to govern until career frustrations lead its members to fragment the legislature once again (Dodd, 1977).

The Organizational Cycle: An Overview

The thrust of the foregoing argument can be summarized in one phrase: professional legislatures are characterized by an organizational cycle. The struggle of legislators for career advancement leads them to press for a fragmentation of legislative resources. This fragmentation eventually cripples the governing capacity of the institution and requires members to reorganize it along more coherent lines. During such cycles the legislature passes through six stages (Figure 5.5):

Stage one:	organizational stability
Stage two:	fragmentation
Stage three:	immobilism and crisis
Stage four:	electoral upheaval and realignment
Stage five:	interventionism
Stage six:	reorganization

This organizational cycle and the six component stages results from the internal politics of the legislature and the effect that such politics has on elections and

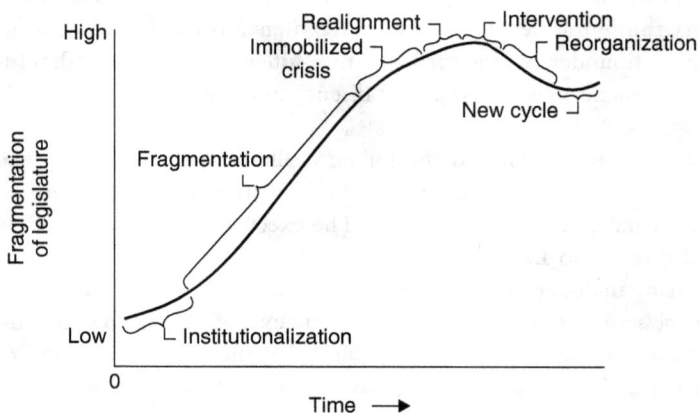

FIGURE 5.5   The organizational cycle.

the broader governing process. This cyclical perspective provides scholars with a theoretical framework they can use to explore legislative change in a more systematic manner.

Conclusions

The value of this theoretical framework depends primarily on its ability to help us explain changes in legislative behavior. A test case is the legislative reforms of the mid-1970s. The prospect that the Congress would centralize itself seemed farfetched to legislative scholars during the postwar years. Legislators preoccupied with reelection would necessarily create a decentralized structure in order to maximize their ability to play constituent politics. They would never create a centralized policy process that could confront them with unpopular policy decisions.

The decisions in the 1970s to strengthen party leadership and create a new budget process proved otherwise. The budget procedures, in particular, built difficult policy choices into the annual roll call votes in Congress. These reforms thus confronted legislative theorists with a challenging task, to explain why a professional legislature of reelection-oriented careerists would enact reforms that could complicate their reelection. The theory of cycles provides such an explanation.

Careerist politicians are drawn to legislative service, the theory argues, not primarily for job security. They are attracted by a desire for policy-making power. Reelection is an essential component of the quest for power. But long-term reelection is in itself rather valueless without power. Members thus must maintain the fundamental policy-making integrity of the institution if their career advancement is to provide them with personal power to make policy.

Throughout the postwar years, the members of Congress pursued their needs for reelection and personal power by fragmenting the committee system and eroding the integrity of the policy process (Dodd and Schott, 1979). They failed to understand that the value of personal power depends on the capacity of the institution to govern. The resulting policy immobilism on issues of civil rights and social welfare provoked the 1964 realignment that produced the Great Society (Burnham, 1970; Sundquist, 1973; Carmines and Stimson, 1986a, 1986b). Yet the coordination and funding of the new policy agenda soon ran afoul of a highly fragmented Congress. The national government, attempting to pursue social and military spending that Congress could not coordinate, faced a growing fiscal crisis (Ellwood and Thurber, 1977; Schick, 1980).

The fiscal crisis provided the executive with a ready-made justification for usurpation of congressional power: the argument that Congress could not coordinate spending in a responsible manner. Richard Nixon embraced this argument to justify unconstitutional impoundments of domestic appropriations (Fisher, 1975). His intervention demonstrated to legislators the institutional and personal price of single-minded careerism. Legislators had crippled the processes of leadership and coordination in Congress much as Fenno's Post Office Committee members had destroyed the policy-making integrity of their committee. Post Office Committee members lost their prized jurisdiction; under Nixon, members of Congress reformed the policy process just in time to defuse presidential cooptation of the budget.

The centralizing reforms of the seventies thus illustrate the explanatory value of the theory. But the theory should fit this case, if no other, since it was created in response to these reforms. The more interesting question is whether the theory can actually be generalized beyond the Congress of the seventies. Can it explain congressional change in earlier decades? Can it explain the widespread pattern of cyclical change among other professional legislatures?

The U.S. House of Representatives, as the world's best-researched legislature, offers us an opportunity to address these questions. In the House the serious growth of legislative professionalism began with the ending of the Civil War. By 1885 Woodrow Wilson could argue that the struggle for power and resources within the House was a central influence on legislative politics. He emphasized the acquisition of resources, particularly committee resources, as a major concern of the members. He also recognized the inherent tension between a central party leadership and fragmented committee politics; he saw this tension as shaping the ongoing life of the institution.

From Wilson's day to the present time this struggle for power has fostered fragmentation, crisis, and reform (Bolling, 1965; Huntington, 1965). Fragmentation in the late nineteenth century centered on the committee system, which grew by approximately 50 percent in size from the 1860s until the reforms of 1920. From 1920 to 1946 congressional fragmentation centered on the proliferation of a variety of special committees and subcommittees, a process reversed by the 1946 Legislative Reorganization Act. And from the early 1950s to the early 1970s, the committee system experienced a growth in the number and autonomy of standing subcommittees and subcommittee chairs. In each of these periods we witness roughly similar sequences of change in which fragmentation is followed by realignment (1890s, 1930s, 1960s) and then reorganization (1910–1920, 1946, 1970–1975).

Our faith in the theory is reinforced by the patterns of countercyclical change that we see in the postwar House. The theory argues that reelection and policy work groups should fragment to a much greater extent than influence and control groups; this is precisely the pattern that emerges when we examine the reelection (constituency), policy, and prestige committees identified by Smith and Deering (1984). From the mid-1950s to the early 1970s, for example, reelection and policy committees increased by approximately 50 percent the average number of members holding committee or subcommittee chairs. By contrast, the more prestigious influence and control committees, such as Appropriations and Rules, experienced no increase in members holding chair positions; the powerful Ways and Means Committee fragmented only with the party reforms of 1974 (Rudder, 1977). These patterns conform to the expectations of the theory.

Micro-level patterns in the House likewise correspond to the general expectations of theory. Career cycles in the House are seen in such empirical patterns as the tendency of junior and senior legislators to concentrate on different electoral strategies (Fenno, 1978; Parker, 1984) and on different types of committee and subcommittee assignments (Smith and Deering, 1984). The linkage between career aspirations and organizational structure is shown by the long-term tendency of the House to fragment as the proportion of careerist members grows (Huntington, 1965; Polsby, 1968). And the linkage between career frustration and fragmentation is shown by the organized efforts of disadvantaged groups such as House liberals in the 1950s to gain personal power and policy influence by pursuing decentralized reforms (Stevens, Miller, and Mann, 1974).

The history of the House thus suggests that the theory has broader relevance than the reforms of the 1970s. In the long term, I hope that the theory also will prove applicable to other legislatures besides Congress. While congressional politics provided the theory's stimulus, its analytic arguments are not necessarily restricted to Congress. Just as Downs could build a general electoral theory by starting with assumptions that resemble British politics, so legislative scholars may find clues in the study of Congress that unlock a general legislative theory. The trick is to discover in Congress phenomena that professional legislatures have in common and to build on this discovery a general theory that is applicable to them all.

The common phenomena I identify is the existence of ambitious career legislators with deep frustrations over the maldistribution of institutional resources (Loewenberg and Patterson, 1979; Schwarz and Shaw, 1976). To the extent that such legislators are present, the concepts and hypotheses of this theory should apply to any legislature. The fragmentation of the British House of Commons over the last 15 years, for example, would seem a possible consequence of the frustrations that a growing number of career members have with the limited resources available to them (King, 1981). Likewise the historic immobilism and cyclical restructuring of the French parliament can be analyzed from the perspective of career ambitions and frustrations of parliamentarians.

The theory thus identifies an extensive research agenda for scholars of professional legislatures, pointing them to such little explored phenomena as goal hierarchies, career cycles, career frustration, cyclical and countercyclical fragmentation, policy immobilism, and organizational reform. It also introduces hypotheses that address some of the most important unanswered questions of electoral and institutional analysis, not only the impact of careerism on institutional change, but the impact of institutional structure on policy immobilism, incumbent security, and electoral realignment.

The answers offered by the theory are necessarily tentative: there are too many gaps in empirical knowledge and theoretical logic for me to argue the theory's general validity. But the theory does provide a foundation, one strengthened by support from the work of Downs, Mayhew, Fenno, Cooper, and others, on which scholars can build.

Empirical efforts to build from this theory will require scholars to modify and interpret the theory before they apply it to a particular legislature. Parliamentarians may be more likely to seek positions in cabinet ministries and party committees, for example, than in standing committees. Parliamentary fragmentation thus may be more adequately measured by examining the cabinet ministries and party committees than the standing committees. Similarly, policy immobilism in a multiparty parliament may not generate an American-type realignment because the electorate may find it difficult both to determine the parties responsible for policy failures and to identify the viable governing alternatives. The realignment that occurs may come in the parliament itself as members fundamentally restructure the parliament's governing coalition.

Efforts at empirical application also require additional developments in the theory itself, one of which I will mention in closing. The cyclical theory treats the legislature's external environment as constant unless the internal decisions of the legislature alter it. In real life, of course, the external environment does change quite independently of a legislature's decision. New technologies can arise, a war can erupt, an international depression can occur, all unprovoked by the legislature.

Such external change can alter the policy problems of a society and confront the legislators with demands to create a new legislative structure designed to address the new policy problems. The legislators themselves, however, have their careers deeply enmeshed in the old structure and may be unwilling to alter it substantially (Davidson and Oleszek, 1976). Reforms pressed by external groups, after all, are primarily designed to help the groups pass their desired policies rather than promote the resources and power of legislators.

This tension between external and internal forces is absent from the cyclical theory and could pose great problems for it. External groups, for example, could force legislators to reform at the "wrong" time in terms of the predictions of the theory. Likewise, legislators could refuse to reform and challengers with "new ideas" could defeat them, thereby causing electoral upheaval and reform that come out of sequence with the theory.

These and other scenarios indicate that theorists must consider closely the interaction of external and internal factors (Strom and Rundquist, 1978). For myself, I believe that the two dimensions can be integrated into an even richer cyclical theory in which the organizational cycle remains the core pattern of legislative change and external factors determine how extensive the process of change will be. Such a theory would explain why some cycles experience greater fragmentation than others, why some realignments are more policy oriented, and why some reforms actually transform legislatures into new policy-making bodies (Dodd, 1986b).

Acknowledgements: I have benefited greatly from the comments of numerous colleagues who read earlier versions of this essay. My special thanks to the panelists who critiqued the original paper, "The Legislative Imperative: Building Broad-gauged Theory," A Paper Prepared for Delivery at the 1983 Annual Convention of the American Political Science Association, Chicago, Ill.: September 3, 1983. The panel discussants were Joseph Cooper, Gary Jacobson, Charles O. Jones, and Kenneth Shepsle; and to those who provided me feedback as this final essay was completed, particularly Michael Berkman, Edward Carmines, Richard Champagne, Carolyn Cooke, Jon Hale, Russell Hanson, Calvin Jillson, Glenn Parker, David Prindle, Leroy Rieselbach, Barbara Sinclair, and Herbert Weisberg. My thanks to Michael Maffie for assisting with the preparation of the essay for publication in *Thinking about Congress.*

Additional Perspective on "Legislative Change"

The Cycles of Legislative Change" develops an institution-centered theory of organizational cycles in Congress. In doing so, it removes the study of change from a particular historical context and seeks to specify in a more systematic and reasoned manner the institutional conditions and logic that can generate organizational cycles across contexts. The reason for focusing on the abstracted logic of cycles is to help analysts see more clearly the common conditions and mechanisms at work in fostering cycles across historical eras. To aid in this effort, the essay nudges into peripheral vision the role that on-going socially-induced institutional change plays in Congress. It highlights the ways in which the institutional ambitions, party-centered politics and organization-based careers of members, operating interactively within Congress, induce institutional change. In doing so, it argues that institutional politics in itself may generate societal crisis, electoral upheaval and subsequent institutional change. The theme of the essay thus is the 'institutional genesis of institutional change.'

The core argument of the essay revolves around the existence of an institutionally-induced *'electoral paradox'* that plays a decisive but largely unseen role in fostering societal crisis and thereby inducing partisan alternation and instituitional reform. In this paradox, the success of a party in capturing majority control of a legislature brings members institutional resources (as in committees and in office staff) to use to generate increased electoral security within constituences (as through casework and pork barrel politics). But over the longrun, the appearance of electoral security leads majority party members to become overconfident of their party's hold on power, lulling them into decreased attentiveness to citizens' broad policy concerns. Overconfidence then sets the majority party and its members up for eventual citizen rebellion and unexpected electoral defeat. This argument underlies much of the author's remaining work on Congress and comes to the fore, in an analysis of inter-generational conflict, in "Congress in a Downsian World (2011)."

The explicit characterization of these arguments as an electoral paradox, and a more extensive development of the paradox, is presented in Dodd (1983a, 1983b). This material was excised from the essay owing to space constraints and reviewers' incredulity with the argument. Reviewers' skepticism resulted from the widespread belief among congressional scholars from the mid-1970s through the mid-1990s that legislators' increased capacity for casework and constituency service had permanently defused the role of policy agendas and issue politics in congressional elections. It was only with the Republican Revolution in 1994 that scholars began to seriously reassess this perspective. The author owes a huge debt to Herbert Weisberg for his decision to publish "Legislative Change" over reviewer objections.

This essay begins a process of explicit theoretical inquiry and empirical assessment that proceeds throughout the remaining essays in this volume. The author engages in theoretical inquiry in order to address concerns about the future of Congress that his early interpretive work on the postwar Congress had generated.

Theoretical inquiry allows scholars to identify empirical processes and implications that are embedded in the logic of politics, and likely to shape future institutional developments, even when immediate events and empirical patterns of the moment suggest otherwise. As the process of theoretical inquiry proceeds in subsequent chapters, the author seeks to clarify with increased breadth and depth of awareness how and why cycles of congressional change occur and what the implications of such awareness are for the way analysts should think about and address change in Congress. Through identifying the conditions and logic generating the cycles, he believes scholars can more readily understand how variation in conditions, constraints, motives and strategies can alter the operation of such cycles. With such awareness, perhaps the nation can better determine how it can turn debilitating cycles of gradual institutional decline into rejuvenating cycles of institutional renewal. In subsequent essays, as in this one, he will move back and forth between theory development and empirical assessment through real-world observation.

Foundation Work: As with all of the author's work on legislative assemblies, the essay benefits from Anthony Downs' classic 1957 masterpiece, *An Economy Theory of Democracy*. The author first read Downs during his initial semester of doctoral work in the fall of 1968. Downs' work has grounded his thinking about legislatures in a goal-oriented and power-centered perspective and has constantly reminded him to be attentive to the critical role political parties play in electoral democracies. That attentiveness comes to the fore in an explicit manner with this essay. The author's attention to party as a central mechanism of contestation and change reflects the growing centrality of ideologically distinct and polarized political parties in Congress in the 1980s. This essay is his effort to clarify the ways such parties were likely to contest for power and influence the cyclical dynamics of Congress in the coming decades.

Dodd's work is also informed in deep background by William Riker, *The Theory of Political Coalitions* (1962), which he read in the spring of 1970. The conception of politics as a game of rational calculation which recurs in his work has its explicit roots in that reading of Riker's pioneering book. This game-theoretic perspective is most clearly delineated in the author's dissertation on the politics of parliamentary assemblies, *Coalitions in Parliamentary Government,* Dodd (1976a). The framework presented in *Coalitions* had a subtle influence on "Quest" and "Legislative Change," particularly their emphasis on legislators' strategic pursuit of power. His work on *Coalitions* also alerted him to the distinctive ways that institutional and societal context, electoral change, society-centered ideological conflict, and party system polarization can shape legislative outcomes, separate from and in interaction with intra-institutional politics. Concern for such broader extra-institutional factors, foreshadowed in Chapters Three and Four, comes to the fore as an explicit theoretical focus in Chapter Six, "Congressional Cycles."

In developing the electoral paradox, the author benefited greatly from Morris Fiorina's classic 1977 study, *Congress: Keystone of the Washington Establishment*, which highlighted the critical role of casework and constituent service in the electoral strategies of post-war legislators; and from John Ferejohn's pioneering study, *Pork Barrel Politics* (1974), which speaks to the multiple kinds of constituent service legislators may pursue. The increased margins of incumbent victory are documented by Mayhew (Mayhew, 1974a; Cover and Mayhew, 1981) and others for the postwar era (Burnham, 1975; Erikson, 1971). For subsequent work on constituent service and the casework thesis, as well as their interaction with factors such as legislative professionalization, see Fiorina (1989, 1995a, 1995b) and Cain, Ferejohn, and Fiorina (1987).

For a discussion of the essay's contributions to congressional studies, see Herbert Weisberg (1986), "Introduction: The Science of Politics and Political Change." See also Mo Fiorina's discussion of the relevance of this essay to understanding the 1994 Republican Revolution, in Morris Fiorina (2001: 149), "Keystone Reconsidered."

Suggested Reading: Works that speak to, build on, test, or assess arguments introduced in this essay include Loomis, *The New American Politician* (1988); Kenneth A. Shepsle, "The Changing Textbook Congress" (1989); David King, *Turf Wars: How Congressional Committees Claim Jurisdiction* (1997); Fiorina, "Keystone Reconsidered," (2001) Diana Evans, *Greasing the Wheels* (2004); David R. Jones and Monika L. McDermott, "The Responsible Party Government Model in House and Senate Elections" (2004); Jones and McDermott, *Americans, Congress and Democratic Responsiveness* (2009); Sean Theriault, *The Power of the People: Congressional Competition, Public Attention, and Voter Retribution* (2005); and Marian Currinder, *Money in the House: Campaign Funds and Congressional Party Politics* (2008), Chapter Two.

Classroom Use: "Cycles of Legislative Change" can be used in the classroom in sections on elections, political parties, legislative–executive relations, and institutional change. It can also be used as a theoretcal foreshadowing of and explanatrion for the 1994 Republican Revolution. The essay thus speaks to the value of theoretical inquiry in the study of real-world politics.

For point/counterpoint contrasts, "The Cycles of Legislative Change" can be usefully paired with *Congress: the Electoral Connection* by David Mayhew (1974b), which stresses a relatively constant and member-centered rather than a cyclical and party-sensitive perspective on congressional elections; and with Morris Fiorina's original version of *Congress: Keystone of the Washington Establishment*, published in 1977, which stresses postwar legislators' growing concern for casework politics and constituent service over agenda politics and policy issues in congressional elections.

6

A THEORY OF CONGRESSIONAL CYCLES

Solving the Puzzle of Change

1986b

Chapter Six expands the cyclical theory of change. It presents legislators as seeking both mastery of organizational politics within Congress and mastery of electoral politics within their constituencies. It sees citizens as narrowly self-interested voters pursuing particularized policies that directly aid them personally—and also as broadly self-interested political actors concerned with collective policy agendas designed to construct the kind of society in which they prefer to live. The interplay of legislators' dual goals and citizens' dual policy concerns yields three processes of cyclical change.

The first generation-long process involves fragmentation and recentralization in the organizational procedures of Congress, and includes shifts in partisan or factional control of Congress. The second multi-generation process involves long-term rigidification of the ideological agenda and governing structure of Congress, followed by periods of transformation in policy agendas, partisan regimes and institutional structure. The third process involves decline in the capacity of Congress to enact major policy initiatives amidst organizational fragmentation and institutional rigidification, followed by a rebound in policy performance in response to partisan realignment, organizational recentralization, and structural reform.

These multiple cycles of change provide mechanisms by which Congress and the national government adapt to social, economic and technological transformations in the nation; restrain presidential aggrandizement of power; and sustain the legitimacy of representative government.

Events of the 1970s caught students of Congress by surprise. Postwar scholars had concluded that the modern Congress was a stagnant and impotent institution,

Lawrence C. Dodd. *"A Theory of Congressional Cycles: Solving the Puzzle of Change."* In Congress and Policy Change, *Edited by Gerald C. Wright, Jr., Leroy N. Rieselbach, and Lawrence C. Dodd. New York, N.Y.: Agathon Press, Inc. 1986, pp. 3–44.*

incapable of rapid change or rejuvenation (Burns, 1963; Huntington, 1965). Yet in the 1970s it suddenly experienced precisely those reforms—the weakening of seniority and the Senate filibuster, the creation of a centralized budget process, the strengthening of the congressional parties—that had previously seemed impossible. These reforms, in turn, produced a dramatic resurgence in the policy activism of Congress (Sundquist, 1981).

This unexpected revitalization of Congress has presented scholars with an intriguing puzzle—the puzzle of change. Scholars can no longer hope to understand Congress fully until they can explain the processes that generate institutional change (Cooper and Brady, 1981b; Huntington, 1971; Polsby, 1975). To understand these processes, and solve the puzzle of change, scholars must construct a theory of Congress that is dynamic in character, plausible, well-grounded in existing knowledge about Congress, and susceptible to empirical test.

This chapter seeks to construct such a theory. It does so by building on empirical discoveries of the 1970s and early 1980s.[1] During this period legislative scholars sought to explain the recent congressional reforms by identifying the historical forces that gave rise to them (Cooper, 1970, 1975; Dodd, 1977, 1981; Huntington, 1981; Strom and Rundquist, 1978; Sundquist, 1981). Scholars found that the upheavals of the 1970s were not a unique occurrence to be explained by special historical circumstance. They were the product of broad and recurring cycles of change that had characterized Congress throughout its existence. These historical patterns suggest that a theory of change, and thereby an explanation of the reforms and policy resurgence of the past fifteen years, lies in developing a theory of congressional cycles.[2]

These cycles of congressional change have occurred at three levels. The first level involves long-term fragmentation and short-term reform of the organizational procedures of Congress, everything from the number of committees and subcommittees to the staff allotments given to members. The second level involves the long-term rigidification of the institutional structure of Congress—the persistence of rules that imposed party government in much of the nineteenth century, for example, or committee government through much of the twentieth century—followed by intense periods of upheaval and structural transformation. The third level involves cyclical change in the policy performance of Congress. This performance declines in periods of fragmentation and rigidification and rebounds in periods of reform and structural reorganization.

The theory presented here argues that these cycles of change, and thus the reforms and policy resurgence of the 1970s, result from legislators' desire to exercise policy making power—to have an autonomous and significant impact on the nation's policy decisions. To attain their primary goal of power, legislators pursue two subsidiary goals: mastery of organizational politics within Congress, and mastery of electoral politics in their external constituencies. A legislator must realize both of these subsidiary goals to exercise sustained policy making power.

The three cycles of change are a product of the pursuit of the two subsidiary goals. The pursuit of organizational mastery generates the cycles of organizational fragmentation and reform. The pursuit of electoral mastery generates the cycles of structural transformation. The organizational and institutional cycles together produce the cyclical changes in policy performance. The remainder of this chapter develops these arguments more extensively, starting with a discussion of the internal changes in congressional organization. Chapter Five on "The Cycles of Legislative Change" elaborates this discussion of internal organizational change in greater detail and with graphic illustrations. The following discussion summarizes the general thrust of the argument in Chapter Five and proceeds to integrate it into the broader three-cycle theory of congressional change developed in this essay.

The Theory of Organizational Cycles

The internal world of Congress is critical to members because it is the arena in which they acquire positions of power and influence. These positions carry with them those organizational resources—staff assistance, access to information, control over parliamentary procedure, and the like—that a member must possess in order to have a significant personal impact on congressional policy making. Power-oriented members thus give considerable attention to the internal politics of Congress (Dodd, 1977; Schwarz and Shaw, 1976; Wolfinger and Heifetz, 1965; Jones and Woll, 1979). Their attention is focused on more, however, than the acquisition of resources. For positions of power such as committee or subcommittee chairmanships to enhance a member's policy impact he or she also needs the respect and support of colleagues (Huitt, 1961a, 1961b, 1965; Manley, 1969; Matthews, 1960; Price, 1972). Only if they respect and trust the member will they listen to her seriously, negotiate with her, and follow her leadership. And only if her colleagues have confidence in her will they award her the additional discretionary positions and resources under their control (Peabody, 1976). The personal support of members thus is just as critical to her organizational career as is the formal acquisition of power positions and resources.

Legislators' personal impact on congresional policy making thus depends on their mastery of organizational politics, that is, on their ability to gain and use the resources and skills necessary both to attain positions of power and influence and to gain the personal trust of colleagues. The struggle to develop organizational skills while competing for the appropriate resources necessarily leads to a great deal of frustration on the part of legislators: few will ever be able to gain resources and skills as rapidly as they desire. Their frustration, or their anxiety over the slowness and tenuousness of career advancement, generates the cycles of organizational fragmentation and reform. To explain the organizational cycles we thus must first understand members' career behavior within Congress, particularly the ways they develop organizational mastery and advance their internal organizational careers.

Organizational Careers and the Stages of Mastery

Career advancement within Congress is the process by which legislators gain mastery of organizational resources and skills (Bardach, 1972; Evans and Novak, 1966; Huitt, 1961a, 1961b, 1965; Manley, 1969; Matthews, 1960; Muir, 1982). To become a successful powerwielder, a legislator must exercise mastery in four areas of organizational life: those that affect member's personal reelection, development of policy expertise, influence over other members, and control over organizational decision making (Dodd, 1977; Fenno, 1973; Mayhew, 1974b). Only when a member masters resources and skills across all four areas can he or she hope to have a strong long-term impact on policy.

To gain organizational mastery, a legislator must develop a personal approach to organizational politics—an organizational style—that will allow her to interact effectively with other members (Davidson and Oleszek, 1981: 98–112; Dexter, 1969b). Development of such a style will earn the legislator the trust and confidence of other legislators. Their trust and confidence, in turn, will help her gain resources and skills she needs to achieve immediate policy objectives and establish a reputation as an effective legislative craftsman. Her achievements and reputation will broaden and solidify her support among members, enabling her to gain more resources and skills and to further advance her career.

Each legislator's style has its own distinctive character, the result of her own unique personality and political circumstance. Yet legislators' styles also share many similarities as a result of the common problems they confront in pursuing their organizational careers. These common problems, and the natural sequential order that legislators follow in addressing them, impose a set of common stages through which members pass as they establish an organizational style and develop their mastery of organizational politics.

On entering Congress, a member's first organizational need is to ensure the electoral support of her constituents so that she can stay in office and pursue a long-term congressional career. As a result, the newly elected legislator must focus extensive attention on gaining those resources and skills in Congress, and developing the organizational style that will best nurture her security in her district (Fenno, 1978; Hershey, 1974, 1984; Jacobson, 1983; Kingdon, 1968). As the legislator acquires the organizational resources, skills, and personal style that can aid her in constituency politics, her concern necessarily turns to policy making—to advocating and presenting specific policy proposals.

Policy making is an immediate concern in part because it is so closely linked to constituent concerns—to fulfilling specific promises (Clausen, 1973; Kingdon, 1973). It is also important, however, because it provides legislators the knowledge and experience they need before they can address broader societal problems and before they can gain legitimacy in the eyes of the legislators they each seek to influence and lead (Manley, 1969; Price, 1972). Thus, as a legislator approaches early midcareer, he or she must devote considerable effort to integrating a strong policy focus into their organizational style, broadening the member's political identity beyond reelection concerns.

As policy expertise develops, the legislators then can concern themselves with influence over other members and control of organizational decision making. Influence, the ability to persuade and bargain effectively with legislators, generally is required before a legislator has enough support from members to win a position of organizational control. Influence will come as a member gains leverage over resources—campaign funds, information, constituency appropriations—that other members want (Fenno, 1973), and as she develops an organizational style and organizational skills that facilitate her use of influence resources (Manley, 1969). Control of the organization—appointments to its committees, scheduling of bills, rulings on parliamentary conflicts, the regulation of policy debates—allows a legislator to shape the policy aganda and policy decisions of the legislature (Cooper and Brady, 1981a; Huitt, 1961a, 1961b; Sinclair, 1983). The acquisition of control resources and the development of the appropriate skills and organizational style are the final tasks of organizational mastery.

Congressional Parties and the Career Cycle

Legislators gain mastery of these four areas of organizational life—reelection, policy making, influence, control—primarily through membership and service in political parties (Jones, 1970; Ripley, 1969a). Since the goal of each party is to govern, each seeks to use the resources and the learning opportunities that it controls to build a large group of supportive legislators who can help it gain and exercise institutional power. As a result, each party spreads its reelection and policy resources widely; each also creates numerous opportunities for members to learn reelection and policy making skills through instruction from more advanced members and through involvement in relevant party activities.

In providing extensive assistance for members' reelection and their development of policy making expertise, the party hopes to ensure members' electoral security and their satisfaction with the party. Yet precisely because a party seeks to govern, it must ensure that party leaders can coordinate the party's members and pursue the party's general interests. It seeks to ensure coordination and leadership by creating a small number of influence and control resources, and by limiting members' access to appropriate apprenticeship opportunities (Masters, 1961; Shepsle, 1978; Westefield, 1974; Nelson, 1977).

The rules and norms of legislative parties thus create a hierarchy of resources and learning opportunities that parallels and reinforces the four stages of organizational mastery that members naturally follow. These rules and norms, moreover, place much greater constraints on the availability of resources and opportunities that aid influence and control than on those that assist reelection and policy making. These constraints make it quite difficult for members to advance into the stages of influence and control. Legislators thus are unable to move through their career path, or career cycle, as rapidly as they would ideally desire (Dodd, 1977).

Legislators seek rapid career advancement for two primary reasons. First, rapid career advancement helps a legislator to create an appearance of achievement and promise, to demonstrate that his or her organizational reputation reflects substance as well as style. This appearance, in turn, helps him/her gain the continuing support of members that is essential if he/she is to gain additional resources, learn new organizational skills, and achieve his/her career objectives. Second, the vagaries of electoral politics, together with the potential success and dominance of other legislators within Congress, may deny any member the opportunity for power. This realization pressures the legislators to seek career advancement and the exercise of power as rapidly as possible.

The ambitious legislative professional thus seeks the desired career cycle illustrated in Figure 5.1, as presented in Chapter Five. He wants to move rapidly through the stages of career development, spending a concentrated amount of time gaining skills and resources necessary to master each stage. The bulk of his career then can be spent in the exercise of policy making power.

In actual practice, the professional legislator spends the bulk of his career not in the exercise of mastery but in its pursuit. The rules and norms of the legislature severely limit the availability of those resources and apprenticeship opportunities that aid influence and control. The relevant positions of power generally are possessed by senior legislators whose electoral and organizational mastery ensures their long term reelection to the legislature and to its positions of power. Young and midcareer legislators thus face a long struggle in the pursuit of influence and control.

Figure 5.2 illustrates the actual career path a professional legislator will experience. While the legislator may move rapidly through the reelection stage and into the policy stage, he then is caught in a midcareer stall that diverts him from influence and control; rather than a career focused on broad policies, he spends the bulk of his time concerned with narrow, middle range issues, always under the influence and control of the more advanced careerists.

The basic message of Figure 5.2 is that the core of a professional legislator's career will be spent in frustration, seeking to fulfill his basic organizational needs but unable to acquire the essential resources and skills. Experienceing such frustration, younger and midcareer legislators will necessarily seek ways out of their predicament, ways to speed up their career advancement. One approach is for junior and midcareer members to unite into informal groups—ideological subcaucuses, regional caucuses, groups of members drawn from the same entering class—and plan strategies and policy initiatives as though they had positions of influence and control (Stevens, Miller, and Mann, 1974; Loomis, 1981). Such efforts help the legislators gain important skills. But informal actions such as this are not enough. Thus a second approach, the acquisition of formal influence and control resources, is also required. The most obvious and direct way to acquire these resources is to change the rules of the legislature to make the resources more available to the less senior members. The consequences of these two approaches are clearest if we examine legislators' behavior beginning with the creation or reorganization of a legislature.

Career Advancement and Organizational Fragmentation

Assume that a legislator enters a professional legislature with a large group of new professionals and at a time when the legislature is reforming. A significant aim of this organizational reform is to streng then the governing capacity of the legislature while securing the broad career interests of its members. The reforms create numerous reelection and policy resources to serve the large junior contingent. They establish a relatively limited number of influence and control resources to meet the career needs of the senior legislators and the coordination and leadership needs of the institution. In addition, the parties establish systematic apprenticeship procedures—opportunities to learn both through observation of senior legislators and through active participation in policy making—to assist legislators in gaining necessary skills so that they can use their resources effectively.

A new legislator will have few initial quarrels with this distribution of resources, and the accompanying apprenticeship structure: it readily fulfills his reelection and policy making interests. But as the new legislator, his cohorts, and succeeding classes seek access to the stages of influence and control, they face more difficult circumstances. The career advancement of the new generation is hindered by the limited number of available resources and learning opportunities, and by the dominance of senior legislators. To end their shared frustration and gain desired resources, these junior and midcareer legislators unite, seek out new apprenticeship arrangements, and gradually introduce reforms that spread resources more widely among all members.

Over time, the legislature will experience the organizational fragmentation pictured in Figure 5.3. The period immediately following the creation or reorganization of the legislature will witness very little fragmentation. The new organizational arrangements and the career interests of legislators mesh fairly well. But with the aging of the new generation, the legislature will witness a steady rise in fragmentation. This fragmentation will occur in two ways. First, the effort to gain organizational skills and personal support will lead junior and midcareer members to create formal and informal groups that provide them special learning opportunities and the chance to work with colleagues who share similar career interests; in doing so the members break down the authority structure of the parties and of the Congress as a whole (Brady and Bullock, 1981; Manley, 1977; Patterson, 1967; Stevens Miller, and Mann, 1974), altering its internal norms and patterns of apprenticeship (Asher, 1973; Rohde, Ornstein, and Peabody, 1985). Second, the junior and midcareer members will use their growing numbers and organizational savvy to challenge existing rules and disperse formal resources more widely.

The result is a breakdown in the mechanisms for coordination and leadership of the Congress. As these mechanisms collapse, the Congress increasingly loses its ability to make policy and govern. The resulting policy, immobilism, makes it difficult for Congress to respond to social, economic, and foreign policy crises; immobilism may even generate such crises. These crises set in motion a period of electoral upheaval during which the public attempts to find legislators who can resolve the crises (Burnham, 1970). Out of this upheaval comes a new majority party, or a new dominant majority party faction, with a mandate to pursue a new direction in public policy. For a more extensive discussion of internal organizational dynamics of Congress generating this upheaval, see the section on "The Institutional Genesis of Party Realignment" in Chapter Five; see also the discussion of 'the electoral paradox' in "Additional Perspective" at the end of the chapter.

Organizing to Govern

On gaining majority status, the victorious party confronts the central dilemma that undercut the former majority party: it must organize the legislature so that it can govern effectively. In approaching this task, the party inherits the fragmented legislature created by the outgoing party. This organization can cripple the new majority party just as it undermined the governing capacity of the old party. Yet the severity of the national crisis demands immediate policy changes and allows little time for organizational reforms.

The new majority party offsets legislative fragmentation initially by drawing on two distinct advantages. It possesses a relatively cohesive party organization from its days as the minority party. In addition, the new party majority contains a large number of new legislators preoccupied with reelection and policy advocacy and not yet concerned with using resources to exercise influence and control. The party thus can govern effectively despite a fragmented legislature. It can move rapidly to enact new policies (Brady, 1978) and defuse the crisis of immobilism.

These early advantages eventually disappear, however, and the new majority party faces the dilemmas of governing. The legislators elected during the realignment gain mastery of reelection and policy making resources. They increasingly pursue the numerous resources available in the fragmented legislature and use these resources to gain influence and control. The capacity of the party to lead and coordinate its members declines and the legislature experiences renewed immobilism (Patterson, 1977).

Policy immobilism after realignment is even more difficult for the legislature to resolve than before. The new majority party is hesitant to deny its members the legislative rewards for which they worked so hard while in the minority. The party members, concerned with their personal career success, fail to connect the policy failures of the party with their pursuit of personal power. The new party thus embraces the politics of fragmentation and watches its governing mandate flouder. Seeing the legislature stiffled, even with a fresh infusion of new members and new ideas, public disenchantment with legislative decision making grows.

Legislative immobilism and the public disillusionment invite the executive to usurp the policy-making power of the legislature and end the national crisis. The executive initially succeeds because the legislature is too fragmented and disorganized to oppose it effectively and because many members of the legislature and the public see executive intervention as necessary to save the Republic. As the executive attempts to consolidate power, however, legislators come to realize that the institution is on the verge of permanently losing its governing power. Such a loss would make members' resources and status in the legislature worthless. The legislators' support for the strong executive thus turns to fear and opposition. They come to recognize that mastery of organizational politics enables them to have an impact on national policy making only so long as Congress itself maintains its policy making integrity.

Executive intervention demonstrates to legislators that they must strengthen the policy making capacity of Congress—both its system of internal leadership and its procedures for policy coordination—if they are to protect and nurture their own personal power. And they must do this even at the expense of some immediate personal sacrifice. They thus respond to executive intervention by reducing fragmentation and creating a more coherent decision making structure. These efforts include the disbanding of informal groups or the more effective integration of them into the formal organization of Congress. They also include efforts to provide a more coherent organization of existing resources. Once such a reformed organization is in place, the new majority party is prepared to govern until career frustrations lead its members to fragment the legislature once again.

The Organizational Cycle: An Overview

The thrust of the foregoing argument can be summarized in one sentence: professional legislatures are characterized by cycles of organizational change. During such cycles the legislature passes through six stages (see Figure 5.5 in Chapter 5 of this volume):

Stage one:	organizational stability
Stage two:	fragmentation
Stage three:	immobilism and crisis
Stage four:	electoral upheaval and realignment
Stage five:	interventionism
Stage six:	reorganization and resurgence

The history of Congress after the Civil War mirrors this cyclical pattern, particularly the history of the larger, elective body, the House of Representatives. Fragmentation in the late nineteenth century, for example, centered on the committee system; the number of committees increased by approximately 50 percent during the two organizational cycles (1860 to the 1880s and the 1880s to 1920). From 1920 to 1946 congressional fragmentation centered on the proliferation of a variety of special committees and subcommittees, a process reversed by the 1946 Legislative Reorganization Act. And from the early 1950s to the early 1970s the committee system experienced a growth in the number and autonomy of standing subcommittees and subcommittee chairs. In each of these periods we witness roughly similar sequences of change in which fragmentation is followed by realignment (party reconstruction in the 1870s; realignment in the 1890s, 1930s, and 1960s) and then reorganization (1880s, 1910s, 1940s, and 1970s).

Microlevel career patterns likewise correspond to the general expectations of the theory. Career cycles in the House are seen in such empirical patterns as the tendency of junior and senior legislators to concentrate on different electoral strategies (Fenno, 1978; Parker, 1984) and on different types of committee and subcommittee assignments (Prindle and Franklin, 1985; Smith and Deering, 1984). The linkage between career aspirations and organizational structure is shown by the long-term tendency of the House to fragment as the proportion of careerist members grows (Huntington, 1965; Polsby, 1968; Swenson, 1982). And the linkage between career frustration and fragmentation appears in the organized efforts of disadvantaged groups such as House liberals in the 1950s to gain personal power and policy influence by pursuing decentralized reforms (Stevens, Miller, and Mann, 1974).

Congressional history thus provides support for the cyclical theory. It must be acknowledged, however, that the theory of organizational cycles fails to account for the substantial differences among the cycles in the extent of change they generate. The reforms of the 1880s were mild adjustments in legislative rules; those of the 1910s crippled the Speakership, made the Senate elective, created the modern revenue and appropriations committees, and instituted committee government. The reforms of the 1940s reduced the fragmentation in committee government that had developed since 1920 but left the fundamental structure and rules of Congress intact. The reforms of the 1970s, not unlike those of the 1910s, once again uprooted existing structure and process.

As these contrasts illustrate, the reform periods in the different historical eras are not equal. Some readjust the existing organizational arrangements inherent in the core structure of Congress; others transform the structure itself. The internal theory, by itself, cannot account for these differences in the extensiveness of reforms across the cycles. The theory likewise provides no explanation for differences between cycles in the magnitude of the electoral realignments, in the severity of executive intervention, or in the extensiveness of the policy changes that occur in Congress. To explain these differences in the cycles we must look beyond internal congressional politics. We must look to the impact that external politics has on congressional change.

The Theory of Institutional Cycles

The external world of Congress is critical to members because it is the arena in which members gain reelection. Reelection, in turn, is essential if members are to stay in Congress and pursue policy making power. Thus members devote considerable attention to their relationship with constituents (Arnold, 1979; Fiorina, 1977b; Jacobson, 1983; Mann, 1978; Mayhew, 1974b). But reelection is not the only dimension of constituent politics that concerns members.

Members' external relations with their constituents also influence the freedom within Congress that members possess as they pursue their career interests (Fenno, 1978). If legislators enjoy strong personal support from a broad range of constituents, they can take those actions that facilitate their acquisition of power—actions such as service on desired committees that provide no immediate particularized benefit to constituents but that aid the members' personal career. Without such freedom, reelection in itself is relatively worthless to legislators concerned with policy making power.

Seen from this perspective, the external politics of Congress centers not on members' struggle for reelection but on their quest for electoral mastery. Such mastery exists when a legislator possess the resources and skills to obtain both the reliable votes she needs to stay in office and the personal trust from constituents she needs to pursue her career interests in Congress. The effort to obtain electoral resources and skills necessarily involves extensive feelings of insecurity on the part of the member: legislators seldom if ever possess sufficient resources and skills to fulfill personally the policy expectations that their constituents hold of them; this knowledge naturally leads them to fear the potential loss of constituent support.

Insecurity about their electoral support—and members' consequent belief that they need special rules and institutional arrangements to help them meet their constituents' expectations—generates the cyclical alteration in the structure of Congress. Thus to explain the institutional cycles of Congress, we first must understand members' behavior in their districts, particularly the processes through which they seek to gain electoral mastery.

Electoral Agendas and Constituent Mobilization

To gain electoral mastery, legislators must accomplish two tasks: they must mobilize reliable support from a winning plurality of district constituents, and they must convince these supporters that their long term personal self-interests depend on the legislators' career advancement within Congress. Since district constituents are policy-concerned individuals who vote in accord with their understanding of personal and group policy interests (Erikson and Wright, 1985; Kuklinski and West, 1981; Wright and Berkman, 1985), constituent mobilization requires legislators to commit themselves to public policies desired by a sizeable body of their constituents.

Legislators make these programmatic commitments in the policy agendas they promise to pursue in Congress. These agendas address four types of policy concerns:

1. Narrow constituent issues that affect the district and its residents in very particularistic ways, including casework service and pork barrel programs;
2. Middle-range policies that address the particularized interests of groups such as farmers, businessmen, teachers and union members;
3. Broad national programs that involve the development of wide-ranging and highly interrelated sets of policies, such as omnibus taxing and spending programs;
4. General political world views that encompass and justify fundamental conceptions of government and society, as expressed in the legislator's personal ideology.

The legislator takes these positions to gain the support of constituent groups. This support includes vital resources that aid her campaign—money, organizational help, and ultimately votes. It also includes assistance in acquiring necessary electoral skills. This assistance comes in two ways. First, groups open themselves to her and allow her to immerse herself in their inner workings so that she can learn their problems, policy goals, and central values. Second, they provide her with key intimates and general advisers who can keep her in touch with the changing concerns and mood of district support groups. The groups thus provide the legislator with opportunities for electoral apprenticeship, opportunities that are essential to her skillful use of resources.

Groups provide the legislator with election support that she needs—both resources and apprenticeship opportunities—so long as she convincingly pursues the policies they desire. To convince constituents of her effectiveness as a representative, and thus to commit them to her career advancement, the legislator seeks to develop an electoral style—a home style—that constituents will find appealing and persuasive (Fenno, 1978). This style—this presentation of self—must help her demonstrate the authentic fit between her values, interests, and agenda commitments and those of her constituents. It must help her convince constituents that their long-term policy interests depend on her career advancement, an advancement that may even require actions at odds with short-term constituent interests. And it must help her make clear the ways that her legislative accomplishments have facilitated and will facilitate the fulfillment of their common goals. Each member's electoral style will be unique, the result of his or her distinctive personality and political circumstance. Yet a member's style will also share much with the styles of other members. In part, this results from a tendency of districts with similar problems and policy orientations to select legislators with similar values, personalities, and styles of communication. But similarities in electoral style also reflect the existence of a common electoral problem and common strategies for resolving the problem.

Electoral Careers and the Stages of Mastery

The overriding electoral problem that legislators face is the hesitancy of constituent groups to provide them electoral support without some clear evidence that they can deliver on their policy promises. Immediate delivery of agenda promises is virtually impossible, particularly for new legislators, both because of the breadth of policy promises candidates must make to attract support and because of the difficulty of enacting policies in Congress. For this reason, legislators follow a sequential strategy in gaining resources and skills and in developing electoral mastery.

Early in their career legislators appeal for constituent support—for access to group advice and for resources from groups—by stressing their commitment to constituent services and to policies that serve specialized groups. They do so in part because these are the issues of most immediate, particularized concern to constituents and thus the ones most likely to generate support from them. But they also do so because these are the promises they can most easily fulfill given the resources to which they have access in Congress.

As the reputation for accomplishment is established through delivery of casework and group services, legislators can widen their focus to emphasize national programmatic concerns and ideological stands. In doing so, they broaden their support base within their constituency and lessen their reliance on groups with specialized interests. They thus gain greater leeway in the specific policy actions that they must take in Congress to keep the support of constituents.

The pursuit of electoral resources and skills thus generates four stages of electoral mastery, together with four related stages in members' home style and electoral skills. Early in their careers members work to acquire district support by extensive attention to constituent service and policies that service specialized district groups, developing electoral skills and a home style that will aid their focus on constituency policies. After legislators have solidified their electoral bases (Fenno, 1978), adjusted to their insider roles as legislators (Fenno, 1986b, 1991a), routinized the delivery of constituent services (Fiorina, 1977b), and learned to communicate their congressional accomplishments to constituent groups, they are free to give greater emphasis to their national policy concerns. They thus move to the more advanced stages of electoral mastery. They seek to adjust their home styles and electoral skills to include greater emphasis on national policy debates and broad ideological controversies. They also broaden their appeal for resources to include a greater stress on individuals and groups concerned with broad-gauged policy issues.

These four stages of electoral mastery parallel the four stages of organizational mastery. Both involve progressive movement from a focus on constituent service activities to group policy issues to general programmatic concerns and finally to broad-gauged ideological politics. Legislators pursue electoral and organizational mastery in parallel stages because each depends so heavily on the other: organizational mastery is required if the legislator is to fulfill his policy promises so that he can maintain his electoral support; and electoral mastery is required if he is to advance in his career in Congress and exercise power.

Electoral and organizational mastery thus come together. And only electoral and organizational mastery together can give the member the legislative mastery that he needs to exercise power. Yet the need for parallel advancement through the stages of organizational and electoral mastery can create some serious problems for the members' long-term electoral success.

Two problems are paramount. The first is the slowness with which a member acquires organizational resources and skills, particularly those necessary for influence and control. The second is the difficulty that a member of a large, complex, and competitive institution such as Congress faces in using his or her resources and skills to gain the policy support of other legislators. These two problems together mean that individual members will face a difficult task in fulfilling the broad-gauged programmatic promises that they must fulfill if they are to maintain electoral support in their district.

Policy Agendas and Congressional Structure

The problems that organizational politics causes for electoral careers generate considerable insecurity among members—anxiety over reelection and maintenance of constituent trust. This insecurity about electoral support leads members to search for ways to ensure that their programmatic promises are fulfilled. Since the legislator cannot fulfill them alone, he must cooperate with other legislators and develop a strategy that can address the programmatic commitments that they share in common. The need for cooperation forces groups of legislators to agree on common policy agendas that they can pursue collectively, and to create rules and institutional arrangements that will help them enact these agendas.

Members are able to agree upon a common policy agenda when their districts confront similar policy problems. Thus legislators from the same region and state, or from districts with similar social and economic conditions, are likely to share common programmatic commitments (Froman, 1963; Clausen, 1973; Kingdon, 1973). Legislators who enter Congress at roughly the same time, and thus build their district coalitions in response to the same historical conditions, are likely to share a common policy agenda. And legislators who have served together during a severe national crisis are likely to have addressed certain common problems and thus to share certain common agenda commitments. The overlap among these various factors means that Congress is composed of a relatively small number of agenda groups.

The structure of Congress is determined, during periods of reform, by the struggle among these policy groups to impose rules and procedures that best serve their policy purposes (Lowi, 1964, 1979; Ripley and Franklin, 1980; Strom and

Rundquist, 1978). Thus groups committed primarily to distributive policies will seek a decentralized structure that facilitates distributive decision making while groups that want redistributive policies will more likely seek a centralized structure capable of coordinated decision making. The actual structure will be determined by the relative strength of the different groups and the skill of group members in negotiating useful compromises with other groups (Bolling, 1965, 1968; Brown, 1922; Davidson and Oleszek, 1977; Hechler, 1940; Patterson, 1967). The groups that finally dominate the creation of the congressional structure will require that the core institutional arrangements enacted by Congress—those rules and procedures which establish the type of individuals and groups that are to exercise central authority—are subject to change only by extraordinary majority votes, or by procedures of analogous difficulty. These institutional rules and procedures impose a dominant policy agenda on Congress—a tendency to facilitate certain types of policy decisions and hinder others.

The design of a congressional structure to facilitate a particular agenda, and the use of extraordinary majority procedures to protect the structure, incorporates into Congress a conservative bias, a tendency to adapt slowly to the rise of new societal problems and new policy agendas. Congress may change its *organizational rules* fairly often, as its members seek to redistribute organizational resources. But change in its *structural rules* will be slow, hindered both by the continuing commitment of legislators to the congressional agenda that underlies the structure and by the requirement of extraordinary majorities to alter core structural rules.

The eventual restructuring of Congress is linked primarily to the generational replacement of legislators (Broder, 1980; Huntington, 1981; Ornstein and Rohde, 1977; Schiff and Smith, 1983). Replacement involves change not only of the members themselves but also of the policy agenda of Congress. This agenda change occurs because new legislators, to win office, incorporate into their constituency coalitions and agendas powerful new groups and policy issues that are salient during their initial campaigns, even though absent in the agenda of the previous incumbent (Hershey, 1984). Each new generation thus follows a different agenda from the last and wants a legislative structure that facilitates the passage of its agenda. The generations differ, however, in the ease with which they can reorganize congressional structure and impose their own agenda on Congress. These differences are tied to the stage in the organizational cycle at which a generation enters Congress.

The Formative Generation and the First Cycle

Legislators who begin service during the formation of a legislative structure—the formative generation—are committed to the institutional structure because they share the same general agenda that underlies the structure's design. They are joined in this commitment by more senior members of the legislature who have actually led the effort to redesign the institution. The relatively close congruence between these senior and junior members exists because they have lived through a period of national crisis that has forced extensive reassessment of the nation's agenda. This reassessment has created an impetus for legislators of all generations to move toward a common set of policy perspectives. This agreement on a common agenda allows them to overthrow the old structure and implement a new one. The extensive support enjoyed by the new structure ensures that it will experience considerable stability in its early years.

In the years following the creation of the structure, the primary conflict will be over the distribution of resources among members rather than the nature of the policy process itself. As the formative generation ages and confronts the limited number of resources for influence and control, it and subsequent generations push to fragment the organization. The stages of organizational immobilism and crisis come during the midcareer phase of the formative generation. The period of reorganization comes as they enter positions of control and power. They will support reorganization that increases the capacity of the existing structure to process the policy agenda for which it was created. But their own commitment to that same agenda leads them to oppose structural changes designed to foster a competing agenda.

The legislative reforms produced by the formative generation thus restore the capacity of the existing structure to facilitate its original agenda. Reorganization may include modest structural changes that prove necessary to win passage of the reforms and that enable the modified congressional structure to process new types of policies produced by societal change. These proposals will be presented by the legislators first elected in the years of fragmentation, who are more sensitive than the formative generation to the emergence of new societal problems and to the need for ameliorative reforms. More extensive structural changes, presented by the newest legislators elected during the periods of crisis and realignment preceding the reform effort, will be opposed and defeated by the congressional leaders.

The organizational cycle following the formation of the congressional structure, referred to hereafter as the "first cycle," will last roughly one legislative generation. It begins when a congressional structure is formally adopted and continues until the generation elected during the formative period gains power and reforms the Congress. The reforms of the first cycle reduce organizational fragmentation and adapt the congressional structure in modest ways to the policy agenda emerging from societal change. But the completion of the first organizational cycle leaves the fundamental structure of Congress—those institutional arrangements based on extraordinary majority rules—basically in place.

The Replacement Generation and the Second Cycle

Fundamental change of congressional structure comes in the second organizational cycle (see Figure 6.1). This cycle follows the same basic pattern of fragmentation, crisis, and reorganization as the first. The institutional conflicts that

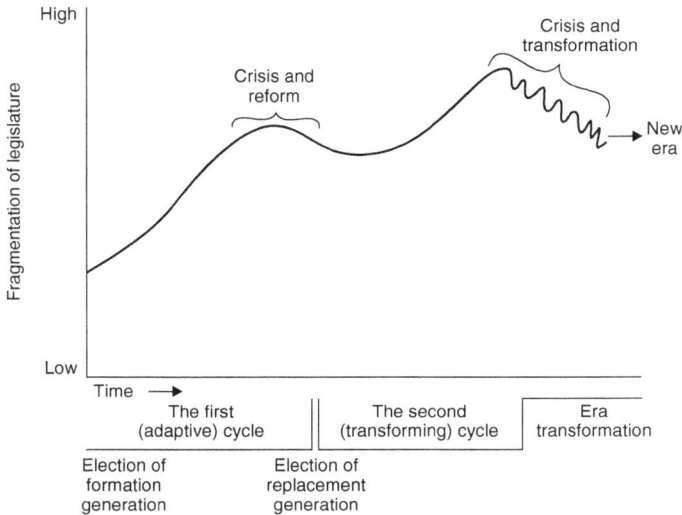

FIGURE 6.1 The institutional cycle.

emerge in the second cycle, however, are more extensive in character and more wide-ranging in their policy impact. This growth in congressional conflict stems from the consequences that societal change and generational replacement have for the career behavior of legislators during the second cycle.

In the first cycle, most legislators generally pursue policy agendas compatible with the agenda structure of the Congress. Their ability to implement their agenda, and thus to succeed within the Congress, does not require them to redesign its structure. The second cycle begins, by contrast, with a number of legislators who support new agendas not reflected in the reformed congressional structure. These legislators, having replaced many of the formative generation during realignment and its aftermath, are the initial generation of the second cycle. These replacement legislators play the major role in shaping the internal politics of the second cycle.

The task facing this replacement generation is more daunting than the task that confronted the members of the formative generation. To succeed, the new members must not only capture organizational resources; they must alter the legislative structure itself so that the institution can process the policies contained in their new agenda. Their career goals thus operate on two levels: they seek personal acquisition of resources so that they will have policy making power; and they seek redesign of the legislature so that they can use the power they acquire to implement the policies contained in their agenda.

Career behavior in the two cycles thus responds to a very different calculus. Whereas the first cycle begins with congruence between the members' policy agenda and the legislature's structure, the second cycle begins with a fair degree of incongruence. The formative generation of the first cycle thus accepts the legislature's structure as compatible with the members' agenda and merely seeks to widen the dispersion of resources within that structure. The replacement generation of the second cycle seeks both a greater dispersion of resources and a new institutional structure appropriate to their new agenda. The differing individual calculus in the two cycles means that the second one will experience different types of change, and more extensive change, than the first cycle.

The preoccupation with a new policy agenda during the second cycle will lead the new generation to concentrate its attention not solely on organizational reforms but also on challenges to the governing structure of Congress. These challenges, while unlikely to succeed in the early years of the new cycle because of the extraordinary majorities required, can introduce extensive conflict between generations. This conflict exacerbates the policy immobilism generated by the growing organizational fragmentation. This deeper immobilism, made worse by the growing incongruence between the national policy agenda and the governing structure of Congress, produces a much broader societal crisis than in the first cycle.

The depth of the policy crisis means that the nation can move forward only by refashioning its governing institutions so that they can address the new policy problems that afflict society. This effort at institutional transformation focuses first on those political institutions most open to democratic control—participatory organizations such as political parties. To maintain public support, these institutions must realign their policy agendas and transform their organizational structures so that they can address the new societal problems. These processes take considerable time and lead to extensive intraparty conflict. As a result, the process of group realignment, particularly party realignment, will be much more extensive and lengthy during the second cycle, when it requires a transformation of the fundamental agendas of the parties, than realignment at the end of the first cycle, which requires only a change of parties.

The ultimate failure of this transforming realignment to ensure the governing effectiveness of Congress, a failure rooted in the continuing fragmentation and rigidification of Congress, leads to extensive executive intervention into congressional policy making. This intervention is much more threatening to the central power of Congress than executive intervention in the first cycle. The severity of the intervention results from the greater policy immobilism of the second cycle and from the executive's fear that his or her party's new coalition will fall apart without policy action of some sort, however achieved.

The congressional reforms of the second cycle that respond to this intervention are necessarily much more extensive than those in the first cycle, involving efforts to transform the structure rather than simply modify existing organizational arrangements (Polsby, 1975). Their extensiveness flows both from the depth of the policy crisis and from the severity of executive intervention. The result is a new congressional structure designed to facilitate a new agenda. The widespread conflict and policy immobilism of the second cycle thus lead to a new institutional era in which Congress is governed by a new agenda, a new structure, and a new party alignment.

As this discussion indicates, the movement from one institutional era to another is an elaborate and lengthy process, taking two political generations and two organizational cycles to complete. The two generations first fulfill policy commitments to a formative agenda and then prepare Congress to pursue a new policy agenda that addresses emerging societal problems. The resulting change is more pronounced in the second cycle, however, reflecting the presence of a new generation of legislators committed to enacting a new policy agenda and a new congressional structure.

Institutional Eras and Historical Change

Congress has experienced three institutional eras during its two hundred year history, and three transformations in its dominant agenda (Dodd, 1981; Huntington, 1974, 1981, Chapter 7; Polsby, 1968). The first era, concerned with an agrarian agenda, employed an elite dominated governing structure. This structure, maintained by a small number of careerists, gave way in the Civil War and Reconstruction period to a postagrarian agenda preoccupied with the expanding economic role of government. This agenda was institutionalized in Congress through party government and a strong Speaker (Brady, 1973; Cooper and Brady, 1981a). The postagrarian era lasted for forty years, until the early 1900s. Its shorter timespan resulted from the rapid growth of careerist legislators during the period and their consequent ability to overwhelm the small group of senior careerists to impose a new structure and agenda.

The third era extended from the 1910s to the 1970s. As the first sustained period of low turnover and high careerism, this era corresponds more closely to the two-cycle theory of institutional change than the two earlier eras. The era began when progressive legislators in 1910, frustrated with the inability of party government to serve the new industrial agenda and assist their career advancement, overturned the governing rules that had dominated Congress since the Civil War (Hechler, 1940). Throughout the 1910s Congress struggled to create a new set of rules and structures—new procedures for appointing committee members and chairs, a cloture rule for the Senate, a new arrangement for the Rules Committee, a new structuring of the jurisdiction over appropriations, and the like—that would facilitate the special distributive agenda of the industrial era (Brown, 1922).

These structural arrangements, and the committee government that they created, remained intact for roughly fifty years, kept in place by complex rules and slow generational change. During this era Congress experienced two organizational cycles. The first one, the adaptive or reinforcing cycle, was from the early

1920s to the mid-1940s. It witnessed extensive fragmentation in the twenties and early thirties, followed by the realignment of the thirties, the interventionist actions of Roosevelt, and then the reforms of the mid- to late 1940s. These reforms, contained in the Legislative Reorganization Act of 1946, streamlined the committee system and rejuvenated its operation while leaving the fundamental structure of committee governing intact (Galloway, 1951).

The second cycle, the transforming cycle, began in the late 1940s and lasted until the reforms of the 1970s. The fragmentation of this cycle involved an expansion in the number and autonomy of subcommittees, a growth in the staff and personal resources of members, and a breakdown in committee jurisdictions (Davidson and Oleszek, 1981; Dodd and Schott, 1979; Fox and Hammond, 1977). This fragmentation grew not simply from the desire by midcareer members for personal resources; it also stemmed from the desire of a new generation of legislators to open up congressional decision making to the postindustrial agenda that had emerged in the postwar years (Bolling, 1965; Stevens, Miller, and Mann, 1974), an agenda that covered new issues such as civil rights, social service delivery, economic planning, and restraints on international involvement. This fragmentation, fueled by well-organized subcaucus activity within Congress, culminated in the electoral upheavals of the mid-1960s, the interventionist efforts of Presidents Johnson and Nixon, and structural transformation in the seventies (Dodd, 1977, 1981; Sundquist, 1973, 1981).

The concern that remains is whether organizational and institutional change, illustrated by the experiences of the industrial-era Congress, produce systematic changes in the policy performance of Congress. Is the long-term decline and short-term resurgence in congressional policy making actually related to alterations in organization and structure? What dimensions of policy making are most likely to be affected, and in what ways? Does the effect differ across different types of policy? To answer these questions, we must examine more extensively the ways in which organizational and structural change can influence policy performance.

The Theory of Policy Cycles

The institutional arrangements within Congress shape its overall policy performance, I will argue, by determining how responsive Congress is to the nation's dominant agenda (Cobb and Elder, 1972, 1981; Cooper, 1975; Huntington, 1965, 1981; Kingdon, 1984; Jones, 1977; Polsby, 1971; Rieselbach, 1978; Sundquist, 1981). When organizational and structural arrangements facilitate innovative decision making—under conditions of low fragmentation and rigidity—Congress can respond to the nation's policy problems in an effective manner. Increases in fragmentation and rigidity, by contrast, decrease the overall policy performance of Congress. These distinct patterns of change can be seen by looking at three separate dimensions of policy performance: policy-making capacity, program innovation, and agenda responsiveness.

Policy Making Capacity

The policy-making capacity of Congress is its ability to enact those decisions that enjoy the clear support of its members. This ability is most likely to exist when Congress is organized in a coherent manner designed to facilitate majority decision making. Such coherence results from the existence of three related conditions. First, Congress must contain the number and type of leadership positions necessary to pursue the desired policies. Too few positions will place undue demands on leaders and dissipate their energies; too many positions will encourage immobilizing conflict among competing legislators. Second, these positions must be accountable to the rank-and-file members. Third, the members who hold these leadership positions must possess the resources and skills they need to gain the enactment of the desired policies.

A major concern during the design or reform of Congress is the creation of a leadership system that will ensure the necessary organizational coherence. The long-term unraveling of organizational coherence comes primarily through fragmentation of the organization—that is, the division of its leadership structure into an ever larger number of positions that possess an ever more equal number of resources. Such fragmentation undermines the decision-making capacity of Congress in four ways (Huntington, 1965; Kingdon, 1984; Sundquist, 1981). It deprives Congress of authoritative leaders who possess sufficient resources to bargain effectively and unite members in policy coalitions. It unravels the apprenticeship structure that underlies the existing leadership system and thereby deprives leaders of the skills they need to use effectively the resources they do possess. It breaks down the rules and procedures for coordinating the policy process. And it confuses the lines of accountability between leaders and rank-and-file members.

The overall decision-making capacity of Congress thus varies in a cyclical fashion, declining as Congress fragments and rebounding when Congress reforms. This close linkage between the organization of Congress and its decision-making capacity is broken only during periods of realignment, when the influx of a new governing majority momentarily breaks the policy deadlocks in Congress. This policy resurgence soon ends, however, when the continuing problems of organizational fragmentation engulf the new majority party. Substantial improvement in decision making will then come only through organizational reform. If this reform comes at the end of the second cycle, it also produces a change in the policy agenda that these decisions address.

This cyclical pattern of policy change is evident, in its broadest outline, in the decline in congressional policy making during the 1920s and early 1930s, and again during the 1950s and 1960s, both periods of organizational fragmentation. The first decline was halted by the Legislative Reorganization Act of 1946, the second by the reforms of the 1970s. Only the realignments of mid-thirties and mid-sixties were able to break the growth of policy immobilism, and only for a

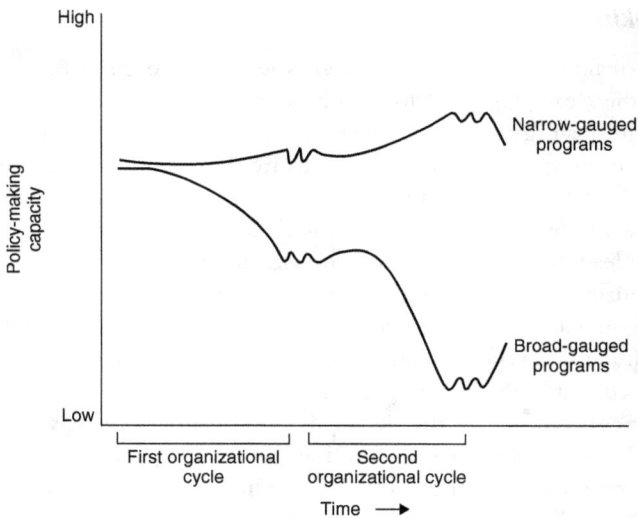

FIGURE 6.2 Change in policy-making capacity.

short period of time. Thus, both Roosevelt in his second term and Johnson and Nixon in the late sixties and early seventies faced renewed problems of congressional immobilism (Patterson, 1967; Sundquist, 1981), problems that were then addressed by congressional reforms.

As Figure 6.2 indicates, this pattern of cyclical decline is most evident in broad national policy making, since deliberation on national problems is likely to require procedures for leading and coordinating a vast array of legislators. The pattern is less likely to exist in the areas of narrow-gauged constituent policy making, such as casework and pork barrel politics, since these can often be handled by the individual actions of members or by norms of reciprocity among members (Fiorina, 1977b; Ferejohn, 1974). In fact, constituent policy making may actually benefit from the uncoordinated spread of resources among members, increasing with fragmentation, declining when reforms impose a new organizational coherence.

These contrasting patterns make the workaday world of Congress difficult to decipher up close. The growth in policy-making activity that results from constituent politics can give Congress the appearance of being an active policy maker. The resulting reelection of members also may give it the appearance of being responsive and popular. These effects of constituent policy making thus may deflect attention from the immobilism that characterizes broad-gauged policy questions. They can thus divert attention from the incapacity of the institution to enact new and innovative programs.

Program Innovation

Program innovation is the process by which Congress initiates and debates new types of policy proposals (Johannes, 1972; Polsby, 1984). Innovation exists even if the programs are not actually enacted into law, so long as new programs are proposed and given serious consideration. The initiation of new types of programs is most likely to come from new legislators committed to a new policy agenda at odds with the agenda of the formative generation.

The continuous replacement of the formative generation by new legislators would seem to guarantee a continuous and cumulative increase in policy innovativeness throughout an institutional era. More new legislators should produce greater innovativeness. An increase in new members fails to guarantee increased innovation, however, if the new members do not possess the resources that they need to gain serious consideration of their proposals. The effect of generational replacement on innovativeness thus depends on how fragmented the resources of Congress are and whether the new legislators have access to existing resources. It also depends on whether one examines resources linked to broad-gauged or narrow-gauged policy making.

Consider broad-gauged national policies. During the first cycle of an era, the new members who seek to develop innovative policy confront four problems. First, they are greatly outnumbered, and even more surpassed in influence, by the members who are committed to the existing congressional agenda. Second, few if any new members will have progressed in their career cycle into the influence and control positions that shape broad-gauged policy. Third, influence and control work groups may actually become more cohesive and inaccessible during organizational fragmentation, more committed to the original agenda, and thus ever greater constraints on broad-guaged innovation. This possibility is discussed more fully in Chapter Five, in 'Countercyclical Fragmentation Among Work Groups," and is illustrated there in Figure 5.4. Fourth, whatever fragmentation occurs throughout the congressional organization is most likely to benefit the members of the formative generation, who are still in mid-career, and to bypass the relatively new members, who are more likely to support a new agenda.

These obstacles to the new members mean that broad-gauged policy innovation actually decreases during the first cycle. The high point for innovation will be the period immediately after the creation of the new structure; the structure facilitates the deliberation of the new ideas associated with the formative agenda. As these ideas are presented and enacted, the policy proposals of the formative generation become more routinized and less original. Yet the new emerging generation is unable to fill the void and initiate a meaningful deliberation of new broad-gauged policies. It is too small in number, too isolated from the centers that control policy making, and too overwhelmed by the growing organizational chaos.

The fate of innovative national programs is quite different in the second cycle. By the second cycle, the death and retirement of older members will have necessitated the broadening of the influence and control groups to include members of the new generation. This replacement generation includes members who entered Congress during the period of crisis, realignment, and reform that ended the first cycle, as well as the growing number of new members elected in the second cycle. The growing size and seniority of the replacement generation enables its members to take increasing advantage of the fragmentation that occurs in the second cycle and to increasingly dominate organizational politics. As the second cycle proceeds this new generation, increasing in size and seniority, will become the dominant group in Congress and the primary beneficiary of resource fragmentation. As their access to resources increases the members of the replacement generation will be in a position to force deliberation of policies that seemed impossible in the first cycle.

The decline in policy innovation during the first cycle thus is followed by its increase during the second. Fragmentation during the first cycle of an institutional era gives power and resources to the supporters of the existing agenda, helps them win continued reelection, and thus enables them to retain power long after their innovative ideas have ended. They use this opportunity to overwhelm new members and override their new agenda commitments. Fragmentation in the second cycle, by contrast, increasingly strengthens the electoral and organizational strength of the new generation, helps them overpower the senior members who oppose the new agenda, and provides them the opportunity for serious efforts to initiate and deliberate national policy.

Fragmentation has a different effect on the innovation of constituent policy during the two cycles. Because fragmentation increases the reelection resources that all members have free access to, it gives members of the replacement generation in both cycles a growing number of resources to use to initiate new types of constituent programs. The replacement generation in the first cycle thus is free to innovate constituent policies—new types of casework or pork barrel activities, for example—as soon as the fragmentation process begins. Innovativeness in narrow-gauged constituent policies thus will grow during both cycles as the number of new members increases and as their personal reelection resources expand.

Program innovation in Congress thus follows the overall pattern outlined in Figure 6.3. Narrow-gauged policy experiences a cyclical rise in innovation, illustrated by the development of new casework and pork barrel projects throughout the postwar years (Fiorina, 1977b). Broad-gauged policy making, by contrast, experiences an initial decline in innovation during the first cycle of an era followed by an increase of roughly equal length in the second.

We see these contrasting patterns during the twentieth century, with the interwar Congress experiencing a steady decline in the initiation of new policy proposals, according to Lawrence Chamberlain (1947), while the postwar Congress experienced a rise in policy initiation (Moe and Teel, 1970). This curvilinear

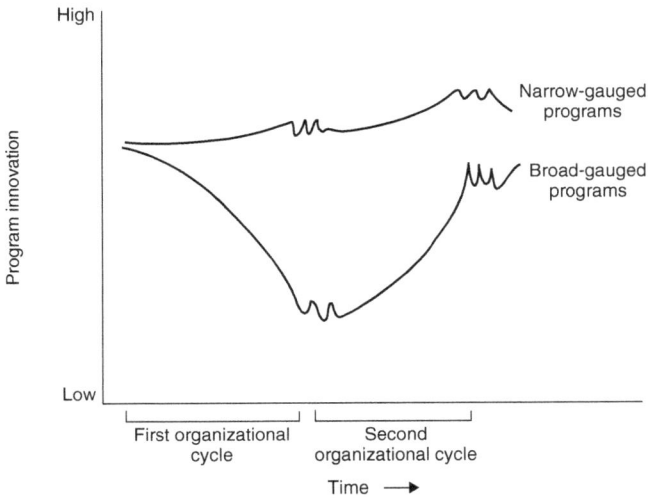

FIGURE 6.3 Change in program innovation

pattern resulted from the interaction between generational change and cyclical fragmentation. The formative generation of the industrial era, solidifying its control of Congress during the period of interwar fragmentation, suffered a decline in new ideas and thus produced a decline in congressional innovativeness. The replacement generation, illustrated best perhaps by Hubert Humphrey, came to power during the period of postwar fragmentation; infused with a new agenda and possessing increasing resources, this generation was able to initiate a growing number of new programs.

There is, of course, an irony in this curvilinear pattern. Congress experiences its most extensive decline in innovativeness in the first cycle, illustrated here by the interwar years, when decision-making capacity is still great. By contrast, Congress experiences an increase in innovative proposals in the second cycle, precisely as its decision-making capacity is in the steepest period of decline. The policy performance of Congress is thus a complex and variable process. This point is reinforced when we consider how the patterns of policy making and innovation combine to shape the overall agenda responsiveness of Congress.

Agenda Responsiveness

Agenda responsiveness is the ability of Congress to produce policy decisions that are congruent with the policy agenda dominant among the nation's citizens. The struggle over the structure of Congress is in large part a battle over which groups in society Congress will respond to and how responsive Congress will be. The formative generation of an era seeks to ensure responsiveness to the groups and agenda dominant at the time of its election; it seeks to ensure responsiveness by institutionalizing the groups' agenda in a new congressional structure.

The close congruence between the congressional structure and the nation's formative agenda ensures that Congress will be a responsive policy maker during the early years following the creation of a new structure. The institutionalization of the structure ensures that Congress will become increasingly unresponsive as a new agenda arises that is less compatible with existing rules and structure.

The rise of a new agenda, and the consequent decline in public support for the formative agenda, is a natural and necessary phenomenon. It occurs in part because congressional implementation of the formative agenda removes it as a pressing public concern and in part because new societal problems emerge that require different types of policies from those advocated in the formative agenda. As this erosion occurs, responsiveness declines.

The decline in agenda responsiveness begins slowly (see Figure 6.4). During the early years of an era, a close congruence between the public agenda and the congressional agenda is virtually guaranteed since an extraordinary public majority must support an agenda before the legislators can reach common policy agreement and implement a new structure. The early decline that does occur in congressional responsiveness—in its ability to deliver policies that the public wants—occurs not because of emerging disagreements between Congress and the majority of the citizens, but because the initial waves of organizational fragmentation in Congress may undermine its capacity to make decisions as rapidly or as satisfactorily as the public desires.

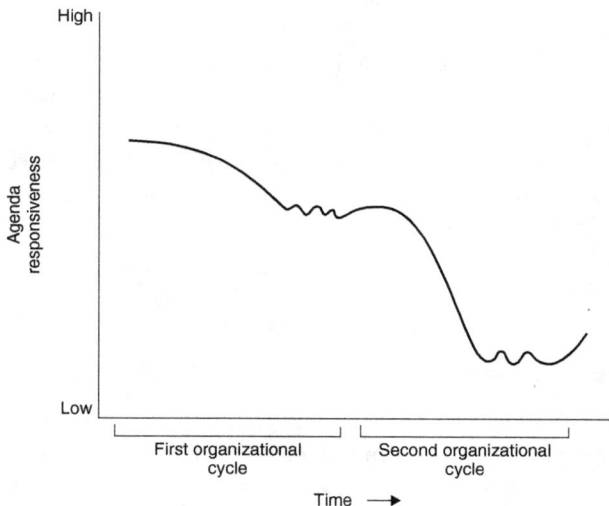

FIGURE 6.4   Change in agenda responsiveness

The crisis that results from this fragmentation centers on the proper way to address the policy choices within an existing agenda, not on the appropriateness of the agenda. During the second cycle, by contrast, the public support for the formative agenda itself will have decayed and congruence between Congress and the public thus will have declined dramatically. This growing incongruence, together with the organizational fragmentation of Congress, produces a dramatic decline in its agenda responsiveness. The resulting crisis centers on the selection of a new policy agenda and the creation of a new congressional structure that can implement it.

Agenda responsiveness during the two cycles thus differs in important ways (Figure 6.4). The first cycle, with a close congruence between the congressional agenda and the public agenda, experiences high overall responsiveness. The crises of the first cycle may be quite severe, aggravated by events beyond the control of Congress. Thus the crisis of the interwar cycle, the first cycle of the industrial period, was the Great Depression, a worldwide phenomenon that was certainly one of the most debilitating experiences in American history. Yet the close congruence between the fundamental agenda orientation of Congress (its amenability to distributive policy making) and the broad agenda concerns of society (the need for new spending programs) meant that the crisis could be handled by a change in parties and by organizational reforms, rather than by long term struggles over the policy agenda and the structure of Congress.

The structure of Congress during the first cycle, in other words, meshes sufficiently with the type of problems society faces that it can facilitate policy responsiveness even to the most severe crisis. The second cycle of an era produces a very different situation. During this cycle, policy responsiveness declines in a very rapid and steady manner. The decline results both from the maintenance of an anachronistic structure, and from the fragmentation of the internal organizational resources. The decline culminates in societal crisis, an agenda realignment among the parties, and structural transformation of Congress.

The societal crisis of the second cycle, even if of less apparent magnitude than that of the first, may well produce a much greater challenge to the responsiveness of the institution. In the first cycle, the structure of Congress, still relatively new, facilitates the policy concerns of most of the public. The structure of Congress in the second cycle, by contrast, facilitates an agenda irrelevant to most citizens and to the critical problems of society. Crisis resolution thus will require much more extensive changes in the agenda orientation and structure of Congress and in the parties that govern Congress. The institutional and policy transformations of the 1970s are an apt illustration.

Explaining the Transformations of the Seventies

The societal crises that led to the reforms of the 1970s—the domestic problems associated with civil rights and social and economic planning, and the foreign problems associated with Vietnam and declining world dominance—lacked the sharp effect on the nation's economic and social life that the Depression had. But whereas the congressional structure of Congress in the 1930s meshed with the policy problems of the period reasonably well, the structure of the sixties and early seventies did not. The later structure, oriented for fifty years to protecting the rights of regional majorities such as whites in the South, to making distributive industrial policy, and to supporting presidential leadership of foreign policy, was unprepared to handle questions of individual liberties, redistributive planning, and the constraint of presidential war making.

The wide gap between the nation's postwar policy problems and its institutional arrangements meant that the resolution of the problems required a greater focus on institutional change than in the thirties and forties. The struggle over party realignment thus was a fundamental change in the agenda orientation of the parties. They had to define themselves not just according to how extensively they would distribute the resources of an industrial nation but also according to how they would manage the transition to a postindustrial order (Carmines and Stimson, 1986a, 1986b; Collie and Brady, 1985; Sinclair, 1982).

The struggle over the policy procedures in Congress likewise involved a prolonged effort to alter the core structure of the institution. The resulting congressional changes—subcommittee government to help facilitate the creation and protection of the new social and economic policies, a new budget process to provide postindustrial planning, the weakening of the Rules Committee, seniority and the Senate filibuster to help decrease the blocking power of entrenched minorities, the War Powers Act to strengthen congressional influence over foreign policy—all of these were major alterations in policy-making structure. These alterations helped ensure responsiveness of Congress to the societal agenda generated by the problems of the new era.

The institutional and policy changes of the 1970s thus can be explained as the product of a long delayed agenda change within Congress. This agenda change was delayed in part by the longevity and political skills of the formative generation of legislators who created committee government in the 1910s. Their long-term dominance of Congress, combined with the extraordinary majority rules that they created, suppressed the restructuring of Congress for over fifty years. This delay was fostered, moveover, by the fragmentation of organizational resources within Congress and the consequent difficulty that reformers faced in gaining support for structural changes from the many legislators who benefited from resource dispersion.

These delays ended in the sixties and early seventies with the occurrence of three critical developments. First, the last members of the formative generation of the 1910s, symbolized by Speaker Sam Rayburn, passed from power. Second, the new generation began to seek a common policy ground, pushed into this endeavor by severe domestic and foreign crises. Third, the interventionist actions of Johnson and Nixon, specifically the unconstitutional impoundments of appropriated funds and the undeclared wars in Vietnam and Cambodia, convinced the members that their personal policy-making power, whether in domestic or foreign policy, required a new congressional structure that would enable Congress to respond more adequately to the nation's policy agenda and thereby protect its policy prerogatives from presidential encroachment.

These three developments made the reforms of the 1970s possible (see also, Rieselbach, 1986). The result is a structure quite different from committee government (Smith, 1985)—a technocratic structure designed to meet the policy needs of the postindustrial era: technical experts in specific policy areas, located increasingly at the subcommittee level (Dodd and Schott, 1979; Smith and Deering, 1984), work with planning experts in the central budget committees, the party leadership and the resource agencies to create explicit budgetary agendas that reflect both the wide-ranging needs of different segments of society and the general collective needs of society as a whole (Ellwood and Thurber, 1977; Schick, 1980; Sinclair, 1983). These technical experts include an increasingly large and influential body of appointed staff (Malbin, 1980). The members and staff face fewer formal hurdles to their policy proposals than did policy specialists in committee government, with Senate cloture having been modified and the Rules Committee brought under greater majority control (Oppenheimer, 1977, 1985). In addition, legislators who are concerned about the lack of policy mastery by particular committee leaders can more easily remove them from their leadership position than in the past, since the seniority norm has been weakened by rules changes (Parker, 1979).

This new technocratic structure has had a significant impact on congressional policy making. Witness the proposals for tax and spending cuts that emerged from Congress in the late seventies, the energy legislation of the mid-seventies (Oppenheimer, 1974, 1981; Sinclair, 1983), the constraints on presidential war making (Art, 1984; Kaiser, 1978), and the adaptation and institutionalization of a variety of domestic programs (Orfield, 1975; Champagne, 1986; Lyons and Taylor, 1981). Perhaps the most notable impact on the nation's governing agenda has been the passage of the 1981 budget, which reduced the annual rate of increase in social spending, expanded the rise of defense spending, and decreased taxes. These decisions would not have been made, certainly not in the extensive form they finally took, without the creation of the new budget process and related structural changes in Congress (Ferejohn and Krehbiel, 1985; Ellwood, 1985). They are a prime example of how structural change facilitates change in the policy agenda of Congress and the nation.

Looking to the future, Congress should now begin to experience renewed fragmentation of its organization and rigidification of the new structure, thereby producing a gradual decline in policy performance. We can thus expect the policy resurgence of the past decade to recede, short of extraordinary circumstances, to be replaced eventually by policy immobilism and executive dominance. The long-term ability of Congress to survive this period of decline and then to rejuvenate itself depends in part, no doubt, on whether the technocratic structure is sufficiently meshed with the nation's policy agenda to maintain a fair degree of social order and political responsiveness despite the inevitable decline in policy performance. Scholars thus must consider whether the reorganization of the 1970s sufficiently transformed Congress so that it can effectively address the postindustrial agenda (Davidson and Oleszek, 1977).

Conclusion

The message of this chapter should be clear: Congress is a dynamic institution characterized by recurring cycles of organizational, structural, and policy change. These cycles are an unintended consequence of the legislators' quest for power. This quest establishes a cyclical rhythm that vibrates across the entire spectrum of congressional life. This rhythm produces periodic reforms and policy resurgence, thereby explaining the institutional and policy changes of the last fifteen years. But the utility of the cyclical perspective goes far beyond the explanation of institutional reform. The cyclical variations detailed here—in the resources and skills of legislators and in the organization and structure of Congress—should help explain change in a wide variety of congressional phenomena, from electoral behavior to committee decision making to legislative-executive relations.

This broad potential significance places a great importance on empirical explorations and tests of the cyclical theory. Immediate topics for investigation range from microlevel studies of members' career cycles, career frustrations, and career agenda to macrolevel analyses of organizational fragmentation, structural rigidification, and agenda transformation. Each of these topics is relatively new to congressional research. The overall theory thus will require extensive empirical work before it can be fully assessed. Efforts to apply the theory to empirical research will also have to revise and refine its concepts and arguments before they can be applied to specific research topics.

The theory developed here, for example, is much too limited historically. Its assumptions, such as the existence of low turnover and high careerism, reflect conditions that were peculiar to the industrial era. Different patterns of turnover and careerism existed in other eras (Bullock, 1972; Fiorina, Rohde, and Wissel, 1975; Polsby, 1968; Price, 1975; Swenson, 1982; Young, 1966), as a result of different social structures and policy agendas, and produced cycles of change somewhat different from those of the industrial era. Thus students of the agrarian or postagrarian period must adjust the theoretical arguments to fit the underlying empirical conditions present in these earlier periods. Students of contemporary and future politics do likewise. They must identify the new patterns of electoral competitiveness and turnover likely to emerge during postindustrialism and determine the types of cyclical change that these new patterns of careerism are likely to produce (Dodd, 1981; Huntington, 1974; Lenchner, 1979).

Other adjustments are likewise needed to refine the theory's applicability. The current theory ignores the bicameral nature of Congress and thus fails to indicate the different patterns of change that might characterize the two houses (Fenno, 1982; Longley and Oleszek, 1983; Carmines and Dodd, 1985; Ornstein, 1981). The theory treats the presidency as a sort of unsung antihero—always the aggressive outsider prepared to intervene in Congress—without considering the ebbs and flows of presidential activism (Barber, 1980; Lowi, 1985; Moe, 1985; Rockman, 1984; Skowronek, 1984). It likewise ignores influence from other actors such as the courts (Scigliano, 1971) and the bureaucracy (Aberbach, 1979; Arnold, 1979; Dodd and Schott, 1979; Ripley and Franklin, 1980). And the theory treats the external changes in societal structure and constituent behavior as a fairly continuous and steady process when in fact it could be, or could become, quite uneven and volitile (Huntington, 1974; Lowi, 1971). These and similar phenomena must be incorporated into the theory if it is to provide a full and accurate explanation of changes in congressional policy making.

These various refinements, however, should not alter the theory's basic argument. It sees political actors—both the legislators and their constituents—as imbued with a vital desire to shape the direction of national policy through the exercise of congressional power. Citizens exercise power by electing legislators who will deliver policies they desire; legislators exercise their power by making policy decisions.

The single-minded pursuit of personal power will foster excessively self-centered and short-sighted behavior—a preoccupation by the citizens with the election of those legislators who can most effectively provide them with immediate personal benefits through constituent services; a preoccupation by legislators with organizational resources and reelection. But such behavior ultimately will give way, in the face of crisis, to a collective realization by constituents and legislators alike that true mastery of the policy process requires the existence of a strong and vibrant Congress. Only when Congress can implement broad-gauged policy decisions can personal power in electoral and institutional decision making translate into significant power over public policy (Maass, 1983).

The cycles of congressional life thus result from a continuing struggle between the desire for personal power and the need for collective cooperation. These cycles have their tragic overtones, witnessed in the destruction of the common welfare that occurs in periods of policy immobilism (Hardin, 1968). Yet such tragedy can be offset over the long run by the capacity of legislators and citizens alike to learn from their collective experiences, adapt the structure of Congress to new societal problems, and thereby redress the public's policy grievances. It is this long term possibility of institutional transformation and rejuvenation that makes the puzzle of congressional change such a central topic in the study of American politics.

Notes

Acknowledgements: My thanks to David Brady, Edward Carmines, Joseph Cooper, Richard Fenno, John Kingdon, Gerhard Loewenberg, Thomas Mann, David Mayhew, Michael Mezey, John Padgett, John Pierce, Leroy Rieselbach, Earl Shaw, and Samuel Patterson for their advice and support at various stages during the development of this work. I am also indebted to the Hoover Institution and to the Dirksen Center for their financial support during the preparation of the essay and to the APSA Congressional Fellowship Program for providing me the first-hand experience in Congress that made the essay possible. My thanks to Michael Maffie for assisting with the preparation of the essay for publication in *Thinking about Congress*.

1. It also builds on the vast literature on Congress (Rieselbach, 1984; Schwarz and Shaw, 1976), drawing particularly on the work of Cooper (1975, 1977), Fenno (1973), and Mayhew (1974b) for the theory of organizational change, the work of Fenno (1978), Huntington (1965, 1981), Kingdon (1968, 1984), Mayhew (1974), Polsby (1968, 1975), and Sundquist (1981) for the theory of institutional change, and the work of Huntington (1965, 1981) and Sundquist (1981) for the theory of policy change. This essay also owes a special debt to Woodrow Wilson's *Congressional Government* (1885), as discussed in Dodd (1980, 1987).
2. The emphasis on a cyclical approach to change is also supported by the work of Blondel (1973). Surveying all contemporary legislatures he found cycles of decline and resurgence to be the single most widely shared characteristic of legislatures and thus the phenomenon around which a theory of legislative change could be most productively constructed.

Additional Perspective on "Congressional Cycles"

The contribution of "Congressional Cycles" lies in highlighting how (1) institu-
tion-generated social crises (resulting from members' organizational ambitions, as
outlined in Chapter Five) interact with (2) long-term societal change (operating
through agenda-centered electoral politics, as discussed extensively in this chapter) to generate two stages in the cyclical change of Congress. In the first stage,
the cyclical swing between organizational fragmentation and centralizing reform
ends in great policy innovation but modest recentralization (as from the 1910s to
the mid-1940s). In contrast, the second stage of cyclical change (as from the late
1940s to the mid-1970s) is less innovative in policy making. Its policy energies are
focused on completing the enactment of the pre-existing agenda and experimental
exploration of a new one. In struggling to enact policy amid heightened institutional fragmentation and in the face of substantial unforeseen developments in the
domestic and international sphere, the second cycle produces substantial recentralization designed to address the institution's policy-making dilemmas. The second
cycle thus creates institutional mechanisms that can aid future policy innovation.

This argument improves the cyclical theory in three critical ways. First,
the two-stage swing highlighted in the argument conforms to the nature of
congressional change, as seen during the early to mid-twentieth century. With
the two-stage swing, the cyclical theory can explain the more centralized nature
of the reforms of the 1970s, as contrasted with those of the 1940s. In the 1940s,
the nation's policy agenda was still focused on distributive policy making, an
agenda that was highlighted by the progressive era. By the 1970s, the nation was
moving to a more redistributive policy agenda, which the decentralized com-
mittee-government based structure of Congress was unprepared to address. Thus
the move to greater centralization. This move would seem to point away from
'decentralization drift' across cycles, as suggested at the end of "Quest" in Chapter
Two. Decentralization drift may nevertheless occur in Congress, but one must
look across multiple two-stage cyclical swings to see it in a dramatic and sustained
manner.

Second, the two-stage argument works because of the ways in which electoral
politics connects the Congress to the broad agenda concerns of citizens and to
the ways societal change affects and alters these citizens' concerns. This helps us
understand the role that citizens and societal change play in shaping the cycles of
congressional change. By the 1970s, citizens had moved well away from concerns
about distributive policy making that dominated electoral politics during the first
half of the twentieth century and were embracing concerns about redistributive
policy, concerns which came to the fore in the 1960s and helped create the environment in which the reforms of the 1970s occurred.

Third, the new expanded theory accounts for variation across cycles and time
in Congress's policy-making characteristics, as with the policy responsiveness and
policy innovation of Congress. The theory thus accounts for the tendency of

Congress to enact limited reforms amid great policy innovation and extensive reform amid limited policy innovation. Waves of great policy change and great reform do not come together but are sequenced in nature. The extensive organizational changes at the end of a two-stage cyclical swing set the stage for the innovative policy-making capacity of Congress in the next phase of cyclical swing in Congress.

The essay leaves unaddressed what happens to the recentralized Congress, once it is in place. The essay intimates that the newly recentralized Congress will move to address the new policy issues emerging in society, issues the previous generation of legislators (and the Congress they inhabited) were unable to address. But it gives little sense of how this renewed policy activism focused on new social dilemmas will occur; at what pace it will happen; and what difficulties it will encounter in seeking to generate great activism.

The essay closes with a recognition that Congress and the nation must engage in social learning in order to aid the capacity of congressional cycles to work effectively in resolving social and institutional problems. Understanding the nature and role of learning in congressional change became the next focus of the author's theoretical inquiries. His attention to issues of learning came to the fore as it became increasingly clear that the nation was facing grave difficulties in addressing the policy challenges of postindustrialism. These difficulties appeared to be permanently upending the constitutional balance between Congress and the presidency, much to the detriment of representative government. This development put at risk the 'automatic' era transformations and institutional resurgence that seemed to flow from the logic of his cyclical theory, as presented in this chapter.

To understand more clearly how it is that the cycles of congressional change can proceed across historical eras, rather than collapsing due to failures in agenda transformation, he turned to focus more directly on how it is that the citizens and leaders of an era "learn" the appropriate ways to address new policy difficulties. His focus on learning, presented in Part III, and his integration of learning with his previous theory of congressional cycles, an integration presented in Part IV, was essential before the author could recognize the critical role of party system polarization in fostering policy innovation in Congress.

Foundation Work: Aside from work listed in *Suggested Reading* for previous chapters, the perspective on electoral politics and agenda shift presented in "Congressional Cycles" benefited greatly from Walter Dean Burnham's 1970 work, *Critical Elections and the Mainsprings of American Politics,* which informed the author's sense of the long-term cyclical rhythm and electoral dynamics of congressional politics. Additionally, Burnham's 1976 article, "Revitalization and Decay," served to underscore the role critical elections and realignment processes play in fostering the adaptive capacities and long-term resilience of congressional politics.

The author's focus on the interplay between Congress and the presidency was greatly aided by the vast work on the presidency, as discussed in *The Politics Presidents Make* by Stephen Skowronek (1993), including particularly Skowronek's pioneering 1984 essay, "Presidential Leadership in Political Time." The author also continued to benefit from the insights of Theodore Lowi, as seen in his provocative 1985 work, *The Personal President: Power Invested, Promise Unfulfilled.* Important as well in fostering the broader interpretation presented in "Congressional Cycles" were David W. Brady (1978), "Critical Elections, Congressional Parties, and Clusters of Policy Change"; and John W. Kingdon (1984), *Agendas, Alternatives and Public Policies.*

Suggested Reading: Works that speak to, build on, test, or assess arguments introduced in this essay include Brady (1988); Elaine K. Swift (1996); Carmines and Stimson (1989); Aldrich (1995); Bensel (2000); Schickler (2001); Baumgartner and Jones (1993, 2002); Raven (2004); Sulkin (2005, 2009); and Theriault (2006, 2008).

Additionally, an assessment of the arguments put forward in the author's work on congressional cycles can benefit greatly from a reading of *Rediscovering Institutions*, by James G. March and Johan P. Olsen (1989, particularly pages 134 to 142). Among their many contributions in this pathbreaking book, March and Olsen provide an insightful discussion of cyclical politics in Western democracies, speaking thereby to the plausibility and value of the cyclical arguments presented in the essays in this volume.

On the move by various scholars, including the author, to integrate behavioral and goal-oriented approaches with an historical-developmental perspective on politics, see Almond, (1990), 214. For a discussion of the development of the author's arguments from "Congress and the Quest for Power" through "A Theory of Congressional Cycles," see Dodd (1987). The essay also presents the author's interpretation of Wilson's argument in *Congressional Government* and the ways that interpretation influenced the development of his work.

Classroom Use: "Congressional Cycles" can be used in the classroom in sections on elections, political parties, legislative–executive relations, changing patterns of congressional policy making, the role of context and generational shift in legislative politics, the politics of agenda shift in Congress, and institutional evolution.

"A Theory of Legislative Cycles" and "Congressional Cycles," together with "Congress, the Constitution, and the Crisis of Legitimation," could be paired with Eric Schickler's masterful study of congressional reform and institutional development, *Disjointed Pluralism.* At issue would be the ways in which the dynamic cyclical logic presented in the essays, together with the historical meaning attributed to congressional change in "Legitimation Crisis," inform the pattern of change witnessed across Schickler's four case studies. Also at issue could be whether adjustments, refinements or reconstructions in the theory, or its replacement, would be required based on Schickler's arguments and evidence.

PART III

Societal Change, Social Learning and Political Renewal

7

CONGRESS, THE PRESIDENCY, AND THE AMERICAN EXPERIENCE

A Transformational Perspective

1991

The chapters in Part II leave the impression that cycles of organizational reform and congressional resurgence occur automatically, insuring congressional adaptation to new historical conditions. But is this really true? Is politics really this predictable and determined? Or is something missing from our cyclical theory that could help us see Congress in a more realistic, open-ended manner?

"Congress, the Presidency, and the American Experience: A Transformational Perspective" argues that the ability of Congress to adapt to new societal conditions depends on the capacity of citizens and politicians to learn ways of understanding social reality appropriate to a new era. This is a daunting task. Learning to see a new social reality requires a willingness to let go of old certainties, experimentation with new governing perspectives, a capacity for creative innovation, some luck, and perseverance. Sometimes citizens and politicians fail in these endeavors, as during the 1850s, with dire national consequences. Other times they succeed, finding a new, more appropriate way of seeing the world that yields a viable policy agenda, a sustained partisan regime, and effective governing processes, as during the New Deal.

Seen in this manner, the most vital cycles shaping congressional politics are the cycles of experimentation with and transformation in the ideas that dominate national politics. Understanding congressional change, including the operation of its long-term institutional cycles, requires close attention to how viable new ideas emerge and the role Congress plays in this process. For the cycles of institutional change to proceed apace in congressional politics, they must mesh with ameliorative cycles of social learning, conceptual shift and agenda transformation in the nation. As they do so, the possibility of renewal in the relevance, authority and legitimacy of Congress emerges.

Lawrence C. Dodd. *"Congress, The Presidency, and the American Experience: A Transformational Perspective."* *In* Divided Democracy: Cooperation and Conflict Between the President and Congress. *Edited by* James A. Thurber. *Washington, D.C.: CQ Press. 1991, pp. 275–302.*

I approach the study of American politics in the midst of an intellectual crisis of faith. The crisis centers on a sense of intellectual powerlessness, a powerlessness to explain and predict politics in the manner that I was taught to expect and with the theories and frameworks that I had come to believe were appropriate. Much of the literature of political science teaches that repetitive and empirically comparable patterns exist in politics, particularly within a stable democracy such as ours. The key to political explanation is to identify these recurring empirical constants and account for them in terms of a general and perhaps universal theory. The goal of political science is to predict future political behavior from historical patterns and explanatory theories.[1]

The patterns to be explained are the recurring empirical manifestations of American politics, particularly the electoral behavior of voters and parties and the policy behavior of presidents and Congress. To explain the behavior of citizens and politicans, one could choose among or blend a variety of theoretical approaches: a realignment perspective, a value consensus perspective, a pluralist perspective, a class struggle perspective, or an institutional conflict perspective.[2] But whatever approach was adopted, it suggested that the future looked roughly like the past in its empirical particulars. We thus should expect realignment approximately every thirty years, say, with innovative policies coming only with strong party government and presidential leadership in the wake of realignment. Likewise, we should expect the constitutionally prescribed relationships among the three governing branches—Congress, the presidency, and the courts—to break apart under the impact of power struggles within and among these institutions. We then should see the return of equilibrium as institutional actors recognize the overriding systemic importance of constitutional roles and creedal values.

The problem was that the closer I looked at the applications of each theoretical approach, the more disappointed I became with its predictive results. Scholars might be able to adjust theoretical approaches and adapt them after the fact to fit particular empirical circumstances, but the theories seemed unable to predict political developments in any precise way. Realignments, for example, do not come when and as expected, though we may develop new concepts of realignment in order to adapt theory to new facts. Policy innovation, as seen in the years of Ronald Reagan's presidency, does not really require party government, though we can suddenly discover the virtues of divided government for certain kinds of innovation, creating the conditions of shared party responsibility for difficult policy decisions. And the power struggles within and among institutions do not end in a return to a predicted and foreseeable constitutional balance but invariably generate new and unforeseen resolutions. Our governing institutions, then, take on new roles, abandon old ones, develop innovative interinstitutional relationships, and establish new power distributions—all in ways that the nomological theories do not foresee.

Such observations create doubts about traditional approaches to the study of American politics. More important, they generate doubts about whether political scientists can ever find general theoretical explanations that will predict the particulars of politics. Decades of empirical research suggest that politics is not a constant and recurring game with simple and recurring patterns that can be discovered and used to predict future occurrences. It is more nearly a process of cyclical transformation in which political actors create, dissolve, and recreate the structure and logic of an evolving game. As they recreate the political game, the future looks different from the past in critical and unpredictable ways.

These conclusions suggest that the reliance on general nomological theories of behavior—based on expectations of a relatively constant recurring order in the empirical substance of political life—is suspect and probably wrongheaded. If wrongheaded, a nomological approach is dangerous. It suggests to actors in the world—to presidents, members of Congress, journalists, political activists, and ordinary citizens—that they should base their expectations and strategic choices about the future on theories that produce vastly inadequate predictions and that scholars keep alive only by post hoc adjustments. Believing in the truth of these empirical theories, presidents, legislators, and public-spirited citizens may make political choices and pursue political actions that have disastrous consequences, all in the name of political science.

Thus the crisis of faith: does one pursue an intellectual strategy that seems suspect, fraught with potentially disastrous consequences if taken seriously by the world at large? No. Far better to give up the preoccupation with nomological theory; acknowledge the variability, evanescence, and openness of the political world; and find a new way to understand that variability if not to predict its empirical content.[3] Far better to acknowledge the creative and evolving character of politics and focus on clarifying its processes, dilemmas, and opportunities. This is the challenge posed by my crisis of faith, a challenge whose elusiveness has preoccupied me for a decade.

In grappling with this challenge, I have come finally to a transformational perspective of American politics. The goal for political science, I believe, is not to discover and predict a recurring constancy in the structure, substance, and logic of political behavior but to clarify the processes whereby political actors create, operate within, dissolve, and recreate new and unforeseeable political worlds. The goal of the political scientist, in essence, is to understand the form, variability, and contingencies of political change, not to predict a content that is unforeseeable and a constancy that is nonexistent in any long-term and substantive sense.

A comparison with other fields of inquiry may help to clarify this goal. Evolutionary theorists in biology give a systematic accounting of how evolution occurs, with its heavy dose of randomness and chance, but they are unable to predict the species that will emerge through evolution.[4] Psychologists identify the processes whereby individuation and personal growth occur and outline the attendant struggles, choices, and constraints, though they cannot predict how each individual will resolve life crises and create a new life structure.[5] Political scientists likewise may be able to identify the processes of choice, experimentation, and struggle through which societies transform and conduct their politics over time, while being unable to predict specific political structures, policies, and behavior patterns that will emerge. By clarifying and theorizing about such processes, scholars bring to the political world not a prediction of its long-term future course but an awareness of its creative processes, dilemmas, and possibilities.[6]

In order to develop a theory of transformation, students of American politics must address a particular puzzle: how and why does American politics experience extended periods of creation, maintenance, dissolution, and recreation in the structure and logic of political behavior? A solution to this puzzle lies in developing a more accurate understanding of individual and group motivations than exists in political science today. It requires that theorists move beyond a rational-choice approach to politics, in which individuals are seen as purposive, self-interested actors pursuing fixed goals and preferences, to a metarational orientation, in which political actors, while often entranced by fixed goals and maximization of short-term interests, ultimately are seen as reflective and responsive individuals capable of shaping their world through experimental and experiential learning. Such metarational reflection and learning come to the fore in periods of crisis produced by a rigid adherence to, and "rational" pursuit of, fixed beliefs and goals that once had been appropriate but that have become outmoded as the world changed. It is the capacity for reflection and learning that enables political actors, who share a collective understanding of political life and operate within it for a sustained period of time, to dissolve existing political structures in the midst of crisis and evolve new governing arrangements appropriate to the emerging world.

A transformational perspective puts American history and contemporary politics in a different light. It requires that we forgo the desire for predictive certainty. In its stead we may come to see more clearly beyond the historical constraints and cyclical catastrophes predicted by nomological theories.[7] We may see instead both the potential for political empowerment and the promise of enlightened and regenerative self-governance.

My goal here is to outline this transformational perspective and demonstrate its applicability to American politics and congressional–presidential relations. It is appropriate that I introduce the theory in a book on Congress and the presidency, not only because they are my areas of primary specialty but because the institutions are critical agents in the American experience. The heart of the chapter is an interpretation of American political history intended to illustrate the transformative nature of political life and to inform our understanding of contemporary politics. In this interpretation, I underscore the role of Congress and the presidency in our political system. I begin, however, by presenting a general theory of transformation based on a metarational approach to the motivational dynamics of politics.

Transformational Politics: A Metarational Approach

Much of the problem with American political studies stems from inappropriate assumptions about human motivational dynamics. Like many others, I brought to the study of American politics, particularly Congress and the presidency, a rational-choice perspective.[8] This perspective entails the belief that the most useful analytic strategy is to assume that presidents, members of Congress, and other political actors share a set of fixed goals and preferences, which they seek to maximize through political action. This is an assumption of substantive rationality in politics, a belief that political actors calculate their self-interest in terms of specific, ordered, and constant preferences about the desired outcomes of politics.[9] Concurrent with this assumption is the expectation that the core structures, procedures, and rules of the political game remain stable over time, with the resources and payoffs being known and limited.

I suspect that essentially every theorist about American politics has been to some extent a closet rational choicer. Whether we explicitly say so or not, we assume that political actors pursue specified goals within an identifiable political game that is, in its most basic form, constant across history. We argue that the efforts of individuals, groups, parties, and institutions to maximize their interests within the context of a constant game set in motion recurring cycles, crises, realignments, and periods of institutional restoration. Since it is assumed that the goals, preferences, and structure of the game remain constant, we predict that change occurs within the parameters of the game itself. Transformation of the game is not possible. Thus the future will look much like the past, even the distant past.

In fact, when the future arrives, it does not look like the past. The substance of politics—the character of the policy agenda, the values of voters and politicians, the system of partisan and group conflict, the power of presidents and members of Congress, and the structure of the state—all change in significant ways unforeseen by our substantive theories.[10] To account for unexpected developments, we modify theories in ad hoc and post hoc ways. We do so from a belief that such theorizing is the best analytic tool we have available and from a desire to bring clarity, however inadequate, to the political world. We believe that we must either choose general predictive theory or become political journalists, content to describe political life void of system. This is the first and perhaps gravest mistake in our effort to understand political change.

The mistake lies in our failure to recognize that we could use other models of microdynamics to understand political change in more accurate and useful ways than the traditional ones.[11] What might such models look like, and what might their implications be? To explore these questions, we can move outside the domain of political science and its expectation of substantive rationality. In the next section I develop an alternative model, building on the approach to human behavior outlined by anthropologist Gregory Bateson, into which I incorporate several related approaches, from Carl Jung to Michael Lerner to Thomas Kuhn.[12]

A Batesonian Perspective

In *Steps to an Ecology of Mind*, Bateson argues that each individual develops a personal epistemology—a conception of how the world operates, including moral and empirical dimensions, collective responsibilities, and individual interests—through early experiences and socialization in the world.[13] These individual epistemologies incorporate fixed goals and preferences in a manner that only approximates the ontology, or reality, of the world. An individual's perception of reality, even at its clearest moment, deviates from reality. The difference between perception and reality forces individuals to become accustomed to some ineffectiveness in their understanding of the world and their action in it. Nevertheless, they hold to their epistemologies for security and order, using them to operate within and exercise power over their world.

Within the confines of their world view, and operating through structures and procedures they have created in pursuit of that world view, individuals take for granted the existence of a collective well-being and stress actions that provide them with or maximize short-term personal gratification. So preoccupied, they overlook behavior necessary to promote longer term and familial, group, or collective well-being. Their focus on short-term interests leads them to epistemological crisis in which short-term behavior generates unpredicted and counterproductive results. The resultant breakdown in social order occurs in part as individuals sabotage those collective structures and processes necessary to sustain interdependent cooperation in ways that blend self-interested pursuits into a common and mutually enhancing enterprise. Epistemological crises generate anxiety as individuals experience growing powerlessness and disorder. They act to reduce this anxiety by renewing their attention to the full range of appropriate epistemological behavior. Their response can be referred to as epistemological rationality, the pursuit of interests in the world in a manner consistent with maintaining their existing world view.

If the ontology of the political world remained constant, substantive theories based on epistemological rationality, as a modified version of substantive rationality, probably would work. Political actors would pursue behavior maximizing their interests, produce crises and anxiety, and then return to political orthodoxy in efforts to reduce anxiety.[14] But because the ontology of the world is not constant, we are led to a more complicated conception of human change.

The great dilemma of human behavior is that the ontology of the world—the way it really is and really operates—can change extensively over time, while the epistemology that dominates human action—beliefs about the way the world is and operates—remains relatively constant, with fixed goals, preferences, values, and moral visions. This is true in part because of the power of habit and because humans value the appearance of order and security. It is true in part because intense focus on short-term maximization within an existing epistemology and corrections in that maximizing behavior are so all-consuming that individuals overlook ontological change. They simply assume that difficulties in manipulating the world are a product of inappropriate behavior within existing world views. Finally, it is true because of the great difficulty and pain involved in reconstructing epistemologies. An individual must be willing to give up the sense of security and order inherent in traditional beliefs. Rather than holding onto traditional beliefs, the individual must try new behavior patterns and beliefs, and, through painful, threatening trial and error, seek forms of action and belief that reduce the sense of powerlessness and thereby seem to fit more clearly with the ontology of the world.

According to Bateson, the insecurity and pain involved in changing epistemologies is so great, and the commitment to and preoccupation with existing world views so extensive, that individuals will allow great gaps to develop between their epistemologies and the ontology of the world.[15] In fact, individuals will not reexamine the accuracy of epistemologies until crises are so great (and the ineffectiveness of epistemological restoration so clear) that they can significantly reduce their pain and powerlessness only by discarding the old world view and developing a new one. I refer to such circumstances as *metacrises*, deep and seemingly intractable dilemmas unresponsive to resolution through the operation of existing epistemological principles, structures, and procedures. When the recognition of metacrises comes—when the individual "hits bottom" so completely that he or she will let go of old assumptions, take responsibility for the self-deception and consequent powerlessness involved in holding to an inappropriate epistemology, and seek to experience the world more directly and experimentally—the process of constructing a new epistemology can begin. I call this act *epistemological reconstruction*.

Epistemological reconstruction occurs through the application of a process I call *experiential rationality*—an individual's experimentation with beliefs, goals, preferences, structures, and procedures until an epistemology of action is found that reduces the experience of powerlessness. Because the gap between an old epistemology and a new ontology can be great, epistemological reconstruction may be long and difficult. The individual may experience feelings of powerlessness and insecurity that arouse irrational fears and unconscious behaviors. Such psychopathological developments, in extreme form, can obstruct the experimentation and reconstruction process, perhaps even sabotaging it so completely that an individual may remain stuck in ineffectual and self-destructive behavior. Alternatively, an individual may create a revised epistemology with significant pathological elements so that, although short-term reempowerment occurs, self-destructive tendencies persist that will subvert long-term empowerment and well-being.[16]

Epistemological reconstruction thus is not assured. It involves trial-and-error experimentation with no guarantee of successful solution. And it may require personal and cathartic confrontation with fears and insecurities that inhibit experimentation. As individuals experience catharsis and experiment with new epistemologies, structures, and procedures, they have the opportunity to construct an epistemology more appropriate to the world than the former one. The new epistemology can empower them to operate in the world as it more truly is.

This, in brief, is a modified and expanded view of Bateson's conception of individual motives and behavior. Central to his thinking is a process I call *metarationality*—the recognition by an individual that adherence to an inappropriate epistemological system engenders a powerlessness and insecurity that is greater in cost than the pain, insecurity, and difficulties involved in creating a new epistemology. Metarational behavior requires an individual to move from epistemological rationality to experiential rationality in order to adjust to ontological change and then to move back to epistemological rationality as a way of regularizing his or her behavior in the world. Ultimately, Bateson suggests, this process occurs in collectivities as well as in individuals and provides us with a way to understand political and social action. Let us turn, then, to the metarational processes as they operate in collectivities.

Metarationality in a Collective World

Like substantive rationality, metarationality posits a world in which political actors relate to one another in terms of a shared understanding of goals, preferences, structures, procedures, and political logic. These shared understandings constitute a collective epistemology of the political world, in a sense a shared imagining of the world.[17] A collective epistemology includes a common understanding of the longterm collective responsibilities of individuals, groups, and institutions (including constitutional roles, moral prescriptions, and social norms) and an understanding of actions appropriate for individual, group, and institutional pursuits of immediate self-interest (whether class and regional interests, electoral success, or political power).

The content of collective epistemologies varies dramatically across historical eras in response to economic, technological, social, and moral possibilities. Before a collective epistemology can be viable, however, social and political actors must recognize that they live in an interdependent world. Because of this interdependence, political actors must act in mutually responsible ways if they are to ensure collective survival and individual enhancement. A viable epistemology thus will entail precepts, structures, and procedures that foster interdependent cooperation and are mutuality appropriate to and possible in a historical time and place. At the heart of a viable collective epistemology lies an ecological vision of political and social life, a sense of the way in which political actors, groups, institutions, and processes fit together in a particular time and place to ensure mutual enhancement and survival.[18] A collectivity may also create a pathological epistemology, one that generates a sense of immediate reempowerment through distorted beliefs that ultimately inhibit political renewal, generate deeper crises, and require more catharsis and experimentation before collective renewal can occur.[19]

Collective epistemologies emerge from deep collective metacrises, which are often evident in revolution; in civil war; in social, moral, and economic dislocations; and in military defeat. Once an appropriate collective epistemology is in place and the crisis wanes (if a viable epistemology is found), the success of the epistemological beliefs and structures lead political actors to accept them as a political orthodoxy that defines their goals, preferences, and political possibilities. Political actors lose their concern for epistemological reassessment. Taking for granted the processes that allow collective well-being, they pursue personal interests within the existing world view. In the process, they lose their sense of the importance of mutuality and interdependence and focus on short-term self-interests.

The pursuit of short-term interests by individuals, groups, and institutions initiates a move from political cooperation to competition in ways that erode the structures, norms, and processes that provide for interdependent and mutual interests. The breakdown eventually produces social and political crises, efforts to strengthen cooperative structures to solve the crises, and reassertions of epistemological orthodoxy. This ongoing process of breakdown and restoration within an era involves shifts in power arrangements and policy concerns because of the various skills of political leaders and activists and because of the shifting policy alignments within the collectivity. Such cyclical political phases occur continually during an epistemological era and constitute the substance of daily politics that journalists and political scientists study. The longer political actors hold to the existing epistemology and allow it to constrain their political responses, the more anachronistic their governing structures and processes become. Holding to the extant world view and pursuing reforms and policy objectives within its constraints thus sets the stage for deep collective metacrises that can be resolved only by epistemological reconstruction.

This perspective suggests that we can think of political life in terms of long-term cycles of epistemological transformation and short-term cycles of political adjustment and reform within a reigning world view. The long cycles consist of the creation, maintenance, dissolution, and reconstruction of a collective epistemology.

The short cycles are the recurring processes of breakdown and restoration that occur within an epistemological era. They are characterized by a variety of cyclical dynamics, including ideological mood swings between collective cooperation and competition, organizational shifts between centralization and decentralization, realignments in the groups and parties that win policy struggles within an era, leadership shifts from creative policy assertiveness to managing and salvaging policy agendas, and the like.[20] As long as cyclical oscillations focus on reforms and adjustments within existing world views, societal change will outpace the ability of governments to respond to national problems effectively. Problems will mount and crises will fester to the point that extensive political restructuring will be necessary for crisis resolution and system survival.

Political restructuring requires extensive experimentation and improvisation. These processes occur throughout society, often coming at local and state levels long before they are evident in national governance.[21] They are generally initiated by dissident groups and individuals, often intellectuals, artists, and social activists outside formal political roles, whose creativity is critical to assessing the nation's problems and "reimagining"—to some real extent, "remythologizing"—its future. Ultimately, however, the collective success of such processes requires an authoritative collective leadership, dialogue, and implementation best found in formal institutions such as Congress, the presidency, and the courts.

A key to successful collective restructuring lies in the ability of the members of the governing institutions to engage in experimentation and improvisation. This ability depends on widespread recognition of the severity of the problems and the failure of existing approaches to solve the problems. It probably also depends on the existence of leaders who are personally grappling with epistemological reassessment and transformation.[22] Successful reimagining—a reshaping of the dominant myths, symbols, and stories through which we understand ourselves and guide our actions[23]—sets in motion a new epistemological era, including new political arrangements and a new set of fluctuations and short-term reform cycles. This pattern of short-term reform cycles nested within longer term transformational cycles is strongly evident in American political history. Four examples are outlined in the next section.

The Cycles of American Politics

I outlined a metarational approach in some detail to provide an analytic sense of how one might envision politics from a transformational perspective. The result is a vision of politics characterized by the cyclical creation and recreation of political reality. These transformative cycles are fueled as much by epistemological rigidification, psychopathological conflict, system-threatening crisis, and experimental improvisation as they are by rational choice of alternative futures based on fixed and shared preferences. It is the long-term preoccupation with rational calculation based on fixed and shared preferences within an epistemological orthodoxy that gives rise to a growing unresponsiveness of government, the eventual development of metacrises, and the struggle to restructure dominant epistemologies and governing arrangements.

This perspective provides a useful framework within which to study American politics. We can think of American history, in simplified terms, as separated into four eras, with each era holding distinct shared epistemologies of politics.[24] We can likewise identify four periods of deep crisis and reconstruction from which arose new epistemologies of action. The four eras of shared epistemologies of politics are the agrarian period of the first half of the nineteenth century, the postagrarian transition of the late nineteenth century, the industrial era of the early to mid-twentieth century, and the current postindustrial transition. The four reconstructive periods are the Revolutionary War and founding period, which gave rise to the agrarian-era politics; the Civil War and Reconstruction, from which arose the postagrarian era; the Progressive upheavals of the early twentieth century, which set in motion industrial-era politics; and the activist politics of the 1960s and 1970s, which shaped the current postindustrial politics.

In each historical era political actors and citizens held a widely shared and seemingly immutable core understanding of politics that gave order to the politics of the day. In the long run, however, the persistence of a collective epistemology and pursuit of immediate interests within it precipitated the crises that sabotaged the political equilibrium of each era. In the following section, I briefly sketch each era, giving a general sense of the way the dominant world view provoked metacrisis and reconstructive struggle. In these sketches, I highlight the role of Congress and the presidency, beginning with the agrarian period, which can be dated roughly from the late eighteenth century to the late 1850s.[25]

The Agrarian Era

The political logic of the agrarian era centered on a limited and constrained government dominated by regional and state elites, a mixed economy balancing the interests of slavery and free labor, and an isolated nationalism. This shared understanding emerged from the Revolutionary War and the postwar effort to find a workable form of governance. It fit conditions of the late eighteenth century and the first decade or so of the nineteenth century rather well. By the 1810s, and certainly by the 1820s, the conditions that had made such epistemological solutions possible were shifting. Agrarianism was yielding to the early stages of industrialization, interstate commerce, and a national transportation network.

The development of a truly national economic system, with its differential effect on states and regions and its impetus toward a growing nationalism and international trade, challenged the nation's compromise on slavery, position on states' rights, and inclination toward isolation. But for another forty years political actors adhered to the old epistemology, seeking to maximize what they thought to be their sectional, economic, and partisan interests. The preoccupation with states' rights and sectionalism is particularly evident in the South, of course, where the politics of slavery intensified in the face of societal change and reinforced the antebellum world view. The South was not alone in the politics of sectionalism and state sovereignty, however, a fact witnessed, for example, in the secessionist sentiments in New England and rabid state loyalties from New York to Ohio to Illinois.

Throughout the agrarian era the political actors thought they were behaving rationally, pursuing sectional interests, partisan advantage, and personal career advancement. And in terms of maximizing short-term interests, they were acting rationally. Their short-term rational pursuits produced the cyclical oscillations to be expected from substantive rationality. Among them were two distinct governing cycles: the Jeffersonian regime from 1800 to the late 1820s and the Jacksonian regime from the 1830s to the late 1850s. Within the broader agrarian mindset, each cycle had its own distinctive policy and power orientations, its own electoral shifts, organizational struggles, and leadership patterns—all of which political scientists can explain to some extent in substantively rational terms.[26] Ultimately, however, understanding agrarian era politics lies not in accounting for these overt actions in "rational" pursuit of an epistemological orthodoxy but in recognizing and understanding the nondecisions, nonactions, and growing sense of collective disempowerment that evolved in the face of mounting societal crisis. Understanding lies in explaining what seems in retrospect to be the country's irrational refusal to let go of an antebellum vision of society, North and South, and to grapple directly with societal and political transformation.

In the verdict of history it was precisely the adherence to an antiquated understanding of politics and society—particularly the pursuit of state and sectional interests through short-term partisan calculations—that was the defining characteristic of the agrarian era. In terms of ultimate consequences it was a characteristic seemingly irrational. After the late 1810s the nation's efforts to salvage the agrarian epistemology and political processes (the Missouri Compromise, the Jacksonian expansion of electoral participation, the nullification doctrine of John C. Calhoun, the Kansas-Nebraska Act, and the Dred Scott decision) merely delayed its confrontation with a new reality. Delay allowed fears and malevolent projections to intensify across the regions and made the confrontation with reality and political restructuring immeasurably more difficult and painful when it came.

During all of this, Congress and the presidency were vital arenas of both decision and nondecision. Their importance lay in their roles in the institutionalization of a founding epistemology in the late eighteenth and early nineteenth centuries, their inventive salvaging of that epistemology throughout the first sixty years of the nineteenth century, and their dramatic efforts in the 1860s and 1870s to save the nation by reinventing the structure of American politics. The great tragedy of the legislative and executive branches was that they were more adept at peaceful adjustments within an existing and increasingly anachronistic world view than at peaceful reassessments of that world view and construction of new structures of policy and governance.

The saving grace of the presidency and Congress came in their providing institutional mechanisms through which the meaning and resolution of civil strife could be addressed in the depth of national self-destruction. Abraham Lincoln, the great imaginer of the new American nation, thus found in the presidency a forum (for example, in the Second Inaugural Address) from which he could articulate the mutual responsibility for and collective costs of civil strife. He could speak to a sense of shared meaning and interdependent destiny and suggest a vision of a people committed to liberty, equality, and compassion. In so doing, Lincoln could address his own transformative struggles between personal ambition and moral purpose. During both the Civil War and Reconstruction, Congress provided the nation with an arena for retribution and catharsis (in the impeachment and conviction trial of Andrew Johnson), for dialogue and negotiation (in the struggle over the shape of Reconstruction), and for experimentation with and eventual restructuring of the constitutional creed and governing arrangements (in the Thirteenth, Fourteenth, and Fifteenth amendments and the implementation of the Compromise of 1876).

The Postagrarian Transition

In the 1870s the nation was freed to pursue a full-fledged transition to industrialization after the slavery issue and the most destructive elements of sectional rivalry were resolved. With this transition evolved a new political logic, an almost unbridled alliance between business and an expansionary government devoted to funding and fueling laissez faire capitalism. Like the agrarian world view, this postagrarian image of politics and society took hold in a deep and ultimately destructive manner. Whereas the business–government alliance (for example, between railroad barons and legislators) may have energized society in the aftermath of the Civil War and Reconstruction, the unregulated pursuit of money and power propelled the nation into some of the worst consequences of capitalist democracy. These ranged from an electoral corruption that left democracy a mockery in much of the country to workplace corruption in which exploitation of child labor and the contamination of food and beverages became the order of the day. Again, political actors seeking to maximize short-term gain in ways justified by an extant epistemology—in this case the world view of social Darwinism—were single-minded in their pursuits, oblivious to the consequences of the action and to changes in societal conditions that had given rise to that world view. Thus they failed to understand that a growing middle class would not support greed and corruption indefinitely. The politicians and business leaders were able to sustain their orgy at the public trough for almost forty years. During the years of the Progressive movement, however, rebellious citizens were so angered by their government that they not only threw the rascals out, but, through electoral, legislative, and bureaucratic reforms, virtually crippled the nation's capacity for deliberative government.

In the Progressive Era a new vision arose of how government might serve the common good. Among the Progressives' ideas were such reforms as conserving the nation's environment, securing clean elections, and regulating industry to ensure safe industrial products and to protect women and children (and men) from the worst abuses of capitalism. Unfortunately, graft and corruption were so rampant and political leaders opposed to Progressive ideas so entrenched in party machines and Congress that the Progressives attacked the very foundations of party and congressional governance in order to implement their policy visions.

In the Progressives' view, party organizations and congressional leadership were major culprits hindering democracy. In contrast, the presidency under Theodore Roosevelt and Woodrow Wilson was democracy's salvation, particularly when the executive controlled a powerful administrative state that could regulate business and society. With the consequent upheavals of the 1900s and 1910s and the struggle to break the trusts and oust corrupt politicians, a new epistemological shift occurred in American politics.

The shift was away from a strong Congress based on cohesive party government and toward a strong, potentially imperial executive supported by presidential rhetoric, bureaucratic regulation, and interest group politics. Reforms to implement this vision eventually produced a fragmented Congress, oriented to seniority, committee government, special interests, and presidential leadership. The presidency was increasingly predominant, judged by its boldness, service to business and labor interests, and social activism and international assertiveness. The price of epistemological rigidification in the late nineteenth century and the deep crisis of confidence that it produced in the early twentieth century thus was a restructuring of the United States' conception of democratic government. The country moved away from deliberative politics toward the politics of rhetoric and personal charisma.

Like the Civil War, the Progressive crisis and the restructuring it provoked were not rational choices by clearheaded actors, nor was the flourishing of creedal passion resolved by the restoration of a pre-existing creedal structure. Rather, they were the irrational and ultimately destructive long-term consequences of "rational" short-term calculations by individuals and groups seeking to maximize immediate self-interests while holding to an outdated and counterproductive world view. The result was as destructive institutionally, if not in terms of lives, as the Civil War. Congressional government was left in shambles, and the foundations were laid for an expansionary executive. In essence, a new balance was created that allowed the government to ensure democratic elections and respond to the demands for industry regulation. But, as with the agrarian era, the long-term adherence to a dominant political orthodoxy and the pursuit of interests within that orthodoxy did damage that had critical long-term consequences. The nation found new epistemological structures that resolved the immediate crisis and provided means for government action. Yet the severity of the crisis left its mark on the political landscape in a way that might have been moderated or prevented with clearer foresight and earlier response than the political actors were able to display.

With the institutional restructuring came a new agenda and a new politics. The new agenda included a socially and internationally activist government committed to a capitalist democracy sustained by domestic government regulation and international interventionism on behalf of American economic interests. The politics centered on universal suffrage and mass democracy, the flourishing of interest group politics, a handmaiden role for Congress in major policy deliberations, and a powerful executive responsible for leading a capitalist democracy.

The Industrial Era

The new structure of politics and policy that arose from Progressive reforms constituted a third American epistemology, a vision of how an interdependent society would work in an era of industrialization. This world view came to dominate the nation just as it entered the "American century," the period in which the country's affluence, domestic resources, and secure and strategic location (together with dynastic reversals in Europe and Asia) helped to ensure its pivotal and even dominant position in the world order.[27] The great architects of this vision were Theodore Roosevelt and Woodrow Wilson, leaders who spoke to issues of mutuality such as conservation, social responsibility, international interdependence, and democratic responsiveness. Hand in hand with their vision, however, came big government, labor and business obsession with controlling government policy, U.S. expansionary intervention abroad, a growing alliance between industry and the military, and the public's disposition to trust presidents as benign protectors of democracy while disparaging Congress in ways that had serious potential consequences for civil liberties and representative government.[28]

During the fifty to sixty years of the industrial era (roughly from the late 1910s into the early 1970s), the nation experienced two broad partisan reform cycles. The first, Warren G. Harding's "age of normalcy," saw Republican dominance, an expansive economy, and economic disaster during a worldwide depression.[29] The second, the New Deal regime that stretched from the presidency of Franklin D. Roosevelt to that of Richard Nixon, saw capitalist democracy saved by the expansion of a bureaucratic state, greater regulation of business, closer attentiveness to the social responsibility of government, and the solidification of an extraordinary military-industrial alliance. The industrial era experienced mood swings, organizational reform cycles, partisan realignments, alterations in leadership patterns, and a sustained period of national economic growth.[30] Yet as the industrial era lengthened, the nation experienced a sense of frustration and powerlessness in the face of problems that seemed unresponsive to the existing political logic.

However appropriate executive government on behalf of capitalist democracy may have been to the policy problems of the early twentieth century, this political epistemology was inappropriate in the second half of the twentieth century. Thus the conflict between labor and business continued to dominate the political parties and the halls of Congress even as the nation moved into a postindustrial service society, leaving unaddressed the issues of social welfare, civil rights, and quality of life endemic to a postindustrial and postmaterialist society. The presidency continued to be seen as relatively benign and relatively unconstrained, particularly in foreign policy, even as the growth of a bureaucratic state and the telecommunications revolution made the executive a threat to civil liberties and democratic government.[31] Congress became fragmented and unresponsive even as the need for a balance to executive power became clear. An interventionist foreign policy continued to dominate American thinking even as the coming of Third World nationalism made interventionism dangerous and counterproductive as a means of ensuring U.S. economic interests. And the country prolonged its economic growth by relying on military and defense spending, even as serious threats to its security decreased and its allies became capable of sharing defense responsibilities. The United States was able to avoid confronting political realities for a remarkably long time—but not forever. The problems seemed to explode almost simultaneously in the 1960s and early 1970s, leaving the nation's self-confidence shaken.

The story of the social breakdown of the 1960s and early 1970s, resulting in the destruction of two presidents, is well known and need not be repeated here. The great tragedy of both Lyndon B. Johnson and Richard Nixon lay in the extent to which they were pursuing, in a classically rational and short-term maximizing sense, the understanding of American politics that they had learned as young politicians. Johnson and Nixon were not aberrations at the end of the American century but its culmination. Their obsession with bold presidential interventionism, at home and abroad, was in the best tradition of Theodore Roosevelt, Woodrow Wilson, Franklin D. Roosevelt, and Harry S. Truman, as were their aggressive partisan politics. Yet approaches to politics and governance that may have worked decades earlier, including military intervention abroad and disingenuous presentation of self and policy actions at home, would not work in a society composed of an increasingly media-oriented and politically sophisticated public.

In essence, by the 1960s there were deep incompatibilities and contradictions between the United States' understanding of itself and the ontological reality of the emerging world, gaps that were leading to metacrisis and disaster, regardless of the individuals in the White House and the partisan control of Congress. The personalities of Johnson and Nixon may have exacerbated matters,[32] and certainly they must be judged as responsible participants in the politics of their time. But the root of the problem was not in Johnson and Nixon but in a broadly shared collective understanding of the world that, for example, expected presidents to act boldly in defense of democracy abroad (and certainly not to lose Southeast Asia to communism) while maintaining order, prosperity, and expanding opportunity at home.[33] In a world of televised war, diminishing resources, and expanding postmaterial expectations, such world view necessarily led to failure, to a sense of growing powerlessness, and eventually to deep and shattering psychopathological crises in which the nation had to face its limits and recognize the need for new policy objectives and governing strategies.

The struggle to visualize a new America was foreshadowed and addressed in an outpouring of social commentaries.[34] The vision of the new character and interdependence of economic, social, political, and international factors emerged most clearly in the late 1960s, however, as leaders such as Martin Luther King, Jr., and Robert Kennedy sought to link concerns for economic and social issues with the United States' approach to world affairs. They created new political strategies that combined collective nonviolence, televised mobilization of mass outrage, and electoral challenge to the status quo (an overall strategy I call movement politics). The message was that the source of America's crises lay not in communist conspiracies and radical protests but in the nation's own failure to assess realistically its domestic problems and foreign commitments.

For a nation addicted after decades of remarkable achievement to believing in its own specialness, righteousness, and ennobled position in the world, the reversals of the 1960s and the suggestion that the nation itself was responsible for its sudden sense of inefficacy and powerlessness were disturbing and threatening. The resulting sense of rage and frustration evoked psychopathological forces that afflicted far more of the country than Presidents Johnson and Nixon and led to a season of attempted and successful assassinations. Among the assassins' targets were John F. Kennedy, Medgar Evers, Malcolm X, Martin Luther King, Jr., Robert Kennedy, George Wallace, Gerald Ford, and Ronald Reagan. The period from 1963 to 1981 was a time of unrest unlike any other two decades in American history. The crisis evoked far more turmoil than the political assassinations. Civil disobedience was widespread, cities were engulfed in race wars and firestorms of destruction, and freedom of speech and free elections were threatened (for example, in the rhetoric of Vice-President Spiro T. Agnew and the Watergate actions of President Nixon). In a way not often recognized, however, the assassinations may have been the greatest tragedy of the period, robbing the nation of individuals who might have served, like Lincoln (and to a lesser extent Theodore Roosevelt and Woodrow Wilson), as transformative leaders who could articulate a vision of interdependence and mutuality and reenergize the public spirit.

The Postindustrial Transformation

A new world view emerged in the 1970s. It was the constrained and confused self-image of a nation adrift, robbed of its historic bearings and sense of limitless possibilities. In their place came a deep sense of malaise, as Jimmy Carter phrased it. The domestic turmoil of the 1960s, the defeat in Vietnam, and the political corruption symbolized by Watergate left the nation bereft of faith in its moral purpose and unsure of its ability to provide its citizens with a viable and rewarding future. During the 1970s and 1980s these doubts were deepened. The oil embargo and the consequent energy crisis demonstrated the nation's growing dependence on increasingly powerful Third World nations. The hostage crisis drove Carter from office and ultimately generated the Iran-contra scandal, which tarnished Reagan's reassertion of American toughness. Inflationary pressures swelled the numbers of American families dependent on two incomes. International borrowing and trade practices left the country one of the world's great debtor nations.

The move to what we can call an epistemology of limits, based on a growing sense of constraints, self-doubt, and retrenchment, constituted in many ways a necessary corrective to the aggressive expansiveness of the American century.[35]

This corrective included elements of true collective learning, ranging from a greater understanding of the disadvantages of presidential imperialism and the value of deliberative decision making to a growing appreciation of the complexity and interdependence of environmental, social, economic, and political forces on a global as well as a domestic scale. With this knowledge came some sense of the United States' responsibility for its weakened condition.

These concerns came to be reflected in structural alterations in the nation's participatory processes and governing procedures during the 1970s.[36] The nation witnessed the rise of a new kind of interest group. This new movement included groups such as Common Cause and "Nader's Raiders" that were committed to the pursuit of collective interests and quality of life across many facets of society. These groups expanded the character of democratic participation, not only by involving minorities and eighteen-year-olds in electoral politics and working for the advancement of women in public office but through a broadened conception of legitimate democratic participation encapsulated in movement politics. In 1973 the nation adopted a war powers act to constrain executive imperialism abroad, and it instituted impoundment procedures whereby Congress could limit executive usurpation of domestic spending powers. And it reformed its Congress. It did so by weakening legislative seniority and spreading power more widely among members, by improving congressional policy-making coordination through a new budgetary process, by creating a stronger leadership structure, and by televising congressional debate.

The new epistemology and governing processes allowed the nation to loosen somewhat its grip on the expectations of the preceding decades and to focus energies on immediate national concerns. The presidencies of Ford and Carter witnessed elements of national renewal: Ford pardoned Nixon, moving the nation beyond its preoccupation with retribution, and Carter rekindled, if only momentarily, a sense of national decency, trust, and mutual respect. By the early 1980s, with Reagan's first term, the nation was able to move on to a "politics of normalcy." It was, of course, a divided politics, with a nation still so unsure of direction that it would set in motion divided party control of Congress and the presidency for the longest time span of modern history.

Under Reagan an ideology of limits dominated the public dialogue. The government's role ideally was limited to defense against "evil empires" and to taxation and expenditures focused on defense-related matters designed simultaneously to secure national defense and to fuel economic growth. It was, as one would expect, a period of epistemological orthodoxy and rigidification in which the pursuit of self-interest generated a disintegration of governing norms and procedures.[37]

The disintegrative impulse can be seen across a variety of dimensions. In Congress, budgetary procedures designed to allow for collective judgment have been subverted by automatic decision processes (such as Gramm-Rudman-Hollings procedures and backdoor spending strategies) that allow politicians to avoid judgment and responsibility. War powers provisions designed to expand legislative control over foreign policy have instead come to be seen as processes legitimizing short-term presidential war making, from Grenada to Panama. The politics of public interest—with a broad vision of the range, complexity, and interdependence of the policy issues confronting the nation—have shattered into a single-interest politics in which special interest groups stress the primacy of individual interest at the expense of a collective policy vision.

Nonviolent collective action, a strategy designed to unite and mobilize a disparate and otherwise powerless citizenry in moral outrage over fundamental issues of national governance, has dissolved into a pressure group tactic employed by often well-funded single-interest advocates (as in the abortion conflict) to immobilize government. Television to some extent became in the 1960s a medium of public dialogue through which disenfranchised, disadvantaged, and disempowered citizens could speak to one another and to the nation's conscience (a role seen recently in the political revolution of Eastern Europe). In recent years, however, it has become a vehicle of mass manipulation through negative campaigning. The politics of negativity and manipulation, fueled by massive corporate and PAC funding of election campaigns, are driving voters away from democratic participation, raising the costs of electoral politics to new heights, and addicting politicians to large corporate clients (such as the savings and loan industry) in a way that blinds them to public interest concerns.[38]

There are, of course, positive signs admist such disintegrative dynamics. Congress continues to reassess budgetary procedures and is even discussing methods of revenue enhancement. Executive officials, such as Lt. Col. Oliver L. North and Adm. John M. Poindexter, have been convicted for their roles in the Iran-contra affair. And legislators, such as the "Keating Five," have been investigated for alleged unethical pursuit of corporate funding.[39] Unfortunately, such developments are the exception rather than the rule. The nation appears trapped in self-interested pursuits that erode the mechanisms and processes which evolved in the 1970s as a means of collective empowerment. Even more troubling, it is trapped in an epistemological vision of American politics that may be inappropriate to international and domestic circumstances.

An epistemology of limits may well have been a necessary corrective to the hubris of the American century, but it is questionable whether a limited vision of the role of government is appropriate as the nation approaches the twenty-first century. Internationally, the world has seen dramatic changes since the early 1970s, most notably the breakdown of Soviet dominance in Eastern Europe, the disturbances in the Middle East, the emergence of Japan as an economic world power, the reunification of Germany, and the possibility of a united Europe. Perhaps the greatest issue facing the nation is whether it can embrace a responsible, interdependent, and cooperative role in the world, or whether it will allow the wounds of Vietnam and the setbacks of the 1980s to fester and push it deeper into a chauvinist mentality in which the world is seen in terms of enemies to conquer and friends to save.

The country faces similar domestic concerns. Americans have learned that government cannot solve all of its citizens' problems, that both tax dollars and planning sagacity are limited. Yet the nation's economic structure and society continue to change in ways that create an interdependent and mobile citizenry in need of mechanisms for collective cooperation and mutual support. The great challenge for domestic politics is to create a model of activism in which the government facilitates collective well-being for its citizens without overreaching its capacities, depriving its citizens of responsibility for their own lives, or creating new foreign enemies to justify defense spending. Discovering such a model will take considerable experimentation, at state and local as well as national levels. It may prove particularly difficult if international developments lead the United States to reduce domestic reliance on a military-industrial complex as the engine of its national economy. Ultimately, it may require an American perestroika that we cannot yet envision.

My concern, in raising these issues, is that the nation not remain so fixated on the politics of limits, so contemptuous of the "vision thing" that once again we let our problems fester until our crises appear unsolvable and psychopathological conflict again engulfs us. However appropriate an epistemology of limits may have been two decades ago, the changes at play in the world today suggest that the United States needs to move beyond a concern with its limits, in which we concentrate on national defense and sustenance of our economy by military and industrial spending, and create a responsible and assertive role both domestically and globally. If we fail to do so, we risk even greater national reversals than we have had in the past. Insofar as we engage in epistemological reassessment and search for a responsible role, we truly sow the seeds of national renewal.

Escaping the Web of History

I have briefly sketched the story of American politics to lend credence to the transformational perspective outlined at the beginning of the chapter. Obviously, my sketch does not prove that such an interpretation is true. I believe, however, that it suggests the plausibility of metarational insights, a plausibility that taken seriously leads one to think differently about American history.

A transformational perspective sensitizes us to the realization that collective disempowerment in the world, and the deep and debilitating crises that come with it, is a product of human choice and political myopia. It is a product of our tendency to embrace as a permanent belief system a collective world view that momentarily empowers us and then to pursue our self-interests within that world view even as ontological reality changes in ways that erode the appropriateness and effectiveness of our beliefs and consequent actions. This is true whether we look at the United States' preoccupation with slavery, sectionalism, and states' rights that led to the Civil War; the social Darwinism that produced the Progressive upheavals; or the fixation on presidential imperialism, U.S. interventionism, and interest group politics that led to the social turmoil and international reversals of the 1960s and 1970s. I suggest that it also is true in the 1990s, insofar as we ignore the changes at play in the world today and hold rigidly to an epistemology of limits.

Within a transformational perspective, the responsibility of each generation is to develop a collective epistemology and governing structures appropriate to the ontological reality of its world. This process is difficult, with reassessment and reconstruction coming only as deep societal crises force us to confront our illusions about the world. My suspicion is that epistemological reassessment and reconstruction is ultimately so difficult that societies will never be able to avoid crises, however reflective and self-aware the citizenry and political leadership may be. Yet a nation attentive to the lessons of history,[40] to the transformational possibilities of political life, and to the message such lessons and possibilities hold for its time and place may become sensitive to the early warning signs of crisis. Such sensitivity can enable its citizens, its Congress, and its president to act responsibly and diligently, even as the shadow of the future descends, to redress its pathologies and disintegrative impulses, even as they threaten to destroy it. This is the challenge of American politics, the challenge to Congress and the presidency, in the 1990s.

Conclusion

These, then, are some thoughts on a transformational interpretation of American politics. I propose that we see American politics as a process in which political actors create, pursue, dissolve, and recreate a collective political epistemology appropriate to a changing world. This process exists because political actors operate in a world of metarationality—a changing world in which the pursuit of fixed goals and preferences leads to long-term powerlessness and metacrises that can be resolved only by reassessing goals, preferences, and values and by reconstructing collective epistemologies in ways appropriate to the emerging world.

The reconstructive and transformational nature of politics works against the long-term existence of recurring substantive patterns in American political life. The structure and procedures of American politics evolve and change so that its logic alters in ways that require a continual deciphering. An understanding of American politics comes thus not through the creation of general theories of party government, congressional reform, realignment, presidential leadership, class conflict, or creedal passions applied as substantive constants across history. It comes through an attentiveness and sensitivity to the ways political actors create and pursue new political epistemologies in new historical eras; in this process, as central agents of authoritative decision making, Congress and the president are critical participants in the transformational struggle.

Scholars can facilitate reconstructive change insofar as they clarify the existence and nature of the reconstructive process. Such awareness empowers political actors to look beyond distortions, orthodoxies, and psychopathological conflicts to experiment with new beliefs and structures and create political world views appropriate to the emergent political world. Conversely, scholars inhibit successful reconstructive politics and disempower political actors insofar as they suggest the existence of general substantive theories and hold to them even as empirical evidence suggests that a changing world operates otherwise. Scholars then become agents of political myopia, the creators of orthodoxies that blind political actors to the changing nature of the world and thus to the necessity of experimentation and epistemological reconstruction.

It is for this reason that I have found it necessary to rethink my approach to American politics. It is not simply that assumptions of substantive rationality and general substantive theories of politics are wrong. It is that they are dangerous. They imply a regularity to history that is not true but that political actors might take seriously. To expect, to believe as a scientific law, that realignments come every thirty years, that political innovation requires realignment, that institutional recentralization is inherent and guaranteed as a cyclical regularity, that the polity always reaffirms its original creedal principles, and so forth, is to hitch one's political and intellectual wagon to a falling star.

What scholars can attempt to do is to decipher the substantive logic of particular eras and thereby understand the political dynamics of a time and place, including, let us hope, our own. We can begin to grasp the ways in which rigid adherence to an existing world view disempowers us and thereby become attentive to ontological change and epistemological reassessment. We can also hope to clarify abstract processes of reconstructive change, realizing that change itself is in no sense assured, that our understanding of the processes of change is approximate at best, and that a degree of experimentation, reflectiveness, and creativity exists in political life that limits our predictive powers. In so doing we can begin to see that the ultimate goal of scholarship is, to paraphrase Marx, not to predict the future but to change it, to so clarify the workings of history that we as a people learn from it in ways that enable us to escape history's relentless machinations.[41]

Such a recognition limits the prospects of a formal science of American politics, if by that we mean a discipline that generates predictive laws subsumed in formalized and trans-historical theory. Yet such a perspective should liberate us to construct a transformational science, a science sensitive to the transformational character of human existence and political life. A transformational vision ultimately is an empowering one, one that helps political actors to recreate and renew politics in ways appropriate to collective self-governance in a changing world.

Notes

Acknowledgements: I wish to thank those who provided written critiques of this work, including Leslie Anderson, Douglas Ashford, Ron Brunner, Richard Fenno, Jeff Fishel, Joan Fiore, Ted Robert Gurr, Calvin Jillson, Peter Katzenstein,

David Mapal, Sidney Milkis, T. J. Pempel, Steven Smith, and Jim Thurber. I am also grateful to the graduate students in my seminar on scope and methods and in my American politics core seminar at the University of Colorado. This essay is dedicated to the memory of my mother, Louise Pierce Dodd, whose encouragement and example instilled in me a belief in the transformational capacities of the human spirit.

1 Eulau (1967); Hempel (1966); Holt and Richardson (1970); Riker (1977, 1982a).
2 Huntington (1981); Alford and Friedland (1985); Seidelman and Harpham (1985).
3 Von Wright (1971); Almond (1990).
4 Mayr (1984); Gould (1989).
5 Erikson (1964).
6 Fay (1975); Winch (1958); Habermas (1973).
7 Huntington (1981); Olson (1982).
8 Fiorina (1977b); Mayhew (1974b); Riker (1977); Riker (1982a). See also Dodd (1977).
9 Simon (1985).
10 Weir, Orloff, and Skocpol, eds., 1988); Inglehart (1989); Mayhew (1986); Sundquist (1981); Skowronek (1982).
11 Lasswell (1970); Brunner (1989).
12 Jung, (1963); Lerner (1986); Kuhn (1970).
13 Bateson (1972).
14 Festinger (1957); Huntington (1981).
15 Bateson (1972): esp. 309–337.
16 Ibid., 469–487.
17 Anderson (1983).
18 Bateson (1972: 469–505); Leslie Anderson (1994).
19 Thus, for example, Bateson argues that the Versailles treaty at the end of World War I, while momentarily empowering France and Britain, was unnecessarily vindictive toward Germany. It engendered pathological conflict within Germany and between Germany and the Western allies that gave rise to Hitler and World War II. In many ways the European world is still involved in experimentation and reconstruction efforts designed to redress the pathologies of the epistemological world view that dominated Versailles.
20 Schlesinger (1986); Dodd (1986b); Rockman (1984); Moe (1985); Key (1955); Burnham (1970); Sundquist (1973); Clubb, Flanigan, and Zingale (1980); Barber (1980); Skowronek (1982).
21 Osborne (1988).
22 Erikson (1970).
23 Jung (1963); Edelman (1985); Reich (1990); Weber (1976).
24 Huntington (1974); Dodd (1981).
25 See also Burns (1963); Dahl (1981); Greenberg (1985); Huntington (1981); Lowi (1979);
26 Riker (1982a).
27 Kennedy (1987).
28 Lasswell (1950).
29 Hill (1988).
30 Stimson (1991); Sundquist (1981); Carmines and Stimson (1986a, 1986b); Skowronek (1984).
31 Neustadt (1960).
32 Barber (1985).
33 Ellsberg (1971).

34 Among the most influential were Myrdal (1944, 1962); Carson (1962); Harrington (1962); and Ward (1966).
35 Thurow (1980).
36 Polsby (1982: 551–570); Harris and Milkis (1987); Smith (1985).
37 Jones (1988).
38 Jacobson (1989); Sorauf (1988).
39 The Keating Five are Republican senator John McCain of Arizona and Democratic senators Alan Cranston of California, Dennis DeConcini of Arizona, John Glenn of Ohio, and Donald W. Riegle, Jr., of Michigan, who reportedly intervened with regulators on behalf of the Lincoln Savings and Loan in early 1987. The five senators received $1.3 million from Charles H. Keating, Jr., and his associates for their reelection campaigns or political organizations with which they were affiliated.
40 Neustadt and May (1986).
41 Weber (1958).

Additional Perspective on "A Transformational Perspective"

"Congress, the Presidency, and the American Experience: A Transformational Perspective" highlights the constantly evolving nature of the social world and the challenge social change poses to governing institutions such as Congress. As new and novel societal conditions continually emerge at home and on the international scene, the nation's citizens and their elected representatives face personal and collective challenges distinctly different from the past. An institution created to address policy challenges in a previous era must address new conditions beyond the imaging of earlier generations. How does it do so? How do the citizens and legislators of a newly emerging era come to recognize the contours of ongoing societal change and grasp the dilemmas associated with them? How does institutional politics adapt in ways appropriate to resolving the pressing dilemmas? And what do these vital questions mean for how students of Congress proceed in studying it?

"A Transformational Perspective" puts these issues front and center for the author and other students of Congress to grapple with and resolve. It asserts that social change and institutional response are not issues to be subsumed by analysts under that broad rubric of *ceteris paribus*, as they craft their models of Congress and test their empirical applicability. Instead, the continuous character of social change, and the need for Congress to adapt to it in effective ways, are central and even defining tenets of the governing purpose of Congress. Theories of its institutional politics thus must directly recognize and address the challenge that change and adaptation pose for it. This chapter seeks to embrace this challenge by presenting a theoretical perspective on the relationship between social change and congressional adaptation built around a social-psychological variant on rational-choice theory.

The social-psychological theory of change presented here argues that social and political actors are engaged in an ongoing process of metarational learning whereby they craft, pursue and recraft their understanding of society and politics. Just as actors engage in short-term forms of rational action to pursue immediate priorities and goals, within a particular understanding of social and political reality, they also engage in longer-term forms of metarational action through which they alter their social understanding, priorities and goal-oriented behavior in light of changing societal conditions. The decision to reassess understanding and reshape priorities comes as citizens and legislators confront festering problems and social crises that demonstrate the inefficacy of existing world views. As a sense of personal and group powerless mounts, they undertake a search for a new understanding of society and politics, thereby transforming their approach to social relations and political action.

The need for actors within the legislative sphere to comprehend new and emerging conditions of society and politics puts a premium on their sensitive capacity to accurately see and interpret the changing nature of social reality.

Those more adept at such sensitive and accurate interpretation will likely embrace substantive understandings and political strategies that empower them as effective participants in legislative politics. In the process they will create new and ameliorative forms of policy agendas and institutional politics more appropriate than past ones to the emerging societal context. As they do so, they renew the promise, power and legitimacy of Congress. Those less adept will more likely fail in these endeavors, perhaps after critical and perhaps sustained periods of resistance to change, and fade in political relevance. And insofar as no group succeeds in these endeavors, the legitimacy, authority and fate of Congress is put at great risk.

Given this prospect, a science of legislative politics must constantly subject itself to renewal in its interpretation and understanding of Congress. In this effort, students of Congress must remain attentive to the prospect that participants within the legislative sphere can fail in efforts at social learning and adaptation, endangerng the survival of representative government, as well as succeed, aiding its adaptation and the nation's rejunevation.

Yet the task of congressional scholars is not simply to recognize and assess the appropriateness of new forms of congressional politics, but (1) to explain how new and ameliorative forms of politics emerge, (2) to identify the factors that aid or hinder the rise of effective forms of action, and (3) to assess how shifts in such ancillary factors may affect the future prospects of adaptive change by Congress. In this effort, they must work to understand whether and how the workaday politics of Congress, and the cycles of institutional change such politics generates, serve to foster and/or hinder its effective metarational response to societal change.

This chapter opens rather than closes the analysis of Congress and social change. The remaining chapters of the book attempt to illustrate the nature, difficulty, and process of effective congressional response to ongoing change, and explore how best to study such processes.

Foundation Work: The development of the perspective presented here benefited, in deep background, from Karl Deutsch's pionerring exploration of the role of information, communication and learning in politics, *The Nerves of Government* (1963), which the author read in the spring of 1969. As he grappled during the mid- to late 1980s with the role of ideas and learning in congressional change and returned to *The Nerves of Government*, he not only benefited again from Deutsch's stimulating perspective, but also discovered the work of Gregory Bateson, an anthropologist and psychologist. Deutsch's discussion of Bateson's seminal 1947 essay on "Deutero-Learning" (or the way in which individuals and organizations 'learn to learn') caught the author's attention (see Deutsch, 1963: 169–171), and he began to delve deeply into Bateson's theoretical work on social change. He found therein a compelling perspective on change that "rang true."

Increasingly considered "one of the great seminal thinkers of the twentieth century," for reasons detailed by Harries-Jones (1995: 14), Bateson has provided the primary lens through which the author has approached the nature and role of learning in congressional politics. The work on which this chapter relies most extensively, and the most famous of Bateson's essays on learning, is "The Cybernetics of 'Self'," (1971: 1–18); it is also reprinted in Gregory Bateson, *Steps to an Ecology of Mind: Collected Essays in Anthropology, Psychiatry, Evolution and Epistemology* (1972: 309–337). The early 1947 essay on "learning to learn" is entitled "Social Planning and the Concept of 'Deutero-Learning'," and it is also reprinted in *Steps* (1972: 159–176).

For the author's discussion of the relevance of Bateson's concept of deutero-learning to the study of the careers of U. S. Senators, see Dodd (1992), "Learning to Learn: The Political Mastery of U. S. Senators." This essay focuses on the way in which those senators who "learn to learn" from past difficulties, as described in the Senate narratives of Richard F. Fenno, Jr. (Fenno, 1989a, 1990, 1991a, 1991b, 1992), can adapt better to the shifting currents of Senate careers than do those senators whose careers give little or no evidence of such deutero-learning.

Suggested Reading: Works that speak to, build on, test, or assess arguments introduced in "A Transformational Perspective" include Hugh Heclo, "Ideas, Institutions and Interests" (1994); Sean Q. Kelly, "Punctuated Change and the Era of Divided Government"(1994); Michael Berkman, *The State Roots of National Politics: Congress and the Tax Agenda, 1978–1986* (1994); Theodore J. Lowi, *The End of the Republican Era* (1995); Fiorina, *Divided Government*, Second Edition (1995a: 176); Douglas L. Koopman, *Hostile Takeover: The House Republican Party, 1980–1995* (1996); Bryan D. Jones, Frank R. Baumgartner, and James L. True, "Policy Punctuations: US Budget Authority, 1947–95" (1998: 1–30); Bryan D. Jones and Frank R. Baumgartner, *The Politics of Attention* (2005); Bryan D. Jones and Walter Williams, *The Politics of Bad Ideas* (2008); and Catherine Rudder, "Transforming American Politics through Tax Policy" (2009).

For an elaboration of the arguments presented in this chapter and their use as a theoretical lens for studying American politics more broadly, see Dodd, "Political Learning and Political Change: Understanding Development Across Time" (1994).

Classroom Use: "A Transformational Perspective" can be used in the classroom in sections as an ideational explanation of patterns of congressional change; as a lens through which to study the contemporary Congress in ways attentive to the role of ideas and societal change; as a way to understand and explain the evolution and shift in issues and agenda politics in the Congress, attentive to their appropriateness to new social conditions; and as a perspective on the social and political upheavals in American politics during the 1960s and 1970s.

A useful scholarly and classroom exercise would be to pair "A Transformational Perspective" with Samuel Huntington's 1981 work, *American Politics: The Promise of Disharmony*, highlighting the complementary and contrasting ways in which they approach the role of ideas and citizen beliefs in politics, and particularly their interpretation of the 1960s and 1970s. Another useful exercise would be to compare the conception of agenda reconstruction presented in "A Transformational Perspective" with the model of issue evolution and agenda change presented by William Riker in *Liberalism Against Populism* (1982a), particularly Chapters Eight and Nine.

8

CONGRESS AND THE POLITICS OF RENEWAL

Redressing the Crisis of Legitimation

1993

"Congress and the Politics of Renewal" examines Congress during the early 1990s and assesses its capacity to embrace a new "logic of politics" appropriate to a postindustrial society. Published twelve years after "Congress, the Constitution, and the Crisis of Legitimation" (Chapter Three), which foresaw an emerging crisis in congressional legitimacy, this chapter depicts a Congress sinking deeper into such a crisis, carrying American state legislatures with it.

The most critical problem facing American legislatures, the essay argues, is finding new ways of envisioning and administering government programs designed to address the nation's growing societal problems within its limited fiscal resources. It proposes experimentation with new forms of private/public cooperation in delivering collective services. Yet the ability of Congress and state legislatures to do so is inhibited by difficulties in their representative and deliberative capacities that emerged during the industrial era.

The essay highlights steps the 'Democratic' 103rd Congress could take to improve representative deliberation of pressing policy concerns, such as creating a joint House/Senate emergency committee. Attention to critical policy problems could also be aided should public debate over government restructuring revitalize the Republican party, generating a more competitive congressional party system. Lacking such developments, the essay foresaw heightened public disenchantment with Congress, increased fury against powerful incumbents, and a crippling of representative government in America, as illustrated by California state politics.

Long-term emasculation of representative government could come through constitutional changes designed to weaken and constrain Congress and state legislatures further. Renewal of representative government could occur through shifts in conceptions of governance and through constitutional revisions designed to strengthen state and national legislatures.

Lawrence C. Dodd. "Congress and the Politics of Renewal: Redressing the Crisis of Legitimation." In Congress Reconsidered, 5th Edition. Edited by Lawrence C. Dodd and Bruce I. Oppenheimer. Washington, D.C.: CQ Press. 1993, pp. 417–446.

For two hundred years Congress has served as the touchstone of American democracy. Always a very human institution, Congress has reflected citizens' base aspirations as well as their noble ones, their calculating natures as well as their capacities for mutual regard. Yet the strength of the nation's democracy ultimately has derived from Congress's ability to identify the common concerns and shared interests of the citizenry amidst the disparate claims for personal advantage and thereby to discover shared principles for collective governance. The discovery of new collective principles of governance has allowed the nation to address the extraordinary challenges that two centuries of societal change have posed: from the struggle over slavery to the rise of industrialization to the coming of global depression and world war. The search for new and broadly acceptable governing principles has enabled Congress to maintain the support of the people and to sustain a sense of governing legitimacy, even in the midst of crises that its shortsighted policies helped induce.[1]

Today the nation faces a new set of governing challenges, posed by the coming of a postindustrial world of expanding service demands and limited resources, and it looks to Congress to chart a new course of common action.[2] Again the public sees a very human institution caught in the clash of opposing interests and shortsighted commitments. Yet as the nation enters its third century, there is another dimension to its governing concerns: a growing apprehension about the capacity of Congress to acknowledge and address the policy dilemmas of the contemporary era.

The public sees a Congress floundering in a policy deadlock unprecedented in modern times. This immobilism is symbolized by the quadrupling of the national debt to four trillion dollars in twelve years and by the emergence of our country as one of the world's largest debtor nations. The immobilism is felt daily in the homelessness, joblessness, or underemployment of much of our citizenry and in the soaring costs of health care that affect us all. It is experienced, most fundamentally, in the absence of the sense of shared community and national purpose that a vibrant legislature would provide. In the face of policy disarray and a lost sense of common identity the public's disillusionment with the government, particularly with Congress, is mounting.[3] For the first time in American history serious efforts to limit the budgetary power of Congress and to impose term limits on its members have received widespread popular support. In the past two elections incumbent reelection margins have fallen after a sustained period of steady increase. And opinion polls report that only 16 percent of the public approve of the job Congress is doing; 69 percent disapprove.[4]

Political analysts generally attribute the nation's disarray and the public's disillusionment with Congress to the divided party government of the Reagan-Bush years; they expect greater policy activism with the coming of united government under President Bill Clinton and a Democratic Congress.[5] I agree that party government matters in American politics. The coming of united party government almost certainly will generate expanded political activism in Washington and on

Capitol Hill. I doubt, however, that united party government alone will reverse the long-term policy drift and institutional crisis engulfing contemporary American politics. The policy immobilism of the modern era and the public's disaffection with Congress have much deeper roots than divided party government.[6]

The source of policy immobilism in American politics, I suggest, lies embedded in the character of contemporary legislative politics. More so than at any other time in the nation's history, Congress is elected and organized to serve the disparate elements of a self-interested public rather than to identify and foster the shared concerns of a public-spirited citizenry. Congress increasingly lacks the ability to recognize the mutual concerns and shared interests of the public and the ability to discover new governing principles that could resolve our policy dilemmas and renew public faith in government. This magnified politics of self-interest came to predominance with the creation of the service state during the advanced industrialism of the twentieth century. In its wake has come a Congress bereft of its representative and deliberative capacities and virtually unable to acknowledge or address the new governing demands of a postindustrial society.

With Congress immobilized and the nation adrift, the public necessarily must doubt the legitimacy of Congress as a policy-making institution and the legitimacy of its members as true representatives of the public interest. This crisis of congressional legitimation, moreover, will fester regardless of united or divided party government as long as it is left unaddressed. Policy change and institutional reform, aided by united party government, together can redress the erosion in representative and deliberative government that gives rise to the crisis of legitimation. With a revitalization of Congress can come a renewed spirit of shared purpose and national community. But first the nation must recognize the deep-seated character of our policy immobilism and the consequent severity of the legitimation crisis that Congress faces.

I first developed this argument in the late 1970s, just before the first election of Ronald Reagan.[7] Writing now in the days immediately following the election of Bill Clinton, as the nation embraces united party government, let me reaffirm and expand the original legitimation thesis and consider its implications for political action.

I

The legitimation thesis rests on a simple assumption: to sustain the long-term support of the public, Congress and its members must demonstrate a reasonable capacity to recognize the fundamental problems of a historical era, deliberate over the proper solutions to these problems, and enact legislation that addresses them in a credible manner.[8] The public does not expect miracles from Congress: people understand that policy solutions will have drawbacks, trade-offs, and unforeseen consequences so that there are limits to what Congress can accomplish. Likewise, the public is aware that Congress alone does not control public policy, that its handiwork may be undercut by a hostile president or a recalcitrant Court. But the public does look to Congress to grapple with the serious issues of the day and to fashion reasonable strategies for addressing them. Insofar as Congress approximates these baseline goals, citizens will give it broad latitude in its policy processes and solid support as a governing institution.[9]

Throughout most of American history, Congress has been "good enough" at problem-solving that it has sustained public belief in its legitimate role in national policy making. Historically, there have been no concerted attacks by the public on its fundamental constitutional powers or decision-making authority. This is not to say that congressional authority has not been seriously tested. The growth of executive power has challenged congressional dominance of policy making, particularly in foreign affairs and budgetary policy, and judicial activism at times has encroached on its domestic policy prerogatives. But through most of American history Congress has been seen as a valuable and legitimate participant in national policy making. More often than not citizens, scholars, journalists, and politicians have considered how to protect and increase the power of Congress in the face of executive imperialism or judicial incursions.[10]

Public support for Congress has derived from two attributes of the institution that citizens value intrinsically and that together allow it to address policy problems in credible ways.[11] First, however imperfectly, Congress has served as our nation's primary *representative* institution—as the central decision-making body whose membership is selected by the enfranchised citizens of a historical era and which reflects in some reasonable manner the citizens' disparate sentiments on the major policy issues of the day. The representative nature of Congress has meant that citizens would have spokespersons in Washington who reflected their broad policy concerns and could speak for them in government. In touch with the central issues preoccupying the citizens, the government could stay abreast of emerging societal problems and reflect the broad range of citizens' concerns about those problems. Moreover, the representative character of Congress, its attentiveness to a broad range of popular sentiment on issues, has lent a special authority to its policy solutions.[12] Policy failures generally have been seen as resulting from an insufficiently inclusive representation of citizens and thereby from a failure to recognize fully the severity of policy problems or the range of policy concerns in society. The most popular reform of Congress thus has been the expansion of voting rights, first to all white males, then to northern blacks, then to women, then to the young, and finally to racial and ethnic minorities.

Second, Congress has served as the nation's primary *deliberative* body—the only institution that addresses national policy questions through open debate and collective policy choice. The deliberative character of Congress has meant that, when faced with severe national problems, citizens could look to Congress to clarify the problems and devise broadly acceptable solutions. Much of the internal history of Congress has been a search to find rules and norms that facilitate deliberative problem-solving. Success in this endeavor has been limited at best.[13]

In creating rules that allow for virtually unlimited debate, the Senate created the opportunity for filibusters, which can make a mockery of efforts at deliberation. The House, in seeking to find mechanisms for regulating debate, created a Rules Committee, which often merely forecloses debate on controversial issues.[14] Nevertheless, throughout most of American history, the House and Senate succeeded well enough in devising workable rules and norms that Congress eventually could address critical policy problems, seek to reconcile the conflicting policy views of a disparate citizenry, and enact credible legislation.

Because Congress has demonstrated a reasonable capacity to act—and to act in a way that reflected both representative and deliberative problem-solving—the public has supported it even in the midst of severe crises. In the first half of the nineteenth century, for example, as westward expansion and regional conflicts raised the issue of slavery to the forefront of national consciousness, it was Congress that reflected the diverse regional concerns of the enfranchised public, debated the moral and political issues, and fashioned the great compromises of the era. Ultimately, congressional efforts at forging compromises over the expansion of slavery failed, in some real degree because the Supreme Court intervened with the *Dred Scott* decision and poisoned the atmosphere of deliberation on Capitol Hill. The issue of slavery thus was decided on the battlefields of the Civil War. Yet the coming of the war did not lead to a loss of faith in legislative decision making but to widespread doubts about the Supreme Court (as a result of the *Dred Scott* decision), the presidency (as a result of tepid leadership before the war), and state government (as a result of the southern secession). Congress emerged from the war with its legitimacy intact and even strengthened. It also won greater legislative powers as a result of the Thirteenth, Fourteenth, and Fifteenth amendments.[15]

During the late nineteenth century, faced with the corporate corruption and collusion associated with rapid industrialization, Congress again became the center of national policy making. At issue was the national government's ability to regulate the worst abuses associated with early industrialization, including corporate trusts, child labor, environmental degradation, and consumer exploitation. Tackling these problems ultimately required that the reformers of the Progressive era attack the power of party bosses, implement extensive new election procedures, and decentralize power within Congress. From these and related efforts came an activist bureaucracy focused on regulating corporate power. Congressional efforts to regulate business had many inadequacies, including the continued and unrestrained power of the stock exchanges, so the end results were mixed. But Congress addressed the general issues of early industrialism and acted in ways that the American public found sufficient for the times. It was not Congress that the public found wanting but the political parties. Congress emerged from the reform era by the 1920s with its power enhanced by the Sixteenth Amendment, which legalized the income tax, and with its representational base expanded through the granting of woman suffrage and the move to an elective Senate.[16]

Finally, with the coming of the Great Depression, Congress confronted the vital issue of ensuring economic stability and individual security during the advanced stages of industrialization. The strategy of choice among industrial nations was to create an extensive government bureaucracy to deliver needed social services and manage the economy. Facing the crisis of the depression and then a world war, Congress embraced bureaucratic service delivery and institutionalized the foundations of the modern service state through a wide range of programs—from farm price supports to Social Security to the Tennessee Valley Authority. Then, with the advent of World War II and the Cold War it embraced a huge military-industrial complex that provided the nation with an economic and research backbone while sustaining a widespread military commitment throughout much of Europe and Asia. Again the congressional response to the central domestic problems of the period had many limitations, including inadequate protection for ethnic and racial minorities. Furthermore, with the waning of the depression Congress became more divided about its general commitment to social programs. But it acknowledged and responded to the depression and did so earlier than the president or the Supreme Court; the election of Franklin Roosevelt in 1932 found a Congress that had already drafted many of the basic statutes of the New Deal's first hundred days. Rather than Congress being seen as the obstacle to change, that stigma fell first to President Herbert Hoover and then to a conservative Court. Out of the Great Depression and World War II, in fact, came not a call for a weakened Congress but for a stronger institution, with larger staffs and more resources, that would be able to restrain the expanding executive branch and oversee the service state. Congress also was given expanded constitutional authority, this time not through constitutional amendments but through the Supreme Court's reinterpretation of the Constitution's interstate commerce clause strengthening the regulatory authority of the legislative branch.[17]

As this brief history suggests, throughout American history Congress has sustained its public support in the face of extraordinary societal crises. In each instance, the nation relegitimated Congress through widespread popular acceptance of constitutional amendments and Supreme Court decisions that expanded its policy-making authority in ways appropriate to the distinctive policy demands of the era. The nation did so, moreover, not because Congress had performed in exemplary ways or even because it had solved the problems of an era. In each era Congress's performance included serious inadequacies and in the mid-nineteenth century proved insufficient to divert the nation from a devastating civil war. But Congress did well enough in its distinctive problem-solving efforts during each era to sustain the support of the public and emerge from each crisis with its formal power increased and its policy-making legitimacy renewed.

Why, then, the disrepute of the contemporary Congress? If Congress could survive a civil war, the coming of industrialization, a global depression, and a world war with its legitimacy intact, why after two hundred years of such resilience has the public begun to forsake it?[18] Instead of calls to expand the power of

Congress to control public policy, there are serious efforts to limit its taxing and spending power by imposing a constitutional amendment requiring a balanced budget. Instead of efforts to increase the institutional resources of its members or to ensure adequate pay, we see attempts to oppose salary increases and to strip away perquisites. Instead of efforts to expand the capacity of citizens to select the representatives they prefer, we find initiative passed now in fifteen states to limit legislators' terms and thereby to limit citizens' choice of representation. Why?

The answer could lie in the unique severity, perhaps even the insolubility, of postindustrial problems. After all, the technological revolutions of postindustrialism are producing a historic shift away from widespread public employment in industrial production and toward a reliance on a knowledge-based economy geared toward scientific innovations, information processing, and systems management. This shift is producing a cruel paradox. The technological advances of postindustrialism are increasing the quality of life to which citizens can aspire, with extraordinary improvements possible in health and longevity, education and self-development, and communication and transportation. Yet these same innovations reduce reliance on a large blue-collar work force involved in industrial production, thus leaving a large class of citizens bereft of the job security, union contracts, and purchasing power that would allow them access to that expanded quality of life. At the same time citizens must cope with the severe social and ecological costs produced by advanced industrialism, including urban decay and violence, the breakdown of the extended (and now the nuclear) family, and the threat to the world's ecological system.[19]

Furthermore, postindustrialism forces the nation to confront severe collective policy problems at a time when the fiscal resources of the nation-state are increasingly limited.[20] On the one hand, because there is fairly broad agreement that a free market economy alone will not redress these collective difficulties, the nation must respond to economic, social, and ecological challenges of postindustrialism through government action. Yet insofar as the government does intervene, the primary strategy that it inherits from the industrial era is reliance on direct bureaucratic provision of necessary services, whether they be jobs, health care benefits, or environmental cleanup. A reliance on bureaucracy, which brings with it management inefficiencies and patronage pressures, magnifies the costs of service delivery immeasurably. Expanding government service delivery in response to postindustrialism thus will greatly increase the fiscal pressures on a service state already burdened by the service programs of the industrial era. It will do so, moreover, at a time when the nation's fiscal resources are increasingly limited because of the depletion of its natural resources, the growing expense of foreign resources, the economic competition from Japan and Europe, and the dislocation costs of the postindustrial transition within the economy.

Perhaps the fiscal limits of the state are so severe that it is impossible for Congress to redress the collective policy problems of postindustrialism. From this perspective, Congress is simply the unwitting victim of the public's growing fury over the inevitability of societal decay and governmental breakdown. As the fury mounts, the public turns against government, particularly against the policy-making institution citizens have most consistently trusted throughout American history. Perhaps representative and deliberative government will simply collapse in the face of an insolvable policy dilemma: expanding collective problems amidst declining fiscal resources.

In truth, the policy problems of postindustrialism are almost certainly not as insolvable as they appear. It is possible, for example, that postindustrial innovations in communications will build cultural awareness and linkages across nation-states and foster the spread of democratic principles in ways that could reduce international military tensions. Reductions in global tensions (seen in the end of the Cold War) then could release the nation from devoting such an extraordinary portion of its national budget to defense spending. Likewise, the economic productivity and quality of life made possible by the technological innovations and knowledge revolution of postindustrialism could create an expanded international demand for high-tech goods and services (particularly for scientific innovations); the resulting employment in scientific and service industries could provide the public with quality jobs, sustain the growth of the nation's economy, and secure resources for the state. Finally, it might be possible for government to move away from reliance on bureaucracy and create cost-effective strategies for ensuring service delivery. Over the past decade, for example, various state and local governments have experimented successfully with the managed use of market competition among private companies and public institutions to ensure collective benefits (city sanitation, economic redevelopment, elementary and secondary education, environmental cleanup) normally considered the primary responsibility of government. Governments, for example, could provide families with vouchers to send children to schools of their choice, thereby bringing competitive pressures on schools to improve their performance and hold down costs. Such experiments have produced collective services with less expense and more efficiency while maintaining or even improving upon levels of quality.[21]

In essence, fundamental restructuring of the national government in ways that could resolve the policy dilemmas of postindustrialism is possible. This restructuring would involve a downsizing of the military-industrial complex, a lessening of the nation's dependence on military spending to sustain the economy, and the freeing of defense funds to be used in programs that help induce a competitive economy and competitive service delivery. It would provide support for educational retraining and high-tech research to help make the nation more competitive in the new global economy. Most critically, government restructuring would shift state activism away from government bureaucracy toward managed competition in the delivery of expanded services. We can refer to this restructured government as an entrepreneurial state—that is, a government that acknowledges its responsibility to address that nation's critical collective problems but seeks to do so by creating incentive structures that encourage publicly managed competition among private as well as public service delivery institutions. The broad goal of the entrepreneurial state would be to ensure the collective goods that a postindustrial society requires without undue dependence on direct government provision of services. The entrepreneurial state would seek to make the problems of postindustrialism manageable and to make possible the vast human opportunities that it offers.[22]

The possibilities afforded by the development of an entrepreneurial state make it difficult to argue that the policy dilemmas of postindustrialism are more severe than those posed by slavery in the early nineteenth century, by the corporate abuses of early industrialization, or by the economic dislocations of advanced industrialism. Each of these policy challenges had a viable solution: the creation of a strong national state to protect each citizen's equal right as a free laborer, the movement to a regulatory state to manage the abuses of laissez faire capitalism, the implementation of a service state to provide for the economic and social security of individuals caught in the economic dislocations of advanced industrialism. So too, it appears, do the policy challenges of postindustrialism: the creation of an entrepreneurial state to ensure the service needs of society while respecting its fiscal limits.[23] The public's disaffection with Congress thus does not appear to result from the inherent insolubility of the policy problems that it faces.

Again I ask: why the growing public disaffection with the contemporary Congress? Why now the moves to restrict its policy-making authority and punish its members collectively through the imposition of term limits? Why now forsake the one governing institution that most empowers the citizenry?

II

The public questions the legitimacy of Congress as a policy-making institution, I suggest, not because it doubts that postindustrial problems can be solved but because it doubts the problem-solving capacities of the contemporary Congress. This perception is an increasingly accurate assessment.

The problem-solving capacities of the modern Congress *are* eroding. Historically, Congress has recognized and addressed the central policy problems of the day, and thereby has sustained its popular support, through reasonably faithful representation and deliberative consideration of the public's general policy concerns. As long as Congress reflected the major policy issues troubling the public and sought to reconcile disagreement through reasoned discussion, the public could forgive the institution's shortcomings and support its continued policy-making power. But what the citizens cannot forgive is a breakdown in the representative and deliberative consideration of their general policy concerns; when that happens the institution loses touch with the people's real-life problems and with the real-life issues that a solution to their problems must address. Yet this is precisely what has happened in contemporary America.

Both the representativeness and the deliberativeness of the modern Congress are in decline. This decline, moreover, is particularly difficult to recognize and address. It is difficult to recognize because it is occurring despite objective appearances suggesting that Congress is doing better rather than worse as a representative and deliberative institution. It is difficult to address because it results from deeply ingrained alterations in the electoral and organizational politics of Congress that occurred during the industrial era and that impede institutional reform and government restructuring. Yet the demonstrable results are a Congress increasingly out of touch with the nation's critical policy problems.

Consider first the changes that are occurring in Congress as a representative institution.[24] When most of us think of political representation, we consider how easy it is for diverse groups in society to gain entrée to our governing institutions; we think about how inclusive an institution is. In terms of inclusiveness the modern Congress is certainly more representative than it was in the past and probably is the most representative institution in American government of the past two centuries. Today the right of all groups in society to vote in congressional elections is essentially assured, and virtually all major ethnic, gender, and class groups in society have at least some presence (if not leadership positions) in Congress. If inclusiveness alone were sufficient to ensure representative problem-solving by Congress, the modern Congress, with its record number of women and minorities, should be the most representative in American history. As such, it should be a widely supported, legitimate, and effective participant in policy making. There is, however, another critical dimension to representation.

To serve as an effective representative of the public, not only must Congress ensure that its members reflect the group diversity of society, but it must ensure that its members speak for a diverse public on the major policy issues of the day. In other words, to be an effective representative institution, Congress must ensure a broadly focused, issue-oriented representation. Insofar as a diverse range of voters can select legislators who are sensitive to their broad issue concerns, Congress can stay attuned to new problems as they arise in society, reflect the intense views of citizens on these problems, and have some chance of finding commonly accepted policy solutions. By contrast, if the voters are constrained in their ability to select legislators based on broad issue concerns, Congress is likely to overlook emerging societal problems and lose its distinctive capacities as a representative problem-solving institution.

The modern Congress's dilemma is that during the industrial era the selection of legislators came to focus not on the broad issue positions of candidates but on their capacity to deliver particular service benefits to constituents.[25] With the coming of the modern service state, we have had a shift away from broadly focused issue representation and toward narrowly focused interest representation. With this shift, legislators have come to build broadly inclusive electoral coalitions within their districts by servicing the particularized interests of all constitutent groups—farmers, bankers, union members, students, the elderly, and so forth. Although such groups may disagree on the broad issues of the day, and would support opposing candidates in an issue-oriented campaign, they agree on the importance of maintaining in office an incumbent who has the power to serve their immediate individual and group interests. Incumbents thus win reelection by large and secure margins, as John Alford and David Brady demonstrate,[26] while their constituents receive the assistance with their service needs that an experienced and powerful incumbent can provide. Such assistance can include the improved processing of Social Security checks and veterans' benefits, intervention with regulatory agencies on behalf of farm price supports or savings and loan negotiations, the building of a local post office or dam, and the awarding of government grants for scientific research and the enactment of defense contracts critical to a local economy.

Over the long run, however, both incumbents and citizens can become so dependent on the politics of service delivery that they overlook the emerging policy problems of a new era. The voters may see the decay of urban infrastructures, sense the declining educational and job opportunities of their children, acknowledge the ecological damage of industrial pollution, and worry about the long-term effects of a mounting deficit. But as they consider their vote for senator and representative, the citizens override any broad concerns they may have with collective issues and vote in accord with ensuring immediate benefits; they do so by voting for the powerful local incumbent who can assist with a desired local defense contract or who can help them with their veterans claims or Medicare benefits. They do so because of the immediate influence that a powerful incumbent legislator can have on their particularized interests. Likewise, the legislators may share a growing concern with collective societal and economic reversals. But their efforts to maintain electoral security and exercise personal influence in Congress are best served by focusing on those particularized programs that mobilize group support, that help them build a solid reputation as effective legislators, and that ensure reelection. The emerging collective problems of the new era thus go unacknowledged and tear away at the fabric of society.

Even when mounting societal problems become so severe that they can no longer be ignored, the politics of the service state can continue to hamstring Congress. Even as societal crises confront the voters with the possibility of serious life reversals, the electorate may demand increased attention to particularized social and economic programs that shield them against personal misfortune. And politicians, faced with rising public discontent, may well increase their emphasis on the strategies of interest representation that shore up their electoral base. Neither the citizens nor the politicians may easily end their obsession with particularized interests and focus on collective issues, such as urban decay, the decline in the nation's economic productivity, environmental pollution, and the deficit. Only with the creation of a "new logic of politics" that helps participants find ways to foster their collective good without unduly harming particularized interests are they likely to face these general issues.[27] The creation of a new and shared logic of collective action generally must come through a process of political deliberation.

Yet, as with political representation, the politics of the industrial era crippled the congressional capacity for deliberation.

Consider the effect of the service state on Congress as a deliberative institution.[28] Most of us think of political deliberation in fairly simple terms. In particular, we tend to think that deliberative policy making occurs when legislators vote on policy decisions after a formal discussion of policy alternatives. If policy discussion and formal votes are our measure of political deliberation, the modern Congress is a deliberative institution par excellence. The modern Congress has created innumerable opportunities for its members to speak about policy matters in committees and subcommittees and on the floor of the House and Senate, with much of their discussion televised; in addition, the right of legislators to initiate formal votes on their bills and amendments is heavily protected in both houses and across subcommittees, committees, and floor action. Judged solely in terms of discussion and formal votes, the modern Congress probably would be the most deliberative in history and, again, should enjoy strong support from the public. Like political representation, however, political deliberation is a complex phenomenon.

To be a truly deliberative institution, Congress must not only ensure debates and votes on policy questions, but it also must facilitate the reasoned search for broadly understood and acceptable policy solutions. The primary emphasis in a deliberative body is not on debate per se, or on majoritarian imposition of policy solutions, but on a dialogue among participants that seeks to find principled agreement on how best to address policy problems. In other words, deliberation is not primarily a strategic game of calculation and maneuvering among supporters of mutually exclusive policy positions, each seeking to impose a preferred policy solution on the other—though such moments may come in the heat of political conflict. Rather, deliberation is a process of learning and discovery in which legislators of vastly different backgrounds and perspectives share concerns about common policy problems and design collective solutions based on principles that virtually all participants can accept.[29] The resulting policies then seek to resolve as many of the separate concerns of participants as possible.

Such deliberative efforts require a broad conversation among all relevant participants; they also require rules and norms that facilitate the collective crafting of commonly acceptable principles of policy action. From such broad conversations and collective choice, it is hoped, will come a clarification of common concerns and principles of action that none of the participants may originally have seen; with such clarification then may come the discovery—the learning—of new and viable policy approaches that virtually all participants can embrace. A deliberative discussion of the problems of postindustrialism might start, for example, with a sense of unreasolvable conflict between the service demands of society and the fiscal limits of the state. Rather than revolving around strategic debates and votes designed to force members to choose between services and fiscal restraint, however, a deliberative process would involve shared acknowledgement of the need for both and a common search for new approaches to governance satisfying both criteria. Participants then might discover the principles of state entrepreneurship. In the process they could create a new collective logic of politics that would influence their specific consideration of a range of policy issues.

Unfortunately, seen not just in terms of strategic debates and formal votes but as reasoned dialogue and collective choice, the deliberative capacities of the modern Congress have eroded at least as much as have its representational capacities. This erosion in deliberative capacities began in the late nineteenth and early twentieth centuries with the internal organization and procedures Congress created to guide the development and implementation of the activist state. Thus Congress expanded the fledgling committee system of the early nineteenth century as a way of marshaling and focusing specialized attention on regulatory and service delivery programs across a wide range of policy domains, from agriculture to education to banking to labor. Likewise, it created an extensive body of rules and norms to help ensure that the work of these committees could proceed in a systematic manner and that the House and Senate could debate the committee proposals in an orderly fashion. As Congress used the industrial-era committee system and policy processes to address the issues of service delivery, a subtle shift took place away from general *dialogic deliberation* over the broad agenda issues and governing principles and toward *strategic deliberation*. Congress designed committee and floor rules and procedures not to facilitate collective conversation and choice but, as the work of Douglas Arnold demonstrates, to foster instrumental manipulation of debating and voting processes in ways that would benefit the passage or defeat of particular policy preferences within a pre-established programmatic agenda.[30]

The move from dialogic to strategic deliberation was heavily shaped and reinforced by the shifting calculus of voters and politicians.[31] Citizens and interest groups wanted the particularized benefits to be derived from the service state and thus came to value members' committee work on service delivery programs and to oppose structures, such as political parties, that would interfere with committee or floor efforts on behalf of particularized interests; they also came to oppose such processes as secret votes that might limit their ability to evaluate legislators' support for major programs. For their part, the legislators, seeking long-term power in government, came to realize that advocating particularized programs in congressional committees, subcommittees, and floor debates could help their reelection and career-advancement efforts while giving them direct personal influence on policy development and agency implementation. Thus they came to support norms such as seniority, which would protect their investment in committee service, and to oppose the power of leaders, who might interfere with their pursuit of particularized interests in the committees or on the floor.

In essence, the voters and the politicians came to assume that the bureaucratic governing principles of the industrial era were a permanent commitment that would not require broad deliberation or review so that congressional attention could shift to the management and implementation of that commitment.[32] As this assumption took hold, Congress weakened the organizational structures concerned with debating and pursuing broad governing principles, such as the political parties and party leaders, and institutionalized the power of committees and subcommittees focused on specific programs. Congress limited open and inclusive debate which could address the broad problems of the nation and the general principles of governance. In its place, as the work of Richard Hall and of George Connor and Bruce Oppenheimer demonstrates, Congress came to rely on narrow specialized debate in committees and subcommittees and time-constrained debate on the House floor.[33] Finally, Congress moved away from rules, norms, and structures that would facilitate the flexible voting processes necessary for fashioning near consensual agreements (as made possible, for example, by extensive closed door meetings or by the "straw polls" that come with voice votes and unrecorded tallies). It moved toward voting arrangements that would allow the processing of a large body of programmatic decisions; that would facilitate members' strategic selection among programmatic alternatives, particularly the increase or decrease in spending commitments and revenue collection; and that would protect members' rights to express their views openly and record their votes so that constituents and lobby groups could gauge their faithfulness to programmatic promises.[34]

The consequent destruction of the structures, rules, and norms that facilitate broad-gauged deliberative dialogue produced a Congress unable to engage in a reasoned and collective consideration of emerging national problems. In other words, Congress so "adapted" its organizational structure and procedures to the strategic processing of an industrial-era agenda that it weakened or lost those institutional mechanisms necessary for a broad discussion of policy problems and governing principles.[35] Lacking such mechanisms, Congress now finds it difficult to discover a new logic of politics that would enable its members to break out of the politics of interest representation and embrace collective solutions to postindustrial policy dilemmas. The irony is that if the legislators were able to focus on such a broad-gauged discussion, they might well move toward a politics of state entrepreneurship that would make it possible to satisfy the concerns of constituents for particularized services while allowing enhanced attention to long-neglected collective problems, such as the nation's infrastructure, environment, and deficit. Such a move could both solidify public support for Congress and protect members' long-term career interests.

In terms of its representational and deliberative capacities, then, the modern Congress is less prepared to address new and general policy issues than perhaps it was at any time in its history. This development is not simply a random and transitory occurrence but is a result of Congress's response to the growth of an activist government, particularly the creation and growth of the service state during the past sixty years. With the coming of the service state, congressional representation has shifted from a broadly focused issue spokesmanship to a more narrowly focused interest servantship; likewise, congressional deliberation has shifted from broad, collegial dialogue over governing principles to a more narrow strategic choice among existing programmatic preferences within the bureaucratic governing principle created by the service state. In identifying these shifts, I do not mean to imply that the historical Congress never engaged in interest representation and strategic choice; the politics of regional interest was a major aspect of nineteenth century policy making. Nor do I suggest that the contemporary Congress never acknowledges general issues and never engages in deliberative dialogue; Congress undertook an extensive discussion of the nation's collective interests in the Persian Gulf before declaring war in 1991.[36] What I do maintain is that decisive movement has occurred in the dominant nature of representation and deliberation.

The result is a *technocratic* Congress devoted to processing incremental and particularized policy choices within the policy agenda of the service state, not a *democratic* Congress in touch with its representational and deliberative roots and capable of restructuring its governing principles and policy commitments.[37] We have a Congress that can manage, oversee, expand, and even contract the service state through strategic response to the shifting demands of interest representation. It is not, however, a Congress that can easily transform the service state through deliberative response to those broad issue concerns of citizens that might require new governing principles and state structures. Congress's disconnection from citizens' emerging issue concerns and its inability to learn new ways of governing in response to these issues has necessarily put in question its value as a problem-solving institution.

Seen from this perspective, the public's loss of faith in Congress may reflect an astute reading on the part of citizens that however well Congress manages the service state and addresses their immediate narrow interests, it is not attentive to the general issues shaping their collective well-being or their long-term future. In the first half of the nineteenth century Congress at least recognized the problems associated with slavery and deliberated their resolution in great debates. In the late nineteenth and early twentieth centuries Congress at least recognized the worst abuses of early industrialization and sought to regulate them. In the mid-twentieth century Congress at least recognized the emerging service needs of an advanced industrial nation and created a bureaucracy to address the most basic public concerns. But as the nation enters the postindustrial era of the twenty-first century, Congress seems oblivious to the limits of the service state as a viable governing approach and to the consequent need for a re-creation of government.

In the face of congressional inaction, the citizens are taking matters into their own hands. Not knowing how else to protect their pocketbooks, much less the fiscal integrity of the state, they support budgetary restraints on Congress. Not knowing how better to produce a more representative and deliberative Congress, they mandate term limits to break the collective dependence on powerful incumbents. And in the interim, faced with a growing economic crisis, they toy with massive rejection of incumbents in general, despite the costs of such rejection to their pursuit of immediate particularized interests.

The public's intervention can have counterproductive consequences that may only make matters worse. Mandatory balanced budgets could cripple the service state and the nation's economy without addressing the service needs of citizens. Term limits deprive citizens even of those seasoned legislators who may truly address the real issues of the day, while leaving lobbyists and bureaucrats as the powers in Washington. And throwing the rascals out may only replace a set of legislators who have valuable experience and knowledge, as John Hibbing demonstrates, with an inexperienced group that lack a genuine understanding of national policy processes.[38]

But what are the citizens to do? They no longer have a truly representative and deliberative Congress that is attentive to their broad issue concerns and presents them with credible solutions to the nation's policy dilemmas. They choose to send a signal—early warning shots—and hope they are heard.

III

So what is to be done? First, the nation must recognize that the crisis of legitimation is real. The public's deep disaffection with Congress is not just a momentary fad to be acknowledged in the midst of the election-year anxiety of incumbents and then ignored as a new administration and united party government make policy activism the topic of the day. Beneath the short-term fluctuations in policy activism in contemporary America is a deep-seated erosion of Congress's representational and deliberative capacities that is crippling its ability to address and resolve the collective policy dilemmas raised by postindustrialism. With the problems of postindustrialism mounting, and with Congress so clearly failing to acknowledge the broad and collective issues and deliberate their resolution, the public must increasingly lose faith in Congress no matter how much particularized legislation it debates and enacts or how diverse a range of particularized interests it reflects and serves.

If the nation can acknowledge the existence of the legitimation crisis, perhaps a strategy can be devised for addressing it. I say perhaps because it is not immediately obvious how Congress can best proceed. On the one hand, it seems that the immediate need is for Congress to become a more representative and deliberative institution in order to recognize and address the general policy issues of postindustrialism. Yet if Congress moves to reform its representative and deliberative capacities without first restructuring government, the politics of the service state almost certainly will sabotage the reform efforts. Moving first to implement entrepreneurial government, thereby fostering conditions that might yield a more deliberative and representative Congress, thus seems the best strategy. But how is Congress to design effective entrepreneurial programs without a truly representative and deliberative policy process? How can it recognize the range of public concerns that such programs need to address or fashion an entrepreneurial agenda that the public can understand and accept? Congress truly seems caught in a bind. But maybe not.

Congress could attempt simultaneously to address the critical issue of postindustrialism—the restructuring of government—and to revitalize its own representational and deliberative capacities. A variety of such strategies might be possible, but consider a direct and simple approach. Congress could acknowledge that it and the nation are in the midst of what is becoming a constitutional crisis. In response, *Congress could create an emergency joint committee on government restructuring*, co-chaired by the Speaker of the House and the majority leader of the Senate, which would meet periodically in televised evening sessions to assess and approve the viable approaches to restructuring and refinancing the service delivery strategies of the federal government.[39] The purpose of the committee would be the creative transition of the government to state entrepreneurship across policy domains and the conversion of government from the wartime programs of the Cold War to peacetime programs. The intent of the committee would be to highlight the issues of government restructuring and state entrepreneurship, thereby making them the central focus of national policy debate. The concerns of the committee would be particularly compelling to the public if such restructuring were tied to the capacity of the government to balance the budget, restimulate long-term economic productivity, and create an expanded and universal health care system.

In creating an emergency joint committee, Congress could move to modernize the nature of representative deliberation on Capitol Hill through the example of the committee itself. The committee could be composed of a small number of members able to undertake collegial discussion and yet include a diversity of members, across ethnic, gender, and ideological lines, reflecting the heterogeneous concerns of all the citizens. Second, the committee could orchestrate the televised discussion of state entrepreneurship to maximize public as well as congressional interest and to generate understanding of programmatic principles and choices. It could even embrace the opportunities opened by the 1992 presidential campaign and engage in public televised town hall meetings around the country. Third, the committee could appear once every four to six weeks in a televised "question hour" before a joint session of the House and Senate to present its findings and propose actions. Such meetings would necessarily be large and would require creative planning. But if the British House of Commons, with more than 600 members, can find ways to meet in collective session and conduct informative and engaging debates between government and opposition leaders, surely American ingenuity can find a way to bring 535 members of Congress together to engage in meaningful joint deliberation. Alternatively, or additionally, the House and Senate could each meet in full session.

This proposal would require a dramatic break with politics as usual and a bold willingness of congressional leaders to acknowledge the severity of the legitimation crisis and pursue creative and innovative solutions to resolve it. During the Civil War and Reconstruction, the greatest previous threat to representative democracy in America, Congress embraced first a Joint Committee on the

Conduct of the War and then a Joint Committee of Fifteen on Reconstruction.[40] During the Watergate crisis, perhaps the greatest modern threat to the legitimacy of the presidency as an institution, Congress authorized highly visible televised investigations into potentially criminal misconduct on the part of the president and his subordinates. It is not unthinkable for Congress to combine these strategies and create a televised joint committee to address what may be the greatest threat to Congress and representative government in the nation's history.

Less dramatic approaches are also possible. The most traditional would be for the leaders of the House and Senate to nudge members toward incremental experimentation with state entrepreneurship and toward gradualist reforms in congressional organization and procedure. With short-term improvements in the nation's economy and a lessening of the sense of national crisis, this strategy would be tempting and yet would be hard to sustain. The politics of the service state— that is, the pressures on legislators to service particularized interests and their desire to do so in order to ensure reelection and consolidate personal power—will likely undercut any such incremental and gradualist efforts outside an atmosphere of national crisis. A highly visible joint committee could dominate and shape the national debate even if the momentary atmosphere of crisis should ebb. Lacking such a highly visible strategy, congressional leaders would have to demonstrate extraordinary leadership skills to sustain incremental congressional activism on government restructuring, and they would become susceptible to cooption by the new president on behalf of strategies that might more nearly reflect the interests of executive dominance. Ideally, Congress would adopt a bold and innovative approach that would solidify its role in policy making, as illustrated by the joint committee, and then would cooperate with the new president from a position of institutional strength.

Whatever strategy Congress adopts, the strategy should be designed *to alter decisively the logic of politics that dominates American public life*. It should shift the public debate away from a focus on the nature and extent of bureaucratic service delivery, and the role of legislators in facilitating that process, and toward an emphasis on government restructuring. It should do so, moreover, through visible efforts of Congress itself that would demonstrate the value and viability of representative deliberation. Congress must demonstrate that representative and deliberative government is not the problem but the solution.

In shifting the logic of politics, Congress and its leaders would change the electoral calculus of voters and thus the political strategies of politicians. By highlighting issues of government restructuring, and the ability of legislators to play a meaningful role in such restructuring, Congress would give the voters a constructive standard by which to evaluate candidates beyond their value in servicing particularized interests. And in creating this standard, Congress would give its members a constructive platform on which to campaign and by which to explain their pursuit of collective rather than (or as well as) particularized interests. The resulting alteration in the logic of politics would not end particularized programmatic concerns or ensure the long-term predominance of collective policy solutions; bureaucratic service delivery would remain a considerable dimension of government even in an entrepreneurial state because there will remain major aspects of collective service delivery that only direct government action can ensure. But a serious congressional focus on governmental restructuring and state entrepreneurship would release such policy concerns to become the central defining and realigning issue of postindustrial politics, rather than the realigning issue being support of or hostility toward representative government.

A change in the logic of politics could set in motion constructive alterations in the government and in Congress. A major issue, for example, might be how best to ensure the effective processing of service delivery within the mix of bureaucratic and entrepreneurial programs that would emerge with government restructuring. Now the role of bureaucratic ombudsman falls primarily to Congress, with each member's office organized to process the casework complaints of constituents. Members of Congress have embraced this role with relish in order to build personal support from constituents—to ensure, as Bruce Cain, John Ferejohn, and Morris Fiorina argue, a personal vote—based not on issue compatibility but on service gratitude.[41] The personal vote then increases legislators' electoral advantage by giving a diverse range of individuals and groups reasons to vote for the incumbent and to contribute massively to campaign war chests. It also creates incentives for members to forgo meaningful reforms of the bureaucracy lest they reduce bureaucratic red tape and lose their personal vote advantage as incumbents.

A public discussion of government restructuring could raise the broad issue of bureaucratic performance to the forefront of national debate and generate consideration of the single reform of government and Congress that might most immediately improve Congress's capacity to focus on issue representation and dialogic deliberation: *the creation of a national ombudsman agency* empowered to oversee the micromanagement of agency services. European nations have experimented with various ombudsman strategies that bypass or limit legislative involvement in casework management. These strategies leave the legislature free to represent constituents on the broad policy issues of government and to focus on broad policy deliberation and government oversight.[42] Likewise, it is possible in the United States to shift the ombudsman role from Congress into a "fourth branch" of government, with that new branch structured to perform its role according to entrepreneurial principles that might involve intra-agency competition.

The implementation of an ombudsman agency could come if the voters saw it as an integral part of government restructuring and evaluated legislators according to their support of it. For their part, legislators might see a loss of casework responsibilities and a decline in their personal vote advantage as preferable to the constitutional imposition of term limits that is likely to occur unless Congress resolves its governing crisis. In conjunction with the creation of a national ombudsman agency, Congress could downsize its own bureaucracy and make it a violation of federal law for any member to intervene on behalf of a constituent with the executive branch. Aside from improving bureaucratic service delivery, such a governmental and congressional restructuring would be intended to free the legislators, organizationally and politically, to focus on issue representation and deliberation.

Were an emergency joint committee able to focus public debate on governmental restructuring and were Congress to let go of its casework responsibilities, a new logic of politics could solidify. This logic would center on the politics of state entrepreneurship—that is, on designing and managing government programs to ensure service delivery through managed use of competitive incentives among and within private and public service institutions. Insofar as a new logic of politics could emerge, and could do so through a process that legitimized congressional policy making rather than reliance on executive intervention, conditions would exist to support additional reforms and adjustments within Congress itself.

For example, as long as the politics of the service state remain the primary focus of the political agenda, it is doubtful that any campaign finance reform can be devised to reduce significantly the special advantage that interest representation gives to incumbents. Organized groups are simply too dependent on the assistance of powerful incumbents (and there are simply too many strategies aside from direct financial contributions by which they can assist incumbents) for campaign finance reforms alone to neutralize incumbents' electoral advantage. In addition, it is extremely difficult to draft finance reform measures that successfully remove the influence of group money from politics; thus political action committee money still plays a vital role in presidential elections (through financial contributions to the political parties and through media campaigns for particular policy positions that aid individual candidates) despite public funding of presidential campaigns. Aside from the difficulty of determining what kind of campaign finance reform might conceivably work, the difficulty of drafting meaningful reform is reinforced by the effort of entrenched incumbents to design reforms that leave them protected and by the pressures of lobby groups to enact reforms in ways that sustain their leverage over politicians.[43]

By contrast, a move toward entrepreneurial government and the ending of casework responsibilities could create an environment that would support meaningful campaign finance reform and help level the electoral playing field. It could do so by lessening the obsession of specialized groups with powerful legislators who intervene with the bureaucracy on their behalf. In fact, a move toward entrepreneurial government could create an incentive for many organized groups to support new legislators with business, scientific, or state government backgrounds who are aware of and experienced with the latest entrepreneurial experiments in a policy arena. Such a shift in the incentives of interest groups could lead to increased support for serious campaign finance reform that would reduce the advantages of longstanding incumbents out of touch with entrepreneurial strategies. A change in the incentives of interest groups, reinforced by serious campaign finance reform, could also help *revitalize the Republican congressional party or third-party conservative movements*. It could do so, first, by lessening the special advantage that the politics of the service state gives to Democrats who support (and thereby claim credit for) bureaucratic service delivery. It could do so, second, by highlighting the value of candidates with experience in the entrepreneurial world of business, an experience designed to give them insights into the creation of state entrepreneurship. Government restructuring and state entrepreneurship, in other words, could help *revitalize a competitive congressional party system while helping to sustain a sufficiently strong Congress* that the spoils of electoral victory would be worthwhile.

A new logic of politics could also help direct the organizational reform of Congress along more constructive paths. My concern at present is that highly publicized reform efforts, without a clear focus on the broad agenda issues whose consideration they are designed to facilitate and without participants having a meaningful grasp of the historical context and implications of reform, are largely a shell game played by professional politicians to gain short-term publicity and career advantage. Such reforms might produce organizational and procedural changes whose ineffectiveness convinces the public that Congress is truly unredeemable.[44] By contrast, if the spotlight of congressional deliberation is placed on the great historic issues of the day, so that the reinvention of government comes clearly into focus, reform efforts in Congress may proceed more productively.[45]

Ultimately, a Congress concerned with the creation of an entrepreneurial state would have to consider how to *design its internal organization to manage a restructured government*; in the process it could strengthen its representative and deliberative character. A redesign of its internal organization, for example, probably would emphasize the need for a more fluid and yet well-coordinated and collective decision structure capable of responding to creative and unpredictable technological innovations and to consequent economic and social restructurings of a postindustrial society.[46] The creation of a more fluid decision structure might come through a reduction in permanent committees and subcommittees accompanied by greater use of special committees with clear policy objectives and limited terms of operation. Such an organizational rearrangement could increase the capacities of Congress to respond to a shifting policy environment. It could also limit members' incentives to build committee power bases and the consequent sweetheart relations with executive agencies and lobbyists that lock existing programs into statutory permanence. Concomitant with such changes, Congress could strengthen the authority of its party leaders, caucuses, and budgetary committees so that they could provide coordination and continuity within a more fluid policy structure; Congress and the nation could then hold them accountable for a lack of institutional responsiveness. Such strengthening could occur through greater leadership authority in the appointment of committee members and leaders and in the creation of special committees. Congress also could experiment with televised question hours attended by all members and with televised town hall meetings. It could hold special deliberation days, when committee and subcommittee meetings would be prohibited, that would be devoted solely to collective debate and votes on critical policy issues. Such organizational changes, if reinforced by the coming of state entrepreneurship, could move Congress a long way toward issue representation and broad-gauged policy deliberation.

Finally, in the effort to solidify a new logic of politics, *Congress should take one major dramatic step: it should seek a formal constitutional reassertion of its legitimacy as the nation's premier democratic institution.* For too long now Congress has ceded the public debate over its future—a debate currently framed by the constitutional efforts to limit terms, to restrain its taxing and spending powers, and to give the president a line item veto—to those who question the value of a strong and independent Congress. In so doing, it has adopted a defensive stance, seeking to defeat or limit constitutional moves against its legislative authority and prerogatives, rather than an assertive stance offering a vision of a revitalized Congress that the public could embrace. To regain the support of the American people, Congress must forthrightly make the case for its legitimate authority and trust the public to understand through open deliberation the current institutional dilemmas and support credible and productive efforts to address those dilemmas.

Congress could make its case by introducing and actively pursuing constitutional amendments that reframe the public debate in ways designed to stress its representational and deliberative roles and strengthen its policy-making capacities. Such amendments might seek to institutionalize the various proposals made in this essay. Amendments could include granting the special policy-making authority that a national legislature in a postindustrial era will need (for example, the creation of a legislative veto power, particularly in the area of international trade agreements negotiated by the executive).[47] And, perhaps most critically, *such efforts could include an amendment protecting the right of citizens to vote for representatives of their choice, without regard to prior legislative service.* In other words, Congress should directly confront the term-limit movement and reframe the issue in a way that emphasizes the special stake that individual citizens have in sustaining unfettered representative government.[48]

In short, *Congress must be willing to engage with the citizens in a national reassessment of the nature and structure of our representative democracy.* Such a reassessment is already underway in the court of public opinion and in the polling booth. But the reassessment is occurring in a deliberative vacuum, with the supporters of Congress failing to join the debate in an aggressive and visible manner—failing to move out of the halls of Congress and offer directly to the citizens and their state representatives a credible set of constitutional choices that the nation could embrace to help solve its governing crisis. For the public to understand the true nature of the current crisis and to engage in a collective process of learning how best to redress the crisis, meaningful public deliberation is necessary. Congress would be well advised to trust the American public, join the constitutional debate over its future, and seek constitutional reaffirmation of its legitimacy as our most representative and deliberative policy-making institution.

IV

This, then, is my assessment of where Congress and the nation are today as we end the Reagan-Bush years and proceed into a new administration. The past twelve years highlighted the drawbacks of divided government. But even more critically, they demonstrated just how vulnerable Congress and American legislatures in general are to a loss of public faith in their capacities for reasoned and responsive policy-making. United party government should produce a short-term surge in policy activism; under skillful leadership it might even generate innovative experimentation with state entrepreneurship and thereby reshape and revitalize the government and Congress. Much depends on how well Congress heeds the early warning signals sent by the voters during the early 1990s.

Should Congress remain frozen in the politics of the past, however, almost certainly we face even greater doubts about its legitimacy as a policy-making institution, and the prospects for continued erosion in our democratic processes of governance will increase. Consider, after all, the bind that will confront both citizens and legislators if Congress as an institution fails to respond to the opportunity for fundamental change that united government and the current atmosphere of crisis together provide.

Left enmeshed in a service state and deprived of a revitalized public agenda, citizens will have an unenviable choice. They can vote for incumbent legislators who serve particularized interests, thereby losing the chance to focus attention on collective issues of state entrepreneurship and institutional renewal. Or they can vote on the broad issues of the day, demanding that candidates look beyond interest representation and speak to diffuse general issues, thereby risking the loss of secure and powerful incumbents who can serve their immediate particularized needs. Caught in such a bind, we should not be surprised if the voters again rebel and turn with more sustained fury against incumbent legislators. Nor should we dismiss the possibility that citizens will continue to support movements against the policy-making power of Congress and the constitutional tenure of members, even at the risk of destroying the very avenue through which they could most directly exercise long-term influence on public policy. Such upheavals would seem most likely in periods of divided party government or institutional conflict, when the president can most aggressively lead public attacks against the legislature. This prospect is illustrated most vividly by the experience of the California state government during the past quarter-century, where Republican governors from Ronald Reagan to Pete Wilson have led direct assaults on the power, resources, and tenure of the Democratic state legislature.[49]

The continued reliance on the service state also gives elected politicians untenable choices. They can speak to the general issues of the day, attempting to redress the nation's collective and long-term problems, and thereby risk the guaranteed electoral support of particularized interests tied to a service bureaucracy, or they can serve citizens' particularized interests, seeking to maintain immediate power but risking eventual repudiation of themselves and of representative government. With politicians caught in this peculiar bind, we should not be surprised to see them yet again blame the institution, their leaders, and each other for the general and collective policy failures of government. At the same time they would reinforce the public's belief that Congress is an unworkable institution.[50] In the grip of severe crisis, and propelled by their own logic of institutional blame, the legislators themselves could become agents of congressional abdication and executive dominance. Such developments may be most likely in periods of united party government, when the president's congressional party, attempting to resolve the national crisis and thereby maintain its short-term electoral viability, chooses to give the president far-reaching authority that Congress subsequently is unable to control or reclaim.

If citizens and legislators see no way out of their political bind except through reliance on the president, the nation's response to the crisis of postindustrialism likely will activate executive control of our national government. Executive control could come through the use of vetoes and political intimidation to force a weakened Congress to accept executive budgetary priorities, through assertive control of international trade negotiations and the use of the resulting trade agreements to abrogate the domestic politics of Congress, and through the increased autonomy of executive agencies that would come with a Congress of inexperienced legislators. Executive dominance would be particularly potent if it were to include a presidential alliance with the conservative business groups that seek to weaken Congress in order to avoid its regulatory power and if it were supported by a conservative Supreme Court. Any moves to consolidate and institutionalize executive power would almost certainly prompt Congress and the public to constrain executive power (such a constraint occurred in the early 1970s after Richard Nixon's impoundment efforts and the Watergate crisis). It is always possible that out of such deep institutional confrontation could come a renewed public commitment to Congress and a renewed effort for it to reassert its authority. Yet one should not discount the possibility that a continued and deepening disaffection with Congress could solidify widespread support for executive government.

The fear is that a loss of faith in Congress might both support the rise of executive government at the national level and reinforce a loss of faith in representative government at the state and local level. Already, because of the development of service bureaucracies akin to those of the national government, many, if not most, state and local assemblies face policy dilemmas and public disaffection analogous to those facing Congress. With these bureaucracies have come a legislative politics characterized by interest representation and strategic deliberation similar to that of Congress. Thus it is not too much to say that a crisis of legislative legitimation is inherent in the coming of postindustrialism at the state and local level as well as the national level. The additional dilemma for subnational assemblies is that Congress's continued reliance on a service state mentality leads it to mandate state and local service delivery programs and to shift fiscal responsibilities to state and local governments, thus further overloading their governing capacities. Congress does so to sustain and expand programs that the federal government cannot fund and in the process to claim credit for the programs. The result is to reduce the autonomy of state and local assemblies, to limit their flexibility in resolving their own governing crises through experiments with state entrepreneurship, and to inter-connect local, state, and national legislatures in a combined governing crisis that could lead—is leading—to general public rejection of the authority of legislatures.

Congress's inability to resolve its own legitimation crisis fuels citizens' general disillusionment with struggling state and local assemblies and reinforces reliance on executive government throughout the system. Thus Congress contributes to the legitimation crisis of subnational systems not only by shifting its policy dilemmas to them but by creating a national atmosphere of hostility toward legislative power which then affects the subnational systems as well. When such developments are combined with serious postindustrial problems endemic to the subnational governments, the result can be a lethal reduction in legislative power. A decline in legislative authority is seen clearly in California, our most postindustrial state. Twenty years ago the California legislature was considered a model institution, but progressively it is being stripped of its policy-making authority, its organizational resources, and its experienced leadership. These developments have come through constitutional initiatives (supported by the governors) mandating limits to the taxing powers of the legislature, to its spending prerogatives, to its staff and operating resources (which were substantially reduced), and to the terms of its members. With the decline in the authority of the legislature has come a shift of power to the executive. Gov. Pete Wilson essentially brought the California legislature to its knees during a 1992 state fiscal crisis by forcing it to accept the bulk of his budgetary priorities despite broad and intense legislative opposition. The California experience should give pause to any observers of Congress who dismiss the severity of the congressional legitimation crisis and discount the possibility of a general breakdown in representative government.

Members of Congress must act before a general crisis of legislative legitimation overwhelms representative institutions throughout the political system. One of the few benefits of the term-limit movement is that, in threatening a near-term end to the career of all members unless they collectively regain the public trust, it may make clear to legislators the linkage between their short-term career interests and the long-term governing capacity of the institution. The message to be gleaned from public support for term limits, however, is not the need for policy activism on behalf of long-neglected particularized interests, but the need for Congress and subnational legislatures to address the collective problems of society in a way that makes possible the long-term availability of particularized services. Short-term activism focused on particularized interests may create a sense of policy movement that dispels public unease for the moment. But if short-term activism leaves unaddressed the deeper institutional and policy dilemmas of postindustrialism, it will set the stage for even greater policy crises in the future and a more dangerous public disillusionment with representative government.

If members of Congress will not act, the public must. Congress, after all, is not the property of its temporary occupants but of the American people. Our investment in representative and deliberative government is a two-hundred-year legacy not to be cast away lightly or allowed to slide silently away in the gradual erosion of congressional policy-making authority. The public has every right to intervene and save Congress, even if its current members, entrapped in the outmoded logic of a passing era, fail to do so. Yet activism by the American public must come in a collective, thoughtful, and deliberative manner that allows for reflective understanding and learning, not through the reactive and angry politics of isolated state initiatives. The Constitution gives us such a collective outlet: the right of the citizenry to demand and participate in a national constitutional convention.

It is arguable that the erosion of the representative and deliberative capacities of Congress during the industrial era occurred because there was no formal and deliberative national reconsideration of how best to restructure the institution with the coming of the service state. Instead, this responsibility was left to Congress. Congress's adapation to the industrial era more nearly served the reelection and power concerns of its members than the representational and deliberative interests of the nation at large. Political activists, myself included, shy away from proposing formal reassessment of our constitutional arrangements, as represented by a national constitutional convention, for fear of the popular passions and uncontrolled assaults on democratic values that such a public reassessment might unleash. But such passions and assaults are already unleashed in our nation and could within two or three decades, and across several cycles of public disaffection, emasculate representative government piecemeal.

In the face of sustained congressional inaction, the nation must trust to a deliberative assembly of citizens to reassess our commitment to a truly representative and deliberative Congress. Only with deliberative reassessment and relegitimation, coming either as a result of congressional leadership or from a constitutional convention, is Congress likely to survive as a vital and democratic policy-making institution. With an open and forthright reassessment, the American people could rediscover the value of representative and deliberative policy making. They could reassert their desire for those institutional processes that identify our shared purpose amidst a diversity of interests and that thereby bond us together as a nation. Congress then could not only survive but flourish. A revitalization of Congress could activate, as I wrote twelve years ago, "a great renewal and expansion of democratic government in America."[51]

Notes

Acknowledgements: For their assistance at various stages in the preparation of this essay, my thanks to Leslie Anderson, Ann Davies, Joan Fiore, Sean Kelly, Carolyn Mohr-Hennefeld, Calvin Jillson, Robert Lopez, Vince McGuire, and David Van Mill. A very special note of appreciation to Cris and Meredith Dodd for their patience and understanding.

1 The argument in this essay builds on Lawrence C. Dodd (1981), "Congress, the Constitution, and the Crisis of Legitimation." This earlier essay, completed in the summer of 1980, raised the prospect that a severe legitimation crisis was likely to descend on the contemporary Congress, given the severity of the postindustrial-era problems confronting it combined with its organizational disarray. For a recent discussion highlighting the emergence of a crisis of congressional legitimacy, see Richard F. Fenno, Jr., "Some Thoughts on Renewing Congress" (Paper presented at the Brookings Institution/American Enterprise Institute Conference on Congressional Reform, Washington, D.C., June 30, 1992).

2 On the coming of postindustrialism, see, for example, Huntington (1974) and Thurow (1980).

3 See, for example, Dionne, Jnr. (1991) *Why Americans Hate Politics*.

4 David S. Broder, "Post-Election News Is Good and Bad for Republicans," Syndicated column, Boulder Sunday Camera, Dec. 6, 1992, 3E.

5 Among journalists the most consistent emphasis on the role of divided government comes from David Broder. See, for example, David S. Broder, "Wreckage of Divided Government," Washington Post, Aug. 30, 1992, C7; see also Broder (1972). Among political scientists emphasizing the role of divided government see, for example, Catherine E. Rudder (1981); David E. Price (1992), *The Congressional Experience*, 108–112; and David W. Rohde (1991), *Parties and Leaders in the Postreform House*. The scholarly debate over the statistical effects of divided government on policy activism is a growth industry. For the most vivid contrast in views, see the debate between Sean Kelly and David Mayhew in Polity, Volume 25 (1993). See also Cox and Kernell (1991); Fiorina (1992); Mayhew (1991); James A.Thurber, "Representation, Accountability, and Efficiency in Divided Party Control of Government," in *PS: Political Science and Politics* 24 (December 1991: 653–657). My own view is that divided government helped fuel the policy gridlock of the Reagan-Bush years but was not the primary source of policy immobilism and the declining public confidence in government. Immobilism and loss of confidence were already apparent during the united government of the Carter years. See James L. Sundquist, "Congress, the President, and the Crisis of Competence in Government," in Dodd and Oppenheimer, eds. (1981); and Peterson (1990: 253–260).

6 For a discussion of the coming of united government, see Lawrence C. Dodd and Bruce I. Oppenheimer, "Perspectives on the 1992 Congressional Elections," in Dodd and Oppenheimer (1993), eds., *Congress Reconsidered*, 5th edition.

7 Aside from "Congress, the Constitution, and the Crisis of Legitimation," see my arguments in "Congress and the Quest for Power." For a recent effort to develop a broader theory of political change to account for the periods of immobilism, within which to place the role of Congress and the presidency, see Lawrence C. Dodd (1991), "Congress, the Presidency, and the American Experience: A Transformational Perspective."

8 For a general discussion of Congress that I find useful as an underpinning to my argument, see Arthur Maass (1983). I shall focus on Congress as a single institution, though of course many of the arguments apply differentially to the House and Senate. For an

earlier attempt to elaborate the contrasting effects of postindustrialism on the House and Senate (arguing that the House would suffer considerably more than the Senate), see Carmines and Dodd (1985), "Bicameralism in Congress: The Changing Partnership."

9 For a discussion of the ups and downs of popular support for Congress, see Davidson, Kovenock, and O'Leary (1966); Fenno, Jnr. (1975); Parker and Davidson (1979); and Parker (1977).

10 See, for example, Fisher (1985); Mezey (1989); Schlesinger (1974); Scigliano (1971); and Sundquist (1981).

11 For an earlier discussion of the distinction between the representational (or electoral) and the deliberative (or governing) dimensions of congressional politics, see Dodd (1988), "The Rise of the Technocratic Congress."

12 Fenno (1977).

13 Polsby (1968); and Matthews (1960).

14 Oppenheimer (1977, 1985).

15 For background discussion of the three historical eras outlined here, see particularly Ackerman (1991); Brady (1988); Greenberg (1985); and Calvin Jillson (1994). On the period leading up to and including the Civil War and Reconstruction, see William W. Freehling, *The Road to Disunion: Secessionists at Bay, 1776–1854* (New York: Oxford University Press, 1990); Merrill D. Peterson, *The Great Triumvirate: Webster, Clay, and Calhoun* (New York: Oxford University Press, 1987); Allan G. Bogue, *The Congressman's Civil War* (New York: Cambridge University Press, 1989); and J. G. Randall, *The Civil War and Reconstruction* (New York: D.C. Heath, 1937). See also Woodrow Wilson's (1885/1973) assessment of Congress in the early and mid-nineteenth century in *Congressional Government*.

16 Brown (1922); and Rothman (1969).

17 See the discussion in Lawrence C. Dodd, "Congress and the Rise of the Activist State, 1933–1964," in *The Encyclopedia of the United States Congress*, ed. Donald C. Bacon, Roger H. Davidson, and Morton Keller (New York: Simon and Schuster, 1995c).

18 For an argument that the current public disaffection is but a continuation of historic patterns of "Congress bashing," see Polsby (1990: 15–23).

19 Reich (1991); and Rivlin (1992).

20 Thurow (1980); Krugman (1990).

21 Eisenger (1988); Osborne and Gaebler (1992); and Chubb and Moe (1990).

22 Restructuring the national government to create an entrepreneurial state could come through a variety of strategies and across a wide range of policy areas. Such experiments are occurring not only in American state and local governments but at the national level in foreign governments as well, from the conservative Britain of the Thatcher era to Social Democratic experiments in Sweden. Aside from the area of school choice, such experiments involve the restructuring of national health systems to force competitiveness among health providers and insurers to hold costs down while making health benefits universally available. The socialist Labor party of New Zealand has even gone so far as to overhaul its entire welfare state, restructuring it according to entrepreneurial principles of competition among private and public sector units. Such restructuring also tends to bring changes in revenue systems and budgetary strategies (including multiyear budgets) designed to foster fiscal responsibility and cost containment. In the best of circumstances, with concerted planning and effective leadership, such restructuring efforts have supported service expansion combined with fiscal realism, they have received broad public support, and they have produced renewed belief in government. See Osborne and Gaebler (1992), esp. 328–330.

23 Congress may need, however, some expansion of constitutional powers to address its role in the new politics of international trade that is emerging with a global economy. See Thurow (1992); and Walter Russell Mead, "Bushism, Found: A Second-Term Agenda Hidden in Trade Agreements," *Harper's*, September 1992, 37–45.

24 This discussion of representation relies particularly on Pitkin (1972). See also Eulau and Karps (1977); Fenno (1978); and Shepsle (1988).

25 See, for example, Huntington (1973) and Fiorina (1977b).

26 See Alford and Brady (1993).

27 See Dodd (1991), "Congress, the Presidency, and the American Experience."

28 See Bernard Manin, "On Legitimacy and Political Deliberation," *Political Theory* 15 (August 1987: 368); Fishkin (1991); Mansbridge (1980); and Quirk (1989).

29 See Lawrence C. Dodd, "Political Learning and Political Change: Understanding Development Across Time," in *Dynamics of American Politics* (1994).

30 Arnold (1990). For a discussion of deliberative versus electoral approaches to congressional policy making somewhat analogous to the distinction here between dialogic and strategic deliberation, see Ferejohn and Shipan (1985). See also Shepsle and Weingast (1987).

31 Mayhew (1974b); Fiorina (1977b, 1980); Dodd (1977).

32 Lowi (1969, 1979); and Dodd and Schott (1979).

33 See the essays by Richard L. Hall and by George E. Connor and Bruce I. Oppenheimer in Dodd and Oppenheimer, *Congress Reconsidered*, Third Edition (1985).

34 Aside from Arnold (1990), *Logic of Congressional Action*, see Bach and Smith (1988); and Smith (1989).

35 For a discussion of the adaptation problems of Congress with the coming of industrialization, see Cooper and Brady (1973). See also Cooper (1977); and Huntington (1965, 1973).

36 Young (1966); and Bensel (1984). See also Swift (1987).

37 See Dodd, "Rise of the Technocratic Congress," Edward Weisband, "Congress, Co-determination, and Arms Control," and Hugh Heclo, "The Emerging Regime," in Harris and Milkis (1987), *Remaking American Politics*.

38 See Hibbing (1993).

39 One of the most successful state efforts in pursuing an entrepreneurial agenda has been in Florida, where the lower house of the state legislature created the Florida Speaker's Advisory Committee on the Future in 1985, composed of forty-five citizens and seven House members. This committee devised significant restructuring proposals that later passed the legislature "despite the political environment" because the Speaker, Jon Mills, "led the effort." See Osborne and Gaebler (1992: 232–236). One should expect no less political courage and boldness from congressional leaders.

40 See W. R. Brock, *An American Crisis: Congress and Reconstruction, 1865–67* (New York: St. Martin's, 1963); see also Sundquist (1981: 26–27).

41 Cain, Ferejohn, and Fiorina (1987). On the localization of congressional elections, see Mann (1978); and Arnold (1981). For a broader discussion of the consequent breakdown of political parties and the process of party realignment that is historically so critical to political transformation, see Burnham (1976).

42 See, for example, Osborne and Gaebler's (1992) discussion of the British Audit Commission in *Reinventing Government*: 328.

43 Gary Jacobson, "Parties and PACs in Congressional Elections," in *Congress Reconsidered*, 4th ed. (1989) and Frank J. Sorauf (1988).

44 Dodd (1977). See also Rieselbach (1986) and Davidson and Oleszek (1977).

45 On the importance of an agenda shift to transformative restructuring of Congress, see Dodd (1986b).

46 There is already evidence that Congress is becoming a more fluid organization. See, for example, Lawrence C. Dodd and Bruce I. Oppenheimer, "The New Congress: Fluidity and Oscillation," in *Congress Reconsidered*, 4th ed. (1989). The multiple referral process and the Speaker's task forces are also evidence of innovative efforts to create a more responsive structure in the House. For discussions, see the essays by Garry Young and Joseph Cooper and Barbara Sinclair in Dodd and Oppenheimer, eds. (1993). See also Mann and Ornstein (1992).

47 On the nature of legislative vetoes and their role in foreign affairs, see Gibson (1992).

48 This proposal thus is in opposition to the position of columnist George Will, who argues that Congress should submit to the states a constitutional amendment imposing term limits. See Will (1992).

49 See, for an illustrative discussion, Robert A. Jones, "California's Bitter Season," *Los Angeles Times Magazine*, (September 27, 1992: 14–18, 40–41).

50 On the politics of blame, see Ken Weaver, "The Politics of Blame Avoidance," *Journal of Public Policy* 6 (October–December, 1986: 371–398); on the general decline in comity that the modern environment has produced, see Uslaner (1993).

51 Dodd (1981), "Congress, the Constitution, and the Crisis of Legitimation," 418. See also Hugh Heclo (1989), "The Emerging Regime," 317–318.

Additional Perspective on "Renewal"

"Congress and the Politics of Renewal" considers the extent to which the Congress of the early 1990s had avoided, resolved or become more deeply mired in a crisis of legitimacy, as forecast in Chapter Three, and how it might proceed in light of the answers to that question. It concludes that the crisis was proceeding apace and that fundamental shifts in ideas about contemporary politics, legislative functioning, policy agendas and regime structure were necessary to address the crisis.

In developing these arguments, the essay focuses attention, in particular, on difficulties in the representative and deliberative capacities of contemporary American legislatures. The essay points to the importance of ideas about governance to the politics of the early 1990s; how outmoded ideas can inhibit renewal of congressional authority and legitimacy; factors that inhibit recognition of, debate over, and embrace of new perspectives on society and politics, particularly factors associated with representation and deliberation; and developments that could generate expanded attention to new perspectives. The essay is thus a natural next step in pursuing the scholarly agenda outlined in "A Transformational Perspective" (Chapter Seven), using the framework presented there to assess how well the Congress of the early 1990s was addressing the governing dilemmas outlined in Chapter Three, "Legitimation Crisis."

Suggested Reading: Works that speak to, build on, test, or assess arguments introduced in this essay include Hibbing and Theiss-Morse (1995); Johnson and Broder (1996); Cooper, ed. (1999); Cooper (2001); Oppenheimer (1997); Mann and Ornstein (2006) and Crenson and Ginsberg (2007).

Classroom Use: "Renewal" can be used in the classroom in course sections contrasting nineteenth and twentieth century politics; sections dealing with the shifting nature and role of representation and deliberation in Congress; sections dealing with the role of interest groups in Congress; sections presenting stages of postwar institutional change, with "Renewal" detailing the structuring of congressional politics in the early 1990s, on the eve of the Republican Revolution; in sections dealing with ways to reform Congress and American politics; and in sections dealing with the shifting relationship between congressional politics and bureaucratic-state structures of national governance.

For point/counterpoint contrasts, "Renewal" could be paired in useful ways with Chapter Three, "Congress, the Constitution, and the Crisis of Legitimation," as an exploration of the trajectory followed by Congress from the mid-1970s to the early 1990s. The two essays could also be paired with Bruce Oppenheimer's 1997 essay, "Abdicating Congressional Power," to compare various of their forecasts to the subsequent behavior of congressional Republicans. These three essays could be combined with Joseph Cooper's 2001 essay, "The

Twentieth Century Congress," to gain a full sense of the causal processes working on contemporary politics. Additionally, the four essays together could be paired with Haynes Johnson and David S. Broder (1996), *The System: The American Way of Politics at the Breaking Point*, in efforts to understand the historical patterning of congressional politics from the 1970s to the early 1990s, as seen through a contemporary lens. In such a pairing, Johnson and Broder provide an in-depth case study to supplement the four interpretive essays by Bruce Oppenheimer, Joseph Cooper, and the author.

9

THE NEW AMERICAN POLITICS

Reflections on the Early 1990s

1995

Published in 1995, "The New American Politics" proposed that historic developments of the late twentieth century—the end of the Cold War, postindustrialism, and the telecommunications revolution— were generating subtle but momentous shifts in how Americans were thinking about politics.

These shifts include (1) a less Olympian and more humanized view of the presidency; (2) a greater concern to find creative ways for private/public cooperation in insuring the economic and health security of citizens, thereby aiding Republicans by highlighting the value of business experience in designing government programs; (3) a growing desire for legislators who act as trouble-shooters in addressing broad policy problems, instead of becoming entrenched careerists serving particularized interests; and (4) an increased reliance on citizen deliberation through the media to set the nation's policy agenda, thereby decreasing the deliberative roles of legislatures.

Each shift, the essay argues, raises serious concerns for students of Congress and American politics: (1) how does one maintain the authority of the presidency while acknowledging the frailty of presidents; (2) how does one maintain a strong activist state while limiting that aspect of the state—the bureaucracy—that is its key defining element; (3) how does one sustain the power of legislatures while limiting the entrenched power of legislators; and (4) how can one rely on citizens for policy deliberation and choice while also recognizing and respecting the need for specialized legislative expertise in policy crafting?

The great social changes of history are those moments when the attitudes or habits of thought of a citizenry shift in some fundamental fashion (Bateson, 1966).

Lawrence C. Dodd. *"The New American Politics: Reflections on the Early 1990s." In* The New American Politics, *Edited by Bryan D. Jones. Boulder, C.O.: Westview Press. 1995, pp. 257–274.*

Such moments may not look dramatic in the immediate alterations they produce in political institutions, public policy, or social relations. The shifts in thought may be subtle and elusive to the participants, such obvious responses to historical developments that citizens have difficulty sensing any "shift" at all, much less foreseeing dramatic long-term consequences. But out of the subtle reformulation of attitudes can emerge new mindsets and behavioral patterns that transform a society and its politics.

One such dramatic shift in attitude during the height of the Cold War came when the Russians launched Sputnik into orbit around the earth and thereby convinced the American public that our educational and research institutions lagged behind those of the Soviets. The increased public support for education and research then helped generate the large national research universities that educate so many of our national citizens and that now, with the Soviet menace gone, are increasingly under attack as unnecessary public investments. Another such shift, identified by Morris Fiorina (1995b), occurred as the states chose to create professionalized legislatures with substantial salary and retirement benefits for members and inadvertently produced an incentive for working-class Democrats to create long-term legislative careers, an incentive less attractive to middle-class Republicans. The new carrerist mindset of Democrats then helped tilt the control of legislatures toward the Democratic Party.

And of course the broadest and most sustained shift in popular mindset in the twentieth century came in the 1930s and 1940s (Lowi, 1979). During that period the depression, World War II, and then, the Cold War led citizens to abandon the laissez-faire and isolationist policies of the early twentieth century and to embrace an activist government at home and abroad. Much that modern political scientists treat as "normal politics"—the strong presidency, a powerful bureaucratic state, incumbent advantage, a professionalized Congress preoccupied with processing casework and controlling entitlement programs—derives from the attitudinal shifts and political experiments of the Roosevelt-Truman era.

I raise the issue of shifting mindsets because it is my belief that a new American politics is emerging in the early 1990s, a politics resulting from subtle shifts in contemporary perceptions and political beliefs of the American public. This emerging mindset, though elusive, is evident in the distinctive and unusual behavior of citizens in the early 1990s, particularly in the nature of the candidates, political movements, and issues positions that they supported during the early and mid-1990s. This behavior suggests that the broad historic developments of the late twentieth century—the end of the Cold War and demise of the Soviet state, the coming of information highways and the interactive telecommunications revolution, the emergence of a postindustrial and postmaterial service society—are generating wide-ranging alterations in how Americans think about politics and society. These alterations may not have come in response to such dramatic events as depression or war; yet they have the potential to transform American politics just as fundamentally as did the depression, World War II, and the Cold War two generations ago (Dionne, 1991; Dodd, 1981, 1993; Fowler, 1994; Huntington, 1974; Inglehart, 1989; Mayhew, 1994; Shefter, 1994).

My purpose here is to identify four shifts in the political mindset of the public that I see occurring in the early 1990s and to discuss some of their general implications. These four shifts—in how we think about the presidency, the functions and structure of government, the nature of political representation, and the character of democratic deliberation—involve some extensive transformations in the nature of American politics. These transformations could ultimately be beneficial, adjusting American political practice to the needs of a postindustrial society. Or they could ultimately be harmful, eroding the institutional and participatory foundations of democratic government. What is important at this point is to recognize the potential transformations that may now be underway in our politics and to begin a systematic assessment of their character and long-term consequences.

The Nature of the American Presidency

Perhaps the most obvious shift during the early 1990s has occurred in the way Americans think about the presidency and current or potential presidents. From the end of World War II onward, the presidency was seen as the institution most responsible for protecting the nation from the onslaught of communism, and the president was the man with his finger on the nuclear button. In this view, candidates for the presidency needed to be tough enough to face down the communists, stable enough to carry the burden of nuclear decision making, and experienced enough in national politics to mind the domestic store while remaining ever attentive to the realities of the Cold War. The presidency was deemed the most powerful office on earth and its occupant thus needed to be an individual of extraordinary character (Barber, 1985; Lowi, 1985; Neustadt, 1960; Rockman, 1984; Schlesinger, 1973; Tiefer, 1994).

In the face of such expectations, candidates for the presidency sought to demonstrate their mettle. Military service, preferably a heroic performance in wartime, became a virtual necessity, such that almost every elected president from Truman through Bush had served in the military, usually with some distinction; the one exception was Ronald Reagan, who made up for this lack of military service by being the greatest Cold Warrior of them all. Potential presidents also sought to demonstrate an incredible capacity for hard work and stamina in the face of adversity, with the country's grueling presidential nomination process often justified as an essential rite of passage that separated the men from the boys; any stumble during the nomination or election process could cast a candidate into oblivion. Personal problems—evident in marital infidelity, divorce, psychological counseling—became stigmas to be avoided or hidden at all costs. And significant symbols of personal success—in national politics, during wartime, or in business—seemed virtually mandatory.

Despite the efforts of candidates and presidents to create heroic images, there was an almost unreal element to these Olympian expectations—expectations that cast presidents as supermen beyond the capacities of ordinary mortals. Their unreality was reinforced by the painful awareness that every president who served out at least one full elective term found himself confronted by scandals, health crises, or misjudgments that brought into question his sufficiency as president. Thus Truman faced charges of corruption among his cronies; Eisenhower confronted heart attacks and accusations of lying to the American public; LBJ faced a credibility gap and the Vietnam fiasco; Nixon, Watergate; Carter, the Iran hostage crisis; Reagan, the Iran-Contra scandal. For his part, George Bush made the mistake of breaking his promise not to raise taxes. Though significant in their own right, each of these problems took on added magnitude because of the exaggerated expectations of postwar presidents and helped produce a growing disillusionment with all aspects of government. Despite the crises, misjudgments, and magnified scandals, the public nevertheless held to an Olympian model of presidents so long as the Cold War continued, the obsession with image over reality most clearly witnessed in the election and reelection of the former actor Ronald Reagan.

With the end of the Cold War and the demise of the Soviet Union in the early 1990s, considerations of the presidency and of presidents are now in transition. The sitting president during the 1992 election, George Bush, fit all the basic characteristics of the postwar expectations. A war hero; a business success during his early years as an oilman; a family man with no evident marital problems; an individual widely experienced in national politics as a member of Congress, a party chairman, a United Nations ambassador, a CIA director and vice-president; the successful commander in chief during the Gulf War—all of these attributes recommended Bush as the epitome of the postwar candidate for reelection. Yet, after flirtations with the unorthodox candidacies of Paul Tsongas, a former senator and cancer survivor, and Jerry Brown, the strange former governor of California, the nation instead focused its prolonged attention on Ross Perot and Bill Clinton.

The candidacies of Perot and Clinton would have been virtually unthinkable during the height of the Cold War. For his part, Perot lacked any major appointed or elected political experience, had a reputation as an eccentric and testy billionaire, was affiliated with no initial political organization, and, during the campaign, exhibited an extraordinarily unstable streak to his personality—entering the campaign on the Larry King talk show, leaving the campaign to avoid complicating his daughter's wedding, reentering the campaign to avoid the appearance of being a quitter. Bill Clinton, in turn, had no military record and was in fact a draft dodger; he had experienced serious marital difficulties and essentially acknowledged his infidelity on national television; he was the governor of a small and historically insignificant state, with very limited business or real-world experience outside of Arkansas politics; and, following his brother's arrest for drug dealing, he had engaged in family counseling with his brother and mother to deal with the consequences of a remarkably dysfunctional early family life. In essence, Clinton entered the race with little that would have recommended him as a man of stature capable of facing down "the evil empire," had the Soviet threat still preoccupied the public. Moreover, like Ross Perot, he possessed a series of shortcomings whose public acknowledgement would have disqualified him in earlier decades. Despite these numerous liabilities, the nation elected Clinton president and gave Perot the largest third-party vote in modern history.

The public fascination with Clinton and Perot, and the rejection of Bush, undoubtedly owes to numerous reasons, including the state of the economy in 1992 and a lackluster Bush campaign; but underlying all such factors, I suggest, was a subtle shift in attitudes about the presidency itself. With the end of the Cold War the public seemed less concerned with the presidency as the most powerful office in a dangerous world, and thus with ascertaining the stable character of potential presidents; citizens seemed more concerned about the presidency as an instrument of change and thus more attentive to candidates' visions of the nation's future. In part, this shift in attitude reflected unhappiness with the nation's economy and a growing concern for domestic policies, with the public anxious to have its president focus attention on the nation's woes. But this shift may well have been more than just a desire to look homeward; it may also have reflected a long-overdue desire on the part of the public to reassess the attributes appropriate to presidents, a reassessment made possible by the end of the Cold War.

In 1992 and thereafter, citizens seemed almost consciously to be scaling down their personal expectations of the president, looking less for blemishes in character than for someone with whom they could personally identify, someone whom they could believe understood them and cared about their real-life problems, someone willing to listen, interact, and empathize, someone for whom health care costs and dysfunctional and violent families were not abstractions but felt realities. It was almost as if the public, soured on supermen, was desperately seeking an everyman who would use the power of the presidency to address the long-neglected problems of real people. In turn, at least during the first two years of Clinton's presidency, the public seemed willing to grant the new president a life, to let him take daily runs in public, to have a strong wife who was clearly his intellectual equal, to protect the privacy of his daughter, to bemoan the unfairness of the Whitewater investigation, and to whine about the suffocating nature of life in the White House. Clinton was permitted to acknowledge publicly that the presidency was a bit daunting, that it took months in office before he became comfortable with the reality that he was the president, that he felt a bit overwhelmed by foreign policy issues and regretted the diversion from domestic policy making.

The flip side of a more human view of the presidency, ironically, has been a willingness on the part of the public to subject the president as an individual to an extraordinary level of unrestrained personal criticism. Conservative talk-show hosts thus have lambasted Clinton in a more virulent, personal, rapid, and dismissive manner than has affected any other postwar president. Even the attacks on Richard Nixon and the Watergate scandal came slowly and were remarkably restrained for almost a year. By contrast, some widely popular commentators rushed to accuse Clinton of complicity in the suicide of White House aide Vince Foster and of murders in his Arkansas years designed to cover up information about his extramarital affairs, with no evidence to support such accusations. Even the highly visible and hysterical nature of the attacks themselves, however, demonstrates a shifting perception of the presidency—underscoring the point that the office itself is not so critical to world security that criticism must be muted until scandals are far advanced, nor are presidents assumed to be superhuman individuals above the crass motives and behavior of the common citizen. Rather, presidents are flawed individuals like ourselves whom we can assume to be subject to common human frailties and flail accordingly.

Whether such apparent shifts in attitudes, in habitual expectations of the presidency and presidents, are real and permanent only time will tell. Perhaps the early patience with Bill Clinton was a result of the public's simple exhaustion with the nuclear nightmares and magnified scandals of the Cold War era. Perhaps with time the Olympian expectations of presidents will yet return, reinforced by the president's role as head of state and thus by a natural expectation that he or she will represent the nation unblemished. Perhaps the very human frailties and political failings of Bill Clinton himself will end the public experimentation with a less grandiose presidency. Certainly one can imagine that the tepid presidency of George Bush and the vascillations of Bill Clinton could tempt the public to return to early Cold War mythology and seek a strong, flawless, and omniscient president whom citizens could blindly trust to do what's best for America. But maybe not.

Possibly the public has learned that the president must be allowed to be human too; that the Cold War belief in superpresidents was a dangerous illusion that magnified rather than defused the dangers of the past fifty years; that character should be gauged less by the appearance of perfection than by the struggle with the wheelchair, the back brace, or the dysfunctional childhood family. Perhaps after fifty years of flawed supermen the public has decided to let go of the president as Olympian warrior and to embrace a new humanized presidency and a new range of standards for presidents: At best, an empathetic and skilled political leader in close and interactive connection with the public; at worst, an everyman beyond his depth. With such a humanized presidency we then could afford to have more daily and personal attacks on the president and, in the process, could confront potential scandals before they engulf our political system; we could use presidents as instruments of change, and then change presidents as a result of policy choice rather than of domestic or international crisis; and we could encourage presidents to interact closely and honestly with citizens and, by this means, provide the depth of explanation and leadership that will allow the public to understand the societal problems and policy choices of a postindustrial and post–Cold War era.

The Functions and Structure of Government

The second habit of thought that may now be shifting is the way citizens think about the nature of government (Chubb and Moe, 1990; Dodd and Schott, 1979; Eisenger, 1988; Osborne and Gaebler, 1992). For most of this century, if not longer, the debate over the role and nature of government has divided between liberals who wanted an activist government committed to solving societal problems and conservatives who wanted a limited and largely passive government; liberal activists supported the creation of a large bureaucracy to deliver government services and engineer social change, whereas conservative advocates of a limited government supported a small bureaucracy that primarily served business growth. The debate was complicated by the suggestion on the part of conservatives that the creation of a large service bureaucracy was a backdoor path to socialism and communism, and by the intimations on the part of liberals that adherence to a passive government demonstrated an inhuman insensitivity on the part of conservatives toward their less fortunate fellow citizens. The bitterness of the debate over the role of the government grew out of the social and economic conflicts that attended the industrial revolution, particularly the division of society into an industrial working class and a capitalist entrepreneurial class.

With the late-twentieth-century arrival of postindustrialism—particularly the move away from a mass-production blue-collar economy toward an urban and suburbanized service society—the industrial-era divisions over what government should do and should be now appear to be shifting. In this new world, most citizens are reasonably well educated and accustomed to material well-being; at the same time, virtually all citizens find themselves vulnerable to job insecurity as technological innovations sweep through all employment sectors and threaten the downsizing of corporate executives as well as service and industrial employees. In the face of such circumstances, there is a growing consensus throughout society that the government has a fundamental responsibility to provide basic economic and health security to all citizens, a consensus that can unite such disparate politicians as Edward Kennedy and Dan Quayle in support of job-training programs and convince Bob Dole and Hillary Rodham Clinton to discuss universal health care (Fenno, 1989a).

One recent sign of the broadening concern for government activism is the preoccupation on the part of virtually all political sides with the issue of government gridlock—the widespread sense that there are fundamental societal problems that the government is failing to address. The concern with gridlock is voiced by the traditional right in assessments by such politicians as Jack Kemp and Dan Quayle; by the traditional left in comments by Bill Clinton, Al Gore, and Jesse Jackson; by political newcomers such as Ross Perot; and by long-standing political commentators such as David Broder. The concern across the political spectrum with the issue of gridlock is a decided break with the past, when large segments of the nation argued that the best government was no government. Whereas a Coolidge,

Hoover, Taft, Eisenhower, or Reagan welcomed government inaction, not only the Kennedys but also the Doles, Kemps, and Quayles today see a need for job training, health care, and urban renewal and lament the gridlock that inhibits their preferred form of action.

The existence of gridlock is attributed most often to divided party government, or to constitutional and congressional arrangements (particularly the existence of bicameralism and the Senate cloture rule) that require super majorities in Congress before united party government can work (Brady and Volden, 1998; Fiorina, 1987; Kelly, 1994; Mayhew, 1991; Quirk and Nesmith, 1994). Thus the politicians suggest that the immediate solution is to put their party in power: In 1992 Quayle used the issue of gridlock to call for a Republican takeover of Congress, whereas Clinton and Gore used it to call for a Democratic White House. Behind the politicians' efforts to use the issue of gridlock for partisan advantage, however, there lurks a growing perception across the parties that the real solution to government inaction may lie less in united party government than in a re-creation of the nature of government itself.

A growing number of political analysts argue that perhaps the government is gridlocked and unable to address critical problems because our historic conception of government is inappropriate to the new realities of the postindustrial era. According to this view, which emerged first at the local, county, and state levels, government has so many responsibilities in a postindustrial era, and bureaucracies are such inefficient and costly strategies for problem solution, that a government that relies on a large bureaucracy to solve societal problems will necessarily become overwhelmed and immobilized. The solution is not to forgo activist government but to find new strategies for government action; to reinvent government. In particular, such advocates argue, an activist government must be willing to downsize bureaucracy and rely increasingly on government creation of incentive systems that encourage the private sector to cooperate with public organizations in addressing societal problems. Again, according to this view, the government neither leaves health care issues solely to the private sector, as conservatives once argued, nor creates a huge national bureaucracy to provide health care benefits directly to all Americans, as liberals once envisioned. Rather, it seeks to create a system of managed competition in which the government provides incentives and guidelines for the private sector to provide universal health coverage to citizens, with oversight and assistance from a limited government bureaucracy. Hence the government plays a strong and facilitative role, rather than the limited and passive role espoused in the past by conservatives; yet in so doing it avoids the interventionist and controlling role espoused by traditional liberals.

The discussion of a reinvention of government, the possibility that there is a third way aside from inactive government or large bureaucracies, came to the nation's attention more forcefully than ever before in the 1992 presidential election. Not only Democrats such as Bill Clinton but Republicans such as Jack Kemp made the restructuring of government a centerpiece of their campaigns, with Clinton's victory attributed in part to his ability to convince the public that his activist policy agenda could be accomplished through strategies of managed competition that would avoid the difficulties associated with a large bureaucracy. Once in the White House, Clinton authorized Vice-President Al Gore to lead the effort at reinventing government and used the principles of managed competition as the core elements of his universal health care plan.

Much like the shift in the public's view of the presidency, the move of the citizens to embrace a re-creation of our conception of government—a view often associated with the term *entrepreneurial government* because it combines activist government with the competitive principles of free enterprise—is a subtle and fragile one. Whether this shift actually solidifies and becomes a fundamental component of our postindustrial politics undoubtedly depends on how successful the early federal experiments with managed competition prove to be. Even if entrepreneurial government is successful in limited policy areas, an extensive move to managed competition as a dominant strategy of activist government probably will take at least a quarter of a century or longer, in part because large public bureaucracies have powerful clienteles that will resist the downsizing of existing bureaucratic agencies. The public acceptance of a new form of government activism—social services sans public bureaucracy—could nevertheless have significant consequences for American politics.

A first consequence is already evident and could dramatically increase—namely, a shift in the public willingness to discuss government responsibility for addressing societal problems. For roughly a quarter-century, since Lyndon Johnson's experiments with the Great Society, the nation has been "gun shy" about discussing government responsibility for societal woes lest doing so ignite another round of bureaucratic programs, federal intervention into state and local government, massive federal budgets, and national tax increases. The experience with the Great Society left the public with a widespread sense that an activist government, however well intentioned, may generate problems worse than the initial ills its programs were designed to address. My own belief is that much of the nation's policy gridlock of the past two decades may truly have been tied to the public's fear that however difficult the nation's social problems may be, action by the national government will create bureaucracies whose expense and inefficiencies only make society worse off than it was before, a fear that political leaders were simply unable to overcome as long as discussion of government action centered on bureaucratic programs.

One of the most significant breakthroughs of the early 1990s was the willingness of the public to envision the possibility that an entrepreneurial form of government activism could address societal problems without a massive increase in bureaucracies and taxes. Thus so long as Clinton's discussion of health care in the 1992 election centered on bureaucratic solutions, the public responded coolly. But when Candidate Clinton introduced the idea of managed competition and the possibility that government could truly address deep-seated problems without creating a new large bureaucracy, the health care issue and his candidacy took off.

Insofar as managed competition works both as an idea and as a form of government action, it could provide a strategy whereby the nation moves beyond its fears of state bureaucracy and broadens its debate over the social responsibilities of government. Clearly, as the subsequent history of Clinton's health care proposals during his first two years in office demonstrated, this process of changing perspectives may prove to be a difficult one, with many pitfalls. Leaders must give attention not just to the rhetoric of reinventing government but also to the drafting of legislation that convinces the public that managed competition without a massive new bureaucracy is possible. Otherwise, public fear of government will resurface and cripple even innovative social programs such as national health care that initially enjoy widespread public support. Although national health care floundered at the end of the 103rd Congress as a result of growing public fear that the Clinton plan was more bureaucratic in nature than he had promised, the ultimate consequence of this defeat may be to encourage leaders to give more sustained attention to the genuine reinvention of government, thereby increasing the long-term possibility of successful social activism at the national level once existing public bureaucracies are downsized and entreprenuerial strategies of government activism are perfected (Dionne, 1994).

A second, ironic consequence of the shift toward an entrepreneurial conception of government may come in the nation's electoral and party politics. One of the reasons that Democrats proved so successful in maintaining control of Congress and most state legislatures over the past forty years was that the ideological opposition of the Republicans to a large state bureaucracy deprived them of the opportunity to claim credit for the social services provided to individual constituents by national or state governments. Democratic legislators, seeking long-term political careers and willing to embrace bureaucratic service delivery, could claim credit for service delivery; the result was a vote advantage for the Democrats, particularly in poorer legislative districts reliant on state bureaucratic services. The irony today is that, although it is a Democratic president, Bill Clinton, who has brought the issue of managed competition most forcefully to the public's attention, it could well be the Republican Party, and conservative movements generally, that benefits in legislative elections. The reason is that the move to an entrepreneurial conception of government may liberate Republican candidates to support activist social policies that utilize principles of free-enterprise competition and to highlight the value of business experience in the design of such policies. Democratic candidates, tied to the bureaucratic clienteles, could prove not only less adept in embracing entrepreneurial government but also, in the process, less competitive in legislative elections.

The prospect for such a Republican resurgence was vividly demonstrated in the 1994 general elections, as the Grand Old Party gained control of both houses of Congress for the first time in forty-two years and increased its strength significantly in state legislatures. The immediate and pressing question is whether the Republicans, particularly in the Congress, can find a way to implement a fundamental and fiscally responsible restructuring of government while ensuring the existence and equitable availability of vital social services, perhaps even including national health care. Clinton found this a daunting task as a Democrat, falling prey to divisions within his party between supporters of bureaucratic service delivery and advocates of managed competition. The Republicans likewise may find long-term and sustainable innovation difficult; they will be torn between old-school conservatives who see government as evil and revisionist conservatives who believe government can do good for society if only it will do so in accord with entrepreneurial principles. Should the Republicans succeed in overcoming this division and provide a restructured government that citizens find both fiscally credible and responsive to human needs, then a prolonged era of Republican rule could unfold. In contrast, a Republican failure could set the stage for a fundamental alteration of our electoral and party politics as new or reinvented parties attempt to fill the void, a possibility already evident in the surprising success of the Perot movement in 1992 and the unease among moderate and conservative Democrats, particularly members of the Democratic Leadership Council, following the 1994 elections.

The shifting conceptions of government evident in the early 1990s thus could have some truly profound consequences for the nature of American government in the twenty-first century. Instead of gridlock and divided party government, the central characteristics of our politics in the next quarter-century could be programmatic innovation and a restructuring of our party system. In the gloom of the early 1990s, preoccupied as we have been by gridlock and a party politics grown exceedingly stale, these possibilities have seemed almost unthinkable. But American politics has experienced renewal and restructuring before; the Jacksonian period and the Progressive era are two obvious examples. One should not underestimate the power of new ideas (Kingdon, 1994) and their capacity to generate partisan realignment and political renewal. Indeed, the idea that one can restructure government, marrying principles of free-enterprise competition with committed government activism, could provide a mechanism for fundamental alterations not only in policy strategies but in the distribution of political power itself. Such alterations might include, moreover, not only electoral restructuring but also a devolution of political power to state and local governments should policy makers in Washington choose to mandate only the general national goals of social policies and then empower local and state governments to choose among a broad range of entreprenuerial strategies in pursuit of such goals, supported in the process by federal funds.

The Nature of Political Representation

A third shift in the public mindset, even more elusive and ill defined than the shift in the conception of government, may be an alteration in our conception of legislative representation (Eulau et al., 1959; Eulau and Karps, 1977; Pitkin, 1972;

Shepsle, 1988). Early in American history, legislators were expected to be citizens who spoke for their fellow countrymen in the general debates over public policy. The primary issue about representation was whether such legislative spokespersons should be trustees—listening to a debate and using independent judgment in speaking for the issue concerns of citizens—or delegates—articulating positions of the electorate as the members understood those positions.

With the coming of industrialization, and the growth of the service state, the meaning of representation began to shift in America. Increasingly, elected representatives were expected to be professional careerists who would gain clout in the state assembly or on Capitol Hill and use their influence to serve the special and particularized interests of individuals, groups, and the constituency as a whole. Thus in a world of Social Security and veterans' benefits, legislators helped ensure that constituents received their checks on time; in a world of agricultural price supports, legislators gained clout on the agriculture committees and ensured that tobacco or dairy or cotton constituents received their price allotments; in a world of international trade, legislators gained influence on the tax and revenue committees to aid the local manufacturers with special trade or tax benefits; and in a world preoccupied by national security and the building of an invulnerable national defense, legislators served on armed services committees to ensure that their local districts had defense contracts and military installations that would help the local economy while aiding national defense. Legislators came to focus, in other words, less on the major national issues of the day and more on the specific needs of constituency clienteles within a broad industrial-era Cold War agenda that seemed essentially permanent in its general characteristics.

Although legislators certainly have pursued local and particularized interests throughout American history (Swift, 1988), the seemingly permanent emergence of the service state and the defense establishment in the mid-twentieth century created such constituent reliance on the national government that service representation came to rival or even surpass spokesperson representation as the basis on which citizens selected their local legislators (Fiorina, 1977b; Cain, Ferejohn, and Fiorina, 1987). The public thus focused not so much on the issue disputes among candidates as on which candidate could best serve the particularized interests of constituent clienteles. This focus gave a distinct advantage to incumbent legislators with seniority and expertise, particularly entrenched Democrats who supported the service state and also desired long-term legislative careers.

The irony of contemporary legislative politics, and the dilemma for many legislators, is that the public now increasingly appears to see entrenched legislators and clientele politics as major obstacles that inhibit the nation from addressing the policy problems of the late twentieth century. In other words, just as the public no longer sees a bureaucratic state as the most desirable way to produce activist government, it seemingly no longer sees the election of long-term careerist legislators as the best way to ensure the public interest. The bureaucracy magnifies the problems it is expected to redress because it introduces inefficiency and high costs into our economic and social programs; entrenched legislators reinforce these problems by defending bureaucratic agencies whose existence gives the legislator clout with particular constituencies. Together the bureaucracy and the career-ist legislators would appear to be making innovative responses to new policy problems virtually impossible, particularly policy solutions that embrace managed competition and the downsizing of public bureaucracies.

The primary response to this dilemma in the 1990s has been widespread sup-port in the public for the imposition of term limits on all legislators. Referenda and initiatives to impose term limits on state and national legislators have now passed in twenty-two states, with some states such as California also voting to reverse the growth of legislative staffs and resources and to move away from pensions for legislators. The effort to change the nature of legislative politics goes beyond these legislative reforms, however, to include widespread efforts to impose bal-anced-budget provisions in state and national constitutions and to ensure that chief executives have line-item vetoes to use in budget battles with legislatures. Behind these moves appears to be a public perception that representative deci-sion making is so undisciplined and irresponsible in American politics today that a broad range of constitutional checks must now be imposed on legislators if the fiscal integrity and general interests of society are to be ensured.

At issue in the public assault on legislatures is the conception of political repre-sentation that will dominate our legislatures in the nation's third century. It could be, of course, that term limits and balanced-budget movements simply reflect a repudiation of professional legislators and service representation and signify a desire for a return to citizen legislators and spokesperson representation. Alterna-tively—and more likely, I suspect—these movements reflect public experimenta-tion with new conceptions of legislative representation that are more attuned to a postindustrial society and entrepreneurial government.

It is difficult to say what the essence of this new conception of representa-tion will be. My guess, based on a limited number of interviews with California state legislators who are experiencing the shift to term limits, is that the language of representation may increasingly center on "problem-solving," with legislators presenting themselves not solely as issue spokespersons in great debates nor as clientele servants focused on particularized interests but, rather, as troubleshooters with the special knowledge and skills to help address the pressing problems of the moment, after which they will then move on to new political arenas and policy challenges. Underlying this conception of representation is the view that good public policy must be a shifting, fluid, and dynamic response to a rapidly changing, technologically driven society, with today's policy solution potentially becoming tomorrow's policy problem if it becomes entrenched through bureaucratic pro-grams and legislative power structures. Thus long-term entrenched legislators are to be avoided, just as are entrenched bureaucratic agencies, with each generation of new legislators having clear budgetary guidelines spelled out (within which they must address pressing societal dilemmas), and with their political careers in future races for other offices dependent on their ability to demonstrate problem-solving capacities in previous offices. In this model of representation, legislatures are legitimized not solely by the citizen connection of their members nor by the members' careerist clout but by the broad task performance of the legislators in addressing pressing societal dilemmas.

As this discussion indicates, I take the movement for term limits and related reforms seriously. The existence of this movement tells us that something potentially quite significant may be occurring in Americans' attitudes about legislative representation, with real implications for the future of American politics. Perhaps out of this experimentation with a new form of representation will come a more responsive form of legislative decision making attuned to the realities of postindustrialism. Perhaps out of it will come the destruction of legislatures as policy-making institutions, as citizens impose such high levels of turnover, and such tight policy-making constraints, that representative assemblies are unable to sustain their policy-making power. These are issues that require serious assessment and debate, with the results to be shaped not only by the conception of representation that is emerging in America but also by a fourth shift in our attitudes toward politics, to which subject we now turn.

The Character of Democratic Deliberation

The final and most elusive shift that I see in American politics concerns the way citizens think about deliberative democracy (Dodd, 1993; Fishkin, 1991; Mansbridge, 1980). This is not to suggest that citizens ever really think about deliberative democracy as a philosophical concept or as part of a full-blown theory of democratic politics. But most citizens, I suspect, do have some sense of the character of democracy that they prefer and of the role of public discussion and debate that is part of that democratic vision. Throughout American history, political deliberation and policy choice were expected to occur primarily among elected or appointed government officials who had been selected for their position in a constitutional manner, with some linkage to a public mandate. Moreover, as the foregoing discussion of representation should have indicated, deliberation and policy choice in the twentieth century have focused increasingly not on broad policy issues but on the particularized interests of constituents. As a result, deliberation has been a heavily institutional-based process, centered particularly in the Congress and in congressional–executive interactions; it has also been primarily a strategic choice by executive and legislative officeholders about which particularized interests should be most strongly supported in return for reelection benefits and political power. As with the public conception of representation, this twentieth-century understanding of political deliberation may also be changing.

In many ways the most remarkable aspect of the 1992 election and the two years following it has been the growing involvement of the average citizen with the daily discussion of candidates, politics, and policy. This involvement is seen in a variety of forums and activities—the radio talk shows that involve interactive conversations of the hosts and guests with listeners; the town hall meetings that involve questions from the audience for political candidates; the televised legislative sessions beamed to many living rooms daily; the expanded use of candidate debates in the nomination process as well as in the general election and in local and state as well as national races; instantaneous polls that determine the public sentiment on controversies of the movement; the growing use of citizen initiatives and referenda at the state and local levels; and the emergence of the Perot phenomenon, with all the earmarks of a new social movement. All of these factors, of course, had roots in past forms of political activity. But in 1992 they seemed to come together in full force, playing a decisive role in the Perot candidacy and, one suspects, in the Clinton victory as well. And in 1994 Republicans were so convinced that the radio and television talk shows helped generate their congressional landslide that, following the general elections, they held a public testimonial in Washington for conservative talk-show host Rush Limbaugh and publicly attributed their victory to him. Such developments, of course, might be reflecting only a passing public fancy. Then again, they could be manifestations of a deeper public shift.

What may be at play in the emergence of this new interactive and electronic politics is a shifting conception of democratic deliberation. The postindustrial problems of our society and the electronic revolution of recent years may have joined together in the early 1990s to shake public commitment to institutional deliberation and to stimulate growing appreciation of the role of citizens themselves in policy debate and agenda choice. In other words, we may be witnessing a shift away from reliance on political institutions for deliberative decision making and toward societal deliberation and citizen agenda setting—with public officials left to solve the technical and instrumental problems of implementing the broad agenda and policy directions that emerge from the national interactive dialogue among the citizenry.

Although a move toward societal deliberation may well not replace institutional deliberation in quantitative terms, it could become quite potent in setting the broad directions of policy and in determining the fate of particular public officials and policy issues. Thus citizens would be able to focus on issues of crime so extensively on talk shows and in polls that they could almost overnight push crime to the forefront of the national agenda and force Congress and the president to respond with new legislation. The public could deem Vice-President Gore's defense of NAFTA more persuasive than Ross Perot's attacks and shift the position of Congress decisively toward the passage of NAFTA. Citizens could turn against the nomination of Zoe Baird, insisting through talk-show conversations on new and high standards for attorney-general, and thereby doom a presidential nomination. Likewise, they could tire of entrenched legislators and pass term limits that essentially vote all the rascals out of office. And as happened in the state of Colorado, citizens could fly in the face of virtually all public officials, tire of taxes, and decree that all new state, local, and county taxes must be approved by the voting public.

How deep and long-lasting the emergence of societal deliberation will be, only time will tell. Hugh Heclo has suggested that the growth of citizen involvement in political deliberation may well reflect a Tocquevillian need for community (Heclo, 1989). In essence, the mobile citizens of a postindustrial society could be creating a kind of interactive and electronic national community that will bind them together through the airwaves as their ties to local communities disintegrate. If in fact we are witnessing a deep-felt reconstruction of community, then the rise of societal deliberation could be a long-lasting shift indeed. Insofar as the move toward societal deliberation succeeds in creating a sense of national community, it could play a vital role in creating a more cohesive postindustrial nation-state. By contrast, agenda setting through societal deliberation may be inherently prone to simplistic, faddish, and uncompromising policy solutions that exacerbate rather than defuse long-term societal problems; certainly the public imposition of tax limitations in states such as California and Colorado has produced serious long-term consequences, particularly for higher education.

The most explosive consequences of a move toward societal deliberation would seem to occur in interaction with changes in the nature of political representation and thus in the character of our representative assemblies. Reliance on societal deliberation for policy directions, when combined with highly restrictive term limits for legislators (particularly restrictions to three two-year terms or less), could produce revolving legislators who engage in limited institutional deliberation and focus primarily on implementing the policy fad of the moment. Such a development, I fear, would leave public policy and deliberative democracy in a shambles. I say this because of my belief that sound policy making ultimately requires a balanced and informed awareness of the multiple consequences that policy decisions can have, an awareness that normally requires more time and attentiveness than the average citizen can give to public issues. Thus, for citizen deliberation to work effectively, it needs to be moderated and guided by seasoned legislators who refine the policy moods of the public and bring to final policy debates a long-term and broad vision of the implications of policy decisions. It probably takes eight to ten years for legislators to gain such seasoned awareness (Hibbing, 1993), so a responsible term-limit provision would probably need to allow legislators at least fourteen to sixteen years of service in order to encourage the presence of legislators capable of generating reasoned institutional deliberation.

Should a move toward highly restrictive term limits be combined with a heavy reliance on citizen deliberation, the nation may experience a very painful learning experience indeed, as citizens support and legislators duly implement faddish popular policies only to realize gradually that with such policies come long-term consequences that the citizens abhor. Of course, legislators have always paid close attention to public-opinion polls. But the very entrenched nature of many legislators has meant in past decades that major policies could not be changed rapidly;

owing to the protection of key legislators, the entrenchment of legislators thus had the ironic consequence of helping to ensure for some time the assessment of the potential consequences of new policies. In a world of highly restrictive term limits, there may exist few such obstacles to rapid shifts in public policy and thus to the embrace of momentary policy fads, even in areas of complex and critical policy making such as taxation. Thus, although there is much that is potentially creative and valuable in the move toward citizen deliberation, as in the move toward a problem-solving vision of representation, there is potential danger as well, a danger that requires extensive recognition and public discussion. Whether the public can learn to engage in extensive societal deliberation productively and safely, particularly in conjunction with changes in political representation, is today an open question (Dodd, 1994).

Conclusions

These, then, are some reflections on changing habits of thought in modern American society and on the ways that they could generate a new American politics. Such shifting attitudes, evident particularly in the distinctive character of the 1992 and 1994 general elections, are made possible by the end of the Cold War and fueled by the coming of postindustrialism and the modern electronic revolution. The single thread running through all four shifts, I suspect, is a broad desire within the citizenry for a more connected and interactive public policy making than existed during the Cold War era, a new politics in which presidents listen, governments facilitate, legislators problem solve, and citizens are heard.

I share these reflections with a note of caution. Attitudinal shifts that today seem fundamental transformations can easily be seen tomorrow as transient fads. Likewise, unforeseeable world events can engulf what otherwise would be significant political developments, such that very real shifts may in fact leave little lasting trace.

It is important, nevertheless, for students of American politics to grapple with issues of change and transformation and to be attentive to imminent possibilities. In retrospect, it seems inexcusable and virtually inexplicable that contemporary scholars of comparative politics and international relations left largely undiscussed and unforeseen the possibility of broad transformations in Soviet politics and the international world order. Thus the breakup of the Soviet bloc and the end of the Cold War caught virtually the entire political and academic world unawares. Perhaps less attention to the repetitive forms of normal Soviet and Cold War politics—and closer attention to possible shifts in the habits of thought within Soviet society (evident, for example, in the role of public opinion in producing the Soviet withdrawal from Afghanistan)—would have led analysts to more rapidly recognize the weakening of the Soviet state, to foresee the demise of the Soviet Union, and to prepare for the end of the Cold War. Just such attentiveness is needed today with respect to the emerging possibilities of American politics, an attentiveness that requires us not only to examine the predominant and repetitive patterns of politics but also to exercise our intuitive imaginations in assessing its new and unusual manifestations.

I offer here my tentative imagining of how the new, distinctive, and unusual events of the early 1990s in America combine into broader patterns of imminent political transformation: ways in which the emergence of a new American mindset may generate distinctly new forms of governmental and political life. At one level these suggestions are empirical possibilities to be examined through systematic observation and testing: Can we find survey evidence over the next decade, for example, that demonstrates shifts in public understandings of the presidency, the nature of government, political representation, or democratic deliberation? At another level my suggested shifts are dilemmas to be resolved: Each of these political transformations, after all, raises serious issues of statecraft—how best to maintain the authority of the presidency while acknowledging the frailty of presidents; how best to maintain an activist and authoritative state while limiting that aspect of the state—the bureaucracy—that analysts often see as its most critical defining element; how best to sustain the power of legislatures while limiting the entrenched power of legislators; how best to engage the public in serious policy deliberation without turning policy making into a faddish electronic game show. Most fundamentally, what I offer here is an interpretation of how politics and society may fit together in the postindustrial aftermath of the Cold War. It is only an interpretation, and an early interpretation at that. But then all of science, all of knowledge, is only an interpretation, subject to debate, probing, testing, and reformulation. In the social sciences, moreover, the most compelling and relentless test is the future itself.

Acknowledgements: My thanks go to Leslie Anderson, Bryan Jones, and Jennifer Knerr for their comments and support.

Additional Perspective on "The New American Politics"

"The New American Politics" attempts to clarify how new international and domestic developments of the late twentieth century were altering American politics, thereby reshaping the political context within which Congress operates. It focuses on how the broad contextual developments were subtly altering the attitudes of American citizens about the nature of their politics and participation within it. It sees the shifting attitudes and perceptions of citizens as potentially transformative in nature, capable of creating new forms of American politics, and looks to the ramifications such shifts could have for political behavior and institutional politics in the coming decades. In doing so, it takes seriously the admonition in "A Transformational Politics" (Chapter Seven) that close interpretation of emerging social and political conditions is an essential part of political science inquiry in a world characterized by continuous change and novel societal developments.

The essay sets the stage for subsequent works in this volume that seek to understand the interplay between the recurring cycles in the organizational and electoral politics of Congress and ongoing process of social learning within society in coming decades. As the politics of Congress unfolds from the mid-1990s onward, will the cyclical dynamics that seem inherent to the institution, as discussed in Parts I and II, mesh in comprehensible and mutually reinforcing ways with processes of novel social learning that appear to be underway, as seen in the essays in Part III? And will the meshing of these analytically distinct processes foster forward movement in the effective adaptation of the nation to postindustrialism, facilitating ameliorative response to the social dislocations it is bringing? Or will disturbances and tensions arise within and across these processes that undercut such adaptation and amelioration? If so, are their remedies at hand that can address the disruptive effect of such factors? And by what standards and through what lens might we bring some detachment and informed judgment to addressing these questions and grapping with the implications of our answers?

The chapters in Part IV address these concerns by considering (1) the extent to which the multiple processes of change outlined thus far in this volume offer a reasonable, and reasonably foresighted, explanation of the Republican Revolution of the mid-1990s, and the ways in which that Revolution appeared to move forward the adaptation of Congress and the nation to postindustrialism; and (2) whether the House and Senate contribute in distinctly different yet constructive ways to the processes of institutional change, social learning and political renewal.

Foundation Work: The interpretive effort presented here was particularly inspired and informed by Gregory Bateson's provocative 1966 essay, "From Versailles to Cybernetics" (Bateson, 1966). That essay stresses the role that attitudes and attitude shift can play in world affairs, with key attitudinal shifts in essence resetting "the bias of the thermostat" that regulates relations in society and politics (476) and thereby setting in motion new forms of human behavior.

Suggested Reading: Works that speak to arguments introduced in "The New American Politics" include the classic work on presidential personalities and presidential power, James David Barber (1985), *Presidential Character*, which continues to be a 'must-read' book for all interested in the topic; for a contemporary discussion, which put recent presidents in perspective, see Fred Greenstein and Stephen Skowronek (2010), "Resolved, A President's Personal Attributes are the Best Predictors of Performance in the White House," in *Debating the Presidency: Conflicting Perspectives*, edited by Richard J. Ellis and Michael Nelson (Washington, D.C.: CQ Press, 2010). On the continuing debate over how to address and structure social benefits essential to individual and collective well-being, see Hacker (2002); for a discussion of how an increased focus on issues such as taxing, government size, and spending came to the fore in the late 1980s and 1990s, see Berkman (1993); and Koopman (1996).

For discussions of the long-term effects of term limits and related attacks on professional legislatures, see Kousser (2005); and Sarbaugh-Thompson et al. (2004). For discussions of the ongoing revolution in media and electronic politics, see Gainous and Wagner (2011); David Barker and Kathleen Knight, "Political Talk Radio and Public Opinion," *Public Opinion Quarterly*, Summer 2000, Vol 64, No 2, pp. 149-170; David C. Barker, "Rushed Decisions: Political Talk Radio and Vote Choice, 1994-1996," *Journal of Politics* (1999), 61: 527-539; and Kensi, Hardy, and Jamieson (2010). On California as an illustration of the difficulties associated with contemporary legislative politics, see Mathews and Paul (2010); and James Q. Wilson et al. eds., Special Issue: "California Budget Quagmire," *California Journal of Politics and Policy*, Vol 2 (2010): #3.

Classroom Use: This essay can be used in courses on American politics, the presidency, Congress or legislative politics, elections, and media and politics, and in sections focused on changing patterns of political behavior in the 1990s and thereafter. For scholarly and classroom purposes, "The New American Politics" could be paired with Kensi, Hardy and Jamieson (2010) *The Obama Victory* for a consideration of the extent to which themes of the essay are present in or obviated by the candidacy and election success of Barak Obama in 2008.

PART IV

The Multiple Dimensions and Processes of Change

10

RE-ENVISIONING CONGRESS

Theoretical Perspectives on Congressional Change–2004

2001/2005

In 1994, Republicans won control of Congress for the first time in forty-two years, confounding observers who believed the Democrats held a secure hold on power. Why?

"Re-Envisioning Congress" draws on and integrates the arguments in previous chapters to explain the Republican Revolution. In doing so, it introduces a multidimensional perspective on Congress. Looking at the foreground game of politics, the Revolution is seen as a stage in an ongoing cycle of partisan change and organizational reform generated by the ways politicians and parties pursue power. Looking at the background context within which the congressional game is played, the Revolution is a product of postindustrial tensions that overwhelmed a Congress and governing party still oriented toward industrial-era politics. And looking at the ideas linking foreground and background actors, the Revolution is an experimental phase in the effort of politicians and citizens to discover principles by which to resolve postindustrial policy problems.

The Republican Revolution demonstrates the continuing resilience of Congress, holding out the prospect that on-going cycles of partisan learning and regime change will enable Congress to adapt to postindustrialism and reassert its governing legitimacy. The essay concludes by highlighting factors evident in 2005 that could undercut Republicans' consolidation of power and generate a new phase of partisan change and institutional learning.

The early twenty-first century has coincided with a time of remarkable change in the U.S. Congress. For much of the twentieth century, from the Great Depression onward, the Democrats were the majority party in Congress, steering the

Lawrence C. Dodd. "Re-Envisioning Congress: Theoretical Perspectives on Congressional Change—2004." In Congress Reconsidered, 8th Edition. Edited by Lawrence C. Dodd and Bruce I. Oppenheimer. Washington, D.C.: CQ Press. 2005, pp. 411–445. This chapter revises and extends Lawrence C. Dodd. "Re-Envisioning Congress: Theoretical Perspectives on Congressional change." Congress Reconsidered, 7th Edition, Edited by Lawrence C. Dodd and Bruce I. Oppenheimer. Washington, D.C.: CQ Press. 2001, pp. 389–414.

country toward an activist social agenda and generating a remarkable amount of institutional and policy innovation. The party's core agenda issues such as Social Security were so popular, and Democratic incumbents paid such close attention to constituents' service needs and to interest groups' programmatic concerns, that the party appeared to have a permanent lock on Congress, particularly the House of Representatives. Thus as Congress entered the 1990s most observers expected Democratic control to continue,[1] despite public opinion polls demonstrating widespread unhappiness with Congress as an institution.[2] Instead, the decade witnessed a dramatic Republican assault on the Democrats and on Congress itself, which culminated in the "Republican revolution" in the 1994 elections.

Once in control of Congress, the Republicans engaged in an aggressive push toward majority party dominance of national government. During the first four years in power they pursued a political and policy struggle of historic proportions with the Democratic president and his congressional party. This struggle included two government shutdowns, the enactment of welfare reform over the objections of most congressional Democrats, and the impeachment of President Clinton. As the struggle went forward, the Republicans maintained control of the House and Senate by slim margins in the 1996 and 1998 elections. The 2000 elections, again generating narrow Republican majorities, extended the Republicans' control into a fourth Congress, delivered the presidency to their nominee, George W. Bush, and gave the party unified control of national government. The 2004 elections then solidified united party control, with expanded Republican majorities in the House and Senate and a popular vote majority for their president. This victory positioned the party to consolidate its long-term dominance of Congress and the presidency and possibly to reshape the Supreme Court for decades to come.

How could this have happened? What does it tell us about Congress as an institution? And what might it tell us about American politics in the first decade of the new century?

In this chapter I address these questions by presenting three theoretical perspectives that, taken together, help us to understand such periods of unexpected change and to clarify the placement and meaning of such changes in contemporary politics. These theories argue that such upheavals, illustrated forcefully by the Republican revolution, can best be understood not as aberrations in our politics but as the natural, long-term outgrowth of three factors: the goals and strategies that politicians bring to congressional politics, the shifting societal contexts that they confront, and the changing ideas about politics that they experiment with as they pursue their goals and address societal problems. To better understand these three theories and their significance for Congress, we will start by considering why the Republican revolution was so puzzling and how the three theories can help us address that puzzle. Then we will examine the three theories, the sense they make out of contemporary politics, and what they together can tell us about the current state of Congress and the nation.

The Puzzle and Explanatory Strategy

What is so puzzling about the Republican revolution is that it occurred at all, given the hold on Congress that the Democrats appeared to enjoy, and that it followed the path it did once the Republicans assumed control of Congress. Three aspects of this overall puzzle require particular attention.

First, the Republican victory came at a time when members of Congress possessed more resources than at any other time in history for conducting constituent service, contacting constituents personally, addressing their specific programmatic needs, and traveling home to meet with them. The incumbent advantage in congressional elections seemed assured, and there appeared little role for national policy agendas or national election forces in congressional elections. These factors seemed to tilt Congress decisively toward Democratic control and to make a serious Republican challenge almost inconceivable, short of conditions such as a major economic crisis. Republican takeover of the House of Representatives seemed particularly unlikely because localized constituent service and targeted federal programs appeared to provide a very special incumbent advantage in the relatively small congressional districts that compose the House. Despite these expectations, in 1994 the Republican Party produced one of the most massive vote swings against an incumbent congressional party in American history.[3] The Republicans captured both the House and Senate and even defeated powerful House committee chairs and the Democratic Speaker, Tom Foley. They accomplished all of this, moreover, in a time of good economic conditions. They did so by stressing a common policy agenda and nationalizing the congressional elections.

Second, as they maneuvered for control of Congress in the decade prior to the 1994 election, and during the 1994 campaign itself, the Republicans systematically attacked the legitimacy of Congress as a governing institution. After gaining control of the Congress that they had worked so hard to capture, Republicans then found themselves constrained by the public distrust of Congress they had helped inflame. Unable to put in place a strong leadership structure, they found themselves blamed for two government shutdowns, embroiled in factional fights, and subjected to three straight elections in which they lost seats in the House and stumbled precariously in the Senate, barely holding on to control of Congress. Their remarkable surge forward in 1994 thus was followed not by the rapid consolidation of a new Republican era that it seemed to portend but by stalemate. This sense of stalemate and tenuousness in the party's hold on power was reinforced by the electoral college controversy surrounding George W. Bush's 2000 presidential victory, which cast a cloud of illegitimacy over the party's claim to unified party control of government once it arrived.

Third, despite the difficulties the Republicans faced as they sought to solidify control of Congress and assert unified party government, their support at the polls did not collapse. They rebounded from the government shutdowns and maintained control of both houses in the 1996, 1998, and 2000 elections, despite a Democratic resurgence. Along the way, the party enacted major new legislation, from reform of welfare laws to trade normalization with China. The Republicans momentarily lost control of the Senate in summer 2001 when Sen. Jim Jeffords, R-Vt., switched to independent status and gave the Democrats chamber control, but the party re-won control at the polls in 2002, while expanding its margin in the House. Then came a major move forward in control of the House and Senate in the 2004 elections, including the defeat of the Democrats' most visible national spokesperson, Senate Minority Leader Tom Daschle of South Dakota. The Republicans' decade-long hold on power, combined with the impressive congressional victories of 2002 and 2004, made clear that the 1994 victory was not a fluke. The Republican revolution had been real, not a momentary electoral anomaly, positioning the party for sustained pursuit of unified and consolidated control of the national government.

In response to these developments, analysts have presented an interpretation of the Republican revolution that stresses its uniqueness and attributes it almost entirely to the hard work and brilliance of one man, Rep. Newt Gingrich of Georgia.[4] The general image conveyed by the converge of events of 1994 and thereafter emphasized the overarching role of Gingrich in orienting congressional Republicans toward a systematic assault on the Democrats in the 1980s and early 1990s, in creating a strategy of attacking Congress in order to discredit the governing Democrats, in aggressively using GOPAC to build a Republican base, in building a "farm team" of Republican challengers, and in creating the thematic focus on a Conservative Opportunity Society and on the Contract with America.

The result has been a kind of "great man" theory of revolution that seems to imply that if only Gingrich had been defeated in 1990, when he faced an extremely close election, the Democrats would have maintained control of Congress and New Deal-Great Society hegemony would have gone unchallenged. This perspective further implies that the Republicans faltered midway through the 104th Congress because Gingrich became overwhelmed with hubris; they recovered in summer 1996 because he recovered; they struggled thereafter because of his ethical struggles and loss of nerve; and they suffered grievously with his miscalculation in relying on impeachment of Clinton to save the Republican Party. Their rebound in the 106th Congress then could be attributed to Gingrich's sagacity in maneuvering Dennis Hastert, Ill., into the speakership as he resigned from the House, putting in place a soft-spoken Gingrich ally who could continue the revolution without generating the negative vibes associated with Gingrich himself. Well served by this leadership transition, congressional Republicans were then positioned to take advantage of the political skills that another great man, George W. Bush, would bring to the head of their national ticket in 2000 and thereafter.

Certainly there is some truth in the emphasis on Gingrich's critical role in the revolution, and on George W. Bush's role in helping realize its longer-term potential. Individuals do matter in politics and history. A gifted politician may see historical dynamics more clearly than others and act in ways that accentuate them. Yet how can an individual overcome "scientific" truths, such as the argument by congressional scholars that citizens' preoccupation with casework politics and public lack of interest in sweeping policy agendas had frozen the Republicans out of contention in the House and limited their future in the Senate? And even if Gingrich, and later Bush, were remarkably adept at sensing the underlying dynamics of history, what was it that they had sensed? What were the historical dynamics that had suggested opportunities to exploit and strategies to pursue?[5]

In contrast to the great man or personalistic perspective, this chapter argues that developments such as the Republican revolution reflect broader dynamics in institutions and societies, and that it is through our identification of such dynamics that we make systematic sense out of critical events.[6] In the short run there are always advantages—city machines in the late nineteenth century, constituent service in the late twentieth century—that benefit one party or group and appear to contemporary observers to make it impregnable to political challenge. But in the long run there are historical processes at work that erode such advantages and subject legislators, their parties, and Congress to new political circumstances. As we understand these dynamic processes, thinking about Congress not by focusing on short-term and static partisan advantages but by assessing long-term dynamic processes, we gain a general sense of how and why surprising upheavals such as the Republican revolution occur. We also learn to focus less on great men and more on the underlying dynamics that help generate and constrain great leadership and in the process change the structure of politics.

To understand the historical processes shaping contemporary politics, this essay looks at Congress through three theoretical perspectives: First, we will employ a *social choice* or microeconomic perspective, which sees the revolution as a predictable stage in a natural and ongoing cycle of organizational and partisan change in Congress, a cycle generated by the strategic ways in which politicians and parties pursue governing power. Second, we will employ a *social structure* or historical-sociological perspective, which sees the revolution as a product of postindustrial societal tensions and public frustrations that overwhelmed a Congress and governing party still oriented toward industrial-era politics. Third, we will employ a cognitive or *social learning* perspective, which sees the revolution as an experimental phase in the effort of politicians and citizens to discover principles and strategies by which to resolve postindustrial policy problems and legitimize a new governing regime.

By looking at congressional politics through these distinct theoretical lenses, we can understand Congress in much the same way as we understand sporting events such as basketball. To some degree we explain which team wins and which loses by focusing on the nature or logic of basketball as a game and the skills, training, personal goals, and team commitment that players bring to it. Invariably, as we do so, we find that one team initially prepares well and works hard to win, but then with success and time it becomes lax and self-indulgent, while another grows strong, leading winners to lose and losers to win. A concentrated focus on the preparation, strategies, and psychology of teams serves us well as we try to explain a basketball game, but few of us rely solely on these "foreground" issues to fully understand teams' successes and failures. We also look at the background context within which games are played: who has the home-court advantage and has best cultivated such advantages; who has the most at stake in a game and may be most willing to take unusual risks or to break normal conventions, as in "talking trash" to gain psychological advantage over another team. Finally, as great teams meet on the court, we invariably consider the philosophies of the game held by the different coaches, schools, and regions of the country: Which philosophy is better, a strong defense or an aggressive running offense? Which philosophy is outmoded and no longer reflects the realities of a new basketball era? Which is innovative and in touch with new strategies and understandings?

In explaining college basketball, or some other sport, we consider each of these factors—the foreground game, the background context, and the overarching philosophies—and then we also look across these dimensions, thinking about their interaction. To what extent, for example, can contextual factors like home-court advantage, or a new and innovative basketball philosophy, make a winner out of a sure loser? As we talk about these issues, each of us has our favorite set of arguments or theories that we debate with others. We do so partly to explain who has won or to predict who will win. But we do so also to understand the essence of the game, to gain perspective on how that essence is changing, and to see how and why the game may change again in the future.

We are following a similar strategy in using a multitheoretical perspective to understand the congressional game and how it changes. Thus the social choice theory is an argument about the foreground of politics—how partisan teams play the game of congressional politics and how maneuvering and jockeying for power lead first one party to succeed and then another. The social structure theory is an argument about the background of contemporary politics, about how societal and institutional contexts influence the way citizens feel about congressional politics and thus shape the strategies and opportunities available to parties as they seek power. Finally, the social learning theory is an argument about how the ideas that politicians bring to the game shape their ability to play effectively, create enthusiasm in their fans, and not only generate victory but make their victory worthwhile.

The remainder of this chapter presents these three theories, one by one, and then concludes with a short assessment of what the theories, taken together, tell us about congressional politics early in the twenty-first century. In particular, we consider several factors that could shape and constrain Republicans' long-term consolidation of their hold on unified national government. In presenting these theories and arguments, I ask the reader not simply to respond to them in terms of partisan or ideological preference but to step back, look beyond which team you prefer, and consider the lessons to be learned about Congress and contemporary politics as we bring into clearer focus the dynamic processes that shape the congressional game. With this understanding, let us turn first to our social choice theory and see how far it goes in explaining the broad patterning of the events of the past decade, and then turn to the social structure and social learning theories, in turn, building a more layered and intertwined perspective as we go.

The Social Choice Theory

The social choice theory is designed to clarify how the political game normally proceeds in the foreground of congressional life, irrespective of historical context.[7] Our concern is with identifying the central goal that drives legislators' behavior, much as the desire to win inspires a basketball team, and with examining how legislators' goal-oriented behavior shapes and alters congressional politics across time. A range of motives exists among legislators, any one of which, separately or in combination with others, could form the basis of a theory of congressional change. These include the reelection motive stressed by Morris Fiorina and David Mayhew,[8] the dual goals of reelection and policy stressed by John Aldrich and David Rohde,[9] and the multiple goals of reelection, policy making, and influence examined by Richard Fenno and Barbara Sinclair.[10] Yet the goal that most universally runs through the discussion of politics, from Machiavelli onward, and that would seem to encompass the other goals, is personal power. Thus it is the concern for governing power around which Anthony Downs builds his classic study of the ways that politicians' goals shape legislative elections and democratic government.[11] It is the concern for personal power that Barry Weingast sees as the basis for reelection activities and norm behavior in Congress.[12] The work of Roger Davidson and Walter Oleszek; C. Lawrence Evans and Oleszek; Glenn Parker; and Raymond Wolfinger and Joan Hollinger provides further evidence that members' concern for personal power or autonomy shapes and constrains party loyalty, resource distribution, and reform on Capitol Hill.[13] Thus the central goal around which we will build our social choice theory of Congress is the quest for personal power.

Our strategy is to specify the logical ways in which legislators' pursuit of power shapes the organizational politics of Congress. Microeconomic theorists argue that the pursuit of profit by individuals and firms ultimately leads to national economic cycles of boom and bust. Does the pursuit of power by legislators and their parties likewise lead to predictable patterns of congressional change? Do such patterns provide a plausible explanation of the contemporary upheavals in Congress? Social choice theory argues that the pursuit of power by members and their parties generates recurring cycles of partisan alternation in Congress. We will look at how well the theory explains contemporary developments.

Congress and the Quest for Power

The foundation of our social choice theory is that the quest for personal power by individual legislators leads them to seek power positions and resources within Congress that provide influence over national policy making.[14] In the pursuit of personal power, members organize into partisan teams composed of like-minded members who would use power to serve similar policy objectives. The majority party will control the major power positions within the legislature, such as committee or subcommittee chairs and the speakership. It will also oversee the organizational resources of the assembly, such as office assignments and staff, and it will largely determine congressional rules and procedures. For these reasons, and in ways discussed more fully by Aldrich and Rohde (2005), the majority's dominance of institutional power and resources gives it the upper hand in policy making and governance.

Being in the majority gives members the chance to exercise personal power by becoming committee or party leaders, by skillfully using resources distributed by the party, and by benefiting from rules and procedures that aid majority party policy making. To attain personal power, members thus must work together to develop political strategies and legislative successes that enable the party and its members to gain public support and consolidate control of the assembly.

The efforts of legislators to gain personal power through service in the majority party involve a special paradox. Members' ability to work together in pursuit of majority party status requires a centralized party leadership that can coordinate their activities. Such coordination helps the party to develop a coherent campaign strategy designed to win a legislative majority, address the central policy problems preoccupying its members and supporters, and demonstrate its effective governing capacities in order to retain power. To ensure effective coordination, a party may want to limit the number of "power positions" and powerful legislators, so that undue resistance to party policy and electoral strategies does not emerge among autonomous power-wielders within the party. Yet the rank-and-file party members will push for the creation of numerous power positions, such as committee or subcommittee chairs, and for special resources such as staff, so that they can have real influence on policy. Such influence renders service in the majority a rewarding experience and also allows members to stress significant personal accomplishments in reelection campaigns. Moreover, the majority party itself will need to spread organizational positions and resources somewhat widely in order to draw on the expertise and energy of members in crafting the details of its policy programs and communicating the programs to constituents. The party also will have incentive to distribute positions and resources widely, so that the resulting incumbent advantage helps the party reelect its members and maintain its hold on power. Doing so, however, carries great risks for the party.

The success of individual members in gaining power positions and resources brings policy making and electoral benefits to the party but also some considerable detriments. For example, the success of members in gaining extensive staff allotments not only helps them perform constituent service, potentially aiding both their reelection and the party's retention of power, but also can enable them to prepare and push bills that party leaders might find objectionable. Similarly, gaining a committee or subcommittee chair may provide a member special advantage when running for reelection, aiding the party's hold on majority status, but it also gives him or her an opportunity to push constituent interests that could undermine the party's program. As members gain such power positions and resources, and the autonomy such success can bring, their personal policy preferences and distinctive pressures of their constituents may push them away from the party's policy stances, thereby undermining party coordination and limiting the ability of the party to campaign or govern as an effective team.

The pronounced tension between centralized party power and autonomous personal power generates long-term cycles of organizational and partisan change in Congress. These cycles result from the contrasting personal calculus and political strategies of majority and minority party members.[15]

The Cycles of Congressional Change

After cooperating to win majority status and consolidate party control of the legislature, members of the majority party naturally push to divide up significant power resources among themselves so that all can benefit from the fruits of victory. They will thus support the creation of increasing numbers of formal and informal power positions within the legislature. They will lobby for greater personal resources such as office staff and travel allotments. And they will seek to establish rules within the party caucus and legislative chamber that respect the personal prerogatives of members. In pursuing these various efforts, they in turn fragment the structure of centralized party authority and undermine the majority party's capacity for internal coordination. These developments weaken their party's ability to respond to new policy problems or political circumstances and can thereby undermine public satisfaction with the party's governing success. Yet the decline in enthusiasm for the party itself will appear to be offset by the growing security of party incumbents, who use their increased autonomy and resources to build incumbent advantage in home districts.[16]

In contrast, members of the minority party have far fewer power resources to divide among themselves and significant incentive to support centralized coordination in order to battle with the majority over control of the assembly. Of course, their party may have suffered such a large reduction when it lost control that a rapid return to majority status appears unrealistic. This can constrain minority party members from an immediate focus on cooperation and party loyalty. But as their sojourn in the political wilderness lengthens, minority party members are far more likely than members of the majority to constrain their desire for immediate autonomy and focus on how best to cooperate in gaining majority party status, since that is their only real avenue to meaningful personal power. They will thus increasingly accept some degree of centralized party coordination.

As the minority party challenges the majority, the latter will appear invulnerable owing to the success of its members in winning reelection, but appearances will be deceptive.[17] The fragmented and uncoordinated nature of majority party governance, which helps generate incumbent advantage, also generates festering policy problems in the nation and a growing sense of governing crisis. The electorate, in response, increasingly focuses on assessing the governing capacity of the majority party rather than the personalized benefits received from its members. It is, after all, a party's ability to use institutional power to respond to policy problems and govern effectively that justifies its hold on majority status. Citizens thus will not indefinitely support majority party legislators simply because they ensure the delivery of benefits from programs that address "old problems." Rather, they will consider punishing majority party legislators for current policy failures.[18] This reaction against the majority party will then be assisted by the strategies and actions of the minority.

The out party, sensing the vulnerability of the majority, will use its centralized capacities to coordinate a national election campaign and to focus its candidates on a clear, unified, and coherent party agenda designed to address governing crises and emphasize its capacity to govern. It also will seek to highlight and magnify particular policy problems and perceived crises, even to the point of ensuring policy immobilism that helps to foster such problems. Meanwhile, the majority party will look to the incumbent advantage enjoyed by its members in order to assure itself that the minority party challenge will be fruitless. Its overconfidence will be reinforced by the vested interests that party members have in maintaining the fragmented status quo within Congress, so that they ignore growing public hostility to their party.

Faced with these circumstances, frustrated voters will revolt against the majority party and install the minority in power, doing so in a manner that appears sudden and unexpected but that is in fact a natural consequence of the ways in which members and parties pursue legislative power across time. The old minority party then will have its opportunity to address societal problems and consolidate institutional control. Buoyed by its momentum and the initial loyalty of members, it will almost certainly experience early policy successes. But the underlying issue is whether the new majority party can reform the legislature in ways that reduce the internal fragmentation that the old majority party had built into organizational rules and arrangements. If the new majority party can implement centralizing reforms appropriate to its governing tasks, it may be able to sustain majority status and operate as a powerful congressional party for some time, perhaps several decades, before the power quests of its members erode its centralized structure. If it fails, it may squander its opportunity and allow the opposing party to regain institutional control. Should the minority party itself remain weak and unable to rally, a cross-party coalition of factions may dominate Congress. The resurgent party, or factional coalition, then would face its own challenge in developing a governing structure that could address societal problems and sustain it in power. In time, any successful governing party or coalition would face magnified tensions between its need for centralized power and the desire of its members for autonomy, experience debilitating organizational fragmentation, and confront an unexpected and surprising minority party challenge.

The success of majority party legislators in fragmenting congressional power, combined with the willingness of minority party legislators to accept centralized party guidance, builds long-term cycles of partisan or factional alternation into the organizational life of Congress, according to our social choice theory. How well does this argument account for the upheavals of the 1990s, particularly the coming of the Republican revolution?

The Revolution as a Cyclical Stage

Seen through the lens of social choice theory, the Republican revolution can be explained as a classic product of the recurring cycles of organizational change. The current organizational cycle of Congress began with electoral upheavals of the 1960s and centralizing reforms of the 1970s that solidified liberal Democratic control. The 1980s and early 1990s were a period of fragmentation and growing immobilism, when the popularity of Democratic incumbents as constituent servants masked growing disenchantment with the party's governing capacities. The sudden and surprising defeat of the Democrats in 1994 was a result of the public's long-term unhappiness with the party. This unhappiness came forth in full fury and produced the defeat of the party's most visible and vulnerable incumbents, at a time when the Democrats had proved unable to address the critical governing items that they had promised the nation in the 1992 elections, such as changing the welfare system and implementing national health care, even when joined by a Democratic president. The defeat was unexpected because politicians and political analysts alike had focused on the incumbent advantages the Democrats enjoyed and discounted the public's growing frustration with political gridlock. The defeat was aided by the efforts of the Republicans to pursue a coordinated campaign strategy that used party resources effectively and presented a compelling image of a party prepared to govern cohesively in pursuit of an agenda widely supported by its candidates.

From the perspective of social choice theory, the brilliant electoral strategies of Republican leaders such as Gingrich were a skillful response to the opportunities afforded them by career ambitions, organizational fragmentation, and policy immobilism within the majority Democratic Party, rather than the machinations of a rare political genius. The early organizational innovations and policy successes of the Republican Party were natural consequences of the internal cohesion it had developed in its pursuit of majority status and of members' concerns to act on its governing mandate. Subsequent factional conflict among Republicans resulted, in part, from the natural reemergence of personal ambitions and power pursuits within a majority party and from frustrations with the realities of governing in a complex policy-making environment.

But the factional conflict was also a consequence of the failure of the party, particularly in the House, to enact reforms that would institutionalize a centralized authority structure. Leaders granted such centralized authority could manage conflict and pursue strategies that would sustain and consolidate the revolution. Rather than decisively strengthening the speakership, the Republicans enacted limits on service as Speaker that substantially weakened party leadership during the Gingrich era, retracting the term limit mandate only in December 2002, long after Gingrich had left the scene. Instead, they relied on the personal power of Gingrich, the good will of members, and debts owed him by members and committee chairs during his speakership. In addition, rather than streamlining the committee system in ways that might make it a more effective policy-making instrument and less a vehicle of member ambitions, for example by strengthening the budget committees and expanding their capacity to constrain and prioritize spending across the federal budget, the Republicans largely kept the old system in place, making changes that were mainly cosmetic and that did little to aid decisive action on their new agenda. The Republicans thus would face a difficult task in consolidating their control, particularly given the electorate's close division between Republicans and Democrats.

The social choice theory of organizational cycles seems to go a long way in accounting for the Republicans' sudden and surprising defeat of a long-term majority party, yet it also has its limits. Why, at their moment of victory, did the Republicans not follow through and implement real reform, choosing instead to undercut the very centralized leadership that had "brought them to the dance"? Why did they maneuver, moreover, for constitutional changes such as term limits and budget constraints that would seem to limit their own power as a majority party?[19] Why did the Republicans themselves so rapidly become the object of public scorn? And why did factional problems emerge so rapidly at the highest levels of leadership activity, so that the Republicans' governing capacities were thrown into serious question despite their great electoral victory?

The social choice theory, focused as it is on the general patterning of congressional change irrespective of historical context, cannot satisfactorily account for these distinctive characteristics and problems of the 1994 revolution. To do so, for reasons illustrated powerfully by Smith and Gamm (2005) and Cooper (2005), we need to shift our conceptual focus to background factors and examine the social context and historical conditions within which it occurred.

The Social Structure Theory

As we shift from the foreground of congressional politics to the background, we will consider how Congress's power struggles and organizational cycles are shaped and altered by the societal conditions within which they occur. In doing so, we will be taking a sociological approach to Congress.

A strong sociological tradition exists in studies of the historical development of Congress. It is exemplified notably by Nelson Polsby's argument that societal modernization generates growing demands on legislatures and induces organizational specialization and institutionalization as they respond, a pattern he demonstrates for the U.S. House of Representatives.[20] We also have insightful sociological analyses of congressional politics during specific eras.[21] Thus James Sterling Young demonstrates how agrarianism, regionalism, and popular suspicion of government generated a passive, factionalized, and constrained early Congress. Woodrow Wilson argues that social changes after the Civil War strengthened the governing role of a centralized, party-driven Congress and pushed the nation toward congressional government. Joseph Cooper and David Brady highlight the ways industrialization and growing careerist politics produced a crisis of adaptation in the early-twentieth-century Congress that undermined strong parties and crippled congressional government. And Theodore Lowi charts the ways that advanced industrialization in midcentury helped create a bureaucratized and clientelist politics that he called "interest group liberalism," solidifying committee government and subsystem politics within a weakened Congress.

Our concern is to assess whether changes in social structure during the contemporary period are having an equally profound impact on Congress and its party politics and whether this shift in context can thereby help us better understand the Republican revolution. This issue requires us first to identify the fundamental changes occurring in the contemporary era and then to consider their potential significance.

The Postindustrial Transition

Historical sociologists have argued that the most critical change among advanced industrial democracies from the 1950s onward has been the move to a postindustrial society driven by a high-tech economy dependent on technological innovation and dominated by service-based employment.[22] The issue facing such nations is whether the policy programs and governing arrangements created to manage industrial-era problems can adapt to this new world.

During the advanced industrial era of the early twentieth century, as the workforce was employed in blue-collar, mass production industry and subject to periods of severe economic dislocations, democracies such as the United States created extensive social service programs. These programs were designed to supplement the health and retirement benefits that blue-collar workers received through union contracts with employers and to aid unemployed workers hurt by the ebbs and flows of the economic cycles associated with modern capitalism. Severe downturns such as the Great Depression not only caused great harm to large groups of individuals (with as many as a quarter of adult Americans unemployed at critical points during the 1930s) but put the stability of the nation and the sustainability of capitalist democracy at risk, thereby reinforcing the need for social programs. Governments also created "safety net" programs such as price supports for the industries. Governments created these programs because large numbers of specialized workers, along with stable manufacturing and agricultural sectors, were essential to the industrial production that generated strong national economies. Such nations also created large bureaucracies to implement the programs and generated political processes such as interest group liberalism and subsystem politics that sustained support for the programs. They also solidified class-based party systems that designed and oversaw the operation of the service programs.

According to social structure theory, the move to a postindustrial society introduces policy problems and political pressures that the governing arrangements inherited from the industrial era cannot address.[23] Although the postindustrialist economy creates high-tech jobs that employ a highly educated and specialized workforce, it also erodes the security of citizens as the new postindustrial employment sectors reduce or eliminate the social benefits provided workers by the union contracts of the industrial era. These citizens turn to government, which is already committed to providing safety nets, and expect it to replace and expand the lost benefits.

In addition, the educated citizens of the postindustrial era expect the national government to address a broadening array of quality-of-life issues overlooked in the industrial era—from racial and gender equality, to consumer protection, to environmental regulation, to quality education, and the list goes on. These "post-materialist" demands[24] put enormous fiscal pressure on the government, pressures not fully offset by growing economic productivity. They also push government into cultural controversies over the values that an activist government should support. These pressures are illustrated by division within the nation over whether abortion should be legal and receive the same kinds of government recognition and funding as other medical procedures, or whether gay couples should have access to benefits and protections the government provides to heterosexuals.[25]

Two political arrangements inherited from the advanced industrial era exacerbate these problems. First, government reliance on expensive and impersonal bureaucracies to implement postindustrial programs further magnifies their cost, while their impersonal nature and intrusiveness accentuate perceptions of cultural insensitivity. Second, electoral rules and interest group politics entrench pre-existing political parties in power, despite their preoccupation with programmatic positions adopted in the industrial era, inhibiting the rise of new parties that might address the new economic and cultural issues.

Social structure theory suggests that citizens faced with such circumstances will question the legitimacy of their government. In particular, they will turn against the democratic institutions most responsible for making public policy and against the traditional parties. Although the severity of public hostility will vary with the boom and bust cycles of national economies, declining somewhat in good times, the public's growing disenchantment with governing institutions eventually should produce a breakdown in democratic government.

This breakdown will occur not because postindustrial citizens are antidemocratic but because the institutional and political arrangements inherited from the industrial era do not provide them with adequate mechanisms with which to generate and legitimate new policy directions and governing regimes. The antiquated structures and procedures of a passing era are instead likely to cripple the capacity of citizens to convey their genuine policy preferences and political loyalties to their elected representatives, leading them to question such democratic procedures. No more vivid illustration of this argument is needed than the crisis over the selection of the new president in the weeks following the 2000 elections. This crisis gave dramatic demonstration of just how debilitated twenty-first-century politics may be when regulated by antiquated procedures, from an eighteenth-century electoral college to nineteenth-century judicial procedures to twentieth-century punch cards, with such procedures throwing the legitimacy of the new president into doubt. The election controversy created issues of legitimacy around the presidency of George W. Bush and Republican control of national government that shadowed the party throughout Bush's first term.

Congress and the Crisis of Legitimation

The social structure argument suggests that disenchantment with the legitimacy of governing institutions should be an integral part of contemporary American politics and that such disenchantment should focus, in particular, on Congress and its two parties.[26] The public would be concerned with Congress because of its powerful role in national policy making, a role greater than that of national legislatures elsewhere. In addition, as Morris Fiorina argued eloquently in *Congress: Keystone of the Washington Establishment*, the electoral and organizational politics of Congress—including the rise of careerist politicians, the prevalence of constituent service activities, engrained norms of seniority, the limited governing capacity of congressional parties, and the veto power of committees—have made it the institution most constrained by industrial-era clientelist and casework politics and by safe incumbents who benefit from such politics.[27] These developments make Congress the national institution most pressured to continue industrial-era policy strategies and reinforce the inclination of citizens to turn their fury against it.

Most important, Congress suffers because it is controlled by parties still rooted in industrial-era politics. Because the Democratic Party created the service state, and thus is the party most constrained by interest group liberalism, public hostility focuses first and foremost on it. This hostility provides strategic opportunities for short-term Republican challenges. But social structure theory questions the long-term capacities of the Republican Party, or any industrial-era party, to solidify public support. Each party will be too beholden to its own industrial-era clientele groups, too blinded by industrial-era programmatic positions, and too compromised by the behavior of its own incumbents to address the problems of postindustrialism in innovative ways.

As we look at the contemporary Congress from a critical sociological perspective, we see an institution out of sync with the emerging postindustrial society and prone to a severe crisis of institutional legitimacy. Power struggles and partisan shifts may be proceeding in the foreground according to normal cyclical patterns predicted by social choice theory. Looking at Congress solely through social choice lenses, we might conclude that nothing truly serious was occurring on Capitol Hill, other than the normal alternation of partisan elites that we occasionally expect. But historical sociologists, looking through the lens of social structure theory, see the Republican revolution as a more momentous development.

The Revolution as a Product of Postindustrial Tensions

The Republican revolution that engulfed Congress in the mid-1990s, as seen from a critical sociological perspective, was a consequence of the growing societal tensions associated with postindustrialism and the legitimation crisis those tensions necessarily generate. In the preceding decades the Democratic Party had held firmly to its orthodox programmatic orientation, the protection and expansion of Social Security, while otherwise failing to provide innovative leadership, when seen against proposals for massive, rapid, and fundamental change. This failure was demonstrated in soaring deficits and in the continuance of festering problems with the environments, poverty, crime, and other quality-of-life concerns. With it came the public's growing disillusionment with Congress and its governing party and the attendant doubts about their governing legitimacy. As a party pursuing power and seeking electoral support, the Republicans embraced the public frustration, gave it public voice, and rode it to power.

The Republican attack began in the 1970s, when President Richard Nixon chided the "credit card Congress" and wasteful Democrats and impounded funds that had been enacted by the Democrats in a constitutionally prescribed manner. Nixon's actions threatened to upend the balance of constitutional power between Congress and the president, before the courts forced him to retreat.[28] The election of Ronald Reagan in 1980 then renewed the Republican assault. Reagan challenged the Democrats' support for "big government" and pushed massive tax cuts, derided their "permissive" stance on cultural issues such as abortion, and scorned their support for "welfare dependency." Reagan also questioned the Democratic commitment to forceful assertion of American interests and power on the international stage and pushed an increase in military spending. His outreach to "Reagan Democrats" in the South and Midwest seemed to portend an imminent Republican takeover of Congress, but the 1982 recession ended such momentum. The Iran-contra controversy in his second term then raised constitutional issues that weakened Reagan's governing authority.

In the end, the concerted and sustained challenge to the Democrats came to the fore in the 1980s within Congress itself, led by young Republicans such as Newt Gingrich and Trent Lott. Convinced that the constituent service activities of incumbent Democrats gave them an unfair advantage that could lock their party in power permanently unless dire measures were taken, Gingrich and his allies engaged in a furious attack that violated the most fundamental norms of comity and decorum within the Congress.[29] In doing so, they highlighted the misdeeds of the Democrats, from Speaker Jim Wright's questionable use of book royalties to members' bounced checks in the House bank, as a way to underscore the sense of a governing party and Congress that were corrupt and illegitimate at the core. To address the problems, they proposed term limits on members, constitutional constraints on Congress's budgetary power, and strengthening the presidency (the institution Republicans had dominated for most of the previous forty years) by granting presidents the line-item veto. And they also questioned the policy positions of the governing Democrats, along the lines of Nixon and Reagan, and proposed the Democrats' removal from power.

These tactics and proposals, attacking not just the policy positions of Democrats but the constitutional authority and governing legitimacy of Congress itself, struck a chord with the public, to a large extent reflecting and magnifying rather than creating public opinion. Coming at a time when the Democrats were vulnerable because of their internal fragmentation, the Republican attack swept the majority party from power in dramatic fashion, appearing to shake the foundations of congressional politics and to mandate dramatic change.

Ironically, and as social structure theory would suggest, once in power the Republicans became victims of the legitimation crisis they had helped to fuel. Early on, as they sought to organize Congress, the party's call for term limits on members (which lost momentum once it became the majority party) became transformed into pressure within the party for imposing term limits on the Republican Speaker and committee chairs in the House, as a way of demonstrating to the public the party's sincerity about reform. Thus did their attack on the instiution boomerang, limiting their own capacity to put in place a governing structure that would help them pursue broad-scale governmental change.[30] Meanwhile, as discussed by Hibbing and Larimer (2005), the public continued to be suspicious of Congress and politicians in general following the Republican takeover. In part this suspicion extended to the Republicans because their earlier investigation of the ethical problems of Democrats (as in the scandal over bounced checks) had also tarnished many of their own colleagues. But the public's wariness of the Republicans had been magnified by the doubts the party had cast on Congress as a governing institution. If Congress was truly as corrupt and outmoded as the Republicans had suggested, it was not clear that they could really improve matters. Citizens thus granted little leeway to the new congressional majority party.

When the Republican Party shut down the government in a budgetary struggle with the president in late 1995, and then proved unable to negotiate with the president because of the weak authority granted to its leadership, the public saw the fiasco as an illustration of the Republicans' own governing incompetence, and the momentum of the revolution stalled. Thereafter, ethical problems associated with Speaker Gingrich, combined with the move of House Republicans to impeach President Clinton despite his public support, deepened citizen disenchantment with Republican governance. It was only the absence of a viable alternative party capable of forcefully moving Congress beyond the Democratic era that kept the Republicans in control during the 1990s. The long-term security of this control then seemed even less certain after the 2000 crisis surrounding Bush's election, particularly when the tax cuts he championed at the beginning of his presidency failed to generate sustained job growth following a cyclical downturn in the economy. Rather, their size and tilt to the wealthy, together with energy and environmental policies favorable to industry, seemed to reinforce the sense that the Republican Party was dominated by its industrial-era clientele groups, just as was the case with the Democrats when they were in power.

From a critical sociological perspective, then, the Republican revolution and its aftermath serve both as a demonstration of the powerful tensions emerging with postindustrialism and as proof of the inability of Congress and the existing congressional parties to address the tensions. This perspective, articulated strongly by Ralph Nader during his 2000 presidential bid, sees the parties and Congress as illegitimate governing instruments destined to lead the nation further astray. Social choice theory then adds the prediction that Republicans' consolidation of their majority will generate renewed pressures toward organizational fragmentation and increased governing problems. The interaction of internal congressional dynamics and external societal tensions seems likely to generate a magnified legitimation crisis, increasing the threat to representative democracy.

These concerns raise serious questions. Is there any model for understanding contemporary politics that might suggest a way to avoid institutional collapse? Is there some ameliorative process at work across the foreground and background of congressional politics that we are simply missing as we look through the lenses of social choice and social structure theories? Moreover, might the Republican revolution be a part of this process, its role helping us to explain the party's continued success in renewing and expanding control of Congress and unified national government in the 2004 elections? These questions suggest that we step back and consider whether there is a broader integrative pattern linking these foreground and background worlds, a shift in which might transform the outcome. Let us now look at Congress through the lens of social learning theory.

The Social Learning Theory

Our goal in turning to social learning theory is to examine how the ideas of citizens and politicians help shape congressional politics and to consider whether new ideas can facilitate the adjustment to a new political era. A cognitive perspective asks that we study Congress by becoming aware of the belief systems and learning processes that characterize society across time and by seeing Congress and its parties as participants in societal learning.

Central to the dominant scholarly conceptions of social learning, particularly as developed by Gregory Bateson and Geoffrey Vickers, is the perception that individuals and groups develop understandings of the world that they share with one another in order to operate effectively.[31] Each generation must develop a realistic understanding of how best to balance personal and collective well-being within its particular historical conditions. Insofar as it does so, its members can compete effectively in pursuit of personal interests at the same time as they address collective social problems and construct viable societies. As the world changes and ideas become outmoded, the ability to accomplish such personal goals and public purposes declines. The solution, from a social learning perspective, is for a new generation to engage in experimental learning of new ideas appropriate to new circumstances. As they discover such ideas and integrate them with orthodox perspectives essential to societal continuity, a more viable social paradigm emerges that can facilitate societal well-being and effective governance.

What might a learning perspective tell us about the capacity of Congress to respond to postindustrialism and the role of the Republican revolution in that process? This requires us first to consider more closely the nature of social learning.

The Process of Social Learning: Crisis, Experimentation, and Paradigm Shift

All of us have experienced the process of social learning in our lives. As an example, think back to sports as a metaphor for understanding politics. Occasionally we see teams that fail to adjust to new circumstances, such as the adoption of the three-point shot in college basketball, and thus lose regularly. The team's coaching staff understands the school's social culture and recruiting strengths, but the coaches learned the game before the new rules were envisioned, so they are committed to an older, more conservative philosophy of basketball. Frustrated after several losing seasons, anxious fans demand change, and college administrators search for a new coaching staff. The college may have to experiment with several coaching arrangements, introducing new members who embrace a more aggressive basketball philosophy while keeping some existing coaches, before it discovers a staff whose approach effectively balances a respect for the program's historic strengths with new ideas about how best to play the game. Once the school finds such a staff, the players learn new strategies of play, and excited fans learn to appreciate the three-point shot. Such a process of social learning, undertaken across several years by administrators, staff, players, and fans, can rejuvenate support for basketball on a campus.

Social learning theory argues that the significant role that ideas and learning play in our private lives, as illustrated here by basketball, also can be seen in politics.[32] An institution such as Congress may have governing problems, not just because of debilitating power struggles or entrenched interests, but because of outmoded thinking. The ideas or social paradigms that dominate congressional politics may once have worked, but times change. Those who learned about politics in the previous era may be so accustomed to thinking within the old paradigm that they fail to comprehend that society is changing and oppose efforts to experiment with new ideas. A social crisis would then lead groups of citizens to demand action and to support ambitious politicians who are willing to experiment and change.

As with finding a successful coaching staff, it may take time, a series of experimental shifts in leaders and programs, and the creative combination of new ideas and orthodox perspectives to find a viable paradigm. It also may take a new generation of politicians and social activists, drawn to service in Congress because of its great constitutional power, who challenge existing arrangements and push new policy perspectives.[33] As the new generation experiments with innovative ideas and constructs a new approach that appears to work, Congress and the nation experience a paradigm shift that can reshape politics and society as powerfully as a new philosophy of basketball can reshape campus sports.

Extensive change in governing paradigms is necessarily slow, in part because of the difficulty of restructuring politics in the midst of complex structures, anachronistic rules, and entrenched alliances but also because social learning itself is a slow process. It requires moments of crisis and recognition of problems, both of which can focus attention on the critical issues, and also incremental processes of experimentation and assimilation.[34] The reliance of Congress on popular elections to select its members helps to make it sensitive to social problems and to the occasional upheavals in the public's partisan loyalties that signal deep societal tensions and crises. The deliberative nature of the committee system and the institution's overall decision-making processes facilitates the informed and methodical reconstruction of paradigmatic understanding in response to crises.

Actual paradigmatic shift comes in phases of innovation followed by assimilative retrenchment, as new ideas break forth amid crisis and then are integrated into pre-existing understandings. These phases bring with them segmented and partial paradigm shifts: Congress and the nation experiment with some ideas central to a new era, see their value and limits when institutionalized in governing strategies, and move on to new problems and paradigmatic adjustment. This pattern of phased and segmented transformation of paradigms can be seen in the response of Congress and its parties to postindustrialism, with the Republican revolution being one such phase of experimental learning.

Congress and the Politics of Renewal: Responding to Postindustrialism

Starting in the 1950s, when the postindustrial transition first began to emerge, we see incremental phases of a paradigm shift across decades of experimentation and assimilation. During the 1950s Congress was still dominated by southern Democrats elected in a segregated political world and was characterized, as it had been since the late 1930s, by a deep resistance to social activism, with the exception of Social Security and occasional increases in the minimum wage. There were few signs of the strong partisan leadership necessary for broad-scale policy innovation. Congressional policy making depended, instead, on a conservative coalition of southern Democrats and northern Republicans committed to the status quo. Congress truly seemed immune to new ideas, social learning, or a transformative response to postindustrialism.[35] But in fact it did change and respond.

In the 1960s, activated by the influx of a new generation of northern Democratic liberals and presidential leadership from two former members, John Kennedy and Lyndon Johnson, Congress broke its policy immobilism and implemented a broad range of programs designed to address postmaterialist policy concerns—including affirmative action for racial and ethnic minorities and women, health care for retired and displaced citizens, environmental and consumer reforms to protect our quality of life, and federal aid to education. This response came amid a growing sense of disorder and crisis over the nation's inability to address vital issues such as civil rights. It also came amid increased belief within the Democratic Party that its traditional commitment to social justice entailed not just the righting of economic wrongs and insecurities induce by modern capitalism, which continued to concern it with respect to fate of the elderly. It also entailed response to such injustices as racial, ethnic, and gender inequality, the inequality in educational opportunities of the young, or the undue social costs accompanying environmental degradation or consumer fraud. This period of expanded activism, highlighted in Sarah Binder's statistical analysis of postwar growth in policy agendas,[36] laid the foundations for a postmaterialist paradigm that moved the nation beyond issues of Social Security and responded broadly to social movements and citizen protests of early postindustrialism. It also moved the Democratic Party beyond attention to, and electoral reliance on, organized labor and connected it to new social movements transforming the face of the nation.

These developments broadened the base of the party and created substantial demands that it fulfill its new postmaterialist agenda. At the same time, such Great Society activism enlarged government bureaucracy and expanded its fiscal commitments in ways that fostered concern about the size, reach, and costs of the national government. It also involved the national government—and thus the governing Democrats in Congress—ever more deeply in cultural and moral conundrums embedded in American society. Such conundrums revolved particularly around the tension between collective responsibility of the nation to ensure social justice and equal opportunity for its citizens, as espoused by the Democrats, and concern that individuals assume primary responsibility for personal well-being, long a foundation principle of the Republican Party.

Growing cultural divisions were augmented by the intrusion of cold war politics into American society, as the Vietnam War led many citizens, particularly liberals and young people within the Democratic Party, to question the extent of their personal obligation to support or be involved with an unjust and costly war. The conflict over the war, combined with the growing concern about the power and reach of the federal government in civil rights and social policy, increased the intransigence of southern conservative Democrats in Congress, who were a minority of the party but held many positions of committee leadership vital to the passage of the party's social agenda. With the loss of the White House in 1968, leadership on behalf of the party's agenda depended on effective action by its majorities in the House and Senate.

In the 1970s the Democrats enacted a wide range of reforms designed to reconstruct their congressional party so as to limit the power of entrenched southern Democrats and ensure the party's sustained commitment to, and effective enactment of, its postmaterialist agenda. These reforms created a new "incentive structure" for career-minded Democratic legislators, in which movement to power and influence in committees and the party rested less on seniority and more on members' commitment to fostering the party's broad policy agenda. By extension, these reforms created disincentives for ambitious politicians to build careers as congressional Democrats in regions such as the South, where constituents were substantially at odds with large elements of the party's new programmatic image. Simultaneously, Democrats joined with reformist Republicans to experiment with new congressional rules and structures that would protect the policy-making authority of Congress in the new era. In doing so they created an innovative new congressional budget process to help Congress maintain fiscal integrity as it pursued its new agenda. This process introduced annual votes on budget resolutions that specified taxing and spending targets for the government, thereby pushing members and the parties to be clearer than in the past about broad priorities and principles. Overall, the reforms of the 1970s encouraged the congressional parties to become more responsible in their articulation of and pursuit of clearly etched policy agendas, a move long espoused by such congressional reformers as Richard Bolling and by academic political scientists.[37]

The Reagan revolution during the 1980s pushed Congress to reassess and reaffirm the extent of its postmaterialist commitments, to experiment with new revenue strategies aimed at ending the economic stagnation that had arisen in a time of expanded spending, and to consider a more muscular approach to foreign policy. It also brought a new generation of southern Republicans into Congress and reinforced ideological shifts within the party toward a more socially conservative stance.[38] This growth of Republicanism in the South had begun in response to the Democrats' paradigmatic shift away from tolerance of southern segregation, a shift counterbalanced by the growing states' rights rhetoric among south-western and western Republicans such as John Tower of Texas, Barry Goldwater of Arizona, and Ronald Reagan of California. The Democrats' embrace of civil rights and voting rights legislation in the mid-1960s, against the opposition of powerful southern congressional Democrats, led many white southerners to begin abandoning the party, voting for southern Republicans and thus slowly shifting southern House and Senate seats to Republican control. This shift was aided over time by the switch of southern Democrats such as Strom Thurmond of South Carolina to the Republican Party and the decisions of young southern white politicians such as Newt Gingrich to build their careers in the Republican Party.

With growing Republicanism in the South, congressional Republicans became more attuned to cultural concerns dominant in the South. This involved not just concerns about the role of the federal government in affirmative action, but also concerns about traditional moral issues and family values associated with fundamentalist Protestant churches of the South. Simultaneously, newly enfranchised southern blacks moved to the Democratic Party, reinforcing its focus on social justice and ensuring that Democrats would continue to hold onto House seats in areas of the South dominated by African Americans. These parallel developments created the sort of deep red Anglo districts and deep blue African American districts in the South, as highlighted in the work of Bruce Oppenheimer (2005), a process somewhat mirrored outside the South as different groups in New England, the Midwest, and the West responded in distinct ways to the repositioning of the parties' policy agendas.

As Congress entered the 1990s it had in many ways become a new institution, which had responded to postindustrialism in ways that would have seemed inconceivable in the mid-1950s. Although it had not embraced a postindustrial paradigm that addressed the full range of problems that the new era posed, Congress had moved the nation in incremental and segmented phases toward new ideas about what government could do. It had also moved to a new vision of how Congress might organize itself and pursue policy implementation, relying more on party discipline and strong party leadership, and on a new congressional budget process, and somewhat less on norms of seniority, specialized policy expertise, and committee government.

As these processes went forward, the parties demonstrated that they were not as entrenched in industrial-era alignments and policy perspectives as social structure theorists had surmised. The Democrats had moved beyond their labor base of the Rooseveltian era and beyond reliance on the safe but segregated South to ensure their national dominance. The party had moved toward a more inclusive stance that reached out to minorities and women and pursued policies, such as environmental protection or consumer safety, that alienated parts of its old labor base. Republicans had moved beyond their benign acceptance of New Deal social activism, beyond their acceptance of permanent minority status that seemed to come with inability to compete in the South, and toward their own version of expanded inclusiveness. Republican inclusiveness entailed an openness to southern social and cultural concerns and to the realignment of political forces inside the party as well as between the two parties.

As additional proof of the adaptive capacities of the parties and Congress, in the early 1990s congressional Democrats abandoned a long-term fascination with deficit spending and embraced a commitment to balanced budgets. While this move had been facilitated by the growing attentiveness to fiscal policy that came with the new budget process put in place in the 1970s and the struggles with deficits in the 1980s, it was given momentum by the new Democratic president, Bill Clinton. He sought to combine the pursuit of postmaterialist programs with fiscal policies that could sustain economic growth and the available revenue for such programs. This move, together with Clinton's repositioning of the party in support of stronger law enforcement, went some distance in addressing fiscal and cultural problems associated with the postmaterialist Democratic agenda that alienated key voters. Yet left unaddressed by congressional Democrats was their undue reliance on the federal bureaucracy to implement activist programs.

During the 1980s and early 1990s, many state and local governments—Democrat and Republican alike—had experimented with new ideas about how to "reinvent government" and avoid excessive bureaucracy. Bill Clinton and Vice-President Al Gore brought this new perspective to the national government in 1993, with the new Democratic administration focused particularly on new "entrepreneurial strategies" for recrafting government programs.[39] These entrepreneurial strategies involved continued government commitment to activist programs such as welfare and public health, but they utilized the private sector to run some aspects of such programs and implemented incentive systems taken from private industry to redesign the government bureaucracies that would oversee them. They also included devolving to states and localities responsibility for the implementation of key social programs and requiring that citizens take significant responsibility for their own personal well-being. The movement to such entrepreneurial strategies thus would reduce the cost of specific social programs to the federal government and had the added benefit of providing ways to limit federal government intrusion into private lives, thereby addressing the cultural issues that concerned voters.

Congressional Democrats, who had done much to address key postindustrial issues, approached these new ideas cautiously and stymied efforts by the Clinton administration to experiment with them in areas such as health care and welfare. These "old" Democratic reformers, elected in the 1960s and 1970s and now heading key committees and subcommittees, continued to support more traditional, bureaucratized approaches to social policy. They were often locked into such commitments by the need to maintain support from groups benefiting from the traditional design of programs and by the need to sustain the personal influence and expertise they had developed within the existing bureaucratic structure and the congressional committee system that regulated it. Yet most also believed that existing arrangements provided a more reliable and equitable way to address policy concerns than a rushed transformation of government, as seen in the Clinton health reforms, with a more gradualist and expertise-informed experimentation being called for. Their strong support for traditional programmatic strategies and gradualism came, however, at a time when citizens were increasingly frustrated by the inability of the government to rein in its bureaucracy. It also occurred at the point where Republicans were mounting their strong assault on the legitimacy of Congress, questioning whether it and the governing Democrats were truly responsive to the interests and values of citizens. At this critical moment, the Democrats' failure to support Clinton's experiments with entrepreneurial reforms provided the congressional Republican Party a historic opportunity to push new entrepreneurial strategies of its own and become a major player in this next phase of postindustrial experimentation and paradigm shift.[40]

The Revolution as a Phase in Experimental Learning

Characterized by greater generational turnover than the governing Democrats, and thus more distant from New Deal and Great Society ideas about government, the congressional Republican Party had by the early to mid-1990s come to contain a growing number of new members willing to challenge existing assumptions about government.[41] With backgrounds in private industry and state legislatures, these young Republicans had their own ideas about reinventing government, accepting the need for social programs but often supporting more radical entrepreneurial strategies than had Clinton and Gore and showing more attentiveness to the ways such strategies helped address cultural and family-value issues salient to regional constituencies. They also tended to be a "post-Vietnam" generation of politicians, often too young to have served in the war or cushioned from it by draft deferments or National Guard service, and thus generally untouched by the personal conflicts and suspicion of militarism associated with it. Rather, as the political heirs of Ronald Reagan, their attention was on limiting national government involvement in domestic life through the reinvention of its social programs, with foreign policy seen more nearly as the area of the national government's legitimate power.

Although the Republican Party continued to be attached to traditional policies, including support for business and low taxes, these new perspectives on reinventing and limiting government in the domestic sphere came to the fore of the party's policy agenda. They provided ways to reframe such traditional party commitments, so that low taxes and the restructuring of the tax system became not just a business-related policy but a by-product of government restructuring to make it more responsive to cultural concerns about government intrusiveness and individual responsibility. Most critically, the party balanced its attack on Congress and the congressional Democrats with innovative proposals for policy reform, so that its candidates did not simply oppose existing programs but had constructive strategies to propose for improving them. As congressional Republicans mounted their 1994 campaign, issues such as welfare reform became core elements of the Contract with America and constituted much of what made it innovative, defining the differences between the congressional parties in some distinctly new ways.

Seen through the lens of social learning theory, what is important about the 1994 election is that it presented a choice between the Democrats' bureaucratized approach to social programs and the new, entrepreneurial approach of congressional Republicans. The Republican victory can be seen as signaling the electorate's frustration with the congressional Democrats' traditionalist perspectives and its willingness to risk experimenting with the Republicans' new direction. The election thus was not just a stage in the normal, cyclical alternation in parties, nor just a product of postindustrial tensions, though both helped make it possible; it was also a phase in the process of experimental learning whereby the nation was incrementally recrafting its governing regime. It was the opportunity to experiment with new ideas and programmatic strategies—with new philosophies of the game—that galvanized the Republican activists, particularly Newt Gingrich, and constituted their contribution to national governance.

Once in power, the Republicans faced the difficulty of learning to govern after forty years as the minority party, while simultaneously pursuing their vision of governmental change.[42] Undermined by a weak leadership structure, by inexperience with the responsibilities of majority party status, and by internal divisions, the Republicans made critical missteps early on that squandered their opportunity to institute fundamental alterations in national government. Yet when the party sought common ground with the president and some Democrats, as on welfare reform, telecommunications restructuring, and the revamping of agricultural policy, congressional Republicans achieved victories that served to actualize their enterpreneurial agenda. Such accomplishments helped the party to demonstrate the promise of its paradigmatic shift and to provide citizens with a reason to maintain it in power, despite a concerted Democratic counterattack in the 1996, 1998, and 2000 elections.

Simultaneously, though less evident to much of the public at the time, congressional Republicans pushed for more forceful assertion of American power on the world scene. In particular, in 1998 they passed the Iraqi Liberation Act at a time when President Clinton could not afford politically to veto it. Asserting that "it should be the policy of the U.S. to remove the Iraqi regime," the act "institutionalized the idea of regime change in Iraq" as U.S. policy and thereby established a justification for its subsequent invasion well before the 2000 elections.[43] The great difficulty for the Republicans, both in pursuing their more assertive ideas about foreign policy and in expanding on their domestic policy successes, lay in the veto power and political skill of the Democratic president and the obstructionist successes of his minority congressional party. To truly pursue their paradigm shift, they needed united control of national government and expanded margins in the House and Senate.

The 2000 and 2004 elections gave the Republicans their great chance to push toward unified control of government and seek consolidation of their national majority status. In George W. Bush they had a gifted politician at the head of the ticket articulating the policy perspectives that had emerged within the congressional party over the previous two decades and representing its conservative southern base. Yet the election also provided Democrats their opportunity for a comeback. The victory of neither party was foreordained in 2000, as the popular vote majority of the Democratic candidate, A1 Gore, demonstrated. Moreover congressional Democrats were sufficiently close to the Republicans in the number of seats they controlled in the House and Senate, particularly through the 2002 elections, that their reassertion of congressional control was not unrealistic.

What was historically determinative with respect to the elections, rather than their prestructured outcomes, was that they pitted two closely competitive parties that had adapted in different ways to postindustrialism. Much of that adaptation had come from within the Congress itself over the previous several decades, rather than being driven by the presidency. Thus, much of the continuing competitiveness of the Democrats resulted from their adjustment in their support base and congressional rules in the 1960s and 1970s, which created a more modern, postsegregationist and postindustrial party, in touch with new forms of progressivism. Similarly, the foundation for the victories of George W. Bush and the growing consolidation of Republican power had been laid by congressional Republicans, as they solidified their competitive stance in the South, challenged Democratic hegemony through aggressive campaigns nationwide, and pushed their entrepreneurial and cultural agendas. Members of Congress responded to and exploited opportunities created by the historical forces at work in the contemporary era, crafting a substantially new party system and new patterns of congressional government as they went.

The elections then provided citizens with critical moments of choice and potential self-correction, as they considered which party could best move the nation forward. Their choice in 2000 was complicated by the cross-pressure citizens felt between the strong economy they attributed to the leadership of the Democratic president and their qualms about the cultural and moral values pursued by his party, qualms his private behavior reinforced. The choice in 2004 was made difficult by the tension between the strong performance of the Republican president and Congress in response to the 9/11 terrorist strikes, as highlighted by the work of Donald Wolfensberger (2005), and questions about the competence of the president and his party with respect to stewardship of the economy and the invasion of Iraq. And across the elections the hold of Republicans on Congress was made questionable by their seeming inability to make the appropriations process work (Gordon, 2005), and by verbal and ethical missteps by leaders such as Trent Lott and Tom DeLay. Yet, impressed by Republicans' resolute response to the terrorist strikes and by their stance on cultural values, the citizens increasingly tilted across the four years toward solidification of Republican control of national government, reinforced in the trend by savvy Republican moves such as the redistricting of House seats by the Republican legislature in Texas. Most fundamentally, the tilt appeared to owe to the desire of citizens for clarity of direction and accountability in performance of the national government, with a majority finally willing in 2004 to give Republicans their clear shot at governing.

This moment of clear choice came slowly and erratically, from the perspective of social learning theory, because reassessment of existing paradigms and experimentation with new ideas is an inherently difficult, lengthy, conflictual, and problematic process. Yet with the 2004 elections, the Republican revolution seems fully realized, and concern turns to how effectively the party can govern, so as to consolidate long-term national majority status. As this transition occurs, and however it may turn out, the essential contributions of the revolution, particularly from the standpoint of the Congress and its institutional legitimacy, need to be recognized.

With the defeat of a long-term governing party in 1994 and the decade-long move to new governing strategies, the Republicans helped to break the sense of paralysis that existed in American politics in the early 1990s and focus the nation on vital issues of deep concern to the citizenry. In doing so, they greatly spurred the process of paradigm reassessment and reconstruction, to such an extent that in the 2000 elections congressional Democrats touted welfare reform, and in 2004 serious proposals for reform of Social Security, long unmentionable in American politics, were commonplace in national debates.

Most critically, as the congressional Republicans faced the opportunity and responsibilities of governing on a sustained basis, which they had not held, in truth, since the 1920s, they came to see more clearly the strengths and contributions of Congress to national governance and even came to defend its prerogatives. They asserted the constitutional role of Congress in annual negotiations with the president, and they asserted their right to impeach a president, drawing on powers that a generation earlier they had denounced when they were used against a Republican president, Richard Nixon. Calls for congressional term limits vanished from party platforms, and the push for constraints on congressional authority decreased. Although Republicans were still struggling to find a vision of Congress that could mesh with their entrepreneurial policy agenda, they were now less prone to emphasize its flaws as justification for reducing its institutional power and constitutional prerogatives.

The Republican revolution thus demonstrates just how critical it is to representative democracy for political parties to alternate in power in legislative assemblies, so that they all will appreciate the complexities and contributions of representative government and will testify on behalf of such assemblies to their diverse supporters. With this testimony from Republicans, American elections have focused less on the legitimacy of Congress as a policymaking institution and more on the principles and strategies that should govern the nation's policy response. This shift surely constitutes a further step toward a viable postindustrial paradigm and the relegitimation of Congress as a governing institution.

Conclusion

Congress is a dynamic institution continually being reshaped by cycles of partisan learning and regime change. For a time it may be dominated by one party or factional coalition, by entrenched societal interests and institutional arrangements, and by an overarching philosophy or governing paradigm. But across time governing groups become overconfident of their mastery of electoral and organizational politics, societal change upends the support bases of the entrenched regime, and innovative ideas and experimental learning allow a new generation of partisans to open pathways to policy responsiveness and institutional renewal. The Republican revolution is a classic instance of these processes at work, as was the rise of liberal Democratic reformers a generation earlier. As Congress and its parties respond to these processes in the contemporary era, they adapt the nation to postindustrialism and incrementally address the issues of governing legitimacy that confront them.

With the 2004 elections, the adaptive processes in Congress and national politics moved the country into a new phase—an effort by Republicans to consolidate their hold on national power through effective performance in governance and skillful crafting of reliable long-term citizen support. The party would now appear to have clear advantages in this effort. With solid majorities in the House and Senate and popular majority support for their president, lingering questions about Republicans' legitimate hold on power are dissipating and they have more room for maneuver as they seek to build policy majorities on Capitol Hill. In doing so, the party has strengthened its dominance in the South, now its core electoral base, while remaining competitive nationally, particularly in the Midwest and West. And it has a message that resonates with voters, that a majority has embraced amid a highly engaged and contested election, signaling some considerable commitment to the party and its principles that may sustain it through difficult times.[44] Moreover, Republicans are poised to exploit potential weaknesses within the Democratic Party. These include the possibility that popular longtime Democratic incumbents in Congress may choose to retire in the face of the Republicans' strength on the Hill, giving the Republican Party an opportunity to expand its majority through capturing contests for open seats previously held by Democrats; the deepening difficulties Democrats have in competing in much of the South, particularly for Senate seats; and the Democrats' ongoing failure to develop a compelling approach to citizen concerns about cultural values and individual responsibility.

The momentary strength of congressional Republicans and the weakness of Democrats, however, should not blind observers to the potential pitfalls that the majority party now faces. Within Congress Republicans continue to struggle with the creation of a policy process that generates responsible and timely decisions and that does so in a way that engages its policy experts within the standing committees. A critical task before Republicans in Congress now is to craft a process that provides members with satisfying and meaningful input into policy decisions and also protects the powers of the institution vis-à-vis the executive. In the short run, in their push to majority status the Republicans in Congress increasingly accepted considerable assertion of policy-making power by party leaders and the Republican president. But with majority status more clearly in hand, members now may come to demand greater personal payoff within the Congress and greater presidential respect for Congress in congressional–executive negotiations. Ensuring that service in Congress is rewarding to members in a Republican era is critical to maintaining quality candidates for office and encouraging them to take seriously the policy-making responsibilities of the institution. Yet should Republicans go too far in spreading power and autonomy among members, that can weaken the party's cohesion and governing capacities. All of this is to say that Republicans now must confront the tensions between individual autonomy and collective governance that come as the rewards and responsibilities of majority party status become increasingly evident.

Within the nation and world at large, Republicans must recognize that societal and international changes continue unabated, so that many of the forces that created opportunities for them to exploit over the past several decades may prove transient and even countervailing in their longer-term consequences. As but one example, the southern realignment could be complicated by a growing Latino population in the South and by movement to the South of the descendants of the African Americans who left it for the North during the era of southern segregation. Both developments could provide Democrats with renewed opportunities in some southern states, including the two largest, Florida and Texas. These opportunities could be magnified by the growing experience and clout of minority members within Congress, as noted by Kerry Haynie (Haynie, 2005) with respect to African Americans. Moreover, insofar as the southern realignment solidifies and southerners dominate the Republican Party, the result could be such a strongly conservative party that more moderate electorates elsewhere in the nation could become alienated from the party's policy stances.[45] As a second example, the forces of globalization could generate growing economic dislocations in the nation that give greater salience and resonance to the Democrats' stress on economic issues. As a third, unpopular or destructive policy actions by Republicans in controversial areas such as judicial appointments, as discussed by Sarah Binder and Forrest Maltzman (Binder and Maltzman, 2005), could reignite concerns about institutional legitimacy, this time perhaps coming forcefully from the left. And as a fourth, the ongoing restructuring of post-cold war power dynamics, including the rise of nonstate terrorism, may continue to pose unforeseen challenges that could test the party in new ways.

Finally, looking to the world of ideas, what ultimately matters with respect to party principles, congressional programs, and paradigm shifts is not just how well they resonate with citizens in the abstract, but how well a party delivers on promises and how effective its programs and principles prove to be in practice. A critical issue in this respect is how accurately a party gauges the true nature of social reality, the viability of programs within that reality, and their long-term side effects. Such concerns, raised forcefully by Catherine Rudder in her discussion of fiscal policy and reform of social programs (Rudder, 2005), pose perhaps the greatest threat to long-term Republican consolidation of power.

Democrats were sustained in power for decades not just because of constituent service prowess or safe southern seats but because their broad principles of social justice seemed appropriate to the Depression era and post-Depression world, and their programs, such as Social Security and price supports, appeared to work in protecting workers and fostering a sound economy. Similarly, their early adjustment to postindustrialism gained broad acceptance, as an increasingly educated, affluent, and informed nation could not tolerate segregation, poverty among the elderly, second-class status for women, and other injustices inherited from industrial-era social relations.

The party's majority collapsed in the face of cultural dilemmas and fiscal pressures that emerged with the longer-term side effects of postindustrialism and Democrats' progressive response to it. The cultural dilemmas are best illustrated by the growing sense that some social programs enacted by Democrats induced an ethic of dependency among recipients of government support and by the moral concerns raised as the party championed women's right to choice with respect to abortion, even including government financing of some such procedures. The longer-term fiscal pressures are illustrated by the anticipation of systemic crises in the maintenance of entitlement programs, such as Social Security and Medicare, as the nation's population ages and by concerns that the tax structure necessary to meet entitlement obligations could undermine the sustenance of an innovative, productive, and growing economy.

Republicans now propose to restructure much that Democrats put in place that appeared to work for considerable periods of time—Social Security, the progressive tax system, Medicare for the elderly, social programs for the poor, privacy in lifestyle choices, and so forth. The restructuring is justified as a response to cultural concerns and family values and also as an attempt to address projected fiscal crises generated by social programs. Republicans also appear prepared to continue the pursuit of a more interventionist approach to international relations than the multilateral strategy long associated with Democratic administrations, with this response justified by the unique threats posed by modern terrorism. The question is how well these initiatives will work in practice, attending to economic and international realities while generating a more moral and fiscally sound nation, and at what social as well as economic price to individual citizens. Additional questions include the price of the Republicans' efforts in terms of constitutional power arrangements, particularly for the sustainability of a strong Congress in the face of growing reliance on party discipline within Congress in support of presidential policy and power.[46] Also of concern is the effect that a muscular foreign policy may have on citizens' personal liberties, particularly insofar as terrorism continues to blur the boundaries between domestic and international security.[47]

As I conclude this analysis in the week following the 2004 elections, it is far too early to know how successful the Republican majority will prove to be in its efforts and how well Congress will serve the nation as these policy struggles proceed. The challenges facing the party and the Congress are substantial. Moreover, as the events of 9/11 demonstrate, history will have its surprises just around the bend, testing the nation's resolve, creativity, and learning capacities anew. Problems with debilitating ambitions, antiquated procedures, and entrenched interests also continue—moderated by waves of reform and change but still capable of inserting themselves destructively into congressional politics and national life. In the face of these concerns, we cannot be sure that our policy experiments and institutional adjustments are adequate to the challenge.

What we know at this point is that we have already adjusted our governing perspectives across a forty-year process of experimentation and governing innovation within Congress, with these adjustments sustaining the nation in past challenges and generating this moment of concentrated attention to new ones. We also know one other thing: that Congress, the parties, and the electorate are capable of rising to the occasion, restructuring political alignments, and learning to address societal problems anew.

To appreciate this capacity, we must attend to the conceptual lenses through which we examine Congress and craft multiple theoretical perspectives that help us envision it more completely. Such perspectives should enable us to look beyond momentary partisan controversies and see the dynamic, historical processes at play in congressional politics. In crafting such lenses, we must bring to the endeavor the commonsense judgment we demonstrate in daily life, taking care to focus on the motives and strategic behavior of participants in the foreground, on the shifting background contexts, and then ultimately on the ideas that participants hold about politics and society.

As we do so, crafting social choice theories to analyze the foreground, social structure theories to interpret the background, and social learning theories to comprehend the role of ideas, we see an overall pattern that no one of our theories could fully illuminate—a multidimensional pattern that helps us understand how Congress can constructively respond to societal problems. Through these multiple lenses, we see the foreground contest for governing power that ensures that partisans will highlight societal problems as they challenge for control of Congress. We see the dynamic societal changes that generate new citizen demands, policy challenges, and electoral coalitions. And we see the coming of a new generation of legislators, social activists, and engaged citizens, who push Congress to experiment with fresh ideas, address the pressing policy challenges, and solve societal problems.

Examining the contemporary Congress through these multiple lenses, we see an institution responding to the problems and opportunities of postindustrialism—gradually, incrementally, and partially, but also in sustained and consequential ways. The concerns to which Congress has responded, though perhaps too limited in number and imperfect in their resolution, are significant ones, and they include such seemingly intransigent problems as racial segregation, gender inequality, poverty among the elderly, urban pollution, budget deficits, economic restructuring, welfare dependency, and international terrorism. Although Congress has not tackled these issues alone, and at times has exacerbated them, it ultimately has contributed to the experimental learning that helped to address them. This capacity of a political institution to contribute to social learning in a sustained and consequential fashion and in a manner ultimately controlled and shaped by a nation's citizens is no small accomplishment.

Time will tell whether the new Republican Congress now helps us learn enough of the right things, and adequately assimilate them with the enduring truths inherited from past generations, to redress the continuing problems associated with postindustrialism. Insofar as it does, it can consolidate a new partisan regime that could conceivably set the direction of the nation for decades to come. And insofar as its experiments fail, we should recall that the essence of policy experimentation within our democracy is the ability of our nation's citizens to learn from error and try again, a lesson Democrats have experienced with growing force over the past decade, to their regret, and that Republicans should keep firmly in mind. This is, after all, the great promise of representative government and electoral democracy—both the ability of a citizenry to find firm footing through the iterative crafting of responsive and responsible new regimes and the ability to hold regimes accountable for their performance. Moreover, Congress is the great stage on which so much of this regime crafting and sustained accountability proceeds. Perhaps this realization will encourage us to embrace the possibilities that this era of Republican experimentation presents and to recognize the vital and legitimate roles that Congress can play—as an arena of majority policy crafting and minority policy challenge—as we approach the challenges ahead.

Notes

Acknowledgements: My thanks to Leslie Anderson, Ryan Bakker, Lance Bardsley, Marija Beckafigo, Shannon Bow, Jim Button, Matt Caverly, Allison Clark, Peggy Conway, Marian Currinder, Wayne Francis, David Hedge, Valerie Heitshusen, David Lee Hill, Josh Gordon, Larry Kenney, Michael Martinez, Seth McKee, Elizabeth Oldmixon, Susan Orr, Beth Rosenson, Jacob Straus, Kevin Wagner, Ken Wald, Fiona Wright, Michael Zarkin for sharing their comments on the various drafts and public presentations of this essay or the original 2001 version.

1 Connelly and Pitney (1994).
2 Cooper ed. (1999); Hibbing and Theiss-Morse (1995).
3 Burnham (1995).
4 For an overview of the Republican revolution and Gingrich's perceived role in it, see Balz and Brownstein (1996).
5 For a revealing look at Gingrich's own take on these matters, see Gingrich and Gingrich (1981).
6 Burnham (1994).
7 On social choice theory, see Riker (1982b); and Shepsle and Bonchek (1997).
8 Fiorina (1974, 1977b); and Mayhew (1974).
9 See, for example, Aldrich and Rohde (2001).
10 Fenno (1973); and Sinclair (1995).
11 Downs (1957).
12 Weingast (1979).
13 Davidson and Oleszek (1977); Evans and Oleszek (1997); Parker (1992); and Wolfinger and Hollinger (1965).
14 Dodd (1977), Chapter Two in this volume.
15 Dodd (1986a), Chapter Five in this volume.
16 Fiorina (1977b).
17 Jacobson (1987); and Mann (1978).
18 This argument reflects the "retrospective voting perspective" developed by Key and Fiorina in their study of presidential elections. See Key (1966); and Fiorina (1981).
19 For a more extensive discussion of this paradox, see Oppenheimer (1997).
20 Polsby (1968, 2004).
21 See Young (1966); Wilson (1885, reissued 1973); Cooper and Brady (1981b); and Lowi (1979). Other important historical analyses that reflect the influence of social context include Swift (1996); and Schickler (2001).
22 For discussion of the "legitimation crisis paradigm" within sociology, see Lehman (1992); for a forceful statement, see Habermas (1973).
23 For a general statement of the powerful influence that antiquated institutions may have on new historical eras, see Oren and Skowronek (1994).
24 On the nature of postmaterialism in the contemporary era, see Inglehart (1989).
25 On the development of such cultural concerns as salient election issues, see Leege et al. (2002). For an analysis of congressional response to the rise of cultural issues, see Oldmixon (2005).
26 Dodd (1981), Chapter Three in this volume. For a broad-gauged historical discussion of the ways in which the organization of the House of Representatives can influence its legitimacy as a policy-making institution, see Cooper (1970: 111–130).
27 Fiorina (1989).
28 For an thorough and insightful discussion of the subsequent quarter-century struggle within Congress over how best to deal with budget policy making and deficit spending, see Farrier (2004).
29 Uslaner (1993).
30 For a discussion of the ways in which term limits on the Speaker, and related factors, helped create a weakened leadership structure, see Peters (1999); see also Dodd and Oppenheimer (1997a), "Revolution in the House: Testing the Limits of Party Government."
31 Bateson (1972); and Vickers (1968). For a useful application of social learning theory to political science, see Hall (1993b). My application of social learning theory to politics, following Hall's lead, restates it in the language of philosopher of science Thomas Kuhn (1970).
32 For my earlier application of social learning theory to Congress, see Dodd (1991),

Chapter Seven in this volume. For my general application of it to Ameican politics, see Dodd (1994).

33 Dodd (1986b), Chapter Six in this volume. .

34 Kingdon (1984); and Mayhew (2000).

35 See Burns (1963); and Huntington (1965).

36 See Binder (2003).

37 Bolling (1965, 1968). See also the discussion in Rohde (1991), Chapter 1. For an innovative theoretical explanation for the long-term historical transition from party government in the late nineteenth century, to committee government in the mid-twentieth century, and now back to party government, see Raven (2004).

38 Black and Black (2002); and McKee (2010).

39 On the emergence of this entrepreneurial perspective and its importance for Congress, see Dodd (1993, 1994), Chapters Eight and Nine in this volume.

40 See, for supportive analysis, Johnson and Broder (1996); see also President Clinton's assessment of this period in Joe Klein, "Eight Years: Bill Clinton and the Politics of Persistence," in *The New Yorker*, October 16–23, 2000, 206–209.

41 Berkman (1993); and Koopman (1996).

42 Fenno (1997b); and Price (2004), particularly Chapters 7, 8, and 9.

43 See Manar El Shorbagy, "The Congressional Dilemma over Iraqi Policy," an unpublished working paper discussed at the Woodrow Wilson International Center for Scholars in November 2003. The quotes are from page three of the discussion paper. El Shorbagy is the Academic Director of the Al Waleed Center for American Studies at the American University in Cairo, Egypt.

44 For an extended discussion of how intense, highly contested and engaged elections can generate strong voter support for parties and regimes, see Anderson and Dodd (2005).

45 Lowi (1995).

46 For an insightful and prescient discussion of the potential threat that a strengthening of party government in the House could pose for its autonomy from the presidency, see Cooper (1970: 128–130).

47 For relevant discussions, see the chapters in Conley, ed. (2005), *Transforming the American Polity: The Presidency of George W. Bush and the War on Terrorism.*

Additional Perspective on "Re-Envisioning Congress"

This essay seeks to explain the Republican Revolution of 1994 through the integration of the author's previous arguments into a more unified and multidimensional metarational (or 'adaptive learning') perspective on studying Congress. The essay can be read both as an explanation of the Revolution and as the introduction of a multidimensional perspective on studying legislative politics.

A. Explaining the Republican Revolution

In explaining the Revolution, the essay stresses three distinct processes at work in and on congressional politics. The first process is the cyclical struggle by individuals and political parties for policy-making power on Capitol Hill, a struggle manifest through electoral and organizational politics; the logic of this struggle is detailed in Chapter Two ("Quest"), Chapter Five ("The Cycles of Legislative Change") and Chapter Six ("Congressional Cycles"). The second process is the ongoing shift in societal conditions that, left unattended through appropriate policy making, creates growing dilemmas for collective well-being of the nation's citizenry; the process is presented in Chapter Three ("Legitimation Crisis"), Chapter Four ("The Shifting Partnership") and Chapter Eight ("Renewal"), which in combination stress a range of dilemmas associated with postindustrialization. The third process is the shifting conceptions of society and its collective dilemmas that are associated with the coming of postindustrialism, a process which also entails shifting perspectives on appropriate governmental strategies for addressing societal dilemmas; this overall process is presented in Chapter Seven ("A Transformational Perspective"), Chapter Eight ("Renewal") and Chapter Nine ("The New American Politics").

Rather than interweaving these processes in an unfolding historical narrative, the essay presents distinct analytic narratives associated with each process, building a more integrative and explanatory meta-narrative as it proceeds sequentially to introduce each separate process-narrative. The resulting analysis emphasizes the contribution of separate dimensions of politics to an explanation of the Revolution. In doing so, it sees the Revolution as a stage in the cycles of partisan contestation and organizational change; as a punctuated electoral and political upheaval resulting from growth in the unaddressed societal and political tensions associated with postindustrialism; and as a phase in societal learning as citizens and the Congress debate, experiment with and assimilate alternative approaches to postindustrialism.

An early statement of this multidimensional perspective and its application to the Republican Revolution is presented in Dodd (1995), "Placing Congress in Theoretical Time."

Suggested Reading: For suggested reading on the Republican revolution, see Burnham (1995); Balz and Brownstein (1996); Fenno (1997b); Gimpel (1996);

Koopman (1996); Dodd and Oppenheimer (1997); Evans and Oleszek (1997); Barnett (1999); Greenberg (2004); Taylor (2005); Jones and Williams (2008); McKee (2010).

Classroom Use: For classroom use in courses on Congress and legislative politics or on American national government, this essay can be employed (1) as a description and analysis of postwar congressional politics; (2) an explanation of the coming of the 1994 Republican Revolution, the progression of Republicans in power across the subsequent ten years, and the threats to Republican control that appeared to confront it as it entered the 109th Congress (2005-06); and (3) as a theoretical framework for assessing other periods of sudden congressional upheaval and change.

B. A Multidimensional Perspective on Legislative Politics: Building on Bateson's Model of Adaptive Learning

In constructing the multidimensional perspective on legislative politics presented here, the author does two critical things. First, he presents a conception of 'multidimensionality' that is, in a sense, a visual one. There is a foreground dimension to empirical awareness and a background dimension, with shifts in attention from foreground action to background context being a natural way in which actors assess the effect of intended foreground action, and by which scholars can do likewise. Additionally, as actors shift attention from background back to foreground, there is a (mental, physical-habitual or social-ideational) assimilative process whereby actors incorporate the perceived outcome of foreground action amid a specific background context into their subsequent awareness; with such assimilation, they can recalibrate foreground strategy and tactics, and improve the effectiveness of intended foreground action within the background context at hand. Scholars should likewise attend to this process of actor assimilation of background outcomes, to understand subsequent actor intentions and strategies.

Second, the author presents a conception of multidimensionality that carries with it a connotation of 'adaptive' actor learning. When an actor or actors discern the consequences that foreground action has within the broader background context, assimilating that awareness, learning occurs. This learning is not just a random shift in ideas and strategies, however, but entails potential adjustment of ideas and strategies to take into account ongoing changes perceived in background context, some of which can be attributed to foreground action. Such learning has the potential to aid actor adaptation to change. This capacity to aid adaptation depends on the extent to which the learning is accurate or inaccurate or, in other words, leads to correction of error (given expectations) or error-reinforcement. Irregardless, the overarching learning process in some subtle or not so subtle manner alters or reinforces actor behavior. This multidimensional perspective conforms to basic notions of human perception and attention shift;

to broadly shared understandings of human learning; and to a conception of collective learning through the interactive crafting and re-crafting of broadly shared ideas about the world.

The effort to construct and utilize an integrated and multidimensional perspective on congressional change was greatly informed by the author's reading of Gregory Bateson and Mary Catherine Bateson (1987), *Angels Fear: Towards an Epistemology of the Sacred*, particularly Chapter Four on "The Model." Based on this work, together with other aspects of Bateson's writing (see, for example, Bateson, *Steps*, 1972), the author began to think about social and political relations in terms of the *foreground* in which an individual or groups 'act'; the constantly-changing *background* within which they 'anticipate and assess' the conditions influencing the outcome of the action; and then the overarching ideas and habituated processes into which they 'assimilate' the awareness of the apparent effect and meaning of their action, given the context in which it occurred. An action/assessment/ assimilation process can be seen as a phase of adaptive or self-corrective learning by individuals and groups, whether that phase occurs in rapid sequence as a hunter shoots at a bird, or in slow, interactive and somewhat overlapping sequences, as in the creation of new social purposes and programs by government.

A long-term, sustained, and interactive phase of action/assessment/assimilation constitutes a kind of meta-process of adaptive learning, that is, a long-term process whereby society adapts to new social and political conditions. "Re-Envisioning Congress" seeks to highlight the existence of such a long-term meta-process during the late twentieth century, as Americans responded to postindustrialism. It does so by highlighting in sequenced manner the three interactive and overlapping social processes that compose adaptive learning. In this effort, it points to an understanding of social and political process that is relevant well beyond the study of the Republican Revolution.

The author's effort in developing this multidimensional perspective, built around Bateson's model of adaptive learning, was aided by his reading of Graham Allison's seminal work (1971, 1999), *The Essence of Decision*, as discussed in Dodd (1997: 1–12).

Suggested Reading and Classroom Use: As an illustrative perspective on multidimensional inquiry, "Re-Envisioning Congress" can be used in the classroom to explore how best to conceptualize, study and explain politics. It would be particularly useful in this respect in advanced courses concerned with congressional studies as an area of scholarly inquiry, courses concerned with the logic of political inquiry, and courses concerned with empirical theories of politics. In such explorations, "Re-Envisioning Congress" could be paired with a reading of Allison's *Essence of Decision*. In advanced classes both could be paired with a reading of Bateson's "The Cybernetics of Self," reprinted in Bateson (1972) or with Chapter Four, "The Model," in Bateson and Bateson (1987). Dodd's rendition of Bateson is greatly simplified, so that there are numerous ways in which attention to Bateson's arguments could move the study of congressional change beyond the framework presented in "Re-Envisioning Congress."

Additionally, "Re-Envisioning Congress" could be paired with portions of Jones (1994) *Reconceiving Decision-making in American Politics* and Jones and Baumgartner (2005), *The Politics of Attention*. In these pairings, the issue is the extent to which the more elaborated conception of decision making and attention shift in these two books informs and alters the arguments in "Re-Envisioning Congress," and the ways in which the framework in the latter can inform the models of change developed in these books.

Finally, Cooper (2009) provides a multidimensional perspective on Congress that seeks to clarify how and why its influence in American politics has changed from the late nineteenth to the late twentieth centuries. "Re-Envisioning Congress" could be paired with Cooper's essay to illustrate different multidimensional perspectives on Congress and to frame a discussion of how different multidimensional perspectives might stress different explanations for the Revolution.

11

MAKING SENSE OUT OF OUR EXCEPTIONAL SENATE

Perspectives and Commentary

2002

How can the small, informal, super-majoritarian Senate function as a viable legislative body? And how can it mesh with the large, formal, majoritarian House of Representatives to insure the adaptation of Congress to new societal conditions?

"Making Sense out of Our Exceptional Senate" proposes that the success of the Senate, coming despite its fluid and permeable organizational life, lies in the efforts of senators to develop extensive social networks among themselves; maintain close communication to make sense out of their unpredictable environment; and improvise new social relations to adapt to their shifting institutional and societal setting. This experience with networking, inclusive communication and improvisation teaches senators to be innovative, live with uncertainty, stay abreast of new societal developments, and appreciate loyalty to the institution. Such learning by senators, as they adapt to the fluidity of the institution, helps the Senate function effectively. The success of the larger and more institutionalized House lies in its members' ability to learn the chamber's routines, generic roles and structured procedures and to operate in predictable, rational ways within its highly regularized politics.

Congress works in normal times because the House provides stability to policy making and keeps the Senate in check in its improvisations and innovations. Yet eventually the House undergoes revolution in its structure to 'catch up' with changes in society. During such periods the better-adapted Senate plays a stabilizing role, giving the House time as it innovates a new internal equilibrium, thereby sustaining the adaptability of Congress.

The essays contained in *U.S. Senate Exceptionalism* mark a turning point in the study of the U.S. Senate. Long considered the world's greatest deliberative body,

Lawrence C. Dodd. *"Making Sense out of Our Exceptional Senate: Perspectives and Commentary." In* U.S. Senate Exceptionalism. *Edited by Bruce I. Oppenheimer. Columbus, O.H.: Ohio State University Press. 2002, pp. 350–363. This essay is the concluding chapter to U.S. Senate Exceptionalism.*

and the object of classic studies during the early postwar years by analysts such as Huitt (1961a, 1961b), Matthews (1960), Ripley (1969b), and White (1956), the Senate nevertheless has taken second place in contemporary empirical research to its larger sister chamber, the U.S. House of Representatives. The broad-ranging research projects reported in the volume (Oppenheimer, 2002a) and the freewheeling discussion at the Vanderbilt conference where these projects were presented make clear that the study of the Senate is no longer an isolated or antiquated phenomenon. Bruce Oppenheimer's excellent introduction that frames these essays (Oppenheimer, 2002b) and David Rohde's probing assessment of new research directions suggested by the essays (Rohde, 2002) point to a strong, innovative, and collective effort now underway among legislative scholars to explore and illuminate senatorial politics. My role here is to conclude with some thoughts about the broader dialogue that took place at the conference about how best to understand and interpret Senate politics, and to speak to the overarching topic of the conference—Senate exceptionalism. In doing so I will focus on one observation that ran throughout much of the discussion at the conference.

The recurring thematic undercurrent was the elusiveness of the Senate as an institution. On the first night, in his keynote address, Richard Fenno opened the conference with a stimulating and reflective overview of his experience and observations across forty years exploring the Senate and interviewing senators (Fenno, 2002). Summing up, Fenno noted that what impressed him most, in retrospect, was how difficult it was to "find the Senate." While we can get a relatively clear understanding of individual members, unlocking a clear and systematic patterning to the Senate itself is more problematic. Two days later the conference closed with a story by Ross Baker in which he shared the observation of a long-term Washington lobbyist who confessed that while he almost always thought he pretty much knew what was happening in the House, he generally had an under-current of apprehension about the more "mysterious Senate"— never really believing that he knew what to expect there.

Between Fenno and Baker came numerous other commentators testifying to the surprising and distinctive character of Senate behavior when contrasted with the House or other legislatures and to the consequent difficulty in interpreting or assessing it. This discussion is illustrated most vividly by Barbara Sinclair's suggestion that policy making in the Senate—given its exceptional institutional characteristics, which virtually mandate supermajoritarian coalitions—is so different from that found in the House and elsewhere as to make theories and explanations derived from study of such majoritarian legislatures untenable when applied to the Senate. In fact, Sinclair suggests, the difficulties created for the Senate by its organizational complexities and supermajoritarian character are so unique, and would seem so debilitating, as to raise fundamental questions about how and why the Senate is able to operate effectively at all (Sinclair, 2002: 260). Sinclair's observations serve to highlight the concern raised by Alford and Hibbing at the end of their essay as to whether the contemporary Senate is capable of playing its most distinctive constitutional role, the moderating of congressional politics and the conserving of stable representative government (Alford and Hibbing, 2002: 107–08).

My effort here, building on the observations of Fenno, Baker, Sinclair, Alford and Hibbing, and others, is to argue that the Senate may well be such a truly exceptional institution that in fact it does require a new form of theoretical analysis if we are to understand it and appreciate its continuing role in American politics.

I

The Senate has proven an elusive institution, I suggest, because the exceptional characteristics of the Senate, operating in combination, have created an institutional context so distinctive that the theoretical lenses needed to see and comprehend the Senate are qualitatively different from the rational-choice lenses that have proven so useful in the study of the U.S. House. In raising this possibility I build on recent empirical and conceptual advances within social psychology.

For several decades, the social sciences have debated how best to understand human behavior.[1] One dominant school of thought maintains that individuals and groups can best be studied from a microeconomic perspective that stresses the primary role of rational-choice calculations in shaping individual and group behavior. According to such a perspective, individuals share common and relatively stable perceptions of the fundamental values and social choices at stake in society and politics; social and political conflict emerges primarily as individuals seek to maximize their personal self-interest in the common pursuit of similar personal goals and social benefits. This approach to politics—which can be characterized as substantive or objective rationality because it assumes general agreement on the interests at stake in social and political life—is illustrated by the work of Downs (1957), Riker (1962), and Olson (1965). In contrast to rational choice, an alternative school of thought argues that social relations are best understood as a process of adaptive social learning. According to this perspective, individuals and groups have quite distinct and often transient perceptions of the values, goals, empirical conditions, and self-interest concerns that dominate social life.

While individuals may each pursue their perceived self-interest, their perceptions of goals, conditions, and interests may be substantially different, so that they lack a shared substantive understanding of the world by which to comprehend each other, interact and negotiate among themselves, and develop expectations about group and institutional behavior. To operate in a world of "multiple realities," social actors devote much of their effort to deciphering each other's worldviews and developing mutually acceptable working arrangements that accommodate their divergent perceptions and substantive orientations. This perspective—which can be characterized as procedural or bounded rationality because it acknowledges that individuals do engage in rational calculations but not necessarily from within the same substantive perspectives on the world—is illustrated by the work of Simon (1985), Berlin (1996), March and Olsen (1989, 1995), Padgett and Ansell (1993), Tilly (1997), and Vickers (1968); see also Adams, Forester, and Catron (1987).

Scholars have generally approached this debate as an all-or-nothing choice and have chosen to stress either a rational-choice or an adaptive learning perspective as the appropriate way to understand society and politics. The early success of political scientists in using rational-choice analysis to develop some powerful parsimonious explanations of political behavior—particularly their success in applying rational choice to the study of legislative behavior—seemed to suggest that a rational-choice perspective was the appropriate approach to politics. Now the growing recognition of the elusiveness and distinctiveness of Senate behavior serves to reopen this debate and does so at a time when the dichotomous choice between a rational-choice and a social learning perspective is increasingly being questioned.

During the 1990s, on the basis of a range of conceptual advances and empirical observations, leading social psychologists such as Michigan's Karl Weick came to conclude that both forms of behavior are prevalent in the world.[2] People are not exclusively narrow rational-choice calculators, preoccupied with self-interested pursuit of a few common and fundamental goals, nor are they exclusively adaptive learners continually crafting and recrafting social arrangements in ways that satisfy divergent styles and multiple perspectives on reality. Rather, they are complex social actors who at times tilt toward shared forms of rational calculation that yield relatively simple, continuous, and predictable group behavior patterns and at other times tilt toward adaptive social action that can yield complex, continually evolving, and idiosyncratic behavior patterns. Which way individuals tilt in their behavioral orientation depends greatly on the context within which they find themselves and the process of sense making—that is, the process of comprehending the context—that best helps them operate within it. This "context-dependent" understanding of human behavior, and its implications for conceptualizing and studying the House and Senate, can be grasped by considering two "ideal types" of social context and the "sense-making" orientation associated with each.

II

Some contexts—type I contexts—are highly structured. Such situations have well-defined organizational arrangements that dominate social life; a large and relatively continuous membership that is divided into clearly identifiable and relatively homogenous subgroups composed of distinctive and predictable types of members; clearly etched status hierarchies among members and organizational positions that serve to create generic roles and organizational goals that predominate group life; formalized rules and procedures that extensively regulate members' organizational activity; and shared identities and characteristics among groups of members that simplify and clarify the character of social life. These and other characteristics generate a regularized world in which a relatively high degree of certainty can exist about how organizational processes will proceed across time, about how participants will behave in their various generic roles and collective activities, and about the consequent outcomes that are likely to characterize collective action or inaction in such contexts.

Because structured contexts yield considerable certainty about organizational processes and group behavior, individuals operating in a structured context can reasonably believe that the principles and social patterns that they have learned through organizational socialization and experience provide a reliable framework through which to make sense out of ongoing events. In other words, structured contexts allow members to develop a shared belief system, based on commonly understood organizational principles and behavior patterns, and to use that belief system for comprehending social life. Little time must be devoted to interpreting, deciphering, reinterpreting, or adapting to social dynamics. Rather, relying on this common belief system, individuals can devote their time and energy to fulfilling the roles they are expected to play and pursuing the individual goals appropriate to such roles. This approach to social life—which Weick calls "belief-driven" sense making—is particularly compatible with the theories of "substantive rationality" that characterize a rational-choice approach to social and political analysis. To explain behavior in a structured context characterized by belief-driven sense making, scholars primarily need to decipher the limited set of shared beliefs that participants hold about the structure of social life and to replicate the calculus that participants use as they determine how best to pursue their roles and goals within that regularized and continuous structure.

Much of the way contemporary scholars approach politics, and certainly the predominant way legislative scholars have approached Congress and other representative institutions, assumes the existence of highly structured contexts likely to generate belief-driven sense making and substantive rationality. In particular, there have been good reasons to assume that the U.S. House is a highly structured or "institutionalized" chamber in which members are socialized into a broadly shared understanding of House politics and pursue shared electoral, organizational, and political goals in a common and calculated manner (Polsby 1968; Asher 1973). Thus, for example, its large size and significant legislative role have fueled the demand for a specialized committee system, relatively strong party organizations, and a formalized system of rules and procedures, thereby helping generate a highly structured politics. Policy specialization among and within committees has helped create generic roles that simplify and regularize House politics. The requirement for reelection every two years creates a common electoral focus among members that facilitates and simplifies their political understanding of each other.

A relatively well-defined status hierarchy of power within and across committees and party organizations structures progressive ambition within the House so that the dominant organizational goals preoccupying its members are relatively clear. The close linkage of personal power in the House with membership in the majority party serves to further simplify and structure House politics. Finally, the fact that the distinctive constitutional power of the House lies in its special role in initiating revenue legislation means that the organizational life of the House is shaped by the annual debates and struggles over taxing and spending, a factor that introduces a strong and routinized regularity to House politics year by year. These and other factors have helped generate a House politics that can be deciphered by participants and scholars in a relatively systematic, straightforward and sustained manner.

The result has been a variety of studies of Congress, based heavily and sometimes entirely on House-centered data or illustrations, that use rational-choice analysis to explain differing aspects of congressional politics. Thus, Mayhew (1974b), Fiorina (1977b), and Arnold (1979) show how members' rational pursuit of reelection drives organizational structure, constitutional service, and congressional-bureaucratic relations. Fenno (1973) demonstrates how members' pursuit of reelection, good public policy, and chamber influence explains the operation and decisions of congressional committees. Cox and McCubbins (1993) and Arnold (1990) argue that strategic maneuvering for majority-party status helps structure committee politics and chamber policy making. And my own work (Dodd 1986a, Chapter Five in this volume) assesses how member concern for personal power conflicts with partisan and institutional power in ways that generate electoral realignments and institutional reform.

An underlying if unspoken assumption of such studies has been that an explanatory strategy that could deliver such systematic results in House-centric studies also provides the way of understanding the Senate, at least once one corrects for the fact that an institution of fewer members would necessarily generate somewhat less statistically powerful results. In point of fact, as the studies in this volume indicate, close examination of the Senate increasingly suggests that it is less a fuzzy shadow of the House and more a different type of institution altogether, with behavior patterns distinctly different from the House. To understand how this could be, it may be useful to recognize, as the work of Weick and others suggests, that social context can shift so dramatically as to actually induce different processes of human sense making and different patterns of human interaction. This can be seen by considering a second type of context.

III

The second type of context—type II—consists of situations that are highly fluid. Such situations can in many ways look like structured contexts, in the sense that there exist systematic organizational arrangements, a stable membership, and some meaningful formal rules. The critical reality in fluid contexts, however, is that the orderliness and regularity of organizational arrangements and rules, and the ways they serve to evoke a simplified and generic reality, are offset by additional conditions and characteristics of the context that complicate, confuse, and even subvert the straightforward operation of the institution. Such additional conditions can include a multiplicity of tasks that a social group must perform to fulfill its social roles and maintain its authority, with the multiplicity of tasks complicating the focus of social life; the unpredictable timing and overlap among tasks, making it difficult to create orderly procedures and rules that easily regulate group life; circumstances that allow individual members to perform a multiplicity of roles and to do so in idiosyncratic and innovative ways that limit the existence of regularized and specialized generic roles; the existence of a small and highly distinctive membership characterized by idiosyncratic motives, goals, and aspirations, thereby limiting the existence of a simple set of identifiable "types" of members that could simplify social life; and arrangements or conditions that allow circumstances external to the organization to dramatically and erratically influence member motives, organizational tasks, or governing activities.

The more complicated and confusing the organizational context is, the less likely it is to generate a continuous and generic structured reality—characterized by clarity and certainty about organizational life—and the more likely it is to generate instead a discontinuous and idiosyncratic fluid reality—characterized by confusion and uncertainty. Because there is no continuous, simple, and generic reality that predominates in such fluid social settings, the real and consequential arrangements that tend to matter are often informal, improvised, and transient behavior patterns that members develop to facilitate the functioning of the organization in response to shifting environmental conditions. As a result, there is no simple substantive understanding of such fluid contexts that members can learn through socialization or experience and use to interpret social life on a continuing and confident basis. Belief-driven sense making and strategic pursuit of interests within a shared substantive understanding of a highly structured reality are thus of limited value.

To function effectively, members in fluid contexts must learn to engage in "action-driven" sense making designed to discover the shifting nature of a complex social reality. Such action-driven sense making includes continuous experimental "action probes" by members designed to discover what the salient conditions of the moment are; extensive social networking designed to understand the distinctive values, goals, and styles of other members of the organization; extensive intragroup communication designed to "update" social awareness in the face of shifting tasks and environmental pressures; and the improvisation of new social relationships and governing strategies that help individuals and groups satisfy their divergent values, styles, and interests while also ensuring the operation of the organization itself as it confronts new circumstances.

The success and power of an organization confronted by highly fluid and permeable contexts, in other words, lies in the long-term and continuing ability of members to improvise social relations within the organization in ways that enable it to adapt to its highly dynamic and unpredictable environment. The tasks for scholars studying fluid contexts is to recognize the complex and shifting conditions that characterize such contexts and to identify the adaptive processes through which participants shape and reshape organizational politics in response to such fluidity. It is difficult enough for scholars to decipher politics in relatively static and structured contexts; it is considerably more challenging to grasp the nature of politics when it is subject to such perpetual change and adaptive transformation, so that the study of organizations in type II fluid contexts is a substantial challenge.

IV

The question confronting congressional scholars is whether there are sufficient reasons to believe that the Senate is best seen as a fluid context so that sustained attention to reconceptualizing senatorial politics, and exploring theories of adaptive process, would seem worthwhile. It seems to me that there are.[3] For example, the Constitution gives to the Senate a greater range of critical governing tasks than is the case for any other major legislature in the world; these include not only a central role in legislation and oversight, and a shared role with the House in the impeachment and conviction of judicial and executive officials, but also critical roles in advice and consent over treaties and over executive, judicial, and ambassadorial nominations; these multiple tasks create an inherent complexity of focus and unpredictability of timing into Senate life. These broad responsibilities then must be handled by a relatively small number of members—two per state for a total of 100 in the contemporary chamber—so that individual members must play a multiplicity of cross-cutting roles for the chamber to manage these tasks; these multiple roles undercut the existence of simple and generic characterizations of senatorial life.

The small size and broad responsibilities of the Senate, moreover, create strong pressures for informal procedures and supermajoritarian decision rules (Matthews, 1960; Binder, 1997; Binder and Smith, 1997), pressures that undercut the existence of the sort of highly structured majoritarian and partisan politics seen in the contemporary U.S. House and that induce fluid cross-partisan coalitions and moderating compromise. The difficulty of developing a simple, generic, and structured understanding of Senate life, and thus the need for ongoing adaptive learning among members, is reinforced by a variety of additional factors: these include the existence of staggered six-year terms for senators and vast differences in the population sizes of senate constituencies, as the research of Lee and Oppenheimer (1999) and Lee (2002) demonstrate; the periodic involvement of senators in campaigns for the presidency, as stressed by Ornstein, Peabody, and Rohde (1985); and the multiple sources of power and career advancement within the Senate that senators enjoy (Matthews, 1960; Ripley, 1969b; Sinclair, 1989). These varying conditions introduce substantial differences in the career goals and political calculations across members year by year so that ongoing informal contact and communication among members are needed for them to understand and respond to each other's distinctive political and career considerations.

These and other conditions would seem, in combination, to create a fluid and action-driven politics within the Senate characterized by multiple realities, procedural rationality, widespread social networking, perceptual and role adjustment, and ongoing organizational adaptation. These expectations of adaptive learning on the part of senators are supported by the pioneering Senate narratives of Richard Fenno, in which he reports on observations of five senators across a decade of Senate life.[4] Fenno's observations suggest a world in which senators proceed, and succeed, not so much according to the pursuit of specific goals, the mastery of specific roles, and the calculation of specific foreseeable career paths, but according to their capacities to comprehend a shifting reality, redefine their roles and goals, and reconstruct political alliances in response to changing times and circumstances, and to do so in nongeneric and idiosyncratic ways largely unforeseen by themselves and others.[5] The expectations of adaptive organizational change are reinforced by Barbara Sinclair's (1989, 2001) broad and dynamic portrait of the Senate across forty years, a portrait that discloses a Senate shifting dramatically from a clubby and closed world of courtly gentlemen to a busy and competitive world of policy entrepreneurs and then most recently to a world of partisan warriors; these changes appear to be explained by the ability of its members to craft and recraft its internal life in response to shifts in its external environment and to do so somewhat informally, without dramatic structural upheaval or political revolution.

Finally, the sense of a highly fluid and adaptive Senate would seem to be greatly reinforced by the essays presented at this conference. For example, the research reported by Abramowitz (2002), Alford and Hibbing (2002), Erikson (2002), Kahn and Kenney (2002), Schiller (2002), and Sellers (2002), in combination, portrays an *institution* so extraordinarily visible and powerful that its members (1) actually experience issue voting and competitive elections when running for reelection; (2) must work both to build highly particularistic electoral coalitions and to coordinate partisan media efforts in order to gain a margin of electoral comfort; and (3) confront regular alterations in their chamber's ideological and partisan majorities and in governing arrangements because of their electoral circumstances. These patterns, taken together, tend to make the Senate much more permeable to outside pressures and developments, and thus to generate a less predictable internal environment, than is generally the case for the highly structured House.

The work of Larry Evans (2002) portrays *senators* who are so distinct in their constituent and political concerns that they must forego cueing off one another when voting and instead develop elaborate staff-based systems to guide them in policy decision processes. This staff-based decision process reinforces the idiosyncratic nature of individual senators, making them extremely sensitive to their unique political circumstances. It also magnifies the unpredictable quality of Senate life.

The essays by Sinclair (2002) and Baker (2002) portray a *policy process* so fragile that the Senate continually operates on the verge of institutional collapse. The Senate appears to avoid this outcome only through the continual construction of new voting alliances in response to the demands of shifting and somewhat unpredictable minorities. It also relies on a deep norm of institutional loyalty that, in moments of extraordinary conflict and tension such as the conviction vote on a president, can introduce shared concern for the institution among an otherwise highly idiosyncratic body of senators. These and numerous other findings point to distinctive qualities of Senate life that are at variance with our expectations derived from the study of the U.S. House and analogous legislatures and that would seem more compatible with the complex and dynamic expectations of a highly fluid world of adaptive learning.

V

The thrust of these observations is to suggest that the Senate has proven elusive because the theories of substantive rationality that legislative scholars have learned to use in extensive study of the highly structured House of Representatives inhibit our ability to comprehend the fluid patterning of senatorial politics. Our problem is not a lack of information about the Senate or research on senatorial politics per se but a lack of appropriate theory. As the essays presented at this conference indicate, scholars are generating a rich body of Senate research. Our problem in seeing the Senate lies in the implicit theoretical frames we bring to it, frames crafted for very different institutional contexts. To see the patterning across new and existing research, and how it fits together to make sense of Senate politics, we need to shift away from theories of substantive rationality, which assume the existence of a regularized, stable, and predictable structure to institutional politics, and toward theories of adaptive learning and procedural rationality, which more nearly anticipate a transient, erratic, idiosyncratic, and improvisational political world.

In raising this possibility, I am not suggesting that senators are not rational individuals capable of identifying and pursuing self-interest: essays such as the one by Bert Loomis (2002) and research by scholars such as Brady and Volden (1998), and Krehbiel (1998) make clear that senators are fully capable of assessing and pursuing self-interest. Nor am I suggesting that the Senate lacks substantial elements of structural commonality with the House and analogous legislatures. The Senate is, in fact, a classic American legislature, composed of professionalized office staffs, powerful committees, meaningful party caucuses, and consequential leadership structures; empowered by constitutional roles and delegated prerogatives; and guided by formal rules, traditions, and precedents. Moreover, as the essays by Gamm and Smith (2002), Cooper and Rybicki (2002), and others make clear, these various arrangements play significant roles in the politics of the Senate.

What I am proposing is that the focus of senatorial politics is so complex, erratic, and uncertain across time, and the focus of rational action generally so varied and idiosyncratic senator by senator, that the predominant concern of Senate life is a crafting, learning, and recrafting of the transient social arrangements that enable it to operate effectively. Such arrangements must respect the broad organizational rules and structure of the chamber and certainly will involve an embrace of substantive rationality when arrangements generate a highly structured moment of political choice. But within these broad parameters, and between these moments of structured choice, senators must continually improvise and adapt an evolving set of interpersonal relationships, personal routines, political alliances, and group norms. It is this process of improvisation and adaptation that enables senators to address the distinctive combination of constitutional tasks, political circumstances, policy problems, and individual ambitions that preoccupy them across time.

Insofar as fluidity is the hallmark of Senate politics, it may well be theories of procedural rationality, satisficing, social learning, social networking, and organizational adaptation that provide us the greatest capacity to comprehend it, rather than theories of substantive rationality and institutional equilibrium. This possibility suggests that considerable debate may be in order over how best to study the Senate in its own right—a debate the essays presented at this conference should serve to stimulate. Such a debate requires us to grapple self-consciously with the deep theoretical assumptions and expectations that we have brought to legislative analysis over the past several decades—assumptions of institutionalized structure, generic roles, identifiable legislative types, common strategic calculations, and regularized political processes—and to imagine the alternative assumptions and theoretical patterns appropriate to a fluid legislative world. As we image such a world, we may more clearly see it. Moreover, an additional and critical concern of such debate must be with the significance that the contrasts between a structured House and a fluid Senate have for the broader functioning of the Congress and the national government. In particular, the perception of such a fluid Senate presented here necessarily forces us to wonder whether and how the Senate today fulfills its most basic constitutional responsibility to moderate and conserve stable representative government.

One possible way to understand how the Senate successfully fulfills its moderating role may lie in recognizing the extraordinary—perhaps even exceptional—ways that the differing institutional contexts and organizational dynamics of the House and Senate fit together so as to facilitate the long-term operation of both chambers. Thus, the House may provide the stabilizing structure and regularity that helps introduce a necessary degree of order and predictability onto bicameral politics during periods of "normalcy," when a dominant policy regime pervades national politics. In so doing the House also defines political and programmatic boundaries that serve to limit and constrain senatorial innovation and improvisation. For its part, the ongoing improvisational quality of senatorial politics may introduce and legitimize political and policy innovations that help generate some

degree of congressional responsiveness to social change, despite the highly structured, stable, and more insulated character of the House.

The ongoing process of procedural and policy innovation in the Senate can
help keep it more contemporaneous in its focus than the more routinized and
insulated House, so that radical change proves less necessary and appealing in the
Senate during periods of national crisis and so that moderation in the face of such
crises appears more politically viable. Simultaneously, the sustained experience
of the Senate with difficulties in governing may generate norms such as institutional patriotism and cross-partisan compromise that in moments of national
crisis help the Congress as a whole maintain a degree of adaptive equilibrium.
The extensive experience of the Senate with uncertainty and adaptive learning
may induce a deep belief among legislators and citizens alike in the ability of representative assemblies to confront governing difficulties and emerge revitalized
and re-empowered. Such experience may also allow members of the Senate to
face system crises with more confidence and to be more open to learning effective strategies for addressing institutional crises than House members accustomed
to a routinized politics of "normalcy." Finally, the very experience of life in the
Senate may enable senators to provide Congress and the nation with broad perspective and steady judgment, guided by the firsthand knowledge that individuals and groups of differing values, goals, and worldviews can nevertheless work
together, learn to accommodate divergent understandings, and find areas of common ground and collective cooperation even in troubled times.

When crises challenge the viability of our bicameral Congress—moments so
often driven by the tendency of citizens to embrace "political revolution" as the
primary way to induce change within our highly insulated House—the conserving, moderating, and stabilizing roles of the Senate come to the fore.[6] Accustomed to improvisation amidst uncertainty and buoyed by norms of institutional
loyalty, a fluid and permeable Senate that appears to operate exceedingly close
to the edge of collapse during periods of normalcy may possess precisely the
capacities for adaptive learning, experienced judgment, policy moderation, and
foresightful leadership that are necessary to cushion and constrain destabilizing
change induced by the House. In doing so, the Senate necessarily engenders
within the nation an appreciation for the power and purpose of its representative
institutions, sustaining popular support for Congress in periods of upheaval and
confusion. If this interpretation is true, then the Senate may be an exceptional
institution indeed, and a truly essential partner in the successful operation of our
bicameral Congress.

Notes

1   Examples of this debate within political science are found in the point/counterpoint
    between William Riker (1982a) and Herbert Simon (1985) in the *American Political Sci-
    ence Review*; in Almond (1990), in Green and Shapiro (1994), and in the extensive dis-
    cussion of Green and Shapiro's book in *Critical Review*, Vol. 9, 31–32, Winter–Spring,

1995. The distinction between substantive and procedural rationality is developed in Simon (1985: 294–98).

2   See, for example, Karl E. Weick (1995, 1979). Other important statements about the role that context and process can play in shaping the nature of rationality and human sense making can be found in Bendor (2001), particularly his suggestion that substantive or objective rational choice is most prevalent when the "game" of politics has narrowed to a few clear strategies and choices, whereas bounded rationality is more prevalent in situations characterized by complexity and multiple paths of action; in Dreyfus and Dreyfus (1986), which suggests that the use of narrow strategic or substantive rationality is primarily confined to simple contexts characterized by easily learned rules and procedures, whereas advanced patterns of procedural rationality and sophisticated or expert learning more nearly characterize complex settings that cannot be managed by simple rules and procedures; and in Flyvbjerg (2001), particularly his extensive discussion of Dreyfus and Dreyfus in Chapter 2 and of the varied ways that "context counts" in Chapter 4.

3   For a more extensive discussion of the general characteristics of the Senate and how they contrast with the House, see Baker (1989) and Oleszek (1996).

4   I refer here to Fenno (1989a, 1990, 1991a, 1991b, 1992a). Fenno's (1986a) presidential address to the American Political Science Association presents a powerful portrait of the Senate as a fluid institution composed of individualistic and idiosyncratic senators. Also illuminating is the distinction that Fenno (1973) makes between "corporate committees," which typify key House committees, and "permeable committees," which appears to typify all Senate committees. Fenno's analysis there suggests the existence, even within an elaborate committee system, of a highly fluid and porous politics within the Senate and thus appear to support the applicability of theories of adaptive learning to the Senate.

5   For a more extensive discussion of the implications of Fenno's narratives for theories of legislative politics, see the "Extension of Remarks" in the November 1992 issue of the *Legislative Studies Section Newsletter*. This issue of "Extensions," entitled "Making Sense Out of the Senate: The Narratives of Richard F. Fenno, Jr.," includes "Introductory Remarks" by Fenno (1992), in which he provides a valuable discussion of the evolution and conduct of his study of senators. Fenno's introduction is followed by five essays that provide varying perspectives on the significant themes and theoretical implications contained in the narratives, with contributions by Donald Matthews (1992), Barbara Sinclair (1992), Bruce Oppenheimer (1992), Steven Smith (1992), and the author (Dodd, 1992). Fenno's introductory remarks and the five essays grew out of a Round-table Discussion of Fenno's narratives held at the Western Political Science Convention in March 1992. "Making Sense Out of the Senate" is available in the Archives for the *Legislative Studies Section Newsletter* on the Legislative Studies Section website of the American Political Science Association (www.apsanet.org), or from the author. The adaptive learning perspective on the Senate developed in the current essay was greatly aided by reading and reflecting on Fenno's Senate narratives and participating in the WPSA Roundtable. The many themes that emerged from the Roundtable include Matthews' stress on the extent to which Fenno's narratives highlight the importance of "sequence" in politics, including (1) the role of pre-Senate careers in shaping senatorial behavior and (2) "the cycle of campaigning, governing and campaigning which dominates the lives of members of the Senate" (Matthews, 1992: 3). Sinclair highlights the ways in which "multiple goals" dominate senators' careers (Sinclair, 1992: 4), with reelection only one of a number of concerns shaping senators' political lives: she calls for building theories focused on "balancing" and "trade-offs" among multiple goals. Oppenheimer notes that these senators, all of whom were observed during the 1980s, "appear to be operating with little concern for party," thereby providing a valuable historical perspective on the role parties played in senatorial careers early in the "Post-

Reform" era of congressional politics (Oppenheimer, 1992: 7). Smith (1992: 8) stresses the extent to which "Fenno's discussion makes plain [that] senators' goals vary with context," so that the very context of the Senate "seems to stimulate a general interest in participating and contributing—for their own sake—that is found less frequently in the House." My own essay lays out an early version of the social learning perspective developed in the current essay, stressing the extent to which "Fenno's narratives...provide a testament to the role of learning and character development in politics"(Dodd, 1992: 10).

6   The periodic tendency of the Congress to experience sudden, unforeseen, and destabilizing upheavals, illustrated by the experience of the "Republican Revolution," is discussed in "Re-Envisioning Congress" (Dodd, 2001a; 2005a, Chapter 10 in this volume), with the logic and illustrations of that essay largely based on the politics of the House. The thrust of the current essay is to suggest that the incremental and adaptive learning processes that "Re-Envisioning Congress" sees as critical to the power and survival of Congress during such crises may derive to a significant extent from the distinctive politics of the Senate. Across time, the differential politics of the two houses may well generate a kind of cybernetic patterning to bicameralism, out of which emerges a dynamic equilibrium between them. Thus, the institutionalized structure of the House provides considerable stability to the Congress in "normal" times, helping to keep the Senate in check and moderated in its action innovations. Yet eventually the institutionalized structure of the House is up-ended by political revolution that comes in response to new social conditions, a revolution that focuses on the House because of its more insulated and less responsive politics. During such periods, the House must undergo substantial procedural, structural, and policy adjustment to "catch up" with the Senate and the social and political world at large. In these adjustment periods, the Senate, being more in tune with and adapted to national currents, may play a special stabilizing, moderating, and conserving role that gives the House some critical time and substantive guidance as it innovates a new policy and structural equilibrium. This interpretation would seem consistent with Mayhew's observations that the Senate generally produces more innovative action than the House, particularly in periods when a dominant regime politics exists in national government. But in periods of extraordinary upheaval such as the Civil War/Reconstruction, the Progressive Era/ World War I, the Depression/World War II, and possibly the contemporary period, the House drives legislative innovation while the Senate shifts into a less action-driven and more moderating stance. See Mayhew (2000: 130–35); see also Carmines and Dodd (1985, Chapter Four in this volume).

Additional Perspective on "Our Exceptional Senate"

"Making Sense out of Our Exceptional Senate" treats the House of Representatives and the Senate as very different kinds of legislative settings that require a distinct theoretical lens by which to understand and explain their politics. In doing so, it develops a "context-dependent" theory of foreground politics in Congress. This theory highlights distinct forms of cognitive sense making and member behavior (particularly networking activity) that characterize the politics of the two houses, given the differences between them created in the Constitution and in their organizational development and evolving role in national politics. These differences enable the House of Representatives and the Senate to play distinctly different roles in the cyclical processes of change detailed in *Thinking about Congress*.

The broader importance of "Our Exceptional Senate" is to suggest that students of legislative politics—and politics more generally—should approach analysis with a more nuanced conception of human sense making and consequent behavior. They should consider the ways in which differences in the context of behavior calls forth different forms of knowing and acting on the part of context-participants. The same individuals, moving from a fluid to a structured context, can instantaneously shift from a more interpretive and proceduralist rationality to a more strategic and substantive rationality. Attention to the context-sensitive understanding of human knowing and acting may well be a key to explaining puzzling behavioral conundrums within and across governing institutions, and to crafting theories that help us to see and explain those conundrums through a simple yet powerful analytic lens.

As an illustration, presidents may inherently face more fluid contexts than do bureaucrats or legislators, so that the former are more improvisational and less predictable in their behavior, whereas the latter are more structured and predictable. Yet presidents may also operate at some times and in some context that are highly structured, with predictable outcomes, and bureaucrats and legislators may operate at times and in context that are fluid, with improvised and less predictable outomes. Alertness to such possibilities may yield more accurate theories that move the study of politics closer to scientific credibility.

Foundation Work: "Our Exceptional Senate" builds, in particular, on Herbert Simon's 1985 distinction between "substantive" and "procedural" rationality and on Karl Weick's 1995 distinction between the "belief-driven" versus "action-driven" processes of sense making that characterize individuals and groups as they operate within social organizations. The essay would not have been possible without these two works, and the scholarly contributions on which they build. For an insightful application of Simon's conception of bounded rationality to political inquiry, see Bryan Jones (2001), *Politics and the Architecture of Choice*. For a historical work highlighting the way in which the late nineteenth century U. S. Senate relied on member networking for organizational functioning, with an underlying contrast with the House of Representatives, see David J. Rothman, *Politics and Power* (New York: Atheneum, 1969). For the postwar literature, studies of Lyndon Johnson's years as Senate Majority Leader offer particularly intriguing insights into the role of networking and sensitivity to context on the part of a great master of senatorial politics. See, for example, Huitt (1961a); McPherson (1972: 11-155); Evans and Novak (1966: 50-194); Caro, (2002).

For a pioneering exploration of the ways in which differing patterns of networking characterize the House of Representatives in the late twentieth and early twenty-first centuries, see Paulina Rippere, "Polarization Reconsidered: A New Take on Congressional Change Over the Last 40 Years" A Paper Presented at the 2011 Southern Political Science Convention, January 5th–8th, New Orleans, La. Looking at patterns of cross-partisan co-sponsorship in the House and Senate during this era, Rippere argues that the appearance of polarized politics in the Senate created by studying roll call votes is belied by the extensive cross-partisan co-sponsorship of bills that occurs during the same period in the Senate; in contrast, partisan patterns of bill co-sponsorship in the House of Representatives reinforce the appearance of high party polarization in the House, as seen in roll call votes for the lower house.

Classroom Use and Additional Reading: For classroom use in courses on Congress, "Making Sense Out of Our Exceptional Senate" can be employed in sections focused on contrasts in the politics of the House and Senate, in sections that examine the logic and characteristics of member behavior, and in sections on theories of congressional politics. It can be paired with Ross Baker's excellent study, *House and Senate*: an interesting exercise would be for students to assess how well the context-dependent theory of congressional sense making explains the range of differences in institutional behavior between the chambers highlighted by Baker (1989, 1995).

The essay can be used in courses on the social psychology of politics and courses on empirical theories of politics to illustrate the empirical utility of Simon's distinction between substantive and procedural rationality and Weick's distinction between belief-driven and action-driven sense making.

It could be interesting to pair "Our Exceptional Senate" with the 2006 essay by Michael Cutrone and Nolan McCarty, "Does Bicameralism Matter?" Utilizing such analytic strategies as spatial modeling, multilateral bargaining theory, and games of incomplete information, Cutrone and McCarty propose that bicameralism makes little difference in legislative politics. Coming out of a social-psychological perspective, "Sensemaking" argues for substantial difference between the House and Senate. Does one essay refute the other, or are they looking at such different dimensions of human experience that both could conceivably be 'true' and offer something useful to consider in studying bicameralism? Could the perspectives even be integrated in some manner? In this regard, see also Jordan Ragusa, "Chamber Hopping in the US Congress: Structure-Induced Learning and the Development of a Partisan Senate." A Paper Presented at the Midwest Political Science Association Annual Meeting, Chicago, IL, April 2010.

BIBLIOGRAPHY

Aberbach, Joel D. (1979). "Changes in Congressional Oversight." *American Behavioral Scientist* 22: 493–515.
——. 1990. *Keeping a Watchful Eye*. Washington, D.C.: Brookings.
Abramowitz, Alan I. 1991. "Incumbency, Campaign Spending and the Decline of Competition in U.S. House Elections." *Journal of Politics* 53: 34–56.
——. 2002. "Party Realignment, Ideological Polarization, and Voting Behavior in U.S. Senate Elections." In *U.S. Senate Exceptionalism*. Edited by Bruce I. Oppenheimer. Columbus, O.H.: Ohio State University Press, pp. 31–44.
Abramowitz, Alan I., and Jeffrey A. Segal. 1992. *Senate Elections*. Ann Arbor: University of Michigan Press.
Abramson, Paul, John H. Aldrich, and David W. Rohde. 1987. "Progressive Ambition among United States Senators: 1972–1988." *Journal of Politics* 49: 3–35.
Ackerman, Bruce. 1991. *We the People: Foundations*. Cambridge: Harvard University Press.
Adams, Guy B., John Forester, and Bayand Catron. 1987. *Policymaking, Communication, and Social Learning: Essays of Geoffrey Vickers*. New Brunswick, N.J.: Transaction Books.
Adler, E. Scott. 2002. *Why Congressional Reforms Fail*. Chicago: University of Chicago Press.
Adler, E. Scott, and John S. Lapinski. 1997. "Demand-Side Theory and Congressional Committee Composition: Constituency Characteristics Approach." *American Journal of Political Science* 41: 895–918.
——. eds. 2006. *Macropolitics of Congress*. Princeton: Princeton University Press.
Aldrich, John H. 1995a. *Why Parties? The Origin and Transformation of Political Parties in America*. Chicago: University of Chicago Press.
——. 1995b. "A Model of a Legislature with Two Parties and a Committee System." In *Positive Theories of Congressional Institutions*. Edited by Kenneth A. Shepsle and Barry R. Weingast. Ann Arbor, M.I.: University of Michigan Press, pp. 173–200.
Aldrich, John H., and Ruth W. Grant. 1993. "The Antifederalists, the First Congress, and the First Parties." *Journal of Politics* 55: 295–326.
Aldrich, John H., and David W. Rohde. 1997. "The Transition to Republican Rule in the

House: Implications for Theories of Congressional Politics." *Political Science Quarterly* 112: 541–67.

——. 2000. "The Republican Revolution and the House Appropriations Committee." *Journal of Politics* 62 (February): 1–33.

——. 2001. "The Logic of Conditional Party Government: Revisiting the Electoral Connection." In *Congress Reconsidered*, 7th ed. Edited by Lawrence C. Dodd and Bruce I. Oppenheimer. Washington, D.C.: CQ Press, pp. 169–92.

——. 2005. "Congressional Committees in a Partisan Era." In *Congress Reconsidered*, 8th ed. Edited by Lawrence C. Dodd and Bruce I. Oppenheimer. Washington, D.C.: CQ Press, pp. 249–70.

Alesina, Alberto, and Howard Rosenthal. 1989. "Partisan Cycles in Congressional Elections and the Macroeconomy." *American Political Science Review* 83: 373–398.

Alford, John R., and David W. Brady. 1993. "Personal and Partisan Advantage in U.S. Congressional Elections." In *Congress Reconsidered*, 5th ed. Edited by Lawrence C. Dodd and Bruce I. Oppenheimer. Washington, D.C.: CQ Press, pp. 141–57.

Alford, Robert A., and Roger Friedland. 1985. *Powers of Theory: Capitalism, the State and Democracy*. Cambridge: Cambridge University Press.

Alford, Robert A., and John R. Hibbing. 2002. "Electoral Convergence in the U.S. Senate." In *U.S. Senate Exceptionalism*. Edited by Bruce I. Oppenheimer. Columbus, O.H.: Ohio State University Press, pp. 89–108.

Allison, Graham. 1971. *Essence of Decision: Explaining the Cuban Missile Crisis*. 1st ed. N.Y.: Harper Collins.

Allison, Graham, and Philip Zelikow. 1999. *Essence of Decision: Explaining the Cuban Missile Crisis*, 2nd ed. New York: Longman.

Almond, Gabriel. 1990. *A Discipline Divided: Schools and Sects in Political Science*. Newbury Park, Calif.: Sage Publications.

Almond, Gabriel, G. Bingham Powell, Russell Dalton, and Kaare Strom. 2009. *European Politics Today*. New York: Longman.

Anderson, Benedict. 1983. *Imagined Communities*. London: Routledge, Chapman & Hall.

Anderson, Leslie. 1994. *The Political Ecology of the Modern Peasant*. Baltimore: Johns Hopkins University Press.

——. 2010. *Social Capital in Developing Democracies: Nicaragua and Argentina Compared*. Cambridge: Cambridge University Press.

Anderson, Leslie E., and Lawrence C. Dodd. 2001. "Nicaragua Votes: The Elections of 2001." *The Journal of Democracy*. Vol. 13 (July): 80–94.

——. 2005. *Learning Democracy: Citizen Engagement and Electoral Choice in Nicaragua, 1990–2001*. Chicago: University of Chicago Press.

——. 2009. "Nicaragua: Progress Amid Regress?" *Journal of Democracy*. Vol. 20 (July): 153–67.

Anderson, Thorton. 1993. *Creating the Constitution: The Convention of 1787 and the First Congress*. University Park: Pennsylvania State University Press.

Ansolabehere, Stephen, James M. Snyder, Jr., and Charles Stewart III. 2001. "Candidate Positioning in U.S. House Elections." *American Journal of Political Science* 45: 136–159.

Arnold, R. Douglas. 1979. *Congress and the Bureaucracy*. New Haven, C.T.: Yale University Press.

——. 1981. "The Local Roots of Domestic Policy." In *The New Congress*. Edited by Thomas E. Mann and Norman J. Ornstein. Washington, D.C.: American Enterprise Institute, pp. 250–87.

——. 1990. *The Logic of Congressional Action*. New Haven, C.T.: Yale University Press.

Art, Robert J. 1984. "Congress and the Defense Budget: New Procedures and Old Realities, 1975–1983. Unpublished manuscript, Brandeis University.

Art, Robert J., Vincent Davis, and Samuel P. Huntington, eds. 1985. *Reorganizing America's Defense: Leadership in War and Peace*. Washington, D.C.: Pergamon.

Asher, Herbert B. 1973. "The Learning of Legislative Norms." *American Political Science Review* 67 (1973): 499–513.

Aydelotte, William O. 1977. *The History of Parliamentary Behavior*. Princeton, N.J.: Princeton University Press.

Bach, Stanley, and Steven S. Smith. 1988. *Managing Uncertainty in the House: Adaptation and Innovation in Special Rules*. Washington, D.C.: Brookings.

Bacon, Donald C., Roger H. Davidson and Morton Keller, eds. 1995. *The Encyclopedia of the United States Congress*. New York: Simon and Schuster.

Bader, John B. 1997. "The Contract with America: Origins and Assessments." In *Congress Reconsidered*, 6th ed. Edited by Lawrence C. Dodd and Bruce I. Oppenheimer. Washington, D.C.: CQ Press, pp. 347–69.

Baker, John D. 1973. The Character of the Congressional Revolution of 1910." *Journal of American History* 60: 679–691.

Baker, Ross K. *House and Senate*. 1989. New York: Norton.

——. 2002. "Examining Individualism versus Senate Folkways in the Aftermath of the Clinton Impeachment." In *U.S. Senate Exceptionalism*. Edited by Bruce I. Oppenheimer. Columbus, O.H.: Ohio State University Press, pp. 305–21.

Balz, Dan, and Ronald Brownstein. 1996. *Storming the Gates: Protest Politics and the Republican Revival*. Boston: Little, Brown.

Bandura, Albert. 1976. "Social Learning Theory." In *Behavioral Approaches to Therapy*. Edited by Janet T. Spence, Robert C. Carson, and John W. Thibaut. Morristown, N.J.: General Learning Press, 1–46.

Barabas, Jason, and Jennifer Jerit. 2009. "Estimating the Causal Effects of Media Coverage on Policy-Specific Knowledge." *American Journal of Political Science*. Vol. 53, No. 1 January: 73–89.

Barber, James D. 1980. *The Pulse of Politics: The Rhythm of Presidential Elections in the Twentieth Century*. New York: Norton.

——. 1985. *Presidential Character*. Englewood Cliffs, N.J.: Prentice-Hall.

Bardach, Eugene. 1972. *The Skill Factor in Politics: Repealing the Mental Commitment Laws in California*. Berkeley: University of California Press.

Barker, David C. 1999. "Rushed Decisions: Political Talk Radio and Vote Choice, 1994–1996." *Journal of Politics* 61: 527–39.

Barker, David C., and Kathleen Knight. 2000. "Political Talk Radio and Public Opinion" *Public Opinion Quarterly*. 64(2): 149–70.

Barnett, Timothy J. 1999. *Legislative Learning: The 104th Republican Freshmen in the House*. New York: Garland Publishing, Inc.

Barry. Brian. 1970. *Sociologists, Economists and Democracy*. London: Macmillan.

——. 1982. "Methodology vs Ideology: The Economic Approach Revisited." In *Strategies of Political Inquiry*. Edited by Elinor Ostrom, Beverley Hills, C.A.: Sage, pp. 92–109.

Bartels, Larry M. 2008. *Unequal Democracy: The Political Economy of the New Gilded Age*. New York and Princeton: Russell Sage Foundation and Princeton University Press.

Bateson, Gregory. 1947. "Social Planning and the Concept of 'Deutero-Learning." In *Readings in Social Psychology*. Edited by T. M. Newcomb and E. L. Harley. New York: Holt, 121–28; it is also reprinted in Bateson. 1972. *Steps to an Ecology of Mind*.

——. 1966. "From Versailles to Cybernetics." An Unpublished Lecture Presented at the "Two Worlds Symposium" at Sacramento State College, April 21, 1966. Published in Bateson. 1972. *Steps to an Ecology of Mind,* 469–477.

——. 1971. "The Cybernetics of 'Self'", *Psychiatry* 34: 1–18; it is also reprinted in Bateson. 1972. *Steps to an Ecology of Mind.*

——. 1972. *Steps to an Ecology of Mind: Collected Essays in Anthropology, Psychiatry, Evolution and Epistemology.* San Francisco: Chandler Publishing Co. Subsequently reprinted by Ballantine Press.

Bateson, Gregory, and Mary Catherine Bateson. 1987. *Angels Fear: Towards an Epistemology of the Sacred.* New York: Macmillan.

Bauer, Raymond A., Ithiel de Sola Pool, and Lewis A. Dexter. 1963. *American Business and Public Policy.* New York: Atherton.

Baumgartner, Frank R., and Bryan D. Jones. 1991. "Agenda Dynamics and Policy Subsystems." *Journal of Politics* 53 (November): 1044–1074.

——. 1993. *Agendas and Instability in American Politics.* Chicago: University of Chicago Press.

——. 2002. *Policy Dynamics.* Chicago: University of Chicago Press.

Baumgartner, Frank R., Bryan D. Jones, and Michael C. MacLeod. 2000. "The Evolution of Legislative Jurisdictions." *Journal of Politics* 62: 321–349.

Bell, Daniel. 1973. *The Coming of Post-Industrial Society.* New York: Basic Books.

Bell, Lauren Cohen. 2002. *Warring Factions: Interest Groups, Money and the New Politics of Senate Confirmation.* Columbus, O.H.: Ohio State University Press.

Bendor, Jon. 2001. "Bounded Rationality in Political Science." In *The International Encyclopedia of the Social and Behavioral Sciences.* Oxford, England: Pergamon.

Benjamin, Gerald, and Michael Malbin, eds. 1992. *Limiting Legislative Terms.* Washington, D.C.: CQ Press.

Bensel, Richard F. 1984. *Sectionalism and American Political Development, 1880–1980.* Madison: University of Wisconsin Press.

——. 1990. *Yankee Leviathan: The Origins of Central State Authority in America, 1859–1877.* New York: Cambridge University Press.

——. 2000. "Of Rules and Speakers, Toward a Theory of Institutional Change of the U.S. House of Representatives." *Social Science History* 24: 2.

Berkman, Michael B. 1993. *The State Roots of National Politics: Congress and the Tax Agenda, 1978–1986.* Pittsburgh: University of Pittsburgh Press.

——. 1994. "State Legislators in Congress: Strategic Politicians, Professional Legislatures, and the Party Nexus." *American Journal of Political Science* 38: 1025–1055.

Berkowitz, Edward D. 2004. "The Great Society." In *The American Congress: The Building of Democracy.* Edited by Julian E. Zelizer. Boston: Houghton Mifflin, pp. 566–83.

Berlin, Isaiah. 1996. "On Political Judgment." *New York Review of Books.* October, pp. 26–30.

Bessette, Joseph M. 1994. *The Mild Voice of Reason: Deliberative Democracy and American National Government.* Chicago: University of Chicago Press.

Bianco, William T. 1994. *Trust: Representatives and Constituents.* Ann Arbor: University of Michigan Press.

Bianco, William T., and Itai Sened. 2005. "Uncovering Evidence of Conditional Party Government: Reassessing Majority Party Influence in Congress and State Legislatures." *American Political Science Review* 99: 361–371.

Bibby, John F., and Roger H. Davidson. 1972. *On Capitol Hill.* 2nd ed. Hinsdale, I.L.: Dryden Press.

Binder, Sarah A. 1996. "The Partisan Basis of Procedural Choice: Allocating Parliamentary Rights in the House, 1789–1900." *American Political Science Review* 90: 8–20.

———. 1997. *Minority Rights, Majority Rule.* New York: Cambridge University Press.

———. 1999. "The Dynamics of Legislative Gridlock, 1947–96." *American Political Science Review* 93: 519–534.

———. 2003. *Stalemate: Causes and Consequences of Legislative Gridlock.* Washington, D.C.: Brookings.

Binder, Sarah A., and Forrest Maltzman. 2004. "The Limits of Senatorial Courtesy." *Legislative Studies Quarterly* 24: 5–22.

———. 2005. "Congress and the Politics of Judicial Appointments." In *Congress Reconsidered*, 8th ed. Edited by Lawrence C. Dodd and Bruce I. Oppenheimer, Washington, D.C.: CQ Press, pp. 297–317.

Binder, Sarah A., and Steven S. Smith. 1997. *Politics or Principle? Filibustering in the United States Senate.* Washington, D.C.: Brookings.

Black, Earl, and Merle Black. 2002. The Rise of Southern Republicans. Cambridge, M.A.: Harvard University Press.

Blondel, Jean. 1973. *Comparative Legislatures.* Englewood, Cliffs, N.J.: Prentice Hall.

Bogue, Allan G., 1989. *The Congressman's Civil War.* New York: Cambridge University Press.

Bolling, Richard. 1965. *House Out of Order.* New York: Dutton.

———. 1968. *Power in the House.* New York: Capricorn.

Bohm, David. 1983. *Wholeness and the Implicate Order.* London: Ark Paperbacks.

Bond, Jon R., and Richard Fleisher. 1990. *The President in the Legislative Arena.* Chicago: University of Chicago Press.

———. 2000. *Polarized Politics: The President and the Congress in a Partisan Era.* Washington, D.C.: CQ Press.

Born, Richard. 1979. "Generational Replacement and the Growth of Incumbent Reelection Margins in the U.S. House. *American Political Science Review* 73: 811–17.

———. 1980. "Changes in the Competitiveness of House Primary Elections, 1956–1976." *American Politics Quarterly* 8: 495–506.

Bosso, Christopher. 1988. *Pesticides and Politics: The Life Cycle of a Public Issue.* Pittsburgh: University of Pittsburgh Press.

Box-Steffensmeier, Janet M., Laura W. Arnold, and Christopher J. W. Zorn. 1997. "The Strategic Timing of Position Taking in Congress: A Study of the North American Free Trade Agreement." *American Political Science Review* 92: 324–38.

Bracher, Karl Dietrich. 1971. "Problems of Parliamentary Democracy in Europe." In *Comparative Legislative Systems.* Edited by Herbert Hirsch and M. Donald Hancock. New York: Free Press, pp. 350–69.

Brady, David W. 1973. *Congressional Voting in a Partisan Era: A Study of the McKinley Houses.* Lawrence: University Press of Kansas.

———. 1978. "Critical Elections, Congressional Parties, and Clusters of Policy Change." *British Journal of Political Science* 8: 78–99.

———. 1988. *Critical Elections and Congressional Policy Making.* Stanford: Stanford University Press.

Brady, David W., Richard Brody, and David Epstein. 1989. "Heterogeneous Parties and Political Organization: The U.S. Senate, 1880–1920." *Legislative Studies Quarterly* 14: 205–23.

Brady, David W., Kara Buckley, and Douglas Rivers. 1999. "The Roots of Careerism in the U.S. House of Representatives. *Legislative Studies Quarterly* 24: 489–508.

Brady, David W., and Charles Bullock. 1981. "Coalition Politics in the House of Representatives." In *Congress Reconsidered*, 2nd ed. Edited by Lawrence C. Dodd and Bruce I. Oppenheimer, pp. 186–203.

Brady, David W., Joseph Cooper, and Patricia A. Hurley. 1979. "The Decline of Party in the U.S. House of Representatives, 1887–1968." *Legislative Studies Quarterly* 4: 381–407.

Brady, David W., and David Epstein. 1997. "Intraparty Preferences, Heterogeneity, and the Origins of the Modern Congress: Progressive Reforms in the House and Senate, 1890–1920." *Journal of Law, Economics, and Organization* 13: 26–49.

Brady, David W., and Mathew McCubbins, eds. 2002. *Party, Process, and Political Change in Congress*, Volume 1. Stanford: Stanford University Press.

———. 2007. *Party, Process, and Political Change in Congress*, Volume 2. Stanford: Stanford University Press.

Brady, David W., and Sean M. Theriault. 2001. "A Reassessment of Who's to Blame: A Positive Case for Public Evaluation of Congress." In *What Is It about Government That Americans Dislike?* Edited by John R. Hibbing and Elizabeth Theiss-Morse. Cambridge University Press, pp. 175–92.

Brady, David W., and Craig Volden. 1998. *Revolving Gridlock: Politics and Policy from Carter to Clinton*. Boulder, C.O.: Westview.

Brenner, David. 1981. "An Approach to the Limits and Possibilities of Congress." In *Congress Reconsidered*, 2nd ed. Edited by Lawrence C. Dodd and Bruce I. Oppenheimer, Washington, D.C.: CQ Press, pp. 371–89.

Broder, David S. 1972. *The Party's Over*. New York: Harper.

———. 1980. *Changing of the Guard: Power and Leadership In America*. New York: Simon & Schuster.

———. 1992. "Post-Election News Is Good and Bad for Republicans." Syndicated Column. *Boulder Sunday Camera*. Boulder, C.O.: Dec. 6, 3E.

Brown, George Rothwell. 1922. *The Leadership of Congress*. Indianapolis: Bobbs-Merrill.

Brunell, Thomas L. 2008. *Redistricting and Representation: Why Competitive Elections Are Bad for America*. New York: Routledge.

Brunner, Ronald D. 1989. *The Policy Movement as a Policy Problem*. Discussion paper 48, Center for Public Policy Research. University of Colorado, Boulder.

Bryce, James. 1924. "The Decline of Legislatures." *Modern Democracies*. Vol. II. New York: Macmillan.

Bullock, Charles S. 1972. "House Careerists: Changing Patterns of Longevity and Attrition." *American Political Science Review* 66: 1295–1300.

Bullock, Charles S., and Burdett A. Loomis. 1985. "The Changing Congressional Career." In *Congress Reconsidered*, 3rd ed. Edited by Lawrence C. Dodd and Bruce I. Oppenheimer. Washington, D.C.: CQ Press, pp. 65–84.

Burden, Barry C. 2007. *Personal Roots of Representation*. Princeton: Princeton University Press.

Burnham, Walter Dean. 1970. *Critical Elections and the Mainsprings of American Politics*. New York: W. W. Norton.

———. 1975. "Insulation and Responsiveness in Congressional Elections." *Political Science Quarterly* 90: 411–32.

———. 1976. "Revitalization and Decay: Looking toward the Third Century of American Electoral Politics." *Journal of Politics* 38 (August): 146–72.

———. 1994. "Pattern Recognition and 'Doing' Political History: Art, Science, or Bootless

Enterprise?" In *The Dynamics of American Politics*. Edited by Lawrence C. Dodd and Calvin Jillson. Boulder, C.O.: Westview, pp. 59–82.

——. 1995. "Realignment Lives." In *The Clinton Presidency*. Edited by Bert Rockman. Pittsburgh: University of Pittsburgh Press, pp. 363–96.

Burns, James MacGregor. 1949. *Congress on Trial: The Legislative Process and the Administrative State*. New York: Harper.

——. 1963. *The Deadlock of Democracy*. Englewood Cliffs, N. J.: Prentice-Hall.

——. 1965. *Presidential Government: The Crucible of Leadership*. Boston: Houghton-Mifflin.

Burrell, Barbara C. 1994. *A Woman's Place Is in the House*. Ann Arbor: University of Michigan Press.

Butler, David. 1981. "Electoral Systems." In *Democracy at the Polls*. Edited by David Butler, Howard R. Penniman, and Austin Ranney. Washington, D.C.: American Enterprise Institute for Public Policy Research, pp. 12–19.

Cain, Bruce, John Ferejohn and Morris Fiorina. 1980. "Legislators v. Legislatures: A Comparative Analysis of Fenno's Paradox." Paper delivered at the Conference on Congressional Elections, Houston, Texas, January 10–12.

——. 1987. *The Personal Vote: Constituency Service and Electoral Independence*. Cambridge: Harvard University Press.

Cameron, Charles M. 2000. *Veto Bargaining*. New York: Cambridge University Press.

Campbell, Donald T. 1970. "Natural Selection as an Epistemological Model." In *A Handbook of Method in Cultural Anthropology*. Edited by R. Narool and R. Cohen. Garden City, N.Y.: Natural History Press: 51–85.

Campbell, James E. 1993. *The Presidential Pulse of Congressional Elections*. Lexington: University Press of Kentucky.

——. 1996. *Cheap Seats: The Democratic Party's Advantage in U. S. House Elections*. Columbus: Ohio State University Press.

Canes-Wrone, Brandice, David W. Brady, and John F. Cogan. 2002. "Out of Step, Out of Office: Electoral Accountability and House Members' Voting." *American Political Science Review* 96: 127–140.

Cann, Damon. 2008. *Sharing the Wealth: Member Contributions and the Exchange Theory of Party Influence in the U. S. House of Representatives*. Albany, N.Y.: SUNY Press.

Canon, David T. 1990. *Actors, Athletes, and Astronauts: Political Amateurs in the United States Congress*. Chicago: University of Chicago Press.

——. 1999. *Race, Redistricting, and Representation: The Unintended Consequences of Black Majority Districts*. Chicago: University of Chicago Press.

Canon, David T., and Kenneth R. Mayer. 1999. *The Dysfunctional Congress? The Individual Roots of an Institutional Dilemma*. Boulder, C.O.: Westview.

Canon, David T., and Charles Stewart III. 2002. "Parties and Hierarchies in Senate Committees, 1789–1946." In *U.S. Senate Exceptionalism*. Edited by Bruce I. Oppenheimer. Columbus, O.H.: Ohio State University Press.

Carmines, Edward, and James Stimson. 1986a. "The Politics and Policy of Race in Congress." In *Congress and Policy Change*. Edited by Gerald Wright, Leroy Rieselbach and Lawrence Dodd. New York: Agathon Press, pp. 70–93.

——. 1986b. *Issue Evolution: Race and the Transformation of American Politics*. Princeton, N.J.: Princeton University Press.

Carmines, Edward, and Lawrence C. Dodd. 1985. "Bicameralism in Congress: the Changing Partnership." In *Congress Reconsidered*, 3rd ed. Edited by Lawrence C. Dodd and Bruce I. Oppenheimer. Washington, D.C.: CQ Press, pp. 414–36.

Caro, Robert A. 2002. *Master of the Senate: The Years of Lyndon Johnson*. New York: Joseph K. Knopf.

Carson, Jamie L., Erick J. Engstrom, and Jason M. Roberts. 2007. "Candidate Quality, the Personal Vote, and the Incumbency Advantage in Congress." *American Political Science Review* 101: 289–301.

Carson, Rachel. 1962. *Silent Spring*. Boston: Houghton Mifflin.

Champagne, Richard. 1986. *The Complex Evolution of U. S. Civil Rights Policy: 1937–1984*. Ph.D Dissertation. Indiana University.

Chamberlain, Lawrence H. 1947. *The President, Congress and Legislation*. New York: Columbia University Press.

Chubb, John, and Paul Peterson, eds. 1985. *The New Direction in American Politics*. Washington, D.C.: The Brookings Institution.

Chubb, John, and Terry Moe. 1990. *Politics, Markets, and America's Schools*. Washington, D.C.: Brookings Institution.

Clark, Joseph S. 1964. *Congress: The Sapless Branch*. New York: Harper and Row.

Clausen, Aage R. 1973. *How Congressmen Decide*. New York: St. Martin's.

Clem, Alan L., ed. 1976. *The Making of Congressmen: Seven Campaigns of 1974*. North Scituate, M.A.: Duxbury Press.

Clubb, Jerome, William Flanigan, and Nancy Zingale, 1980. *Partisan Realignment*. Beverly Hills: Sage.

Cobb, Roger W., and Charles D. Elder. 1972. *Participation in America: The Dynamics of Agenda-Building*. Boston: Allyn and Bacon.

———. 1981. Communications and public policy. In *Handbook of Political Communications*. Edited by Dan Nimmo and Keith Sanders. Beverly Hills: Sage, pp. 121–40.

Collie, Melissa P., and David W. Brady. 1985. "The Decline of Partisan Voting Coalitions in the House of Representatives." In *Congress Reconsidered*, 3rd ed. Edited by Lawrence C. Dodd and Bruce I. Oppenheimer. Washington, D.C.: CQ Press, pp. 272–87.

Collie, Melissa P., and Brian E. Roberts. 1992, "Trading Places: Choice and Committee Chairs in the U.S. Senate, 1950–1986." *Journal of Politics* 54: 231–245.

Conley, Richard S. 2005. *Transforming the American Polity: The Presidency of George W. Bush and the War on Terrorism*. Upper Saddle River, New Jersey: Longman.

Connelly, William F., and John J. Pitney, Jr. 1994. *Congress' Permanent Minority?* Landham, M.D.: Rowman & Littlefield.

Cook, Elizabeth Adell, Sue Thomas, and Clyde Wilcox, eds. 1994. *The Year of the Woman: Myths and Reality*. Boulder, C.O.: Westview.

Cook, Rohdes. 1980. "National Committee Given Major Roll in Fall Campaign." *Congressional Quarterly Weekly Report*. July 19: 2011.

Cooper, Joseph. 1970. *The Origins of the Standing Committees and the Development of the Modern House*. Houston: Rice University Studies.

———. 1975. "Strengthening the Congress: An Organizational Perspective." *Harvard Journal on Legislation*. 12: 307–368.

———. 1977. "Congress in Organizational Perspective." In *Congress Reconsidered*, 1st ed. Edited by Lawrence C. Dodd and Bruce I. Oppenheimer. New York: Praeger Publishers, pp. 140–59.

———, ed. 1999. *Congress and the Decline of Public Trust*. Boulder, C.O.: Westview.

———. 2001. "The Twentieth-Century Congress." In *Congress Reconsidered*, 7th ed. Edited by Lawrence C. Dodd and Bruce I. Oppenheimer. Washington, D.C.: CQ Press, pp. 335–66.

———. 2009. "From Congressional to Presidential Preeminence: Power and Politics in

Late Nineteenth-Century America and Today. In *Congress Reconsidered*, 9th ed. Edited by Lawrence C. Dodd and Bruce I. Oppenheimer. Washington, D.C.: CQ Press, pp. 361–91.

Cooper, Joseph, and David Brady. 1973. "Organizational Theory and Congressional Structure." A Paper Delivered at the Annual Meeting of the American Political Science Association. New Orleans, Louisiana, September 4–8.

———. 1981a. "Institutional Context and Leadership Style: The House from Cannon to Rayburn." *American Political Science Review* 75: 411–425.

———. 1981b "Toward a Diachronic Analysis of Congress." *American Political Science Review* 75: 988–1006.

Cooper, Joseph, and G. Calvin Mackenzie. 1981. *The House at Work*. Austin: University of Texas Press.

Cooper, Joseph, and Elizabeth Rybicki. 2002. "Analyzing Institutional Change: Bill Introduction in the Nineteenth-Century Senate." In *U.S. Senate Exceptionalism*. Edited by Bruce I. Oppenheimer. Columbus, O.H.: Ohio State University Press, pp. 182–211.

Cooper, Joseph, and Garry Young. 1997. "Partisanship, Bipartisanship, and Crosspartisanship in Congress since the New Deal." In *Congress Reconsidered*, 6th ed. Edited by Lawrence C. Dodd and Bruce I. Oppenheimer. Washington, D.C.: CQ Press, 246–73.

Cooperman, Rosalyn, and Bruce I. Oppenheimer. 2001. "The Gender Gap in the House of Representatives." In *Congress Reconsidered*, 7th ed. Edited by Lawrence C. Dodd and Bruce I. Oppenheimer. Washington, D.C.: CQ Press, pp. 125–40.

Cover, Albert D. 1980. "Contacting Congressional Constituents: Some Patterns of Perquisite Use." *American Journal of Political Science* 24: 125–134.

Cover, Albert D., and David R. Mayhew. 1981. "Congressional Dynamics and the Decline of Competitive Congressional Elections." In *Congress Reconsidered*, 2nd ed. Edited by Lawrence C. Dodd and Bruce I. Oppenheimer. Washington, D.C.: CQ Press, pp. 62–82.

Cox, Gary W., and Jonathan N. Katz. 2002. *Elbridge Gerry's Salamander*. Cambridge: Cambridge University Press.

———. 2007. "Gerrymandering Roll Calls in Congress, 1879–2000. *American Journal of Political Science* 51: 108–119.

Cox, Gary W., and Samuel Kernell, eds. 1991. *The Politics of Divided Government*. Boulder, C.O.: Westview Press.

Cox, Gary W., and Mathew McCubbins. 1993. *Legislative Leviathan: Party Government in the House*. Berkeley: University of California Press.

———. 2005. *Setting the Agenda: Responsible Party Government in the U.S. House of Representatives*. New York: Cambridge University Press.

Cox, Gary W., and Keith T. Poole. 2000. "On Measuring Partisanship in Roll Call Voting: The U.S. House of Representatives, 1877–1999." *American Journal of Political Science* 46 (2002): 477–489.

Cox, James, Gregory Hager, and David Lowery. 1993. "Regime Change in Presidential and Congressional Budgeting: Role Discontinuity or Role Evolution?" *American Journal of Political Science* 37: 88–118.

Crenson, Matthew, and Benjamin Ginsberg. 2007. *Presidential Power: Unchecked and Unbalanced*. New York: W. W. Norton.

Critchlow, Donald T. 2004. "When Republicans Become Revolutionaries." In *The American Congress: The Building of Democracy*. Edited by Juliam E. Zelizer. Boston: Houghton Mifflin, pp. 703–28.

Cummings, Milton C. 1966. *Congressmen and the Electorate*. New York: Free Press.

Currinder, Marian. 2009. *Money in the House: Campaign Funds and Congressional Party Politics*. Boulder: Westview Press.

Cutrone, Michael, and Nolan McCarty. 2006. "Does Bicameralism Matter?" In *Oxford Handbook of Political Economy*. Edited by Donald Wittman and Barry Weingast. New York: Oxford University Press, pp. 180–95.

Dahl, Robert A. 1956. *A Preface to Democratic Theory*. Chicago: University of Chicago Press.

———. 1981. *Democracy in the United States*, 4th ed. Boston: Houghton Mifflin.

Davidson, Roger H., ed. 1992. *The Postreform Congress*. New York: St. Martin.

Davidson, Roger H., David M. Kovenock, and Michael J. O'Leary. 1966. *Congress in Crisis*. North Scituate, M.A.: Duxbury Press.

Davidson, Roger H., and Walter J. Oleszek. 1976. "Adaptation and Consolidation: Structural Innovation in the U.S. House of Representatives." *Legislative Studies Quarterly* 1: 37–65

———. 1977. *Congress against Itself*. Bloomington: Indiana University Press.

———. 1981. *Congress and Its Members*. Washington: D. C.: Congressional Quarterly.

———. *Congress and Its Members. 1996*. 5th ed. Washington, D.C.: CQ Press.

Davidson, Roger H., Susan Webb Hammond, and Raymond W. Smock, eds. 1998. *Masters of the House*. Boulder, C.O.: Westview Press.

De Boef, Suzanna, and James A. Stimson. 1993. "The Dynamic Structure of Congressional Elections." *Journal of Politics* 55: 630–48.

Deering, Christopher J., and Steven S. Smith. 1997, *Committees in Congress*. 3rd ed. Washington, D.C.: CQ Press.

DeGregorio, Christine, and Kevin Snider. 1995. "Leadership Appeal in the U.S. House of Representatives: Comparing Office-holders and Aides." *Legislative Studies Quarterly* 20: 491–511.

Destler, I. M. 1997. *Renewing Fast Track Legislation*. Washington, D.C.: Institute for International Economics and Policy Analysis, no. 50 (September).

Deutsch, Karl. 1963. *The Nerves of Government*. New York: Free Press.

Dexter, Lewis A. 1969a. *How Organizations Are Represented in Washington*. Indianapolis: Bobbs Merrill.

———. 1969b. *The Sociology and Politics of Congress*. Chicago: Rand McNally.

Diamond, Jared. 1999. *Guns, Germs and Steel: The Fate of Human Societies*. New York: W. W. Norton.

———. 2005. *Collapse: How Societies Choose to Fail or Succeed*. New York: Viking.

Diermeier, Daniel. 1995. "Commitment, Deference, and Legislative Institutions." *American Political Science Review* 89 (2): 344–355.

Dion, Douglas. 1997. *Turning the Legislative Thumbscrew: Minority Rights and Procedural Change in Legislative Politics*. Ann Arbor: University of Michigan Press.

Dion, Douglas, and John Huber. 1996. "Procedural Choice and the House Committee on Rules." *Journal of Politics* 58: 25–53.

Dionne, E. J., Jr. 1991. *Why Americans Hate Politics*. New York: Simon and Schuster.

———. 1994. "The Not-So-Inevitable Republican Landslide." *Daily Camera*. Boulder, C.O.: October 7, p. 3C.

Dodd, Lawrence C. 1972. "Committee Integration in the Senate: A Comparative Analysis." *Journal of Politics* 34: 1135–71.

———. 1974. "Party Coalitions in Multiparty Parliaments." *American Political Science Review* 68: 1093–17.

——. 1975. *Congress and Public Policy*. Morristown, NJ: General Learning Press.

——. 1976a. *Coalitions in Parliamentary Government*. Princeton: Princeton University Press.

——. 1976b. "The Emergence of Party Government in the House of Representatives." *DEA News* (A Publication of the American Political Science Association). Summer.

——. 1977. "Congress and the Quest for Power." In *Congress Reconsidered*, 1st ed. Edited by Lawrence C. Dodd and Bruce I. Oppenheimer. New York: Praeger, pp. 269–307.

——. 1978a. *"Review of Congress: The Electoral Connection." American Political Science Review* 72: 693–95.

——. 1978b. "Congress and the Cycles of Power." *Society*. Vol. 16 #1 (November). A revised and expanded version appears in *The Presidency and Congress: A Changing Balance of Power*. Edited by William S. Livingston, Lawrence C. Dodd, and Richard L. Schott. Austin, TX: Lyndon Baines Johnson Library, pp. 46–69.

——. 1979. "The Expanding Roles of the House Democratic Whip System." *Congressional Studies* 6: 27–56.

——. 1980. "Congress, the Presidency and the Cycles of Power." In *The Post-Imperial Presidency*. Edited by Vincent Davis. New Brunswick: Transaction, Inc., pp. 71–100.

——. 1981 "Congress, the Constitution, and the Crisis of Legitimation." In *Congress Reconsidered*, 2nd ed. Edited by Lawrence C. Dodd and Bruce I. Oppenheimer. Washington, D.C.: CQ Press, pp. 390–420.

——. 1983a. "The Calculus of Legislative Change." A Paper Prepared for Presentation at the 1983 Midwest Political Science Convention, Chicago. Illinois, April 20.

——. 1983b. The Legislative Imperative: Building Broad-guaged Theory. A Paper Prepared for Delivery at the 1983 American Political Science Convention. Chicago, September 3.

——.1983c. "Coalition-Building by Party Leaders: A Case Study of House Democrats." *Congress and the Presidency Journal* 10 (Fall): 145–168.

——. 1884. "The Study of Cabinet Durability: Introduction and Commentary." *Comparative Political Studies* 17: 155–61.

——.1986a. "The Cycles of Legislative Change." In *Political Science: The Science of Politics*. Edited by Herbert F. Weisberg. New York: Agathon Press, pp. 82–104.

——. 1986b. "A Theory of Congressional Cycles." In *Congress and Policy Change*. Edited by Gerald Wright, Leroy Rieselbach, and Lawrence C. Dodd. New York: Agathon Press, pp. 3–44.

——. 1987. "Woodrow Wilson's Congressional Government and the Modern Congress: The 'Universal Principle' of Change." *Congress and the Presidency* 14 (1): 33–49.

——1988. "The Rise of the Technocratic Congress." In *Remaking American Politics*. Edited by Richard Harris and Sidney Milkis. Boulder, C.O.: Westview Press.

——. 1991. "Congress, the Presidency, and the American Experience: A Transformational Perspective." In *Divided Democracy*. Edited by James A. Thurber. Washington, D.C.: Congressional Quarterly, pp. 275–302.

——. 1992. "Learning to Learn: The Political Mastery of U.S. Senators." In *Extension of Remarks: Legislative Studies Newsletter*. (November): 10–11.

——. 1993. "Congress and the Politics of Renewal: Redressing the Crisis of Legitimation." In *Congress Reconsidered*, 5th ed. Edited by Lawrence C. Dodd and Bruce I. Oppenheimer.

——. 1994. "Political Learning and Political Change." In *The Dynamics of American*

Politics. Edited by Lawrence C. Dodd and Calvin Jillson. Boulder, C.O.: Westview Press, pp. 331–64.

——. 1995a. "The New American Politics: Reflections on the Early 1990s." In *The New American Politics*. Edited by Bryan D. Jones. Boulder, C.O.: Westview Press, pp. 257–74.

——. 1995b. "Placing Congress in Theoretical Time." In *Extension of Remarks: Legislative Studies Newsletter*. December: 331–64.

——. 1995c. "The Rise of the Modern State: 1932–1964." In *The Encyclopedia of the United States Congress*. Edited by Donald C. Bacon, Roger H. Davison and Morton Keller. New York: Simon and Schoster, pp. 1023–32.

——. 1997. "Re-Envisioning Congress: Theoretical Perspectives on Congressional Change." A Paper Prepared for Delivery at the 1997 American Political Science Convention. Washington, D.C. (August).

——. 2001a. "ReEnvisioning Congress: Theoretical Perspectives on Congressional Change." In *Congress Reconsidered*, 7th ed. Edited by Lawrence C. Dodd and Bruce I. Oppenheimer.

—— 2001b. "Comments on David Mayhew's Congress: The Electoral Connection." In *PS: Political Science and Politics*, Vol. 34, No. 2 (March): 262–264.

——. 2002. "Making Sense Out of Our Exceptional Senate: Perspectives and Commentary." In *U. S. Senate Exceptionalism*. Edited by Bruce I. Oppenheimer.

——. 2005a. "Re-Envisioning Congress: Theoretical Perspectives on Congressional Change 2004." In *Congress Reconsidered*, 7th ed. Edited by Lawrence C. Dodd and Bruce I. Oppenheimer. Washington, D.C.: CQ Press, pp. 411–45.

——. 2005b. "Entrapped in the Narrative of War." In *Transforming the American Polity: The Presidency of George W. Bush and the War on Terrorism*. Edited by Richard Conley. Upper Saddle River, N.J.: Pearson/Prentice Hall, pp. 149–64.

——. 2011. "Congress in a Downsian World." A Paper Prepared for Presentation at the 2011 Annual Meeting of the American Political Science Association, Seattle, W.A. (September).

Dodd, Lawrence C., and Calvin Jillson, eds. 1994a. *The Dynamics of American Politics*. Boulder, C.O.: Westview Press.

——, eds. 1994b. *New Perspectives on American Politics*. Washington, D.C.: CQ Press.

Dodd, Lawrence C., and Bruce I. Oppenheimer, eds. 1977. *Congress Reconsidered*, 1st Ed. New York: Praeger.

——, eds. 1981 (2nd ed.), 1985 (3rd ed.), 1989 (4th ed.), 1993 (5th ed.), 1997 (6th ed.), 2001 (7th ed.), 2005 (8th ed.), 2009 (9th ed.). *Congress Reconsidered*. Washington, D.C.: CQ Press.

——. 1977. "The House in Transition." In *Congress Reconsidered*, 1st ed. Edited by Lawrence C. Dodd and Bruce I. Oppenheimer. New York: Praeger, pp. 21–53.

——. 1981. "The House in Transition: From Albert to O'Neill." In *Congress Reconsidered*, 2nd ed. Edited by Lawrence C. Dodd and Bruce I. Oppenheimer. Washington, D.C.: CQ Press, pp. 31–61.

——. 1985. "The House in Transition: Partisanship and Opposition." In *Congress Reconsidered*, 3rd ed. Edited by Lawrence C. Dodd and Bruce I. Oppenheimer. Washington, D.C.: CQ Press, pp. 34–64.

——. 1989. "Consolidating Power in the House: The Rise of a New Oligarchy." In *Congress Reconsidered*, 4th ed. Edited by Lawrence C. Dodd and Bruce I. Oppenheimer. Washington, D.C.: CQ Press, pp. 34–64.

———. 1993a. "Perspectives on the 1992 Congressional Elections." In *Congress Reconsidered*, 5th ed. Edited by Lawrence C. Dodd and Oppenheimer. Washington, D.C.: CQ Press.

———. 1993b. "Maintaining Order in the House: The Struggle for Institutional Equilibrium." In *Congress Reconsidered*, 5th ed. Edited by Lawrence C. Dodd and Bruce I. Oppenheimer.

———. 1997a. "Revolution in the House: Testing the Limits of Party Government." In *Congress Reconsidered*, 6th ed. Edited by Lawrence C. Dodd and Bruce I. Oppenheimer. Washington, D.C.: CQ Press.

———. 1997b. "Congress and the Emerging Order: Conditional Party Government or Constructive Partisanship?" In *Congress Reconsidered*. 6th ed. Edited by Lawrence C. Dodd and Bruce I. Oppenheimer. Washington, D.C.: CQ Press, pp. 390–413.

———. 2001a. "A House Divided: The Struggle for Partisan Control." In *Congress Reconsidered*, 7th ed. Edited by Lawrence C. Dodd and Bruce I. Oppenheimer. Washington, D.C.: CQ Press, pp. 21–44.

———. 2001b. "Congress and the Emerging Order: Assessing the 2000 Elections." In *Congress Reconsidered*, 7th ed. Edited by Lawrence C. Dodd and Bruce I. Oppenheimer. Washington, D.C.: CQ Press, pp. 367–388.

———. 2005. "A Decade of Republican Control: The House of Representatives, 1995–2005." In *Congress Reconsidered*, 8th ed. Edited by Lawrence C. Dodd and Bruce I. Oppenheimer. Washington, D.C.: CQ Press, pp. 23–54.

———. 2009a. "The Politics of the Contemporary House: From Gingrich to Pelosi." In *Congress Reconsidered*, 9th ed. Edited by Lawrence C. Dodd and Bruce I. Oppenheimer. Washington, D.C.: CQ Press, pp. 23–51.

———. 2009b. "Congressional Politics in a Time of Crisis: The 2008 Elections." In *Congress Reconsidered*, 9th ed. Edited by Lawrence C. Dodd and Bruce I. Oppenheimer. Washington, D.C.: CQ Press. pp. 419–441.

Dodd, Lawrence C., and John C. Pierce. 1975. "Roll Call Measurement of Committee Integration." *Polity* 7: 386–401.

Dodd, Lawrence C., and Richard L. Schott. 1979. *Congress and the Administrative State*. New York: John Wiley.

Dodd, Lawrence C., and Scot Schraufnagel. 2008. "Congress and the Polarity Paradox." A paper presented at the 2008 Midwest Political Science Convention, Chicago, Illinois (April 3).

———. 2009a. "Reconsidering Party Polarization and Policy Productivity: A Curvilinear Perspective." In *Congress Reconsidered*, 9th ed. Edited by Lawrence C. Dodd and Bruce I. Oppenheimer. Washington, D.C.: CQ Press, pp. 393–418.

———. 2009b. "Rethinking Legislative Productivity: Commemorative Legislation and Policy Gridlock." In *Congress and the Presidency*. (May): 132–147.

Dodd, Lawrence C., and Terry L. Sullivan. 1981. "Majority Party Leadership and Partisan Vote Gathering: The House Democratic Whip System." In *Understanding Congressional Leadership*. Edited by Frank H. Mackaman. Washington, D.C.: Congressional Quarterly.

Downs, Anthony. 1957. *An Economic Theory of Democracy*. New York: Harper and Row.

Dreyfus, Herbert, and Stuart Dreyfus. 1986. *Mind over Machine: The Power of Human Intuition and Expertise in the Era of the Computer*. New York: Free Press.

Durst, Samantha. 1991. "Delay, Deadlock, and Deficits: Evaluating Congressional Budget Reform." In *Federal Budget and Financial Management Reform*. Edited by Thomas D. Lynch. Westport, C.T.: Greenwood Press.

Eckhardt, Bob, and Charles L. Black, Jr. 1976. *The Titles of Power: Conversations on the American Constitution*. New Haven, C.T.: Yale University Press.

Edelman, Murray. 1985. *The Symbolic Uses of Politics*. Urbana: University of Illinois Press.

Ehrenhalt, Alan. 1983. "The Moulting Season in the U.S. Senate." Congressional Quarterly Weekly Report. March 15, p. 535.

Eisenger, Peter K. 1988. *The Rise of the Entrepreneurial State: State and Local Economic Development Policy in the United States*. Madison: University of Wisconsin Press.

Ellis, Joseph J. 2001. *Founding Brothers: The Revolutionary Generation*. New York: Alfred A. Knopf.

Ellis, Richard J., and Michael Nelson, eds. 2010. *Debating the Presidency: Conflicting Perspectives*. Washington, D.C.: CQ Press.

Ellsberg, Daniel. 1971. "The Quagmire Myth and the Stalemate Machine," *Public Policy* 19 (Spring): 217–274

Ellwood, John W. 1985. "The Great Exception: the Congressional Budget Process Decentralization." In Dodd and Oppenheimer, *Congress Reconsidered*, 3rd ed. Washington, D.C.: CQ Press, 315–342.

Ellwood, John W., and Thurber, James A. 1977. "The New Congressional Budget Process." In *Congress Reconsidered*, 1st ed. Edited by Lawrence C. Dodd and Bruce I. Oppenheimer. New York: Praeger Publishers, pp. 163–192.

——. 1981. "The Politics of the Congressional Budget Process Re-examined" In *Congress Reconsidered*, 2nd ed. Edited by Lawrence C. Dodd and Bruce I. Oppenheimer. Washington, D.C.: CQ Press, pp. 246–71.

Elster, Jon. 1982. "Marxism, Functionalism and Game Theory." *Theory and Society*. Vol. 11: 453–82.

Endersby, James W., and Karen M. McCurdy. 1996. "Committee Assignments in the U.S. Senate." *Legislative Studies Quarterly* 21: 219–234.

Epstein, David, and Peter Zemsky. 1995. "Money Talks: Deterring Quality Challengers in Congressional Elections." *American Political Science Review* 89: 295–308.

Erikson, Erik H. 1964. *Childhood and Society*. New York: Norton.

——. 1970. *Gandhi's Truth*. New York: Norton.

Erikson, Robert S. 1971. "The Advantage of Incumbency in Congressional Elections." *Polity* 3: 395–405.

——. 1972. "Malapportionment, Gerrymandering, and Party Fortunes in Congressional Elections." *American Political Science Review* 66.

——. 1976. "Is There Such a Thing as a Safe Seat?" *Polity* 8: 623–632.

——. 1988. "The Puzzle of Midterm Loss." *Journal of Politics* 50: 1011–1029.

——. 1990. "Roll Calls, Reputations, and Representation in the U.S. Senate." *Legislative Studies Quarterly* 15: 623–42.

——. 2002. "Explaining National Party Tides in Senate Elections: Macropartisanship, Policy Mood, and Ideological Balancing." In *U.S. Senate Exceptionalism*. Edited by Bruce I. Oppenheimer. Columbus, O.H.: Ohio State University Press, pp. 70–85.

Erikson, Robert S., Michael B. MacKuen, and James A. Stimson. 2002. *The Macro Polity*. New York: Cambridge University Press.

Erikson, Robert S., and Gerald C. Wright. 1985. "Voters, Candidates and Issues in Congressional Elections." In *Congress Reconsidered*, 3rd ed. Edited by Lawrence C. Dodd and Bruce I. Oppenheimer. Washington, D.C.: CQ Press, pp. 87–108.

——. 2009. "Voters, Candidates, and Issues in Congressional Elections. In *Congress Reconsidered*, 9th ed. Edited by Lawrence C. Dodd and Bruce I. Oppenheimer. Washington, D.C.: CQ Press, pp. 71–95.

Eulau, Heinz. 1967. *The Behavioral Persuasion in Political Science.* New York: Random House.

Eulau, Heinz, John C. Wahlke, William Buchanan, and Leroy C. Ferguson. 1959. "The Role of the Representative: Some Empirical Observations on the Theory of Edmund Burke." *American Political Science Review* 53 (September): 742–756.

———. 1963. *The Behavioral Persuasion in Politic.* New York: Random House.

Eulau, Heinz, and Paul Karps. 1977. "The Puzzle of Representation." *Legislative Studies Quarterly* 2: 233–254.

Evans, C. Lawrence. 1991. *Leadership in Committee.* Ann Arbor: University of Michigan Press.

———. 2002. "How Senators Decide: An Exploration." In *U.S. Senate Exceptionalism.* Edited by Bruce I. Oppenheimer. Columbus, O.H.: Ohio State University Press, pp. 262–82.

———. 2009. "The Whip Systems of Congress." In *Congress Reconsidered*, 9th ed. Edited by Lawrence C. Dodd and Bruce I. Oppenheimer. Washington, D.C.: CQ Press, pp. 189–215.

Evans, C. Lawrence, and Walter J. Oleszek. 1997. *Congress Under Fire.* Boston: Houghton Mifflin.

Evans, Diana. 1994. "Policy and Pork: The Use of Pork Barrel Projects to Build Policy Coalitions in the House of Representatives." *American Journal of Political Science* 38: 894–917.

———. 2004. *Greasing the Wheels: Using Pork Barrel Projects to Build Majority Coalitions in Congress.* Cambridge: Cambridge University Press.

Evans, Rowland, and Robert Novak. 1966. *Lyndon B. Johnson: The Exercise of Power.* New York: New American Library.

Fair, Ray C. 2009. "Presidential and Congressional Vote-Share Equations." *American Journal of Political Science.* Vol. 53, No. 1 (January): 55–72.

Farrier, Jasmine. 2004. *Passing the Buck: Congress, the Budget, and Deficits.* Lexington: University of Kentucky Press.

———. 2010. *Congressional Ambivalence: The Political Burdens of Constitutional Authority.* Lexington: University of Kentucky Press.

Fay, Brian. 1975. *Social Theory and Political Practice.* Boston: Allen & Unwin.

Fenno, Richard F., Jr. 1965. "The Internal Distribution of Influence: The House." In *The Congress and America's Future.* Edited by David B. Truman. Englewood Cliffs, N.J.: Prentice-Hall.

———. 1966. *The Power of the Purse.* Boston: Little, Brown.

———1973. *Congressmen in Committees.* Boston: Little, Brown.

———1975. "If, as Ralph Nader Says, Congress Is 'The Broken Branch,' How Come We Love Our Congressmen So Much?" In Norman J. Ornstein.1975. *Congress in Change: Evolution and Reform.* Edited by Norman Ornstein. New York: Praeger Publishers, pp. 277–87.

———. 1977. "Strengthening a Congressional Strength." In *Congress Reconsidered*, 1st ed. Edited by Dodd and Oppenheimer. New York: Praeger Publisher, pp. 261–307.

———. 1978. *Home Style: House Members in Their Districts.* Boston: Little, Brown.

———. 1982. *The United States Senate: A Bicameral Perspective.* Washington, D.C.: American Enterprise Institute.

———. 1986a. "Observation, Context and Sequence in the Study of Politics." *American Political Science Review.* 80: 1–15.

——. 1986b. "Adjusting to the U.S. Senate. In *Congress and Policy Change*. Edited by Gerald Wright, Leroy Rieselbach, and Lawrence C. Dodd. New York: Agathon.

——. 1989a. *The Making of a Senator: Dan Quayle*. Washington, D. C.: Congressional Quarterly Press.

——. 1989b. "The Senate through the Looking Glass: The Debate over Television." *Legislative Studies Quarterly* 14: 313–48.

——. 1990. *The Presidential Odessey of John Glenn*. Washington, D. C.: Congressional Quarterly Press.

——. 1991a. *The Emergence of a Senate Leader: Pete Domenici and the Reagan Budget*. Washington, D. C.: Congressional Quarterly Press.

—— 1991b. *Learning to Legislate: The Senate Education of Arlen Specter*. Washington, D. C.: Congressional Quarterly Press.

——. 1992a. *When Incumbency Fails: The Senate Career of Mark Andrews*. Washington, D. C.: Congressional Quarterly Press.

——. 1992b. "Introductory Remarks for Making Sense Out of the Senate: The Narratives of Richard F. Fenno, Jr." In *Extension of Remarks: Legislative Studies Section Newsletter*. (November): 2.

——. 1992c. "Some Thoughts on Renewing Congress. Paper Presenting at the Brookings Institution/American Enterprise Institute Conference on Congressional Reform. Washington, D.C., June 30.

——. 1997a. *Senators on the Campaign Trail: The Politics of Representation*. Norman: University of Oklahoma Press.

——. 1997b. *Learning to Govern: An Institutional View of the 104th Congress*. Washington, D.C.: Brookings.

——. 2002. "Looking for the Senate: Remniscences and Residuals." In *U.S. Senate Exceptionalism*. Edited by Bruce I. Oppenheimer. Columbus, O.H.: Ohio State University Press, pp. 12–27.

——. 2003. *Going Home: Black Representatives and Their Constituents*. Chicago: University of Chicago Press.

Ferejohn, John A. 1974. *Pork Barrel Politics*. Stanford: Stanford University Press.

——. 1975. "Who Wins in Conference Committee?" *The Journal of Politics* 37 (November): 1033–1046.

——. 1977. "On the Decline in Competition in Congressional Elections." *American Political Science Review* 77: 166–76.

Ferejohn, John A., and Charles R. Shipan. 1985. "Congressional Influence on Administrative Agencies: A Case Study of Telecommunications Policy." In *Congress Reconsidered*, 3rd ed. Edited by Lawrence C. Dodd and Bruce I. Oppenheimer. Washington, D.C.: CQ Press, pp. 393–410.

Ferejohn, John A. and Keith Krehbiel. 1985. "Reconciliation and the Size of the Budget." *Working Papers in Political Science No. P-85–2*. The Hoover Institution, Stanford University.

Festinger, Leon. 1957. *A Theory of Cognitive Dissonance*. Evanston, I.L.: Row, Peterson.

Fessler, Pamela. 1982. "Spending Cuts, Record Tax Hike Pass Senate." *Congressional Quarterly Weekly Report*. July 24, p. 1747.

Fiorina, Morris P. 1974. *Representatives, Roll Calls, and Constituencies*. Lexington, Mass.: Lexington Books.

——1977a. "The Case of the Vanishing Marginals: The Bureaucracy Did It." *American Political Science Review* 71: 177–81.

———. 1977b. *Congress: Keystone of the Washington Establishment*. New Haven, C.T.: Yale University Press.

———. 1980. "The Decline of Collective Responsibility in American Politics." *Daedalus* 109 (Summer).

———. 1981. *Retrospective Voting in American National Elections*. New Haven, C.T.: Yale University Press.

———. 1987. *Divided Government*. New York: Macmillan.

———. 1989. *Congress: Keystone of the Washington Establishment*. 2nd ed. New Haven, C.T.: Yale University Press.

———. 1995a. *Divided Government*. 2nd ed.. New York: Allyn and Bacon.

———. 1995b. "Political Change in the States: Another Example of Unintended Consequences?" In *The New American Politics*. Edited by Bryan D. Jones. Boulder, C.O.: Westview Press, pp. 122–31.

———.1995c. "Rational Choice, Empirical Contributions, and the Scientific Enterprise." *Critical Review* 9(1–2): 85–94.

———. 2001. "Keystone Reconsidered." In *Congress Reconsidered*, 7th ed. Edited by Lawrence C. Dodd and Bruce I. Oppenheimer. Washington D.C.: CQ Press, pp. 141–62.

———. 2004. "Keystone Reconsidered." In *Congress Reconsidered*, 8th ed. Edited by Lawrence C. Dodd and Bruce I. Oppenheimer. Washington, D.C.: CQ Press, pp. 159–79.

Fiorina, Morris P., David W. Rohde, and Peter Wissel. 1975. "Historical Change in House Turnover." In *Congress in Change*. Edited by Norman J. Ornstein. New York: Praeger Publishers, pp. 24–57.

Fiorina, Morris P., with Samuel J. Abrams and Jeremy C. Pope. 2005. *Culture War? The Myth of a Polarized America*. New York: Longman.

Fishel, Jeff. 1973. *Party and Opposition*. New York: David McKay.

Fishkin, James S. 1991. *Democracy and Deliberation: New Directions for Democratic Reform*. New Haven, C.T.: Yale University Press.

Fisher, Louis. 1975. *Presidential Spending Power*. Princeton, N.J.: Princeton University Press.

———. 1978. *The Constitution between Friends: Congress, the President, and the Law*. New York: St. Martin's.

———. 1985. *Constitutional Conflicts Between Congress and the President*. Princeton: Princeton University Press.

———. 2000. *Congressional Abbdication on War and Spending*. College Station, T.X.: Texas A & M Press, 2000.

Flavin, Patrick, and John D. Griffin. 2009. "Policy, Preferences, and Participation: Government's Impact on Democratic Citizenship." *Journal of Politics*. 71, No. 2 (April): 544–59.

Fleisher, Richard, and Jon R. Bond. 2004. "The Shrinking Middle in the U.S. Congress." *British Journal of Political Science* 34 (July): 429–451.

Flemming, Gregory N. 1995. "Presidential Coattails in Open Seat Elections." *Legislative Studies Quarterly* 20: 197–211.

Flyvbjerg, Bent. 2001. *Making Social Science Matter*. New York: Cambridge University Press.

Formisano, Ronald P. 1971. *The Birth of Mass Political Parties: Michigan, 1827–1861*. Princeton, N.J.: Princeton University Press.

———. 1974. "Deferential-Participant Politics: The Early Republic's Political Culture, 1789–1840." *American Political Science Review* 68: 473–87.

Fowler, Linda L. 1993. *Candidates, Congress, and American Democracy*. Ann Arbor: University of Michigan Press.

———. 1994. "Political Entrepreneurs, Governing Processes, and Political Change." In *New Perspectives on American Politics*. Edited by Lawrence C. Dodd and Calvin Jillson. Washington, D.C.: CQ Press, pp. 291–310.

Fowler, Linda L., and Robert D. McClure. 1989. *Political Ambition: Who Decides to Run for Congress?* New Haven, C.T.: Yale University Press.

Fox, Harrison W., Jr., and Susan Webb Hammond. 1977. *Congressional Staffs: The Invisible Force in American Lawmaking*. New York: Free Press.

Franklin, Daniel P. 1993. *Making Ends Meet*. Washington, D.C.: CQ Press.

Frantzich, Stephen E. 1979. "Computerized Information Technology in the U.S. House of Representatives." *Legislative Studies Quarterly* 4: 255–280.

Freehling, William W. 1990. *The Road to Disunion: Secessionists at Bay, 1776–1854*. New York: Oxford University Press.

Freeman, J. Leiper. 1955. *The Political Process*. New York: Random House.

Friedman, Sally. 2007. *Dilemmas of Representation*. Albany: State University of New York Press.

———. 1996. "House Committee Assignments of Women and Minority Newcomers." *Legislative Studies Quarterly* 21: 73–82.

Frisch, Scott A., and Sean Q. Kelly. 2006. *Committee Assignment Politics in the U.S. House of Representatives*. Norman: University of Oklahoma Press.

———. 2006. *Jimmy Carter and the Water Wars*. Amherst, N.Y.: Cambria Press.

———. 2011. *Cheese Factories on the Moon: Why Earmarks are Good for American Democracy*. Boulder, C.O.: Paradigm Press.

Froman, Lewis A., Jr. 1967. *The Congressional Process: Strategies, Rules and Procedures*. Boston: Little, Brown.

———. 1963. *The Congressmen and Their Constituencies*. Chicago: Rand McNally.

Gailmard, Sean, and Jeffery A. Jenkins. 2007. "Negative Agenda Control in the Senate and House: Fingerprints of Majority Party Power." *Journal of Politics* 69: 689–700.

Gainous, Jason B., and Kevin Wagner. 2011. *Rebooting American Politics: The Internet Revolution*. Lanham, M.D.: Rowman & Littlefield.

Galloway, George B. 1946. *Congress at the Crossroads*. New York: Crowell.

———. 1951. "The Operation of the Legislative Reorganization Act of 1946. *American Political Science Review* 45: 41–68.

Gamm, Gerald, and Kenneth Shepsle. 1989. "The Emergence of Legislative Institutions: Standing Committees in the House and Senate, 1810–1825." *Legislative Studies Quarterly* 14: 39–66.

Gamm, Gerald, and Steven S. Smith. 2002. "Emergence of Senate Party Leadership." In *U.S. Senate Exceptionalism*. Edited by Bruce I. Oppenheimer. Columbus, O.H.: Ohio State University Press, pp. 212–38.

Gershtenson, Joseph, Jeffrey Ladewig, and Dennis L. Plane. 2006. "Parties, Institutional Control, Trust in Government." *Social Science Quarterly* 87(4) (December): 882–902.

Gibson, Martha. 1992. *Weapons of Influence*. Boulder, C.O.: Westview Press.

———. 1995. "Issues, Coalitions, and Divided Government." *Congress and the Presidency* 22: 155–166.

———. 2000. *Conflict amid Consensus in American Trade Policy*. Washington, D.C.: George-town University Press.

Gilmour, John B. 1990. *Reconcilable Differences*. Berkeley, C.A.: University of California Press.

Gilmour, John B., and Paul Rothstein. 1996. "A Dynamic Model of Loss, Retirement, and Tenure in the U.S. House." *Journal of Politics* 58: 54–68.

Gimpel, James A. 1996. *Fulfilling the Contract: The First 100 Days*. Needham Heights, M.A.: Allyn and Bacon.

Gingrich, Newt, and Marianne Gingrich. 1981. "Postindustrial Politics: The Leader as Learner." *The Futurist* (December): 30–32

Glazer, Amihai, and Bernard Grofman. 1987. "Two Plus Two Plus Two Equals Six: Ten-ure of Office of Senators and Representatives, 1953–1983." *Legislative Studies Quarterly* 12: 555–563.

Goehlert, Robert U., and John R. Sayre. 1982. *The United States Congress: A Bibliography*. New York: Free Press.

Goodwin, George, Jr. 1970. *The Little Legislatures*. Amherst: University of Massachusetts Press.

Gordon, Joshua B. 2005. "The (Dis)Integration of the House Appropriations Commit-tee: Revisiting *The Power of the Purse* in a Partisan Era." In *Congress Reconsidered*, 8th ed. Edited by Lawrence C. Dodd and Bruce I. Oppenheimer. Washington D.C.: CQ Press, pp. 271–95.

Gould, Stephen J. 1989. *A Wonderful Life: The Burgess Shale and the Nature of History*. New York: Norton.

Green, Donald P., and Ian Shapiro. 1994. *Pathologies of Rational Choice Theory*. New Haven, C.T.: Yale University Press.

———. 1995. "Pathologies Revisited: Reflections on our Critics." *Critical Review* Vol 9, Nos. 1–2: 235–276

Green, Michael N. 1978. *The Federal New Towns Program Policy Making in a Subgovernment in Flux*. Master's Report, University of Texas-Austin.

Greenberg, Edward S. 1985. *Capitalism and the American Political Ideal*. New York: M. E. Sharpe.

Greenberg, Stanley. 2004. *The Two Americas: Our Current Political Deadlock and How to Break It*. New York: Thomas Dunne Books.

Greenstein, Fred, and Stephen Skowronek. 2010. "Resolved, A President's Personal Attributes are the Best Predictors of Performance in the White House." In *Debating the Presidency: Conflicting Perspectives*. Edited by Richard J. Ellis and Michael Nelson. Washington, D.C.: CQ Press, pp. 121–29.

Griffin, John D. 2006. "Senate Apportionment as a Source of Political Inequality." *Legisla-tive Studies Quarterly* 31: 405–432.

Grose, Christian R., and Bruce I. Oppenheimer. 2007. "The Iraq War, Partisanship, and Candidate Attributes: Variation in Partisan Swing in the 2006 U.S. House Elections." *Legislative Studies Quarterly* 32: 559–595.

Groseclose, Timothy, and Keith Krehbiel. 1994. "Golden Parachutes, Rubber Checks, and Strategic Retirements from the 102nd House." *American Journal of Political Science* 38 (February): 75–99.

Gross, Bertram M. 1953. *The Legislative Struggle*. New York: McGraw-Hill.

Guelzo, Allen C. 2003. *Abraham Lincoln: Redeemer President*. Grand Rapids, M.I.: Wm B. Eerdmans Publishing Co.

Habermas, Jurgen. 1973. *Legitimation Crisis*. Boston: Beacon Press.

Hacker, Jacob. 2002. *The Divided Welfare State: The Battle over Public and Private Social Benefits in the U.S.* New York: Cambridge University Press.

Hager, Gregory, and Jeffery Talbert. 2000. "Look for the Party Label: Party Influence on Voting in the U.S. House." *Legislative Studies Quarterly* 25: 75–99.

Hall, Peter. 1993a. "Policy Paradigms, Social Learning and the State." *Comparative Politics* 25: 75–96.

Hall, Richard L. 1993b. *Participation in Congress.* New Haven, C.T.: Yale University Press.

Hall, Richard L., and Frank W. Wayman. 1990. "Buying Time: Moneyed Interests and the Mobilization of Bias in Congressional Committees." *American Political Science Review* 84(3): 797–820.

Hamilton, Alexander, James Madison, and John Jay, 1961. *The Federalist Papers.* Edited by Clinton Rossiter. New York: New American Library.

Hammond, Susan Webb. 1997. *Congressional Caucuses in National Policymaking.* Baltimore: Johns Hopkins University Press.

Hardin, Garrett. 1968. "The Tragedy of the Commons." *Science* 162: 1242–1248.

Harries-Jones, Peter. 1995. *A Recursive Vision: Ecological Understanding and Gregory Bateson* Toronto: University of Toronto Press.

Harrington, Michael. 1962. *The Other America.* New York: Macmillan.

Harris, Joseph. 1964. *Congressional Control of Administration.* Washington, D.C.: Brookings.

Harris, Richard, and Sidney Milkis, eds. 1987. *Remaking American Politics.* Boulder, C.O.: Westview Press.

Harrison, Robert. 2004. *Congress, Progressive Reform, and the New American State.* Cambridge: Cambridge University Press.

Hawkesworth, Mary. 2003. "Congressional Enactments of Race-Gender: Toward a Theory of Raced-Gendered Institutions." *American Political Science Review* 97: 529–550.

Haynie, Kerry L. 2005. "African Americans and the New Politics of Inclusion: A Representational Dilemma?" In *Congress Reconsidered*, 8th ed. Edited by Lawrence C. Dodd and Bruce I. Oppenheimer. Washington D.C.: CQ Press, pp. 395–409.

Hechler, Kenneth W. 1940. *Insurgency: Personalities and Politics in the Taft Era.* New York: Columbia University Press.

Heclo, Hugh. 1977. *A Government of Strangers: Executive Politics in Washington.* Washington, D.C.: Brookings Institution.

——. 1989. "The Emerging Regime." In *Remaking American Politics.* Edited by Richard A. Harris and Sidney Milkis. Boulder, C.O.: Westview Press, pp. 289–320.

——. 1994. "Ideas, Interests, and Institutions." In *The Dynamics of American Politics.* Edited by Lawrence C. Dodd and Calvin Jillson. Boulder, C.O.: Westview Press, pp. 366–92.

Heitshusen, Valerie. 2001. "The Allocation of Federal Money to House Committee Members: Distributive Theory and Policy Jurisdictions." *American Politics Research* 29: 80–98.

——. 2000. "Interest Group Lobbying and U.S. House Decentralization: Linking Information Type to Committee Hearing Appearances." *Political Research Quarterly* 53: 151–176.

Heitshusen, Valerie, and Garry Young. 2006. "Macropolitics and Changes in the U.S. Code: Testing Competing Theories of Policy Production, 1874–1946." In *Macropolitics of Congress.* Edited by E. Scott Adler and John S. Lapinski. Princeton: Princeton University Press, pp. 129–30.

Hempel, Carl. 1966. *The Philosophy of Natural Science*. Englewood Cliffs, N.J.: Prentice-Hall.

Hero, Rodney. 1992. *Latinos and the U.S. Political System: Two-Tiered Pluralism*. Philadelphia: Temple University Press.

——. 1995. "Two-Tiered Pluralism: Race and Ethnicity in American Politics." In *New Perspectives on American Politics*. Edited by Lawrence C. Dodd and Calvin Jillson. Washington, D.C.: CQ Press, pp. 47–57.

——. 1998. *Faces of Inequality: Social Diversity in American Politics*. New York: Oxford University Press.

——. 2007. *Racial Diversity and Social Capital: Equality and Community in America*. New York: Cambridge University Press.

Herrnson, Paul S. 1988. *Party Campaigning in the 1980s*. Cambridge: Harvard University Press.

——. 1995. *Congressional Elections: Campaigning at Home and in Washington*. Washington, D.C.: CQ Press.

Herrnson, Paul S., and James M. Curry. 2009. "Issue Voting in the 2006 Elections for the U. S. House of Representatives." In *Congress Reconsidered*, 9th ed. Edited by Lawrence C. Dodd and Bruce I. Oppenheimer. Washington, DC.: CQ Press, pp. 97–118.

Hershey, Marjorie.1974. *The Making of Campaign Strategy*. Lexington, Mass: Lexington Books.

——. 1984. *Running for Office: The Political Education of Campaigners*. Chatham, N.J.: Chatham House.

Hibbing, John R. 1991. *Congressional Careers*. Chapel Hill: University of North Carolina Press.

——. 1993. "Careerism in Congress: For Better or For Worse?" In *Congress Reconsidered*, 5th ed. Edited by Lawrence C. Dodd and Bruce I. Oppenheimer. Washington, D.C.: CQ Press, pp. 67–88.

Hibbing, John R., and Christopher W. Larimer. 2005. "What the American Public Wants Congress to Be." In *Congress Reconsidered*, 8th ed. Edited by Lawrence C. Dodd and Bruce I. Oppenheimer. Washington, D.C.: CQ Press, pp. 55–75.

Hibbing, John R., and Elizabeth Theiss-Morse. 1995. *Congress as Public Enemy: Public Attitudes toward American Political Institutions*. Cambridge: Cambridge University Press.

Hill, Kim Q. 1988. *Democracies in Crisis: Public Policy Responses to the Great Depression*. Boulder, Colo.: Westview Press.

Hinckley, Barbara. 1970a. "Incumbency and the Presidential Vote in Senate Elections." *American Political Science Review* 64: 836–842.

——. 1970b. "House Reelections and Senate Defeats: The Role of the Challenger." *British Journal of Political Science*, 10: 41–60.

——. 1971. *The Seniority System in Congress*. Bloomington: Indiana University Press.

Hirschman, Albert O. 1982. *Shifting Involvements: Private Interests and Public Action*. Princeton: Princeton University Press.

Hoadly, John F. 1980. "The Emergence of Political Parties in Congress, 1789–1803." *American Political Science Review* 74: 757–779.

Hobbes, Thomas. 1962. *Leviathan*. Edited by Michael Oakeshott. London: Collier Books.

Hofstadter, Richard. 1969. *The Idea of a Party System: The Rise of Legitimate Opposition in the United States, 1780–1840*. Berkeley, C.A.: University of California Press.

Holt, Michael. 1978. *The Political Crisis of the 1850s*. New York: John Wiley & Sons.

Holt, Robert T., and John M. Richardson. 1970. "Competing Paradigms in Comparative Politics." In *The Methodology of Comparative Research*. Edited by Robert T. Holt and John E. Turner. New York: Free Press, pp. 21–24.

Howe, Daniel Walker. 2007. *What God Hath Wrought: The Transformation of America, 1815–1848*. New York: Oxford University Press.

Howell, William G. 2003. *Power without Persuasion*. Princeton: Princeton University Press.

Howell, William, Scott Adler, Charles Cameron, and Charles Riemann. 2000. "Divided Government and the Legislative Productivity of Congress." *Legislative Studies Quarterly*. 25: 285–312.

Howell, William C., and Jon C. Pevehouse. 2007. *While Dangers Gather: Congressional Checks on Presidential War Powers*. Princeton: Princeton University Press.

Huder, Joshua C. 2011. "Cycles of Opposition: Reform Politics and Legislative Development, 1878–1996." A Paper Prepared for Delivery at the 2011 Southern Political Science Association Annual Meeting, New Orleans, LA (January).

Huitt, Ralph K. 1961a. "Democratic Party Leadership in the Senate." *American Political Science Review* 55: 333–44. Reprinted in Huitt and Peabody. 1969. *Congress: Two Decades of Analysis*. New York: Harper.

———. 1961b. "The Outsider in the Senate." *American Political Science Review* 55: 566–75. Reprinted in Huitt and Peabody. 1969. *Congress: Two Decades of Analysis*. New York: Harper.

———. 1965. "The Internal Distribution of Influence in the Senate." In *Congress and America's Future*. Edited by David Truman. Englewood Cliffs, N.J.: Prentice-Hall, pp. 52–76.

Huitt, Ralph K., and Robert L. Peabody. 1969. *Congress: Two Decades of Analysis*. New York: Harper.

Huntington, Samuel P. 1965. "Congressional Responses to the Twentieth Century." In *The Congress and America's Future*. Edited by David B. Truman. Englewood Cliffs, N.J.: Prentice-Hall, pp. 5–31.

———. 1973. "Congressional Responses to the Twentieth Century." In *Congress and America's Future*. 2nd ed. Ed. David B. Truman. Englewood Cliffs, N.J.: Prentice Hall, pp. 6–38.

———. 1971. "The Change to Change: Modernization, Development and Politics." *Comparative Politics* 3: 283–322.

———. 1974. "Postindustrial Politics: How Benign Will It Be?" *Comparative Politics* 6: 163–192.

———. 1981. *American Politics: The Promise of Disharmony*. Cambridge, Mass.: Harvard University Press.

Hurley, Patricia. 2001. "David Mayhew's Congress: The Electoral Connection After 25 Years." P *SOnline*, (June): 259–261: www.apsanet.org.

Hurley, Patricia, and Kim Quaile Hill. 2003. "Beyond the Demand-Input Model: A Theory of Representational Linkages." *Journal of Politics* 65: 304–326.

———. 1980. "The Prospects for Issue Voting in Contemporary Congressional Elections." *American Politics Quarterly* 8: 425–448.

Hurwitz, Mark S., Roger J. Moiles, and David W. Rohde. 2001. Distributive and Partisan Issues in Agriculture Policy in the 104th House." *American Political Science Review* 95: 911–922.

Inglehart, Ronald. 1989. *Culture Shift in Advanced Industrial Societies*. Princeton, N.J.: Princeton University Press.

Jackson, John. 1974. *Constituencies and Leaders in Congress*. Cambridge: Harvard University Press.

Jacobson, Gary C.1980. *Money in Congressional Elections*. New Haven, C.T.: Yale University Press.

———1983. *The Politics of Congressional Elections*. Boston: Little Brown.

———. 1987. "The Marginals Never Vanished: Incumbency and Competition in Elections to the U.S. House of Representatives, 1952–81." *American Journal of Political Science* 31: 126–141.

———. 1989. "Parties and PACs in Congressional Elections." In *Congress Reconsidered*, 4th ed. Edited by Lawrence C. Dodd and Bruce I. Oppenheimer. Washington, D.C.: CQ Press, pp. 117–52.

———. 1990. *The Electoral Origins of Divided Government*. Boulder, C.O.: Westview.

———. 2004. *The Politics of Congressional Elections*. 6th ed. New York: Pearson Longman.

Jacobson, Gary C., and Samuel Kernell. 1983. *Strategy and Choice in Congressional Elections*. New Haven, C.T.: Yale University Press.

Jensen, Laura. 2003. *Patriots, Settlers, and the Origins of American Social Policy*. New York: Cambridge University Press.

Jensen, Merrill, John P. Kaminski and Gaspare F. Saladino, eds. 1976. *The Documentary History of the Ratification of the Constitution*. State Historical Society of Wisconsin. Vol. 10.

Jewell, Malcolm E., and Samuel C. Patterson. 1977. *The Legislative Process in the United States*. 3rd ed. New York: Random House.

Jillson, Calvin C. 1988. *Constitution Making: Conflict and Consensus in the Federal Convention of 1787*. New York: Agathon.

———. 1994. "Patterns of American Political Development" In *The Dynamics of American Politics: Approaches and Interpretations*. Edited by Lawrence C. Dodd and Calvin Jillson. Boulder, C.O.: Westview Press, pp. 24–58.

Jillson, Calvin C., and Rick K. Wilson. 1994. *Congressional Dynamics: Structure, Coordination, and Choice in the First American Congress, 1774–1789*. Stanford: Stanford University Press.

Johannes, John. 1972. *Policy Innovation in Congress*. Morristown, N.J.: General Learning Press.

———. 1984. *To Serve Our People*. Lincoln, N.E.: University of Nebraska Press.

Johnson, Haynes, and David Broder. 1996. *The System*. Boston: Little, Brown.

Jones, Bryan D. 1994. *Reconceiving Decision-Making in Democratic Politics: Attention, Choice, and Public Policy*. Chicago: University of Chicago Press.

———, ed. 1995. *The New American Politics*. Boulder, C.O.: Westview Press.

———. 2001. *Politics and the Architecture of Choice*. Chicago: University of Chicago Press.

Jones, Bryan D., and Frank R. Baumgartner. 2005. *The Politics of Attention: How Government Prioritizes Problems*. Chicago: University of Chicago Press.

Jones, Bryan D., Frank R. Baumgartner, and James L. True. 1998. "Policy Punctuations: U.S. Budget Authority, 1947–1995." *Journal of Politics* 60: 1–33.

Jones, Bryan D., and Walter Williams. 2008. *The Politics of Bad Ideas*. New York: Pearson, Longman.

Jones, Charles O. 1961. "Representation in Congress: The Case of the House Agricultural Committee." *American Political Science Review* 55: 358–67.

———. 1967. *Every Second Year*. Washington, D.C.: Brookings Institution.

———1970. *The Minority Party in Congress*. Boston: Little, Brown.

——. 1977. "Will Reform Change Congress?" In *Congress Reconsidered*, 1st ed. Ed. Lawrence C. Dodd and Bruce I. Oppenheimer. New York: Praeger, pp. 247–60.

Jones, Charles O., ed. 1988. *The Reagan Legacy*. Chatham, N.J.: Chatham House.

Jones, David R., and Monika L. McDermott. 2004. "The Responsible Party Government Model in House and Senate Elections." *American Journal of Political Science* 24: 1–12.

——. 2009. *Americans, Congress and Democratic Responsiveness*. Ann Arbor, M.I.: University of Michigan Press.

Jones, Rochelle, and Peter Woll. 1979. *The Private World of Congress*. New York: Free Press.

Jones, Robert A. 1992. "California's Bitter Season." *Los Angeles Times Magazine* 27: 14–18, 40–41.

Jung, Carl. 1963. *Memories, Dreams, Reflections*, recorded and edited by Aniela Jaffe. New York: Pantheon.

Kahn, Kim Fridkin, and Patrick J. Kenney. 1999. *The Spectacle of U.S. Senate Campaigns*. Princeton: Princeton University Press.

——. 2002. "Ideological Portrayals during U.S. Senate Campaigns." In *U.S. Senate Exceptionalism*. Edited by Bruce I. Oppenheimer. Columbus, O.H.: Ohio State University Press, pp. 45–60.

Kaiser, Fred M. 1978. "Congressional Change and Foreign Policy." In *Legislative Reform* Edited by Leroy Rieselbach. Lexington, M.A.: Lexington Books, pp. 61–72.

Kaplan, Abraham. 1964. *The Conduct of Inquiry: Methodology for Behavioral Science*. San Francisco: Chandler Press.

Kassel, Jason S. 2008. *Constructing a Professional Legislature: The Physical Development of Congress, 1783–1851*. Ph.D. Dissertation in Political Science. University of Florida.

Katz, Jonathan, and Brian Sala. 1996. "Careerism, Committee Assignments, and the Electoral Connection." *American Political Science Review* 90: 21–33.

Kazee, Thomas, ed. 1994. *Who Runs for Congress? Ambition, Context, and Candidate Emergence*. Washington, D.C.: CQ Press.

Kelly, Sean Q. 1993. "Divided We Govern: A Reassessment." *Polity* 25: 475–484.

——. 1994. "Punctuated Change and the Era of Divided Government. In *New Perspectives on American Politics*. Edited by Lawrence C. Dodd and Calvin Jillson. Washington, D.C.: CQ Press, 162–90.

——. 1995. "Democratic Leadership in the Modern Senate: The Emerging Roles of the Democratic Policy Committee." *Congress and the Presidency* 22: 113–140.

Kennedy, Paul. 1987. *The Rise and Fall of the Great Powers: Economic Change and Military Conflict from 1500 to 2000*. New York: Random House.

Kennedy, Roger G. 2003. *Mr. Jefferson's Lost Cause: Land, Farms, Slavery, and the Louisiana Purchase*. New York: Oxford University Press.

Kensi, Kate, Bruce W. Hardy, and Kathleen Hall Jamieson. 2010. *The Obama Victory: How Media, Money and Message Shaped the 2008 Election*. Oxford: Oxford University Press.

Kernell, Samuel 1977. "Toward Understanding 19th Century Careers, Ambition, Competition and Rotation." *American Journal of Political Science* 21: 669–693.

Kerr, K. Austin. 2004. "Railroad Policy." In *The American Congress: The Building of Democracy*. Edited by Julian E. Zelizer. Boston: Houghton Mifflin, pp. 285–97.

Key, V. O. 1955. "A Theory of Critical Elections." *Journal of Politics* 17:3–18.

——. 1961. *Public Opinion and American Democracy*. New York: Knopf.

——. 1966. With the assistance of Milton C. Cummings, Jr. *The Responsible Electorate:*

Rationality in Presidential Voting, 1936–1960. Cambridge, M.A.: Belknap Press of Harvard University Press.

Kiewiet, Roderick, and Mathew D. McCubbins. 1991. *The Spending Power*. Berkeley, C.A.: University of California Press.

King, Anthony S. 1981. "The Rise of the Career Politician in Britain—and Its Consequences." *British Journal of Political Science* 11: 349–285.

King, David C. 1997. *Turf Wars: How Congressional Committees Claim Jurisdiction*. Chicago: University of Chicago Press.

Kingdon, John W. 1968. *Candidates for Office*. New York: Random House.

——. 1973. *Congressmen's Voting Decisions*. New York: Harper.

——. 1984. *Agendas, Alternatives and Public Policies*. Boston: Little Brown.

Klein, Joe. 2000. "Eight Years: Bill Clinton and the Politics of Persistence." In *The New Yorker*. October 16–23: 206–9.

——. 1994. "Agendas, Ideas, and Policy Change." In *New Perspectives on American Politics*. Edited by. Lawrence C. Dodd and Calvin Jillson. Washington, D.C.: CQ Press, pp. 215–29.

Koopman, Douglas L. 1996. *Hostile Takeover: The House Republican Party: 1980–1995*. Lanham, M.D.: Rowman & Littlefield.

Kostroski, Warren Lee. 1973. "Party and Incumbency in Postwar Senate Elections: Trends, Patterns, and Models." *American Political Science Review* 67 (December): 1213–1234.

Kousser, Thad. 2005. *Term Limits and the Dismantling of State legislative Professionalism*. New York: Cambridge University Press.

Kramnick, Issac. 1987. "Editor's Introduction." In *The Federalist Papers*. Edited by Isaac Kramnick. London: Penguin Books, pp. 11–82.

Krasno, Jonathan S. 1994. *Challengers, Competition, and Reelection: Comparing Senate and House Elections*. New Haven, C.T.: Yale University Press.

Krehbiel, Keith. 1990. *Information and Legislative Organization*. Ann Arbor: University of Michigan Press.

Krehbiel, Keith. 1993. "Where's the Party?" *British Journal of Political Science*. 23:235–266.

——. 1998. *Pivotal Politics: A Theory of U.S. Lawmaking*. Chicago: University of Chicago Press.

Krehbiel, Keith, Kenneth A. Shepsle, and Barry R. Weingast. 1987. "Why Are Congressional Committees Powerful?" *American Political Science Review* 81: 929–948.

Krugman, Paul. 1990. *The Age of Diminished Expectations: U.S. Economic Policy in the 1990s*. Cambridge, Mass.: MIT Press, 1990.

Kriner, Douglas L., and Francis X. Shen. 2007. "Iraq Casualties and the 2006 Senate Elections." *Legislative Studies Quarterly* 32: 507–530.

Krutz, Glen S. 2001. *Hitching a Ride: Omnibus Legislating in the U.S. Congress*. Columbus: Ohio State University Press.

Kuklinski, James H. 1977. "District Competitiveness and Legislative Roll Call Behavior: A Reassessment of the Marginality Hypothesis." *American Journal of Political Science* 21: 627–638.

Kuklinski, James H., and Darrell West. 1981. "Economic Expectations and Mass Voting in United States House and Senate Elections. *American Political Science Review* 75: 436–447.

Kuhn, Thomas. 1970. *The Structure of Scientific Revolutions*. Chicago: University of Chicago Press.

Lasswell, H. D. 1950. *National Security and Individual Freedom*. New York: McGraw-Hill.

———. 1970. "The Developing Science of Democracy.," In *The Analysis of Political Behavior*, ed. H. D. Lasswell. Hamden, C.T.: Archon Press, pp. 1–28.

Lawless, Jennifer, and Richard Fox. 2005. *It Takes a Candidate: Why Women Don't Run for Office*. New York: Cambridge University Press.

Lawrence, Eric D., Forrest Maltzman, and Paul J. Wahlbeck. 2001. "The Politics of Speaker Cannon's Committee Assignments." *American Journal of Political Science* 45: 551–562.

Layman, Geoffrey C., Thomas M. Carsey, and Juliana Menasce Horowitz. 2006. "Party Polarization in American Politics: Characteristics, Causes, and Consequences." *Annual Review of Political Science* 9: 83–110.

Lebo, Matthew J., Adam J. McGlynn, and Gregory Koger. 2007. "Strategic Party Government:
Party Influence in Congress, 1789–2000." *American Journal of Political Science* 51: 464–481.

Lee, Frances E. 2000. "Senate Representation and Coalition Building in Distributive Politics." *American Political Science Review* 94: 50–72.

———. 2002. "Representational Power and Distributive Politics: Senate Influence on Federal Transportation Spending." In *U.S. Senate Exceptionalism*. Edited by Bruce I. Oppenheimer. Columbus, O.H.: Ohio State University Press, pp. 283–301.

———. 2010. *Beyond Ideology: Politics, Principles and Partisanship in the U.S. Senate*. Chicago: University of Chicago Press.

Lee, Frances E., and Bruce I. Oppenheimer. 1999. *Sizing Up the Senate*. Chicago: University of Chicago Press.

Leege, David C., Kenneth Wald, Paul Mueller, and Brian Krueger. 2002. *The Politics of Cultural Differences: Social Change and Voter Mobilization Strategies in the Post–New Deal Period*. Princeton: Princeton University Press.

Lehman, Edward W. 1992. *The Viable Polity*. Philadelphia: Temple University Press.

LeLoup, Lance T., and Steven Shull. 1979. "Congress versus the Executive: The 'Two Presidencies' Reconsidered." *Social Science Quarterly* 59: 704–719.

Lenchner, Paul 1979. "Postindustrialization and the New Congress." Paper presented at the Annual Meeting of the Southern Political Science Association, Atlanta.

Lerner, Michael. 1986. *Surplus Powerlessness*. Oakland, C.A.: Institute for Labor and Mental Health.

Light, Larry. 1980. "Republican Groups Dominate in Party Campaign Spending." *Congressional Quarterly Weekly Report*. November 1, pp. 3235–39.

Lipinski, Daniel. 2004. *Congressional Communication*. Ann Arbor: University of Michigan Press.

Livingston, William S., Lawrence C. Dodd, and Richard L. Schott. 1979. *The Presidency and Congress: A Changing Balance of Power*. Austin, T.X.: Lyndon Baines Johnson Library.

Loewenberg, Gerhard. 2011. *On Legislatures: The Puzzle of Representation*. Boulder: Paradigm Publishers.

Loewenberg, Gerhard, and Samuel Patterson. 1979. *Comparing Legislatures*. Boston: Little, Brown.

Longley, Lawrence D., and Walter J. Oleszek. 1983. "The Three Contexts of Congressional Conference Committee Politics: Bicameral Politics Overviewed." Paper presented at the Annual Meeting of the American Political Science Association, Chicago.

Longley, Lawrence D., and Walter J. Oleszek. 1989. *Bicameral Politics: Conference Committees in Congress*. New Haven, C.T.: Yale University Press.

Loomis, Burdette A. 1981. "Congressional Caucuses and the Politics of Representation." In *Congress Reconsidered*, 2nd ed. Edited by Lawrence C. Dodd and Bruce I. Oppenheimer.

——. 1982. "Congressional Careers, Legislative Behavior and Policy Outcomes." Paper Prepared for the 1982 Midwest Political Science Convention.

——.1988. *The New American Politician: Ambition, Entrepreneurship, and the Changing Face of Political Life*. New York: Basic Books.

——. ed. 2000. *Esteemed Colleagues: Civility and Deliberation in the U.S. Senate*. Washington, D.C.: Brookings.

——. 2002. "Explaining Impeachment: The Exceptional Institution Confronts the Unique Experience." In *U.S. Senate Exceptionalism*. Edited by Bruce I. Oppenheimer. Columbus, Ohio: Ohio State University Press, pp. 322–28.

Lowi, Theodore J. 1964. "American Business and Public Policy, Case Studies and Political Theory." *World Politics* 16: 677–715.

——. 1969/1979. *The End of Liberalism: The Second Republic of the United States*. New York: Norton.

——. 1971. *The Politics of Disorder*. New York: Basic Books.

——. 1972. "Four Systems of Policy, Politics, and Choice."*Public Administration Review* 32: 298–310.

——. 1985. *The Personal President*. Ithaca: Cornell University Press.

——. 1995. *The End of the Republican Era*. Norman: University of Oklahoma Press.

——. 2009. *Arenas of Power*. Edited and Introduced by Norman K. Nicholson. Boulder, C.O.: Paradigm Publishers.

Lupia, Arthur, and Mathew D. McCubbins. 1994. "Who Controls? Information and the Structure of Legislative Decision-Making." *Legislative Studies Quarterly*. 19:361–384.

Lyons, Michael, and Taylor, Marcia Whicker 1981. "Farm politics in transition: The House Agriculture Committee." *Agricultural History* 55: 128–146.

Maass, Arthur. 1983. *Congress and the Common Good*. New York: Basic Books.

MacRae, Duncan, Jr. 1970. *Issues and Parties in Legislative Voting*. New York: Harper and Row

Maestas, Cherie. 2000. "Professional Legislatures and Ambitious Politicians: Policy Responsiveness of State Institutions." *Legislative Studies Quarterly* 25:663–690.

——. 2003. "The Incentive to Listen: Progressive Ambition, Resources, and Opinion Monitoring among State Legislators." *Journal of Politics* 65: 439–456.

Maisel, Louis S. 1982. *From Obscurity to Oblivion: Running in the Congressional Primary*. Knoxville: University of Tennessee Press.

Malbin, Michael. 1980. *Unelected Representatives*. New York: Basic Books.

——. 2003. *Life after Reform*. Lanham, M.D.: Rowman & Littlefield.

Maltzman, Forrest. 1997. *Competing Principals: Committees, Parties and the Organization of Congress*. An Arbor: University of Michigan Press.

Maney, Patrick. 2004. "The Forgotten New Deal Congress." In *The American Congress*. Edited by Julian E. Zelizer. Boston: Houghton Mifflin, pp. 428–45.

Manin, Bernard. 1987. "On Legitimacy and Political Deliberation." *Political Theory* 15: 368.

Manley, John F. 1965. "The House Committee on Ways and Means: Conflict Management in a Congressional Committee," *American Political Science Review* 59: 927–939.

——.1969. "Wilbur Mills: a Study in Congressional Influence." *American Political Science Review* 53: 442–464.

——. 1970. *The Politics of Finance*. Boston: Little, Brown.

——. 1977. "The Conservative Coalition in Congress." *Congress Reconsidered*, 1st ed. Edited by Lawrence C. Dodd and Bruce I. Oppenheimer. New York: Praeger Publisher, pp. 75–95.

Mann, Thomas E. 1978. *Unsafe at Any Margin: Interpreting Congressional Elections*. Washington, D.C.: American Enterprise Institute.

Mann, Thomas E., and Norman J. Ornstein, eds. 1981. *The New Congress*. Washington, D.C.: American Enterprise Institute for Public Policy Research.

———. 1992. *Renewing Congress: A First Report*. Washington, D.C.: American Enterprise Institute.

———. 2006/revised 2008. *The Broken Branch: How Congress Is Failing America and How to Get It Back on Track*. Paperback ed. Oxford: Oxford University Press.

Mann, Thomas E., and Raymond E. Wolfinger. 1980. "Candidates and Parties in Congressional Elections." *American Political Science Review* 74 (September): 617–632.

Mansbridge, Jane. 1980. *Beyond Adversary Democracy*. New York: Basic Books.

March James G., and Johan P. Olsen. 1989. *Rediscovering Institutions: The Organizational Basis of Politics*. New York: Free Press.

———. 1995. *Democratic Governance*. New York: Free Press.

Marcus, George E., and Michael B. MacKuen. 1993. "Anxiety, Enthusiasm, and the Vote: The Emotional Underpinnings of Learning and Involvement during Presidential Campaigns." *American Political Science Review* 87: 672–85.

Marcus, George E., Russell Neuman and Michael Mackuen. 2000. *Affective Intelligence and Political Judgment*. Chicago: University of Chicago Press.

Maass, Arthur. 1983. *Congress and the Common Good*. New York: Basic Books.

Madison, James. 1969. *Notes of Debates in the Federal Convention of 1787*. New York: W.W. Norton.

Masters, Nicholas. 1961. "Committee Assignments in the House of Representatives. *American Political Science Review* 55: 345–357.

Matthews, Donald R. 1960. *U.S. Senators and Their World*. New York: Vintage Books.

———. 1992. "Understanding the Transformed Senate: The Role of Sequence." In *Extension of Remarks: Legislative Studies Section Newsletter.*(November): 3.

Matthews, Joe, and Mark Paul. 2010. *California Crackup: How Reform Broke the Golden State and How We Can Fix It*. Oxford: Oxford University Press.

Matthews, Richard K. 1995. *If Men Were Angels: James Madison and the Heartless Empire of Reason*. Lawrence, K.S.: University of Kansas Press.

Mayer, Kenneth R. 2001. *With the Stroke of a Pen*. Princeton: Princeton University Press.

Mayer, Kenneth R., and David T. Canon. 1999. *The Dysfunctional Congress? The Individual Roots of an Institutional Dilemma*. Boulder, C.O.: Westview.

Mayhew, David R. 1966. *Party Loyalty among Congressmen*. Cambridge: Harvard University Press.

———. 1974a. "Congressional Elections: The Case of the Vanishing Marginals." *Polity* 6: 295–317.

———1974b. *Congress: The Electoral Connection*. New Haven, C.T.: Yale University Press.

———. 1986. *Placing Parties in American Politics*. Princeton, N.J.: Princeton University Press.

———. 1991. *Divided We Govern*. New Haven, C.T.: Yale University Press.

———. 1993. "Let's Stick with the Larger Question." *Polity* 25: 489–490.

———. 1994. "U.S. Policy Waves in Comparative Perspective." In *New Perspectives on American Politics*. Edited by Lawrence C. Dodd and Calvin Jillson. Washington, D.C.: CQ Press, pp. 325–40.

———. 2000. *America's Congress: Actions in the Public Sphere, James Madison through Newt Gingrich*. New Haven, C.T.: Yale University Press.

Mayr, Ernst. 1984. *The Growth of Biological Thought*. Cambridge, M.A.: Harvard University Press.

McClosky, Herbert, and John Zaller. 1984. *The American Ethos: Public Attitudes Toward Capitalism and Democracy*. Cambridge, Mass.

McConachie, Lauros G. 1898. *Congressional Committees*. New York: Crowell.

McCubbins, Mathew D., and Thomas Schwartz. 1984. "Congressional Oversight Overlooked: Police Patrols versus Fire Alarms." *American Journal of Political Science* 2: 165–79.

McKee, Seth. 2010. *Republican Ascendancy in Southern U.S. House Elections*. Boulder, C.O.: Westview Press.

McPherson, Harry. 1972. *A Political Education*. Boston: Little, Brown.

McPherson, James M. 1988. *Battle Cry of Freedom*. New York: Oxford University Press

Mead, Walter Russell. 1992. "Bushism, Found: A Second-Term Agenda Hidden in Trade Agreements." Harper's, September: 37–45.

Mezey, Michael L. 1989. *Congress, the President, and Public Policy*. Boulder, C.O.: Westview.

Miller, Warren E., and Donald E. Stokes. 1963. "Constituency Influence in Congress." *American Political Science Review* 57: 45–56.

Miller, William Lee. 1995. *Arguing About Slavery: John Quincy Adams and the Great BattleIn the United States Congress*. New York: Vintage Books.

Moe, Ronald C., and Teel, Steven C. 1970. "Congress as Policy-maker: a necessary reappraisal." *Political Science Quarterly* 85: 443–470.

Moe, Terry M. 1985. "The Politicized Presidency." In *The New Direction in American Politics*. Edited by John E. Chubb and Paul E. Peterson. Washington, D.C.: Brookings Institution, pp. 235–71.

———. 1987. "An Assessment of the Positive Theory of Congressional Dominance." *Legislative Studies Quarterly* 12: 475–520.

Moe, Terry M., and William G. Howell. 1999. "Unilateral Action and Presidential Power: A Theory." *Presidential Studies Quarterly*, 29: 850–74.

Mondak, Jeffery, and DonaGene Mitchell, eds. 2008. *Fault Lines: Why the Republicans Lost Congress*. London: Routledge.

Monroe, Nathan, Jason M. Roberts, and David W. Rohde, eds. 2008. *Why Not Parties? Party Effects in the United States Senate*. Chicago: University of Chicago Press.

Muir, William K., Jr. 1982. *Legislature: California School for Politics*. Chicago: The University of Chicago Press.

Muthoo, Abhinay and Kenneth Shepsle. 2008. "The Constitutional Choice of Bicameralism." In *Institutions and Economic Performance*. Edited by Elhanan Helpman. Cambridge, M.A.: Harvard University Press, pp. 249–282.

Mycoff, Jason 2007. "Committee Ambition and Congressional Oversight." A Paper presented at the American Political Science Convention (September).

Myrdal, Gunnar. 1944, 1962. *An American Dilemma*. New York Harper & Row.

Namenwirth, J. Zvi. 1973. "Wheels of Time and the Interdependence of Value Change in America." *Journal of Interdisciplinary History*, Vol. 3, No. 4: 649–684.

Neale, Thomas H. 1995. " Voting and Suffrage." In *The Encyclopedia of the United States Congress*. Edited by Donald C. Bacon, Roger H. Davidson and Morton Keller, New York: Simon & Schoster, pp. 2070–80.

Neely, Mark E., Jr. 2004. "The Civil War." In *The American Congress: The Building of Democracy*. Edited by Julian E. Zelizer. Boston: Houghton Mifflin, pp. 207–18.

Nelson, Garrison. 1977. "Partisan Patterns of House Leadership Change, 1789–1977." *American Political Science Review* 71: 918–939.

Neustadt, Richard. 1960. *Presidential Power: The Politics of Leadership*. New York: John Wiley.

Neustadt, Richard E., and Ernest R. May. 1986. *Thinking in Time: The Uses of History for Decision-Makers*. New York: Free Press.

Norpoth, Helmut. 1976. "Explaining Party Cohesion in Congress: The Case of Shared Party Attributes." *American Political Science Review* 70: 1157–1171.

Ogul, Morris S. 1976. *Congress Oversees the Bureaucracy*. Pittsburgh: University of Pittsburgh Press.

Oldmixon, Elizabeth A. 2005. *Making Moral Decisions: God, Sex and the U.S. House of Representatives*. Washington, D.C.: Georgetown University Press.

Oleszek, Walter J. 1996, 2001. *Congressional Procedures and the Policy Process*. 5th ed. Washington, D.C.: CQ Press.

Olson, Mancur, Jr. 1965. *The Logic of Collective Action*. Cambridge, M.A.: Harvard University Press.

——. 1982. *The Rise and Decline of Nations*. New Haven, C.T.: Yale University Press.

Oppenheimer, Bruce I. 1974. *Oil and the Congressional Process: The Limits of Symbolic Politics*. Lexington, M.A.: Lexington Books.

——. 1977. "The Rules Committee: New Arm of Leadership in a Decentralized House." In *Congress Reconsidered*, 1st ed. Edited by Lawrence C. Dodd and Bruce I. Oppenheimer. New York: Praeger Publishers, pp. 96–116.

——. 1981. "Congress and the New Obstructionism: Developing an Energy Program." In *Congress Reconsidered*, 2nd ed. Edited by Lawrence C. Dodd and Bruce I. Oppenheimer. Washington, D.C.: CQ Press, pp. 275–95.

——. 1985. "Changing Time Constraints on Congress: Historical Perspectives on the Use of Cloture."In *Congress Reconsidered*, 3rd ed. Edited by Lawrence C. Dodd and Bruce I. Oppenheimer. Washington, D.C.: CQ Press, pp. 393–413

——. 1989. "Split Party Control of Congress, 1981–1986: Exploring Electoral and Apportionment Explanations." *American Journal of Political Science* 33: 653–669.

——. 1992. "Career Development in the Senate: Re-election as an Auxiliary Goal." In *Extension of Remarks: Legislative Studies Section Newsletter*. (November): 6–7.

——. 1997. "Abdicating Congressional Power." In *Congress Reconsidered*, 6th ed. Edited by Lawrence C. Dodd and Bruce I. Oppenheimer. Washington, D.C.: CQ Press, pp. 371–89.

——, ed. 2002a. *U.S. Senate Exceptionalism*. Columbus, O.H.: Ohio State University Press.

——. 2002b. "Let's Begin With the Senate: An Introduction to U.S. Senate Exceptionalism." In *U.S. Senate Exceptionalism*.Edited by Bruce I. Oppenheimer. Columbus, O.H.: Ohio State University Press, pp. 3–11.

——. 2005. "Deep Red and Blue Congressional Districts: The Causes and Consequences of Declining Party Competitiveness." In *Congress Reconsidered*, 8th ed. Edited by Lawrence C. Dodd and Bruce I. Oppenheimer. Washington, D.C.: CQ Press, pp. 135–58.

——. 2009. "The Process Hurdles: Energy Legislation from the OPEC Embargo to 2008." In *Congress Reconsidered*, 9th edition. Edited by Lawrence C. Dodd and Bruce I. Oppenheimer. Washington, D.C.: CQ Press, pp. 285–309.

Oppenheimer, Bruce I., and Christian R. Grose. 2007. "The Iraq War, Partisanship, and Candidate Attributes: Explaining Variation in Partisan Swing in the 2006 U.S. House Elections." *Legislative Studies Quarterly* 32: 531–558.

Oren, Karen, and Stephen Skowronek. 1994."Beyond the Iconography of Order: Notes for a 'New Institutionalism.'" In *The Dynamics of American Politics*. Edited by Lawrence C. Dodd and Calvin Jillson, Boulder, C.O.: Westview Press, pp. 311–30.

Orfield, Gary. 1975. *Congressional Power: Congress and Social Change*. New York: Harcourt.

Ornstein, Norman J. 1975. *Congress in Change: Evolution and Reform*. New York: Praeger.

———.1981. "The House and Senate in a New Congress."In *The New Congress*. Edited by Thomas Mann and Norm Ornstein. Washington, D.C.: American Enterprise Institute Press, pp. 365–89.

Ornstein, Norman J., Thomas E. Mann, and Michael J. Malbin. 1995. *Vital Statistics on Congress, 1995–1996*. Washington, D.C.: Congressional Quarterly.

Ornstein, Norman J., Robert L. Peabody, and David W. Rohde. 1985. "The Senate through the 1980s: Cycles of Change." In *Congress Reconsidered*, 3rd ed. Edited by Lawrence C. Dodd and Bruce I. Openeheimer. Washington, D.C.: CQ Press, pp. 13–33.

Ornstein, Norman, and David Rohde.1977. "Revolt from within: congressional change, legislative policy and the House Commerce Committee."In *Legislative Reform and Public Policy*. Edited by Susan Welsh and John G. Peters, New York: Praeger Publishers, pp. 54–72.

Osborne, David. 1988. *Laboratories of Democracy*. Cambridge, Mass.: Harvard Business School Press.

Osborne, David, and Ted Gaebler. 1992. *Reinventing Government: How the Entrepreneurial Spirit Is Transforming the Public Sector*. Reading, M.A.: Addison-Wesley.

Ostrom, Elinor, ed. 1982. *Strategies of Political Inquiry*. Berverly Hills, CA.: Sage.

Ostrom, Vincent. 1971. *The Theory of A Compound Republic*. Blacksburg, V.A.: Public Choice.

Owens, John E. 1997. "Curbing the Fiefdoms: Party-Committee Relations in the Contemporary U.S. House of Representatives." In *The Changing Roles of Parliamentary Committees*. Edited by Lawrence D. Longley and Attila Agh. Appleton, Wis.: Research Committee of Legislative Specialists, pp. 96–123.

———. 2003. "Explaining Party Cohesion and Discipline in Democratic Legislatures: Purposiveness and Contexts." *Journal of Legislative Studies* 9(4): 12–40.

Padgett, John F., and Christopher Ansell. 1993. "Robust Action and the Rise of the Medici, 1400–1434." *American Journal of Sociology* 98: 1259–1319.

Parker, Glenn R. 1977. "Some Themes in Congressional Unpopularity." *American Journal of Political Science* 21: 93–109

———. 1979. "The Selection of Committee Leaders in the House of Representatives." *American Politics Quarterly* 7(January): 71–93.

———. 1984. "Stylistic Changes in the Constituency Orientations of U.S. Senators: 1959–1980." Paper prepared for Presentation at the 1984 Midwest Political Science Convention.

———, ed. 1985. *Studies of Congress*. Washington, D.C.: Congressional Quarterly.

———.1986. *Homeward Bound: Explaining Changes in Congressional Behavior*. Pittsburgh: University of Pittsburgh Press.

———. 1992. *Institutional Change, Discretion and the Making of the Modern Congress*. Ann Arbor: University of Michigan Press.

Parker, Glenn R., and Roger H. Davidson. 1979. "Why Do Americans Love Their Congressmen So Much More Than Their Congress?" *Legislative Studies Quarterly* 4: 53–61.

Patashnik, Eric, 2005. "Budgets and Fiscal Policy." In *The Legislative Branch*. Edited by Paul J. Quirk and Sarah A. Binder. Oxford: Oxford University Press, pp. 382–406.

Patterson, Samuel C. 1978. "The Semi-sovereign Congress." In *The New American Political System*. Edited by Anthony King. Washington, D.C.: American Enterprise Institute, 125–177.

Patterson, James T. 1967. *Congressional Conservatism and the New Deal*. Lexington: University Press of Kentucky.

Payne, James L. 1980. "The Personal Electoral Advantage of House Incumbents, 1936–1976." *American Politics Quarterly* 8: 465–482.

Peabody, Robert L. 1976. *Leadership in Congress: Stability, Succession, and Change*. Boston: Little, Brown.

Peabody, Robert L., Norman J. Ornstein, and David W. Rohde. 1976. "The United States Senate as Presidential Incubator: Many Are Called But Few Are Chosen." *Political Science Quarterly* 91 (Summer): 237–258

Peabody, Robert L., and Nelson W. Polsby, eds. 1977. *New Perspectives on the House of Representatives*. 3rd ed. Chicago: Rand McNally.

Pearson, Kathryn, and Eric Schickler. 2009. "Discharge Petitions, Agenda Control, and the Congressional Committee System, 1929–1976." *The Journal of Politics* 71(4): 1238–1256.

Peters, Ronald M., Jr. 1990. *The American Speakership*. Baltimore: Johns Hopkins University Press.

——. 1999. "Institutional Context and Leadership Style." In *New Majority or Old Minority?* Edited by Nicol C. Rae and Colton Campbell. Lanham, M.D.: Bowman & Little Field, pp. 43–65.

Peterson, Mark A. 1990. *Legislating Together: The White House and Capitol Hill from Eisenhower to Reagan*. Cambridge: Harvard University Press.

Peterson, Merrill D. 1987. *The Great Triumvirate: Webster, Clay, and Calhoun*. New York: Oxford University Press.

Pierson, Paul. 2004. *Politics in Time: History, Institutions, and Social Analysis*. Princeton, NJ: Princeton University Press.

Pitkin, Hannah. 1972. *The Concept of Representation*. Berkeley: University of California Press.

Pimlott, Jamie. 2010. *Women and the Democratic Party: The Evolution of Emily's List*. Amherst, N.Y.: Cambria Press.

Pinderhughes, Dianne. 1987. *Race and Ethnicity in Chicago Politics: A Reexamination of Pluralist Theory*. Champaign-Urbana: University of Illinois Press.

——. 2011. *Black Politics After the Civil Rights Revolution*. New York: Routledge.

Pfiffner, James P. 1975. "Congressional Budget Reform, 1974: Initiation and Reaction." Paper Prepared for Presentation at the American Political Science Convention. San Francisco, CA., September 2–5.

Polsby, Nelson W.1968. "Institutionalization in the U.S. House of Representatives." *American* Political *Science Review*. 62: 144–168.

——. 1971. "Strengthening Congress in National Policy Making." In *Congressional Behavior*. Edited by Nelson Polsby. New York: Random House.

——. 1975. "Legislatures." In *Handbook of Political Science: Government Institutions and Processes*. 5. Reading, Mass.: Addison-Wesley.

——. 1982. "Contemporary Transformations of American Politics: Thoughts on the Research Agenda of Political Scientists." *Political Science Quarterly* 96 (Winter): 551–569.

Polsby, Nelson W. 1984. *Political Innovation in America.* New Haven, C.T.: Yale University Press.

——. 2004. *How Congress Evolves.* New York: Oxford

——. 1990. "Congress Bashing for Beginners." *Public Interest* 100 (Summer): 15–23.

Polsby, Nelson W., Miriam Gallagher, and Barry Rundquist.1969. "The Growth of the Seniority System in the House of Representatives." *American Political Science Review* 63: 787–807.

Polsby, Nelson W., and Eric Schickler. 2002. "Landmarks in the Study of Congress since 1945." *Annual Review of Political Science.* 5: 333–67.

Poole, Keith T., and Howard Rosenthal. 1997. *Congress: A Political-Economic History of Roll Call Voting.* New York: Oxford University Press.

Potter, David M. 1976. *The Impending Crisis.* New York: Harper Torchbooks.

Powell, Lynda W. 1982. "Issue Representation in Congress." *Journal of Politics* 44: 658–678.

Pressman, Jeffrey L. 1966. *House vs. Senate.* New Haven, C.T.: Yale University Press.

Pressman, Jeffrey L., and Aaron Wildavsky. 1973. *Implementation.* Berkeley, C.A.: University of California Press.

Price, David E. 1972. *Who Makes the Laws?* Cambridge, M.A.: Schenkman.

——. 1992. 2000. 2004. *The Congressional Experience.* Boulder, C.O.: Westview Press.

Price, H. Douglas. 1975. "Congress and the Evolution of Legislative Professionalism." In *Congress in Change.* Edited by Norman J. Ornstein. New York: Praeger Publishers, pp. 2–24.

——. 1977. "Careers and Committees in the American Congress: The Problem of Structural Change." In *The History of Parliamentary Behavior.* Edited by William O. Aydelotte. Princeton: Princeton University Press, pp. 28–62.

——. 1985. "Congressional government and the Politics of the Late 19th Century: A Retrospective View." Paper presented at the Annual Meeting of the American Political Science Association.

Prindle, David T., and Franklin, Daniel P. 1985. "Testing two purposive theories of congressional behavior." Paper presented at the 1985 Meetings of the Western Political Science Association, Las Vegas, Nevada (March 28–30).

Quirk, Paul. 1989. "The Cooperative Resolution of Policy Conflict." *American Political Science Review* 83 (September): 905–921.

Quirk, Paul, and Bruce Nesmith. 1994. "Explaining Deadlock: Domestic Policymaking in the Bush Presidency." In *New Perspectives on American Politics.* Edited by Lawrence C. Dodd and Calvin Jillson. Washington, D.C.: CQ Press, pp. 191–211.

Rae, Nicol C., and Colton Campbell, eds. 1999. *New Majority or Old Minority?* Lanham, M.D.: Rowman & Littlefield.

Ragsdale, Lyn, and Jerrold G. Rusk. 1995. "Candidates, Issues, and Participation in Senate Elections." *Legislative Studies Quarterly* 20: 305–328.

Ragusa, Jordan. 2010. "Chamber Hopping in the US Congress: Structure-Induced Learning and the Development of a Partisan Senate." A Paper Presented at the Midwest Political Science Association Annual Meeting, Chicago, I.L., April.

——. 2011. Resolving Differences: Bicameral Disagreement and Reconciliation in the Postreform Congresses. Doctoral Dissertation. University of Florida.

Randall, J. G. 1937. *The Civil War and Reconstruction*. New York: D.C. Heath.

Rauchway, Eric. 2004. "The Transformation of the Congressional Experience." In *The American Congress: The Building of Democracy*. Edited by Julian E. Zelizer. Boston: Houghton Mifflin, pp. 319–34.

Raven, Thomas. 2004. "Institutional Development in the House of Representatives, 1890–2000." A Paper Presented at the Annual Meeting of the American Political Science Association, Chicago, Illinois (September 1–5).

——. 2010. *Czars, Kings, and Barons: Understanding Institutional Transition in the House of Representatives*. Unpublished manuscript provided by the author.

Reich, Robert. 1990. *Tales of a New America*. New York: Random House.

——. 1991. *The Work of Nations*. New York: Vintage.

Rieselbach, Leroy N.1966. *The Roots of Isolationism*. Indianapolis: Bobbs-Merrill.

——, ed. 1970a. *The Congressional System*.

——. 1970b. "Introduction: Congress as a Political System." In *The Congressional System*. Edited by Leroy Rieselbach. Belmont, C.A.: Wadsworth Publishing Company, pp. 3–22.

——. 1973. *Congressional Politics*. New York: McGraw-Hill.

——. 1977. *Congressional Reform in the Seventies*. Morristown, N.J.: General Learning Press.

——. 1978. *Legislative Reform: The Policy Impact*. Lexington, M.A.: Lexington Books.

——. 1984. "The Forest For the Trees: Blazing Trails for Congressional Research." In *Political Science: The State of the Discipline*. Edited by Ada W. Finifter. Washington, D.C.: American Political Science Association, pp. 241–73.

——. 1986. *Congressional Reform*. Washington, D.C.: Congressional Quarterly.

——. 1994. *Congressional Reform: The Changing Modern Congress*. Washington, D.C.: CQ Press.

——.1995. *Congressional Politics: The Evolving Legislative System*. 2nd ed. Boulder, C.O.: Westview.

Riker, William H. 1962. *The Theory of Political Coalitions*. New Haven, C.T.: Yale University Press.

——. 1977. "The Future of a Science of Politics." *American Behavioral Scientist* 21 (September): 11–38;

——. 1982a. "The Two Party System and Duverger's Law: An Essay on the History of Political Science." *American Political Science Review* 76: 753–766.

——.1982b *Liberalism Against Populism*. San Francisco: Freeman.

——. 1986. *The Art of Political Manipulation*. New Haven, C.T.: Yale University Press.

——. 1992. "The Justification of Bicameralism." *International Political Science Review* 13:101–116.

Ripley, Randall B. 1969a. *Majority Party Leadership in Congress*. Boston: Little, Brown.

——1969b. *Power in the Senate*. New York: St. Martin's.

Ripley, Randall B., and Franklin, Grace A. 1980. *Congress, the Bureaucracy and Public Policy*. Homewood, Ill.: Dorsey Press.

——. 1991. *Congress, the Bureaucracy, and Public Policy*. 5th ed. Belmont, C.A.: Wadsworth.

Ripley, Randall B., and James M. Lindsay, eds. 1993. *Congress Resurgent: Foreign and Defense Policy on Capitol Hill*. Ann Arbor: University of Michigan Press.

Rivlin, Alice. M. 1992. *Reviving the American Dream*. Washington, D.C.: Brookings Institution.

Roberts, Jason M., and Steven S. Smith. 2003. "Procedural Contexts, Party Strategy, and

Conditional Party Voting in the U.S. House of Representatives, 1971–2000." *American Journal of Political Science* 47: 305–317.

Robinson, Michael. 1981. "Three Faces of Congressional Media." In *The New Congress*. Edited by Thomas E. Mann and Norman J. Ornstein. Washington, D.C.: American Enterprise Institute, pp. 55–96.

Rockman, Bert. 1984. *The Leadership Question: The Presidency and the American System*. New York: Praeger.

Rogers, Lindsay. 1926. *The American Senate*. New York: Knopf.

Rohde, David W. 1979. "Risk-bearing and Progressive Ambition." *American Journal of Political Science* 23: 1–26.

———. 1991. *Parties and Leaders in the Postreform House*. Chicago: University of Chicago Press.

———. 2002. "Seeing the House and Senate Together: Some Reflections on the Research on the Exceptional Senate." In *U.S. Senate Exceptionalism*. Edited by Bruce I. Oppenheimer. Colombus, O.H.: Ohio State University Press, pp. 341–49.

Rohde, David W., Norman J. Ornstein, and Robert L. Peabody. 1985. "Political change and legislative norms in the U. S. Senate, 1957–1974." In *Studies of Congress*. Edited by Glenn E. Parker. Washington, D.C.: CQ Press, pp. 147–88.

Rohde, David W., and Kenneth A. Shepsle. 1973. "Democratic Committee Assignments in the U.S. House of Representatives." *American Political Science Review* 67: 889–905.

———. 1985. "The Ambiguous Role of Leadership in Woodrow Wilson's Congress." Paper presented at the Annual Meeting of the American Political Science Association.

Rosenson, Beth A. 2005a. *Shadowlands of Conduct: Ethics and State Politics*. Washington, D.C.: Georgetown University Press.

———. 2005b. "Costs and Benefits of Ethics Laws." *International Public Management Journal*. Part of Symposium: Ethics, Governance and Democracy. Vol. 8, No. 2: 209–224.

———.2007. "Explaining Legislators' Positions on Outside Income Limits: Voting on Honoraria in the U.S. Senate, 1981–1983." *Public Choice*, Vol. 133, Nos. 1–2)(October): 111–128.

———. 2009. "Congressional Frequent Flyers: Demand and Supply Side Explanations for Privately Sponsored Travel." *Legislative Studies Quarterly*. Vol. 34. No. 2 (May).

Rossiter, Clinton. 1956. *The American Presidency*. New York: New American Library.

Rothman, David J. 1969. *Politics and Power*. New York: Athenaeum.

Rudder, Catherine E. 1977. "Committee Reform and the Revenue Process." In *Congress Reconsidered*, 1st ed. Edited by Lawrence C. Dodd and Bruce I. Oppenheimer. New York: Praeger Publishers, pp. 117–39.

———. 1985. "Fiscal responsibility and the revenue committees." In *Congress Reconsidered*, 3rd ed. Edited by Lawrence C. Dodd and Bruce I. Oppenheimer. Washington, D.C.: CQ Press, pp. 319–42.

———. 1993. "Can Congress Govern?" In *Congress Reconsidered*, 5th ed. Edited by Lawrence C. Dodd and Bruce I. Oppenheimer. Washington, D.C.: CQ Press, pp. 365–74.

——— 2005. "The Politics of Taxing and Spending in Congress: Ideas, Strategy and Policy." In *Congress Reconsidered*, 8th ed. Edited by Lawrence C. Dodd and Bruce I. Opppenheimer.

——— 2009. "Transforming American Politics through Tax Policy." In *Congress Reconsidered*, 9th Edition. Edited by Lawrence C. Dodd and Bruce I. Oppenheimer. Washington, D.C.: CQ Press, pp. 263–83.

Saloma, John S. III. 1969. *Congress and the New Politics*. Boston: Little, Brown & Co.

Sarbaugh-Thompson, Marjorie, Lyke Thompson, Charles D. Elder, John Strate, and Richard C. Elling. 2004. *The Political and Institutional Effects of Term Limits*. New York: Palgrave-Macmillan.

Schick, Allen. 1980. *Congress and Money*. Washington, D.C.: The Urban Institute.

———. 1983. *Making Economic Policy in Congress*. Washington, D.C.: American Enterprise Institute.

Schickler, Eric. 2001. *Disjointed Pluralism*. Princeton: Princeton University Press.

———. 2000. "Institutional Change in the House of Representatives, 1867–1998: A Test of Partisan and Ideological Power Balance Models." *American Political Science Review*. 94: 269–288.

———. 2007. "Entrepreneurial Defenses of Congressional Power." In *Formative Acts: American Politics in the Making*. Edited by Stephen Skowronek and Matthew Glassman, pp. 293–315.

Schickler, Eric, and Andrew Rich. 1997. "Party Government in the House Reconsidered: A Response to Cox and McCubbins." *American Journal of Political Science* 41: 1387–1394.

Schickler, Eric, and Kathryn Pearson. 2009. "Agenda Control, Majority Party Power, and the House Committee on Rules, 1937–65." *Legislative Studies Quarterly* 34(4): 455–491.

Schiff, Steven H., and Smith, Steven S. 1983. "Generational change and the allocation of staff in the U.S. Congress." *Legislative Studies Quarterly* 8: 457–467.

Schiller, Wendy J. 1995. "Senators as Political Entrepreneurs: Using Bill Sponsorship to Shape Legislative Agendas." *American Journal of Political Science* 39: 186–203.

———. 2000. *Partners and Rivals: Representation in U.S. Senate Delegations*. Princeton: Princeton University Press.

———. 2002. "Sharing the Same Home Turf: How Senators from the Same State Compete for Geographic Electoral Support." In *U.S. Senate Exceptionalism*. Edited by Bruce I. Oppenheimer. Columbus, O.H.: Ohio State University Press, pp. 109–31.

Schlesinger, Arthur M., Jr. 1973. *The Imperial Presidency*. New York: Popular Library.

———. 1986. *The Cycles of American History*. Boston: Houghton Mifflin.

Schneider, Jerrold E. 1979. *Ideological Coalitions in Congress*. Greenwood, C.T.: Greenwood Press.

Schudson, Michael. 2004. "Congress and the Media." In *The American Congress: The Building of Democracy*. Edited by Julian E. Zelizer. Boston: Houghton Mifflin, pp. 650–63.

Schwarz, John E., and L. Earl Shaw. 1976. *The United States Congress in Comparative Perspective*. Hinsdale, Ill.: Dryden Press.

Scigliano, Robert. 1971. *The Supreme Court and the Presidency*. New York: Free Press.

Seidelman, Raymond, and E. J. Harpham. 1985. *Disenchanted Realists*. Albany: State University of New York Press.

Seidman, Harold. 1975. *Politics, Position, and Power*. 2nd ed. London: Oxford University Press.

Sellers, Patrick J. 2002. "Winning Media Coverage in the U.S. Congress." In *U.S. Senate Exceptionalism*. Ed. Bruce I. Oppenheimer. Columbus, O.H.: Ohio State University Press, pp. 132–53.

———. 2010. *Cycles of Spin: Strategic Communication in the U.S. Congress*. New York, N.Y.: Cambridge University Press.

Shefter, Martin. 1994. "International Influences on American Politics." In *New Perspectives on American Politics*. Edited by Lawrence C. Dodd and Calvin Jillson. Washington, D.C.: CQ Press, pp. 311–24.

Shepsle, Kenneth A. 1978. *The Giant Jigsaw Puzzle.* Chicago: University of Chicago Press.

——.1988. "Representation and Governance: The Great Trade-off." *Political Science Quarterly* 103 (Fall): 461–484

——.1989. "The Changing Textbook Congress." In *Can the Government Govern?* Edited by John E. Chubb and Paul E. Paterson. Washington, D.C.: Brookings Institution, pp. 238–67.

Shepsle, Kenneth, and Mark S. Bonchek. 1997. *Analyzing Politics: Rationality, Behavior, and Institutions.* New York: W. W. Norton.

Shepsle, Kenneth, and Barry R. Weingast. 1987. "The Institutional Foundations of Committee Power." *American Political Science Review* (March): 85–104

——, eds. 1995. *Positive Theories of Congressional Institutions.* Ann Arbor: University of Michigan Press.

Shipan, Charles R. 2003. "Regulatory Regimes, Agency Actions, and the Conditional Nature of Congressional Influence." *American Political Science Review* 98: 467–480.

Shribman, David M. 1999. "Insiders with a Crisis from Outside." In *Congress and the Decline of Public Trust.* Edited by Joseph A. Cooper. Boulder, C.O.: Westview Press, pp. 27–42.

Simon, Herbert. 1985. "Human Nature in Politics: The Dialogue of Psychology with Political Science." *American Political Science Review* 81: 85–104.

Sinclair, Barbara. 1981. "The Speaker's Task Force in the Post-Reform House of Representatives." *American Political Science Review* 75 (2): 397–410.

——. 1982. *Congressional Realignment, 1925–1978.* Austin: University of Texas Press.

——. 1983. *Majority Leadership in the U.S. House.* Baltimore: Johns Hopkins University Press.

——. 1989. *The Transformation of the U.S. Senate.* Baltimore: Johns Hopkins University Press.

——. 1992. "Framing, Interpreting and Explaining Senate Behavior: The Importance of Looking Up-Close-and-Personal." In *Extension of Remarks: Legislative Studies Section Newsletter.* (November): 4–5.

——. 1995. *Legislators, Leaders, and Lawmaking: The U.S. House of Representatives in the Postreform Era.* Baltimore: Johns Hopkins University Press.

—— 1999. "Coequal Partner: The U.S. Senate." In *Senates: Bicameralism in the Contemporary World.* Edited by Samuel C. Patterson and Anthony Mughan. Columbus, O.H.: Ohio State University Press, 32–58.

——. 2001. "The New World of U.S. Senators." In *Congress Reconsidered,* 7th ed. Edited by Lawrence C. Dodd and Bruce I. Oppenheimer. Washington, D.C.: Congressional Quarterly Press, pp. 1–19.

——. 2002. "The 60-Vote Senate: Strategies, Process, and Outcomes." In *U. S. Senate Exceptionalism.* Edited by Bruce I. Oppenheimer. Columbus, O.H.: Ohio State University Press, pp. 241–61.

——. 2006. *Party Wars: Polarization and the Politics of National Policy Making.* Norman: University of Oklahoma Press.

——. 2007. *Unorthodox Lawmaking: New Legislative Processes in the U.S. Congress.* 3rd ed. Washington, D.C.: CQ Press.

Skocpol, Theda. 1992. *Protecting Soldiers and Mothers: The Political Origins of Social Policy in the United States.* Cambridge: Belknap Press of Harvard University Press.

——. 1994. "Early U.S. Social Policies: A Challenge to Theories of the Welfare State." In

New Perspectives on American Politics. Edited by Lawrence C. Dodd and Calvin Jillson. Washington, D.C.: CQ Press, pp. 367–87.

Skowronek, Stephen. 1982. *Building a New American State.* Cambridge: Cambridge University Press.

——. 1984. "Presidential Leadership in Political Time." In *The Presidency and the Political System.* Edited by Michael Nelson. Washington, D.C.: CQ Press, pp. 115–59.

——. 1993. *The Politics Presidents Make: Leadership from John Adams to Bill Clinton.* Cambridge Ma.: Belknap Press of Harvard University Press.

Skowronek, Stephen, and Matthew Glassman, eds. 2007. *Formative Acts: American Politics in The Making.* Philadelphia: University of Pennsylvania Press.

Smith, Steven S. 1985. "New Patterns of Decisionmaking in Congress." In *The New Directions in American Politics.* Edited by John E. Chubb and Paul E. Peterson.

——.1989. *Call to Order: Floor Politics in the House and Senate.* Washington, D.C.: Brookings.

——. 1992. "Policy Leadership in Fenno's Senate Studies." In *Extension of Remarks: Legislative Studies Section Newsletter.* (November): 7–9.

——. 1995. *The American Congress.* Boston: Houghton Mifflin.

——. 2007. *Party Influence in Congress.* New York: Cambridge University Press.

Smith, Steven S., and Christopher J. Deering, 1984. *Committees in Congress.* Washington, D.C.: CQ Press.

Smith, Steve S., and Gerald Gamm. 2005. "The Dynamics of Party Government in Congress." In *Congress Reconsidered,* 8th ed. Edited by Dodd and Oppenheimer. Washington, D.C.: CQ Press, pp. 181–205.

Snyder, James, and Tim Groseclose. 2000. "Estimating Party Influence in Congressional Roll Voting." *American Journal of Political Science.* 44: 193–211.

Sorauf, Frank J. 1988. *Money in American Elections.* Glenview, I.L.: Scott, Foresman.

Squire, Peverill, 2005. "The Evolution of American Colonial Assemblies as Legislative Organizations." *Congress and the Presidency.* 32: 109–131.

——. 2006. "Historical Evolution of Legislatures in the United States." *Annual Review of Political Science* 9:19–44.

Stein, Robert M., and Kenneth N. Bickers. 1995. *Perpetuating the Pork: Policy Subsystems and American Democracy.* New York: Cambridge University Press.

Stevens, Arthur G., Arthur H. Miller, and Thomas E. Mann. 1974. "Mobilization of liberal strength in the House, 1955–1970: the Democratic Study Group." *American Political Science Review* 68: 667–681.

Stewart III, Charles. 2001. *Analyzing Congress.* New York: W.W. Norton.

Stimson, James A. 1999/1991. *Public Opinion in America.* Boulder, C.O.: Westview Press.

Stimson, James A., Michael B. MacKuen, and Robert S. Erikson. 1995. Dynamic Representation." *American Political Science Review* 89: 543–565.

Stone, Walter J. 1980. "The Dynamics of Constituency: Electoral Control in the House." *American Politics Quarterly* 8: 399–424.

Strom, Gerald S., and Barry S. Rundquist. 1977. "A Revised Theory of Winning in House-Senate Conferences." *American Political Science Review* 71 (June): 448–453

Strahan, Randall. 1990. *New Ways and Means: Reform and Change in a Congressional Committee.* Chapel Hill: University of North Carolina Press.

——. 2007. *Leading Representatives: The Agency of Leaders in the Politics of the U. S. House of Representatives.* Baltimore: Johns Hopkins University Press.

Strom, Gerald, and Barry S. Rundquist. 1978. "On Explaining Legislative Organization." Paper presented at the Annual Meeting of the American Political Science Association.

Sulkin, Tracy. 2005. *Issues in Congress*. New York: Cambridge University Press.

——. 2009. "Promises Made and Promises Kept." In *Congress Reconsidered*, 9th ed. Edited by Lawrence C. Dodd and Bruce I. Oppenheimer. Washington, D.C.: CQ Press, pp. 119–39.

James L. Sundquist. 1968. *Politics and Policy*. Washington, D.C.: Brookings.

——. 1973. *Dynamics of the Party System: Alignment and Realignment of Political Parties in the United States*. Washington, D.C.: Brookings Institution.

——. 1977. "Congress and the President: Enemies or Partners?" In *Congress Reconsidered*, 1st ed. Edited by Lawrence C. Dodd and Bruce I. Oppenheimer. New York: Praeger Publisher, pp. 222–43.

——. 1981. *The Decline and Resurgence of Congress*. Washington, D.C.: Brookings.

Swain, Carol M. 1993. *Black Faces, Black Interests: The Representation of African Americans in Congress*. Cambridge: Harvard University Press.

——.1997. "Women and Blacks in Congress: 1870–1996." In *Congress Reconsidered*, 6th ed. Edited by Lawrence C. Dodd and Bruce I. Oppenheimer. Washington, D.C.: CQ Press, pp. 81–99.

Swenson, Peter. 1982. "The influence of recruitment on the structure of power in the U.S. House, 1870–1940." *Legislative Studies* Quarterly 7: 7–36.

Swift, Elaine K. 1987. "The Electoral Connection Meets the Past: Lessons from Congressional History, 1789–1899." *Political Science Quarterly* 102: 625–45.

——. 1996. *The Making of an American Senate: Reconstitutive Change in Congress, 1787–1841*. Ann Arbor: University of Michigan Press.

——. 1998. "The Start of Something New: Clay, Stevenson, Polk, and the Development of the Speakership, 1789–1869. In *Masters of the House*. Edited by Roger H. Davidson, Susan Webb Hammond, and Raymond W. Smock. Boulder, C.O.: Westview Press, pp. 10–32.

Tacheron, Donald G., and Morris K. Udall. 1970. *The Job of the Congressman*. Indianapolis: Bobbs-Merrill.

Talbert, Jeffrey, Bryan D. Jones, and Frank R. Baumgartner.1995. "Nonlegislative Hearings and Policy Change in Congress." *American Journal of Political Science* 39: 383–405.

Tate, Katherine. 2003. *Black Faces in the Mirror: African Americans and Their Representatives in the U.S. Congress*. Princeton: Princeton University Press.

Taylor, Andrew. 2005. *Elephant's Edge: The Republicans as a Ruling Party*. Westport, Connecticut: Praeger.

Theriault, Sean M. 2005. *The Power of the People: Congressional Competition, Public Attention, And Voter Retribution*. Columbus, O.H.: The Ohio State University Press.

——. 2006. "Party Polarization in the U.S. Congress: Member Replacement and Member Adaption." *Party Politics* 12:483–503

——. 2008. *Party Polarization in Congress*. New York: Cambridge University Press.

Thomas, Sue. 1994. *How Women Legislate*. New York: Oxford University Press.

Thurber, James A., ed. 1991a. *Divided Democracy*. Washington, D.C.: CQ Press.

——. 1991b. "Representation, Accountability, and Efficiency in Divided Party Control of Government." In *PS: Political Science and Politics* 24: 653–57.

——, ed. 1996. *Rivals for Power: Presidential Congressional Relations*. Washington, D.C.: CQ Press.

——. 1997. "Centralization, Devolution, and Turf Protection in the Congressional Budget Process." In *Congress Reconsidered*, 6th ed. Edited by Lawrence C. Dodd and Bruce I. Oppenheimer. Washington, D.C.: CQ Press, pp. 325–46.

Thurber, James A., and Roger H. Davidson. 1995. *Remaking Congress: Change and Stability in the 1990s*. Washington, D.C.: CQ Press.

Thurber, James A., and Colton Campbell, eds. 2002. *Congress and the Internet*. Upper Saddle River, NJ: Prentice-Hall.

Thurber, James A., and Candice Nelson, eds. 2004. *Campaigns and Elections American Style*. Boulder, C.O.: Westview Press.

Thurow, Lester. 1980. *The Zero Sum Society*. New York: Basic Books.

———. *Head to Head: The Coming Economic Battle Among Japan, Europe, and America*. New York: Morrow, 1992.

Tiefer, Charles. 1994. *The Semi-Sovereign Presidency: The Bush Administration's Strategy for Governing without Congress*. Boulder, C.O.: Westview Press.

Tilly, Charles. 1997. *Roads from the Past to the Future*. Lanham, M.D.: Rowman & Littlefield.

Tocqueville, Alexis de. 1835/1969. *Democracy in America*. Edited by J. P. Mayer and translated by George Lawrence. Garden City, NY: Doubleday, Anchor Books.

Truman, David B. 1951. *The Governmental Process*. New York: Knopf.

———, ed. 1965/1973. *Congress and America's Future*. Englewood Cliffs, N.J.: Prentice-Hall.

Tufte, Edward R. 1978. *Political Control of the Economy*. Princeton, N.J.: Princeton University Press.

Turner, Julius. 1970. *Party and Constituency: Pressures on Congress*. Rev. ed. by Edward V. Schneier Jr. Baltimore: Johns Hopkins University Press.

Unekis, Joseph, and Leroy N. Rieselbach. 1984. *Congressional Committee Politics: Continuity and Change*. New York: Praeger.

Uslaner, Eric M. 1978. "Policy Entrepreneurs and Amateur Democrats in the House of Representatives." In *Legislative Reform: The Policy Impact*. Edited by Leroy. Rieselbach, Lexington, M.A.: Lexington Books, pp. 105–16.

———. 1993. *The Decline of Comity in Congress*. Ann Arbor: University of Michigan Press.

———. 2000. "Is the Senate more civil than the House?" In *Esteemed Colleagues: Civility and Deliberation in the Senate*. Edited by Burdett Loomis. Washington, D.C.: Brookings Institution, pp. 32–55.

Vickers, Geoffrey. 1968. *Value Systems and Social Process*. London: Tavistock.

Volger, David J. 1971. *The Third House*. Evanston, Ill.: Northwestern University Press.

von Wright, Georg Henrik. 1971. *Explanation and Understanding*. Ithaca, N.Y.: Cornell University Press.

Ward, Barbara. 1966. *Spaceship Earth*. New York: Columbia University Press.

Wawro, Gregory J. 2000. *Legislative Entrepreneurship in the U.S. House of Representatives*. Ann Arbor: University of Michigan Press.

Wawro, Gregory J., and Eric Schickler. 2006. *Filibuster: Obstruction and Lawmaking in the U.S. Senate*. Princeton: Princeton University Press.

Wayne, S. J. *The Legislative Presidency*. New York: Harper.

Weaver, Ken. 1986. "The Politics of Blame Avoidance." *Journal of Public Policy* 6: 371–98.

Weber, Max. 1976. *The Protestant Ethic and the Spirit of Capitalism*. New York: Scribner's.

———. 1958. "Science as a Vocation." In *From Max Weber*. Edited by H. H. Gerth and C. Wright Mills. New York: Oxford University Press, pp. 129–56.

Weick, Karl E. 1979, 1989. *The Social Psychology of Organizing*. New York: McGraw-Hill.

———. 1995. *Sensemaking in Organizations*. Thousand Oaks, C.A.: Sage Publications.

Weingast, Barry R. 1979. "A Rational Choice Perspective on Congressional Norms." *American Journal of Political Science* 23: 245–62.

——.1989. "Floor Behavior in the U.S. Congress: Committee Power under the Open Rule." *American Political Science Review* 83: 795–815.

Weir, Margaret, Ann Shola Orloff, and Theda Skocpol, eds. 1988. *The Politics of Social Policy in America.* Princeton, N.J.: Princeton University Press.

Weisberg, Herbert F. 1978. "Evaluating Theories of Congressional Roll Call Voting." *American Journal of Political Science* 22: 554–577.

——. 1986. "Introduction: The Science of Politics and Political Change." In *Political Science: the Science of Politics.* Edited by Herbert F. Weisberg, New York: Agathon Press, pp. 3–23.

Weisberg, Herbert F., Eric S. Heberlig, and Lisa M. Campoli. 1999. *Classics in Congressional Politics.* New York: Longman.

Welsh, Susan, and John G. Peters, eds. 1977. *Legislative Reform and Public Policy.* New York: Praeger.

Westefield, L. P. 1974. "Majority Party Leadership and the Committee System in the House of Representatives." *American Political Science Review* 68: 1593–1604.

White, William S. 1956. *Citadel: The Story of the United States Senate.* New York: Harper.

Whittington, Keith E., and Daniel P. Carpenter. 2003. "Executive Power in American Political Development." *Perspectives on Politics* 1(3): 495–513.

Wildavsky, Aaron. 1964. *The Politics of the Budgetary Process.* Boston: Little, Brown.

Will, George F. 1992. *Restoration.* New York: Free Press.

Wilson, James Q., Jack Citrin, Bruce Cain and Jerry Lubenow, eds. 2010. "Special Issue: California Budget Quagmire." *California Journal of Politics and Policy.* 2: 3.

Wilson, Woodrow. 1885. *Congressional Government.* 1885. Reprint, Gloucester, Mass.: Peter Smith, 1973.

Wills, Garry. 2002. *James Madison.* New York: Times Books, Henry Holt and Co.

Winch, Peter. 1958. *The Idea of a Social Science.* London: Routledge & Kegan Paul.

Wirls, Daniel, and Stephen Wirls. 2004. *The Invention of the United States Senate.* Baltimore: Johns Hopkins Press.

Wolbrecht, Christina, Alvin Tillery, Peri Arnold and Rodney Hero. 2005. *The Politics of Democratic Inclusion.* Philadelphia: Temple University Press.

Wolfensberger, Donald R. 2000.*Congress and the People: Deliberative Democracy on Trial.* Baltimore: Johns Hopkins University Press.

——. 2005. "Congress and Policymaking in an Age of Terrorism." In *Congress Reconsidered, 8th ed.* Edited by Dodd and Oppenheimer. Washington, D.C.: CQ Press, pp. 343–62.

Wolfinger, Raymond E., and Joan Heifetz Hollinger. 1965. "Safe Seats, Seniority, and Power in Congress." *American Political Science Review* 59: 337–349.

Wood, Gordon S. 1969. *The Creation of the American Republic, 1776–1787.* Chapel Hill: University of North Carolina Press.

——. 1992. *The Radicalism of the American Revolution.* New York: Alfred A. Knopf.

Wright, Fiona A. 2000. "The Caucus Reelection Requirement and the Transformation of House Committee Chairs, 1959–94." *Legislative Studies Quarterly* 25:469–480.

Wright, Gerald C., Jr., and Berkman, Michael B. 1985. "Candidates and policy in the 1982 U. S. Senate elections: a comparative state analysis." Paper presented at the 1985 Annual Meeting of the Western Political Science Association, Las Vegas, Nevada.

——. 1986. "Candidates and Policy in United States Senate Elections." *American Political Science Review* 80: 567–588.

Wright, Gerald C., Leroy Rieselbach, and Lawrence C. Dodd, eds. 1986. *Congress and Policy Change.* New York: Agathon.

Wright, John. 1985. "PACs, Contributions, and Roll Calls: An Organizational Perspective." *American Political Science Review* 75: 400–414.

———. 1996. *Interest Groups and Congress: Lobbying, Contributions, and Influence.* New York: Allyn and Bacon.

Young, Garry.1996. "Committee Gatekeeping and Proposal Power under Single and Multiple Referral." *Journal of Theoretical Politics* 8: 65–78.

Young, James S. 1966. *The Washington Community, 1800–1828.* New York: Columbia University Press.

Zelizer, Julian E. 2004a. *On Capitol Hill: The Struggle to Reform Congress and Its Consequences, 1948–2000.* New York: Cambridge University Press.

———, ed. 2004b. *The American Congress: The Building of Democracy.* Boston: Houghton Mifflin.

PERMISSIONS

"A Theory of Congressional Cycles: Solving the Puzzle of Change." In *Congress and Policy Change*. Edited by Gerald C. Wright, Jr., Leroy N. Rieselbach, and Lawrence C. Dodd. New York, NY: Agathon Press, Inc. 1986, pages 3–44. Reprinted with permission of Agathon Press.

"Bicameralism in Congress: The Changing Partnership." In *Congress Reconsidered*, 3rd edition. Edited by Lawrence C. Dodd and Bruce I. Oppenheimer. Washington, D.C.: CQ Press. 1985, pages 414–436. Reprinted with permission of CQ Press.

"Congress and the Politics of Renewal: Redressing the Crisis of Legitimation." In *Congress Reconsidered*, 5th Edition. Edited by Lawrence C. Dodd and Bruce I. Oppenheimer. Washington, D.C.: CQ Press. 1993, pages 417–446. Reprinted with permission of CQ Press.

"Congress and the Quest for Power." In *Congress Reconsidered*, 1st Edition. Edited by Lawrence C. Dodd and Bruce I. Oppenheimer. New York, NY: Praeger Publishers. 1977, pages 269–312. Reprinted with permission of the author.

"Congress, the Constitution, and the Crisis of Legitimation." In *Congress Reconsidered*, 2nd edition. Edited by Lawrence C. Dodd and Bruce I. Oppenheimer. Washington, D.C.: CQ Press. 1981, pages 390–420. Reprinted with permission of CQ Press.

"Congress, The Presidency, and the American Experience: A Transformational Perspective." In *Divided Democracy: Cooperation and Conflict Between the President*

INDEX

Note: The following abbreviations have been used: *f* = figure; *n* = note

For Product Safety Concerns and Information please contact our EU
representative GPSR@taylorandfrancis.com
Taylor & Francis Verlag GmbH, Kaufingerstraße 24, 80331 München, Germany

www.ingramcontent.com/pod-product-compliance
Lightning Source LLC
Chambersburg PA
CBHW050558270326
41926CB00012B/2104